Third Edition

A MANAGERIAL INTRODUCTION TO MARKETING

Thomas A. Staudt
Director of Marketing
Chevrolet Motor Division
General Motors Corporation

Donald A. Taylor
Professor and Chairman
Department of Marketing and Transportation
Michigan State University

Donald J. Bowersox
Professor
Department of Marketing and Transportation
Michigan State University

PRENTICE-HALL, INC., Englewood Cliffs, New Jersey

Library of Congress Cataloging in Publication Data

STAUDT, THOMAS A.
   A managerial introduction to marketing.

   Includes index.
   1. Marketing management.   2. Industrial management.
3. Marketing research.   I. Taylor, Donald Arthur,
(Date)   joint author.   II. Bowersox, Donald J.,
joint author.   III. Title.
HF5415.13.S87   1976   658.8   75-22114
ISBN   0-13-550186-5

© 1976, 1970, 1965 by Prentice-Hall, Inc.,
Englewood Cliffs, New Jersey

All rights reserved.
No part of this book may be reproduced
in any form or by any means
without permission in writing from the publisher.

Printed in the United States of America

10   9   8   7   6   5   4   3   2   1

Parts of Chapters 2 and 3 appeared previously
in Lazer and Kelley's *Managerial Marketing:
Perspectives and Viewpoints,* rev. ed.
(Homewood, Ill.: Richard D. Irwin, Inc. 1962).

    To Elaine, Shirley, and Carol
    for reasons they full well understand.

    Prentice-Hall International, Inc., *London*
    Prentice-Hall of Australia, Pty. Ltd., *Sydney*
    Prentice-Hall of Canada, Ltd., *Toronto*
    Prentice-Hall of India Private Limited, *New Delhi*
    Prentice-Hall of Japan, Inc., *Tokyo*
    Prentice-Hall of Southeast Asia (Pte.) Ltd., *Singapore*

Contents

PREFACE xi

Part I

MARKET ORIENTATION AND ENTERPRISE ADJUSTMENT 1

Chapter 1

COMPETITIVE SOCIETY AND MARKET AFFAIRS 3

Competition as a Process of Adjustment
Competitive Uncertainty
Uncertainty—A Permanent Factor
Market Decision Making in a Competitive Environment
Summary

Chapter 2

**MARKET ORIENTATION
AS A PHILOSOPHY OF BUSINESS MANAGEMENT** 20

Profits Guide the Effective Functioning
  of the Firm as a Whole
Market Veto Power and Management Action
Application of the Marketing Philosophy
Competition for Differential Advantage
Cooperative Marketing Actions
What is Marketing?
Market Leadership and Managerial Marketing Activities
Summary

Chapter 3

THE MANAGERIAL FUNCTIONS OF MARKETING   35

    Functions Related to Market Opportunity Assessment
    Functions Related to Product-Service Market Matching
    Functions Related to Marketing Programming
    Functions Related to Execution
    A Systems Integration of the
        Managerial Marketing Functions
    Summary

Chapter 4

ENVIRONMENTAL MONITORING AND STRATEGY FORMULATION   55

    Environmental Monitoring
    Corporate Growth
    Development of Marketing Strategy
    One Strategy or Many?
    Strategic Planning in Action
    A Composite View Thus Far
    Summary

Part II

MARKET OPPORTUNITY ASSESSMENT   85

Chapter 5

CONSUMER MARKET DELINEATION   87

    Environmental Monitoring
    Identification of Marketing Objectives
    Selecting Market Targets
    Summary

Chapter 6

FOUNDATIONS OF CONSUMER BEHAVIOR   113

    Classification of Consumer Choice Decisions
    An Interdisciplinary Framework
        for Understanding Consumer Choice
    Summary

Chapter 7

PURCHASE BEHAVIOR ANALYSIS   138

    A Learning Perspective of Consumer Behavior
    A Framework for Qualitative Market Investigation
    A Purchase Motivation Study on Automobiles
    Some Practical Considerations
    Summary

Chapter 8

INTERMEDIATE MARKETS   152

    The Market for Intermediate Goods
    A Classification of Intermediate Goods
    Special Characteristics of Intermediate Goods
        and Their Markets
    Opportunity Assessment in Intermediate Markets
    Summary

Chapter 9

INTERNATIONAL MARKETS   175

    Various Forms of Participating in Foreign Markets
    Characteristics of Markets Outside the United States
    Market Feasibility Study
    Summary

Part III
PRODUCT-MARKET MATCHING   197

Chapter 10
PRODUCT PLANNING ENVIRONMENT   199

Elements of Product Planning Risk
Product-Market Matching
Fundamental Matching Strategies
Patterns of Product Diversity
Typical Product Planning Problems
Summary

Chapter 11
STAGES OF PRODUCT-MARKET DEVELOPMENT   221

The Product Life Cycle Concept
Life Cycle Stages and Competitive Conditions
Opportunities and Need for Changing Marketing Strategies
   from Time to Time
Some Limitations and Benefits
   of the Product Life Cycle Concept
Summary

Chapter 12
FRAMEWORK FOR PRODUCT PLANNING   246

Stage I—Corporate Research
Stage II—Feasibility Research
Stage III—Development
Stage IV—Test Marketing
Stage V—Market Introduction
Commercialization or Kill?
Combining the Elements of Analysis
Summary

Part IV
MARKETING PLANNING   271

Chapter 13

MARKETING CHANNEL STRUCTURE   273

    The Overall Nature of Marketing Channels
    The Process of Sorting
    The Role of Marketing Intermediaries
    Channel Separation
    Summary

Chapter 14

TRANSACTION CHANNEL DESIGN   287

    Interorganizational Behavior
    Conglomerate Market Competition
    Criteria for Selecting Transaction Channel Structure
    Direct Versus Indirect Channels
    Summary

Chapter 15

PHYSICAL DISTRIBUTION CHANNEL DESIGN   315

    Physical Distribution in a Logistical Perspective
    Pressures for Improved Physical Distribution Performance
    Operating Areas of Physical Distribution
    Total Cost—The Integrating Concept
    Customer Service Performance
    Summary

Chapter 16

ADVERTISING   344

    A Communications Model
    The Terminology of Advertising
    The Objectives of Advertising
    Factors Affecting the Successful Use of Advertising
    The Selection of Media
    Determination of the Advertising Appropriation
    Cost of Advertising to the Consumer
    Summary

Chapter 17

PERSONAL SELLING   373

    Nature and Importance of Personal Selling
    Management of Employee Sales Force
    The Use of Manufacturers' Agents
    Manufacturer-Dealer Arrangements
    Summary

Chapter 18

PRICE   412

    The Role of Pricing
    Theoretical Concepts of Price Determination
    Pricing to Achieve Corporate Objectives
    New Product Pricing
    Alternative Price Structures
    Legal Implications of Price Determination
        and Administration
    Summary

Chapter 19

MARKETING STRATEGY PLANNING   448

   The Planning Sequence
   Formulating Specific Marketing Objectives
   Selection of Market Targets
   Formulation of the Marketing Mix
   Summary

Part V

EXECUTING THE MARKET PLAN   485

Chapter 20

ORGANIZATION   487

   Major Influences Leading to Organizational Modification
   Concepts of Organizational Design
   Evolution of an Organization
      Embracing a Concept of Market Orientation
   Criteria for Effective Organizational Design
   Organizational Directions for the Future
   Summary

Chapter 21

ADMINISTRATION   512

   Marketing Control
   Performance Measurement
   Marketing Information Systems
   Integrated Marketing Administration
   Summary

Part VI
THE UNIVERSALITY OF MARKETING   557

Chapter 22
MARKETING IN NONCOMPETITIVE SYSTEMS   558

What Is a Nonprofit-Making Institution?
The Importance of Noncompetitive Institutions
A Format for Noncompetitive Marketing
Summary

Chapter 23
THE FIRM AS A MARKETING AND SOCIAL ENTITY   572

The Firm as a Market Entity
Contemporary Issues Related to Marketing Practice
Conclusion

Appendix A
RETAIL AND WHOLESALE TRADE   579

Retailing
Wholesaling

INDEX   587

Preface

We believe marketing to be fully worthy of the best intellectual competence that can be brought to bear on the complex aspects of competition and competitive strategy. We have sought to convey this complexity while simultaneously seeking clarity of exposition and understanding. We have introduced conceptual and theoretical notions not normally associated with initial instruction in the field. We have done so while relying on continued example and illustration to facilitate comprehension. Experience has shown that it is easy to underestimate students—to talk down to them. That is what makes for a dull subject, dull students, and dull faculty. We genuinely believe the level of this book to be within the grasp of those receiving their first exposure to the field, and it is so intended. Finally, we believe that marketing, properly conceived, can attract and challenge the keenest minds among the student population.

A market orientation as a philosophy of business management has been developed and articulated as the cornerstone of this treatment. Too often in the past, students have been exposed to a catalogue-like coverage of the varied aspects of marketing. In these attempts to be comprehensive, so much detail has been presented that the student often fails to master either a coherent point of view or a body of knowledge. We hope an integrated philosophy is clearly perceivable here. One may contest its adequacy or validity, but its presence cannot be denied. Each part introduction reverts to the beginning and builds upon the emerging structure. Each chapter is summarized to stress the broader context.

In this third edition, we have preserved the point of view expressed above while expanding and articulating our commitment to competitive strategy. Marketing management is primarily concerned with the formulation of a competitive strategy to guide the firm. Capitalizing on those resources of a company which give it competitive distinctiveness, the firm is viewed as perpetuating its existence in an uncertain environment by virtue of gaining a differential advantage over rivals.

In order to further clarify this conceptual base and elaborate the integrated performance of the enterprise, several changes have been made in this edition. The number of chapters has been reduced from thirty-three to twenty-three. However, the noteworthy changes are found in the substantive additions and their sequential development.

In Part One, Market Orientation and Enterprise Adjustment, a cornerstone is set. The macro-marketing beginning of the second edition has been expanded to include the managerial mandates imposed by the dynamic competitive environment in which the enterprise functions. The firm is positioned as a participant in an ecological system of competitive behavior. Such notions as market leadership, its meaning, importance, and achievement through creative entrepreneurship are stressed as fundamental objectives of managerial marketing. The remainder of the book is structured by identification of four managerial activities universal to marketing. These *managerial activities*—market opportunity assessment, product-market matching, marketing planning, and execution—form the major parts of the text treatment. Within these four managerial activities, the performance of nine *managerial functions* of marketing is developed as the specific action by which leadership is sought and achieved. The perspective of seeking differential advantage through a five-step marketing strategy planning sequence provides a road map to guide the reader through the content of the various parts.

Part Two, Market Opportunity Assessment, has been expanded to stress the increasing emphasis given to the behavioral aspects of the consumer, intermediate, and international markets. Part Three, Product-Market Matching, has been condensed, while at the same time preserving the essential features of product strategy formulation in the establishment of the marketing mix.

In Part Four, Marketing Planning, the selection of the distribution, communications, and price mix has been changed by extensive additions in the area of marketing channel structure and design as well as physical distribution design. The part ends with an exploration of Marketing Strategy Planning, which is designed to integrate the material into a managerial commitment. This chapter purposely parallels the road map established in Part One. Part Five, Executing the Market Plan, emphasizes the role of organization and administration in resource allocation and mobilization. The area of marketing administration stresses control and performance measurement in the context of pretransaction, transaction, and posttransaction feedback. The administrative process is geared to stress the need for continuous performance monitoring to complete the circular process of managerial marketing. As such, Part Five concludes our scenario from the viewpoint of a profit-seeking enterprise.

Part Six, The Universality of Marketing, is new to the third edition.

Its objective is to expand the horizon of traditional managerial marketing by exploring the application of marketing strategy planning to institutions which operate in noncompetitive systems. The book concludes with a summary of the essential features of our approach and identifies selected issues confronting contemporary marketing management. We are of the firm belief that the very presence of a marketing orientation is a significant force to help solve today's emerging problems.

Three qualifications are appropriate regarding this major revision. First, we have strived to insure that managerial considerations are identified and integrated throughout the text. Such considerations consistently involved in private enterprise are critical to survival and societal growth. They are not something to be added at the end of selected chapters or simply treated in a separate chapter. Second, although a managerial approach is stressed, we have at the same time emphasized the aggregative economic and societal results of managerial marketing as practiced by the many institutions in the private and public sectors. Third, because of the dynamics of a competitive system, we have emphasized at each appropriate stage the need for continuous and innovative adjustment to the ever-changing requirements of the marketplace. We feel the welfare of a free market society rests with private enterprise. This mission is judged worthy of the best effort we can all conceptualize and implement.

Finally, it is our belief that the changes included in this edition take a step toward a broader and more relevant understanding of marketing, and at the same time have added to the conceptual depth and logical presentation.

It would be impossible to mention all the individuals who have made significant contributions to this book.[1] Special mention, however, should be made of our earlier mentors, particularly Professors Phelps, Davisson, and Griffin of the University of Michigan, Professors Haring, Mee, and Edwards of Indiana University, Professor Arthur E. Warner of the University of Alabama, and Walter L. Jeffrey, Vice Chairman of the E. F. MacDonald Company. Also, the early professional association with Wroe Alderson and Robert E. Sessions of the (then) Alderson and Sessions consulting organization is evident. In fact, the true influence of Professor Alderson may never be adequately measured, for he was the brilliant innovator of much

---

[1] As authors of the first two editions, we wish to express our pleasure and thanks for the addition of Professor Bowersox as a member of this writing team. His insights, experience, and untiring dedication have contributed immeasurably to the completion of this third edition.

T.A.S.
D.A.T.

of the theory and methodology that is current in marketing. We also wish to express our thanks to Ms. Felicia Kramer for the endless hours of editing, manuscript preparation, and general assistance in this undertaking.

Most of all, the professional capital for this book comes from the by-now-quite-sizable number of senior executives of some of the nation's great enterprises, who in providing an almost unlimited variety of professional assignments, have made it possible to maintain a personal touch with the problems, meditations, and behavior of top management in its periods of competitive readjustment. Many of the examples and concepts throughout the book are direct evidence of these involvements. The professional enrichment of rigorous problem-solving is of enduring value to an educator.

Finally, we are grateful for the support of our colleagues at Michigan State University, whose advice and timely assistance made it possible to finish this venture. We express, also, gratitude to our wives and families, who, for the most part, were able to sustain a patient encouragement throughout.

While many have contributed to this book and it has been greatly improved by their contributions, we, however, take responsibility for any of its faults.

THOMAS A. STAUDT
DONALD A. TAYLOR
DONALD J. BOWERSOX

Part I

MARKET ORIENTATION AND ENTERPRISE ADJUSTMENT

Many approaches have been taken to the study of marketing. They range from an analysis of the specific activities performed during the flow of a single commodity from producer to consumer; to a study of the business institutions participating in the creation and delivery of our standard of living; to a delineation of universal functions that must be completed to achieve a flow of goods from production to consumption. An important development of the past 25 years has been the blending of these approaches into managerial marketing. The managerial orientation is concerned with the way in which the enterprise conducts its market affairs and the way in which these actions contribute to the competitive posture, growth, and perpetuation of the enterprise.

This book follows a managerial orientation to marketing. It is concerned with the development of policies, strategies, and operations of a competitive enterprise. Three basic premises underlie the presentation.

First is the premise that *marketing activity as we know it is a result of our political-economic orientation for production and consumption and the resulting competitive society such an orientation creates.* The myriad of independent actions taken by decision makers in supplying firms and purchasing units is the substance of competition—the normal state in a free society. An understanding of this environment within which the decision maker functions is crucial to understanding both the objectives of the individual enterprise and the societal objectives of the overall marketing system. The need for the decision maker continuously to assess the future action of competitive firms and purchasing units can only be appreciated if the system of competition is understood. For a firm to enjoy longevity, its management must respond to competition with creative and innovative action to insure differential advantage. The striving for market leadership on the part of firms is the energizing force in a competitive market system.

Second is the premise that *a market orientation provides a philosophy of business management.* As such, a market orientation must pervade the entire enterprise. Each firm engages in a number of contributory functions: research and development, personnel management and industrial relations, financial planning, logistics, production, and marketing. Although all these are important, a more generalized description of the firm considers it as engaged in two interconnected basic functions: production and marketing. These functions are complementary, for unless goods are produced they are not available for consumption, and unless they are available and desired for consumption there is no justification for their production. It is the market, however, that sanctions all the steps that precede consumption. The market holds veto power over the total enterprise. For this reason, a market orientation is essential for the enterprise. More specifically, the competitive actions of the firm should derive from market forces and opportunities. Once this concept is grasped it is possible to think of the enterprise as an integrated production-marketing system that mobilizes all of its resources toward meeting the requirements of effective competition and the fulfillment of market potentialities.

Third is the premise that *the enterprise is a total system of action.* This management perspective demands that responsibility concerning market affairs be concentrated organizationally on an integrated systems basis. With competition for differential advantage as the basis for a market orientation, it is possible to delineate enterprise goals, managerial activities, and managerial functions of marketing. These managerial activities and functions must be blended into a total system of action if the goals of the enterprise are to be achieved.

The purpose of Part One is to explore the competitive environment within which the firm functions, the way in which this environment is dependent on a market orientation, the identification of managerial activities and functions, and the integration of managerial activities and functions into a total system of competitive action. To accomplish this objective, Part One contains four chapters. Chapter 1 provides a broad, or macro, orientation to the interrelated nature of competition and market affairs. Chapter 2 continues the discussion at the macro level by describing the fundamental need for developing a market orientation as the guiding business management philosophy. At the conclusion of Chapter 2, the materials presented thus far are summarized in Figure 2-3. Four managerial activities are introduced in Figure 2-3 as the bridge between a macro orientation to marketing and the managerial functions of the marketer. Chapter 3 further refines the managerial orientation by introducing specific functions required for successful marketing. The treatment is further operationalized by Chapter 4, which introduces the development of marketing strategy.

Chapter 1

Competitive Society and Market Affairs

This book is concerned with the way in which a firm conducts its market affairs and how such actions contribute to the competitive posture, growth, and perpetuation of the enterprise. The decisions made by millions of independent firms throughout the economy, combined with the purchase behavior decisions made by the consuming public, create the competitive environment.

No decision maker functions solely within the narrow confines of the firm represented. Every decision maker is influenced by and influences the myriad decisions made by others. The single most important characteristic of this process of independent decision making is the *uncertainty* created. Not only is uncertainty the constant adversary of the decision maker, it is our basic contention that *uncertainty is the major factor responsible for the manner in which a firm conducts its market affairs, and the principal element of an intensely competitive economic system.*

The market affairs of the firm are so closely related to the existing competitive state that it is almost impossible to distinguish cause and effect —that is, to assess whether action in the marketplace is determined by or is a determinant of the level of competition. To make good decisions concerning market affairs managers must understand the competitive environment in which they must take action. Only by such understanding can they assess the forces affecting the outcomes of their decisions and exercise creativity in a continuous process of innovative and retaliatory actions.

In this chapter, we examine the nature of competition. To understand competition, one must develop an appreciation for both the structure and the behavior of competitive markets. Next, the prevailing condition of uncertainty is examined in detail. We conclude with a discussion of market decision making within the competitive environment. The chapter serves as a prelude to examining the fundamental need for a marketing orientation as a philosophy of business management.

COMPETITION AS A PROCESS OF ADJUSTMENT

The environment in which the firm functions has been characterized as competitive, free enterprise, and market oriented. These terms are frequently used, and much lip service is given to the desirability of the organizational forms and patterns of action they represent. Everyone has some notion of what these terms mean, but the intricacy of the mechanisms through which society fulfills its needs and desires is not generally conveyed. Too frequently, *competition* signifies a haphazard, unorganized approach to the economic affairs of society, one in which something akin to a "law of the jungle" prevails. In reality, competition is a complex, delicately balanced mechanism through which society satisfies its needs and desires.

Many analyses have been made concerning the degree of competition existing in the economy.[1] For the most part, they have been concerned with the number of buyers and sellers, their size, and the relative concentration of power. These studies are concerned with the *structure* of competition.

Another definition of competition is a rivalry between two or more for the patronage of another. This definition treats competition as a form of *behavior,* rather than as the *structure* of the behaving units.[2] Both views are helpful in understanding the competitive environment. Fortunately, both treat competition as a *process of adjustment,* and it is in this context that we shall examine each.

THE STRUCTURE OF COMPETITION

An objective of economic activity is to maximize satisfaction from scarce means. This is best accomplished through a division of labor (specialization). The most primitive societies resort to a division of labor to gain the greatest benefit from limited resources. The moment a division of labor exists, some members have more than they need of those things in which they specialize and less of other desired objects. Exchange of sur-

---

[1] See B. Imel, M. Rehr, and P. Heimberger, *Market Structure and Performance: The U.S. Food Processing Industries* (Lexington, Mass.: Lexington Books, 1972); William G. Shepherd, *Market Power and Economic Welfare* (New York: Random House, 1970); and B. Bock, *Restructuring Proposals: Measuring Competition in Numerical Grids* (New York: The Conference Board, 1974).

[2] A classical treatment of competition may be found in J. M. Clark, "Toward a Concept of Workable Competition," *American Economic Review,* Part I (June 1940), p. 241.

plus is essential, for it is the means by which individuals in a free society satisfy their economic wants.

In our society, goods are made available through a very complicated industrial-marketing complex, in which specialization exists in different ways. Enterprises in the extractive industries are, of course, specialized in the raw material they are equipped to extract. For example, some lumbering operations are confined to timber for pulp, and others confined to hardwood. Agriculture is specialized in dairying, grain products, beef cattle, truck gardening, and so on. With a high degree of specialization among the producers of goods *exchange* is an important function in our economy. In fact, so important is it that one economist states:

> Indeed it is hardly too much to say that the study of exchange comprises nine-tenths of the economist's dominion.[3]

It is through the process of exchange that value is created in a specialized economy. Goods do not have intrinsic market value. Even finished goods stored in a warehouse have only potential value. It is true they are assigned a value in accounting records because it is anticipated they will be exchanged in the near future, but they have no value until they are made available for use both physically and legally. Even then, value emerges only when they are made available to a buyer and an exchange actually takes place. The availability of the goods and the "wantingness" of the buyer determine the value of the goods exchanged.

Another characteristic of exchange is important. The term "wantingness" in the preceding paragraph was deliberately selected to describe a mental state among buyers. Before an exchange takes place, both parties must feel that they will benefit from the transaction. There is no equality in the minds of the participants concerning the two items that are exchanged: the buyer must want the item he is buying more than he wants the money he must pay for it; the seller must want the money more than the item. The intensity of desire on the part of the participants is what determines value. This characteristic of inequality is important to marketers, for the wantingness of the subject is stimulated by the different means of market cultivation.

In a highly specialized economy such as ours, in which money is used as a medium of exchange, we do not normally think of the seller as having varying intensities of desire for money. He is usually offering goods for exchange; this is his business. The desire he has for money determines the amount of goods he will make available for exchange. You will recall from

[3] Kenneth E. Boulding, *Economic Analysis,* 4th ed. (New York: Harper and Row Publishers, 1966), p. 4.

economics that this is known as *supply*. The wantingness of the buyer is also determined by how many such items he has, and his interpretation of the value of obtaining additional items. His willingness to give up money for additional items is known as *demand*.

The single most dominant characteristic of supply and demand in a specialized economy is *heterogeneity*. We can think of the supply segment as made up of a large number of geographically concentrated, specialized producers providing different types of goods. Approximately 9.2 million establishments (total industrial goods buyers less retailers and wholesalers) are responsible for the supply of all goods and services. Because they are specialized, supply is heterogeneous.

Demand consists of the wants of approximately 66.6 million households in the consumer market and about 11.8 million establishments in the intermediate market.[4] Each buying unit is searching for an assortment of goods that will satisfy anticipated needs and wants. The desire to acquire a unique assortment is not confined to the millions of households in the consumer market; it is equally a characteristic of the intermediate goods buyer. The latter must assemble all the goods necessary to carry out the functions of the enterprise. Each assortment requires a much wider variety of products than any one producer can provide, and the quantity demanded is usually much smaller than those offered by any single producer.[5] Demand is therefore also heterogeneous.

So important is the heterogeneity of demand and supply created by the division of labor, that some define marketing as "the set of activities that make possible (and in turn are made necessary) by the intricate division of labor that characterizes our economy."[6] Not only do we have a need to match a heterogeneous supply with heterogeneous demand, we can also be certain that the composition of the heterogeneity of demand and supply will change through time. Therefore, any society in which work specialization exists requires a market mechanism "to guide the choices economic specialists make among alternative uses of their resources and to exchange among them the goods and services they produce."[7]

In a society in which producers are relatively free to determine what to produce, and consumers relatively free to purchase that which they want and have the capacity to command, an adjustment process takes

---

[4] Compiled from data in *Statistical Abstract of the United States*, 1974.

[5] There are exceptions to this, as in those cases where one manufacturer contracts to take the entire output of another manufacturer.

[6] Reavis Cox, *Distribution in a High-Level Economy* (Englewood Cliffs, N.J.: Prentice-Hall, Inc., 1965), p. 14.

[7] Ibid., p. 14.

place. Adjustment is required on both the part of the supplier and the purchasing unit.

Rarely do we know in advance of purchase just exactly what we want. For us to be able to do so would require a production-to-order economy, with attendant diseconomies. Fortunately, we ordinarily enjoy the shopping experience of seeking out those things that we, at the time, think will satisfy us most. Supplying firms do, however, make many adjustments to satisfy purchasing units. This is evident in the parade of new products made available each year and in the wide variety of a given item marketed. The actions each supply firm engages in to make appropriate adjustments are the responsibility of its management, and the actions of all firms is the substance of competition.

For one approach to describe the adjustment process let's review *economic equilibrium analyses*. The economist describes the result of aggregated adjustment action taken by supplying firms and purchasing units. In Figure 1-1, a set of relationships between supplying firms and purchasing units is identified. The relationships are expressed in flows quantified in both real and monetary terms. The demand is based upon hypothesized relationships between price and quantity, with psychological forces expressed in the utility and productivity curves assumed. At each corner of the diagram, the marginal curves which theoretically determine the size of the flows are shown. The marginal cost curves determine the quantity of goods offered at various prices in the marketplace. The marginal cost curves are in turn determined by the marginal production curves, or the amount of productive services that will be forthcoming to produce the supply at various payment levels. The marginal productivity curves are determined by the marginal disutility curves, which describe the psychological disutility incurred as more units of effort are provided for different payments. The marginal disutility curves determine the marginal utility curves. The satisfaction to be derived from additional units declines as the disutility associated with earning the means to purchase increases. In equilibrium, the sum total of curves for each buyer, supplier of productive services, and seller represents the supply and demand for productive services, the supply and demand for goods at different prices. In equilibrium, the prices determine the monetary flows in terms of revenues, expenditures, and incomes, and a balance exists between supply and demand for productive services and goods.

Underlying the entire analysis is a system of conflict between firms as they vie for the purchasing unit's patronage. Conflict also exists between supply firms and purchasing units as they negotiate along the demand curves. Finally, conflict exists between purchasing units as they bid for scarce resources in the marketplace. Equilibrium is simply that state which results from resolving such conflicts. It is a tight theoretical treatment of the way purchasing units and supply firms complete the adjustment process.

FIGURE 1-1
A Marginal Diagram of the Economy

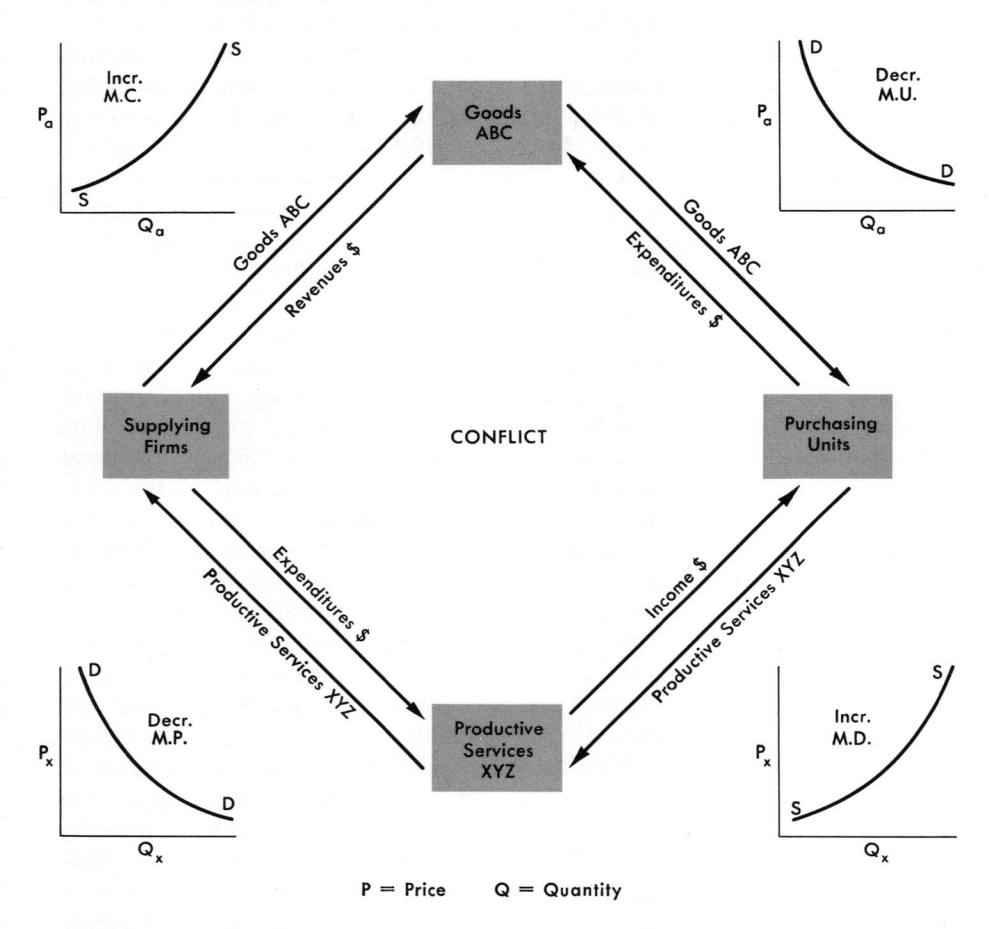

P = Price   Q = Quantity

    Equilibrium reflects adjustment in terms of the number of buyers and sellers and the size of various flows. The number of buyers and sellers is often used to classify market structures as *pure competition, pure monopoly, monopolistic competition,* or *monopoly.* Each is characterized by assumptions concerning the intensity of competition. The approach attempts to describe the actions taken by the participants during the exchange. Although these four states of competition are usually used to describe pricing practices, some knowledge of market structure is useful to understanding competition.

    In *pure competition,* the number of sellers is so large and the output of each so small that no single firm can influence price. The product sold is assumed to be completely homogeneous. Each buyer and seller is viewed as having complete knowledge of conditions in the marketplace. In such a structure, the demand curve is a horizontal straight line. That is, if a firm raised its price over the market price it would sell nothing. Since each firm can sell all it makes at the market price, there is no tendency to lower price. Under conditions of pure competition, supply makes a quantity adjustment to prevailing market price in a manner that maximizes profits. Cases of pure competition are rare, with the agricultural commodity markets coming closest. But even in agricultural markets there is so much governmental manipulation of supply and demand that they are not purely competitive in the classical sense.

Pure monopoly is the reverse of pure competition in that adjustment is dominated by a single firm. There are no product substitutes. Because no competition exists, the demand curve of the supplier is the same as the industry curve, and slopes to the right. Any increase in price decreases the volume that will be purchased, and any decrease in price may slightly increase the volume. The pricing problem of the supplier given this competitive structure is to determine the best combination of price and quantity to achieve the goals of the company. These prices are often called business-controlled prices because the firm does control the price it will ask. Sometimes, as in the case of public utilities, the price is set by a governmental agency and is called a government-controlled price. Similar to pure competition, it is doubtful whether there is such a thing as a pure monopoly, as the supplying firm must still compete for a share of the consumer's disposable income. From a theoretical point of view, pure competition and pure monopoly represent polar extremes.

In *monopolistic competition,* the most typical market structure, there are a large number of suppliers, each having a slightly different offering. In effect, each firm is a small monopolist. On the other hand, the offerings of rivals are to a significant degree substitutes from the buyer's viewpoint. The demand curve slopes to the right but is not as steep as in the case of the pure monopoly. The television industry with its large number of brands, each slightly differentiated yet each substitutable in most cases, is representative of a monopolistic market structure. The price under monopolistic competition is the result of a quantity, price, and cost adjustment by the seller firm. Because of substitutability, each competitor will incur costs such as advertising and personnel selling in an effort to increase the quantity sold. The alternative also exists to reduce prices in an effort to increase the quantity sold. An optimum balance is ideally achieved among the quantity, price, and associated cost which results in satisfactory profits. Prices in this kind of market structure are also called business-controlled prices, as the firm does control the price. However, the control is less than in the case of pure monopoly because of the close substitutes.

A few large sellers characterize *oligopoly*. Because of the fewness of sellers, the actions of any one have a direct effect on the others. In selecting prices, each competitor in an oligopoly must carefully consider retaliatory actions on the part of other sellers. If the product is homogeneous, there will be a tendency toward price uniformity. To the extent that products are differentiated, different prices may prevail among substitute sellers. The demand curve under differentiated oligopoly in this kind of a structure is known as a *kinked demand curve*. That is, the demand curve will slope gently to the right to the prevailing price and steeply to the right below the prevailing price. The significance of a kinked demand curve is that there is little tendency to decrease price below the prevailing price because all sellers will follow, resulting in no change in market share but lower total revenue. If a firm were to increase price above the prevailing price, the other firms would not likely follow. Thus, unless substantial difference in offering exists, the firm increasing price stands to lose a considerable share of market. In oligopolistic industries, prices tend to be stable over time. When adjustments are necessary, all firms increase price together, thereby establishing a new market price. The steel industry is an example of oligopoly. The automobile industry may be classified as a differentiated oligopoly.

These then are descriptions of competitive states derived from the economists' equilibrium model. Emphasis is placed upon the price-quantity relationships underlying exchange. This structural approach does not describe the motivating forces underlying the behavior of both supplying firms and purchasing units.

THE BEHAVIOR OF COMPETITION

From the viewpoint of managerial marketing it is more useful to describe competitive adjustment in a behavioral sense. The behavioral approach views competition and adjustment in an ecological and systems framework. There are certain general advantages to using a systems approach to describe competition and particular advantages in comparing it with an ecological system.

A system is an aggregation or assemblage of things so combined, by man or nature, as to form an integral and complex whole. The systems approach is a way of examining a complex whole by studying the parts and their relationship to each other. When applied to socioeconomic systems, this approach concentrates on the relationships between the participants, and postulates that all action is a result of the relationships between them.

A systems approach has two distinct advantages. First, a dynamic element is introduced as it is necessary to study changes in relationships as the participants adjust to each other and create new relationships with each act. Second, the systems approach can be applied to any level of generalization. For example, the human body is a homeostatic system made up of a number of subsystems, such as the circulatory, digestive, and nervous systems. A disturbance in any one of the subsystems will trigger a change in the functioning of the other subsystems and the system as a whole. The entire body may be studied as a system, also any one of the subsystems or, even more minutely, the organs in a subsystem may be studied as a system. We can examine the whole economy as a system or we can just as appropriately examine an industry, a company, or a division or department within a company.

An ecological analogy provides an appropriate way to describe our competitive system. An ecological system is illustrated by a pond in a forest. The pond is composed of a number of participants, such as fish life, insect life, and plant life. In a state of equilibrium the participants are in a perfect balance; with just the proper amount of each life form and all biological and zoological functions operating. If the conservation department adds fingerlings to the pond, a new set of relationships will exist between the life forms. Automatically the pond will start in motion a process of adjustment to realize equilibrium. When equilibrium is restored, the composition of the life forms is different and the pond is structurally changed.

The competitive system behaves in similar fashion. We can visualize a set of purchasing units and supplying firms with a set of relationships between each and also between groups of supplying firms or industries and purchasing units. All the supplying firms are attempting to adjust to the needs and desires of the purchasing units by making a variety of offerings available in the marketplace. At any given time, the offerings are such that a given share of the market exists for each grouping of firms and for each firm within the grouping. Then a new firm may enter the market or an existing firm may change its offering. Immediately the system accommodates the change. A process of adjustment takes place which redistributes the market shares and establishes a new equilibrium. Then the new equilibrium may once again be disturbed by supplying firms attempting to recoup their lost position or perhaps to improve an already superior position.

A simple example will illustrate this point. Every Friday evening, a mass exodus of students traveled both east and west from a large midwestern university to spend the weekend at home. Some traveled by private automobile, some hitchhiked, and some went by Greyhound bus. The proportions traveling by each method of transport were fairly fixed over time. Thus, each method of transport enjoyed a reasonably constant market share, and a state of equilibrium existed. However, the equilibrium was disturbed by the addition of AMTRAK train service. The train fare was sufficiently low so that many students who used to hitchhike or drive now took the train. As a countermeasure, Greyhound doubled the number of buses running in both directions and reduced the price. The result was a rearrangement of market share with more total students riding trains and buses. To illustrate the dynamics of this system, two years later the railroad cancelled the passenger run, causing a new set of adjustments. With the advent of the energy crisis of the mid-1970s, rail service was once again initiated due to the gasoline shortage. Thus, once again a disequilibrium was experienced which resulted in adjustment and a new set of market shares followed.

A disturbance can have its roots in a behavioral change initiated by a purchasing unit and does not necessarily result from managerial action among suppliers or governmental decisions. The automobile-consuming public's immediate response to the energy crisis forced auto manufacturers within weeks to cut production of large cars, to increase production of small cars immediately, and to speed up plans to introduce high gas mileage cars. This disturbance not only changed the market shares for different size autos, but, depending upon the speed with which the principal manufacturers were able to respond, had an effect on the market shares of each. For a short period in early 1974, American Motors was the only domestic manufacturer who enjoyed a sales increase.

The above examples illustrate the ecological nature of our competitive system. It is a closed system; it must be closed to function. However, it has the capacity to open up and admit new participants—new supplying firms and purchasing units—or to eject old ones.[8] It has the capacity to adjust to any new set of relationships between the participants. The system is dynamic in nature, since any change results in a new equilibrium unsatisfactory to some participants. As participants attempt to improve their positions, new sets of adjustments are called for. Thus, the competitive system is in a continual state of adjustment to the many changes thrust upon it.

COMPETITIVE UNCERTAINTY

So far we have not explained the motivation for change, which is an integral part of our competitive system. These motivational forces are found in the *uncertainty* present in the system. So central is the presence of uncertainty to the market affairs of the firm and so tremendous is its effect on the firm's competitive posture that a thorough understanding of uncertainty

---

[8] For a more complete discussion of the paradox of openness and closure at the same time, see Wroe Alderson, *Marketing Behavior and Executive Action* (Homewood, Ill.: Richard D. Irwin, Inc., 1957), pp. 117–20.

is essential. Uncertainty exists because of the division of labor and because we politically and economically uphold freedom of choice in both consumption and production. These characteristics of our society are highly prized, and it is not our purpose to examine their merits; however, it should be pointed out that alternative ideologies do not minimize uncertainty.

The uncertainty present is of three types: that related to time and space, that caused by the inability to aggregate purchasing unit preferences, and that resulting from freedom of choice in the producing sector.

TIME AND SPACE

Because of specialization output is generally for sale at a future time and in a market geographically distant. A farmer plants winter wheat in the fall for harvesting and sale in late summer. At the time of planting he has incurred much out-of-pocket cost, but he has no way of determining what price his wheat will command several months later. Even when the time of sale approaches, information received on the radio midday crop report does not entirely remove the uncertainty of the best day on which to sell. Prices are quoted in fractions of a cent and they change frequently throughout the day. Uncertainty is perhaps even greater for the manufacturer of nonstandardized goods.

A Detroit toy manufacturer starts production in March on toys to be sold in June, for October delivery to businessmen in Los Angeles. The latter will sell to consumers in November and December. Any number of events over which the manufacturer has no control may influence ability to dispose of the inventory at the predetermined time. Whenever production is completed in anticipation of sale during a future period, costs must be incurred and the risk of recouping them, along with profits for the effort, is always present. There is no way of knowing that the output will be sold at the anticipated prices and time. Regardless, management must make every effort to assess the probabilities of favorable outcomes before committing corporate resources.

INABILITY TO AGGREGATE PURCHASING UNIT PREFERENCES

Even if the uncertainty of time and space could be overcome, the inability to predetermine purchasing unit preferences would still remain as a source of uncertainty for managers. As long as purchasing units are free to choose those products which most closely match their needs and desires, the information requirements of the decision maker are dispersed among individuals he is seeking to satisfy. There is no known method of delving into the minds of the millions of purchasing units to determine precisely what they desire or upon which fundamental points they agree. In our high-level economy the desires of the consuming public are extremely meticulous. At times they appear almost whimsical. Purchasers today examine a wide range of products available, and select from among the many brands the one they think will most closely satisfy their preferences. There are those who would have us believe that business does have the means to determine precisely what the customer wants and the means to "manage" his wants in one direction or another.[9]

It is true that to some extent the purchaser can be influenced if the offering happens to parallel his latent desires. But the number of business failures each year gives testimony to the inability to manipulate the consuming public. Granted, the causes of business failure are many, but the unacceptability of the product in the marketplace is surely a major one. Even giant corporations possessed of all the skills and abundant talent are not immune to the fickleness of the marketplace.

Many a new offering, such as General Electric's Eletrak (battery-powered garden tractors), H. J. Heinz's concentrated tomato juice, and Du Pont's Corfam, failed to develop sufficient customer acceptance to sustain production. The financial commitments in these ventures varied in size, but all were sufficiently large to justify the most sophisticated research available. Such failures are discouraging but should be expected. They help instill respect for the risks connected with the uncertainty of consumer acceptance. To assess the probabilities of success, every effort must be made to analyze market desires as completely as possible. Managerially, the enterprise must tackle this problem with vigor, while at the same time recognizing that complete success in aggregating purchasing preference is as yet unattainable.

FREEDOM OF CHOICE IN PRODUCTION

The converse of freedom of choice in consumption is freedom of choice in production. The production structure compatible with a free society is one in which there is an absence of barriers to entry or exit. Freedom exists on the part of all participants to decide what they will offer for sale. It should be recognized that, in reality, in our economy various barriers to entry do exist. Some, such as the granting of public utility franchises, are consciously imposed by the government. Others are imposed by the large-scale concentration of economic power by specific firms

---

[9] John K. Galbraith, *The New Industrial State* (Boston: Houghton-Mifflin Company, 1967).

and the heavy investment requirements prior to market entry. The magnitude of these barriers varies. In addition, government has attempted to disburse excessive concentrations of power through judicial and administrative processes. Notwithstanding such limitations, there is relative freedom of entry and exit in our economy's production structure.

In entering a new product on the market, even though the management of a firm is able to make fairly accurate predictions about events related to time and space and purchasing unit preferences, they still must consider potential retaliatory actions by other firms unfavorably influenced.

The speed with which other firms follow successful moves makes the calculation of lead time and pay-out periods an extremely important part of the decision to introduce a new market offering. For example, recall the speed with which General Motors followed Ford's Pinto with the Vega, and how quickly every major brewery followed Drewry's with a bottled draft beer. We call this rapid adjustment *neutralization*. Because the possibility of rapid neutralization exists, the gains realized by the innovator must be swift because competitors can be expected to react in an effort to redivide market shares.

An example from the transportation industry illustrates the validity of concern with the speed of competitive reaction. Prior to 1970, most agricultural chemicals were moved by train. Around 1971, the river barge system, with its favorable cost structure, virtually took over this movement. By 1973, the rails had regained the chemical traffic share by virtue of new equipment and price innovations coupled with the potential pollution danger of continued river movement.

Since uncertainty concerning competition is diffused among all purchasers and supplying firms, it is impossible to eliminate and difficult to bring within tolerable limits for managerial decision purposes.

UNCERTAINTY—A PERMANENT FACTOR

The sources of the uncertainty we have been discussing have an enduring quality. Although many advances have been made in managerial tools in the last thirty years, such as the development of refined consumer research techniques, rapid information retrieval systems, computer simulations, and an improved body of decision-making theory, little has been accomplished in removing the sources of uncertainty. In 1945 the problem faced in a free society was stated as follows:

> If we possess all the relevant information, *if* we can start out from a given set of preferences and *if* we command complete knowledge of available means, the problem that remains is purely one of logic.

> ... The peculiar character of the problem of a rational economic order is determined precisely by the fact that the knowledge of the circumstances of which we must make use never exists in concentrated or integrated form, but solely as the dispersed bits of incomplete and frequently contradictory knowledge which all the separate individuals possess.[10]

Again in 1965 the problem was presented:

> The exact number of agencies required by the country and their assortment by type, size, location, and the like could no doubt be worked out mathematically under two conditions:
> (1) If we had complete and detailed data concerning the choices consumers would make for themselves as to what goods and services the economy should produce. ... The problem would be eased for the engineers, of course, if an all-powerful rationing board were to standardize choices for consumers. Whether the consumer would be better off is less certain ...
> (2) If the standards of service to be met also were fixed and specified. ... Here again an administrative decision would simplify the mathematicians' problem, but we cannot arbitrarily assume that it would serve the consumer better.[11]

The increase in social and geographic mobility, the general affluence within the economy, the wide range of customer choices, and the great variety of competitive strategies by an increased number of firms have probably caused an increase in uncertainty over the past thirty years.

The normal competitive condition in the mid 1970s is characterized as a state of pervasive uncertainty. For our purposes the more crucial issue relates to how the firm rationalizes uncertainty and reduces the inherent risk of related decisions.

MARKET DECISION MAKING IN A COMPETITIVE ENVIRONMENT

The decision maker must use every means possible to reduce the uncertainty faced in the marketplace. This means a continuous monitoring of market trends to anticipate future events and sustained investigation of markets to assess purchasing unit preferences more accurately. Also, the

---

[10] F. A. Hayek, "The Use of Knowledge in Society," *The American Economic Review,* XXXV (September 1945), 519.

[11] Cox, *Distribution,* pp. 78–79.

retaliatory actions of competitors must be continuously anticipated. One of the more difficult problems today is to determine or identify the competitors for strategic purposes. For example, is a manufacturer of outboard motorboats competing solely against other makers of outboard motorboats or against producers of all types of power pleasure boats; makers of any kind of boat, including row boats, sailboats, and canoes; all businesses offering recreational services or products; and any enterprises offering any product or service used to occupy leisure time? Identification of the market is crucial. Is the manufacturer in the outboard motorboat market, the power boat market, the boating market, the recreation market, or the leisure market? In reality, he functions, in part, in all of these markets.

Since competition is a dynamic process, the firm must be prepared to watch old decisions lose their effectiveness. Management must be innovative enough to renew its vitality constantly. The speed with which successful offerings are neutralized by competing firms makes necessary a willingness continually to change product-service offerings if the firm is to be successful in capitalizing on market opportunity. There are complex competitive issues related to instances in which a firm can appropriately provide market leadership. In contrast there are other occasions when it should follow the leadership of rival firms. In either case, there is little place for corporate nostalgia if the firm is to grow, survive, and perpetuate itself. All actions taken by the firm should be predicated on an appraisal of how purchasing units will react to the total market offering and of what retaliation can be expected from rivals. Managements vary in their ability to cope with uncertainty. It is such management variation that results in a competitive environment made up of profits and losses and market leaders and market followers.

With this understanding of the environmental field in which the firm conducts its affairs, we next examine the importance of a market orientation as a philosophy of business management.

SUMMARY

The environment within which a business enterprise functions influences, and is influenced by, the myriad of choices made by independent decision makers in the millions of business enterprises making up our economy and those made by the many more millions of purchasing units. Those actions in which the particular firm participates constitute the competitive state. Only through understanding the competitive environment can the decision maker assess the forces affecting the outcomes of his decisions and the need to exercise creativity in a continuous process of innovative and retaliatory actions.

Competition is a process in which purchasing units adjust to supplying firms and supplying firms adjust to purchasing units. This process of adjustment is orderly and systematic. One way to describe the system is by the equilibrium analysis of economics. Under a structural economic approach, conflict between participants is resolved through a balancing of supply and demand for goods and the factors of production. The resulting market structures, pure competition, pure monopoly, monopolistic competition, and oligopoly were reviewed from the point of view of their structural characteristics and resulting intensity of price competition. The major limitation to such a structural approach is that it describes a result rather than the actions taken to arrive at the new equilibrium state.

Another way to view the competitive process is as an ecological system. The systems approach is a way of studying a complex whole by studying the individual parts and their relationships. An ecological system is one in which the relationships existing between various parts determine the actions taken individually, and the interaction continues until an equilibrium is achieved. An ecological system has the capacity to admit new parts or eject old ones, and it immediately sets in motion a set of actions to restore equilibrium once there has been a change in relationships. In an ecological approach to the competitive system, the participants are the supplying firms and the purchasing units. Each is adjusting to the other, and as the supplying firms strive to improve their position, new sets of adjustments take place. The motivational forces stimulating departures from equilibrium are found in the uncertainty present in the system.

Uncertainty in the system is related to the unpredictability of time and space factors; in our inability to anticipate behavior of purchasing units; and our inability to forecast retaliatory action of competitors.

The normal competitive condition in the mid 1970s is characterized as a state of pervasive uncertainty. Decision making in a competitive environment requires a continuous monitoring of market trends to anticipate future events and a sustained investigation of markets to assess purchasing unit preferences. It requires as well a recognition of the dynamic character of competition and a creative, innovative capacity to maintain the competitive posture of the enterprise.

QUESTIONS AND PROBLEMS

1. Explain how competition is a process of adjustment.
2. In what way does the division of labor create a need for adjustment?
3. What is an ecological system? How can the ecological approach be used to describe our competitive economy?

4. Explain how the ecological system is open and closed at the same time.
5. How does uncertainty stimulate firms to act in the marketplace?
6. What are the sources of uncertainty in a free economy?
7. Why is uncertainty still a problem with all our advanced technological and scientific breakthroughs?
8. How does freedom of choice in production create uncertainty?

Chapter 2

Market Orientation as a Philosophy of Business Management

Business management in the contemporary world economy is a highly complex process that cannot be easily characterized. Stated succinctly, business management involves the planning, organizing, and controlling of a combination of "inputs" to achieve a predetermined series of "outputs." This means that the administration of the firm should be a goal-directed effort, letting objectives guide the way in which men, materials, machines, and money are combined into operating systems. Although objectives influencing the administrative behavior of a firm are extremely diverse, they share a common orientation. Most generally, *a firm seeks to grow and to perpetuate itself, in addition to earning for its owners, managers, and employees an ever-improving return for effort.*

Business management is also a dynamic process. Faced with rigorous competition, accelerating technology, and a continuously changing operating environment, management must stand ready to make adjustments in its goals, organization, policies, and systems. Above all, the firm must maintain competitive vitality in the marketplace.

A business firm is organized to produce and distribute goods and services of economic value. In a free market economy, for any good or service to have value, it must have want-satisfying power called utility, and it must be scarce. A good which has utility but which is abundant, such as air, is a "free good," and hence has no or limited market value. Once produced, goods must be made available to consumers via the exchange process. The essential end of all production—both for the individual firm and for the economy as a whole—is consumption. Finance is a facilitative function basic to the whole business process. From a managerial point of view, however, *the firm is engaged in integrated production* (creation of utility) *to serve most profitably an area of market opportunity.*

Markets are the lifeblood of the business. They represent the firm's principal source of revenue. It is in satisfying the needs and performances of buyers constituting the market that a firm finds economic justification for its existence. A realization of the importance of the market substantially sharpens the focus of the whole business process. It properly presents a market orientation as the cornerstone in a managerial philosophy to guide the actions of the firm. Firms are often characterized as machine tool manufacturers, food processors, dressmakers, steel fabricators, or heating and air-conditioning assemblers. These characterizations that emphasize the principal employment activity of the firm are descriptively helpful. Yet such classifications do not adequately convey the managerial orientation of the firm. Such activities are only preparatory to achieving the main goal of the firm, which is *profitably serving markets in which these products are consumed.*

We have purposely cast a market orientation as a philosophy of business management in a competitive framework. The way in which an enterprise implements a market orientation is also useful to institutions operating outside the competitive system. Such institutions as agencies of government, churches, hospitals, and labor unions have substantial reason to implement a market orientation to guide managerial action. The universality of marketing and specific application in the public and non-business sectors is treated in Part VI.

Our objective in Chapter 2 is to elaborate the basic reasons that a market orientation is essential in a competitive economy. First, the firm is presented in an overall perspective in order to stress the interrelationship of all parts that make up the enterprise. Next, the concept of market veto power is developed. The philosophy of a market orientation and its managerial implications from both a competitive and cooperative perspective is discussed in the following two sections. The chapter concludes with a formal definition of marketing.

PROFITS GUIDE THE EFFECTIVE FUNCTIONING OF THE FIRM AS A WHOLE

If the dominant goal of the enterprise is to serve profitably an area of market opportunity, then the firm must fully capitalize upon those of its assets and distinctive qualities that make for lasting competitive superiority. In carving a niche for itself in the market, each firm must employ its resources in such a way as to develop a total "personality" for competitive purposes that gives it the greatest economic power and that rivals will find hardest to neutralize. In this mission, all resources of the firm are pertinent, including its research and development talents, engineering skills, production efficiency and know-how, and the effectiveness of its marketing organization.

When one thinks of all the factors that can make for competitive superiority, it becomes obvious that the operation of the firm as a *whole* must be considered primary, rather than the functioning of any one of the parts. Moreover, in striving for profit maximization, management's problem is one of effective integration and combination of all the parts of the enterprise. In this sense, then, it cannot be said that marketing is more important than any other functional part of the firm, any more than it can be said that the carburetor is a more important part of a gasoline engine than the ignition system. The efficient functioning of the engine depends upon the optimum operation of each of the parts in a mutually dependent way. Translating this systems notion into management terms, we can think of the firm as consisting of a profit pipeline, into one end of which flows a series of inputs, ultimately being transformed into a series of outputs at the other end. In between, acting as successive valves or gates in the profit pipeline, are the principal functional phases of operations which account either directly or indirectly for this transformation. For profits, which are the energizing force within the business, to flow in an optimum way, all gates must be open. Close any one gate and the profit pipeline becomes clogged. Figure 2-1 is a pictorial illustration of the pipeline.

FIGURE 2-1
Business Functions in the Profit Pipeline

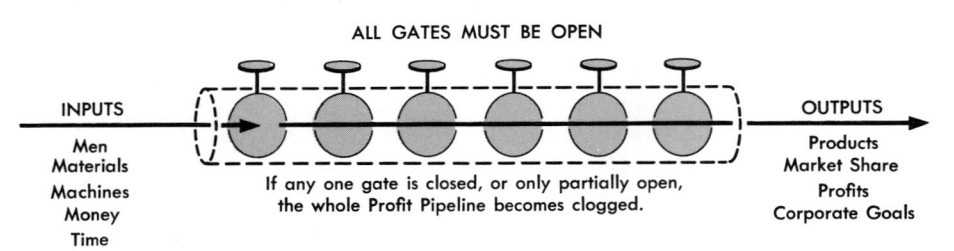

ALL GATES MUST BE OPEN

INPUTS

Men
Materials
Machines
Money
Time

If any one gate is closed, or only partially open, the whole Profit Pipeline becomes clogged.

OUTPUTS

Products
Market Share
Profits
Corporate Goals

The operations of most enterprises center around functional relationships such as production, shown as gates in the illustration. When performance in any area is inferior, the firm as a whole may be incapable of achieving its overall objectives. A few selected examples will illustrate the point.

The crucial importance for many firms of research and development is evidenced by the fact that many companies project that a major proportion of their sales in the next ten years will come from new products. American industry more and more is dependent upon technological development for its well-being. Product replacement has become more rapid. The profitable length of life of many products is consequently much shorter than once was the case. For instance, in the electronics industry, three years is believed to be a long period of time for any firm to expect to have a preferred technological position with a product before competitors offer improved replacements. This means that firms are required to spend an increasing number of dollars for research and development if the overall goal is to be realized.

The coordination of personnel management and industrial relations is very important to attainment of goals. Human resources are perhaps the most significant asset of any firm. The success of the firm, to a great extent, depends upon the quality of its people and their effective utilization. Indicative of this is the current widespread management interest in executive development programs, to provide able administrators to keep pace with industrial growth and decentralization, and provide a continuous supply of top management personnel. In the industrial relations area, consider the cost to any manufacturer of a prolonged strike. Millions of dollars in profits are lost directly by shutdown, and more millions indirectly before overall market position can be recaptured. To estimate accurately the total real cost of such a strike is almost impossible.

The importance to the firm of sound financial management is obvious. Capital budgeting and financial controls are a normal part of day-to-day operations in any soundly managed enterprise. Moreover, with the current rate of industrial expansion, long-range financial planning is increasingly essential if growth opportunities are not to be lost. It has been said that the end result sought for any business is financial, and all other activities are merely a means to the end. While such a position overstates the case and is also oversimplified, none would deny the key influence to business welfare of good financial planning and control.

Production for many enterprises accounts for the bulk of personnel and the major expenditure of funds. In some industries, such as the manufacturing of fractional horsepower electric motors, the ability to match competitors' costs in automated line production is a prerequisite to engaging in serious competition. That production is closely interdependent with marketing should also be noted at this point. Actually, one finds its meaning in the other. The major dichotomy between the two so often found in industry is neither sound nor practical. This viewpoint will be expanded later on.

These selected examples and comments are intended to stress the need for integration of a firm as a whole rather than any of its operational parts. The chief executive officer of the company cannot become preoccupied with the overriding importance of any one functional area as compared with another. While some companies are primarily oriented in one particular way—such as soap companies being primarily merchandising organizations and scientific instrument companies being oriented to technical research and engineering—the point still holds: the operation of the firm should be looked at as a total system of action. Consequently, the gasoline engine analogy holds. In this sense no one functional area of the firm is more important than any other functional phase of company operations. There is one overriding and all-powerful consideration: *it is the force of the marketplace that provides the focus for management action.*

MARKET VETO POWER AND MANAGEMENT ACTION

While all individual actions taken in the functional areas can be considered as within management discretion, *it is the market which sanctions all the preceding steps prior to the making of a sale. This is to say that the market holds at least veto power over the entire system.* What is done in research and development, production design, production scheduling, quality control, inventory control, and the like must ultimately meet the test of the marketplace: Do buyers give their approval through allocating their own resources for the purchase of the product in sufficient quantities and at adequate prices? Since this veto power exists, and since the firm is organized for the purpose of profitably serving market opportunity, it follows that the adjustments the firm makes should be market oriented. The synthesis of this point of view is conceptually diagrammed in Figure 2-2.

The flow diagram, Figure 2-2, shows raw materials (or in whatever state purchased by the firm) entering the enterprise, and through design, equipment, human effort, and organizational systems and procedures being transformed into products destined for ultimate use. The managerial adjustments underlying the system as a whole are shown to be market oriented, or based on market requirements and specifications. Conviction to this fundamental notion is basic to any soundly managed, mature enterprise in a competitive free market economy. Value added to the product increases with each succeeding phase of operations within the system.

The philosophical objective of this system of action is maximum impact at the point of ultimate sale to precipitate purchase action within the boundary of cost and revenue relationships. The qualification is important. Maximizing impact alone is not the objective. Reaching profit goals is a prime target. Stated differently, this means *matching total effort with market opportunity.* The effort in terms of manpower and dollars should be only as much as the market justifies. Also, this effort must not only be of the right quantity, but of the right quality and character for greatest market influence. Operationally, this precise point is extremely difficult to determine, much less reach. To approach this ideal, an optimum combination of all cost centers wherever they exist is necessary (be they manufacturing or distributive), and the combination should be focused on market requirements. It is basically less time-consuming—and more profitable—for management to adjust its offering to the market environment, rather than to try to change the market environment to be responsive to what management prefers to supply. The old adage "You can have any color you want so long as it is black" may represent a happy state of affairs for a production executive, but it is as out of date as a sound business philosophy as the Model T Ford to which it was applied.

FIGURE 2-2
Integrated Production-Marketing System

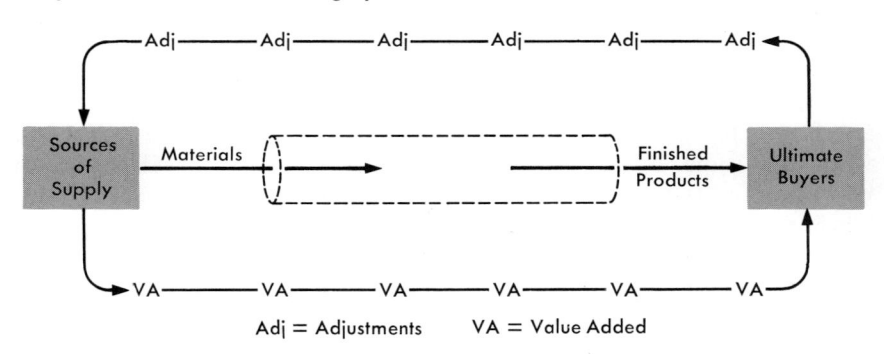

Adj = Adjustments   VA = Value Added

There are, however, circumstances when a firm cannot focus all effort on satisfying market requirements. For example, after a large fixed investment has been made to produce a specific product to meet market requirements, a firm may be confronted with a rapid shift in demand preference. Under such conditions, it may be necessary for the short run to involve every ounce of ingenuity and marketing capability to bend demand to available supply.

APPLICATION OF THE MARKETING PHILOSOPHY

Given that the dominant goal of a private enterprise is to serve profitably an area of market opportunity, the two most important functions of the firm are *negotiation* and the *seeking of market leadership*. Each is discussed below. A third function important to application of a marketing philosophy, *seeking cooperative relationships,* is discussed in a later section of this chapter.

NEGOTIATION

In any system in which there is a division of labor, exchange is mandatory and must be preceded by negotiation. In a very simple economy, negotiation can be seen in the haggling over price that goes on between the buyers and sellers in the marketplace. In our economy the act of negotiation is not so evident. Rarely do you have an opportunity to bargain with the salesperson in a retail store over the price you are willing to pay. There are cases, however, when you do, such as in the purchase of an automobile. When one businessman is buying from another, a fair amount of negotiation over price, terms, delivery dates, and service arrangements often takes place. In general, however, units purchasing for personal or household consumption do not negotiate in an overt manner.

Another kind of negotiation, however, does take place. It consists of a series of actions taken by a supplying firm to adjust whatever it is offering to more closely match the expectations of the purchasing unit. The firm is trying to ensure that it has the right product in the right place at the right time. If experience proves that it has failed, it will engage in another round of actions to influence the purchasing unit more favorably. Consider the number of ways a typical department store tries to negotiate with you as a customer. First, it tries to offer an assortment of merchandise which is complete and has depth in variety; then, it displays this merchandise in an attractive setting, hires and trains a competent sales staff, offers convenient parking, delivers merchandise to your home, lets you pay thirty days later, and at least once a week informs you in its advertising of any special purchases it has made or special prices at which it will offer merchandise. The store is negotiating with you for your patronage. You, in turn, negotiate, and your ability to do so effectively depends upon your knowledge of alternative sources of supply and your ability to select that merchandise which most closely fits your needs and desires. Although bartering is not practiced in our economic system, ultimate consumers are exceptionally skillful in the way they negotiate with supplying firms. The amount of interstore and also intrastore shopping done for some products illustrates some consumers' negotiating capacity. Sometimes alternatives are limited, and this is a weakness of the system. Sometimes there are so many items to choose from that it is difficult to select. But what an advantage this condition is over the opposite state of affairs!

SEEKING MARKET LEADERSHIP

Market leadership is sought because it provides the foundation for negotiation. What is market leadership? Market leadership consists of four capabilities:

1. The capability to enter selected markets.
2. The capability to achieve a large market share rapidly.
3. The capability to maintain market share over time.
4. The capability to exit or deviate when desired.

Although the *capability to enter selected markets* may be taken for granted, some of the most successful marketing organizations in the country have been unsuccessful. Even a giant like RCA was unable to penetrate the computer market successfully and had to drop out.

The *capability to achieve a large market share rapidly* cannot be understated in a competitive economy in which neutralization is swift and costs of product development and entry must be recouped quickly. Bombadier was one of the first in the snowmobile market with its line of Skidoo machines. Although competitors entered the market, the large share achieved by Skidoo endured for many years. Once a market share is achieved, displacement by new entrants is difficult.

The *capability to maintain market share over time* requires careful monitoring of trends and constant adjustment in offerings. There is ample evidence that after a few years of success, a complacency sets in and managements often take success for granted. Coca-Cola, long a leader in the soft drink field, was one of the last to enter the diet drink field, and then only after it had lost its overall dominant market share position.

The *capability to exit when desired* is one of the most difficult aspects of leadership. In a dynamic environment in which management must be constantly innovating, mistakes are bound to be made. Unless a product mistake is recognized early and management takes corrective action, leadership positions in other products and markets may be drained. An example of an exit decision is Du Pont dropping Corfam after millions of dollars were spent and many years of development went into market development.

If these four features are the characteristics of market leadership, how is it obtained in a competitive economy? In any negotiation, a certain amount of conflict exists, as each party is attempting to fare better than the other. Of course, no exchange takes place until each feels he is gaining. Throughout the negotiation, each will try to favorably resolve the conflict. Yet the supplying firm cannot legally exert pressure on the purchasing unit. As we have discussed, the purchasing unit is sovereign!

The purchaser selects from the array of offerings provided by a number of competing firms. It is the capability of the purchasing unit to either accept or reject offerings that creates the uncertainty and competition in a free society. The leadership of any single supplying firm is weakened if the purchasing unit elects to patronize another firm. Consequently, leadership results from purchasing unit preference. The only way leadership can be achieved by a supplying firm is through establishing loyalty among purchasing units. When such loyalty is established, the firm is said to have found an ecological niche. This is a position of market strength based on purchase unit loyalty. If the loyalty is strong a firm will be in a position to exercise leadership. Rarely is such leadership enduring. The very success of a firm will trigger a series of actions by competitive firms attempting to recoup their lost position—or if they are particularly aggressive, to improve an already strong position.

COMPETITION FOR DIFFERENTIAL ADVANTAGE

Leadership is obtained through differentiation. Differentiation allows the supplying firm to identify its product-service offering by giving it some distinction. The objective is to create a preference among purchasing units that is sufficiently strong to withstand the negotiating efforts of other firms seeking the purchasing unit's patronage. The number of ways a firm may differentiate its offering is endless, and requires maximum creativity of those responsible for the market affairs of the firm. Most means of differentiation can be easily copied by competition. The task is to seek differentiation that cannot be readily duplicated. Some of the more common forms of differentiation are (1) physical differentiation of the product, (2) psychological differentiation through communication, (3) differentiation in the purchase environment, (4) differentiation by virtue of physical distribution capability, (5) differentiation in after-purchase assurances of satisfaction in use, and (6) differentiation in price and terms of sale.

Physical differentiation of the product is a most common form. Even a Heinz bottle of tomato ketchup looks considerably different than a bottle of Hunt's ketchup. It is difficult to imagine an Audi looking exactly like a Datsun. Even though a large amount of money is spent on physical product differentiation, additional sums are expended to communicate these real, and to a degree imaginary, differentiations to the marketplace. Copywriters in advertising agencies are paid large salaries to ensure that the advertising copy of the client is different from that of the client's competition. Considerable effort and expense is incurred to make sure a K-Mart store does not look the same as a Woolco, and who would expect a Ford dealership to be identical to that of a Chevrolet dealership? Considerable difference exists between order processing time and degree of product delivery consistency between major competitors in an industry. The differentiation in after-purchase assurances of satisfaction in use is vividly illustrated in the service organization of Westinghouse elevators. Equally important is provision for repair parts and trained service personnel for practically all machinery. Price and terms of sale are, of course, differentiating elements that can be very important. They are listed last because they are a form of differentiation most easily duplicated by competition. An interesting exercise is to select any basic product, then three or four brand names, and write down the various ways in which the suppliers try to achieve distinction by differentiation.

Differentiation is aimed at obtaining purchasing unit loyalty. Loyalty in turn reduces risk. The process of seeking differential advantage creates competition. Because the actions taken are designed to differentiate between sellers, the interaction can be viewed as a *competition for differential advantage*. Because these actions affect the relationships between firms and purchasing units, they constitute the competitive market affairs of the enterprise.

In summary, through negotiation and differentiation a firm seeks market leadership. The successful firm reduces risk. Profits are, in part, a payment for risk. Thus, firms should not always seek the lowest risk alternatives—not if growth of profitability is a powerful objective for the enterprise (which it normally is). Profits generally reflect the degree of risk entailed in any venture. With staple food products, for which demand does not fluctuate widely, profit as a percent of sales is generally low. In contrast, profit-sales ratios on many durable goods are relatively high because durables suffer from wide fluctuations in sales volume due to consumers' capability to postpone purchases. The opposite way the market reacted for recreation vehicles and economy cars during the initial months of the energy crisis illustrates the inherent risk involved in marketing.

Thus, management is always concerned with the substance of the resources that can be mobilized to achieve market leadership. The objective is to gain a differential advantage over rivals, which is hard to emulate and of enduring value. A firm must acquire and nurture a distinctive competence that is the foundation of differential advantage. This relatively complex underpinning to the notion of market orientation is important, and we shall explore and illuminate it throughout this book.

COOPERATIVE MARKETING ACTIONS

Although the greatest share of a decision maker's time is concerned with competition for differential advantage, not all actions related to the market are competitive.[1] A great many activities are *cooperative*.

---

[1] See Chapter 22 for a discussion of marketing in noncompetitive systems.

Cooperation is frequent among agricultural producers. On both a formal and informal basis, select farmers pool output of a standardized commodity and rely on a cooperative association to market it. Cooperation between firms in the channel of distribution is essential if a broad assortment of different manufacturers' products are to be found at a single retail store. We also can observe examples of industry-wide cooperation in advertising campaigns conducted by trade associations—for example, "Every litter bit helps." Some cooperative advertising conducted by trade associations is designed to increase demand for a class of product or service rather than for a single competitor. For example, the American Railroad Association and the American Trucking Association conduct extensive image advertising to explain to the public the many virtues of their respective members' services.

Integration is another form of cooperative action. This technique involves tying together different parts of the production and marketing process through outright ownership or on the basis of a contractual and administrative arrangement. The franchise agreements binding together the numerous Holiday Inns within the United States are representative of such integration.

Another departure from competitive action is the assumption by government of certain activities affecting relationships between buyers and sellers. Illustrative is the regulation of rates in the public utilities and transportation industries. Other examples are the production control and market support programs in agriculture and petroleum. Another circumstance of cooperative behavior, although imposed, is the compliance actions dictated by the government agencies and courts in behalf of consumer and environmentalist groups. All of the above forms of behavior must be combined with the process of competition for differential advantage in order to understand the full range of affairs involved in managerial marketing.

WHAT IS MARKETING?

The definition of marketing has deliberately been avoided up to this point because of the necessity for placing the role and function of marketing in the perspective of a total system of action carried on by the firm. The Committee on Definition of the American Marketing Association defines marketing as "those activities which direct the flow of goods and services from production to consumption."[2]

---

[2] R. S. Alexander, et al., *Marketing Definitions* (Chicago: American Marketing Association, 1960).

This definition, although widely accepted, does not emphasize either the competitive role of marketing in the total economy, or the scope of managerial responsibility for a specific firm's marketing activity. Rather, the AMA definition implies a physical process of matching the heterogeneity of supply and demand. From a managerial viewpoint, two specific notes of caution are urged in using this definition. First, those charged with marketing responsibilities within the firm dare not think of their job as *starting* with goods on the shipping platform. Secondly, and at the other end of the spectrum of responsibilities, executives cannot consider their job as *finished* when the cash register rings at the retail level or point of ultimate sale. Effective and creative marketing encompasses a broader area of activities at both ends of the scale. Because of our concern with viewing marketing as an integral part of competition and our emphasis on the managerial actions necessary for the firm to function in a competitive society, we prefer to define marketing managerially as *"the maintenance of profitable market leadership through responding to buyers' needs and wants."* What then is involved in the process at the firm level?

MARKET LEADERSHIP AND MANAGERIAL MARKETING ACTIVITIES

To this point we have been dealing with marketing at different levels of abstraction. We have described a competitive society and established the need for a market orientation as a philosophy of business management. Within this philosophy, we have suggested the two major functions of a firm are negotiation and the seeking of market leadership. Both are basic to the process of competition for differential advantage. To negotiate well and achieve market leadership requires management involvement in four basic activities:

1. Market Opportunity Assessment.
2. Product-Service Market Matching.
3. Marketing Programming.
4. Execution.

Although these four areas of activity constitute the remainder of this text, we shall discuss them very briefly relative to our understanding thus far. Market leadership is achieved through building loyalty relationships with potential purchasers and careful assessment of market needs and wants. *Market opportunity assessment* and selection of those markets in which the firm wishes to operate is the appropriate starting point. Once the target markets are selected there is a need to make a *product-service market match*. That is, the offering must match the needs and wants of the market if a differential advantage is to be achieved. Customer wants and needs are far more basic than products and services offered by sellers. The firm that can clearly perceive customer wants and needs and can translate these requirements into products and services has taken a long step toward achieving market leadership.

The old adage "If a man can write a better book, preach a better sermon, or make a better mouse trap than his neighbor, though he builds his house in the woods, the world will make a beaten path to his door," is nowhere less true than in modern competition. For a product or service to enjoy profitable market longevity, it must be available, communicated, and properly priced. Unless the managerial activities involved in marketing are properly programmed, profits may be jeopardized. This activity is described as *marketing programming*. Many a well-conceived product with a carefully designed market plan has failed in the marketplace because of poor *execution*. Thus, the managerial responsibility of "putting it all together" is equally important as the first three managerial activity areas. It is within each of these activity areas that we now explain in the next chapter the managerial functions of marketing.

SUMMARY

In order to visualize the logic of the first two chapters, examine Figure 2-3. In this figure, we can see the relationships existing between the competitive state in which we live and the two basic freedoms present in our society—freedom in production and freedom in consumption. Because of freedom in production, we have a division of labor or specialization and a heterogeneity of supply. Because of specialization and freedom in consumption, exchange is mandatory for individuals to participate in the economic process, thus a heterogeniety of demand. In the process of matching a heterogeneous demand with a heterogeneous supply, uncertainties for the supplying firms emerge. Because of specialization and freedom in consumption, an uncertainty concerning time and space arises. Because of freedom in production, an uncertainty concerning competitor retaliation is present. Because of freedom in consumption, uncertainty stemming from the supplying firm's inability to aggregate purchasing unit preferences enters the picture.

In a free society, the market has a veto power over the entire system. To affect these uncertainties, the supplying firm engages in two primary

FIGURE 2-3
Competition in a Free Society

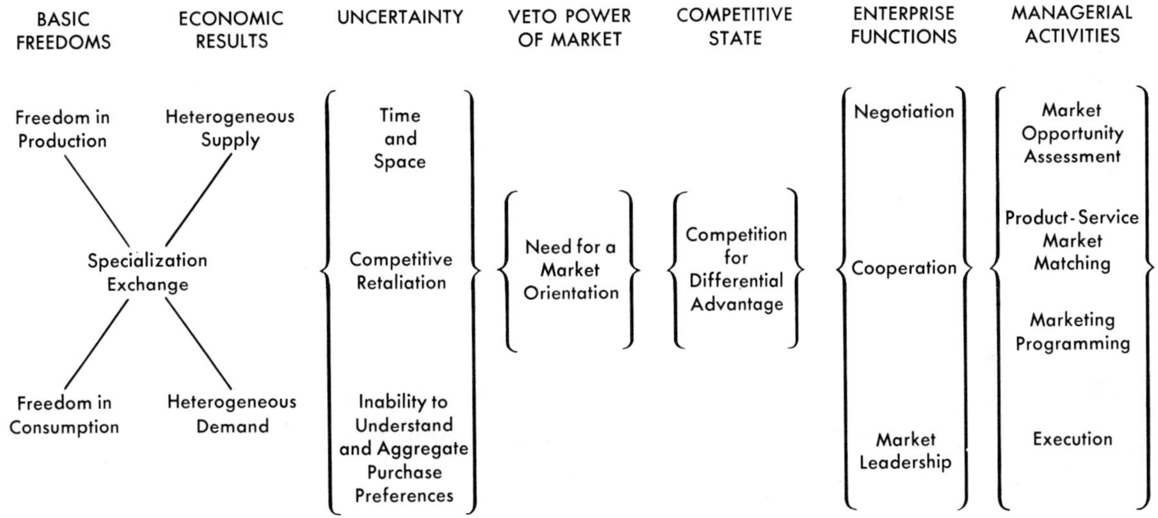

BASIC FREEDOMS	ECONOMIC RESULTS	UNCERTAINTY	VETO POWER OF MARKET	COMPETITIVE STATE	ENTERPRISE FUNCTIONS	MANAGERIAL ACTIVITIES
Freedom in Production	Heterogeneous Supply	Time and Space	Need for a Market Orientation	Competition for Differential Advantage	Negotiation	Market Opportunity Assessment
Specialization Exchange		Competitive Retaliation			Cooperation	Product-Service Market Matching
						Marketing Programming
Freedom in Consumption	Heterogeneous Demand	Inability to Understand and Aggregate Purchase Preferences			Market Leadership	Execution

functions. First is negotiation with the supplying firm hoping to come out of the exchange more successfully than his competition. Second is the search for market leadership through differentiation to build loyalty relationships with purchasing units. Also of importance to marketing are the cooperative affairs of the firm that influence managerial discretions.

So important is the search for market leadership that it becomes the substance of our managerial definition of marketing—*the maintenance of profitable market leadership through responding to buyers' needs and wants.* From a marketing action point of view, market leadership is achieved through managerial action in four activity areas—market opportunity assessment, product-service marketing matching, market programming, and execution. These activity areas structure the subject matter of each part of this book.

QUESTIONS AND PROBLEMS

1. What is meant by *integrated production?*
2. What are the principal common goals toward which all enterprises tend to strive?
3. Think of all the different roles of *profit* in our economy. What is its managerial significance?
4. Defend the notion that marketing is no more important than any other major function in the successful management of an enterprise.
5. How does the firm seek market leadership?
6. Select any product and write down the ways in which the manufacturer of a single brand of that product seeks market leadership.
7. What is competition for differential advantage?
8. What is the alternative to competition for differential advantage? Do you think it would be socially desirable?

Chapter 3

The Managerial Functions of Marketing

The profit orientation discussed in Chapter 2 requires the enterprise to function as a total system of action. That is, no single area of managerial action—research and development, purchasing, personnel management, labor relations, finance, production, or marketing—is more important than any other area. The need for a market orientation as an overall philosophy of business management results from the fact that markets hold veto power over all competitors. A specific firm achieves its goals through profitably serving selected areas of market opportunity. To enjoy success the firm must realize a differential advantage in the eyes of a significant share of the total market. An enterprise achieves such differential advantage as a result of its *overall* capability to negotiate, seek cooperative arrangements, and realize market leadership within the competitive market structure.

One should not mistake the fundamental need for an overall enterprise market orientation as being synonymous with the process of managerial marketing. Marketing management is a subject of total corporate management that contributes to the overall quest for differential advantage by the performance of market opportunity assessment, product-service matching, market planning, and execution, shown in Figure 3-1. In order to clarify further this abstract construct of the managerial marketing actions necessary to gain differential advantage, we now turn our attention to specific functions which must be performed within each activity area. This we identify as the *managerial functions of marketing.*

It is important to realize that the managerial functions of marketing are distinct from the functions of the firm—negotiation, cooperation, and market leadership—in a competitive environment. The latter are adequate to describe the role of the enterprise in the total economy, but are too general to give operational direction to marketing managers. Thus, in this chapter we complete the transition from *macro* marketing to *micro* managerial marketing. The first part of the chapter identifies the specific managerial functions of marketing. The final part considers the coordination of managerial marketing from a systems perspective.

FIGURE 3-1
Managerial marketing activities

[Diagram: Four circles arranged in a cycle — Opportunity (top), Product (right), Program (bottom), Execution (left) — with arrows flowing clockwise, and "Leadership" in the center.]

The following managerial functions of marketing are set forth with the view that they apply to any enterprise. They provide a basis for auditing, through functional analysis, the efficiency of a firm's marketing effort. Such is the prime requisite for classifying marketing functions.[1]

---

[1] Considerable debate has taken place over the years with regard to the functions of marketing. Although there is no common agreement as to what these functions are, perhaps the most widely accepted breakdown is the following: (A) Exchange functions: (1) Buying; (2) Selling—(B) Physical supply functions: (1) Transportation; (2) Storage—(C) Facilitating functions: (1) Finance; (2) Risk taking; (3) Standardization and grading; (4) Marketing information. This classification is useful when thinking in aggregate economic terms. It points up the fact that these functions cannot be eliminated from the total marketing process. But although these functions cannot be eliminated, they *can* be shifted back and forth among institutions—e.g., retailers such as supermarkets shift a part of the transportation function to consumers. This functional classification, however, has several limitations from a managerial marketing point of view.

FUNCTIONS RELATED TO MARKET OPPORTUNITY ASSESSMENT

The overall objective of opportunity assessment is to isolate target markets that have the sales potential to meet corporate objectives. Opportunity assessment involves two managerial functions: *market delineation* and *purchase behavior motivation*.

MARKET DELINEATION

Every seller must ascertain in some way or other the potential buyers for his product. This is the first requisite for effective marketing performance.
The market may be delineated by as simple a device as hanging a sign out close to a farmhouse, "FRESH EGGS 89¢ A DOZEN," which automatically tends to sort out the potential buyers from among the general population of passersby. At the other extreme, an elaborate market research program may be employed to determine carefully the potential buyers. Broadly understood, market delineation includes not only determining who the potential buyers are but also the other relevant quantitative factors that serve to delineate or define the market. For example: Where are the buyers located? When do they buy? How frequently do they purchase, and in what quantities? Truly effective performance of this function presumes a precise delineation of the market. The marketing affairs of the firm cannot be guided wisely on the basis of a generalized description of the market. It is not helpful to an appliance sales executive to be told that the potential market for dishwashers consists of owners of all wired homes with plumbing facilities. Nor could a motorcycle sales manager intelligently direct his marketing effort if the only definition of the market to guide him indicated that buyers were predominantly from the male population sixteen years of age and over. A more precise delineation is needed that defines the market by such specific factors as age groups, income levels, educational backgrounds, marital status, geographic areas, urban or rural areas, and perhaps past ownership behavior.
In the formulation of the marketing effort, a first consideration is: *Does the firm know the markets for its products and their makeup with reasonable depth and precision?* Such an evaluation includes consideration of whether the market is sufficiently large and of appropriate character to support profitable operations. A firm might know in detail the market for a given product, and it might be cultivating the market in an ideal way, but an adequate market may not exist to justify competing for available

purchasers. Thinking of this function with respect to the introduction of a new product, a measure of market potential and the feasibility of market entry is a first consideration.

On the basis of the above discussion, *the market delineation function is defined as the determination and measurement of potential purchasers and their identifying characteristics.* Chapters 5, 8, and 9 examine in detail the dimensions of market delineation from the viewpoints of consumers and other business enterprises.

PURCHASE BEHAVIOR MOTIVATION

In presenting a product or service for sale, every firm inherently does so with some major underlying assumptions with regard to purchase behavior. These assumptions may be consciously calculated, and tested with the aid of sophisticated psychological research techniques or based on an inadvertent and perhaps unconsciously reached conclusion. Regardless, the universality of this function is evident. Some notion about what motivates buyers is inescapable.

In the rudimentary marketing approach for selling eggs, cited earlier, the sign read "FRESH EGGS 89¢ A DOZEN." Such factors as size, color, grade, packaging, and convenience, among others, are ignored. This sign implies that the two most influential factors that can be used for attracting buyers are *freshness* of product and the *price*. This may or may not be so, but it represents the position taken by our farmer-marketer. At the other extreme, pharmaceutical producers spend large sums of money on motivation research to find out what factors underlie and influence the prescription habits of physicians beyond the obvious therapeutic effects of one drug over another. In between these extremes, a number of examples could be used to illuminate the need to understand purchase behavior motivation.

Such merchandising slogans as "good to the last drop" and "I can't believe I ate the whole thing" represent important assumptions about the best way to gain a favorable consumer response to the product. In a broader sense, any message that is transmitted to potential buyers necessarily contains information with motivational overtones. Inspection of advertising copy in any magazine quickly reveals the range and variety of appeals used for market cultivation. Actually, even the mere announcement of a product for sale, with no apparent attempt at persuasion, still involves purchase motivation. In such a case, the marketer may have concluded that the motivational variables were so diverse that each potential buyer would be more effectively influenced when left to his or her own devices. One could argue perhaps that cost considerations in a case such as this preclude any verbalized attempt at motivation. However, such a position in itself is a motivation conclusion—namely, that cost is the predominant or sole motivational force.

Historically, marketing campaigns have been based predominantly on the perceptive judgment and keen insight of executives. More recently, research techniques have become available to measure motivational forces more scientifically.

In formulating the marketing affairs of the firm, then, the second important functional consideration would be *whether the firm knows what the most significant forces are that underlie purchase behavior.* The purchase behavior motivation function, therefore, builds naturally upon market delineation. One would not have the means for understanding the forces that underlie purchase behavior without first knowing the potential buyers of the product. The relationship is thus a sequential one. The two functions combine to create market targets.

The second managerial function of marketing is *purchase behavior motivation, which is the assessment of those direct and indirect factors that underlie, impinge upon, and influence purchase behavior.* Chapters 6 and 7 and selected sections of Chapter 8 present the foundations and a framework for approaching the study of consumer and intermediate purchase behavior motivation.

FUNCTION RELATED TO PRODUCT-SERVICE MARKET MATCHING

To understand market need is not adequate. The realization of corporate objectives requires that the firm offer products and services that will satisfy customer wants and needs. *Product-service matching* is the managerial function that links an enterprise with its potential market.

PRODUCT-SERVICE ADJUSTMENT

A business needs to stay in an effective state of adjustment to its market environment. In a major way, this means keeping the product line in harmony with market characteristics, preferences, and expenditure patterns. Few businesses can prosper through time with a static product line. Since markets are dynamic, product policy with respect to goods to be consumed in those markets must be dynamic. Reflecting this consideration, the product line should be periodically reviewed to see how well it is meeting its intended purposes.

Effective performance of the product-service adjustment function depends to an important extent on how well the preceding two functions have been conducted. A product mix is well adjusted only in the context of the specific market delineated for its acquisition and consumption and the motivational forces. So, again, the function is sequentially related to, and builds upon, those mentioned earlier. While this is true, it must be recognized that both markets and their motivational forces are characterized by change.

Market change results from fluctuating income levels, population growth, new-family formation, population mobility, and the like. Cultural and social forces influence consumption patterns, as does the changing nature of individual tastes and esthetic preferences. As a nation becomes more prosperous, people's wants become more specific in terms of their demand for products of precise characteristics. Markets that were once quite homogeneous or uniform tend to become more segmented. This movement toward segmentation has had the effect of making a broader assortment of goods available to consumers to draw on in the marketplace for replenishing and extending their inventories of goods. As a result of all these factors, a given offering may be very much "in tune with the times" at one point, and poorly adapted to the market at another. Finally, the marketer finds his product-service problems complicated, in addition, by competitors' actions.

Although we have stressed tangible products in our discussion, marketing of services is equally important. Books, insurance companies, finance companies, and athletic team owners are constantly assessing market targets and adjusting their offerings to the buying groups they wish to cultivate. If they do not, new competition, such as the World Football and World Hockey leagues, materializes.

The product-service adjustment function is thus important managerially to insure that the marketing system is functioning effectively in the pursuit of corporate goals. Marketing executives must be continuously alert to opportunities in individual products to achieve a more entrenched market position. No amount of otherwise astute or skillful marketing can make up for a product (or product line) which is basically unacceptable to purchasers at the price that must be paid to acquire it.

In formulating the marketing affairs of the firm, an important consideration is *the mix of the different products and services in the line and their relative share of the total sales volume through time.*

This third managerial function is defined as including *those activities required to match the product-service offering with the market in which it is to be purchased and consumed.* Because of the fundamental importance of product-service adjustment, various aspects of this managerial function are discussed in Chapters 10, 11, and 12 of Part Three.

FUNCTIONS RELATED TO MARKETING PROGRAMMING

Marketing programming is concerned with operationalizing enterprise effort to exploit market opportunities. Once product-service capabilities have been matched with market opportunity, the enterprise must mobilize resources toward selected targets. The programming of operations involves managerial decisions in *channel selection, physical distribution, communication,* and *pricing.* These four managerial functions are discussed below.

CHANNEL SELECTION

Once markets in which the firm elects to operate have been identified and appropriate product-service matches selected, the complex of marketing institutions through which most of the marketing effort is channeled and the product-service is offered to the marketplace must be programmed. This complex network of organizations is known as the *channel of distribution.* A channel of distribution is defined as a combination of institutions through which a seller offers his products to the user or ultimate consumer. Each institution, such as retailers, wholesalers, and other types of middleman institutions, represents a composite of specialized marketing capabilities. The institutions selected to form the channel of distribution might be considered as an external or extraorganizational unit hired to assist a specific enterprise in gaining differential advantage. The number of potential channel combinations are unlimited. In programming activities the selection of any particular combination to realize market penetration should result from careful analysis.

The policy of Electrolux to sell vacuum cleaners direct from the factory to the consumer through a force of house-to-house salesmen is very different from Hoover's decision to market through a network of carefully selected department, hardware, and appliance stores. The rationale behind each is sound and is based upon the manufacturer's interpretation of such factors as the degree of market coverage and control desired plus the desired aggressiveness of marketing effort. A vacuum cleaner has a high cost and is a technical product that requires demonstration at the point of sale. Electrolux believes that a direct to home and service organization can provide the marketing effort better than relying on independent retailers. Hoover, on the other hand, believes the careful selection of retailers better satisfies marketing requirements. Provision is made for demonstration of the product in the store and assurances of service are provided either by the store or through a listing of authorized service organizations. Such considerations as the product, market, and manufacturers' characteristics that affect the selection of marketing channels are the subject matter of Chapters 13 and 14. Appendix A reviews marketing channel alternatives.

In formulating the market affairs of the firm, a major question is *the review of alternative channel structure and is the selection of a combination based upon a logical analysis.* Like everything else in marketing, the predominant channels used at one time lose their vitality, requiring a mandatory change to new channels in order to maintain market leadership.

The fourth managerial function of marketing is *the channel selection function which is the selection and organization of institutions through which the product-service offering is made available to the marketplace.*

PHYSICAL DISTRIBUTION

Physical distribution concerns the actual movement of goods from points of production to points of consumption. This function thereby attacks the problem of physical transfer in time and space. Physical distribution differs from channel selection in that there is no need for the physical product to flow through the same complex of institutions selected to channel the marketing effort toward buyers. It may do so, but economics are often achieved by separating the two flows. The product must be moved to the market in the most economic way that will satisfy customer service availability requirements. The makeup of the market and its dispersion are obvious factors in designing a physical distribution system. The product itself is also an important factor in the selection between alternative paths of physical movement. Considerations of perishability, fragileness, bulk, weight, handling, and potential damage through multiple handling are quite naturally pertinent. Not so obvious is the relevancy of the purchase motivational function. This has a bearing on physical movement in that it relates to how, when, and why people want to buy goods. For example, if industrial buyers would accept 72 hours for delivery of parts, as compared with 24 hours, a strikingly different and perhaps more economical physical distribution system might be appropriate. Consequently, the means employed in making the products available must reflect such considerations. The variety of circumstances influencing product movement account for the sequential position of the physical distribution function within overall listing of managerial functions.

While Chapter 15 is devoted to physical distribution in substantial detail, several observations with respect to delivery performance are appropriate here. First, the physical distribution objective is to integrate transportation, warehousing, and inventory economics into a balanced effort. Secondly, achieving efficient and effective physical distribution requires the economic integration of production points, warehousing locations, and market areas. Third, within this framework, four basic decision areas call for careful programming. These areas are: (1) choice of the basic unit of shipment; (2) selection of the mode and method of transportation to and from customer service locations; (3) determination of product storage layouts and systems for movement through physical distribution support facilities; and (4) adoption of procedures and policies for customer order processing and inventory replenishment. These are principal elements in designing an efficient physical distribution channel.

Physical distribution is an important managerial consideration because a sizeable part of total marketing cost is involved in this function. Thus, in formulating the marketing affairs of the firm from a managerial perspective, a pertinent question for the analyst is: *"How efficient and effective is the physical distribution of products?"*

The fifth function, *the physical distribution function, is concerned with the actual movement of goods from points of production to points of consumption.*

COMMUNICATION

Unless communication occurs between the marketer and the potential buyer, no transaction can take place. A buyer must at least be aware of the availability of a product-service offering and its price. Sellers, on the other hand, are not merely interested in seeing that this minimum information reaches buyers. It is also important to supply pertinent information which leads to a favorable attitude toward the product and its sponsor, an overt purchasing decision, and satisfaction from the product when placed in use.[2]

Traditionally, marketers have been preoccupied with the individual problem areas of personal selling, advertising, publicity, and sales promotion as tools of demand cultivation. In a broader sense, while each of these has some individual status, they are all parts of a market-communications system. Viewing the problem in this way tends to open new vistas to thinking about informational requirements. From a managerial viewpoint, the principal question in selecting and coordinating the various demand cultivation components is a communication opportunity—namely: *How can consumers or buyers be most effectively reached in terms of the*

---

[2] Communication is not the mere transmitting of messages containing information. There can be no communication until these messages are received and understood at the destination and a sense of psychological need is aroused. The essential requirements of an effective communication process are taken up in detail in Chapters 16 and 17, Advertising and Personal Selling.

kind and quantities of information that will have the most powerful influence in inducing them to purchase?

The communication function clearly draws upon functions previously enumerated. Any program for communicating with buyers must take into account data gathered in delineating the market, the purchase behavior motivational forces in the market, the way the product mix has been adjusted to the market, the channels used, and the physical distribution system deployed.

Communication is basic to marketing. Its principal purpose is demand cultivation. However, market communication is not merely a bargaining instrument used in bringing buyer and seller together. Many other communication needs beyond this important one exist in a marketing system. From the layman's view, most of the activities called selling would be a part of the communication function. If gratifying sales are not forthcoming for the firm, one factor that could account for the difficulty might be the ineffectiveness of the nature, scope, and frequency of information reaching the market. Making a sales force more productive may in fact be a matter of making communication impact more effective at the buyer or purchasing unit level. The same could be said for other forms of demand-cultivation activity. Communication as a part of marketing programming is treated in Chapters 16 and 17.

In formulating the marketing affairs of the firm *managers must periodically review how effectively the firm is communicating with potential buyers to assure that the most favorable climate exists for serving company purposes.*

The purpose of communication is to precipitate in the marketplace action that serves the seller's purpose. The sixth managerial function, *communication, thus consists of the design and transmitting of information and messages between buyer and seller to the end that the most favorable climate for the seller is created in the marketplace.* The performance of the communication function engages advertising and personal selling.

PRICE

Price is frequently considered an element of the product-service activity, since in the buyer's eyes it places a value on the total bundle available for purchase. We prefer to consider it a separate managerial function of marketing because it tends to place a value perspective on all other functions presented thus far. In a monopolistically competitive market structure, the most commonly experienced situation, the firm has some control over the price placed on products offered for sale. Thus, price determination is a managerial function. Pricing is an important alternative tool of market cultivation to such activities as advertising, sales promotion, and personal selling. For example, a low price may offer a substitute for large advertising expenditures.

No matter how carefully the product-service offering has been matched to market needs, channels selected, physical distribution systems developed, and communication alternatives blended into an information system, the setting of the wrong price can nullify the combined impact. For example, a manufacturer developed a new piece of street cleaning equipment utilizing an entirely new operational principle. In keeping with environmental interests, the device used regenerated air. Instead of moving street dirt around the street with a brush, it shot a jet of air onto the street and then immediately sucked the disturbed debris into a hopper with a vacuum process. The air was then regenerated. The problem was how to price such a product. In one sense the new process was properly viewed as being in competition with conventional street cleaning equipment. In another sense, potential buyers were expected to be willing to pay some premium for the new principle which offered ecological benefits. But how much? The company started out with a rather substantial premium in their price only to learn they immediately had to reduce price to generate market demand. Fortunately, the cost structure did not prohibit price reductions.

The problem of price determination is not confined to new products. The dynamics of the marketplace require constant evaluation of prices through time. We saw this happen in the rapid price adjustments on petroleum and beef products during the shortage periods of the 1970s.

The pricing decision is not confined only to the determination of price for a specific product. Once determined, a price must be administered as the same product is often sold under a wide variety of conditions. For example, when the product is sold in very large quantities, and a savings in cost to the seller can be demonstrated, there is justification for a quantity discount structure which lowers price as quantities purchased increase. If different middlemen, such as retailers or wholesalers, in the channel of distribution perform some of the marketing activity, they also deserve reductions in price, known as trade discounts. There are also questions of prices to be set for goods sold in different geographic locations to reflect differentials in cost of physical distribution.

In programming the marketing affairs of the firm, a major consideration is: *Do the prices charged for products reflect the best combination of revenues generated and costs expended to meet the objectives of the enterprise?*

The seventh managerial function of marketing, *the price function, is the determination and administration of prices that meet the objectives of the enterprise.* Chapter 18 is devoted to price determination and administration. Chapter 19 provides a summary and intergration of managerial functions related to marketing programming discussed in Chapters 13 through 18.

FUNCTIONS RELATED TO EXECUTION

Two managerial functions are related to the execution of the marketing plan. They are *organization* and *administration*. These execution functions have somewhat of a different orientation than the functions discussed previously, since they are not unique to marketing. Aspects of organization and administration are universal to all functional areas of management. Building upon the principles of management that are universal throughout the enterprise, we discuss these two functions from the vantage point of specialized marketing considerations.

ORGANIZATION

Organization determines how functions, facilities, and people are arranged, and their relationships to one another. We are principally concerned with organization structure, which groups similar functions, maintains proper balance between them, and provides integration in a way that facilitates cooperation and performance. Authority and responsibility in any organization should be delegated according to functional groupings. Proper organization is important in developing a coordinated competitive effort. Without it, we have merely a number of individuals and groups functioning independently. Most units of today's large businesses are wholly or partially dependent on broader system requirements.

The organizational aspects of mobilizing resources is a matter of both structure and incentives. The proper structural design provides for coordination of activities, planning effectiveness, and clarity in decision when dealing with the competitive affairs of the firm. Unlike other organizational parts in the business, marketing has both an internal and an external organizational relationship. All firms that join together in either a channel of distribution or physical distribution do so in anticipation of joint behavior that will lead to satisfaction of enterprise goals. Thus, marketing organizations by definition must extend beyond the single enterprise to include extra-organizational relationships.[3]

The organizational structure should basically reflect the tasks required in markets and the basic approach to be used in reaching those markets. Organizational studies frequently start at the president's office

---

[3] This concept is developed in Chapter 13.

and work down through the organization. The pattern urged here is that the analysis start with the market and work back and up. In other words, market affairs should be organized before factories, product development groups, and the like are organized. The organizational aspects of market affairs are treated in detail in Chapter 20.

If the firm has good people and good facilities, and both are well organized in a structural sense, it has most of the ingredients for effective job performance. Properly organized, however, only a *potentially* effective force exists. This potential energy must be released through proper incentives and channeled in productive ways through proper operational arrangements. Incentives are of special significance, for when broadly conceived and carefully implemented, they lead to a hard-hitting and aggressive organization, with high morale. Incentives include job opportunity, practices in job rotation and advancement, proper recognition for achievement, equal opportunity, and numerous other variables, as well as compensation. Once again these matters should be based on market objectives. A sales compensation study or program should proceed only after the marketing job to be accomplished is identified, the specific tasks of salesmen determined, the capabilities required of salesmen to perform those tasks evaluated, and the selection of salesmen geared to these needs.

An illustration of this viewpoint concerns the case of a producer of ethical drugs (prescription items) and proprietary (nonprescription) pharmaceuticals who invited four consulting organizations to submit proposals for a compensation-of-salesmen study. Three firms submitted cost estimates ranging from $20,000 to $25,000 for the study. The fourth submitted an estimate of $90,000. When asked to defend the seemingly excessive bid, the fourth explained that the study required intimate knowledge of markets, purchase behavior, and the payoff to the company of having salesmen spend their time in alternative ways between different classes of customers. The firm further indicated that if these factors were already known, then the study could be completed within the equivalent cost estimates of the other three organizations. The fourth firm received approval of its proposal after management agreed to the need for the broader study.

Thus, in formulating market affairs of the firm, a pertinent question is: *"Is there a rationale for the internal and external marketing organization?"* The eighth managerial function, *organization*, deals with the structuring and incentive of human resources.

ADMINISTRATION

The managerial function of marketing administration is concerned with the continuous control and measurement of marketing operations.

Following the finalization of marketing plans and organizational arrangements selected to execute these plans, two general areas of administrative concern remain: (1) to *control* performance through formulation and implementation of programs to guide pretransaction and transaction operations, and (2) to *measure* performance and provide feedback to realize more effective marketing operations on a continuing basis. It is through marketing administration that closure is achieved for the total competitive effort of the enterprise.

The administrative process is centered around three aspects of marketing transaction: (1) pretransaction, (2) transaction, and (3) posttransaction. Each aspect of transaction analysis is integral to marketing administration.

The *pretransaction* aspect of marketing concerns all activities necessary to *create* a meeting of the minds among parties favorable to ownership transfer. This control aspect of marketing administration is pervasive throughout the marketing system. Aspects of pretransaction control involve internal operations of the firm as well as the interaction of the firm in a dynamic channel context.

The *transaction* aspect of marketing administration concerns all activities that must be performed *between* the time a meeting of the minds occurs among parties and the actual transfer of ownership. Control of the transaction process is essential if the enterprise is to capitalize upon its expenditures made to obtain market penetration.

The *posttransaction* aspect of administration is concerned with the state of affairs that exists between buyer and seller *after* the ownership transfer is completed. Marketing responsibility does not stop until the merchandise provides satisfactory performance in use. Posttransaction performance measurement and feedback is integral to marketing administration because it assists management in achieving a desired state of competitive and buyer adjustment in marketing penetration. The performance measurement function provides information concerning how well the planned activity has achieved expectation, a diagnostic evaluation of reasons for deviation from expectation and information to anticipate environmental change.

In evaluating the marketing affairs of the firm, pertinent questions are: *What standards are used to measure performance and what procedures are used to measure buyer satisfaction?*

Thus, the final managerial function of marketing, *administration, is the formulation of operating procedures and standards to control pretransaction and transaction performance and the measurement of posttransaction feedback to generate satisfactory marketing performance on a continuing basis.* The performance measurement and feedback aspect of the administrative function of managerial marketing clearly illustrates that marketing systems are circular. Market opportunity assessment and its related functions of market delineation and purchase behavior motivation directly link to performance feedback. Effective marketing is a process that must be constantly evaluated and modified. Such continued adjustment means that past experience must be incorporated in future opportunity assessment. Chapter 21 treats the overall administration of marketing affairs.

A SYSTEMS INTEGRATION OF THE MANAGERIAL MARKETING FUNCTIONS

In Chapter 2, the coordinated behavior of all aspects of an enterprise were viewed from the perspective of an integrated production-marketing system. A systems integration is also essential to understanding the interrelated nature of the managerial functions of marketing.

To accommodate change, marketing systems and the focus of marketing effort must also change. This implies that a marketing system must be a circular rather than a linear system, be "open circuit," and provide feedback to improve the functioning of the system in the next round of operations. These notions are further developed to provide perspective for the integration of the managerial functions of marketing.

Different systems may perhaps be best understood by comparing their nature with the operations of a furnace. The furnace example, which is presented in the next few pages, also will serve to show why a marketing system should not be linear.

THE LINEAR SYSTEM

Picture a hot-air coal furnace, fired by hand, that has a series of ducts leading to a number of floor registers throughout the house. When coal is burned, hot air rises and is distributed by the ducts, providing comfortable temperatures to the various rooms. After the fire dies down, the rooms cool off, and the whole heating procedure must be repeated. This furnace works on a *linear system;* its components form a *line*. It has a beginning and an end. The system itself has no way of responding to changes that affect it. The inputs (coal) cannot be adjusted to varying outputs (heat) by the system to accommodate different requirements in different parts of the house.

You can see that this isn't a very efficient system. First, it requires a highly skilled operator, one who knows just the right amount of coal to add for a desired increase in temperature, how much draft (air) will be needed, what the usual time lags are between "firing-up" and obtaining heat, how to bank the fire at night to conserve fuel, and how to handle any special idiosyncrasies of the furnace. But even with a skilled operator there are likely to be drafty rooms, uneven temperatures, and excessive fuel consumption.

By the same token, a marketing system that is merely an adjunct to a factory will also prove inadequate. The marketing system in this case would play a role similar to the ducts of the furnace, which simply carry heat to the rooms in the hope that occupants will find the temperature satisfactory. By analogy, the marketing system would merely carry to the market what the factory had produced with the expectation that all would be well. Now an extremely perceptive factory management with a keen intuitive sense of market characteristics and preferences might get along reasonably well for a period of time, much as a highly skilled furnace operator might with his furnace, but the same kinds of limitations are likely to exist. In both cases, necessary adjustments may occasionally be overlooked until it is too late for effective action. Our furnace operator may fail to notice the gradual drop in the temperature of the living room until it actually becomes chilly. When he rushes downstairs to shovel more coal into the furnace, he finds that the fire is out. Our factory operator could discover at the end of an apparently good first quarter an alarming pileup of finished goods inventories. In both cases, it could be too late for minor corrective changes.

THE CLOSED-CIRCUIT SYSTEM

A more efficient and more satisfactory heating system could be obtained by placing a thermostat in the living quarters and adding a stoker to the furnace. With these built-in devices, the furnace will function in a better state of adjustment to its environment. The desired temperature is selected by the homeowner. After the furnace has dispensed enough heat to reach this temperature, the thermostat is actuated; this transmits an electrical impulse to the furnace, shutting it off. The electrical circuit connecting the thermostat and furnace is a closed circuit; it provides a continuous, closed path for current flow (the thermostat opens and closes the electrical circuit).

Automatic temperature control in a closed-circuit system is called *feedback*. The action of the thermostat depends on the action of the furnace. Conversely, the action of the furnace depends on the action of the thermostat. Each is both cause and effect of the behavior of the other. Each is both output and input—all the forces affecting the closed-circuit system are built into the system itself. Consequently, heating system operation is not subject to change from unexpected or random external forces over which it has no control—for example, an impending drastic drop in outside temperature because of a storm that has yet to arrive over the area. Likewise, it cannot raise the inside temperature a degree or two for psychological purposes because overcast, windy weather outside makes it seem colder in the house than it actually is.

The system we now have is reasonably satisfactory. It can, however, become still more effective. While it is possible to strike an average temperature for the house that partially suits the needs of varying quarters, a single temperature is not fully satisfactory. For example, activity quarters such as the kitchen or game room do not require as high a temperature as sitting areas such as the living room or study. Also, sleeping areas would be more comfortable with a third temperature. *This demonstrates a basic consideration in programming marketing effort (almost an axiom): One expenditure of effort can seldom be all things to all people.* To remedy this situation, several thermostats may be placed strategically throughout the house and the necessary modifications made in the heating plant in order to render the furnace capable of maintaining a better state of adjustment to the total household environment.

The marketing counterpart of our furnace at this point has several ramifications. First, "sensing devices" (such as the thermostat) are needed to insure that the overall market is reached and served with reasonable precision. The total market must be focused on initially, as it is the market that the system must satisfy. Next, feedback is important, so that adjustment in operations can take place on a continuing basis, as warranted by the market response to the firm's marketing activities. Finally, there must be an awareness of the various segments of the market and their accompanying variations if precise adjustment is to be achieved. Many firms have recognized this need. As it is impossible to be all things to all people with a single marketing effort, many methods are used to adjust to different segments of the market.[4] A familiar one is the offering of "good, better, and best" product qualities in a single merchandise line.

THE OPEN-CIRCUIT SYSTEM

Returning to the furnace analogy, we might think that there is limited improvement possible since the system has progressed from a linear one to a closed-circuit one with feedback. To take into account external forces that influence its internal functioning, the system can be made *open-circuit*. For example, a rapid change in the outside weather will play a part in how well the furnace does its job because of the time lag between the moment when the furnace gets a signal to change operations (shut off or come on) and the effect of the signal to change the temperature of the rooms. If a

[4] See Chapter 19 for a discussion of the means used to adjust to different segments of the market.

severe cold front is moving into an area, the furnace will have no specialized mechanism to anticipate a desired change in temperature. Not until the temperature inside the house suddenly drops will the room thermostat actuate the furnace to provide more heat. Alternatively, an outdoor thermostat could have "sensed" anticipated requirements and signaled the furnace of radical temperature changes in advance. Such a sensing system is called *open-circuit feedback* because the outside thermostat can actuate the furnace but the furnace has no impact on the themostat. The two units are no longer mutually cause and effect, as was the case with the inside thermostat and the furnace.

Now we have attained our prime goal, devising a nearly perfect system for keeping the furnace in an effective state of adjustment to its complete operating environment. The occupants will not be obliged to change or adapt their preferences for hot or cold rooms or their attitudes toward what constitutes a comfortable temperature in different rooms within the house. Nor are they forced to live with an inefficient system. The furnace adjusts to the family's needs regardless of whether the need for change comes from a change in desires of the inhabitants or from outside forces.

What, then, is the marketing analogy? "Outside" environmental forces over which the firm itself has no control are frequently crucial in maintaining an effective marketing effort. Technological change, creative invention, competitive forays of new institutions (discount houses, for instance), and the ever-changing desires of the market all exert significant weight on the marketing system employed by the firm to meet corporate objectives. For this reason, a linear marketing system cannot be satisfactory; the system must have open-circuit feedback characteristics.

In summary, a marketing mechanism is needed which not only maintains a reasonable state of adjustment to the existing overall market environment (single thermostat in the house), but which also takes account of the varying needs of particular market segments (a thermostat in various quarters of the house), and which can anticipate impending outside events or forces which should be taken into account (outside thermostat). A marketing system must be of this sort because all the forces which influence the system cannot be "internalized"—that is, outside factors over which the firm has no control will inevitably influence the character of its marketing effort. Consequently, a circular-flow system is needed that can best be characterized as an open-circuit feedback system.

SUMMARY

The chapter has extended our treatment of managerial marketing to the specific functions which must be completed to assure that an enterprise maintains a proper state of adjustment to its marketing environment. These functions are philosophically in harmony with the firm's goal of gaining a differential advantage with respect to a significant share of the total market. In total, the following managerial functions were defined:

1. The market delineation function—the determination and measurement of potential purchasers and their identifying characteristics.
2. The purchase behavior motivation function—the assessment of those direct and indirect factors that underline, impinge upon, and influence purchase behavior.
3. The product-service adjustment function—those activities required to match the product-service offering with the market in which it is to be purchased and consumed.
4. The channel selection function—the selection and organization of institutions through which the product-service offering is made available to the marketplace.
5. The physical distribution function—the actual movement of goods from points of production to points of consumption.
6. The communications function—the design and transmitting of information and messages between buyer and seller to the end that the most favorable climate for the seller is created in the marketplace.
7. The pricing function—the determination and administration of prices that meet the objectives of the enterprise.
8. The organization function—the structuring and incentive of human resources.
9. The administration function—the formulation of operating procedures and standards to control pretransaction and transaction performance and the measurement of posttransaction feedback to generate satisfactory marketing performance on a continuing basis.

A marketing mechanism is desired that can anticipate impending outside events or forces which should be taken into account in formulating marketing action. A marketing system must be of this sort because all the forces which influence the system cannot be "internalized." Outside factors over which the firm has no control will inevitably influence the character of the marketing effort. Consequently, a circular flow system incorporating feedback is needed to integrate the managerial functions of marketing. The managerial functions provide a sequence of specific tasks that management must perform and evaluate in order to operationalize marketing. It is against this concept of circular flow that we turn to the operationalization of marketing action in the next chapter.

QUESTIONS AND PROBLEMS

1. How would you conceptually define when a business is operating efficiently?
2. "Effective business management is a continuous process of adaptive behavior." Elaborate on this statement, using your own terms.
3. Why can a business *system* never be fully a closed system?
4. Why does a business system need to have feedback? What are some of the elements of informational feedback needed?
5. Explain how the managerial functions of marketing provide a basis for auditing the efficiency with which a firm is conducting marketing activity.
6. How does the communications function draw upon the performance of the market delineation and purchase behavior motivation functions?
7. Distinguish between pretransaction and transaction marketing administration.
8. How does a marketing organization differ from organization of other functional parts of an enterprise?

Chapter 4

Environmental Monitoring and Strategy Formulation

To operationalize the study of marketing we now turn our attention to how a manager establishes objectives and then formulates a program to achieve such objectives. We have characterized the overall task of managerial marketing as one of allocating scarce corporate resources as inputs to achieve a predetermined series of objectives or outputs. We have also stated that such managerial action involves interrelated managerial functions that must be coordinated within a framework of uncertainty. The firm that achieves its predetermined objectives is viewed as gaining a differential advantage over competition. This advantage results from the firm's capability to mobilize instrumental or meaningful action in specific target markets. The essence of long-term growth and survival is to maintain such differential advantage over time by making necessary adjustments.

In order for an enterprise to maintain the proper state of adjustment across time, it must develop "sensing" devices to provide continued surveillance of critical or prime markets and to give early warning of their pending and changing characteristics. Markets reflect extremely dynamic forces and qualities. Never static, markets are constantly changing in their makeup as a reaction to their underlying behavioral foundations. The marketing manager must "catch the pulse" of such change and formulate a course of action to maximize success.

In this chapter we first introduce *environmental monitoring* as an example of the type of early warning surveillance that must precede executive commitment to a specific program of adjustment. The competitive environment is viewed in terms of its most volatile and meaningful dimensions of change. Next, the appraisal of *resources* available for the firm to use in pursuit of differential advantage are discussed. All resources are scarce and therefore should be deployed to maximum benefit. The matching of resources to environmental opportunities is viewed as the firm's *marketing strategy plan.* The chapter concludes with several basic concepts that underly such strategy formulation.

ENVIRONMENTAL MONITORING

The challenges of marketing are found within the environment that surrounds all activities of the firm. The environment represents both opportunity and threat. Innovative management must constantly be sensing environmental change in an effort to avoid the impacts of nondesirable threats while developing the proper competitive position to capitalize on opportunities. No specific firm has a mandate to stay in business. As market needs change, emerge, or diminish, so must the firm adapt its assortment of products and services. For example, while one 6-oz. size of Coke was adequate for many years, and still is adequate to meet the market needs of many developing countries, a proliferation of different sizes and package combinations was necessary to satisfy the United States market.

Many different types of change are involved in environmental dynamics. Some changes are minor with respect to their impact upon the firm, providing ample time for adjustment. Such evolutionary change must be accommodated. However, the impact at any time does not constitute a major adjustment on the part of the firm. In contrast, revolutionary change can require an all-out adjustment by a firm within a matter of hours, days, or weeks. The change in family size preference among the newly married had a specific impact upon subsequent demand for 9-passenger station wagons. However, the change occurred over time, allowing ample time to convert production to other models and styles. In contrast, the major shift in the buying public's demand for automobiles offering high gasoline economy literally occurred overnight. The shift in demand preference was so rapid that almost all firms in the industry were forced to convert manufacturing facilities and redirect production schedules within the 1974 model year. While a consumer demand shift for automobiles offering gasoline economy was clearly predicted, few if any anticipated the magnitude of the preference shift. Despite ample early warning in sales trends, dealer inventories of middle-size and luxury autos reached an all-time high before production schedules could be modified.

Through perpetuation of a system of competition, society has set in motion some of the forces that call forth the level of innovation needed for economic progress. As we observed in Chapters 1 through 3, a state of competition for differential advantage prevails, and it is the totality of market actions engaged in by the industrial and distribution complex that provides whatever growth pattern we ultimately enjoy. Marketing is an integral part of competition and is a mandatory management responsibility if the firm is to operate successfully and survive in a competitive environment. As such, marketing is very closely tied to both corporate survival and economic growth. One writer views the relationship as follows:

> The very essence of our competitive system is the pressure placed on an individual business to produce better products at lower cost. . . . Businessmen therefore are constantly seeking new techniques, new products, and new ideas in all fields to give them competitive advantages. The marketplace today clearly is a place where a businessman innovates or fails.[1]

In order for a business to survive it must monitor its operating environment.

The process of *environmental monitoring consists of a systematic review, appraisal, and projection of all aspects of the environment that involve existing and potential firm operations.* The objective of such monitoring is to avoid the pitfalls of becoming so engulfed with day-to-day operations that we fail to calibrate properly the impact of overall change that will influence future success. Environmental monitoring involves traditional marketing research and a great deal more. Environmental monitoring includes all aspects of information gathering. While many different classifications of environmental change exist, we have selected to illustrate and group change areas critical to marketing management into six sub-environmental categories:

1. Economic environment.
2. Competitive environment.
3. Technological environment.
4. Support environment.
5. Political and legal environment.
6. Cultural and social environment.

To a significant extent the dimension and magnitude of change within each category of the overall environment is beyond the short-range control of a specific firm. While the individual firm is a participant and may be to a degree a change agent, no single firm or even all firms collectively can control the direction or rate of overall environmental change. From the viewpoint of any single firm the rate of overall environmental change may far exceed the firm's capability or willingness to adapt to or exploit the opportunities encompassed within the change. Thus, the purpose of

---

[1] George A. Steiner, "Improving the Transfer of Government-Sponsored Technology," *Business Horizons,* IX (Fall 1966), Graduate School of Business, Indiana University, 60.

environmental monitoring is to develop an informed basis for taking selective initiative in a changing environment.

ECONOMIC ENVIRONMENT

Over the past two hundred years the United States economy has experienced tremendous growth. There is no need to substantiate this fact by assembly and display of massive statistical data. The essence of economic growth is the existence of a population with the capability and willingness to purchase productive output. In a few words, growth seems to depend on the level of desire within the culture in question and the system used for accomplishing that level. Over the modern history of the world, it is a reasonable hypothesis that all societies strive for a higher level of material well-being. Although the composition of output may vary, few are satisfied for any length of time with their economic lot.

An explanation of growth may be found in the system used to accomplish it. A prominent business leader expressed the proposition during the late 1960s as follows:

> Few seriously doubt any longer our ability to avoid another depression of 1929 proportions.
>
> But it seems to me that while adroit fiscal and monetary policy can help to create a climate for progress, the needed economic growth rate can best be achieved by an intensified use of competition—among nations, among their institutions, and particularly among their various industries.
>
> If there is a distinguishing economic characteristic that sets the 20th century apart from all that has gone before, the intensity and creative breadth of modern competition is surely it.
>
> The real question is how to use both competition and the diversified corporation to best speed the economic growth of the entire world.[2]

The 1970s truly became the decade of worldwide marketing and competition. For prolonged periods of time during the early 1970s, the United States experienced a deficit of trade. It was not until the wheat trade with the Soviet Union and the price-wage controls of 1973–74 that the United States as a nation began once again to export in total more goods than it imported.

[2] John B. McKitterick, "New Markets and National Needs," *The General Electric Forum,* X (April–June 1967), 8.

From the viewpoint of the individual enterprise, it is essential to take a position with respect to the short- and intermediate-run economic outlook for specific products and markets. Mere speculation on the level of gross national product, the rate of inflation, or the level of unemployment is not adequate to guide marketing planning. Monitoring and projecting the economic environment necessitates an appraisal of the aggregate impact of all economic variables upon specific market segments. In a complex economy the fate of specific industries and market segments may be different than that of the total economy. For example, increased interest rates may mean unexpected profits for specific financial institutions, while they may simultaneously result in significant slowdowns for home construction and supporting industries.

The widespread material and capital shortages of the mid-1970s unquestionably influenced industries and markets in a substantially different manner. To some, the impact of fuel shortages was limited to higher costs of operation and distribution. To others, the shortage of energy necessitated massive changeovers in manufacturing facilities in order to protect future growth capability. Still others faced such significant shortages in petroleum products that they were forced to suspend or curtail operations and allocate output.

It is significant for the marketing student to realize that while shortages may dominate specific industries and markets, a growth economy simultaneously has significant pockets or areas of abundance and expanding opportunity. The purpose of economic environmental monitoring is to appraise the overall business outlook and to interpret the significance of economic change upon the specific product-service ventures of the firm. The physical attributes and behavioral characteristics of purchase units are examined in detail in Part Two of this book dealing with market opportunity assessment. These attributes and characteristics constitute the *potential* behavior of consumer and industrial purchase units. The current and expected levels of economic activity influence the *capability* and *willingness* of the purchase unit to fulfill its potential.

COMPETITIVE ENVIRONMENT

Throughout the first part of this text we have stressed the central importance of a competitive environment to both economic growth and marketing behavior. In Chapter 1 traditional economic models were highlighted and reviewed to illustrate the structure of competition for differential advantage. From this basic review it was stressed that competition for differential advantage represents a combination of price and nonprice behavior that exists within the framework of an imperfect market structure. In other words, resources are allocated and loyalties realized in a competitive process characterized by uncertainty.

In addition to a competitive environment of firms engaged in direct confrontation—for example, manufacturer to manufacturer and retailer to retailer—we must realize that competition exists between channels of distribution. The term *conglomerate market competition* describes competition between firms engaged in marketing identical products. This process of mixing a wide variety of products within one retail store as opposed to specialization is sometimes referred to as *scrambled merchandising*. Scrambled merchandising gained momentum well before World War II, accelerated rapidly in the postwar years, and currently shows no signs of abating. It is important to understand that one's customer in a channel of distribution may also represent major competition. For example, national branded food products find significant competition in retail food chain supermarkets from private label items. Likewise, American Hospital Supply is both a significant customer and competitor of national branded health care products.

Similar to all other forms of environmental change, the structure and behavior of competition are always undergoing modification. Marketing plans must be formulated with insight into the competitive equilibrium that exists within the specific industry. While the most direct course to realizing differential advantage may be one of exploiting opportunities, such bold moves must be calibrated to capitalize on the trend of competitive structure and behavior and with appraisal of probable retaliation. Assessment of the competitive climate is central to overall environmental monitoring.

TECHNOLOGICAL ENVIRONMENT

It is inappropriate to examine the marketing effects of competitive behavior on economic growth without considering the function of technology. An intensely competitive state may exist without new technological developments, but it is not likely to be a growth economy in the sense that more and better products are made available for mass consumption. The new product, the improved quality, or the new way of doing business is far more enduring as a competitive weapon than engaging in a series of artificial and often superfluous differentiations. The latter may be tolerated if in the long run substantive improvements, as judged by the marketplace, are forthcoming. It is doubtful whether we could or would tolerate an automobile industry that offered nothing but changes in body styling year after year if it did not on occasion give us major functional improvements, such as automatic transmission. In the ladies' garment industry we perhaps do tolerate inconsequential differentiation from year to year, interspersed with substantive fabric changes from the textile industry. In an affluent society, however, the aesthetic values associated with changing styles can be very functional. We must provide for new technology, for without it the competitive posture of the economy is wasteful, and the desired end result—growth—is not attained.

Technology funding comes from two sources, private industry and the government. While basic technology has long been largely financed by government, research and development expenditures of the private sector have increased at an accelerating rate. Even a great deal of government funded research and development is conducted by private industry and universities on a contractual basis. The rapid rate at which patentable inventions are generated is not a very good measure of the rate at which they will be converted into commercially marketable products and consequently find their way into the prevailing standard of living. The role of private enterprise in economic growth is, in part, to assume the risks inherent in making change palatable to the consuming public.

Among others, two conditions must be met to make effective use of technology for economic progress. First, some enterprising management must become aware of the new technology. Second, it must assess the market feasibility of the technology and be willing to incur the risks commercialization entails. Awareness of technology is not always easy. Although research activity is generating a large number of patentable inventions, what firm is organized to scan the thousands of technical journals in which new technology is reported? The time lapses between invention and first use are often long. So great is the federal government's concern over the loss of technology that many agencies, such as the National Aeronautics and Space Administration, Department of Defense, National Science Foundation, and the Atomic Energy Commission, have established technology communication programs. The Technical Services Act is specifically designed to make the output of the federal government's research activities available to small and medium-sized business.

Once a decision is made to explore a new technology further, the entire new product development and market introduction process begins. Clewett makes a distinction between the R & D concept of integrating technology and marketing. He concludes that the latter focuses more on human want satisfaction, whereas the former focuses on transforming the technology into new products. The entrepreneurial concept, because of its difference in emphasis, is more productive of growth in the economy than the R & D approach.[3] It is in the commercialization attempt that we find a

[3] See Robert L. Clewett, "Integrating Science, Technology, and Marketing: An Overview," *Science, Technology, and Marketing,* ed., Raymond M. Haas, 1966 Fall Conference Proceedings, American Marketing Association, pp. 11–20.

conjunction of marketing and technology. The management of opportunity and risk was discussed in Chapter 2 and there is no need to repeat it here. It should be clear, however, that technology delivered to the marketplace is essential for economic progress. The incessant pressure of competition, which forces firms to seek differential advantage through continually capitalizing on market opportunity in their innovative action, is a major factor in causing firms to grow, flourish, and perpetuate themselves. At the same time the economic system provides society with a growing and improved stock of goods from which its members may satisfy their needs and desires.

While the federal government has created an office of technology assessment, every firm must mobilize their own assessment effort.[4] Evaluation and prediction of technological development is an essential ingredient of environmental monitoring.

SUPPORT ENVIRONMENT

No individual firm in the marketing process is self-sufficient. Each must depend upon the resources and capabilities of numerous other firms in order to survive. As noted earlier in the discussion of conglomerate competition, many firms are simultaneously partners and competitors.

Specialization in manufacturing creates problems of both time and space in the process of matching supply and demand. To facilitate specialization and to achieve matching, a number of unique marketing firms have developed. These firms, commonly referred to as *institutions, middlemen,* or *intermediaries,* combine to form a *distribution network or channel* through which goods and services are matched with customers. At any given time a specific firm may well be a member of numerous different channels of distribution.

While a firm cannot dramatically alter the nature of the support environment, it can encourage structural change, and it must select a combination of support arrangements in order to function. Like all other aspects of environment, the structure of support is constantly changing. For example, while a few years ago the main purpose of a frozen food warehouse was to pool shipments in order to realize freight savings, today nationwide networks of distribution warehouses exist which offer a full line of specialized services on a single system basis.

While support relationships cannot be modified with reckless abandon, care must be taken to assure that sufficient modification is introduced to enjoy new innovations. Thus, the support environment must be constantly monitored to appraise the quality of existing relationships and the potential cost-benefit of modification. Over time the support capability of specific firms can be expected to deteriorate. An aggressive firm will not

[4] The Office of Technology Assessment was created by Congress in 1973.

permit its market share to deteriorate with the decay of a support institution. The function of support monitoring is to assure that the firm is fully appraised of all options available.

POLITICAL AND LEGAL ENVIRONMENT

It was not too many years ago that business advertisements and media slogans were populated with such forms of puffery as the *jumbo pound,* the *giant quart,* or the *big gallon.* Despite the existence of a history of federal regulation of commerce dating from the 1890 passage of the Sherman Antitrust Act, it has only been during the decades of the 1960s and 1970s that business has felt the *full regulatory influence* of the political and legal environment.

The political and legal environment of business is properly viewed in the broadest terms to include all formal and informal constraints on business behavior. Thus, full regulatory influence spans from formal legislative acts of government to include judicial and bureaucrat interpretation of programs as well as voluntary compliance and action initiated by business associations. While free market competition is permissive, competition for differential advantage must be exercised within a well-defined set of "rules of the game."

The federal government, with the passage of the Sherman Antitrust Act, became committed to the protection of the consuming public from the potential evils of business. Protection of the public interest from business behavior has continued to represent the main thrust behind federal and state legislation to the present-day series of acts and administrative rules dealing with credit, packaging, and advertising.[5]

To support and accelerate the formal regulation of business, the entire 20th century has been characterized by a series of consumer movements aimed at marshalling public opinion against specific business behavior and practices.[6] Most business students are familiar with the widely acclaimed books that criticize business practice.[7] Works of this type clearly illustrate the *power of viewing with alarm* as one type of regulatory behavior.

---

[5] See George S. Day and David A. Aaker, "A Guide to Consumerism," *Journal of Marketing* (July 1970), 12–19; also David A. Aaker and George S. Day, *Consumerism: Search for Consumer Interest* (New York: The Free Press, 1971).

[6] Ibid.

[7] Vance Packard, *The Waste Makers* (New York: David McKay, 1960); Rachel Carson, *Silent Spring* (Boston: Houghton-Mifflin, 1962); Senator Warren Magnuson and Jean Carper, *The Dark Side of the Marketplace* (Englewood Cliffs, N.J.: Prentice-Hall, 1968); and Ralph Nader, *Unsafe at Any Speed* (New York: Pocket Books, Inc., 1966).

Few marketing experts doubt the fact that consumerism was an inevitable phase of economic development and that it will endure during the foreseeable future.[8] The fact that consumer protection is now fully institutionalized will continue to cast this form of regulation critical to business planning.

The task of cataloguing the total span of regulatory influence upon private enterprise would constitute a voluminous book in itself. The marketer cannot escape an evaluation and interpretation of legal and political currents. This naturally is a vital aspect of overall environmental monitoring. However, prior to leaving the area of legal and political change, a few concluding remarks may be helpful.

First, the student of marketing should realize that despite all federal and state legislature, judicial and administrative action, and with full benefit to consumerism and ecology movements, the real burden of improving the quality of life rests upon business leadership. It is the business enterprise that invests the resources and talents to realize broad-scale improvement.

Second, not all legal and political change is rapid and prohibitive. We have learned to think in terms of the dramatics of safety recalls, cyclamates, monosodium glutamates, and cranberries. Many true, and some exaggerated, cases of food deterioration and contamination have created an atmosphere of violation of the public trust on the part of business. In fact, private research and development leads to as many recalls as any other organized effort. In many cases, new and better products result. To illustrate, the packaging of frozen can soups did not protect cream soups because the cans could not breathe. The introduction of pouch packaging not only solved the problem but also improved product profitability and price.

Finally, the student of marketing should realize that all forms of regulation are not necessarily antimarketing. Consumerism does not automatically mean formal regulation of business interests. In many cases, an improved societal orientation may create new product opportunities. Modern marketing has been preoccupied with satisfying consumer wants. Expansion of the marketing concept to include societal needs opens the door to offering products that satisfy both needs and desires; for example, nutritious and tasteful foods.

Few would argue against the extreme importance of environmental monitoring of political and legal activities. A firm finds survival in the marketplace as a result of customer choice. The opportunity for the customer

---

[8] See C. B. Weiss, "Is Consumerism Giving Up the Ghost? Not Quite!" *Advertising Age* (April 30, 1973), p. 47. Also C. B. Weiss, "Marketers Fiddle While Consumers Burn," *Harvard Business Review,* 46 (July–August 1968), 45–53.

to make a selection only comes after most costs of business have been experienced. Few if any revenues are realized until the transaction is completed. The risks of neglecting aspects of full regulatory influence can be fatal to the long-run survival of the enterprise.

CULTURAL AND SOCIAL ENVIRONMENT

The marketing philosophy of business is predicated on an indepth understanding of the quantitative and qualitative aspects of customer purchase behavior. Such purchase behavior, regardless of its nature as to consumer, industrial or international orientation, must be viewed in a social-cultural setting. The impacts of *social stratification* and *cultural heritage* upon purchase behavior are extremely important aspects of consumer behavior.

In any society the beliefs, values, attitudes, habits, and behavior patterns represent the framework within which market opportunities must be identified and evaluated. Such characteristics vary between cultures and change within any given culture. For instance, the so-called Protestant Ethic which dominated western culture for most of the 19th century had no counterpart in eastern culture. Over the years, the Protestant Ethic has been at least temporarily replaced in significant portions of the Western Hemisphere, including most of the United States.

Recently, we have observed the full-scale development of minority equal opportunity and women's liberation movements as major thrusts of modern cultural change. The desire for security has to a degree replaced the spirit of entrepreneurial behavior. The individual has become more organizational in orientation. Expression has replaced suppression. In short, the predominant characteristics of a culture change with time. Such change, while never homogeneous among all members of a society, has been accelerating in comparison to previous time periods. Ultimately social-cultural characteristics will be manifest in purchasing behavior. While future chapters deal specifically with market delineation and purchase behavior motivation, it is important to single out the need for continuous monitoring of this critical aspect of the overall environment.

CORPORATE GROWTH

Our study of marketing to this point is based on the belief that the key to corporate growth is maintaining competitive superiority through a continuous process of matching market opportunities with total corporate resources. There are a number of ways of measuring corporate growth. Among these are change in profitability, return on investment, return on net assets, sales volume, share of market, or the company's share of its industry's sales.

Even the best managed corporations sometimes lose their superior positions for a period of time—or forever. There are a number of cases of firms that slipped backward after achieving unbelievable goals. Coca-Cola, Singer Sewing Machine, American Motors, Penn Central Railroad, and Studebaker are examples of companies that have at one time or another lost some or all of their momentum. The causes are many, and the road back is difficult. Perhaps success breeds complacency. In any event, no corporation, even giants, are immune to economic failure. While failure may appear to represent economic waste, such waste is minimal when compared to the gains realizable by those innovators who have displaced the failing enterprise. Fortunately, there is a process of either self-renewal or self-destruction. As some firms drop from positions of leadership, others take their places. Which firms provide economic growth is of little concern to society as a whole, so long as a sufficient number of firms are stimulated to grow.

From the viewpoint of the individual firm, self-renewal is essential if the enterprise is to endure. At least two pressures act upon the firm to stimulate growth. One is the competitive environment and the other is the structure of ownership. The pressures exerted by competition on the market affairs of the firm have a profound influence on the firm's aggressiveness in seeking differential advantage through innovation. The normal mentality of management would be to achieve a position of prominence in selected markets and then to hope that no moves were made by competitors to endanger their position or, at worst, dislodge them. As we have seen, the process of competition affords no luxury of complacency. The dynamic nature of competition forces firms to continue to innovate. Growth goes hand in hand with the process of self-renewal.

It has been suggested by Baumol that it is the structure of ownership in the corporation that stimulates innovation and corporate growth.[9] Since ownership is held through stock certificates, management must continually pay out sufficient yields to keep the owners happy. It would be relatively easy to provide a satisfactory yield year after year; however, the fact that ownership is constantly changing complicates matters. Each time a share of stock is bought, the purchaser pays for past successes, since these are reflected in the purchase price of the stock. The new owner anticipates either a similar yield or an appreciation in value, or both. To meet these

---

[9] William J. Baumol, *Business Behavior Value and Growth* (New York: The Macmillan Co., Inc. 1959), pp. 93–95.

demands, the company's growth is mandatory. Add to this pressure the pressures of competition, and it seems clear that the environment within which the firm functions acts to promote the growth of the enterprise.

DEVELOPMENT OF MARKETING STRATEGY

Thus far, we have deliberately avoided the use of the term *strategy*. The reasons are twofold. First, the notion of strategy is generally overused, thus tending to dilute the critical importance of its meaning to marketing planning. Second, a firm in fact has limited strategic commitment. Most managerial functions are engaged in operational or tactical implementation of a singular or limited strategic plan.

Marketing strategy consists of a predetermined plan to guide the deployment of resources in an effort to generate growth. The formulation of a strategy consists of five interrelated steps:

1. Environmental monitoring.
2. Identification of objectives.
3. Selection of target markets.
4. Formulation of the marketing mix.
5. Resource allocation and mobilization.

The central notion involved in *marketing strategy planning* is that a significant change in orientation is required from time to time in order to realize self-renewal. A growth firm cannot rely on traditional or historical practices because of environmental change. Each step involved in the formulation of marketing strategy is discussed below. The first step, environmental monitoring, was discussed earlier in this chapter. We now direct our attention to an overview of the remaining four steps in marketing strategy planning.

IDENTIFICATION OF OBJECTIVES

Earlier we noted that at a reasonably high level of abstraction any firm's growth and effort to perpetuate itself can be measured. Highly generalized or aggregate measurements are not sharp enough to give specific guidance or a clear sense of direction to administrative action. More explicit statements of objectives are needed for the formulation of marketing strategy. There are two broad categories in which objectives should be cast—the financial and operational areas.

Financial Objectives

Since profits are the energizing force within the business, profit targets are a common starting point in planning. The word *profit* by itself is not very precise, particularly when various segments of a company's business are being analyzed for profitability. Moreover, since profitability is a major yardstick for judging management performance, it is of special significance that the profit standards used to evaluate the degree to which this objective is achieved be undersood. Different profit standards are used in business for planning purposes. Perhaps the most important measure of profitability is *return on investment.* One large, rather widely diversified industrial goods manufacturing enterprise expects a potential return of at least 15 percent on its invested capital before committing its limited managerial resources to any new area of operation. This is perhaps the most relevant measure of the achievement of profit objectives because it measures the efficiency with which capital is utilized. A variation of this standard that is used in a relatively few cases is profits as a return on stockholders' equity. The grounds for the use of this standard is that a major business purpose is to maximize returns on stockholders' investments, as distinct from other forms of long-term capital, such as borrowings.

The second major profit standard frequently used is *the ratio of profits to sales volume.* A specialty foods packer characteristically sets a profit target of 10 percent on sales volume. The significance of this standard is that it measures profitability related to volume of operations necessary to produce particular profit levels. In some cases, profit goals are stated in absolute amounts, often based on past years' results.

A third measure used that should be mentioned is *earnings per share of stock outstanding.* When a company has paid an historic dividend over many years without interruption, such as in the case of one of the large utility companies, then planning may well start with the pool of revenue necessary to meet this requirement.

It should be noted that profitability targets can be established for various company divisions, product lines, classes of customers, or geographic areas. The true complexity of profit evaluation becomes apparent when this is done. For instance, suppose profit standards are applied to particular products for both planning purposes and evaluation of management performance. Cost-revenue analysis (of a simplified nature for illustrative purposes) for three products shows the following results: the sales of product A cover all direct costs incurred in conjunction with the production and marketing of the product and all fixed costs allocated to the product with some amount left over. From an accounting point of view, this is a clearly profitable product on a full-cost basis.

Product B's sales cover all direct costs and an additional increment for covering some, but not all, of fixed costs. For operations as a whole, it is more profitable to retain this product than to drop it (even though it shows an "accounting" loss) because it makes a contribution to overhead that would go on with or without the product. Product C's revenue does not even cover direct costs, and is therefore seemingly totally unprofitable even from an "out-of-pocket cost" point of view. Proper policy would seem to indicate that profitability would be maximized from concentrating effort on A, continuing B, and dropping C. Suppose, however, that the sales manager argues that he must continue product C because it is necessary to offer in order to sell some of the A product. If this argument is really valid, then C may be "actually" profitable, even though it shows a considerable "accounting" loss. That is, some of the costs associated with C are really incurred to sell A, and therefore perhaps some of C's costs actually should be borne by A. The point of the illustration is to show the complexity of profit and profit standards. Even more severe problems are encountered by management in attempting to accommodate both short- and long-run opportunities and evaluations.

While profitability goals are the most significant financial objectives, others of importance can be specified which have planning relevance. For instance, under certain circumstances, management may wish to conserve working capital, or, even more stringently, prevent a net outgo of cash. A packing company president, on assuming office, issued a statement relating to corporate expenditures, designed to conserve the cash position of the company. The previous president had depleted cash with a number of equipment purchases that had not yet been reflected in cost savings that more than offset the increased depreciation charges. So, on an interim basis, a key objective became to conserve cash, and this was reflected throughout the total planning of the firm.

Another example of a financial objective that could influence planning would be to raise the market value of stock. An electrical goods manufacturing company, in formulating its long-term product strategy, determined it needed to acquire a company as a means of diversifying its rather narrow consumer goods product lines. The president accepted this proposal, but wished to delay its implementation until the price of his stock could be raised so as to obtain a more desirable relative basis for acquiring a company by trading of stock. This meant that company planning would reflect short-term programs that would have the effect of raising the market price of the stock in the relatively near future.

Operating Objectives

Objectives other than those immediately and directly associated with profit are significant for planning purposes. (The examples given here are meant to be merely illustrative rather than definitive or exhaustive.) For instance, such an operating objective might be to achieve a particular balance between defense and commercial business.

An electronics company had 80 percent of its sales from governmental purchasers—mostly for defense—and only 20 percent in normal commercial markets. The president, believing the company lacked appropriate control over its own destiny because of the continuing potentiality of cancellation of government contracts, explicitly desired more nearly to equalize the proportions. In a somewhat similar way, the management of a photographic equipment company desired a better balance of business, from the high-priced equipment market and the lower-priced equipment market. Having previously been in professional level equipment, the firm recognized its greater vulnerability to recessions because such purchases were more postponable in nature than tended to be true of lower-priced equipment.

A major appliance manufacturer desired a better balance between foreign and domestic sales. This firm was anxious to achieve a rather sharp rate of growth, and recognized that certain foreign markets were growing at a rate appreciably more rapid than U.S. markets. Accordingly, it established specific targets in terms of the balance it hoped to achieve in future years between the two major operating components, overseas and domestic.

Another kind of operating objective might be to broaden the customer base of the company. This objective was established in the case of an industrial chemicals company which received such an extremely heavy proportion of its sales from just five customers that the loss of any one of them would have had a serious effect on the business as a whole.

In certain instances a firm might have an explicit objective of maintaining a specific minimum rate of utilization of a key facility. An industrial products company, with key technological interests in metallurgy, maintained a relatively high-cost steelmaking capacity of its own. It wished to operate these facilities as a hedge against steel strikes or a mobilization period in which steel might be in short supply, and also for its own research and development interests. Careful planning was required, however, to maintain effective utilization of the facilities to keep costs within reasonable limits.

Objectives related to growth rates and industry position or leadership are often expressed in terms of share of market to be achieved.

To a casual observer some of these objectives may appear to go well beyond marketing considerations, and in some cases this is certainly true. However, all of them have market manifestations and provide initial considerations for programming of corporate effort, if in fact that effort is to be goal directed. A final example illustrates this point.

To assure regular employment for the labor force could be another kind of operating objective. The president of one of the nation's largest paper mills indicated that one of his two key objectives was to be sure that each employee then working for the company would have a job ten years hence. Fulfillment of this objective required that the sales of the company's products be forecast that far ahead, and then that the level of labor utilization required for that volume of operations be forecast, with allowances for forseeable production automation. Any discrepancies from the size of the existing labor force would have to be made up from new products or new areas of operations.

This procedural point raises the question: How are the different objectives established? Defining objectives clearly is not always an easy task; often it requires considerable analysis of the problems and environment of the business. Certain objectives may be formulated primarily as management policy—earning a stated minimum return on the invested capital or maintaining regular employment for the labor force. Other objectives can be identified only after intensive study and evaluation of the firm's competitors and of the existing economic situation. Reasonable goals for planning are based on a thorough study of the business and the factors that affect it. Also, objectives, as well as the total planning process, must reflect a time perspective. As a matter of fact, *every* factor in the planning process has a time dimension. What may be suitable in the way of facilities, personnel, and organizational structure today, for example, may be poorly suited to corporate needs next month, or next year, or in longer-term periods as the operating variables change.

SELECTION OF TARGET MARKETS

The second aspect of formulating a marketing strategy involves the selection of target markets. Objectives can be achieved only through action in specific markets. No matter how dispersed the activities of the firm are, and regardless of the number and variety of different markets in which it engages, operating effort must ultimately be reduced to the level of specific markets. The isolation of specific markets is referred to as *market segmentation.*

Two features concerning market segmentation are important to understand clearly. First, the process of segmentation is essential to planning marketing strategy since the isolated segment is the target for marketing effort. Thus, the market segment offers an arena for concentration of marketing resources. Second, the result of segmentation is unique to the firm that defines the segment. Since markets can be viewed from a number of different vantage points, no two firms will view segmentation in the same perspective. The following quote illustrates the essence of the role of segmentation in formulating marketing strategy:

> Segmentation implicitly means identifying competitors, and their resources relative to yours, for each relevant market-product pairing. Successful market strategies in effect segment the total market in a way that minimizes competitors' strengths while maximizing yours. The parallel in military strategy is "isolating the battlefield." Control Data's spectacular success in entering the computer market against IBM is a classic example of astute segmentation. Most dramatically successful business strategies are based on market segmentation and concentration of resources in that segment.[10]

The sale of automobiles amounts for billions of dollars annually, yet they are largely sold one at a time to individuals. There really is no such thing as the *electronics* market or *paper* market or *chemicals* market. Each of these markets has many, many segments. The marketer needs to understand the requirements of effective competition in the specific markets in which action will take place.

Specific market segments may be isolated on a wide variety of different criteria. Figure 4-1 provides a classification of potential segments based on possible physical attributes of the market and behavorial characteristics of purchasers. For any segmentation of a market to be useful in strategic planning, it must have the following characteristics. First, the segment must contain sufficient revenue potential to justify financial objectives. Second, the segment must have sufficient stability to allow adequate time to achieve both financial and operating objectives. Third, the selected segment must be accessible so as to assure effectiveness of marketing efforts. Finally, the market segment should be capable of potential measurement so as to provide a basis for judging marketing efforts.

Market segments selected for exploitation become target markets. The target market is an extension of the objectives contained in the first step of formulating the marketing strategy. Targets identify the arena within which objectives must be realized.

FORMULATION OF THE MARKETING MIX

Depending upon the objectives and target markets selected, the manager must develop the correct combination of marketing effort to serve each specific segment effectively. This combination of efforts is frequently

---

[10] "The Strategic Perspective," *Perspectives,* No. 38 The Boston Consulting Group, Inc., Boston, Massachusetts, 1968.

called the *marketing mix*. The essence of formulating a marketing mix is found in alternative ways a firm can differentiate aspects of its marketing activities. Since the firm is viewed as engaging in competition for differential advantage, the actual differential between firms engaged in a specific segment can be traced to the marketing mix formulation.

The marketing mix is composed of four subcombinations called the *product mix,* the *distribution mix,* the *communication mix,* and the *price mix.* These several mixes that combine to form the overall marketing mix are the principal linkages between the firm and its selected target markets. The marketing mix refers to the actual work that must be realized in each target market to reach corporate objectives.

The task of adjusting products to specific target markets is known as *product-market matching.* The determination of the number of product lines is referred to as the *strategic product adjustment.* Determination of the variations to be offered within each line is identified as the *tactical product adjustment.* The actual product assortment that is matched to the market segment is known as the *product mix.*

Once appropriate products are selected, provision must be made to link the highly specialized market segments with the producing firm. An

FIGURE 4-1
Criteria for Market Segmentation

Physical Attributes of the Market

Size of Market	Geographic Location	Demographic Description of Purchasers	

No. of units sold
Dollar sales
Share of market
  held by each
  competitor
	Sales by region
	Sales by county size
	Sales by city size
	Specific locations
	Kinds of stores where
	  stores are made
		Sex
		Age
		Income
		Occupation
		Marital status
			No. of persons
			  in family
			Race
			Religion
			Education

Behavioral Characteristics of Purchasers

When Purchases Are Made	Reasons for Purchasing	Social-Psychological Classification of Users	Purchasing Influences	How Buying Is Done

Month
Week
Season
Day of week
	Obvious utility
	Psychological
	Major and
	  minor uses
		Social class
		Value differences
		Introvert-extrovert
		Others
			Who uses product
			Who buys product
			Who influences
			  buying
				Impulse or
				  by brand
				  request
				Unit sizes
				  bought
				No. of units
				  bought
				Frequency

Source: Adapted from Jack Z. Sissors, "What is a Market?" *Journal of Marketing,* Vol. 30 (July 1966), p. 21, published by the American Marketing Association.

elaborate organization of institutions has developed to help in the process of exchanging ownership and of physically moving goods to market segments. These institutions assist in the overall marketing process by assembling unique assortments of goods to match different demand segments. They also assist the marketing process by stimulating the exchange process. To implement a marketing strategy, different combinations of these institutions must be selected and organized into functioning units. The particular combination selected is known as the *distribution mix*.

Communications is vital in bringing about the exchange of commodities in a free society. Without communications the consumer would not be aware that products are available. Furthermore, in a free society each firm competes for the consumers' favors through communicating with them in a persuasive way. Such activities as personal selling, advertising, sales promotion, dealer training, and so on must be organized into a unified force to help achieve target markets. The combination of means selected is known as the *communication mix*.

Finally, the price and terms of sale must be delineated. The price places a value on the overall marketing mix in the eyes of the potential buyer and constitutes the *price mix*. While all aspects of the marketing mix are capable of significant differentiation, price is not. In essence, given all other factors, price encourages or discourages transaction.

RESOURCE ALLOCATION AND MOBILIZATION

The final step of formulating the overall market strategy consists of the mobilization and allocation of physical and human resources. The objectives combined with the marketing mix to be executed govern the resources needed to meet the requirements for effective competition. When all elements of the marketing strategy are aligned and properly balanced, performance should lead to the achievement of objectives. Stated somewhat differently, it should lead to a matching of effort with opportunity.

Physical facilities and human resources should be considered together because both provide the necessary means for the execution of the marketing mix. Human resources are the more important of the two, however, since frequently they cannot be purchased on the open market as can plants and equipment. The term *human resources* is used to describe the innate capacity, knowledge, experience, and skill which individuals and groups must have if they are to execute effectively the task required. Human resources are placed at this point in the planning sequence because if the firm is to be effective in the specific markets selected and achieve its objectives, the fundamental characteristics of individuals and groups must be determined by the tasks they are expected to accomplish. Thus, the planner must consider two principal factors here: (1) the kinds of skills and capabilities required in the people who carry out the job to be done, and (2) the number of people needed to do this work.

The term *physical facilities* is used in a broad sense to describe the equipment, supplies, and buildings needed to compete effectively in particular markets. The term covers all marketing facilities and may include the supporting production facilities required to produce the selected product mix. In general, physical facilities are designed to help individuals and groups either directly or indirectly to perform their functions with economy and effectiveness.

ONE STRATEGY OR MANY?

Since marketing strategy involves a basic five-step planning procedure, can a firm have more than one strategy at a time? The answer is yes. The overall strategic perspective of an individual firm is based on the number of market segments selected as targets and the degree to which one or more aspects of the marketing mix are varied in an effort to differentiate the firm from competition. The range of available strategies can be classified as *segmented* and *nonsegmented* marketing. Simply stated, the key to implementation of multiple marketing strategies is the selection of more than one target market. Each strategy is briefly reviewed.

Nonsegmented marketing strategy views the full range of potential buyers as a single group for purposes of programming marketing mix effort. No significant change in the marketing mix is programmed to appeal to the needs of specific buyer segments. In contrast, the communication effort programmed into a nonsegmented strategy usually strives to influence potential purchasers toward the virtue of the single offering. The strategy followed by Volkswagen in the North American market up until the introduction of United States subcompacts is a good example of a nonsegmented strategy. The product offering was essentially held constant over a number of model years, while the remainder of the marketing mix effort was directed to any or all potential buyers. No attempt was made to identify or appeal to different buyer groups. It is important to note that the strategy of nonsegmented marketing does not imply a small or limited market. Indeed, the Volkswagen "segment," or target, was North America. Rather, nonsegmented marketing reflects an attitude on the part of management that no specific benefit would result from further refinements in target market groupings.

Segmented marketing, as the name implies, reflects a strategy in which the total potential market is subdivided for purposes of marketing mix programming. You will recall from earlier discussions that the major way a firm can differentiate from competitors is by virtue of marketing mix adjustment. Within the category of segmented marketing, we can identify two subclassifications—*limited-line* and *broad-line*.

The most radical adjustment is to modify or differentiate a firm's product-mix in an effort to appeal to a specific target market. For example, a firm may select to manufacture tapes for the consumer and industrial market in a wide variety of different sizes, grades, and even under different labels. A food or appliance manufacturer may select to sell the same basic product under two different labels or brands. This form of segmented marketing is identified as broad-line because the product-mix is being substantially altered to accommodate different market segments. To support the variation in a broad-line offering, substantial modifications can be expected in other areas of the overall marketing mix.

The second category of segmented marketing strategy is referred to as limited-line because the product-service offering is only modified as absolutely necessary to accommodate specific segment requirements. However, distribution, communication, and even price offerings of the firm may be substantially altered between market segments. The product may be offered for sale in a variety of different marketing channels so as to reach the purchase potential of a number of different segments. Personal selling and advertising efforts may be modified to reach multiple segments. Finally, price variations to reflect purchase at different times or places may be introduced to the segmented strategy.

In summary, a firm that selects to follow a single strategy is viewed as being engaged in nonsegmented marketing. The identification of multiple target markets requires multiple marketing strategy. The selection of multiple strategies is referred to as segmented marketing. Two categories of segmented marketing reflective of the degree of product differentiation were identified. If the product-service offering is subject to substantial differentiation as a major aspect of the strategy, we refer to this type of segmented marketing as broad-line differentiated. If the marketing mix is subject to modification between market segments but primary emphasis is *not* placed on the product-mix, we refer to the strategy as limited-line. Significant differences in flexibility to adjust offerings rapidly exist between firms following a broad as compared to a limited-line strategy. This aspect of strategy formulation is further developed in Chapter 10.

STRATEGIC PLANNING IN ACTION

Our discussion of strategic planning has been placed early in the book because it offers a practical conceptual structure for the development of marketing effort. It also provides a philosophy through which one may observe a wide variety of marketing systems in action. The following example is given in order to test the relevance of this planning structure in analyzing a basic adjustment made by management in competitive strategy.

THE ILLUSTRATION OF THE XYZ PAPER COMPANY

The XYZ Paper Company, a midwestern paper mill, had been known for many years as a leading producer of kraft papers used in making various kinds of bags, such as grocery and shopping bags. The mill was nonintegrated, meaning that the pulp- and paper-making were separate operations, not linked in one continuous process. Rival southern mills, having an important competitive advantage because of newer and faster equipment, lower taxes, cheaper labor, and greater efficiency because of integrated pulp-paper operations, had seriously infringed on XYZ's market position. A number of different changes were made by XYZ management in an attempt to regain sales. Colored papers were introduced, lighter weight papers were developed, and a larger proportion of output was allocated to high-grade specialty papers. When the new kinds of papers failed to bring a substantial increase in sales, management finally concluded that a major new product would have to be added.

It had been observed that the use of plastic-coated papers, for which the company produced the base stock, had expanded considerably in both the industrial (for example, food packaging) and consumer (for example, paper picnic plates) areas. Statistics confirmed the accuracy of this observation: use of plastic-coated papers *had* increased tremendously in the most recent five-year period. Convinced that this was an attractive new area for expansion, the XYZ Company purchased the most modern coating equipment available. Recalling the advantage enjoyed by some southern mills because of their larger, faster equipment, XYZ purchased a high-speed coater which, at the time of installation, was one of the largest in the industry. Crews from the paper machines were trained to operate the coating machine—but they experienced considerable difficulty in getting it to perform properly. The sales force, at its annual sales meeting, was told about the installation of the new machine, and the technical research director described what grades of paper could be coated on the machine, and some of the important uses of the various grades. The sales manager delivered an inspired talk to the sales force on the growth potential of plastic papers; then he distributed price sheets. Shortly afterward, advertisements were run in the trade press, announcing the new operations, and the new program was put into effect.

Question: What do you think of the company's strategy up to this point? Was the expansion program soundly conceived? Can you spot any weaknesses in the approach taken by XYZ? Try to arrive at some tentative conclusions before reading further.

Sales response to XYZ's new program was poor. The coating machine was in use only about 10 hours a week, although fixed charges on the machine amounted to $25 per hour on a 24-hour-a-day, 5-day-a-week basis. There seemed to be two chief reasons for the disappointing results. First, the sales force had difficulty in selling the product. Potential buyers asked many technical questions that the salesmen were unable to answer. For example, one prospect wanted to know the temperature at which the plastic would be formed on the paper. To ease this problem of providing technical information, two men from the technical department were designated to help the salesmen on important or difficult calls. The second chief reason for disappointing results was that when orders were received, the coating machine operators had difficulty meeting the product specifications, which resulted in a high quantity of scrap and many delays in delivery. To combat the situation, the technical director of the company was asked to take charge of the equipment temporarily, and regular test runs were made at times when orders were not being filled, to augment the training of operating crews. Management felt that these changes would help the situation.

Question: How do you regard the program now? Have your earlier views been borne out? Do you see other mistakes made by the XYZ Company? What should the company have done when it discovered the two major difficulties in its program? Think about this before proceeding.

Although somewhat helpful, these changes did not materially improve the situation. Several months later two salesmen were hired to handle plastic-coated paper on a full-time basis in the principal markets, which centered around New York and Chicago. These important markets had not been adequately covered because the regular salesmen were kept busy with their usual accounts, and also, it seemed, because they were less enthusiastic about the coating phase of the business.

A short time later, management concluded that a reorganization of the coating operations was necessary. The company president decided to put a general manager in charge of all operations, to avoid divided responsibility and buck-passing. Since the technical director had been put in charge of coating production temporarily (replacing the general production manager), it meant that the same group was responsible for making the product and for judging whether it met quality standards. The sales manager criticized this arrangement, saying that quality control was one of his big problems in satisfying customers. He also criticized the company for failing to develop specific grades of coated papers for particular product applications. In response, the product development manager explained that the technical department was often unable to formulate the grades of paper the sales manager proposed. Even when the technicians were successful in using pilot equipment in the laboratory, he said, there were numerous delays before the product could actually be made on the high-speed coater.

The president thought the new general manager of coating operations should have a sales background, primarily since he considered the problem mostly one of marketing. Because no one in the organization appeared qualified, the assistant general sales manager from one of the larger plastic-coating firms was hired as general manager of coating operations. After working a few weeks for XYZ, the new manager asked to have a study made of specific markets within the general coated papers field, to determine which grades the company was best equipped to make and which were the most attractive from the standpoint of sales potential.

Question: Now do you begin to see more clearly some of the difficulties? How should management have approached this new area? Try to think through as complete an answer as possible before proceeding.

When the market study was completed, management realized that the company was in an unfavorable position to compete effectively in any of the markets that had originally appeared attractive. In the high-profit-margin specialty papers, XYZ was outclassed by the superior technical skill and specially designed equipment of the custom coaters. Specialty papers usually were produced in short runs, which would negate the tremendous speed of the XYZ coater. Moreover, the downtime that would be needed between each run to ready the machine for the next job was economically unsound.

It was also discovered that the large tonnage grades which could be coated on the large machine could not use paper milled at XYZ. This meant that the basic paper stock had to be purchased on the outside, which completely canceled one of the company's original objectives in setting up the program—to place the paper mill on a better competitive footing. Ultimately, management concluded that the paper facilities and the coating facilities were basically incompatible. For that matter they were doubtful about XYZ's attempt to get into the coated-paper field. The coating operation was apparently destined to use only a very small amount of paper compared to the mill's capacity. Basically, the characteristics of the two businesses differed. Paper was sold to a relatively few large customers, who were in close liaison with the mill and who carried their own inventories. Coated paper, on the other hand, went to many small concerns, resulting in complicated ordering systems, extensive bookkeeping, and a major inventory to be carried by the XYZ Company.

Since business had materially improved in paper operations as the economy turned sharply upward, and since the coating machine had been operating only about one day per week, management decided to concentrate on the other phases of the business, and let the manager of coating operations do the best he could, recognizing that opportunity for profitable operation of this facility was extremely unlikely.

Question: What was wrong with the planning approach followed by the XYZ Company? What approach should have been taken?

We will concede that hindsight is better than foresight and that it is always easier to be critical than creative; nevertheless, it is obvious that many fundamental errors in programming were made by this company. Notice that for all practical purposes the programming began with the purchase of equipment. All that preceded this decision was the recognition that paper sales were declining because of southern competition and that the *generalized* coating field was growing. The initial error was inevitably compounded. In summary, let us look at some of the factors in this case.

1. Objectives were never clearly established. These would have been derived in part from a careful analysis of southern competition. This could have demonstrated what specific operational goals, for example, would have to be accomplished.

2. Only the *generalized* coating market was considered by XYZ, although marketing action inevitably takes place in *specific* markets.

3. Because it failed to identify the character of the market and the factors influencing purchase action, the XYZ Company was unable to establish market targets or to determine whether marketing effort would provide adequate opportunity for achieving management goals.

4. The necessary marketing mix was not adequately established and assigned; that is, what would salesmen be called upon to do? What would be required in the way of product development or technical activity? The proper moves for each area could only have been determined by knowing market characteristics.

5. Personnel were selected on the basis of their availability rather than on the basis of the skills needed to perform the necessary activities; that is, crews from the paper machines and regular salesmen were assigned to the coating operation. Requisite qualities of human resources were woefully lacking in almost every segment of operations.

6. Machinery was selected without regard for the specific requirements to compete effectively in a particular phase of the coating markets. Rather, it was purchased because it was big and high-speed. The really relevant issues, related to the kind of facilities needed and their capacity, were not considered.

7. The organization structure failed to relate and integrate functions, facilities, and personnel. This is reflected in part by the subsequent changes that were made. Notice, for example, the difficulties encountered

in selling; the regular paper salesmen were not organized and perhaps could never be organized to do a truly effective job.

8. Operating procedures were noticeably lacking. Product development, production, and order handling difficulties are illustrative. Standards of performance were almost nonexistent.

On the basis of these observations, the general process of planning should now be clearer in terms of its usefulness for bringing about major changes in competitive strategy and adjustment.

A COMPOSITE VIEW THUS FAR

Throughout the first four chapters, the firm as a competitive entity in a free market society has been introduced and discussed. To illustrate the need for a market orientation as a philosophy of business, a series of four *managerial activities* were introduced in Chapter 2. Within the four managerial activities in Chapter 3 we identified nine *managerial functions of marketing* which were universal to firms engaged in competition for differential advantage. In Chapter 4 the formulation of a marketing strategy was introduced in terms of five interrelated planning steps.

In each situation we were discussing the responsibilities and duties of marketing management from a different perspective. Naturally, the way you treat a specific item at a specific point depends upon the relevant perspective to capture properly the subject at hand. However, in the event that confusion was introduced by nature of the selected treatment, each

FIGURE 4-2
Managerial Actions and Functions in Marketing Strategy Planning

Managerial Activities	Managerial Functions	Marketing Strategy Planning
Market opportunity Assessment	Market delineation Purchase behavior motivation	Environmental monitoring Identification of objectives Selection of target markets
Product-service Market matching	Product service adjustment	Formulation of the marketing mix
Marketing programming	Channel selection Physical distribution Communication Price	
Execution	Organization Administration	Resource allocation and mobilization

perspective is illustrated and managerially related in Figure 4-2. Figure 4-2 should be viewed by the reader as a logical extension of Figure 2-3.

SUMMARY

The contemporary marketing management process has been characterized as a goal-directed effort in which the total system of action is mobilized to accomplish specific objectives. To afford the maximum opportunity for success, management must combine a series of inputs in order to achieve a predetermined series of outputs. This is achieved by continuous environmental monitoring and the formulation of a marketing strategy to guide managerial action.

The purpose of environmental monitoring is to provide a systematic review, appraisal, and projection of all aspects of the environment that involve existing and potential firm operations. Such sensing requires monitoring of six subenvironmental categories: *economic, competitive, technological, support, political and legal,* and *cultural and social.* The end result of environmental monitoring is to develop an informed basis for taking selective initiative in a changing environment. This selective initiative should provide the corporate self-renewal necessary for growth.

The process by which management plans the deployment of resources to assure growth was identified as *marketing strategy planning*. Strategy formulation consists of five interrelated steps. The planning process begins with *environmental monitoring* and results in the establishment of *objectives*. The objectives are achieved through purposeful action in *specific target markets*. The process of market segmentation is critical to strategic planning. The fourth is to determine the requirements of effective competition in terms of the *marketing mix* that must be provided to reach the targets selected. The final step in strategic planning is *resource allocation and mobilization*.

A firm may select to engage in *segmented* or *nonsegmented* marketing depending upon the number of target markets selected. If segmented marketing is the order of the day, multiple strategies will be required. If such strategy adjustment involves changes in product-service offerings, the firm is engaged in broad-line segmented marketing. If strategic modifications are limited to marketing mix areas other than the product-service offering, the multiple strategy is called limited-line segmented marketing.

When planning is undertaken with sufficient research, marketing performance should achieve the desired objectives. Planning skill is essential to the successful marketing executive in today's complex business environment.

QUESTIONS AND PROBLEMS

1. What areas are of concern in the process of environmental monitoring?
2. What conditions must be met to make effective use of technology for economic progress?
3. Consumerism is a public reaction to the failure of marketers to supply goods and services wanted by consumers. Explain.
4. Explain the major pressures for growth on the corporation.
5. What is a marketing strategy?
6. Explain the relationship between selecting market targets and market segmentation.
7. Discuss the different bases for segmenting a market.
8. Explain the difference between limited-line and broad-line segmented marketing.

BIBLIOGRAPHY

ALDERSON, WROE, *Marketing Behavior and Executive Action.* Homewood, Ill.: Richard D. Irwin, Inc., 1957.

BAUMOL, WILLIAM J., *Business Behavior Value and Growth.* New York: Macmillan Publishing Co., Inc., 1959.

BECKER, HAROLD S., "Technology Assessment: Another View," *Business Horizons* (October 1973), pp. 58–60.

COX, REAVIS, *Distribution in a High-Level Economy.* Englewood Cliffs, N.J.: Prentice-Hall, Inc., 1965.

FRANK, R. E., W. F. MASSY, and Y. WIND, *Market Segmentation.* Englewood Cliffs, N.J.: Prentice-Hall, Inc., 1972.

GREYSER, STEPHEN, A., and STEVEN L. DIAMOND, "Business Adapting to Consumers," *Harvard Business Review* (September–October 1974), pp. 38–58.

KOTLER, PHILIP, *Marketing Management* (2nd ed.). Englewood Cliffs, N.J.: Prentice-Hall, Inc., 1972.

LAZER, WILLIAM, *Marketing Management.* New York: John Wiley & Sons, Inc., 1971.

LEVITT, THEODORE, "Marketing Tactics in a Time of Shortages," *Harvard Business Review* (November–December 1974), pp. 6–7.

MCCARTHY, E. JEROME, *Basic Marketing: A Managerial Approach* (5th ed.). Homewood, Ill.: Richard D. Irwin, Inc., 1974.

SHUBIK, MARTIN, *Strategy and Market Structure.* New York: John Wiley & Sons, Inc., 1971.

Part II

MARKET OPPORTUNITY ASSESSMENT

We have seen in Part One that a market orientation as a philosophy of business management places the customer as the focal point of marketing strategy planning. If the enterprise is to function effectively, it must maintain a proper state of adjustment to its operating environment. In fact, knowledge of that environment is the beginning point of all sound marketing effort. The operating environment within which the enterprise functions is a reflection of the interactions among the institutions and individuals that make up the environment. An understanding in depth of these interactions is the pivot around which all economic life revolves.

Performance of the first two managerial functions of marketing, market delineation and purchase behavior motivation, are the cornerstones of opportunity assessment. Part Two examines the means used to monitor the environment, identify marketing objectives, and select target markets. The quantitative dimensions of the market are referred to as market delineation and are treated in Chapter 5. Through economic monitoring, it is desirable to track potential growth opportunities and assess current markets to identify possible declines. Only in this way can the mission of the enterprise be determined. As new areas of market opportunity are identified, they are singled out for more intensive study. These studies are necessary to determine the feasibility of entry, and in order to establish marketing objectives. As opportunity assessment proceeds and more precise knowledge is gathered, specific target markets are identified which constitute the goals of marketing strategy planning.

Equally as important as the quantitative measurements made in the performance of the market delineation function are the more subjective or qualitative analyses made in the performance of the purchase behavior motivation function. In Chapter 6, existing theories concerning consumer behavior are explored to provide a framework for understanding the complex of psychological and sociological forces at work in the marketplace. In Chapter 7, we examine the kinds of analyses that may be made to provide answers to the underlying motivations concerning why different consumers buy the products they do, where they do, and when they do. With the use of such techniques to break down the market into unique cells, the kind of product adjustments, communication messages, channel structures, and prices needed can be identified and implemented.

To expand our overall understanding of opportunity assessment, the measurement of intermediate and international markets is treated in Chapters 8 and 9. Although we are only devoting one chapter to each of these areas, their importance and difference in comparison to consumer markets should not be overlooked. The intermediate market is much larger in dollar volume than the consumer market. It also has a number of characteristics that are significantly different than those found in the consumer goods market. These differences affect the formulation of marketing strategies. Although quantitative measurements of the intermediate market have been used extensively, purchase motivation analysis is of more recent vintage. Nonetheless, they are as important as in the consumer goods market. In Chapter 8, we explore the kinds of studies needed and the pioneering work to be done in the intermediate area.

In contemporary times, more and more marketers have extended their market horizon beyond the domestic market to the world as their area of market opportunity. Although the need exists for market delineation and purchase behavior motivation, and much the same techniques are used, there are special circumstances in international markets that merit our attention. There is a special need to assess the long- and short-run political risk. To formulate an international strategy, there is a need to understand the cultural and economic characteristics, such as literacy levels, living habits, income levels, credit availability, distribution structures. The area of international markets is discussed in Chapter 9.

Our description of the forces influencing market behavior is of necessity generalized and somewhat simplified. The reader should not lose sight of the complexity of forces that interact in the consummation of any transaction. The objective in our treatment is to introduce the many dimensions of market opportunity assessment.

Chapter 5

Consumer Market Delineation

The initial step in opportunity assessment is the identification of market growth areas to provide alternatives for the establishment of corporate objectives. This is realized through environmental monitoring. A second step is a quantitative delineation of alternatives to assess their relative feasibility and to select specific marketing objectives. It is in terms of the marketing objectives selected that we are able to plan marketing strategy. More detailed quantitative analysis of selected growth opportunities constitutes a third step in which the marketer identifies unique target markets from which he may select those he wishes to cultivate. Only in this way can he determine which markets are large enough to permit profitable operations. Based on the size of these targets, it is possible to identify what production facilities are needed, what inventory levels are necessary, and how many distributors and dealers are needed to reach the market.

Equally important, quantitative identification of the market is needed before purchase motivation investigations can be conducted. Until the market is delineated, it is impossible to determine whether it is worth entering or what kinds of marketing effort and resources will be necessary to serve it profitably. The overall task, then, is to develop a quantitative measurement of product quantities that may be sold in the selected target markets. In addition, it is necessary to delineate identifying characteristics of the purchasing units.

In this chapter, we examine the use of environmental monitoring to identify market opportunities. The techniques used to identify marketing objectives quantitatively and to delineate target markets in the consumer goods market (those used for personal or household consumption) are also examined.

ENVIRONMENTAL MONITORING

In Chapter 4 we described several environments that may be monitored to sense the dynamics of the marketplace at any particular time. These studies may be very extensive or somewhat restricted in scope. A minimal monitoring system would be the surveillance of demographic characteristics of the consuming public and their ability and willingness to purchase. After all, a market is made up of people with money and a willingness to spend.

POPULATION CHARACTERISTICS

The work of the demographer—which involves the statistical study of populations—may have considerable bearing on the selection of appropriate objectives. Changes in the absolute population size have drastic effects on the age composition of the population, the rate of new family formations, and the long-run market opportunity for selected types of goods.

In 1973, the United States population was 211 million. If the birth rate stays at the current level of 2.05 children per woman, population in 1980 will be approximately 230 million.[1] An examination of the age composition of this population is useful in identifying market opportunities. In Figure 5-1, one estimate of the population profile by age and sex is illustrated. In 1968, the age group between 30 and 40 was much smaller than it will be in 1980 because of the decline in births during the thirties. Throughout the decade of the seventies, there will be a very large bulge in the 20 to 40 age bracket, a decline in the 40 to 50 age bracket as the 30 to 40 age bracket deficit moves up, and in the 5 to 15 age bracket because of the lower birth rates in the sixties.

Beyond 1980 there is much conjecture with respect to population increases. In Figure 5-2, a projection of United States population to the year 2020, based on different fertility rates, is shown. Most demographers expect that the rate will not turn up and might even turn down. If the rate stays at 2.05, we can expect 264 million by the year 2000, and about 250 million if the fertility rate drops to 1.8. If the fertility rate drops to 1.8, we can expect zero population growth in approximately 2025.[2] Assuming no change in current rates of fertility, a comparison of numbers in each

---

[1] Reprinted from "Population Slowdown—What It Means to Us," *U.S. News & World Report,* December 25, 1972, p. 59. Copyright 1972. U.S. News & World Report, Inc.

[2] Ibid., p. 59.

age bracket and the product and service categories affected is shown in Figure 5-3.

Relative demand for youth-oriented goods, popular housing, economy autos, and household equipment will increase. As older people acquire more income they will upgrade their standard of living, resulting in

FIGURE 5-1
Population by Age and Sex

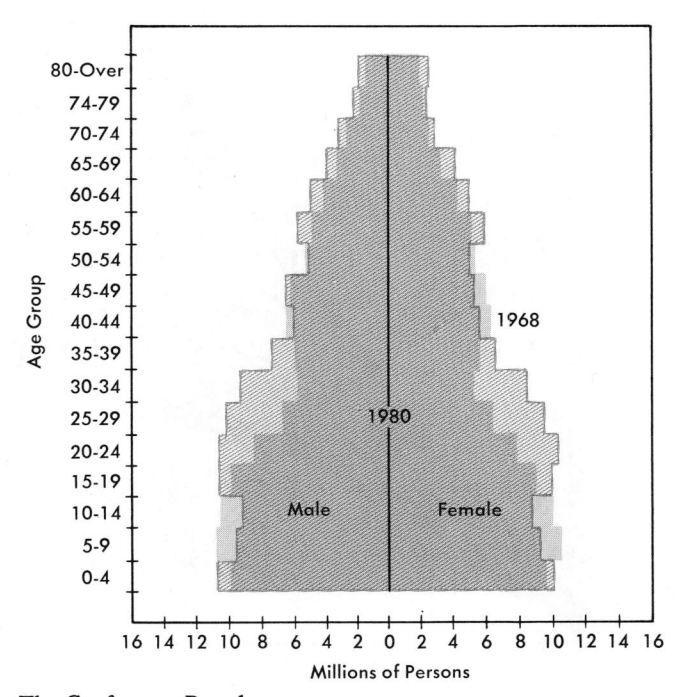

Courtesy: The Conference Board.

an increase in demand for more expensive housing, autos, travel, leisure and luxury goods, medical care, retirement homes, and apartments.

FAMILY FORMATION

Equally as important as population and its age distribution is how that population forms itself into consuming units. In Figure 5-4 we can see the increase in number of families formed up to 1980. By 1980 there will be about 10 million more families than in 1970. This is a larger in-

FIGURE 5-2
Will U.S. Population Level Off?

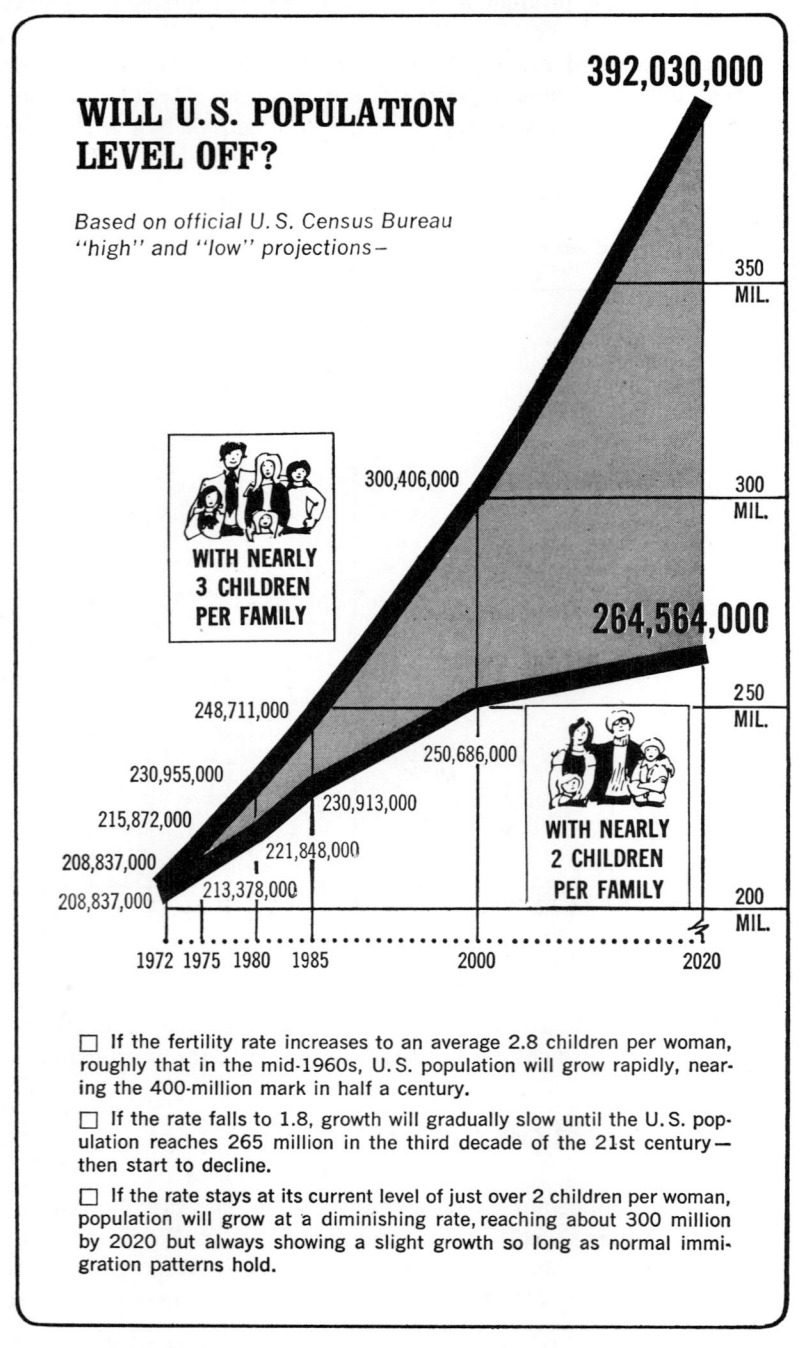

WILL U.S. POPULATION LEVEL OFF?

Based on official U.S. Census Bureau "high" and "low" projections—

392,030,000
350 MIL.
300,406,000
300 MIL.

WITH NEARLY 3 CHILDREN PER FAMILY

264,564,000
250 MIL.
248,711,000
250,686,000
230,955,000
230,913,000
215,872,000
221,848,000
208,837,000
213,378,000
208,837,000

WITH NEARLY 2 CHILDREN PER FAMILY

200 MIL.

1972 1975 1980 1985   2000   2020

☐ If the fertility rate increases to an average 2.8 children per woman, roughly that in the mid-1960s, U.S. population will grow rapidly, nearing the 400-million mark in half a century.

☐ If the rate falls to 1.8, growth will gradually slow until the U.S. population reaches 265 million in the third decade of the 21st century—then start to decline.

☐ If the rate stays at its current level of just over 2 children per woman, population will grow at a diminishing rate, reaching about 300 million by 2020 but always showing a slight growth so long as normal immigration patterns hold.

Source: Reprinted from *U.S. News and World Report,* December 25, 1972, p. 59. Copyright 1972 U.S. News and World Report, Inc.

crease than existed during the 1960–70 decade. New family formation has a large impact on residential construction, credit, and all products required for household establishment. As we have seen from population projection to the year 2000, these markets will begin to show less than average gains after 1980.

FAMILY INCOME

Since markets are made up of people with capacity to buy, incomes by family group are an appropriate measure for environmental monitoring. In 1967 average family income was $9,300 in 1966 dollars. This figure is expected to reach $13,800 by 1980 in 1966 dollars.[3] The number of families in different income categories has changed drastically. Figure 5-5 shows the inverted pyramid of income that will prevail during the decade of the 70s. In 1966 about 15 million families, or almost 30 percent of total families, had incomes of $10,000 or more, representing 55 percent of all income. In 1980 it is expected that about 35 million, or almost 55 percent of all families, will have incomes of $10,000 or more, representing 80 percent of all income in constant 1966 dollars. The extremes of income distribution are no less impressive. Those at the lower income group are declining and the $15,000 and over group are swelling.[4]

Closely allied to absoute family income is the amount of money left over for spending on luxuries once essential needs are satisfied. If we define discretionary income as earnings of families in excess of $10,000 in 1968, the discretionary income pool equaled about $50 billion, or 10 percent of total income. In 1980 this is expected to reach $350 billion in 1968 dollars, or 30 percent of total family income.[5]

WHO CONTROLS THE PURSE STRINGS?

Given the fact that we are moving toward a relatively affluent society, how can we characterize the consuming units quantitatively? Two measures provide an indication as to the types of goods and services that will be demanded. First is the age of the head of the household and second is the educational level. Both of these measures influence the kind of products demanded, and to some extent the best manner to appeal to these buyers.

---

[3] "The Consumer of the Seventies," *National Industrial Conference Board, Inc.,* p. 50.

[4] Ibid., p. 54.

[5] Ibid., p. 58.

FIGURE 5-3
Population Projection to Year 2000

HOW THE AGE MIX OF AMERICANS WILL CHANGE

If Current Trends Hold...

If the fertility rate stays at this year's level — just over 2 children per woman — U.S. population will rise slowly, from 209 million now to 264 million by the year 2000. But major shifts would take place in the age mix, with far-reaching impact on almost all aspects of American life.

CHILDREN AND TEEN-AGERS
NOW   76,849,000
2000   80,743,000

CHANGE: UP 5%

With only a slight increase in numbers, American youth would make up a shrinking share of total U.S. population by century's end—31 per cent, down from 37 per cent now. Relative demand for teachers, school buildings, wide variety of youth-oriented goods would slacken.

YOUNG ADULTS, 20-34
NOW   45,572,000
2000   54,925,000

CHANGE: UP 21%

Now the fastest-growing age group, young adults will show less-than-average gains in numbers by 2000. This is the age bracket that now is the main target of the marketing efforts of business — the group in which people take their first jobs, start families, look for homes, spend and borrow freely.

Family Income and Age of Head

An increasing proportion of income during the decade of the 70s will accrue to households in which the head is under 35 years. In constant 1967 dollars, about 23 percent of total income accrued to households in which the head is under 35. By 1980 this proportion will reach about 33 percent. Households in which the head is over 35, about half of total households by 1980 will have about 66 percent of total income.[6]

Education by Age

In the late 60s about 20 percent of the United States population received some college education, with about 10 percent completing college. By 1980 these relative shares are projected to be 25 percent exposed to some college and 15 percent completing four-year degrees. The change in high school exposure is even more dramatic. In the late 1960s less than

[6] Ibid., p. 28.

FIGURE 5-3
(Continued)

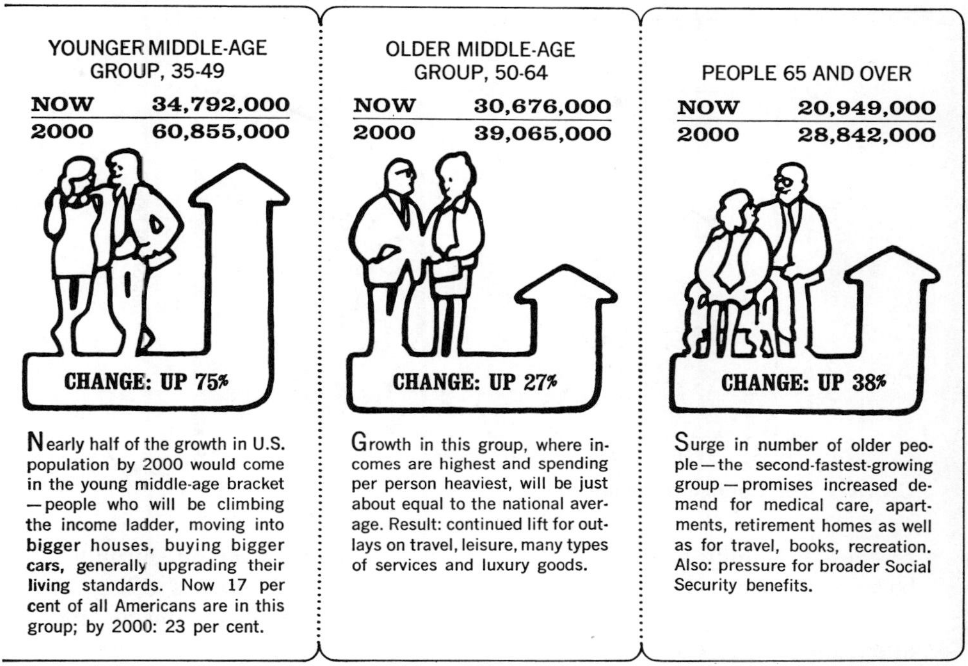

YOUNGER MIDDLE-AGE GROUP, 35-49	OLDER MIDDLE-AGE GROUP, 50-64	PEOPLE 65 AND OVER
NOW 34,792,000	NOW 30,676,000	NOW 20,949,000
2000 60,855,000	2000 39,065,000	2000 28,842,000
CHANGE: UP 75%	**CHANGE: UP 27%**	**CHANGE: UP 38%**
Nearly half of the growth in U.S. population by 2000 would come in the young middle-age bracket — people who will be climbing the income ladder, moving into **bigger** houses, buying bigger **cars**, generally upgrading their living standards. Now 17 per cent of all Americans are in this group; by 2000: 23 per cent.	Growth in this group, where incomes are highest and spending per person heaviest, will be just about equal to the national average. Result: continued lift for outlays on travel, leisure, many types of services and luxury goods.	Surge in number of older people — the second-fastest-growing group — promises increased demand for medical care, apartments, retirement homes as well as for travel, books, recreation. Also: pressure for broader Social Security benefits.

Source: Reprinted from *U.S. News and World Report,* December 25, 1972, pp. 60–61. Copyright 1972 U.S. News and World Report, Inc.

33 percent finished high school. By 1980 this proportion is projected at 40 percent.[7]

The education explosion is greatest in the 25–44 age bracket, the fastest growing group during the decade of the 70s. Households earning $10,000 or more with a head in this age group will command 40 percent of all income compared with about 25 percent in 1967.[8] Households in this age group need different kinds of products and likewise demand different kinds of products than households with older heads.

THE EFFECTS OF AFFLUENCE AND YOUTH

At least during the 70s, the fastest growing market is a relatively affluent young adult, well-educated household. As a result, some product sectors can be expected to grow faster than others. As the youth group

[7] Ibid., p. 30.
[8] Ibid., p. 60.

FIGURE 5-4
Marriages and Husband-Wife Families

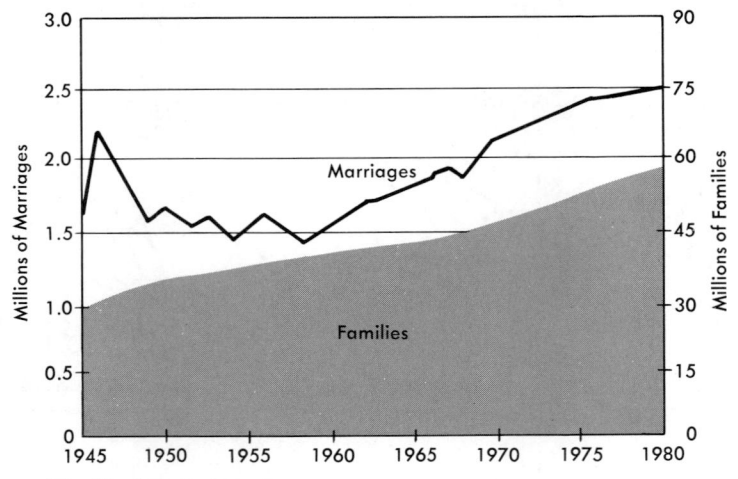

Courtesy: The Conference Board.

reaches the family formation stage, demand for housing, credit, furniture, basic appliances, household items, electric power, and services will grow at an accelerated rate. In addition, demand for upgraded housing and attendant products and services is expected to be strong from the over-35 household heads, who represent about one half of all households but 66 percent of total income.

The affluence level has still another impact on product and services demanded. Engle's Law states that as incomes rise the proportion of total income spent on necessities such as food, housing, and household operations decreases, and expenditures on luxuries increase.[9] We can therefore expect bigger than average growth rates in the luxury category of products. In Figure 5-6 growth rates for selected product sectors have been calculated by applying consumer responses to rising incomes over the past ten years to the projected incomes for the decade of the 70s. As can be seen, the luxury categories show substantial market opportunity.

The above type of economic monitoring is relatively simple to conduct. There is no excuse for corporate surprise when markets begin to shrink. The early warning signals are prevalent long before the changes take place. Although the above may hold for the decade of the 80s, the

---

[9] For a review of Engle's Law, see Hendrik Houthakker, "An International Comparison of Household Expenditure Patterns Commemorating the Centenary of Engle's Law," *Econometrica* (October 1957), pp. 532–51.

FIGURE 5-5
Distribution of Families and Income by Income Group
All Figures in 1966 Dollars
Percent Distribution

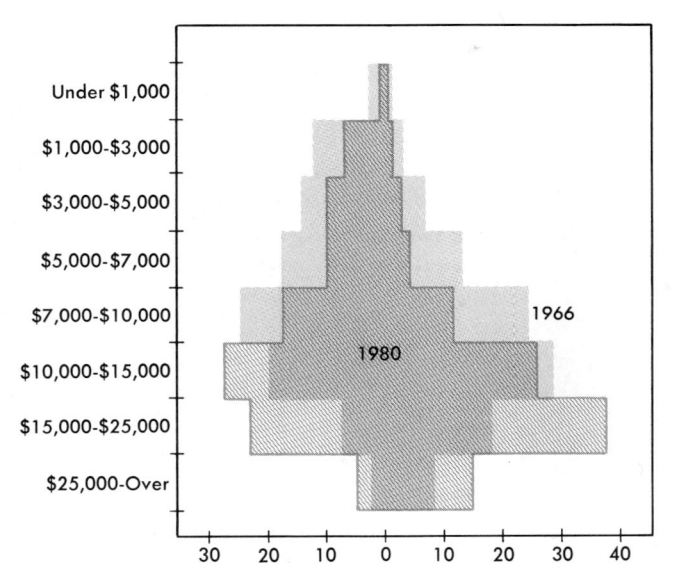

Courtesy: The Conference Board.

population projections shown in Figure 5-3 clearly show that the growth markets of the 70s will not endure as we move toward the year 2000. As companies must plan many years in advance, changing directions for the future should be in the formulative stage today.

Although such aggregative measures of opportunity are useful in giving overall direction, they are not specific enough for identifying corporate marketing objectives or selecting target markets for strategy planning. Nor do they give any hint as to willingness to buy or how these units may be appealed to with marketing effort. This last need must await more qualitative evaluation of markets as described in Chapters 6 and 7. We now turn our attention to more specific analysis of broad opportunity areas identified by such economic monitoring.

IDENTIFICATION OF MARKETING OBJECTIVES

A distinction must be made between the various levels at which objectives may be stated. For example, it may be a financial objective of the corpora-

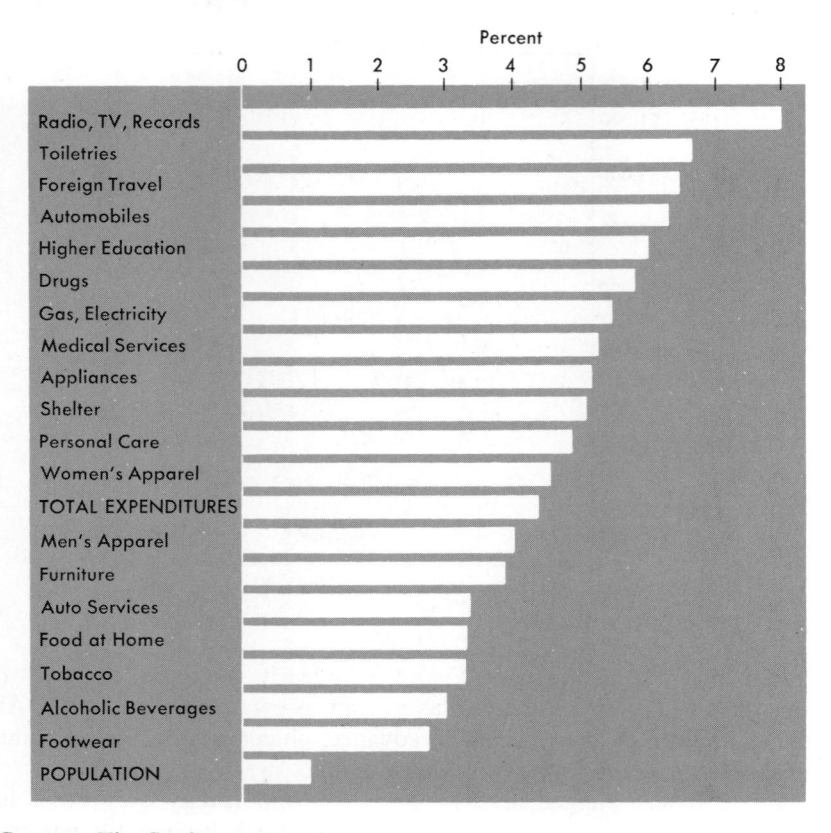

FIGURE 5-6
Projected Growth by Sector
Average Annual Growth Rates: 1968–1980

Sector	Percent
Radio, TV, Records	~8
Toiletries	~6.5
Foreign Travel	~6.3
Automobiles	~6.2
Higher Education	~5.8
Drugs	~5.6
Gas, Electricity	~5.4
Medical Services	~5
Appliances	~5
Shelter	~4.8
Personal Care	~4.6
Women's Apparel	~4.5
TOTAL EXPENDITURES	~4.2
Men's Apparel	~3.8
Furniture	~3.8
Auto Services	~3.4
Food at Home	~3.2
Tobacco	~3
Alcoholic Beverages	~2.8
Footwear	~2.5
POPULATION	~1.2

Courtesy: The Conference Board.

tion to earn a 14 percent return on investment or a stated percent net profit after tax, or a stated earnings per share. These, however, are of no value in giving direction for marketing strategy planning. If these same financial measures are to be achieved in specific markets, such as the recreational equipment market or the transportation market, they provide a beginning for marketing strategy planning.

Statements of marketing objectives should be broad guidelines of marketing policy as shown in Table 5-1. Although an excellent statement of how a diversified corporation executes its market affairs it is not intended as a specific guide to marketing strategy formulation. The individual businesses perform this task as part of the corporate planning process.

TABLE 5-1
The Westinghouse Marketing Purpose

1. To maintain a continuously high level of marketing strategy, practice and cost efficiency which will contribute significantly to the corporation's goals for return on investment and its first in performance objectives.
2. To provide an effective commercial climate for doing business by continuing to promote the corporation's reputation as a vital, dynamic enterprise offering a wide range of quality products and services.
3. To achieve steady growth in profitable sales volume through effective marketing programs that intelligently advertise, promote, distribute and sell the corporation's products and services worldwide.
4. To attain optimal price realization on the sale of the corporation's products and services.
5. To develop, through market research, accurate business forecasting information to assist the corporation in planning people, product, and facility needs.
6. To act as an "early warning system" to detect new and profitable markets for the corporation's present products and services and to act as a "feedback" from current markets on what new products and services should be developed to meet changing needs.
7. To encourage employees in all functions to respond accurately and quickly to customer needs by helping them understand the markets in which the corporation competes, the kind of competition we face there and the needs of the customers in those markets.
8. To provide fast, reliable and economical after-sale service for the corporation's products.
9. To maintain the highest ethical standards in all the corporation's dealings with other organizations and the public.
10. To make sure the corporation has a continuous supply of the best marketing personnel available and that the selection, development and utilization of these employees enables them to perform at their highest potential of efficiency and satisfaction.

Courtesy: Westinghouse Electric Corporation.

An example of marketing objectives cast in more operational terms is shown in Figure 5-7. In this case, a railroad includes in its statement of objectives specific target markets within which improved performance is desired.

FIGURE 5-7
Annual Marketing Objectives for Major U.S. Railroad

1. Increase share of present rail traffic.
2. Develop new traffic by recapture from competing modes and joint arrangements with other modes.
3. Develop new traffic through industrial development projects, both market oriented and resource based.
4. Develop new revenues from nonrail sources which are related to transportation of freight.
5. Increase profitability of presently marginal traffic.

The formulation of overall marketing objectives should be developed in a means-end chain. A financial objective to realize an increase in absolute dollar profit after tax is initially stated. Through environmental monitoring two *means* may be identified: marketing products in the recreational equipment market or marketing products in the precision machine tool market. The latter is selected and the financial objective (the end) is to be achieved in the precision machine tool market (the means). The *means* then becomes an *end*. In order to achieve this end, alternatives (means) could be identified as a change in the channel of distribution or a more intensive use of the company's direct sales force. If the means, a change in channel of distribution, is selected, this now becomes an end. Thus, the new end is to establish a revamped channel of distribution to reach the precision machine tool market. Two alternatives—means—may be identified to be the development of a new dealer structure or more intensive use of the present dealers. If the first means is selected, it then becomes an end, and alternative means to obtain new dealers must be evaluated. The process can go on and on.

When we speak of identifying marketing objectives in opportunity assessment, which objectives are we referring to? If ends are synonymous with objectives it is clear that a $3.5 million profit after tax in the precision machine tool industry is an objective for marketing strategy planning. The development of a new distribution channel is an objective of the distribution mix formulation. Recruitment of new dealers to develop the new channel is an objective of the communications mix formulation.

In this section, reference is to the first level of objectives—which markets are we going to operate in. In this respect, the objective is to delineate markets capable of yielding financial objectives. Consequently, we must precisely describe the overall opportunities identified in order to select potential markets to operate in and those segments of the total market we wish to evaluate as target markets.

There is an overlap in selecting marketing objectives and target markets. Precise information is needed on all market opportunities identified in environmental monitoring to determine which are worthy of cultivation. As this decision is made the overall marketing objectives can then be stated. For example, the marketing objective stated in Figure 5-7—develop new revenues from nonrail sources related to transportation of freight—could not have been stated without a precise delineation of the market for physical distribution performance.

Our examples have stressed the need for precise delineation of new market opportunities. The need continuously to evaluate existing markets in which the corporation is currently operating for year to year formulation of marketing strategy should not be overlooked.

Attention is now directed to methods available to delineate more precisely those areas of market opportunity identified by environmental monitoring. Although there are many different types of market investigations, we shall limit our discussion to two: (1) the historical method, and (2) the buildup method. In the following section we shall not describe in detail the statistical and marketing research techniques used; rather, we shall examine the concepts used.[10]

THE HISTORICAL METHOD

The historical method relies on past events as a guide to future behavior. Some of the past events of particular interest to the marketer are those related to income and expenditure as income changes. The information used in historical studies is confined to collected and published data, sometimes known as secondary data, supplemented by internal company records.

For estimating purposes, the relationship between income level and actual expenditure must be extended to include future income level. Since detailed income data are gathered only once every ten years, at the time the census is taken, the marketer must be able to estimate income in the intervening years. There are several sources from which he can secure information, such as that described at the beginning of this chapter, on income levels.[11]

Data on consumption expenditures for differing household incomes are not as easy to obtain. Detailed studies of this type have not been con-

---

[10] For a discussion of techniques used, see David J. Luck, Hugh G. Wales, and Donald A. Taylor, *Marketing Research,* 4th ed. (Englewood Cliffs, N.J.: Prentice-Hall, Inc., 1974).

[11] "The Consumer of the Seventies."

ducted on a regular basis.[12] Fortunately, consumption patterns do not change rapidly and consumption expenditure data of relative vintage may be used for making a first estimate of market size. For example, a corporation may be satisfied with the growth rate projection of 8 percent given in Figure 5-6 for radios, television sets, and phonographs, but they might want to know the actual dollar market size as well. Past studies reveal that of the total expenditures on recreation in 1975 (6.5 percent of all consumption expenditures), 25 percent will be spent in the brown goods market, the name given to this class of product.[13] Thus, if total consumer expenditures in the United States are estimated to be $1,205.5 billion in 1980,[14] a first estimate of the radio, television, and phonograph market would be $19.589 billion (25 percent of 6.5 percent of $1,205.5 billion). This provides a quantitative estimate of the size of the market, but gives no indication of the different kinds of communication equipment purchased, the number and strength of competitors, or the market share that any one company might expect to capture. Nevertheless, it may be enough of a delineation for a company to state a preliminary marketing objective as "to achieve a 12 percent market share of the radio, television, and phonograph market over the next two years."

It is not always necessary to have estimates of past expenditure patterns. If industry sales figures are available, either through trade associations or government reports, these may be related to any number of statistical series that are forecast on a regular basis. Some of the more widely used series are gross national product, per capita income, population, new housing starts. Through comparing past industry sales over time with these indices, relationships can be developed in the form of regression equations which can then be applied to estimates of future markets. For example, aggregate hotel income shows a very close relationship to national income, as shown in Figure 5-8.

If one is lucky enough to find an index that leads industry sales, that is, that changes before industry sales change, it is possible to use actual data in making the projection. For example, residential building permits lead the index of sales of home heating equipment by several months. Since building permits are reported frequently, it is relatively easy to estimate sales for relatively short periods of time in the future.

---

[12] An original study was conducted by *Life* in 1957, entitled *Life Study of Consumer Expenditures*. In 1965 the Conference Board published *Expenditure Patterns of the American Family,* and in 1967, *Market Profiles of Consumer Products.*

[13] National Economic Projection Series, *Study of Consumer Expenditures,* Report No. 71-N-2 National Planning Association (November 1971), p. S.14.

[14] Ibid., p. S.9.

FIGURE 5-8
Relationship Between Hotel Income and National Income

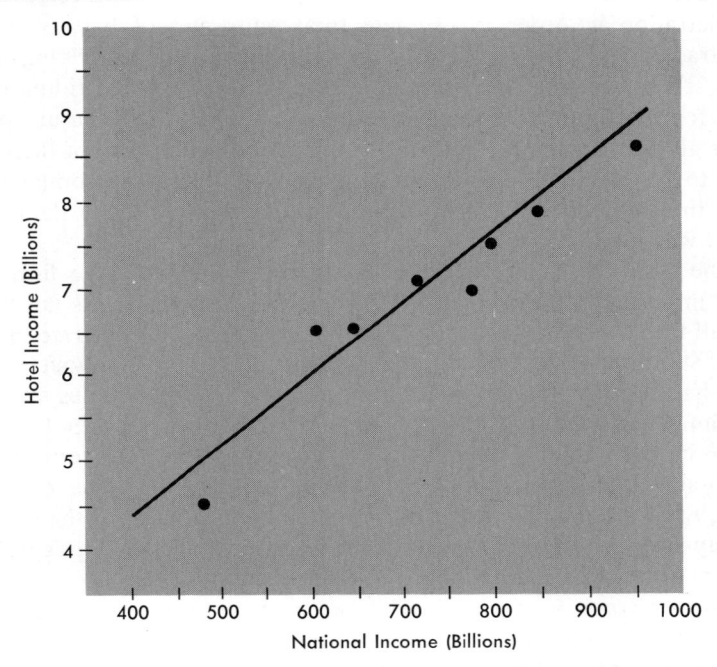

Source: Compiled from *Statistical Abstracts of the United States,* 1963 to 1973.

If industry sales are not available, past sales of a company may be used to determine relationships with such market indices. For example, through an analysis of warranty cards a manufacturer of farm tractors found that the company was selling an increasingly large number of units to nonfarm buyers for nonfarm purposes—to factories, mines, airports, and municipalities. By analyzing these nonfarm buyers more closely, management was able to classify them into ten different types of business. Further analysis identified indices such as number of employees and kilowatt hours used by each type of business. Past sales were related to these indices to develop a purchase ratio for each type of business. These ratios were then applied to the indices for each business type by geographic region, thus giving a first estimate of market opportunity by each of 10 nonfarm businesses.

Another form of historical projection is the use of time series analysis. For example, in an attempt to make an aggregate estimate of the battery-powered riding tractor market, sales by units of riding tractors of all types were plotted by years to determine the actual trend. The past trend discovered is then simply projected into the future for estimates of the total riding tractor market. New products can make the projection more difficult. In this case, management needs to appraise competition and relative market penetration in order to estimate total unit sales of battery-powered riding tractors and express it as a percentage of the total riding tractor market. To arrive at a first estimate of the battery-powered riding tractor market for the future, the same percent was applied to the future projection for all riding tractors. In this case, the crude delineation of the market proved to be too small for profitable expansion. Thus, the company conducting the study deleted this market as an opportunity area at the time the analysis was made.

The need for market delineation is not limited to large firms. It is equally important for the small firm. The cost of delineation is not beyond the small firm's means. An example in the retail field will illustrate the case.

A suburban drugstore on the outskirts of a city of about 150,000 people has been in operation for nine months. Monthly sales volume is approximately $34,000. The owner has established a goal of a 10 percent increase in sales volume over the next two years. Two questions confront him: First, is the location such that he can expect a 10 percent increase? Second, what are the characteristics of potential customers of the store and how may they best be influenced? Some knowledge of the store's potential market is necessary to answer both of these questions.

From records kept of prescription customers, the owner found that 70 percent of prescription sales were to people living within a three-block radius of the store. Working on the premise that prescription sales, the most profitable part of the business, are usually made to those customers who also buy the more frequently purchased drugstore items in the same location, he designated this three-block radius as his "primary trading area." Similar primary trading areas were identified for seven competitors. This left another section, designated a "secondary trading area," to the west of the store's location. Within the primary and secondary trading areas are 2,200 households. From *Sales Management,* 1973 Survey of Buying Power,[15] the drugstore owner found the average expenditure by household per year on drugs to be $217. Multiplying the $217 by 2,200 households suggests a potential market of $477,400, an estimated potential volume large enough to achieve the sales volume goal.

The answer to the druggist's second question, which concerned the identifying characteristics of consumers, was simplified because of the relatively small number of customers and the owner's constant contact with

---

[15] *The Survey of Buying Power* is published annually in July by *Sales Management* magazine.

them. Since he was personally acquainted with many people in the area, he began to identify formally the characteristics of his potential customers and to tailor a marketing plan to influence them to trade at his store rather than at his competitors'.

Although we have not exhausted the many ways in which the historical method can be used, it is appropriate to mention some of its limitations. The method is useful for determining how consumers allocate their expenditures. It records past events and assumes that these same decisions will be made in the future. Although it is true that for many classes of products consumers do not change their expenditure patterns quickly, we have already seen that in the long run changes do occur. In spite of these limitations, the historical approach is widely used. However, many adjustments should be made in historical projections, particularly in the durable goods markets. The marketer using this method should be aware of the kinds of adjustments needed.

The Survey Research Center of the University of Michigan has pioneered in consumer attitude studies. These studies were developed out of the recognition that historical relationships between the purchase of durable goods and income are unreliable. The ability of consumers to postpone purchases of durable goods influences the amount they spend and save and the way they allocate that which they do spend. Consumer surveys have been used with some success more accurately to predict consumers' intentions with respect to durable goods purchases.

The consumer attitude studies conducted are based on the following propositions:

1. The basic problem is that of determining the general levels of spending and saving.
2. Consumer decisions to spend or save are dependent upon: (a) the basic needs of individuals as represented by aspiration levels, status, security, and group conformity; (b) individual decision-making characteristics, such as problem-solving ability and information level; (c) constraints arising out of situational variables, such as income, family size, prices, and assets, as well as status roles and accepted patterns of activity; and (d) consumer attitudes with respect to the expected outcomes from one pattern of action versus another.
3. Since previous research has demonstrated the dynamic character of consumer choice, any inquiry must focus on those influencing variables which change through time.
4. Since the basic needs of individuals as well as the decision-making characteristics of individuals are rather stable personality variables, they do not materially influence changes in consumer behavior.

5. Although the situational variable in part may change over time, it represents no serious problem since the variable may be handled empirically with little difficulty.
6. The remaining variable, consumers' attitudes with respect to the expected outcome from one pattern of action versus another, is the area that may possibly explain the dynamic nature of consumer decisions with respect to how much to spend and how much to save.
7. It is known that much consumer spending is habitual and relies on expectations from similar courses of action taken in the past. On the other hand, much consumer action requires extensive deliberation, for example, in purchasing durable goods. Therefore, the significant changes in the spend-save pattern must be determined by changes in consumers' expectations concerning the outcome of different courses of action with respect to durable goods purchases.
8. Study of attitudes in relation to expectations will shed light on consumer's decisions to purchase durable goods or to save.
9. More specifically, the survey technique is used to measure, as frequently as possible, consumers' attitudes concerning expected outcomes from one course of action versus another. Changes in consumers' attitudes are then related to changes in the spend-save pattern of the group.[16]

The findings to date may be divided into two types: First, the level of saving versus spending seems to be directly related to consumers' past income and expected future income; and second, the purchase of durable goods is dependent upon past income and expected future income.

In general, the method, through assessing the consumers' outlook, attempts to judge the direction of change in spending decisions and attempts to relate consumers' outlook to changes in intention to purchase specific products. The method does not study specific products. The method does not study the specific forces generating a change in attitudes. It identifies these attitudes.

[16] For complete descriptions of the purpose and method, see James Morgan, "A Review of Recent Research on Consumer Behavior," in *Consumer Behavior: Research on Consumer Reactions,* ed. Lincoln H. Clark, (New York: Harper & Row, Publishers, 1958), pp. 118–20. Also George Katona, "The Predictive Value of Data on Consumer Attitudes," in *Consumer Behavior,* II, *The Life Cycle and Consumer Behavior,* ed. Lincoln H. Clark (New York: New York University Press, 1955), 66–74. Also George Katona, *Psychological Analysis of Economic Behavior* (New York: McGraw-Hill Book Company, 1951), Chap. 8. Also Klein, Katona, Lansing, and Morgan, contributors to *Survey Methods of Economics* (New York: Columbia University Press, 1954).

THE BUILDUP METHOD

In the buildup method, the marketer tries to measure the demand of each individual purchasing unit and then add them together for an aggregate measure of the market. This is obviously much easier to accomplish if the number of potential customers is small. For this reason, the buildup method is used widely in industrial markets but has limited application in the consumer goods field. For example, in measuring the need for and actual use of hospital services, market research surveys are often used. In these studies an area's population is classified by socioeconomic groupings on a sampling basis to determine actual need, willingness, and capacity to use hospital services. Once determined, these measurements are projected to the total population for each socioeconomic grouping. The capacity of existing facilities can be measured, and the gap represents the market opportunity.

The task of market delineation is extremely complex when trying to appraise the market for new products. The problem is that it is even more important in the case of new products to judge market potential accurately. The large financial investment that precedes the introduction of a new product can be justified only if the market is sufficiently broad to generate adequate profits. For new products, estimates of total demand have to be estimated from analysis of particular uses, users, or individual market requirements. In such situations, the buildup method may be the only applicable technique of estimating market size. In some cases, total demand cannot be estimated accurately, but analysis proceeds until sufficient potential purchasers have been identified to reach a necessary threshold for commercially profitable operations in the new product field.

Consider the problems facing the producers of nylon. The potential number of household and personal uses had not been completely identified, and the size of the market was unknown. As another example, the manufacturers of automatic water softeners had very little to go on in the early days. Each case represented an entirely new product whose market opportunities depended upon how well and how quickly need could be demonstrated and behavior patterns of the public could be influenced.

Another example is the mass introduction of the motorcycle into the American scene. In this case, market opportunity depended on whether or not the attitudes of the consuming public could be changed with respect to this form of transportation and recreation. In fact, in more than one case, failure to make any analysis of this market resulted in failure to enter the market and the attendant loss of a major market opportunity.

Businesses launching new products of these kinds risk a substantial amount of money in virtually unknown markets. Any information that can be obtained regarding the size of the market is of value to the decision maker.

In most instances, research programs aimed at new product development are based upon some hypothesis regarding the public's desire for or ability to use a new product. That is, there is usually some recognition of a market demand before time, energy, and money are directed toward the development of a product to satisfy that demand.

Frequently the end product developed is a different sort of thing than originally intended. It may turn out that it will not serve the intended purposes but may conceivably serve other purposes. At this point, additional hypotheses are made concerning the product's usefulness. It is in the analysis of these hypotheses that a means is found for interpreting markets for such products.

For example, the makers of automatic washing machines hypothesized that if the washing and drying mechanism could be combined into one unit, the space-saving characteristics of the product would open a market among residents of compact dwelling units. The increasing cost per square foot in residential construction puts space saving devices at a premium. What other hypotheses might have been used? The reduction in production cost may enable a price differential over the separate washer and dryer, and aid in displacing competitors. This then assumes that the market for automatic laundry equipment would respond favorably to a price decline. Another would be the desire on the part of housewives to have a one-operation washday. All these hypotheses can be checked through market research to determine their validity. Space does not permit us to examine the specific techniques used for verifying the hypotheses, but once they are verified, the number of people that may be influenced by, let us say, the space-saving features of the product can be determined and projected for the entire marketing area. The buildup method is not as accurate as the previous approaches, yet where other methods cannot be used it is much better than nothing. The firm may never know accurately the total quantity that the market will absorb, but at least it is fairly certain that the market will not reject the product to the point where the investment is lost.

Aggregate market delineation characteristic of the historical and buildup methods is a managerial function to be performed continuously. It must be performed on existing products and on new areas of opportunity as identified by environmental monitoring. Only in this way can the enterprise begin to formulate its marketing strategy objectives for each planning period. You will recall we stated earlier that there was an overlap between formulating marketing objectives and selecting target markets. Attention is now directed to the selection of target markets, in which we will continue to examine the use of the historical and buildup methods in the performance of the market delineation function.

SELECTING TARGET MARKETS

In an earlier example, we determined that radios, television sets, and phonographs represented a substantial market opportunity in the future, and that a preliminary marketing strategy objective might be "to achieve a 12 percent market share over the next two years." This generally directs a marketing effort, but a much finer delineation would be helpful in formulating marketing strategy objectives. Many questions may be asked concerning the projected market estimate of 12 percent. In what household income levels are these products purchased? What is the education and occupation of the household head? What is the stage in the family life cycle (age and number of children) of the household? In what regions are these products sold? In what kind of outlets are the products sold? What are the relative shares for radios, television sets, and phonographs? Given these facts, it may not be wise to try to gain a market share among all potential buyers, but rather select certain segments of the market upon which to concentrate marketing efforts.

The historical method can be applied to the analysis if we are willing to project past behavior into the future. Using data from past studies, we can construct a market profile as in Table 5-2 to answer some of the above questions. In using the data in Table 5-2, we are assuming that the percentage share of the market coming from each cell does not change drastically over time, but that the changing base (total consumer expenditures) reflects the change in numbers in each cell as we move through time. Notice that the data in Table 5-2 go beyond quantitative expression of the market and provide information on its more subjective characteristics. For example, there is a difference in the consumption of radios, television sets, and phonographs between households in which the head finished high school and those in which the head finished grade school. There is also a difference in the consumption of the same product between different occupational groups. These differences will influence the kinds of outlets that can most satisfactorily handle the product for different kinds of purchasers, the kinds of appeals made in all communications to the market, and the organization and manpower requirements necessary to reach the market.

Add to this information the facts we have learned from our environmental monitoring—namely, by 1980, 55 percent of all households will have incomes of over $10,000, representing 80 percent of all income. Also, the fastest growing group is the 25-44 age group, which will command 40 percent of all spending—and we begin to see well-defined market targets appearing. A manufacturer of brown goods may elect to concentrate his marketing effort in one distinct market, the 25-44 over $10,000 market, and forego the 44-65 and over, over $10,000 market. With this in

TABLE 5-2
Market for TV, Radios, Musical Instruments
Based on Buyer Characteristics (In Percentage)*

Income	Total Market	Occupation of Household Head	Total Market
Under $3,000	4.5	Professional, technical	16.5
$3,000–$5,000	10.0	Manager, official	16.0
$5,000–$7,500	17.5	Clerical, sales	12.0
$7,500–$10,000	21.5	Craftsman, foreman	19.0
$10,000 and up	46.5	Operative	16.5
		All other	20.0

Geographic Location	Total Market	Market Location	Total Market
Northeast region	27.0	Metropolitan areas	
North central region	27.0	Central cities	32.0
Southern region	26.0	Urban fringe	35.5
Western region	20.0	Other areas	6.5
		Outside Metropolitan areas	
		Urban	24.5
		Rural	11.5

Education of Household Head	Total Market	Age of Head	Total Market
Grade school or less	20.0	Under 25 years	6.0
Some high school	18.5	25–34 years	21.0
High school graduate	31.0	35–44 years	27.5
Some college	12.5	45–54 years	23.0
College graduate or higher	18.0	55–65 years	14.0
		65 years and up	8.5

Stage in Family Life Cycle	Total Market
Families with child under 6	
Some under 6	16.0
All under 6	12.0
6 and over only	
All 6 to 11	6.0
Any 12 or over	36.0
No children	
Husband/wife	20.5
Other	9.5

* In 1980 six and one-half percent of personal consumption expenditures will be spent on recreation and recreation equipment; 25 percent of recreation and recreation equipment expenditures will be for TV, radios, and musical instruments.

Source: Compiled from "Market Profiles of Consumer Products," Fabian Linden, ed., The Conference Board, 1967.

mind, his marketing objective to achieve a 12 percent market share in the radio, television, and phonograph market over the next two years is verified. A specific target market to which all effort must be directed may be stated as follows:

> To concentrate marketing effort among the 25–44 age group, families with incomes of over $10,000.

As the marketer continues to analyze the market, he may conclude that although the market is much larger in metropolitan areas, it is also much more competitive. As a relative newcomer he may wish to achieve his objectives in nonmetropolitan markets. Thus, another target market may be identified as follows:

> To concentrate marketing effort in nonmetropolitan areas throughout the United States.

The number of potential targets can go on and on. Each must meet the characteristics of a viable segment if it is to be selected as an integral part of the firm's marketing strategy.[17]

Where there is no historical data available, it may be necessary to conduct one-time analysis using the buildup method to delineate the market more precisely. For example, the Whirlpool Corporation, manufacturer and marketer of its own brand of household appliances (refrigerators, washers, dryers, ranges, and the like), was concerned about changing patterns in retailing of these so-called white goods.[18] Although Whirlpool's market is the ultimate consumer, it reaches consumers through an assortment of different types of retailing institutions. In an effort to determine what mix of retail outlets would attain and maintain a balanced retail distribution system in the future, the corporation conducted a study of both the number of stores and the number of brands shopped by socioeconomic grouping of recent appliance purchasers in a selected market. It reasoned that a change in consumer behavior with respect to location of purchase would be manifest in a change in the relative strengths of brand loyalty and store preference, as both are significant elements in the purchase decision. As such, the stronger a preference for a particular store or store

---

[17] The characteristics of a market segment are discussed in Chapter 19.

[18] This study was conducted under the direction of Sol Goldin, Director of Retail Marketing, Whirlpool Corporation, and is used with the permission of the Whirlpool Corporation.

FIGURE 5-9
Loyalty by Product Group

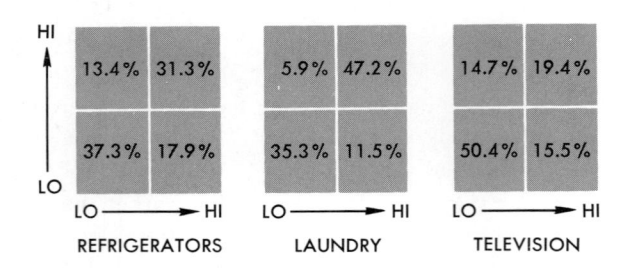

	REFRIGERATORS	LAUNDRY	TELEVISION
HI	13.4% 31.3%	5.9% 47.2%	14.7% 19.4%
LO	37.3% 17.9%	35.3% 11.5%	50.4% 15.5%
	LO → HI	LO → HI	LO → HI

Courtesy: The Whirlpool Corporation.

type, relative to brand loyalty, the greater the need for the manufacturer to pay close attention to the mix of retail outlets. Conversely, where consumers have strong brand loyalties but weak store preferences, the manufacturer can be highly selective about what store type handles his product and not be concerned about shifts in retail store-type strengths.

One finding is shown in Figure 5-9. In this example, there is a difference between the way in which buyers purchase refrigerators, laundry, and television. Buyers are much more store and brand loyal when buying refrigerators or laundry equipment than when buying televisions. Laundry equipment has a slight advantage in terms of store and brand loyalty than do refrigerators in the purchase process. Of particular importance in identifying target markets is to determine if there is a difference in the people in the four cells. In the case of laundry equipment, buyers in the HI-HI cell were long-term residents, nonlabor, older families, with low incomes. Those in the LO-LO cell were long-term residents, younger families, with low incomes. Those in the LO-LO cell, when they purchase televisions, show no significant differences on any demographic variable over those in the HI-HI cell. In fact, that such a large proportion fall in the LO-LO cell signifies very little brand or store loyalty among television buyers.

The significance of this finer breakdown is to allow the marketer to select those target markets he wishes to concentrate on and to adjust his marketing effort accordingly.

Target markets help us to refine more aggregative marketing objectives. They indicate what must be accomplished so that the planner's view of the future may be achieved through marketing action.

With the selected target markets well defined, we turn our attention to the behavioral aspects of these targets—the performance of the purchase behavior motivation function—in the next two chapters.

SUMMARY

Environmental monitoring is a first step in assessing potential markets and establishing overall corporate marketing objectives. Although there are many aspects of the environment to be monitored, a minimum economic monitoring is imperative. Analysis of aggregate population growth and composition, such as family formation, family income, age, and education of household head, reveals market trends for different industries. On the basis of these analyses, selected markets may be more thoroughly analyzed for purposes of establishing more specific marketing objectives.

Two methods, the historical and the buildup, are used in the performance of the market delineation function. The historical method relies on past events as a guide to future action. Of particular interest is the relationship between past income and consumption, and the allocation of consumption expenditures to various product categories. In addition, simple time series projections of past sales may be used for arriving at a first estimate of market opportunity. The historical method assumes past decisions of consumers will continue in the future. Although consumers do not change expenditure patterns rapidly, the ability to postpone durable goods purchases makes it necessary to make adjustments in historical projections in this product market. Research has demonstrated that consumers' evaluations of past experiences and expected future experiences with respect to their financial conditions are important in their decisions to purchase durable goods. Therefore, an assessment of consumers' general optimism or pessimism may be used to modify historical durable goods expenditure patterns.

The buildup method relies on measuring the demand for individual purchasing units by market surveys that can be projected to the entire population. In the case of new products it may be necessary to identify potential use at the time of product development and then measure consumers' opinions concerning intended use to build up an estimate of market size.

Once aggregate markets have been appraised by performance of the market delineation function, they must be analyzed in much more detail to select those target markets, or parts of the aggregate market, that the firm wishes to cultivate. The historical and buildup methods can also be used for this fine line analysis. In all methods, ingenuity and imagination are required to devise ways and means to secure information about potential buyers.

QUESTIONS AND PROBLEMS

1. How does the age composition of the population affect predictions of market size for specific products?
2. Marketing objectives are developed along means-end chains. Discuss.
3. Describe the historical method of quantitatively measuring markets.
4. In what ways can complete past sales records of a company be used in applying the historical method to market measurement?
5. Explain the difference between a marketing objective and a market target.
6. How might the buildup method be used to quantitatively measure the market for educational records with a complete set of lectures on a given topic?
7. What is meant by the inverted pyramid of family income?
8. Why is market delineation necessary for marketing strategy planning?

Chapter 6

Foundations of Consumer Behavior

In the last chapters we described the demographic and demand determinants that constitute market delineation of consumer markets. Such demand determinants represent potential product purchases. However, until a consumer makes a decision to purchase a specific product for consumption, nothing of significance has resulted from the marketing process. Because of this basic importance of the consumer to the marketing system, we established in Chapter 2 the importance of a market orientation as a philosophy of business management. To have a market orientation is to appreciate *why* consumers purchase and to understand *what* consumers need. It is important to keep in mind that the real and perceived needs of customers are of far more fundamental importance than specific products or services. It is the customer by virtue of purchase behavior that renders some firms a differential advantage.

In this and the next chapter we are concerned with developing an understanding of consumer behavior. How does a consumer make specific choices in the market? How is a specific product perceived? Why and how is a decision made to purchase or reject a specific product? What are the foundations of brand loyalty? Understanding at least partial answers to such questions provides insights into marketing opportunities not obtainable from market delineation studies.

In this chapter, attention is first directed to the decisions a consumer makes during the purchasing process. Next, we present an interdisciplinary framework that summarizes a variety of vantage points from which purchase behavior has been examined. In total, the chapter provides the foundation for better understanding of consumer behavior motivation.

CLASSIFICATION OF CONSUMER CHOICE DECISIONS

The consumer in the marketplace is faced with a range of choices. The critical choices concern the following decisions:

1. Deciding how much to spend and how much to save.
2. Deciding which products and services to buy.
3. Deciding the specific sources from which to purchase.
4. Deciding the conditions of purchase.

Fundamental to understanding purchase behavior is a realization of the nature of choice decisions faced by the consumer. Thus, each is briefly described.

THE SPEND-SAVE DECISION

Through its productive activity, the economy in any given period generates a certain amount of consumer income that is available for the purchase of the commodities and services produced. The proportion of income that consumers elect to spend is important in three ways. First, the amount of current income consumers choose to spend, along with their access to credit and the condition of their savings and other assets, determines the quantity of goods and services they will purchase. Second, the amount of savings in any one period significantly affects the level of income out of which their future purchases will be made. Third, evidence indicates that there are reasonably stable relationships between the amount of income earned and the amount consumers will spend on different kinds of products. Throughout this section this choice problem is called *the spend-save decision.*

DECIDING WHICH PRODUCTS AND SERVICES TO BUY

How much of the income for any period will be spent on food, how much on housing, how much on recreation? The magnitude of the choice is tremendous. Consider the housewife with X dollars to spend for food. How much of the total will she spend on meat, on bread, on milk, on other items? Women's magazines frequently feature suggested household budgets for families in various income brackets. In real life, the household budget is more often a *result,* made out after the money has been spent, not a plan made in advance. Consumers appear to make haphazard independent decisions on each product. Nevertheless, consumers, when purchasing, do give consideration to those purchases that have been made before and those contemplated in the future. Obviously, more will be spent on food than on recreation, but how can the marketer of frozen orange juice get a larger portion of the total breakfast expenditure? This problem of determining the most advantageous assortment to offer the market is called the *product-mix decision.*

Deciding which products and services to buy is equally important to the businessman. The wholesaler and the retailer must make decisions on what assortments they will stock. Should the hardware retailer stock transistor radios? The bank owner and the manufacturer have similar choice problems. Should the manufacturer replace old machinery or add additional warehouse space in a given budget period? Although the businessman's decisions are dictated by supposedly more rational considerations, he too is usually confronted with a number of alternatives.

DECIDING THE SPECIFIC SOURCES FROM WHICH TO PURCHASE

Since most consumer goods are identified by brands, this choice of sources is referred to as the *brand-choice*. Once the decision has been made to spend so much on food and a certain proportion of that on breakfast cereal, which of several available brands of cereals will be purchased? Or, if brands are not important in the purchase under consideration, which source of supply shall be patronized? For example, in buying coal, which of three dealers will receive the order?

DECIDING THE CONDITIONS OF PURCHASE

This decision is closely associated with the brand-choice decision. The source of supply selected by an industrial buyer is often determined by the conditions under which he is able to purchase. Speed of delivery, quality of material, and price may all be determinants. Likewise, for a housewife purchasing milk, source of supply is frequently based on conditions of purchase. Milk may be delivered to the home, purchased in the nearby supermarket, at the neighborhood grocery store, or at the vending machine. In another product category, an automatic washer could be bought in a crate at the discount house in the next community, or from the local department store. In the first instance, the purchaser must provide transportation, undertake installation of the machine, and assume responsibility for repairs. In the second, the department store will deliver, install, and demonstrate the machine in the home, and often supply a year of free service along with the purchase.

Although we have discussed the choices in a set order, it would be a mistake to assume that they are independent of each other or that they always occur in a given sequence. The decision on how much to spend and how much to save may influence both the kinds of products that are purchased, the brand chosen, and the conditions of purchase. The thrifty family that saves a large proportion of its income may go without many luxuries, shop for high-quality merchandise at lower prices, and purchase goods with a minimum of costly service features. Conversely, the family that spends up to the limit of income and beyond may purchase a variety of luxury products and generally prefer to purchase in full service establishments at slightly higher prices. For many families the product-mix decision may come first and the spend-save decision is a result; however, there are limits to how far one may go.

AN INTERDISCIPLINARY FRAMEWORK FOR UNDERSTANDING CONSUMER CHOICE

Now that we have reviewed the kinds of choice decisions buyers face, we can ask: "How do they solve them?" To help achieve an understanding of consumer purchase behavior, market analysts have adopted an interdisciplinary approach. The process of understanding why a consumer makes a specific choice requires a simultaneous examination of human behavior from a variety of vantage points. Thus, the disciplines of economics, sociology, cultural anthropology, and psychology all provide insights useful to understanding consumer purchase behavior. Although marketers, economists, sociologists, and psychologists have for many years been attempting to identify the forces influencing buyer choice, their findings are still inconclusive. Nevertheless, there is a classification of influencing forces that the practicing marketer will find helpful. Influencing forces may be divided into three groups:[1]

1. Enabling conditions.
2. Environmental conditions.
3. Individual motivations.

This classification is convenient for study purposes since it interrelates economic, sociological, cultural anthropology, and psychological approaches to consumer behavior.

ENABLING CONDITIONS

Income, assets, and access to credit are important in determining how much consumers will spend and how much they will save. Likewise, expectations of future income are determinative. Any decision to purchase a new

[1] This classification is modified from George Katona and Eva Miller, "A Story of Purchase Decision," in *Consumer Behavior,* I, ed. Lincoln H. Clark (New York: New York University Press, 1954), 30–36.

home, for example, is directly influenced by the expected future income of the buyers. The general business atmosphere and its anticipated future are important factors in determining the level of employment. Businessmen's suppositions concerning future profit temper their current employment commitments. Employment levels, in turn, influence consumer choices both current and future. The short-term decline in economic activity associated with the energy crisis of the mid-1970s is a pointed example.

A complete analysis of enabling conditions is usually imperative in an attempt to measure how much in the aggregate consumers will purchase. To determine the quantity the market will purchase, we must first know how much purchasing power is available and where it is located. These aggregate determinants of demand were discussed in the last chapter devoted to market delineation. However, delineation of purchasing power is not sufficient to understand how the consumer will select among choice alternatives. Thus, a deeper look into enabling conditions on an individual consumer basis is necessary. To review one perspective of this insight we turn to the discipline of economics.

Economists were among the first social scientists to examine consumer choice behavior. In terms of interdisciplinary classification the economists' theory of consumer choice behavior is the oldest approach and provides a high degree of theoretical consistency. The economic theory of consumer behavior traces from the writings of Adam Smith and Jeremy Benthan.[2] Modern treatments of consumer behavior can be classified as either the marginal utility or the indifference approach. Each approach is briefly reviewed to refresh the reader's memory of the basic underlying postulates. This section on the *why* of enabling conditions is concluded with a brief evaluation of the value of the economists' approach for the marketing practitioner.

Marginal Utility Approach

During the latter half of the 19th century a number of economists began to formulate and present the theory of approaching individual choice from the viewpoint of marginal value of utility. This early work, and its subsequent refinement by Alfred Marshall[3], has resulted in an explanation of choice that is firmly embedded within the framework of modern microeconomic theory.

---

[2] For a brief but interesting review of the history of the economic theory of consumer behavior, see Peter D. Bennett and Harold H. Kassarjian, *Consumer Behavior* (Englewood Cliffs, N.J.: Prentice-Hall, Inc., 1972), Chap. 2, pp. 11–26.

[3] Alfred Marshall, *Principles of Economics* (London: The Macmillan Company, 1927).

The basic postulate of the marginal utility approach is that value in an economy characterized by specialization of trade is reflected by the consumer's consumption choice. Each consumer is assumed to make choices on a basis that will maximize overall utility. To the degree that utility is maximized, the consumer is viewed as receiving maximum satisfaction or value. Thus, utility is viewed as the measure by which the consumer achieves the most satisfactory choice.

To explain how a consumer selects among a variety of goods and services, the economists reasoned the *law of diminishing marginal utility*. The essence of diminishing marginal utility is based on the belief that total utility derived from increased quantities of a specific good or service increases at a decreasing rate. Thus, the notion of *marginal utility* is operationalized in terms of the additional satisfaction realized by each unit of consumption from 1 to n. To illustrate: assume a child enjoys ice cream cones and has a father who purchases one per week. If grandpa purchases a second ice cream cone, the child enjoys it but not as much as the first cone. If a race starts between father and grandfather to see who can buy the most ice cream cones for the child, pleasure is soon replaced with pain. The child may get to the point where no additional satisfaction or utility is realized by an additional ice cream cone. In fact, the child may even lose or experience negative marginal utility.

From the viewpoint of overall choice, the consumer is viewed by the economist as having limited income. In addition, as noted earlier, the consumer must make a decision between spending and saving. Thus, among the finite income available to be spent, a choice must be made concerning how to spend. The economist solves this aspect of the overall choice problem by application of the *law of equal marginal utility per dollar spent*. Thus, the consumer is viewed as purchasing a mix of products and services that result in the greatest overall or total utility. This point of maximum utility is an equilibrium between the weighted marginal utility from among all products consumed.

As the reader can easily determine, the economist approach based on marginal utility is founded on a rational and somewhat hedonistic approach to consumer behavior. The problem traditionally confronted by the economist was the inability to measure utility in order to accumulate empirical justification of the marginal allocation approach.

The Indifference Approach

A second and more contemporary attempt by economists to explain consumer behavior is the indifference approach. A complete development of consumer indifference theory is not justified given the current objectives.[4] The main advantage of the indifference approach is that the overall consumer choice problem is structured as a relative choice between product alternatives within constraints related to price, income, and the available budget. Thus, the consumer is structured as being indifferent to choice between two products or services given specific conditions. At least on a conceptual level, the need for cardinal measurement of utility is replaced by relative indifference measurement.

The Economists' Contribution to Understanding Purchase Behavior

From the viewpoint of market delineation the economist offers a useful appraisal to understanding enabling conditions that permit consumer purchasing. To support the necessary linkage between individual demand and market demand, the economist has long sought a further explanation of choice beyond the spend-save decision. The results depict a rational goal-directed consumer who allocates income between consumption alternatives with computer-like precision to the point where the most satisfactory results are realized.

The simplicity of the economists' concept of purchase behavior and the mathematical exactness is appealing. Indeed, the logic used to support choice decisions offers at least a partial explanation of why consumers behave as they do. Bennett and Kassarjian have summarized three major reasons why the traditional approach of the economist falls short of an adequate explanation of consumer behavior.[5]

1. The model is not operational.
2. The theory is centered on the product and not the consumer.
3. The theory is simply incomplete.

The criticism that the model is not operational has already been noted in terms of measurement difficulties. The other two criticisms of the economists' approach are worthy of brief comment since these deficiencies constitute the fundamental reasons for examining environmental conditions and individual motivations to provide an additional perspective of consumer behavior.

The criticism that economic theory is centered on products and not consumers constitutes a fundamental difference between the disciplines of marketing and economics. If the consumer purchases a product to

[4] For the original treatment, see J. R. Hicks, *Value and Capital,* 2nd ed. (New York: Oxford University Press, 1948). For a contemporary treatment, see Richard H. Liftwich, *The Price System and Resource Allocation,* 5th ed. (Hinsdale, Ill.: Dryden Press, 1973).

[5] Bennett, *Consumer,* pp. 23–25.

achieve satisfaction or to satisfy a need, a useful distinction can be made between the goal of need satisfaction and the object that helps the consumer achieve the goal. To a significant degree, objects that help consumers achieve goals can be substituted. Needs are fundamental to the purpose of purchase behavior. Thus, earlier in the chapter we warned that the marketer must clearly understand that consumer needs are more basic than products. Consumer needs create product opportunities.

The criticism that the economists' theory of consumer behavior is incomplete is true and reflects the reason why the marketer has turned to an interdisciplinary approach to seek an understanding of consumer choice. Perhaps the greatest area lacking in the economists' explanation is the fundamental assumption that all consumers will act in a uniform and rational manner given the same set of enabling conditions and constraints. The facts of market life reject this comfortable notion.

The economist, in summary, has provided a logic that should not be dismissed because of its deficiencies. Indeed, if the economists' contribution is rejected on the grounds of not being empirically operational, we will soon be forced to reject most explanations of buyer behavior. The economist does provide a fundamental understanding of the aggregate market demand or total purchasing power. The logic of individual consumer choice is helpful in providing a normative choice model. We now turn to the behavioral fields of sociology, cultural anthropology, and psychology better to describe consumer needs and motives.

ENVIRONMENTAL CONDITIONS

Individuals do not live in isolation nor do they consume in isolation. Mobility, stage in family life cycle, age, social class, and even culture all have a bearing on the products and quantities of each that consumers will purchase. To illustrate: a dishwasher manufacturer added a portable dishwasher to round out his line, and sales of this item far exceeded his expectations, particularly in one large upper-middle-income sector of an eastern city. Investigation revealed that most purchasers were junior executives who, in the course of their careers, purchased middle-priced housing on each assignment, knowing that they would most probably have to leave the community in about two years. Rather than purchase a standard dishwasher in each home, the junior executive preferred a portable one that could be taken with him.[6] From the viewpoint of rational purchase behavior, the decision to purchase a portable dishwasher could be adequately

---

[6] William H. Whyte, Jr., "The Consumer in the New Suburbia," in *Consumer Behavior*, I, ed. Lincoln H. Clark (New York: New York University Press, 1954), 109. Also see Lewis Alpert and Ronald Galty, "Product Positioning by Behavioral Lifestyles," *Journal of Marketing*, 33 (April 1969), 65–69.

explained in terms of mobility, life cycle stage, or even age. The more fundamental decision on the part of the junior executive to purchase a portable dishwasher of any variety or model might require much deeper examination.

Sociologists and cultural anthropologists have long studied the influence of groups upon human behavior. The group represents a number of people who share a common ideology concerning mutual behavior. The intensity of this common ideology creates an integrating force among individuals who perceive themselves as current or aspiring group members. Thus, the group has an explicit social psychological relationship among members that can be expected to influence behavior.

From a structural viewpoint groups may be voluntary or involuntary with respect to member participation. In cases where the common ideology is intensely felt by members, such as a family, it can be demonstrated that the group behavior norm will result in conformity among members. In other levels of social interaction the explicit psychological relationship may be vague and at best characterized as a social organization as opposed to a group. Thus, social organizations require less behavioral conformity than do groups.

The sociologist and cultural anthropologist study human behavior from the vantage point of examining the way in which an individual's environment influences action. For purposes of examining the environmental conditions that influence consumer behavior, we will briefly examine the concepts of family, reference group, social class, and culture.

Family Unit

In contemporary western society, the immediate family is the fundamental group influence upon human behavior. Because of the intensity of this basic relationship, most forms of overt behavior stem from either the desire to conform to or reject family norms. Thus, at least during the early years of life, the family dominates the formulation of behavior patterns among children.

In different cultures, the structure of the family will take different forms. Regardless of the specific structure, one universal characteristic of the family group is the assignment of member roles. The role of each family participant limits the type of behavior and influence that a member can play in the formulation of behavior patterns. Thus, the husband as "breadwinner" or "head of house" plays a different role than either the mother or any of the children. From the viewpoint of purchase behavior, three concepts are of critical importance to marketing:

1. Relative roles in purchase behavior.
2. Formulation of sanctioned behavior.
3. Modification with time.

Among family groups, different positional roles result in various members of the family being the "prime influences" of specific types of product purchases. For example, the "mother" role clearly makes the housewife the dominant resident expert in matters related to household living consumption. Thus, food, furniture, preschool clothing are examples of purchase areas clearly influenced by the mother. Likewise, similar resident purchase behavior expertise is delegated by virtue of the family structure to participants playing specific roles in the group. As a general rule the family membership is expected to conform to the purchase behavior advice of their resident experts. Within this elaborate structure, many joint decisions exist with respect to purchase behavior. For example, automobiles and boats may be purchased only after consultation among family members. However, while the family structure seems to encourage joint participation in selected decision making, the role structure casts one participant in the dominant role as a result of resident expertise.

A second concept of interest to the marketer is the formulation of behavior norms within family structures. While those family participants playing specific roles can be expected to influence purchase behavior, the norms of overall family-sanctioned behavior result from the interaction of all members. Thus, the family "direction" is the product of member interactions, both internal and external to the family. To the extent that the family is a cohesive group, the cooperative formulation of sanctioned behavior can greatly influence purchase behavior. For example, families may "like" or "dislike" specific products as a composite or conglomerate of separate preferences rather than an expressed preference of an individual. Conformity, because of expectation and sanction, dominates the pattern of expressed family member purchase behavior.

Finally, it is important to stress that family structures, with respect to consumer purchase behavior, change with time. The overall family is viewed as being engaged in a life cycle that extends from formation until the group dissolves. Thus, families as a purchase group are in the market to satisfy specific needs at specific times. These needs will greatly influence which products and services are selected for consumption. To illustrate: families with children five years old and under purchase various chest rubs at an 80 percent greater rate than do other families. Waffles are cooked most often by those in the 35–44 age bracket. First-born babies are fed an average of 50 percent more processed baby foods than are later-born babies among parents of the same age.[7]

[7] See James H. Myers, Roger R. Stanton, and Arne F. Haug, "Correlates of Buying Behavior: Social Class vs. Income," *Journal of Marketing,* 35 (October 1971), 8–15. The quoted examples are from S. G. Barton, "The Life Cycle and Buying Patterns," in *Consumer Behavior, II,* ed. Lincoln H. Clark (New York: New York University Press, 1955), 30–36.

Without question, a study of family relationship is essential to understanding purchase behavior. The family is the dominant social group in society and also the primary purchase consumption group. A marketer must be familiar with consumption needs as manifest in family interrole behavior. These needs explain why consumers buy specific products or why markets exist for specific products. The simple contrasting role of a family preference for onion flavor and the modern mother's distaste for cooking raw onions is the reason why instant onion products have rapidly gained household preference. However, the complete answer to consumer behavior patterns and choice over time is not found within the family structure.

Face-to-Face Reference Groups

The family as a reference group was singled out for special treatment because of the initial and persuasive influence placed on a consumer by virtue of his or her family role. Beyond the family, many additional face-to-face groups influence behavior of all forms. Indeed, as already noted, family direction, to a degree, results from the degree to which members are deeply involved in other groups. Overall behavior is influenced by the composite of groups to which the individual belongs or aspires to belong. An explanation of reference groups is found in the following quotation.

> Descriptions of the manner in which individuals are influenced by group norms sometimes employ the term "reference group." This expression refers to the fact that people evaluate themselves and orient their behavior by reference both to (1) the groups in which they hold official membership, and (2) others to which they aspire or hope to belong in the future. A reference group is thus any group with which a person psychologically identifies himself or in relation to which he thinks of himself. It is implicit in this idea that his existing group memberships may be relatively meaningless to the person whose primary "ego anchorages" are established with reference to groups with which he is not formally or objectively linked. This type of anticipatory allegiance is especially noticeable in a mobile society in which the ambition to raise one's status is characteristically encouraged.
>
> Reference groups are thus said to establish the individual's organizing conceptions or frames of reference, for ordering his experiences, perceptions, and ideas of self.[8]

---

[8] For basic contributions in the impact of reference groups, see A. R. Lindesmith and A. L. Strauss, *Social Psychology* (New York: Holt, Rinehart & Winston, Inc., 1956), and Leon Testinger, "A Theory of Social Comparison Processes," *Human Relations,* 7, (May 1954), 117–40.

The stimulus of the reference group depends on the degree of psychological identification which the individual has with the group. Sometimes the identification is called *ego involvement*. As suggested in the quotation, some reference groups may be ego involving and some may not. Let us use a simple example to explain this idea. If a plumber is walking down the street and the local attorney, with whom he has had an occasional business contact in the last six months, fails to speak to him, it is not likely he will engage in any behavior to gain recognition. In other words, the attorney does not represent a reference group with which the plumber is ego involved or one to which he aspires. On the other hand, if a plumber acquaintance from his own reference group fails to recognize him, he probably is ego involved and will engage in behavior calculated to gain recognition. A complicating factor is that the reference groups that are ego involving and those that are not are in a constant state of change. Let us suppose the same plumber to be strongly influenced by the family reference group. In an effort to improve the living standard of his family, he enters the contract plumbing business and is very successful. There is a possibility that the plumber now will shift his allegiances from his former occupational group to that of the attorney's reference group. Now he may engage in behavior designed to gain recognition by the attorney.

As the name implies, the term *reference group* provides the individual with a "point of reference" from which to align or differentiate behavior. Thus, while an individual's reference to selected groups might well be characterized by ego involvement in terms of other groups, the reference might be rejection or complete nonconformity. However, from the viewpoint of marketing, the essential point is that individual purchase behavior is influenced by reference groups and the attitudes of specific reference group members.

In practice it is difficult to identify reference groups. For market predicting purposes, the ego-involving reference groups must be identified beforehand. Unfortunately, when reference group theory is applied to market behavior, the only way to identify the influential group is to study past behavior, as well as the reference groups to which the individual belongs or aspires to belong. A cause-and-effect relationship is then made between the two sets of data. There is a serious limitation to this procedure. When one tries to identify influential reference groups *before* purchases are made, it is soon discovered that it is impossible to identify behavior.

Because of the above limitation, reference group theory in the form described does not provide an approach that is widely used in marketing. However, an understanding of the theory is important, because a modification of it is used in market investigation. To avoid the problem of specifying an actual group, there has been a tendency to refer to *status roles* rather than reference groups.

The term *status role* seems to have no existence in the literature of social psychology. Yet it is used in marketing literature and apparently combines two ideas. The word *status* refers to position within a group. The idea assumes that every person has some position within the groups to which he or she belongs. For example, a mother has position within a family. Also, she is expected to engage in certain activities to fulfill that position. These activities are known as *roles*. In general, the activities necessary to fill a position are determined by the particular reference group in which the position exists.

It is important to understand that in filling a role no two people will engage in exactly the same activities, for two reasons. First, action is not solely determined by the expectations of the reference group, but also by personality traits and physiological needs. Since these may vary, considerable literature is available on the way in which a person fulfills a status position he or she occupies. Second, a person may aspire to another reference group and play a role which is more in keeping with the manner in which the status position is filled in that group. Even though the dynamic aspects of status role are recognized, there is a belief that people will generally perform in a given status position by playing a role which is dictated by the reference group within which the position exists.

From a marketing point of view, it is thought that if segments of the market can be identified in terms of individuals' perception of the status roles they engage in, it is possible to infer the reference groups to which they belong or aspire to belong and the kinds of market choices they will make to fulfill their status roles.

Social Class

Society in general tends to be structured into social stratifications. That is, the society tends to rank order individuals in terms of their importance in the eyes of all members of the society. The attorney and the plumber discussed earlier each play an important role in society. However, their roles are not only *differentiated* in the eyes of society, but a significant degree of differential value or importance is assigned each role.

The above is not to imply that occupation is the sole determinant of social class. It does serve to identify the prime nature of social stratification. A society is classified as *closed* or *open* depending upon the opportunity that exists for mobility between classes.

The concept of class comes from research completed by W. Lloyd Warner.[9] Professor Warner hypothesized that social status, interacting

[9] W. Lloyd Warner, *Social Life of a Modern Community* (New Haven: Yale University Press, 1941).

with personality components, results in a grouping of *social classes* whose attitudes toward spending and saving differ and whose retail store loyalties and attitudes toward different products also differ. The Warner system classified United States society into six classes: (1) Upper-Upper, (2) Lower-Upper, (3) Upper-Middle, (4) Lower-Middle, (5) Upper-Lower, and (6) Lower-Lower.

While Warner's class stratification represents an important contribution to overall behavioral studies, we are concerned with the degree to which the class concept helps to explain the why of consumer purchase behavior. To this end numerous studies have been centered around class stratification.[10] For example, in one study consumers were divided into six different classes that represented different personality, cultural value, and reference groups. The purpose of the class stratified sample was to test the hypothesis that class differences influence family spending patterns, retail store loyalties, and specific product selection. Some of the contrasts between two of the groups follow.

Middle-Status

1. Pointed to the future.
2. Viewpoint embraces a long expanse of time.
3. More urban identification.
4. Stresses rationality.
5. Has a well-structured sense of the universe.
6. Horizons vastly extended or not limited.
7. Greater sense of choice making.
8. Self-confident, willing to take risks.
9. Immaterial and abstract in his thinking.
10. Sees himself tied to national happenings.

Lower-Status

1. Pointed to the present and past.
2. Lives and thinks in a short expanse of time.
3. More rural in identification.
4. Essentially nonrational.
5. Vague and unclear structuring of the world.
6. Horizons sharply defined and limited.
7. Limited sense of choice making.

[10] The following example is drawn from a classical study reported by Martineau. See Pierre Martineau, "Social Class and Spending Behavior," *Journal of Marketing*, 23 (October 1958), 121–30. For a more recent study, see H. Lee Mathews and John W. Slocum, Jr., "Social Class and Commercial Bank Credit Card Usage," *Journal of Marketing*, 33 (January 1969), 71–78, and James H. Myers and John F. Mount, "More on Social Class vs. Income as Correlates of Buying Behavior," *Journal of Marketing*, 37 (April 1973), 71–73.

8. Very much concerned with security and insecurity.
9. Concrete and perceptive in his thinking.
10. World revolves around his family and body.

Behavior in each of these two groups was examined. One of the conclusions is as follows:

> Middle-Status people usually have a place in their aspirations for some form of saving. Thus, saving is most often in the form of investment, where there is a risk, long-term involvement, and the possibility of higher return. . . . The aspirations of the Lower-Status are just as often for spending as they are for saving. This saving is usually a noninvestment saving where there is almost no risk, funds can be quickly converted to spendable cash, and returns are small.[11]

Other interesting differences between the groups are as follows: Upper-Lower status consumers have many more household appliances than Lower-Lower status. The inferential explanation of the finding is that "Upper-Lower status man sees his home as his castle . . . and he loads it down with hardware—solid heavy appliances—as his symbols of security. The Lower-Lower status individual is far less interested in his castle, and is more likely to spend his income for flashy clothes or an automobile."[12]

Different social classes appear to choose department stores according to social class. In shaping her store image, a shopper will consider the other customers in the store, the type of treatment received, familiarity with surroundings, and a number of other variables. The strictly economic characteristics of the store, such as price and quality, are important, but the shopper will not patronize a store willingly if the store does not fit her social class. A store wishing to cater to all segments of the market must take care not to exclude some segments unwittingly through poor social class identification. Likewise, the manufacturer must take care to place his goods in those outlets which have social class images compatible with the market he wishes to reach.

Social class is a broader concept than reference group. The class concept serves as an integrative framework within which the environmental conditions influencing purchase behavior choice can be synthesized. The class stratification structure provides a means of predicting purchase behavior through social class identification. It also suggests differences in product objects and appeals that will satisfy consumer needs.

[11] Martineau, *Social Class,* p. 129.
[12] Ibid.

Culture and Subculture

It is desirable to complete a review of environmental conditions that influence consumer behavior passing reference to the impact of culture and subculture. At a broad level, *culture* represents the accumulated and shared learning of a society. This learning constitutes a society's heritage that is passed from generation to generation in the form of beliefs, attitudes, values, habits, and knowledge. The shared learning that constitutes a society's culture influences to a significant degree the actions that individuals and groups can publicly perform.

The notion of *subculture* is, as the name suggests, a subdivision within the broader concept of culture. By subcultural classifications, accommodations in learned behavior can be made on the basis of nationality, race, or religion.

It is difficult to generalize the pointed value of cultural and subcultural considerations to the practical study of consumer behavior. At the cultural level, most learned behavior is taken as a given which is the foundation of the competitive system. To be sure, culture represents an environmental influence on consumer behavior. However, cultural differences are hard to operationalize toward the understanding of consumer choice. The subset of cultures does offer a useful motivational perspective. There is little doubt that subcultural classifications do represent significant markets and that learned behavior can influence purchase behavior. The opportunities represented by the black consumer market in the United States are a prime example of the importance of understanding the heritage of a subcultural division.

Conclusion—Environmental Influences

The environmental influences upon purchase behavior have been examined from the vantage point of the face-to-face relationship characteristic of the family to the broad range of learned heritages transmitted by cultural association. There is no doubt that social interaction influences purchase behavior. Indeed, a significant degree of consumer behavior can be attributed to the environmental setting of the purchase choice.

Unlike the concept of the economist, the explanations offered by the sociologist and cultural anthropologist cannot be rejected on the basis of simplicity. The study of purchase environment can be operationalized at least on a fragmented basis, and empirical support for numerous basic assumptions is accumulating. In addition, the sociological and anthropological approach to consumer behavior theory does not, similar to the economists' contribution, make the critical error of concentrating on products at the neglect of fundamental need.

What is missing from an environmental orientation to explaining consumer behavior is a completed treatment of the foundations of individual purchase motivation. Thus, rather than a complete approach to understanding, we must view the environmental orientation as one more leg on the stool. Once again, existing environmental theories simply cannot be judged complete. Therefore, our attention is now directed to various attempts to understand the individual motivation underlying purchase behavior.

INDIVIDUAL MOTIVATION

Thus far, we have reviewed approaches to the study of consumer behavior that concentrate on enabling and environmental influences upon individual choice. In this section, motivational aspects of an individual's purchase behavior are examined.

Traditionally, there has been disagreement among researchers concerning the basic nature of consumer purchase motivation. The following quote summarizes the disagreement:

> There are two broad classifications of theory with respect to the motivation of consumer purchases. One holds that the aspect of consumer behavior under study is in some sense irrational. Members of this school do not believe that buying behavior can be adequately explained on the assumption that the buyer is acting on the basis of a clear conception of ends he is seeking and means which are appropriate to these ends. The opposing school believes in the essential rationality of consumer behavior in solving individual household problems in the purchase of goods.[13]

We shall use the term *nonrational* rather than *irrational* because the second term is often used to describe those acts not accepted by the group to which the individual belongs. According to this definition, all acts which are acceptable to the group are rational.

Any charge that consumers have acted in a nonrational way must be based on an outsider's judgment of what constitutes a rational action and what does not. Since the individual engaged in the action is the only one truly capable of rendering such a judgment, this charge is subjective and easily open to error. The charge "nonrational" frequently arises when sensory perception provides the basis for making a particular purchase. But it is quite possible to rationalize within the sensory aspects of personality. We cannot say that purchasing a pound of coffee because of its extremely

---

[13] See "Cost and Profit Outlook," Vol. 7 (March 1954), prepared by Alderson and Session Associates.

pleasant odor is a nonrational act. Neither can we label nonrational an act in which certain subconscious forces have played a part. These subconscious forces may simply influence the nature of the conscious process that takes place before a purchase is made. If an irate wife calls her husband a miser for refusing to buy her a new winter coat, she may in fact be correct. But we cannot say that the husband's subconscious leanings toward thrift make his refusal a nonrational act. His refusal may be the result of a very rational process. For instance, he may reason that her old coat is still good and that, with some remodeling, it could very well serve her for another year. His tendency to thrift is a deeper need, forcing him to reason in a certain way.

Frequently the charge of nonrational behavior is based on a consumer's own admission that he has acted in a nonrational way. Obviously, a consumer may sometimes feel that he has made a mistake, but this can usually be explained in other ways. A desirable end last week may not be so next week. Take the case of a young lady who spends a week's salary on Monday for a new evening dress to wear to the dinner-dance on Saturday. The following Monday she may seriously question the appropriateness of her ends. It was therefore impossible for her to determine the proper means at the time of purchase. Uncertainty is present in all purchases, since consumers must match anticipated ends with alternative means available to them. The problem is magnified when we recognize that there is a difference between buying and consuming. The purchaser is usually buying for others in the household as well as for himself, and so he must anticipate their ends in addition to his own, and also the capacity of a number of means to satisfy them.[14]

While some purchases are clearly means to ends, many are made without any apparent deliberation. Katona suggests making a distinction between the types of problems consumers face in the marketplace—those that call for real decision making and those that are handled on a habitual, routine basis.[15] The routine type of problem-solving behavior hardly suggests the presence of rational behavior. But this criticism is countered with the argument that rational insight, having once solved the problem, is no longer necessary after a habitual, routine behavior pattern has been established.

There may be other cases in which a given purchase does not contribute significantly to the purchaser's well-being. Then the person does not

---

[14] For a more detailed explanation, see Wroe Alderson, *Marketing Behavior and Executive Action* (Homewood, Ill.: Richard D. Irwin, Inc., 1957), pp. 165–66.

[15] George Katona, *Psychological Analysis of Economic Behavior* (New York: McGraw-Hill Book Company, 1951), p. 49.

trouble himself to identify the appropriate means, but follows a trial-and-error procedure. For example, a person selecting a magazine at a railroad station newsstand may reason along two or three different lines. Instead of buying one magazine, he may choose two in the hope that one will suit him. If both prove unsatisfactory, he can buy another on the train or, as a last resort, look out the window if none of the magazines prove satisfactory. A casual observer would fail to detect any sign of rational behavior as he observed this action.

Many impulse purchases appear to be devoid of any rational process. Actually, impulse purchases may be the result of habitual, routine behavior of the type described above; they may take place on a trial-and-error basis, or a rational process may occur instantaneously at the time of purchase. Another type of impulse purchase is the result of a rational process that has taken place previously. Much Christmas gift shopping would come in this last category.

To sum up, it seems that there is no clear-cut evidence that consumer behavior is nonrational. Claims made for such behavior can just as easily be used to provide evidence for rational behavior. It is unfortunate that the terms *rational* and *nonrational* are used. From a marketing point of view, it is important to recognize that consumers engage in some kind of *deliberate process* before purchasing. It matters little whether the deliberation is extensive, based on habit, governed by the senses, or influenced strongly by subconscious forces. The chief point is that a deliberate process is involved. Of course, some consumers have more capacity for matching means with ends, and the degree of deliberation for different kinds of products varies. However, once we know that such a process exists, the appropriate task is to identify the various elements in the process.

Different explanations of individual motivation toward purchase behavior have been suggested by psychologists and social psychologists. To examine the basic concepts of motivation we have selected three explanations for review: (1) Need-Satisfaction; (2) Psychoanalytic; and (3) Cognitive.

Need-Satisfaction Foundation

The examination of purchase motivation from the viewpoint of need satisfaction is one of the oldest attempts to explain why an individual performs a specific act. This approach has been extensively used by laboratory or experimental psychologists, who study the basic needs of living organisms and observe how they establish behavior patterns to satisfy these needs. The subjects of such experiments are usually animals. Perhaps the most widely quoted experiment of need-satisfaction behavior was the dog feeding and bell association research of Ivan Pavlov.

The foundation of need-satisfaction motivation is the existence of a stimulus-response type of relationship. The individual is viewed as having basic drives, such as survival, self-protection, relief from heat and cold, need for love. Several different classifications of need have been suggested that formulate a complex grouping of biological, social, and psychological drives which motivate behavior. Maslow has suggested a hierarchical classification of needs into five basic categories:[16]

1. *Physiological*—the most basic needs of an individual required for biological survival.
2. *Safety*—the need for security and basic peace of mind.
3. *Love*—the need for affection and togetherness or belongingness.
4. *Esteem*—the need for prestige and recognition by others.
5. *Self-Actualization*—the need to do one's own thing.

In the Maslow scheme of explaining motivations, the basic categories represent an interdependent hierarchy since each preceeding level of need must be satisfied prior to a drive materializing at a more advanced level. As one author summarizes the Maslow hierarchy, it "reaches from the belly to the brain."[17]

While one cannot argue with the existence of drives, the need for stimulus, a reaction on the part of the individual and, given sufficient repetition, a form of reinforced behavior, it is difficult to generalize need satisfaction into a meaningful approach for marketers to use in examining purchase behavior. To state it briefly, the basic propositions make sense but they are difficult to operationalize.

Psychoanalytic Foundation

Sigmund Freud introduced the field of personality as the motivating force behind human behavior. To Freud, the biological origin of man resulted in three interdependent psychological forces that combined to formulate the individual's behavior patterns. The foundations of behavior in the psychoanalytic approach stem from:

1. *The Id*—the basic biological impulses that man is born with.
2. *The Superego*—the internal filter that presents to the individual the behavioral expectations of society.
3. *The Ego*—the rational control device that reconciles conflicts between the Id and the Superego and results in a defensible behavior pattern.

---

[16] Abraham H. Maslow, *Motivation and Personality* (New York: Harper & Row, Publishers, 1954), and "A Theory of Human Motivation," *Psychological Review*, 50 (1943), 370–96.

[17] Bennett, *Consumer,* p. 63.

Following Freud, the basic concepts of biological origin of all drives were substantially modified by followers of the psychoanalytic school to include socially generated drives.[18] However, the central feature of the psychoanalytic explanation of motivation is the belief that all physiological and psychological needs cannot be completely satisfied within the bounds of society. Consequently, such needs create tensions within the individual that must be repressed. Although they lurk in the subconscious, they remain a factor that influences purchase behavior.

Repressed needs may influence the conscious needs of the individual and the behavior he indulges in to satisfy these needs. An interesting example of the application of this theoretical structure is found in a study of businessmen's reluctance to use air travel for business purposes. After psychoanalytical techniques had been used to probe the subconscious of a small sample of businessmen, it was concluded that their reluctance was a result of "posthumous guilt complexes." This means that subconsciously they were fearful, in event of a fatal accident, of what their wives would say about them afterward. Since this complex was so strong, it could not be removed and had to be compensated for.

One company's advertising appealed to the desire to get home from a business trip sooner so the businessman could have more time with his children. Most printed advertising copy showed pictures of young children running down the walk with outstretched arms to greet Daddy on Friday night instead of Saturday noon. This approach was used to compensate for the guilt complex, as it is believed anything to do with the love of children is one of the strongest appeals that can be made.[19]

Psychoanalytic explanations of individual behavior motivation offer interesting speculation concerning the forces that channel purchase selection. However, similar to the concept of need-satisfaction motivation, the basic tenets of psychoanalytic explanations are difficult to operationalize in the formulation of marketing activities.

Cognitive Foundation

A cognitive approach to motivation is based on the assumption that the individual learns desired behavior as a result of past experience and understanding. Thus, basic behavior is the result of the consumer attempting to achieve certain goals by virtue of purchase activity.

[18] For example, see Calvin S. Hall and Gardner Lindzey, *Theories of Personality* (New York: John Wiley & Sons, 1957), and Charles D. Schewe, "Selected Social Psychological Models for Analyzing Buyers," *Journal of Marketing,* 37, (July 1973), 31–39.

[19] Perrin Stryker, "Motivation Research," *Fortune* (June 1956), p. 226.

An early orientation to the learning and understanding of cognitive structures was contributed to the study of human behavior by Gestalt psychology.

The Gestalt psychologists employ a more inclusive approach to human behavior. Behavior is not explained by one set of forces only, as in the case of the psychoanalytic school, but rather by many forces. The word *gestalt* means "configuration" or "pattern," and Gestalt theorists see human beings as acting in goal-directed patterns. People identify their own needs and follow conscious paths toward satisfying them.

Gestalt psychology today views the individual as existing in a *life-space* (the atmosphere within which he lives and acts).[20] The goals he seeks and the means selected are not determined by physiological needs and inner personality variables only, but also by environment. This interaction between the person and his environment has caused social psychologists to place much emphasis upon the combination of Gestalt psychology and sociological concepts of reference group influence.

From the cognitive viewpoint of consumer behavior the decision choices to spend money or to save it, the allocation of expenditures to specific products, the brands purchased, and the conditions of purchase are all made with some end in mind. Thus, this orientation to understanding behavior is characterized by a means-end or problem-solving motivation. The consumer is viewed as engaging in planned activity to attain a specific goal. To operationalize this notion of perceived need and conscious goal-directed behavior, marketers have developed the notion of self-image, product-image, and image matching.

The concept of *self-image* is explained in the following quotation:

> Human beings characteristically act with self-awareness, exercise self-control, exhibit conscience and guilt, and in the great crises of life make decisions with reference to some imagery of what they are, what they have been, and what they hope to be.[21]

Marketers believe that by understanding the self-image they may obtain clues to the ends consumers are seeking. For example, conspicuous consumption may be interpreted as an attempt by the consumer to achieve a certain position in the community. This position is the consumer's image of himself at some point. More recently the notion of inconspicuous consumption has been popularized. Conspicuous consumption, in which the

---

[20] Kurt Koffka, *Principles of Gestalt Psychology* (New York: Harcourt, Brace, and World, Inc., 1935), and Wolfgang Köhler, *Gestalt Psychology* (New York: Liveright Publishing Corporation, 1947).

[21] Lindesmith, *Psychology,* p. 413.

consumer purchases in a manner which sets him apart from the group, is explained by the consumer's desire to achieve an image which distinguishes him from the group. With inconspicuous consumption the image the consumer wishes to achieve and the position he wishes to occupy is one of the conservative, intelligent class. The fact that these two descriptions of the images people wish to achieve are at opposite extremes is not a contradiction. It does illustrate, however, that the images consumers have are in a constant state of change and are, in part, a result of the changing cultural environment.

Products, brands, and conditions of purchase are viewed through the consumer's eyes as a means of achieving the self-image. In effect, a *product-image* is created in the mind of the consumer. The tastes in furniture of two groups of people may well vary considerably. One group may prefer bright-patterned, massive furniture, extreme in design. The forces that shape the self-images in this group construct a compatible product-image for this type of furniture. The other group may be completely repelled by this type of furniture. It in no way contributes to an achievement of the self-image, and the product-image will reflect this.

It must be understood that a product as viewed by the consumer has many dimensions, and the product-image incorporates all of them. A product generally includes a particular brand; and consumers may have a favorable product-type-image, although a given brand-image does not satisfy their self-image. This is particularly true of gift merchandise. Sears Roebuck bath towels may generate a compatible product-image for most consumers for their own use, but Cannon towels are more likely to be bought as gifts.

Another dimension is the environment in which the product is offered for sale. Sterling silverware available only in leading high-quality jewelry and department stores may shape a product-image compatible with the self-image of most buyers. If the same product is available in a less fashionable environment, at cut prices, the product-image may change enough to be incompatible with their self-images.

From the foregoing discussion it is clear that the consumer sees a product as more than an object providing a certain objective utility. In his eyes it is a means to psychological as well as material ends. He looks beyond the immediate utility of the product, forms an image of the product, and intuitively if not consciously compares this image with his desired self-image. An automobile provides objective utility—transportation—but it is more than this; it is a means of achieving ends that are determined by the buyer's desired self-image. The reputation of the brand (the brand-image), the purchase environment, and even assurances in the use of the product, all contribute to the product-image—the psychological utility of the product or brand.

Image matching relates to how compatible the consumer perceives a product-image to be with the desired self-image.[22] If the two images are not viewed as compatible, in all likelihood no sale will result. Considering the wide variety of purchases made by individual consumers, it is not logical to assume that each must be preceded by a conscious marketing process. A great deal of consumer behavior is learned from past experience and associations. Thus, many products, such as light bulbs and spark plugs, may be purchased solely for their functional value with little thought of the way in which they contribute to one's self-image. However, in the establishment of purchase behavior patterns an image match for all product requirements which is psychologically rewarding must be achieved by virtue of search or learned experience.

Conclusion—Individual Motivation

In an effort to understand patterns of purchase motivation, we reviewed three explanations of how consumers formulate choice patterns. Among the three approaches, the cognitive explanation is appealing to marketers for two reasons. First, the basic assumptions of conscious goal-directed behavior appear to offer the greatest measurement potential. Second, the cognitive approach to explain motivation draws upon the basic contributions of all disciplines reviewed throughout this chapter.

The combination of cognitive psychological motivation within the constraints of economic capability and sociological environment offer a complete framework for investigation of consumer behavior. The cognitive approach to motivation places direct emphasis on the satisfaction of basic needs, therefore overcoming earlier noted deficiencies of the economic approach. The orientation on the individual offered by the cognitive approach balances the social emphasis of the environmental contributions. From within the combined disciplines of economics, the study of purchase environment, and the explanation of individual motivation, the marketer can logically forge an understanding of how an individual learns to consume. From this understanding products can be conceived and marketing activities can be formulated. The fundamental concepts of learning to consume are discussed in the next section.

SUMMARY

This chapter has presented the basic choice decisions a consumer must make in selecting a behavioral pattern. Contributions of multiple disci-

---

[22] For expansion, see Ira J. Dolich, "Congruence Relationships Between Self-Images and Product Brands," *Journal of Marketing Research,* 6 (February 1969), 80–84.

plines that offer insight into the way consumers make choices were also reviewed. In total, the material presented provides the foundation of consumer behavior. The implications of the material presented in Chapter 6 will not be fully summarized until the end of Chapter 7.

QUESTIONS AND PROBLEMS

1. In programming marketing effort, how can management use information on what, how much, and under what conditions the market will purchase?

2. In what way do problems faced by the consumer in purchasing products influence the marketing of these products?

3. Name at least two products, the purchase of which would be influenced by stage in the family life cycle and social class of the consuming unit. Discuss the way in which these environmental conditions will influence purchase.

4. In attempting to understand consumer behavior for marketing purposes, it has been said that "it is only necessary to work at immediate levels of causation." Explain this statement.

5. What is meant by reference group theory? How is it relevant to marketing?

6. Why is Gestalt psychology particularly useful in analyzing consumer behavior?

7. Explain how different stages in the family life cycle can influence purchasing.

8. "Consumers, in their purchase patterns, intrinsically attempt to express a station in life." Do you agree? Elaborate on this statement.

Chapter 7

Purchase Behavior Analysis

In this chapter we continue our review of consumer behavior by looking at the way in which consumers make decisions and some of the implications involved in qualitative market investigation. With all the enabling environmental and individual motivational forces at work, how does the consumer eventually make a purchase decision? The precise answer to this question has long been sought, and perhaps we shall never know the explicit nature of the total choice process. While marketers would like to understand consumer behavior fully, an important qualification should be kept in mind. The market planner is most interested in *what* action consumers will take in solving choice problems versus *why* they take specific actions. In other words, the marketer is more interested in understanding and predicting consumer behavior patterns than in seeking a full explanation of what motivates a specific pattern. You will recall from Chapter 1 that the "inability to understand and aggregate purchase preferences" was one of the major areas of uncertainty confronted in a free society.

The initial part of the chapter introduces a learning perspective as one way better to understand consumer behavior. Next, a framework to guide qualitative market investigation is presented. To illustrate the type of information that can be obtained from behavior research, the third part of the chapter reviews a motivation study related to automobile purchase. The treatment is concluded by a review of some practical aspects of purchase behavior research.

A LEARNING PERSPECTIVE OF CONSUMER BEHAVIOR

During the last decade a number of theoretical models have been developed to help explain to marketers the process of consumer purchase selection.[1]

[1] Among the most widely circulated are John A. Howard and Jagdish N. Sheth, *The Theory of Buyer Behavior* (New York: John Wiley & Sons, Inc., 1969);

Most such models build upon the basic belief that purchase actions are a form of *learned behavior*. In other words, consumers learn over time how best to behave with respect to their choices in consumption. A learning orientation to consumer behavior starts with the assumption that individuals have a number of basic drives, motives, and needs that must to some degree be satisfied. Some drives are biological in origin. However, most drives, motives, and needs of interest to consumers are learned as a result of social and psychological interaction. Thus, most significant consumption drives are based upon individuals' current array of needs and are not the product of a long history of experiences.

As consumers we learn through continuous consumption that selected products satisfy our needs. Given a perceived need, a potential consumer is stimulated by either the product, from commercial activities of sellers, or from social interaction to "give the product a try." It is important to realize that marketing activities, such as advertising, represent only one form of *stimulus* or *information cue* that may influence consumer evaluation. The consumer, because of restrictions or constructs, may or may not select to purchase the initial product observed. If the product does not appear to offer the desired benefits, the consumer may search for a better product self-image fit.

Learning occurs from search and consumption. If stimulated to consume by a specific phenomenon, the consumer will experience some degree of satisfaction or reward. It is important to understand that learning results from environmental influences and from the individual cognitive appraisal of the situation confronted. Thus, learned behavior can be articulated by consumers in the form of attitudes and opinions concerning specific acts, events, or products. To illustrate: a student needs food for survival. Among available alternatives, steak may be viewed as the socially accepted "best food," but the student might prefer hamburger given all constraints. The situation wherein steak is selected is clearly not always one based on nutrition or financial requirements. The football team that wins the grudge contest eats steak while the loser eats hamburger. Having *learned* that steak is generally held in high esteem, it hardly follows that an eligible bachelor will be served hamburger by an available young lady. Regardless if we were to ask the football players, the bachelor, or the lady, all could clearly articulate their preferences for steak over hamburger. They

---

Francesco M. Nicosia, *Consumer Decision Processes* (Englewood Cliffs, N.J.: Prentice-Hall, Inc., 1966); James F. Engel, David T. Kollat, and Roger D. Blackwell, *Consumer Behavior* (New York: Holt, Rinehart and Winston, Inc., 1968); and Frederick E. Webster, Jr. and Yoram Wind, "A General Model for Understanding Organizational Buying Behavior," *Journal of Marketing,* 36 (April 1972), 12–19.

might have a great deal of difficulty explaining the real *why* behind their choices.

An important concept of learning is the notion of *reinforcement*. Given a specific form of behavior the act will be judged by the consumer. If the experience is rewarding, the selection of a specific product will be reinforced. Positive reinforcement may result from either or both personal self-satisfaction or peer group appraisal. To realize the highest degree of reinforcement, both social and personal appraisals must support or reinforce the purchase behavior. To illustrate: a young man may purchase a "10-gallon Texas style" hat, which he personally feels makes him look very dapper. However, if the hat is the object of considerable ridicule at the football game, and his date is embarrassed, he may have second thoughts concerning how well the product fits his desired self-image. Despite the fact that he likes the hat, in order to get social reinforcement he may need to transfer from Harvard to the University of Texas. In this case, both forms of reinforcement were not positive.

The essence of learning to consume rests in sufficient reinforcement of behavior so as to develop the capability to *generalize* and *discriminate*. Given the wide variety of behavior decisions a consumer must make and the countless information cues experienced, the individual does not have time to engage an overt search prior to each purchase action. *Generalization* occurs when the consumer begins to respond to a new situation in a manner similar to the way he responded in past situations. If a particular activity was rewarding and positive reinforcement occurred, there is no need to change behavior when confronted with similar or near similar circumstances. To the degree that consistency exists in behavior the burden of consumption is reduced, allowing cognitive capabilities to be concentrated on decisions of personal or social importance. To overgeneralize could be dangerous. The capability to *discriminate* is to override previous generalizations when the results may not be reinforcing.

The foundations for evaluating *brand loyalty,* or for that matter *institutional loyalty,* are directly related to reinforcement, generalization, and discrimination. If a person finds positive reinforcement at both the personal and social appraisal levels of reward, it logically follows that the specific purchase behavior is a strong candidate to be repeated. In essence, the consumer becomes committed.

From the viewpoint of market planning, cognitive commitment on the part of consumers to a specific brand or outlet represents a most desirable result of purchase behavior. If commitment is not realized, then a neutral reaction is superior to rejection or even extinction of a previously satisfactory experience. Thus, loyalty is not permanent and it is relative. Intense loyalty can lead to habit. For a particular activity to remain habitual it must continue to be reinforced.

Brand loyalty offers a good basis for illustrating generalization and discrimination. A woman may have consumed Nabisco crackers for years with satisfactory results. Such reinforcement could well have reached a habitual stage early in her married life, so, acting as family purchase agent, her brand choice without deliberation is always Nabisco crackers. It is not difficult under such a situation for the housewife to generalize from soda crackers to Ritz or even to Oreo cookies on the basis of positive reinforcement. In fact, she may view all Nabisco bakery products as "good values," only selecting among flavors on the basis of her family's taste preferences. It is important to note that while the housewife's family may not like Fig Newtons, she has a positive attitude that they "are good if you like figs."

If asked by a market researcher, there can be little doubt that the housewife described would offer positive endorsement to Nabisco products. For her face-to-face reference groups, she is bound to cast an influence upon product choice. For example, she may bound into the kitchen of a new neighbor, observe a Jane Parker package of cookies, and without hesitating ask why the woman doesn't buy Oreo. The fact that the housewife generalizes positive experience across product lines is one reason that marketers develop *brand names, symbols,* and *trademarks* to identify a family of products. Such names as Libby, Kellogg's, Heinz, GE, RCA, General Motors, and Whirlpool help consumers to generalize cognitive acceptance.

Discrimination is the limiting factor. The fact that in the eyes of a consumer Nabisco makes the best bakery products available does not mean carte blanche acceptance of Freezer Queen meats, Chuckles candy, or Aurora toys—all also made by Nabisco. Indeed, the consumer may react in a negative way to a baker freezing TV dinners, making candy, and selling road racers. For some, this change of "image" could tend to weaken or even make extinct the positive attitude toward crackers. For most, the process of discrimination would require the building of a separate and independent set of opinions and attitudes concerning each product family. The fact that outboard motors built by Mercury were held in high esteem by large segments of the sporting market did little to help Mercury's entrance into the snowmobile market.

A learning perspective of consumer behavior provides marketers with a basic understanding of the way in which specific purchases are made. The detailed study of the consumption phenomenon as one aspect of overall human behavior is properly the dominion of other social sciences. In most cases, it is not necessary for the marketer to understand fully why consumers hold certain attitudes and opinions toward various products. Rather it is sufficient that the opinions and attitudes prevailing among a large segment of consumers be identified so that market offerings can be matched to potential customer needs and wants.

A FRAMEWORK FOR QUALITATIVE MARKET INVESTIGATION

From the foregoing we may conclude that the key element in understanding consumer choice is to identify the ends or goals of consumers. Once self-images are pinpointed among a segment of the market, it is necessary to estimate how consumers will react to the different means by which they can gain desired ends. The problem is complicated by the fact that means and ends are different for each consumer choice problem.

For example, consider the case of a young couple deciding what to do with a $500 Christmas bonus. Their first choice is to put the money in a savings account, since both have always desired some financial reserve in case of an emergency. The dominant end here is a desire for security, which may be related to a self-image of a responsible citizen with the foresight to provide for emergencies. This choice—to save money—may be in sharp conflict with another end, the couple's desire to purchase a stereophonic record player to use at their house party on New Year's Eve. This end is related to the self-image of a socially gifted hostess known for successful parties.

But perhaps they can realize both ends. They could purchase a $300 record player and save $200. In shopping for the stereo, however, they learn that only the lower-quality makes are available for $300, and that in tone these cannot measure up to the better sets. After comparing many brands, the couple prefers a $600 XYZ. This is unquestionably the best set. Having decided on an XYZ, the search for a source of supply begins. The end in mind at this point is to buy from the cheapest possible source. They find a discount house where they can buy a set in the crate on a cash-and-carry basis for $480, and the purchase is made.

This case illustrates several ends and several means. In the first choice problem, the end is security, and the means is saving $500. In the second choice problem, the end is a desire for social acceptance, and the means is a stereophonic record player. In the third problem, the end is a stereophonic record player, and the means is one of the many different brands available. In the last choice, the end is purchasing the selected brand at the lowest possible price, and the means is the discount house.

The marketer's task is to cater to any and all of the several ends through providing market offerings in which the perceived images are compatible with the desired self-images.

This discussion should not leave the impression that marketing is an entirely passive process; that is, that marketers should restrict their efforts to seeking out consumers' self-images, adjust their products to them, and in this way insure success. If this were possible there would be little occasion for failure, but two circumstances prevent such a neat solution. First, at this time we do not have the means to delineate precisely the different self-

Purchase Behavior Analysis 143

images composing the market. We do recognize the presence of differences and undertake by various means to arrive at offerings that will hopefully precipitate purchase. Second, this solution assumes that marketing can do nothing about conditioning the consumer with respect to both the self-image he creates for himself and the product-image he envisions. Through time, and with the appropriate marketing effort, society can be conditioned to the point where various images and attitudes are restructured as related to market behavior.

Although many purchases are not based upon matching self-image with product-image, we do believe that the matching of self-image with product-image does provide a conceptual framework for the study of consumer decision making in regard to a wide array of products offered in the marketplace.

To examine a market potential in terms of qualitative factors, we proceed with the assumption that product-image will reflect the product, the brand, and the condition under which it may be purchased. If the product is perceived in such a way that purchase will allow the consumer to achieve his desired self-image, purchase is likely to follow. Given the purchase behavior, learning experience will be generated to assist in the next round of choice decisions.

Figure 7-1 provides a schematic of decision areas involved in consumer choice. This diagram is not presented as a model of consumer behavior. Rather, it illustrates areas where the market researcher can concentrate research efforts in order better to understand consumer needs and predict reactions to alternative market actions.

Most market investigation of consumer behavior may have a splin-

FIGURE 7-1
A Schematic Structure for Qualitative Market Investigation

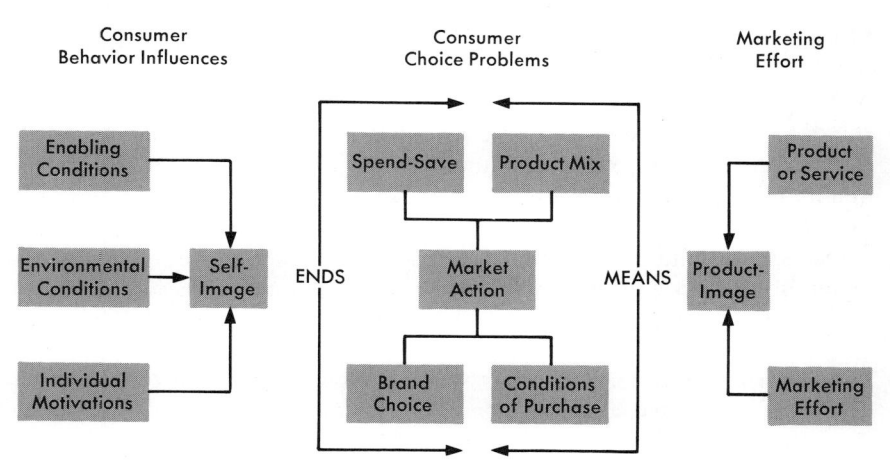

tered appearance to the uninitiated. Very few investigations could be structured from a time or cost perspective that would seek to explore all aspects of the framework presented in Figure 7-1. There are two ways to gather information about consumers. Behavior can be *observed* or information can be *acquired* by questioning. When overt behavior is observed or straightforward factual questions are asked, the results have a quantitative feature that may be statistically evaluated.

When information is gathered by more subtle means, such as depth interviewing or the use of projective techiques, the interpretation with respect to behavior influences is always inferential. Under such conditions, the number of consumers subjected to analysis is limited by time and cost. Conclusions obtained by behavioral research rarely are experimentally or statistically proven. Thus, to employ behavioral research results effectively in the formulation of plans, marketers must be willing to work on limited results and small samples of respondents to identify potential market segments and related appeals. Using behavioral techniques, cause-and-effect relationships must be established on an inferential basis. The following section illustrates a behavioral study.

A PURCHASE MOTIVATION STUDY ON AUTOMOBILES[2]

A few years ago the National Broadcasting Company began a series of studies to determine the value of television as a medium for the promotion of heavy duty consumer goods. The automobile was selected for these studies. One aspect of the project was to gain an understanding of the buying process in the purchase of automobiles. A study was undertaken to determine the self-images of the buyers of cars in general and the self-images and the product-images found in the buyers of different brands and types of cars. More specifically, the study dealt with the differences existing between (1) buyers of different brands in the same price class; (2) buyers of different price classes; (3) potential buyers of the small American car and the standard American car; and (4) potential buyers of the small American car and the small foreign car. This illustration is used to show the kind of qualitative information necessary to match marketing effort with opportunity. It illustrates the way in which differences in self-images affect product choice and also the way in which differences in product-image require adjustments in product and marketing efforts to accommodate these differences.

The study included a sample of the general public in addition to new

[2] This illustration is adapted from "Auto Motives, A Study in Customer Acceleration," sponsored by the National Broadcasting Company.

buyers and old buyers. The following findings are based on a sample of 11,000 interviews distributed over the entire country.

Each new car buyer and each old buyer was asked to check from a list of personality traits those which he felt described himself. This information was used to develop self-images of buyers of different makes of automobiles. These self-images were then compared with the self-images of the general public regardless of make of car owned, and the results expressed in percent differences between the buyer of a specific make and the general public. That is, the number of buyers of a specific make declaring a certain trait were expressed as a percentage of total buyers. Likewise, the number of people in the general public declaring a specific trait were expressed as a percentage of the total. Differences between the percentage of total for buyers of car B and D and the percentage of total for the general public for each trait identified are shown in Table 7-1.

Car B and car D are low-priced cars of different brands. In general, Table 7-1 shows that buyers of low-price car B thought they were more daring, unpredictable, and impulsive than the general public and less sociable and sentimental. The buyers of low-priced car D displayed the opposite characteristics. Both groups believed they were more ambitious and thrifty than the general public. Although the product-image for each of the two brands was not determined, we can infer that if purchase shows compatibility between the self-image and product-image, the latter must be considered different for each brand. From a marketing standpoint, it would be fruitful for manufacturers of both cars to analyze buyers more deeply to determine which characteristics of their cars appeal to which characteristics of their customers' self-images. Changes in the product in advertising appeals and in purchase environment may be necessary to tap the different segments of the market.

Table 7-1 shows a further refinement of the data in which self-images

TABLE 7-1
Self-Image of the Buyer

	Relative Difference Between Buyers and General Public	
	Car B	Car D
Daring	+27%	−40%
Unpredictable	+21	−16
Impulsive	+11	−15
Sociable	−10	+14
Sentimental	− 8	+ 6
Ambitious	+21	+20
Thrifty	+16	+20

Courtesy: National Broadcasting Co.

are related to price classes. Buyers of all three price classes consider themselves more efficient and adventurous than the general public. Many more buyers of high-priced cars believe themselves to be more efficient and adventurous than buyers of low- and medium-priced cars. All buyers consider themselves as less soft-hearted, sensitive, and shy than the general public, but more high-priced buyers than low- or medium-priced buyers profess an absence of these characteristics. With respect to thrift and practicality, buyers of low-priced cars consider themselves above average, medium-priced about average, and high-priced below average. The type of marketing effort needed to cultivate the market for differently priced cars must be tailored to these differences in self-image.

Since the small car question was a crucial one in the automobile industry at this time, NBC also developed a profile of customers' product-images for small cars, both foreign and American-made, and for standard American-made cars. As shoppers were examining standard American-made cars in a showroom, they were shown a number of adjectives that might be used to describe a car and were asked to select those adjectives that best expressed their opinion of the particular car they were looking at. They were also asked to do the same for an illustration of a small American-made car. Car buyers, interviewed in the home, were shown a small car illustration. To one-half of this group the car illustration was described as a new small American-made car, and to the other half a new small foreign car. The old buyers were also asked to select those adjectives that best expressed their opinions of the standard American car they had already purchased. The data shown in Figure 7-2 is limited to that given by the shoppers in the showroom and that given by the old buyers, to whom the illustration was identified as a new small American-made car.

Figure 7-2 shows the difference in the percentage of people applying

TABLE 7-2
Self-Image by Price Classes

	Relative Difference Between Buyers and General Public		
	Low-Price	Medium-Price	High-Price
Adventurous	+ 9%	+25%	+77%
Efficient	+13	+17	+29
Cautious	+ 9	+ 9	−25
Soft-hearted	−16	−13	−22
Sensitive	− 6	−15	−54
Shy	−22	−29	−69
Thrifty	+14	− 1	−32
Practical	+10	+ 2	−25

Courtesy: National Broadcasting Co.

particular adjectives to the standard American-made car and the percentage of respondents applying the same adjectives to the new small American-made car. For example, 64 percent more people thought the small American-made car was more economical than the standard. A glance at the chart indicates that the product-image of these two cars is quite different. These differences should be capitalized on in personal selling and advertising by emphasizing in each car the qualities most often attributed to it.

In comparing the small American-made car with the small foreign car, the data collected from old buyers were used. To one-half of this group the illustration was identified as a new small American-made car and to the other half a new small foreign car. The differences in the percentage of people applying an adjective to the new small American-made car illustration over the percentage of respondents applying the same adjective to the new small foreign car illustration are shown in Figure 7-3.

The small American-made car is felt to be superior to the foreign car in such characteristics as convenience in servicing, comfort, trade-in value, and "a lot of car for the money." The small foreign car is definitely considered more daring and exciting. Relating this information to the self-images of buyers of different makes shown in Tables 7-1 and 7-2, the

FIGURE 7-2
Image of American Small Car Versus Standard

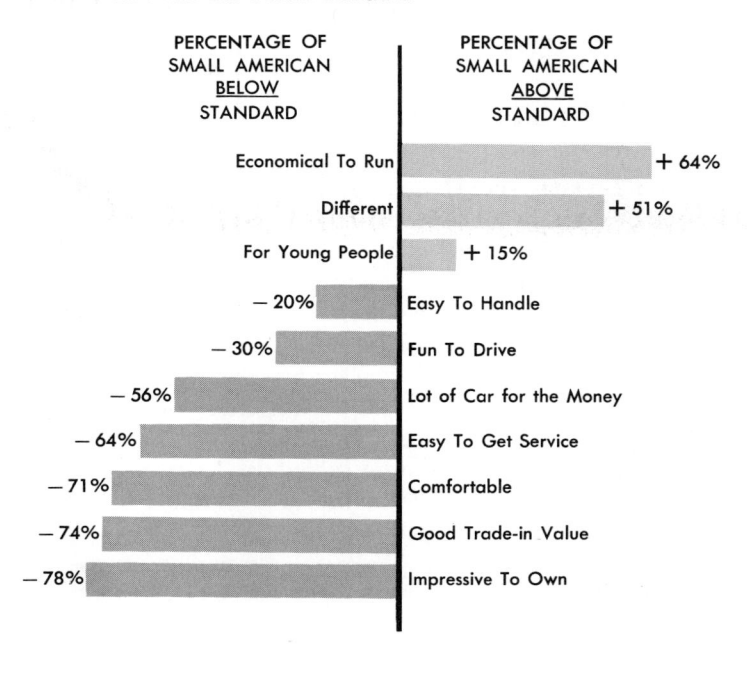

PERCENTAGE OF SMALL AMERICAN BELOW STANDARD		PERCENTAGE OF SMALL AMERICAN ABOVE STANDARD
	Economical To Run	+64%
	Different	+51%
	For Young People	+15%
−20%	Easy To Handle	
−30%	Fun To Drive	
−56%	Lot of Car for the Money	
−64%	Easy To Get Service	
−71%	Comfortable	
−74%	Good Trade-in Value	
−78%	Impressive To Own	

FIGURE 7-3
Image of American Small Car Versus Foreign

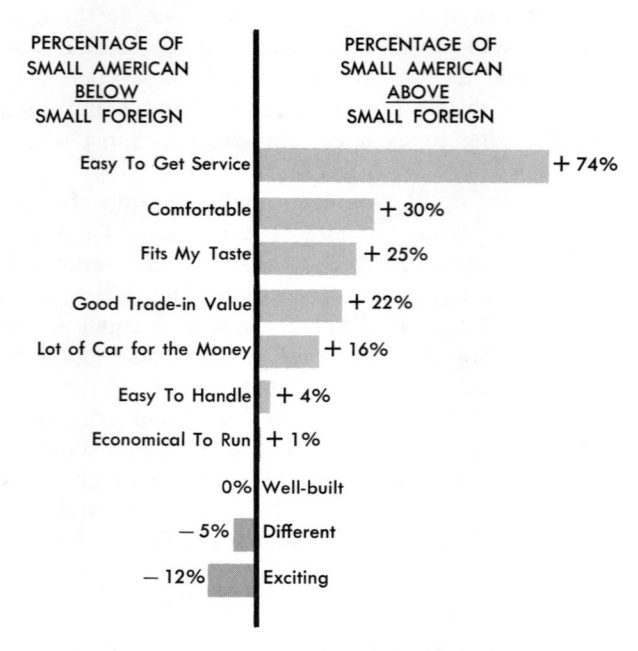

	PERCENTAGE OF SMALL AMERICAN BELOW SMALL FOREIGN	PERCENTAGE OF SMALL AMERICAN ABOVE SMALL FOREIGN
Easy To Get Service		+74%
Comfortable		+30%
Fits My Taste		+25%
Good Trade-in Value		+22%
Lot of Car for the Money		+16%
Easy To Handle		+4%
Economical To Run		+1%
Well-built	0%	
Different	−5%	
Exciting	−12%	

small foreign car will appeal most likely to the high-priced buyers and the buyers of low-priced car B.

SOME PRACTICAL CONSIDERATIONS

You may wonder how success can ever be achieved without detailed analyses of the subjective characteristics of markets. Many companies know very little about what motivates consumers. They are unquestionably successful without this detailed knowledge. But the more precise a firm's knowledge of markets, and the deeper its understanding of purchase motivation, the greater the expectation that its marketing effort will be successful.

The real role of knowledge concerning purchase motivation is in designing programs that are competitively superior and contribute most effectively to the achievement of corporate objectives. If none of the rival firms is adjusting to the market's more subjective desires, competition will assume many other forms, but the ability of consumers to achieve their ends in the marketplace will be reduced.

Although the advantages of this kind of market investigation are many, there are limitations to its use in practice. Let us look at some of them.

COST

Practically all of the studies described involve very costly collection and interpretation procedures. One researcher reports:

> Any competent motivation research report is primarily an interpretive (rather than statistical) analysis of the data in which the researcher draws conclusions and presents them in the report. This interpretation of the data usually requires many man hours of time of highly trained analysts. In analyzing our time sheets we find that professional time in hours on a study runs much higher than the clerical time and is only exceeded by the interviewer man hours.[3]

Most companies today are either unwilling or unable to incur the expense of this kind of research.

TIMING

Regardless of cost, the value of motivation studies is rather short-lived. As influencing conditions change, so do self-images. Technological improvements and marketing innovations by competitors create changes in product-images. Consequently, studies must be conducted at frequent intervals to be reliable. In extremely competitive industries, moreover, there is frequently no time for a full-scale study of consumer behavior; in order to compete successfully the manufacturer must get new products on the market as quickly as possible. With many product types, a few months are all the head start that can be hoped for.

PERSONNEL

There is a shortage of personnel trained to do motivation research. Much that passes for scientific inquiry is conducted by incompetent individuals using poorly designed research techniques. Businessmen must rely on the services of outside organizations to conduct this research. Even when competent analysts are used, the lack of knowledge by management about the theoretical orientation upon which much research rests and about the techniques used constitutes a barrier to acceptance by management.

[3] Burleigh B. Gardner, "The ABC of Motivation Research," *Business Topics*, Vol. 7 (Summer 1959).

METHODOLOGY

One of the greatest limitations of behavioral research is the lack of useful techniques for analyzing consumer behavior. Techniques are still far from adequate for determining the nature of the buying process in detail. Moreover, as pointed out earlier, theories differ; and the different theoretical orientations can lead to different and sometimes conflicting interpretations of the same findings. Since the only source of information is the consumer himself, this research effort is trying to understand the most complex phenomenon in the universe—man.

Of necessity then, this section ends on a note of caution. Nevertheless, although the problems of determining purchase motivation are many, awareness of the subjective elements in consumer behavior is of fundamental—perhaps paramount—importance to the businessman. Moreover, although it may not always be possible to conduct elaborate, costly, and time-consuming studies, the competent manager, with his many years of experience in the marketplace, will often be able to deduce the possible effects of these subjective elements and make a shrewd guess at how the consumer will behave. This kind of thinking combined with the findings of quantitative market investigations will result in more effective marketing programs.

Finally, there are situations—for example, when the undertaking is such that rather large losses may be incurred if mistakes are made—in which the high absolute cost of an elaborate study may be relatively small.

SUMMARY

Sound market planning requires answers to several questions: *What will the market purchase? How much will the market purchase? Under what conditions* will the market purchase? Since the answers to these questions are dependent upon consumer behavior in the marketplace, they can only be secured through an understanding of the way in which consumers act. Consumers are faced with four choice problems in the marketplace: (1) deciding how much to spend and how much to save (*the spend-save problem*); (2) deciding which products and services to buy (*the product-mix problem*); (3) deciding on the specific sources from which to purchase (*the brand-choice problem*); and (4) deciding on the conditions of purchase.

Purchase behavior with respect to consumer choice is influenced by three types of forces. *Enabling conditions* set the foundation for purchase behavior. While it is adequate to examine income, assets, and credit as a measure of aggregate market size, little if any insight is provided into individual consumer choice by economic analysis. *Environmental* conditions that influence purchase behavior range from family reference groups to cultural associations. Consumption in modern society is not a private or isolated behavior. Thus, the influence of family, face-to-face reference groups, social class, and cultural associations represents prime determinants of purchase behavior. Finally, purchase behavior is influenced by *individual motivation*. Three approaches to understanding motivation—*need-satisfaction, psychoanalytic,* and *cognitive*—were reviewed in an effort to determine purchase behavior patterns. The study of purchase behavior from the combined viewpoints of enabling conditions, environment, and individual motivation was labeled as interdisciplinary because contributions were selected from a broad range of social sciences.

The process of consumption was viewed as a *learning* experience. For purposes of understanding the foundations of consumer brand and institution loyalty, the basic concepts of *reinforcement, generalization,* and *discrimination* were introduced. The relationship between marketing activities of a seller and the perception of potential consumers was developed and illustrated as a result of examining the learning-to-consume process.

For purposes of operationalizing buyer behavior research as an input to market planning, a schematic structure to guide behavioral market investigation was presented. This research orientation was followed by an illustration of a buyer behavior study and a review of some practical aspects of behavioral research.

QUESTIONS AND PROBLEMS

1. Is it always necessary to know *why* a person buys as he or she does?
2. Explain: "Most models of consumer behavior build upon the basic belief that purchase actions are a form of *learned behavior.*"
3. What is reinforcement? How does it relate to consumer purchase behavior analysis?
4. How do you explain *brand loyalty* in terms of learning theory?
5. Illustrate the capability to *generalize* and *discriminate* in terms of several choices you have made in the marketplace in the last week.
6. Relate the concepts of *product-image* and *desired self-image.*
7. "After enough motivation analysis, it should be relatively easy for the marketer to manipulate consumers to his own ends." Do you think this statement is valid?
8. What factors tend to limit the extent and usefulness of formal purchase-motivation analysis? What alternative approaches are open to the marketer working in this area?

Chapter 8

Intermediate Markets

So far we have dealt with the performances of the market delineation and purchase motivation functions in the markets for consumer goods—goods bought for personal or household consumption. But there must also be the plant, equipment, and materials to produce consumer goods, as well as all of the equipment necessary to make them available for consumption. These goods and services destined for use in producing other goods and services are known as industrial goods.[1] The term *industrial goods* connotes manufacturing and, as we shall see, a large proportion of these kinds of goods are consumed in nonmanufacturing companies. For this reason we prefer to call them intermediate goods or intermediate markets.

Intermediate goods are used either directly in the production and distribution of other goods and services, or indirectly to facilitate production and distribution. The market is called the *intermediate market* and includes businesses in the extractive industries—agriculture, manufacturing, distributive trades and services, transportation, communication and utilities, and governmental agencies such as schools, hospitals, and prisons.

The approaches to market delineation and purchase motivation presented in Chapters 5, 6, and 7 apply to the intermediate market, but there are differences in the characteristics of buyers and sellers, as well as differences in the forces influencing purchasing behavior. These differences have an effect on the way in which intermediate goods are marketed. As we examine the characteristics of the market we shall see the way in which they affect policies regarding price, channels of distribution, and communications.

In this chapter we shall describe the intermediate market by explaining its complexity, the number and type of intermediate buyers and sellers, and the size of the market. Intermediate goods are then classified and the

---

[1] R. S. Alexander, et al., *Marketing Definitions* (Chicago: American Marketing Association, 1960), p. 14.

characteristics of the market examined. Approaches to the performance of the opportunity assessment functions are explored.

THE MARKET FOR INTERMEDIATE GOODS

In this section the nature of the intermediate goods market is examined. First, the complexity of the intermediate market is reviewed. Next, attention is directed to an examination of participants who buy and sell in intermediate markets. The final section deals with the size of intermediate markets.

THE COMPLEXITY OF THE INTERMEDIATE MARKET

The industrial and commercial organization that makes possible the vast array of consumer goods is a highly specialized one. In the production sector are a number of specialized plants that produce parts of the final finished consumer products. In the commercial sector is a similar specialization. We find wholesalers buying from manufacturers and selling to distributors, and we observe purchases and sales between the many different types of facilitating agencies—banks, advertising agencies, hotels, restaurants.

There are many specialized suppliers of materials in such categories as farm materials, minerals, utilities, durable and nondurable manufacturing, and imported materials. Purchases and sales between these specialized units are necessary to produce consumer goods, equipment, and construction (plants, commercial buildings, and residential houses). All of the equipment, much of the farm and imported materials, and much of the construction must find its way back to the material supplier specialists. There is also a large market among the materials suppliers; for example, the steel ingot plants must have instrument parts and the mineral suppliers must have shipping containers.

If we were to include those establishments responsible for the distribution or use of intermediate goods, as well as the facilitating establishments, such as banks, transportation companies, and advertising agencies, we would have a picture of the buyers and sellers in the industrial market.

BUYERS AND SELLERS OF INTERMEDIATE GOODS

In this subsection buyers of intermediate goods are grouped and briefly discussed. The number of establishments in each of these categories is shown in Table 8-1.

As stated earlier, it is normal to think of the market for intermediate

TABLE 8-1
Number of Industrial Goods Buyers by
Kind of Business (In Thousands)

Agriculture, Forestry, and Fisheries	3,179
Mining	79
Construction	875
Manufacturing	309
Distributive Trades and Services	
Retailers	2,210
Wholesalers	470
Service Establishments	2,964
Transportation, Communication, Utilities	380
Financial, Insurance, and Real Estate	1,292
Government	78
TOTAL	11,836

Source: Compiled from U.S. Bureau of the Census, *Statistical Abstract of the United States: 1973* (94th ed.), Washington, D.C., 1973, p. 471.

goods as made up of manufacturers. In terms of number of buyers, however, the manufacturer segment is relatively small. The other sectors of this market constitute a large potential market for a wide array of goods. For example, the fishing industry needs such products as boots, tackle, radios, cold storage facilities, and the lumbering and extractive industries need a wide variety of machinery, as well as materials handling equipment, to move raw materials from their source to processing points. A walk through any retail supermarket, hotel, or restaurant reveals the various kinds of equipment necessary to the conduct of a retailing or service establishment. The various transportation companies, television and radio stations, magazines, and newspapers all require specialized equipment, as do the public utilities engaged in the production and distribution of electric power. The construction industry represents a large market for a wide array of raw materials and the equipment necessary to assemble the end product. The finance, insurance, and real estate companies, as well as the government, represent a large market for such things as office supplies, reproduction equipment, and computers. This is a numerically large group and is frequently overlooked as a part of the intermediate goods market.

Each segment of the intermediate goods market is both a seller of the specialized goods and services it produces and a buyer from other segments of the goods and services necessary to produce the vast array of consumer goods and services to which we have become accustomed.

THE SIZE OF THE INTERMEDIATE MARKET

A mistaken conception often exists that the market for intermediate goods is smaller in dollar size than the consumer goods market. From a marketing point of view the size of the intermediate market is the total dollar value of all transactions that take place between various intermediates. Marketing is involved in the consummation of each of these transactions. There are no reliable estimates of the total dollar value of all transactions in the intermediate market, but a simple example will illustrate why this market is larger than the consumer goods market.

Let us assume a very simple transaction in which 100 units of product A are produced and consumed. The final price to consumers from the manufacturer is $1 per unit, which covers all costs and the profit necessary to bring product A to the market. Consumer expenditures in this case are $100 (100 × $1). In our complex industrial structure, in which specialization plays an important role, let us say that four specialized enterprises are necessary to bring this product to the consumer: the mine, the processor, the fabricator, and the manufacturer of product A. The processor purchases raw materials from the mine at 30 cents a unit. Thus, the mine has a market of $30 (100 × .30). The processor uses equipment and labor, and sells the processed product to the fabricator at 50 cents a unit. His market is valued at $50. The fabricator takes the processed material and, using equipment and labor, fabricates it and sells it to the manufacturer of product A for 60 cents a unit, the market being valued at $60. The total intermediate market, then, is equal to $140 ($30 + $50 + $60), in comparison to a consumer market of $100. The example illustrates how specialization causes the intermediate goods market to engage in numerous transactions that in turn make it larger in aggregate dollars than the consumer market.

A CLASSIFICATION OF INTERMEDIATE GOODS

Industrial goods can be classified into three categories: (1) capital goods, (2) components and materials, and (3) supplies. While it is not always possible to fit every product neatly into one of the above categories, such a classification provides a basis for developing important characteristics of the intermediate goods market.

CAPITAL GOODS

Capital goods include such items as *plant and equipment,* which are used in the production and distribution of other goods but which do not become a part of the goods produced. The plant category includes factories, warehouses, retail stores, and wholesale structures. The equipment category includes all production machinery, materials handling equipment,

TABLE 8-2
Distribution of Capital Outlays—1973

	Billions	Percentage
Manufacturing	37.0	36.7
Durable	18.7	18.6
Nondurable	18.3	18.1
Nonmanufacturing	63.6	63.3
Mining	2.6	2.6
Transportation, communication, utilities	38.8	38.6
Commercial and other	22.2	22.1
TOTAL	100.6	100.0

Source: Compiled from data in *Statistical Abstract of the United States, 1973,* p. 476.

and furniture and fixtures, as well as transportation and communication equipment. These goods are used in manufacturing and distributing but are not a part of the product. Capital goods may be thought of from an accounting standpoint as assets that are capitalized in accounting records and amortized over their economic lives.

Table 8-2 shows the very substantial size of the capital goods market in 1973 and the shares going to different segments of the total market. An important item is the size of the nonmanufacturing and the utilities market. There is a tendency to think of the capital goods market as made up of manufacturers. However, this segment represents only 36.7 percent. Nonmanufacturing constitutes 63.3 percent.

COMPONENTS AND MATERIALS

Components and materials differ from capital goods in that they become part of the total product the consumer purchases. *Components* are partially or wholly manufactured or processed goods. Tires, batteries, and spark plugs are components in the auto industry, as well as car frames, textiles, and engine blocks. *Materials* may be wholly or partially processed and include such goods as iron ore, copper, coal, lumber, and wheat. The distinction between components and materials is not always clear. In the baking industry, flour processed from wheat might be considered a component, but in fact it is considered a raw material.

SUPPLIES

Supplies include goods used to facilitate production and distribution processes. Like capital goods they do not generally become a part of the finished goods, but unlike capital goods they are used up in production, and from an accounting viewpoint are considered as an expense rather than a capital investment. This category includes such goods as industrial cleaning compounds, lubricating oils for equipment, and stationery supplies.

SPECIAL CHARACTERISTICS OF INTERMEDIATE GOODS AND THEIR MARKETS

Although there are many similarities between the marketing of intermediate goods and consumer goods, the differences are sufficiently great to call for modification in marketing strategy formulation. At the root of these differences are special characteristics of the products, the market structure, the market demand, and the purchasing process.

THE PRODUCT

There are three major differences between consumer goods and intermediate goods: (1) homogeneity of product, (2) technical considerations, and (3) high average value of sale.

Homogeneity of Product

A good many industrial products tend to have a high degree of similarity with the products of competing manufacturers. For example, all fractional horsepower electrical motors are built to common National Electrical Manufacturers Association (NEMA) specifications and are, therefore, markedly similar. There are even fewer differences among competing materials. Steel of a given technical grade is steel, and, likewise, all cement is cement, regardless of the source of supply. Skilled purchasing agents interested in performance buy to basic specifications. This is contrary to the situation among many consumer goods; for example, cigarettes, where competing brands that are substantially similar are made to appear very different through skillful packaging and heavy advertising. New product variations in the intermediate market tend to be adopted quickly by competitors. This results because of the characteristically high level of technical research and development expenditures among rival firms, and the fact that often slight changes in a product's design will obviate the danger of patent infringement and allow a competitor to adopt an improvement in his own product.

But ease and speed of copying do not mean that product improvements bring no competitive advantage, only that the advantage will be short-lived and that new improvements must be constantly sought if a competitor wishes to maintain his market position. This overall homogeneity of product tends to place a great deal of importance on delivery performance and customer service.

Technical Considerations

Industrial goods are characteristically more complex than consumer goods. Since they are used in complex industrial processes, the marketing of them differs from that of consumer goods. Capital goods—electronic computers, textile machinery, automatic screw machines, turbines—are obviously complex. However, this complexity can extend to components and materials as well as to some supplies. The sale of electric motors to original equipment manufacturers, such as tool manufacturers, is frequently on a specification basis. In marketing such goods, many more technical features of the product come into the negotiations. The sale of lubricating oils in the supply group is a highly technical job. There are as many as 300 different grades of lubricating oils, and much skill is needed to determine the proper grade for each machine and for the operation it is performing.

This complexity of form and application means that a close relationship between buyer and seller is usually established to assure that the product meets the needs of the buyer. Technical assistance is needed at many points in the buyer-seller relationship. In many products, it is needed before the sale, particularly when the goods are not standardized but are formulated to consumer specifications. This is the case for most capital goods, such as electronic data processing systems, electric generators, stamping equipment, and large presses used in manufacturing. Many components, such as automobile carburetors, batteries, and electric motors, require before-sale service. Postsale service is needed in the form of training operators for new equipment.

Personal representation over a rather long period of negotiation is usually necessary to work out the details of each sale. The skill required of the salesman in many cases calls for engineers or highly trained representatives to perform the selling job. The need for personal selling and the nature of the negotiation process make advertising and sales promotion less important in marketing many industrial goods. Advertising is usually placed in specialized trade journals, or direct mail advertising is used. Its major purpose is as a prospecting device for the personal salesmen and as information dissemination. Sales promotion for the most part is confined to conventions and trade fairs.

To back up the sales that have been made, it is necessary to maintain adequate supplies of repair parts and to have the facility to expedite repairs if necessary. Unless repairs can be made rapidly, the breakdown cost to the buyer may be high. Often the product may be so technical that skilled repairmen must be readily available. For example, elevator manufacturers must provide trained maintenance personnel wherever they make installations. Service on some intermediate goods is so important that its adequacy is often the deciding factor in the buyer's choice from among several competing products.

The technical nature of intermediate goods and the technical uses of them require that the distribution mix and communications mix be adjusted to the needs which these technical considerations dictate.

High Average Value of Sale

Intermediate goods usually have a high unit value. If the unit value is low, such goods are often purchased in large quantities, resulting in a high average sale. It is common for capital goods to cost hundreds of thousands of dollars. The average dollar size of sale is important because it is the base that must absorb all marketing costs. If the average value of a sale is high, the marketer can afford the high costs of skilled representation and the long periods of negotiation necessary to adjust the product to the customer's needs. If the average value of the sale is low, not as much can be spent in marketing to consummate the sale.

THE MARKET STRUCTURE

The word *structure* is used here to refer to the form of the market—the number and geographic location of buyers.

Limited Number of Buyers

The number of intermediate goods buyers in the United States is much smaller than the number of consumers. In 1973 there were 211 million consuming individuals as compared to the 11.9 million intermediate goods buyers shown in Table 8-1. For the individual producer of intermediate goods the number of potential customers is further reduced by buyer specialization. Whereas every consumer buys shoes, only textile manufacturers will buy textile machinery. Probably no producer of intermediate goods will find customers in all segments (agriculture or manufacturing, for example) of the market. If the individual intermediate marketer sells mainly or exclusively to manufacturing enterprises, he finds still another factor restricting the number of customers. Buying power is concentrated in the hands of a few buyers. Approximately 9 percent of the manufacturing firms in the United States account for about 80 percent of value added by manufacturing.

The number of buyers who must be contacted reduces the cost of personal selling. It is much less expensive to cultivate a few potential buyers personally than it would be to contact personally the large number in the consumer goods market. The number of buyers has implications for the marketing strategy selected.

Geographic Concentration of Buyers

Considerable geographic concentration in manufacturing exists within the United States. Two hundred and sixteen manufacturing centers account for almost 80 percent of the manufacturing labor force, and 25 of these absorb 45 percent of the total force.[2] There is also geographic concentration in agriculture and the extractive industries.

Geographic concentration is not characteristic of all intermediate goods buyers. We find distributive trades, service establishments, transportation, communication, and utility enterprises scattered all over the country. Nevertheless, there is more geographic concentration among intermediate goods buyers than among ultimate consumers.

Whenever there is geographic concentration among the buyers of intermediate goods the task of contacting the potential buyer is much easier and much less costly. Couple this characteristic with the limited number of buyers, and the overall task of contacting the market is much simpler than in the case of ultimate consumer buyers. Of course, marketers of less specialized goods or of goods going to specialized but dispersed industries do not benefit from geographic concentration. Industrial cleaning compounds, for example, can be used by a variey of intermediate goods buyers, and the market is almost as dispersed geographically as the market of the retailing industry.

Nevertheless, many marketers are confronted by geographically concentrated markets, and this fact is particularly influential in determining the directness of distribution and the means of solicitation used. When we examine the distribution and communications mixes in Part Four, the influence of these characteristics will be more evident.

MARKET DEMAND

Three characteristics of the demand for intermediate goods are different from the demand for consumer goods. They are: (1) wide fluctuations in demand, (2) relative inelasticity of demand, and (3) infrequent

[2] "Location of Key Manufacturing Market Centers," U.S. Department of Commerce.

purchase. Each of these characteristics should be understood in conjunction with the marketing of intermediate goods.

Wide Fluctuations in Demand

The intermediate goods market is for a number of reasons much more erratic than is the consumer goods market. One reason for this irregularity in demand is that increases or decreases in consumer goods demand, on which the demand for intermediate goods depends, cause much wider fluctuations in the demand for intermediate goods. This is called the *acceleration principle* and can be illustrated by reference to our hypothetical example on page 155. Suppose that the demand for product A is cut 10 percent and only 90 units are demanded instead of 100. Total consumer demand is now valued at $90, or a cut of $10. The processor needs only $27 (90 × 30 cents) of the raw material; the fabricator needs only $45 (90 × 50 cents) of the processed raw material; and the manufacturer of product A needs only $54 (90 × 60 cents) of the fabricated part. We have a $14 decrease in the demand for intermediate goods along with the $10 decrease in the demand for consumer goods.

Although the absolute decrease is greater in the intermediate goods market, the proportionate decrease is the same—10 percent, if no adjustments are made in inventory levels. Typically, however, retailers and distributors reduce their average inventories, which has an accelerating effect back through the distribution channels.[3]

This situation is also intensified when we consider the role of capital goods in our economy, something overlooked in our simple example. Suppose the manufacturer of product A requires 10 machines, each of which will produce 10 units of product A. Also assume that all machines have the same physical life span and that their age differences are such that one wears out each year and is normally replaced.

In the first year the demand for product A is 100 units; the manufacturer has 10 machines and one will wear out each year and will be replaced if necessary. The schedule in Table 8-3 illustrates the demand for machines by the manufacturer of product A and the percentage of change in demand under different consumer demand conditions.

A small change in the demand for consumer goods caused a greater than proportionate change in the demand for capital goods.

The acceleration effect on capital goods can be erratic, as one might expect. In our example we assumed a fixed ratio between the number of machines needed and output, but in reality there is usually some "slack." The manufacturer of product A might be able to absorb an increase in

---

[3] The inventory "shiplash" or acceleration effect is explained in Chapter 15.

TABLE 8-3
Example of Variations in Capital Replacement

Year	Consumer Demand Product A (Units)	Percentage Of Change	Machines Needed (Units)	Industrial Demand for New Machines (Units)	Percentage Of Change
1	100	0	10	1	0
2	100	0	10	1	0
3	110	+10	11	2	+100
4	130	+18.1	13	3	+ 50
5	130	0	13	1	− 66.6
6	100	−23	10	0	−100

consumer demand in the seventh year by putting on an extra shift and increasing capacity. The acceleration effect would thus be eliminated. We also assumed the same physical life span for each machine and a machine age distribution that resulted in one machine wearing out each year. Neither assumption is entirely accurate. The rapid rate of technological development has forced many buyers to think of the economic rather than the physical life span of their equipment. Thus, technological advances tend to reduce replacement schedules and create nonuniformity in machine age.

The fact that the demand for intermediate goods fluctuates so widely has three implications for marketing. First, the buyer of intermediate goods exercises extreme care before funds are committed for plant and equipment. The seller of intermediate goods has the problem of adjusting supply to demand. Second, since the seller is faced with a fluctuating market, measurement of the market from year to year is even more important than in the consumer goods field. Because of the fluctuations, it is almost impossible to employ the historical approach so often used in the consumer goods field for predicting markets. All indications are that the most important influencing force is the buyer's expectation of future business conditions. The buildup approach is more frequently used. Third, the wide fluctuations in demand have some influence on the elasticity of price demand. This characteristic of the market demand for intermediate goods will now be examined in detail.

Inelasticity of Demand

The problems of adjusting supply to demand are aggravated by the fact that demand will not significantly expand with lower prices. In the consumer goods market, when demand falls off and inventories consequently pile up, price reduction is an effective competitive weapon. But in the intermediate market a price reduction does not usually generate a proportionate increase in sales. This inelasticity of price demand is a result of the dependence of the demand for intermediate goods on the demand for consumer goods. The buyer of intermediate goods will hesitate in spite of price reductions if there is an anticipated drop in consumer demand.

It is sometimes argued that a reduced price on intermediate goods would allow a reduced price on consumer goods, which generally will respond to price reductions. But since many components from different sources are used to produce a single consumer product, a slight change in the price of any one of them contributes so little to the total cost of the consumer product that the buyer of intermediate goods is not influenced by the price change.

Another factor that contributes to the relative inelasticity of demand for intermediate goods is the ability of the buyer to postpone purchases. This is clearly so in the case of capital goods. When future business expectations are not favorable, the buyer can generally postpone the purchase of a new plant and equipment and get along with the old. In the upswing, price increases within limits do not reduce demand. The potential buyer is interested in making ready for the expected increase in his own market demand.

The demand faced by a single marketer of intermediate goods in competing for a share of a given market is more elastic than that of its total industry. For example, total demand for a given product may be cut back, but individual marketers competing for the demand that remains face buyers who are responsive to price reductions. However, two factors—the homogeneity of product in intermediate goods and the paucity of competitors—make it difficult to use price as a competitive weapon. If a significant marketer of an intermediate good were to lower his price, so would his major competitors, and all would maintain market share—but at lower total revenues.

The homogeneity of product makes it difficult for competitors not to follow the price reduction. The limited number of marketers makes it possible for all to retailate quickly. The general result is uniformity among prices.

This tendency toward uniformity of prices is more true of capital goods and components than it is of materials. The materials market as a rule has many suppliers; consequently there is a tendency for more price competition. However, the fact that many materials are sold on a contractual basis impedes price fluctuations, except at the time of contract renewal.

Infrequent Purchase

In comparison with consumer goods, the purchase of intermediate goods is often infrequent. This is particularly true of capital goods, because they last longer and because replacement can be postponed. If the financial condition of the user is not sound, he usually can make his old equipment do until he is able to purchase new equipment.

However, as noted earlier, there is a trend among many forward-looking purchasers of plant and equipment to think of the economic rather than the physical life span of capital goods. Thus, they may have equipment with a physical life span of ten years, but if technology after four years has produced more efficient cost-saving equipment, they will replace immediately. The economic life span of the old equipment is four years. This has given special impetus to manufacturers of capital goods to seek technological improvements that shorten the economic life span and step up the replacement cycle. Continuous appraisal of the product mix is an important aspect of this development.

Components, materials, and supplies are more frequently purchased than capital goods. However, in many cases once an acceptable supplier is found, purchases are on a contract basis and contact between buyer and seller is not as frequent as if original sales had to be closed each time a delivery was made.

THE PURCHASING PROCESS

The process of purchasing in the intermediate market is significantly different than in consumer markets. Four significant characteristics of intermediate purchasing are discussed below.

Purchase on a Performance Basis

Intermediate goods are bought to produce other goods or services that must be sold at a profit. For this reason, performance of intermediate goods in the buyer's operation is the important consideration. Psychological factors play a minor role. Buyers of intermediate goods must know what will best satisfy their performance requirements and be able to determine which products meet their requirements most fully. Frequently the purchasing enterprise must prepare specifications for producers of intermediate goods. To be sure that expert knowledge is available, most companies have established an *organized purchasing unit,* composed of trained specialists who are aware of price trends, sources of supply, and new products, and who know their company's needs exactly. These buying specialists often use elaborate tests to compare the merits of competing products. The buyers of intermediate goods may often have more technical knowledge than the salesmen selling them. Under such conditions a great deal of emphasis is placed upon product and physical distribution performance.

Emotional Appeals

Although the emphasis in purchase of intermediate goods is on performance, emotional appeals should not be ruled out completely. Color and design of equipment are important. Such product attributes seem to have greater appeal when related to performance—for instance, to their effect on worker morale, fatigue, and productivity. But appeals to plant appearance or to the desire to be technologically progressive are also effective.

It is also possible to appeal to personalities of influential persons in the buying organization. Individuals are concerned about their positions in the company and are desirous of initiating or influencing the purchase of industrial goods that will demonstrate their value to the firm. If new equipment, components, or materials result in cost savings, the individual initiating the change has an objective measure—savings in cost—to demonstrate personal value.

Diffusion of Purchase Influence

Influences on buying are much more diffused than the specialized purchasing department might lead one to imagine. The department may have final responsibility for choosing the supplier, but unusual situations often arise, requiring the special knowledge of other departments. Research into the actual purchase process is relatively new. Enough, however, has been done to demonstrate that there is a wide variation depending upon the industry, type of product purchased, and the reason for purchase. In 1970, *Scientific American* conducted a study among 3,400 intermediate goods buyers in eleven industries to determine what management functions participate in a purchase decision.[4] The study was further broken down to determine who participates in the purchase of three different product types —capital goods, components, and supplies—in three different stages of the purchasing process—initiating project motive, determining kind, and deciding on the supplier.

Figures 8-1 through 8-3 show the importance of different management functions for one product type—component goods. These figures illustrate that the organized purchasing function is not very important except in the last stage—deciding on supplier. Although space does not permit including the charts for the different decisions in each stage of the purchasing process, the differences in functional participation are substantial. For example, in the stage of initiating project motive, five different motives are treated: new price differential, innovation in component design, change in design of product, change in production process, and new product. In

[4] "How Industry Buys," *Scientific American*, 1970.

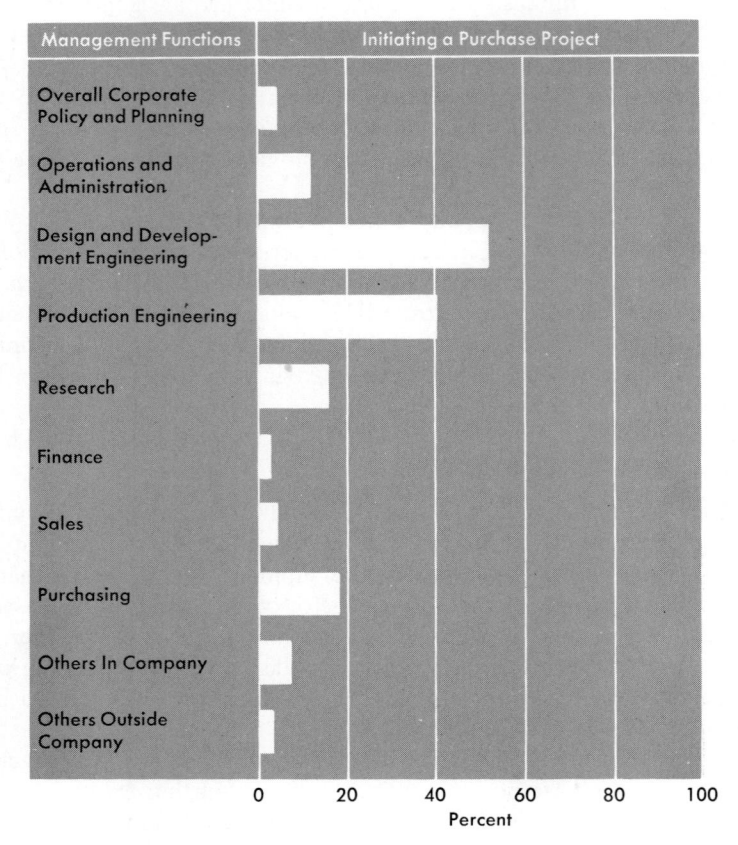

FIGURE 8-1
The Purchasing Process: Component Parts

Management Functions	Initiating a Purchase Project (Percent)
Overall Corporate Policy and Planning	~3
Operations and Administration	~8
Design and Development Engineering	~55
Production Engineering	~42
Research	~18
Finance	~3
Sales	~8
Purchasing	~20
Others In Company	~8
Others Outside Company	~5

Source: From "How Industry Buys/1970," by Research Department of SCIENTIFIC AMERICAN. Copyright © by Scientific American, Inc. All rights reserved.

each case, the participation of different managerial functions changes. Likewise, there is considerable difference in participation from industry to industry and among the three product types.

The type of research reported above provides a long needed look at the nature of purchasing behavior. The study demonstrates the variability in buying practice and points the direction for additional research in this market.

The diffusion of purchase influence characteristics presents some unusual problems for the marketer. The salesman must know the decision-making process of the buying company and establish close relationships

Intermediate Markets

FIGURE 8-2
The Purchasing Process: Component Parts

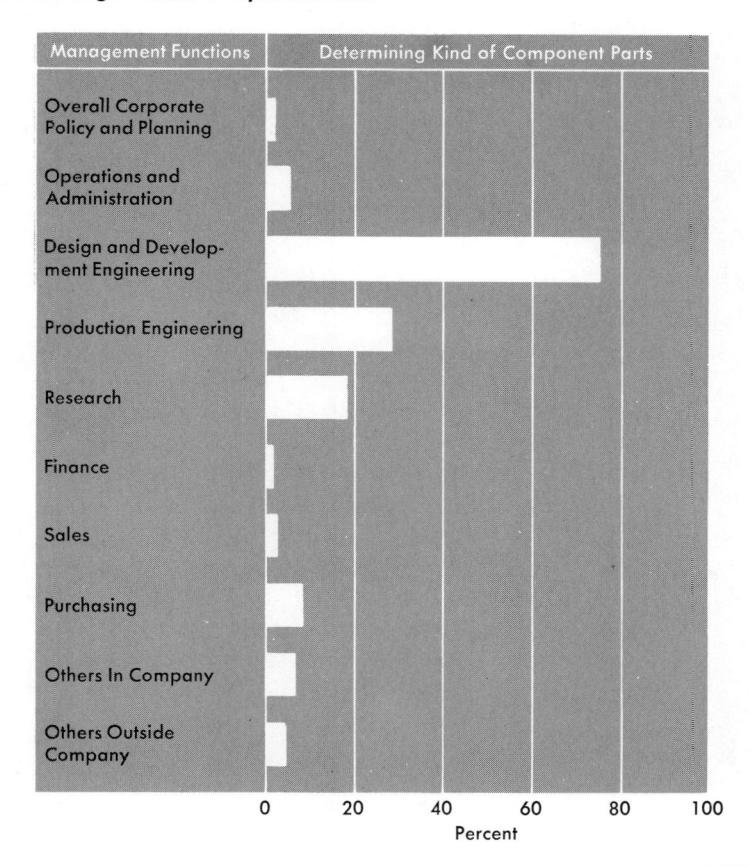

Management Functions	Determining Kind of Component Parts (Percent)
Overall Corporate Policy and Planning	~2
Operations and Administration	~5
Design and Development Engineering	~75
Production Engineering	~28
Research	~20
Finance	~2
Sales	~5
Purchasing	~8
Others In Company	~10
Others Outside Company	~5

Source: From "How Industry Buys/1970," by Research Department of SCIENTIFIC AMERICAN. Copyright © by Scientific American, Inc. All rights reserved.

with important personnel. Even if the salesman is successful in identifying influential personnel, they are not always accessible to him, especially if they are high-ranking officers. The number of people who must be convinced makes the sales task more difficult.

Reciprocity

Although currently most intermediate buyers are predominantly influenced by performance, a few are strongly influenced by reciprocal arrangements—"you buy from me and I'll buy from you." These reciprocal arrangements can include more than two buyer-sellers. For example, Buyer

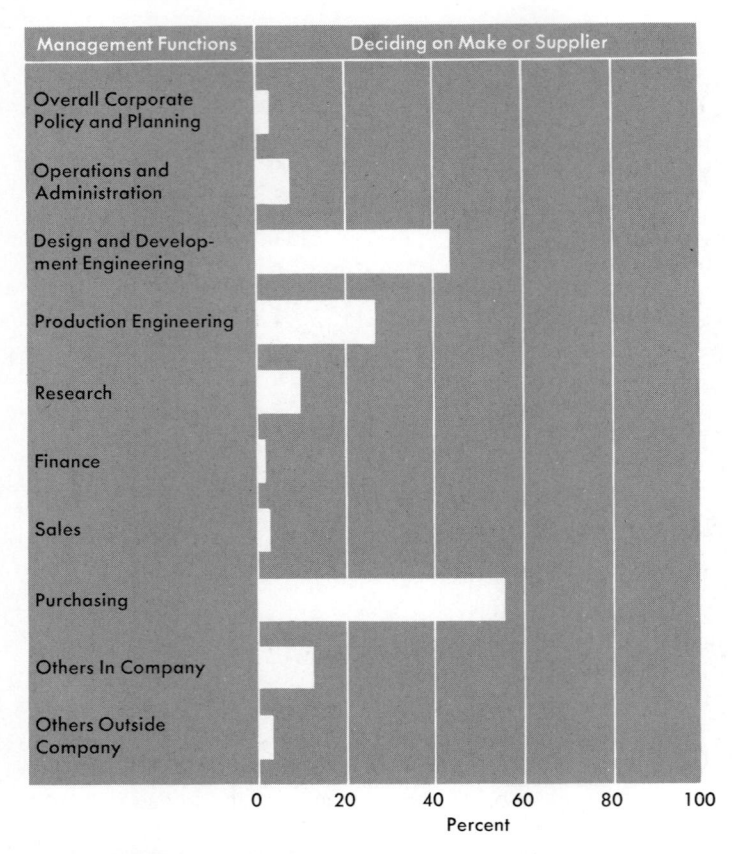

FIGURE 8-3
The Purchasing Process: Component Parts

Management Functions	Deciding on Make or Supplier (Percent)
Overall Corporate Policy and Planning	~2
Operations and Administration	~8
Design and Development Engineering	~42
Production Engineering	~25
Research	~10
Finance	~2
Sales	~7
Purchasing	~55
Others In Company	~13
Others Outside Company	~4

Source: From "How Industry Buys/1970," by Research Department of SCIENTIFIC AMERICAN. Copyright © by Scientific American, Inc. All rights reserved.

A may refuse to buy from B unless B buys from C, who is the customer of A. Such an arrangement prevents buying according to performance and substitutes an altogether different basis for the choice of supplier. Reciprocity does not allow the purchasing department always to purchase the best value, and it restricts the market available to competitive marketers. In some cases there is no effective means of breaking these relationships. The marketer's only recourse is to maintain a relationship with the buyer until such time as the reciprocal relationship with a competitor shows signs of weakening. Although reciprocal relationships are not widespread, some marketers of intermediate goods must contend with them.

These then are the special characteristics of intermediate goods and their markets. The analysis of any intermediate good in terms of the product, the market structure, the demand for intermediate goods, and the purchasing process will provide useful information when developing the marketing mix.

OPPORTUNITY ASSESSMENT IN INTERMEDIATE MARKETS

As mentioned previously, the wide fluctuations in demand for intermediate goods make it difficult to adjust supply to demand. Market delineation is very important, because the best way to prevent inventory buildups in the downswing is the continuous and accurate forecasting of market opportunity. The wide variations in buyer purchase behavior make the performance of the purchase motivation function equally important as in the consumer goods market.

MARKET DELINEATION

A good way to measure market opportunity quantitatively is to analyze each buyer's demand. In the intermediate market the number of consuming units is usually much smaller than in the consumer market, and this procedure is often practicable. For example, in the sale of agrichemicals each distributor sells in an area encompassing a radius of 15 miles from his location. This includes, depending on the size of farms, about 300 potential customers. In such a case, it is relatively easy to maintain a continuous census of opportunity. Since salesmen travel through the area two to three times a month, are adept at judging acreage, and have use ratios for different crops, it is relatively easy, using a form such as in Figure 8-4, to acquire a precise delineation of the market. From such cards a salesman can select those buyers or target markets he wishes to concentrate on in any season.[5]

This same method can be used when the marketing area is much larger, if the sales force is carefully trained to ferret out the kind of information needed on every potential buyer. However, when the number of potential buyers is too great for this buildup procedure, the demand estimate may be made by much the same means as used in the consumer goods market. That is, past buyers are classified according to objective character-

---

[5] Adapted from Donald A. Taylor, "Development of Marketing and Promotional Programs," 1972. Courtesy of Agricultural Chemical Division, Ciba-Geigy Corporation.

FIGURE 8-4
Farmer Buyer Profile

Name: _____ Year: _____

Address: _____ Credit Rating: _____

Total Acreage by Crop

Crop	Acreage	Use Rate
_____	_____	_____
_____	_____	_____
_____	_____	_____
_____	_____	_____
_____	_____	_____
_____	_____	_____

Total Product Needs

	Fertilizer			Pesticides			Seeds			Feeds		
	This Year	Last Year	Gr. Opp.	This Year	Last Year	Gr. Opp.	This Year	Last Year	Gr. Opp.	This Year	Last Year	Gr. Opp.
	___	___	___	___	___	___	___	___	___	___	___	___
	___	___	___	___	___	___	___	___	___	___	___	___
	___	___	___	___	___	___	___	___	___	___	___	___
	___	___	___	___	___	___	___	___	___	___	___	___
	___	___	___	___	___	___	___	___	___	___	___	___

Special Needs: _____

Psychological Type: _____

Estimate Made By: _____

Courtesy: Agricultural Division of Ciba-Geigy Corporation, U.S.A.

istics, such as number of employees, kilowatt hours used, and in the case of retailers and wholesalers, square feet of selling space. These characteristics are related to past sales. For example, on the average, buyers with between 500 and 700 employees purchased 300 units of product A last year. Next, all potential purchasers with 500 to 700 employees are identified. The relationship between past sales and the number of employees characteristic for actual purchasers in the past is applied to all potential buyers, and a total market demand figure is established. From this figure, the marketer must determine that portion which he wishes to set as a marketing objective.

PURCHASE MOTIVATION

Purchase motivation studies in the intermediate market are relatively new. The dollar size of the market and the complexity of selling have recently stimulated a great deal of interest in intermediate purchase behavior. In contrast to the development of consumer purchase models discussed in Chapter 7, organizational buying models are just beginning to emerge.[6]

One such model is shown in Figure 8-5.[7] It suggests that a study of intermediate buyer behavior should pursue four different areas—organizational technology, organizational structure, organizational goals and tasks, and organizational actors. Organizational technology refers to the management and information systems that are involved in the buying process. What kind of analyses are used before a "make or buy" decision is made? What computer simulations are used to determine the best transportation mode for shipments of finished goods to the market? To what extent does present manufacturing technology in a buying organization affect the demand for specific raw materials or component parts? Often marketers attempt to sell products to buyers in whose organization current technology determines the desire and willingness to buy.

Organizational structure is composed of the subsystems of communication, authority, status, rewards, and work flow. It is absolutely essential to understand how the different actors are informed of product availability, who has decision capacity, and to what extent does he rely on inputs from other participants in the buying organization, as well as the reward systems, for those who contribute to buying decisions.

Organizational goals and tasks refer to the actual tasks in a buying situation. These include identification of need, establishment of specifications, identification of alternatives, evaluation of alternatives, and selection

---

[6] F. E. Webster and Yoram Wind, "A General Model for Understanding Organizational Buyer Behavior," *Journal of Marketing* (April 1972), pp. 12–19.

[7] Ibid., p. 13.

FIGURE 8-5
A Model of Organizational Buying Behavior

THE ORGANIZATION (ORGANIZATIONAL DETERMINANTS OF BUYING BEHAVIOR)
The Organizational Climate: Physical, Technological, Economic, Cultural

ORGANIZATIONAL TECHNOLOGY	ORGANIZATIONAL STRUCTURE	ORGANIZATIONAL GOALS & TASKS	ORGANIZATIONAL ACTORS
Technology Relevant for Purchasing	Organization of the Buying Center and the Purchasing Function	Buying Tasks	Members of the Buying Center

THE BUYING CENTER

| Technological Constraints and Technology Available to the Group | Group Structure | Group Tasks | Member Characteristics and Goals, Leadership |

| TASK | Activities Interactions Sentiments | NON-TASK | Activities Interactions Sentiments |

GROUP PROCESSES

THE INDIVIDUAL PARTICIPANTS   Motivation
Cognitive Structure, Personality, Learning Process, Perceived Roles

BUYING DECISION PROCESS: 1. Individual Decision-Making Unit   2. Group Decision-Making Unit

BUYING DECISIONS

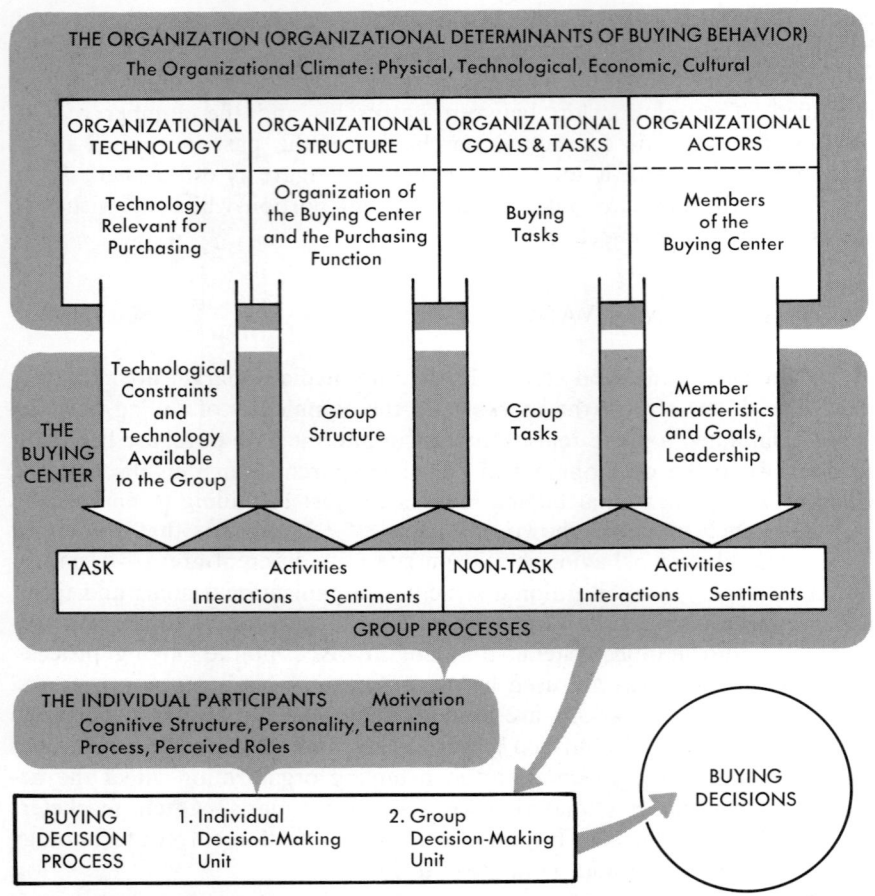

Source: Reprinted from Webster, F. E. and Yoram Wind, "A General Model for Understanding Organizational Buying Behavior," *Journal of Marketing,* April 1972, pp. 12–19, published by the American Marketing Association.

of suppliers. They are similar to those tasks specified in Figures 8-1 through 8-3.

The organizational actors are the users, influencers, deciders, buyers, and gatekeepers. In this sense, the marketer must begin to attach names to those in the organizational structure if he is to influence the buying process.

This model is based on the premise "that organizational buying is a decision-making process carried out by individuals, in interaction with other people, in the context of a formal organization."[8] Although it is conceptual, it demonstrates that to understand and influence the buying process, a complex situation must be identified and understood.

SUMMARY

The intermediate goods market deals in goods and services used, directly or indirectly, to produce other goods and services. Manufacturers, agriculture, the extractive industries, the distributive trades, service industries, and government and quasi-government institutions are all important segments of this market.

Intermediate goods may be divided into *capital goods, components,* and *materials and supplies.* Capital goods are those essential to efficient production and distribution, but are not part of the final product. Components and materials are parts of the final product. Supplies do not enter the final product, but facilitate the efficient operation of production and distribution and are used up in the process.

Many similarities exist between intermediate and consumer markets, but there are differences in products, market structure, market demand, and the purchasing process that require different marketing methods. The most important product characteristics are: (1) homogeneity, (2) technical considerations, and (3) high average value of sale. Market structure is characterized by a limited number of, and geographic concentration of, buyers. Market demand suffers from wide fluctuations, inelasticity, and infrequent purchases. Purchase on a performance basis, diffusion of purchase influence, and reciprocity are important characteristics of the purchasing process.

Analyses of product, market structure, market demand, and the purchasing process are necessary to determine the requirements for effective competition. Market delineation is perhaps more important in intermediate markets than in consumer markets. Because of the ability to postpone purchase for many intermediate goods, the historical method is not favored. As a result of the specialization of sellers, their small number and geographic concentration, the buildup method of market delineation is more widely used. Purchase behavior motivation studies of intermediate buyers are of recent vintage and concentrate on understanding the buying process—the technology, structure, tasks, and actors in the organized buying unit.

[8] Ibid.

QUESTIONS AND PROBLEMS

1. Define intermediate goods.
2. Compare the size of the intermediate market and the consumer market.
3. What are capital goods? What is included in this broad classification?
4. What is included in components and materials? From a marketing point of view, does it make a difference if some components or fabricated parts are identifiable in the end consumer product of which they are a part, while others are not? (Briggs & Stratton engines for power lawn mowers versus Tecumseh compressors for window air conditioners.) Elaborate and explain.
5. How are intermediate markets different from consumer markets?
6. What are the marketing implications of wide fluctuations in demand? Be comprehensive in your answer.
7. What marketing implications, in terms of strategy for meeting downturns in business conditions, follow from a combination of relatively inelastic demand, relatively homogeneous products, and industrial purchasing against known future requirements?
8. "The basic philosophy of marketing and the approach to strategy formulation are the same for both industrial and consumer goods; yet the specific nature of marketing activity is quite different." Agree or disagree. Defend your position.

Chapter 9

International Markets

Market opportunity has a way of transcending national boundaries. Marketers today must be less provincial in their thinking and outlook than were their historical counterparts. There has been increasing initiative on the part of business firms in pursuing overseas opportunities. For this reason we wish to treat some of the dimensions of international markets and the ways in which they depart from usual practices in the performance of the market delineation and purchase motivation functions.

The careful market analyst intently pursues the same mission in evaluating both domestic and international market opportunities. That is, he seeks to evaluate all factors in the environment that are germane to the conduct of operations in particular markets. The specific factors to be considered and the level of uncertainty will vary from case to case. The objectives, conceptual structure, principles of research design, and use of scientific method are in large measure universal. It is on these grounds that some writers omit any special treatment of markets in international environments. There are, however, a number of differences that marketers generally experience in doing business outside the United States. In this chapter, we begin with the meaning of foreign operations. Next, emphasis is placed on the differences in international operations, and we conclude with the need for highly specific market feasibility studies in assessing overseas opportunities.

VARIOUS FORMS OF PARTICIPATING IN FOREIGN MARKETS

Foreign, as the term is generally used, means "related to or dealing with another nation." The means by which business may be conducted and markets cultivated when "dealing with another nation" are many and varied. The spectrum of organizational and operational involvement in international marketing runs all the way from the relatively simple licensing of patent rights for use in another country to (at the other extreme) a few truly international companies that do not hold a prime loyalty to any one country and are not concerned particularly with the expatriation of profits in a given currency.

Let us now examine briefly some of the principal means for engaging in international marketing.

EXPORTING

Exporting is perhaps the easiest and most common form of participation by American companies in foreign markets. It is also the least risky, for investments in the other country are not necessarily entailed, in export operations, nor must the company's own personnel be employed extensively. Instead of the company's sending its own personnel to conduct the sale and distribution of products in the importing country, commission agents can be engaged. Virtually all activities can be carried on from the domestic location and are largely concerned with securing proper licensing, insurance, and transportation, and preparing the necessary trade documents. Because of the relatively limited risk and expenditure of funds involved, market feasibility studies for evaluating the availability of export profit opportunities can be minimal—in contrast to those that involve substantial investment commitments and physical facilities in potentially alien environments. Moreover, the increasing attractiveness of American products in many markets and the desire of established market representation agencies to handle these products make such export possibilities good for a wide range of both large and small U.S. companies. If sales in the foreign countries are made through wholesalers, the transactions normally take place in U.S. dollars, avoiding the more complicated aspects of fluctuations in exchange rates and currency conversion. On the other hand, the exporter loses a large measure of control over servicing and other factors connected with the sale of his product, as well as the product's market identity.

FRANCHISING ARRANGEMENTS

Franchising arrangements have many similarities to licensing arrangements, but the terms are not synonymous. Franchising is particularly relevant in the service industries, whereas licensing is more prominent in product-oriented enterprises. Holiday Inn's motel expansion in other countries is illustrative of franchising. It enables the company to control carefully the nature of operations and the specific elements in the market offers made to potential customers in the host country, while not requiring heavy investments. Revenue is increased from royalty payments made by host country franchise owners. Licensing agreements, on the other hand, characteristically provide great freedom for the licensee in how he will use the patent right he has secured. That is, the grantor makes no significant effort to control the nature of market cultivation strategies to be employed, leaving such matters to the discretion of the licensee.

TRANSNATIONAL MONOLITHIC COMPANIES

The transnational company is one which conducts operations across national boundaries and employs its own personnel in a number of countries and markets. It usually has sales offices in the countries in which it does business, but it may or may not have plants and warehouses. A variation to this pattern is companies having their own sales offices in major countries and using agents in minor markets. The approach is monolithic in that the same products and/or services are marketed in each country and generally the same approach to the market is followed; there is also a high degree of control from the home headquarters. This pattern was rather common as American businesses expanded overseas and exported their marketing methods and philosophies into other countries, while retaining control with their own personnel and operating their own facilities whenever the product was produced outside the United States. This pattern is still probably the most common one, but it is becoming less practical under rising pressures of nationalism and the need to adapt overseas operating entities more closely to host country environments.

JOINT VENTURES

The increase in joint ventures has been a response to the growing difficulty and risk in operating wholly owned subsidiaries in some countries. The joint venture constitutes a separate company owned by two or more companies, one of which represents host country investors. The joint venture permits the pooling of know-how existing between the two companies; tends to minimize adverse market acceptance that could derive from any anti-American feelings in the country; reduces the potential threat of expropriation of assets by hostile governments; promotes the prospect of adaptation of the enterprise to the cultural environment; and increases the likelihood that the enterprise will be geared, at least in part, to the national needs of the host country. The joint venture frequently reflects specialized contribution by the participating ownership groups. The host country enterprise would normally accept prime responsibility for establishing manufacturing processes and for production. The labor force thereby is largely made up of host country nationals. Characteristically, such complex matters as labor customs utilization, restrictions, legislation, and negotiation are better handled by nationals. Frequently, the American enterprise contributes the marketing competence and modern management processes. The companies joining in the venture frequently share in financial administration and in the conduct of the research and development function. The future will probably see a considerable expansion in this type of overseas involvement (closely akin to multinational companies) on the part of U.S. enterprises, as well as the development of the truly international company.

MULTINATIONAL COMPANIES

The multinational firm carries on its foreign operations in several countries through separate subsidiary companies, each managed on a relatively autonomous basis. The subsidiary companies may be wholly or partially owned or both. In that respect they may, but do not necessarily, constitute a number of joint ventures. The parent company acts more as a holding company with foreign as well as domestic investments. Each unit in a foreign country has a separate board of directors and its own president or managing director. While each unit functions under a high degree of decentralization and autonomy, some planning and control is normally exercised by the parent company.

In the multinational enterprise each unit establishes its own product line, determines its own channels of distribution, carries on separate advertising campaigns, follows its own pricing policy, and mobilizes its resources to meet its own objectives in the context of the competitive forces and total environment peculiar to that country. The parent company, however, seeks the eventual "expatriation" of profits to its own country and is basically oriented to its own currency and loyal to its own stockholders, who for the most part are citizens of the country of corporate origin. In these respects, it differs from the truly international company. Ford and General Motors are examples of multinational companies.

INTERNATIONAL COMPANIES

The truly international company is virtually a world enterprise without tying loyalty to the interests of any one country. It does not function in terms of national sovereignty, and its own board of directors and stockholders are truly international in character. Its liquid assets are held in many currencies and in the negotiable instruments of numerous countries. Its long-term objective is not to expatriate profits into the country of headquarters location. From time to time it suffers disruption in its operation from the expropriation of some of its properties, but it seeks to remain aloof from political entanglements that reflect a highly partisan or nationalistic view. In contrast to the multinational company, in which stability in local management is maintained through using nationals as chief executives, the managing directors of the international company are shifted from country to country. Its top board of directors is made up of individuals who have had experience as directors in several units functioning in different parts of the world. The international company maintains a degree of planning and control at headquarters similar to that of the multinational company, but it seeks an almost total rationalization of its worldwide operations, whereas in the multinational company, the several units operate more as individual total systems in their own country than as subsystems in a broader functioning complex. If the scale of operations of a multinational company should grow, its success would logically tend to lead it toward becoming an international company. Some examples of truly international companies are Lever Brothers, Royal Dutch Shell, and Phillips Electrical Company.

The concept of international marketing is thus seen to embrace a wide variety of "foreign involvements." Feasibility studies for assessing non-domestic market opportunities need to vary considerably in scope, detail, and precision, depending on the type of foreign involvement contemplated, because risks and investment requirements vary considerably. Of course, the value of information is greater and the forecasting precision more critical in the riskier venture entailing larger scale investment.

CHARACTERISTICS OF MARKETS OUTSIDE THE UNITED STATES

American marketers engaged in foreign operations can expect to run into a number of marked differences in markets that will influence their efforts to achieve satisfactory commercial results. The differences could be almost endless, ranging from prevailing business philosophies to the minutiae of variations in life styles. While not exhaustive, the factors listed here cover a number of different areas, and they vary in degree among the emerging and developing nations. The extremes of these factors will be found in the underdeveloped nations, but all appear in some measure in contrast to standards prevailing in the United States.

LITERACY RATE AND EDUCATION

The United States has the most educated population in the world and one of the highest literacy rates. While other advanced western cultures exceed the U.S. literacy rate, worldwide literacy ranges from a high of about 98 percent in some highly developed nations to a low of 5 or 6 percent in some of the underdeveloped countries. In some areas, literacy is defined as the ability to write one's name. It is hard for the American marketer to comprehend the difficulty of doing business where only 10 percent of the people can read and write. His marketing communications often must put great reliance on pictures, diagrams, and simplicity of language in space advertising, billboards, packages, labeling, and other communication forms. The lower level of education also has distinct implications for the adoption of innovations and potential changes in purchasing patterns.

We must also not overlook the substantial differentials, beyond the level of simple literacy, in cultures other than our own. Better educated people tend to have more appreciation for sanitation, personal hygiene, and personal use products. However, this is not always independent of the influences of custom and habit.

POPULATION AND LIFE SPAN

The United States, with only a little over 6 percent of the world's population, enjoys approximately 30 percent of the world's income.[1] These proportions can be expressed in reverse: While the United States has five times the income in proportion to its population, other countries have one-fifth of the income in proportion to the sizes of their populations. Population density is not to be overlooked either. The United States has 57 people per square mile; Great Britain has 593; Japan, 736; Belgium, 824; the Netherlands, 840; and Poland, 273. The Soviet Union has only 29 people per square mile; Australia and Canada both have 5.[2]

Expected life span also varies substantially from nation to nation. In the United States, it is roughly 70 years. In some of the Middle East countries, it is as low as 34 years. Shorter life spans can affect stages in the life cycle and exert corollary influences on expenditure patterns. These population factors materially alter market demand over time, as well as the suitability of products for particular markets. For instance, they help to ex-

[1] *Statistical Abstract of the United States,* 1974.
[2] Ibid.

TABLE 9-1
GNP Per Capita for Different Regions of the World—1970 (Billions of Dollars)

World	$ 881
Developed countries	2,701
Developing countries	208
North America	4,670
Europe	1,948
Latin America	510
Far East	290
South Asia	103
Near East	366
Africa	202

Source: U.S. Bureau of the Census, *Statistical Abstract of the United States: 1973* (94th ed.), Washington, D.C., 1973, p. 813.

plain why the automobile market in most of the world has been oriented to small cars rather than to the larger cars for so long characteristic of the United States.

INCOME

Markets reflect the amount of money people have. The United States mass market reflects the generally high incomes earned by American workers. Table 9-1 shows the GNP per capita for different regions of the world.

PROMOTIONAL MEDIA

The range of promotional media available in markets outside the United States is typically much smaller than it is here. The number of publications reaching all segments of the population, the existence and number of radio and television stations, and the availability of facilitating organizations for such things as direct-mail advertising result in the marketer's having many fewer alternative choices open as market cultivation media. For instance, most foreign government-owned telephone companies do not accept advertising, so there are no yellow pages. And even where a particular promotional medium, such as television advertising, may be available, it is likely to have a different structural form from that prevailing in the United States.

To illustrate: Switzerland, which allowed its first television commercial in 1965, was forced to ration time among 170 requesting firms.

France limits television ads to ten minutes a night. Japanese television time is now so valuable that sponsors are limited to 15 seconds each or to "crawl-along slogans" that slither along the bottom of the tube while a program is in progress. Belgium, Holland, and the three Scandinavian countries allow no television commercials at all. In Switzerland, television ads are never shown on Sunday, and in Italy all the ads are run together in one eleven-minute advertising segment.

MARKET INFORMATION AND DATA

Typically, outside the United States there is a distinct paucity of market data to guide the actions of firms in their cultivation of markets and in their evaluation of competitive performances. We are accustomed to the availability of a considerable quantity of market information from a variety of published sources and governmental agencies. In many countries, there are no publications comparable to American census volumes or to the *Statistical Abstract of the United States.* Government agencies frequently do not have the requisite resources or skilled personnel for preparing these types of publications, nor do they recognize any special need for providing business firms with such useful information. When data are published, their reliability is hard to judge, and in some cases, they may be quite misleading. The general scarceness of information makes the performance of the market delineation function and other elements of scientific marketing immeasurably more difficult.

CREDIT AVAILABILITY

In a number of countries market expansion suffers from a lack of readily available credit. Consumer credit and installment buying were not very common in the past. This significantly affected the potential market otherwise available for consumer durables. Trade credit in the business sector has also been quite limited, with custom favoring cash transactions. In a number of countries today (particularly in the more developed nations), there is a trend toward more widespread use of consumer credit, but as yet the lack of availability is still a major limiting factor constraining marketers in the durable goods area.

OWNERSHIP OF CONSUMPTION EQUIPMENT

In addition to the lack of credit, the lack of widespread ownership of equipment essential to other forms of consumption puts a constraint on market expansion in a number of product categories and market areas. For instance, in a recent year 948 radios were owned for each 1,000 persons in the United States, against 123 per 1,000 in Italy. The ratios for washing machines, refrigerators, and ranges are equally or more dramatic. The scarcity of refrigerated storage space makes the sale of economy-size packages of perishable foodstuffs difficult; necessitates frequent trips to the market to replenish stocks; increases small orders and congestion in retail stores; and increases the overall cost of distribution.

BUYING HABITS

All of the above factors, plus custom and tradition, help to produce striking differences in buying habits in overseas markets. Buying habits should not be seen as a snapshot but more as a motion picture. Purchase behavior habits are rapidly changing worldwide. Research has shown the kinds of differences in buying habits that have affected the character of marketing institutions, marketing practices, and the nature of competition.[3] Some of these differences may be seen from the following illustrations:

1. The European housewife and her counterparts in other nations of the world regard daily shopping expeditions as customary social events and opportunities to intermingle and communicate with friends and shopkeepers. The market as an institution is thereby distinctly different from that common to this country, with its orientation to efficiency and customer problem solving.

2. Lack of income and ownership of consumption equipment such as refrigerators force consumers to buy in very small quantities. High unit prices reflecting high unit costs further support the daily shopping custom.

3. Consumers are slow to accept innovation in services while being more receptive to changes in products.[4] Bargaining over price between buyer and seller, for instance, has long been a market tradition and is still common. However, it is disappearing in Western Europe and declining elsewhere. Also, after a history of parsimonious shopping behavior, of cash-only purchases, or barter, consumers are now buying on credit. Innovations in marketing services have been needed more than product innovations to accelerate market growth. But because customers have been slower to accept the former than the latter, most supplying firms have been product-oriented, and competition has been quite sharply product-focused. Considerable change from this historical orientation is now evident, and marketers in the future will need to be alert to market opportunities that

---

[3] See Robert Bartels, "Are Domestic and International Marketing Dissimilar?" *Journal of Marketing,* 32, (July 1968), 55–61.

[4] George Fisk, *Marketing Systems* (New York: Harper and Row, Publishers, 1967), p. 751.

a few years ago would have seemed strongly counter to established patterns of serving customers and to traditional buying habits.

MARKETING INSTITUTIONS

By and large, the rest of the world in comparison to the United States is characterized by small, highly specialized service retailers who are a vital part of the trade and social structure. This reflects years of custom and tradition, ingrained shopping habits, limited incomes, and, in some cases, legislation. For example, in Italy, restrictive legislation has resulted in special shops for poultry, different shops for beef, and still others for veal. Licensing arrangements have been such that large volume, one-stop shopping was curtailed, even as the weakening of custom, rising income, and increasing automobile ownership might have encouraged it. In some countries self-service supermarkets have been making striking headway, but they are nevertheless subordinate to the small specialized service establishments characterized by a larger number of employees per unit of output, higher gross margins, and lower stock turnover.[5]

BUSINESS PHILOSOPHIES

Essentially, American marketing development has been characterized by low prices, high volume, rapid stock turnover, and narrow gross margins. In contrast, a much different philosophy has operated in many other parts of the world, and only recently has been changing. The essential difference has been a preference for profit maximizing on a per unit basis, or (by indirection) a low volume-high profit philosophy. While this philosophy is moderating under the pressure of intensified competition resulting from a reduction of trade barriers, the lack of an expansionist policy continues to be reflected on a widespread basis. Even among the more progressive European firms, a conservative philosophy concerning marketing prevails.

MARKET FEASIBILITY STUDY

Feasibility studies for assessing profit opportunities in nondomestic markets need to be tailored to the objectives, the program contemplated,

[5] See Arieh Goldman, "Outreach of Consumers and the Modernization of Urban Food Retailing in Developing Countries," *Journal of Marketing,* 38, (October 1974), 8–16. Also William Cunningham, R. Moore, and I. Cunningham, "Urban Markets in Industrializing Countries: The Sao Paulo Experience," *Journal of Marketing,* 38, (April 1974), 2–12.

the country involved, and the particular situation facing the marketer. By way of illustration: a major tire company did not need a particularly elaborate feasibility study for deciding to bid, at a carefully determined price, on a large volume of truck and passenger car tires of given technical specifications, solicited by the government of one of the Eastern European Socialist states. The tire manufacturer, however, required an extremely thorough, elaborate, and detailed study in deciding whether to locate a manufacturing plant in the same Socialist state. As a matter of fact, domestic trade and public opinion were so strongly antagonistic that the manufacturer elected to withdraw, or at least delay, its announced plan for market entry. This illustration highlights the range of additional factors that must be considered in contemplating involvement in international markets in contrast to domestic markets. The extremes of extraproject considerations will vary from country to country, as environmental factors will differ from those in the United States. While a complete inventory of the special factors in feasibility studies for international marketing operations is beyond our scope, certain minimum areas of consideration are noted. At a minimum, the following broad extraproject factors should be investigated.

POLITICAL ENVIRONMENT

Political trends and stability of government importantly affect the level of risk and the degree of market uncertainty relative to a venture contemplated in another country. Consideration should be given to: (1) whether the swings of the foreign government are toward more state ownership or freer functioning of the private sector of the economy; (2) the government's policy toward acquisition, mergers, or any special alignments with particular competitors; (3) the concerned country's relations with its neighbors and with the United States; and (4) the government's policy toward profit repatriation. In most countries, rather detailed governmental approval must be granted to foreign enterprises wishing to enter a particular market sector, and the host government's attitude toward United States firms or domestic competitors is important.

SPECIAL INCENTIVES

Closely related to the political situation is the foreign government's attitude toward attracting outside investments. Market opportunities vary depending on the country's view of its own development problems and market needs. For example, most Western European nations have specifically stated those areas in which they actively solicit foreign capital. These can be in importation of technical know-how favoring such areas as electronics, precision opticals, and automated industries. In South America, Brazil has actively solicited foreign capital to bridge its capital gap since about 1965. In fact, incentive programs are such that in certain industries it is possible to enter Brazil with a very limited capital input. In 1974 any company that produced goods "essentially" for export could acquire the right to import a complete plant and receive a 42 percent tax incentive on all goods sold for export. On the other hand, Argentina, although favorable to foreign investment, has not been able to control some elements of its citizenry, as evidenced by the number of American executives kidnapped by guerrillas during the mid-1970s. A thorough review of incentive programs is a must in assessing market opportunity. In fact, in many countries the willingness to look upon the public sector as a partner is essential to successful operations.

TAXES

Taxes reflect the existence of special incentives as well as the restriction of outside enterprises in certain markets. The particular type of taxes levied on foreigners, their rate and historical patterns, are important considerations. Also relevant is the possibility of crediting local taxes against the United States taxes, and vice versa, because American firms often ship component parts of final products into our domestic market from overseas producing points. Taxes on conversion to foreign exchange are pertinent, given the American enterprise's objectives and policies of conducting its business in dollars and bringing home profits. Import and export tariff restrictions and quota must also be taken into account. In some cases these restrictions, which are used to control the volume of business done from foreign markets, can be more or less offset by the degree of national participation in the project.

CURRENCY AND AVAILABILITY OF CAPITAL

Foreign exchange is largely handled in gold, dollars, or pounds; these latter currencies are known as reserve currencies. In converting local currencies to foreign exchange the degree of freedom is important. The value of currency in free markets, as well as official government rates, and the stability of both rates should be evaluated. Because of efforts to hold down dollar outflows for a more favorable balance of payments, American businessmen are increasingly turning to overseas capital markets to finance their entry into and growth in international markets. Borrowing outside the United States has increased sharply, but typically at considerably higher interest rates. The premiums stand to reduce United States companies' foreign earnings.

Interest on international loans in Brazil, for example, in 1974 amounted to an effective 10.5 percent. Although written at a nominal 6 percent, an interest payment tax of 25 percent and an intermediary bank service charge of 3 percent resulted in a much higher effective cost of money. Since so much of Brazil's capital is foreign, it cannot adjust interest rates for inflation control. It can and does, however, for indefinite periods require a 25 percent deposit of any international loan in the central bank, thus raising the effective cost of money once again. Insofar as possible, these features must be assessed for their effect on profitability of any anticipated ventures.

SOCIAL ENVIRONMENT AND CUSTOMS

Besides the legal and economic barriers that confront an outside company doing business in international markets, there are formidable social constraints. Knowledge of local customs, buying and work habits, and local conditions for doing business are vital in bringing about a profitable performance in foreign operations. The nation in question may have different customs affecting work and sales patterns that, while subtle, have a pronounced impact on management processes and results. For example, it is customary and acceptable in some countries to provide extra payments to certain trade officials in return for various amenities and privileges. Such practices will affect profits and may have an important effect on morale, company ethics, and employee attitudes as well.

The overseas enterprise must be environmentally suitable to the host nation as well as to the firm's owner. To ensure that the national interests are met, some countries impose restrictions on the employment of management and operating personnel who are noncitizens. Even without such restrictions, United States companies seeking to effect a good state of adjustment to the local environment extensively use foreign nationals in their operations.

INVESTMENT FEASIBILITY STUDY

A United States corporation, marketing a broad product line of poultry and hog-raising equipment, had considerable technical know-how in design of equipment and had developed a worldwide reputation for its marketing expertise in the introduction of such sophisticated equipment. In 1973, the company embarked on a project to evaluate the possibility of entering the Brazilian market. The first step, after a very preliminary review of the Brazilian environment was completed, was to outline and conduct a market feasibility study. In Figure 9-1 the outline of the study is reproduced to illustrate the nature of international opportunity assessment.

FIGURE 9-1
Investment Feasibility Study

    I. EXECUTIVE SUMMARY
        A. Scope of Investment Feasibility Study
           1. Objectives
           2. Coverage
           3. Report Structure
        B. Key Findings
           1. Brazil: Social/Political/Economic
           2. Brazilian Agricultural Market
           3. Market Trends and Forecasts
               a. Poultry
               b. Eggs
               c. Red Meat
           4. Outlook for Equipment Industry
        C. Market Opportunity: 1975–1980
        D. Proposed Method of Entry
        E. Projected Investment and Return
   II. BRAZIL: SOCIAL/POLITICAL/ECONOMIC
        A. Historical Perspective
        B. Political Stability
        C. Economic Growth
        D. Incentives and Attitudes Toward Foreign Investment
  III. BRAZILIAN AGRICULTURAL MARKET
        A. Industry versus Agriculture
        B. Importance of Agricultural Growth
        C. Monoculture to Multiculture
  IV. MARKET TRENDS AND FORECASTS
        A. Broilers
           1. Trends and Forecasts
               a. Production (Geographic Patterns)
               b. Per Capita Consumption
               c. Consumer Price Index
               d. Import/Export
           2. Producer Characteristics
               a. Size and Location
               b. Financial Factors
                  —Credit Sources
                  —Profitability
               c. Feeding Practices
               d. Confinement Practices
           3. Supplier Relations
               a. Stock
               b. Feed
               c. Equipment

4. Processor Relations
   a. Identity of Processor
   b. Degree of Vertical Integration
      —Producer/Cooperative
      —Producer/Independent
   c. Quality Grading Practices
B. Eggs
  1. Trends and Forecasts
     a. Production (Geographic Patterns)
     b. Per Capita Consumption
     c. Consumer Price Index
     d. Import/Export
     e. Industrial Demand
  2. Producer Characteristics
     a. Size and Location
     b. Financial Factors
        —Credit Sources
        —Profitability
     c. Feeding Practices
     d. Confinement Practices
  3. Supplier Relations
     a. Stock
     b. Feed
     c. Equipment
  4. Processor Relations
     a. Identity of Processor
     b. Degree of Vertical Integration
        —Producer/Cooperative
        —Producer/Independent
     c. Quality Grading Practices
C. Turkeys
  1. Trends and Forecasts
     a. Production (Geographic Patterns)
     b. Per Capita Consumption
     c. Consumer Price Index
     d. Import/Export
  2. Producer Characteristics
     a. Size and Location
     b. Financial Factors
        —Credit Sources
        —Profitability
     c. Feeding Practices
     d. Confinement Practices
  3. Supplier Relations
     a. Stock
     b. Feed
     c. Equipment

4. Processor Relations
   a. Identity of Processor
   b. Degree of Vertical Integration
      —Producer/Cooperative
      —Producer/Independent
   c. Quality Grading Practices
D. Hogs
   1. Trends and Forecasts
      a. Production (Geographic Patterns)
      b. Per Capita Consumption
      c. Consumer Price Index
      d. Import/Export
   2. Producer Characteristics
      a. Size and Location
      b. Financial Factors
         —Credit Sources
         —Profitability
      c. Feeding Practices
      d. Confinement Practices
   3. Supplier Relations
      a. Stock
      b. Feed
      c. Equipment
   4. Processor Relations
      a. Identity of Processor
      b. Degree of Vertical Integration
         —Producer/Cooperative
         —Producer/Independent
      c. Quality Grading Practices
E. Breeder Stock
   1. Chickens
      a. Production
      b. Producer Characteristics
         —Size and Location
         —Financial Factors
         —Feeding Practices
         —Confinement Practices
      c. Equipment Source
   2. Turkeys
      a. Production
      b. Producer Characteristics
         —Size and Location
         —Financial Factors
         —Feeding Practices
         —Confinement Practices
      c. Equipment Source
F. Red Meats—Trends and Forecasts

V. OUTLOOK FOR EQUIPMENT INDUSTRY
   A. Growing Equipment: Feeding Equipment, Cages, Environmental Equipment
      1. Unit Sales Trends (Historic) by Selected Products
         a. Domestic Production
         b. Importation
         c. "On Farm" Assembly
      2. Channel Overview
         a. Manufacturer Practices
            —Labeling
            —Terms of Trade
            —Margins/Prices
         b. Channel Interconnections
            —Distributors
            —Cooperatives
            —Direct-to-Users
      3. Competition
         a. Name/Location
         b. Financial Strength
         c. Estimated Market Share
         d. Service/Quality Ranking
         e. Existing Channel Pattern
      4. Qualitative Evaluation of Equipment Supply
      5. Unit Sales Forecast by Selected Products
   B. Breeding Equipment
      1. Unit Sales Trends (Historic) by Selected Products
         a. Domestic Production
         b. Importation
      2. Channel Overview
         a. Manufacturer Practices
            —Labeling
            —Terms of Trade
            —Margins/Prices
         b. Channel Interconnections
            —Distributors
            —Cooperatives
            —Direct-to-Users
      3. Competition
         a. Name/Location
         b. Financial Strength
         c. Estimated Market Share
         d. Service/Quality Ranking
         e. Existing Channel Pattern
      4. Qualitative Evaluation of Equipment Supply
      5. Unit Sales Forecast by Selected Products

VI. MARKET OPPORTUNITY: 1975–1980
   A. Prime Product Category Targets
   B. Market Share
      1. Unit Sales
      2. Revenue
VII. PROPOSED METHOD OF ENTRY
   A. Alternative Legal Structures
      1. Wholly Owned Subsidiary
      2. Joint Venture (Nonpublic)
      3. Open Company
   B. Alternative Operating Structures
      1. Contract Manufacturing
      2. Owned Manufacturing
   C. Recommended Entry Method
VIII. PROJECTED INVESTMENT AND RETURN
   A. Investment Detail
      1. Initial Investment
         a. Startup Cost
         b. Fixed Assets
      2. Working Capital
         a. Cash
         b. Accounts Receivable
         c. Inventory
   B. Profitability Analysis
      1. Operating Costs
         a. Cost of Goods
         b. Operating Costs
            —Fixed
            —Variable
      2. Revenue
      3. Pro Forma Analysis
         a. Profit (Loss)
         b. Balance Sheet
         c. Cash Flow
   C. Investment Analysis
      1. Return on Investment
      2. Pay Back Period
   D. Credit Sources

This outline was designed to focus on the details of data requirements. Space does not permit an elaboration of each section. It is evident that Part II inquires into the extra project features described above; Part III evaluates the market trends in agriculture; Part IV evaluates the market trends in user production and prevailing business practices; Part V projects user output to equipment demand to arrive at a market opportunity in

Part VI; Part VII explores the legal aspects of alternative entry means and operating structures; and Part VIII is a financial evaluation of the venture.

Considerable detail is required in the preparation of such an analysis. Evaluations must be developed concurrently with searches to assess the availability of data. The responsibility for performing the managerial functions of market delineation and purchase behavior motivation not only exist in international opportunity assessment but they may be even more essential to success than in domestic situations.

SUMMARY

Foreign operations cover a variety of forms, ranging all the way from relatively simple exporting by a largely domestic enterprise, on the one hand, to the truly international company without special allegiance to any one country on the other.

As international markets increase in dollar importance, their differences in comparison to domestic markets become more critical to marketing strategy. These include such characteristics as: (1) lower literacy rates, (2) shorter life spans and more rapid life cycles, (3) restricted purchasing power, (4) limited promotional media, (5) a paucity of market information and data, (6) restricted credit availability, (7) limited ownership of consumption equipment, (8) different buying habits, (9) differing marketing institutions, and (10) divergent business philosophies.

International risk, uncertainty, and profit relationships are considerably different than in domestic operations. A number of extraproject features, such as (1) political environment, (2) special incentives, (3) taxes, (4) currency and availability of credit, and (5) social environment and customs, vary extensively from country to country. These differences make it imperative that market feasibility studies be tailored to the particular project and country contemplated. The performances of market delineation and purchase motivation are difficult in international situations, but they are essential to effective opportunity assessment.

QUESTIONS AND PROBLEMS

1. Identify the principal methods of international marketing. Discuss the characteristics of each method.
2. How will the economic development of other countries affect international market opportunities of United States companies?

3. What is meant by the term *expropriation of assets?* What methods of international marketing are most likely to prevent this from happening?

4. What is a market feasibility study? Illustrate its importance in international marketing.

5. What are the essential elements of any international market feasibility study?

6. What are the marketing implications of the differences in buying habits between domestic and international markets?

7. What are the distinguishing characteristics of international markets which produce the differences in buying habits in these markets?

8. "The difference between domestic market characteristics and international market characteristics is one of degree." Comment.

BIBLIOGRAPHY

ALPERT, LEWIS, and RONALD GALTY, "Product Positioning by Behavioral Lifestyles," *Journal of Marketing,* 33 (April 1969), 65–69.

BARTELS, ROBERT, "Are Domestic and International Marketing Dissimilar?" *Journal of Marketing,* 32, no. 3 (July 1968), 55–61.

BENNETT, PETER D., and HAROLD H. KASSARJIAN, *Consumer Behavior.* Englewood Cliffs, N.J.: Prentice-Hall, Inc., 1972.

CLARK, LINCOLN H., ed., *Consumer Behavior: Research on Consumer Reactions.* New York: Harper & Row, Publishers, 1958.

CUNNINGHAM, WILLIAM, R. MOORE, and I. CUNNINGHAM, "Urban Markets in Industrializing Countries: The Sao Paulo Experience," *Journal of Marketing,* 38 (April 1974), 2–12.

ENGLE, JAMES F., DAVID T. KOLLAT, and ROGER D. BACKWELL, *Consumer Behavior* (rev. ed.). New York: Holt, Rinehart and Winston, Inc., 1972.

GARDNER, BURLEIGH B., "The ABC of Motivation Research," *Business Topics,* vol. 7 (Summer 1959).

HOWARD, JOHN A., and JAGDISH N. SHETH, *The Theory of Buyer Behavior.* New York: John Wiley & Sons, Inc., 1969.

KATONA, GEORGE, *Psychological Analysis of Economic Behavior.* New York: McGraw-Hill Book Company, 1951.

KOFFKA, KURT, *Principles of Gestalt Psychology.* New York: Harcourt, Brace and World, Inc., 1935.

KÖHLER, WOLFGANG, *Gestalt Psychology.* New York: Liveright Publishing Corporation, 1947.

LINDESMITH, A. R., and A. L. STRAUSS, *Social Psychology.* New York: Holt, Rinehart and Winston, Inc., 1956.

LUCK, DAVID J., HUGH WALES, and DONALD A. TAYLOR. *Marketing Research* (4th ed.). Englewood Cliffs, N.J.: Prentice-Hall, Inc., 1974.

MARTINEAU, PIERRE, "Social Class and Spending Behavior," *Journal of Marketing,* 23 (October 1958), 121–30.

Maslow, Abraham H., *Motivation and Personality*. New York: Harper & Row, Publishers, 1954.
Nicosia, Francesco M., *Consumer Decision Process*. Englewood Cliffs, N.J.: Prentice-Hall, Inc., 1966.
Schewe, Charles D., "Selected Social Psychological Models for Analyzing Buyers," *Journal of Marketing*, 37 (July 1973), 31–39.
Sheth, Jagdish N., "A Model of Industrial Buyer Behavior," *Journal of Marketing*, 37 (October 1973), 50–56.
Warner, W. Loyd, *Social Life of a Modern Community*. New Haven: Yale University Press, 1941.
Warner, W. Loyd, Marchia Mecker, and Kenneth Eells, *Social Class In America*. New York: Harper & Row, Publishers, 1960.
Webster, F. E., and Yoram Wind, "A General Model for Understanding Organizational Buyer Behavior," *Journal of Marketing* (April 1972), pp. 12–19.
Woods, Walter A., "Psychological Dimensions of Consumer Decision," *Journal of Marketing*, 25 (January 1960), 15–19.

Part III

PRODUCT-SERVICE-MARKET MATCHING

The combination of products and services offered by a firm should result from a deliberate plan to match offerings with the markets it wishes to cultivate. The combination of products and services offered by a firm is referred to as the *product mix*. The plan for matching product mix and markets constitutes a major aspect of marketing strategy planning.

Planning of this sort is a natural result of what we observed in Parts One and Two to be the firm's goals, and the behavior required to achieve them. In Part One we observed that the main goal of the firm is profitably to serve markets in which products are *consumed*. The firm does this through offering buyers better "bundles" of utility (products) than its rivals. Because the marketplace is constantly changing, Part Two followed with an investigation of the forces that shape the diverse and changing wants of buyers. In spite of the many forces working on buyers, we found that it was possible to group them according to similar wants and needs.

As it is possible to characterize markets available, the firm can choose from them and build or modify the product mix to meet specific demands. In short, the firm can begin to formulate a product strategy.

Determining the most profitable product mix to market is one of the most important and most complex management problems. This area of management action reflects factors both within and external to the firm. The total market offering includes such things as convenience of purchase, package attractiveness, brand image, services rendered, the reputation of the company, and other elements that are clearly supportive of, and integrated with, the product. Externally considered, the product is such a large proportion of the total market offering that it can be considered as the bridge that links the producing enterprise with the consuming market. As a consequence, the product mix offered provides the principal component of competitive adjustment through which the firm aligns its corporate resources with its market environment in an effort to achieve its goals.

Internal to the firm, the product mix serves as the common element that binds together the diverse interests of all operating departments, such as production, finance, marketing, purchasing, research and development, personnel-management and industrial relations. The product mix is the hub of the wheel around which the firm as a whole revolves.

In Part Three we examine alternatives available to the firm in product-market matching. Although the firm must adjust its offering to its market environment, other considerations sometimes condition the selection of product mix. As a result, different patterns of product diversity emerge. The reasons for inherent risks and problems related to product-market matching patterns are examined in Chapter 10. Chapter 11 presents the stages of product-market development that are characteristic of a typical product life cycle. While not all products pass through the typical life cycle, the model is useful for planning marketing strategy. The final chapter of Part Three presents a framework for new product review. The need for continuous new product introductions requires screening of ideas and careful analysis of the feasibility of candidates. The procedures used in this phase of matching are explored.

Chapter 10

Product Planning Environment

Formulation of product plans has always been a critical aspect in effective market performance. In the American economy we have reached a stage in which future economic growth will largely depend upon the introduction of new products. This trend has been evident for the past 25 years as an increasing proportion of sales and profits have come from new product development. However, the risks associated with new product development have also increased. In consumer goods, changing life styles have virtually upset the stability of product offerings. If corporations are to adjust adequately to dynamic markets, their product lines must reflect new consumer demands. A firm's product images play a vital role in shaping its overall corporate image. The customer's perception of a firm's vitality, progressiveness, service, and customer orientation results primarily from product adjustments.

In this chapter we turn our attention to the environmental setting for product-service adjustment. The first part of the chapter reviews nine of the most significant elements of risk related to product planning. Next, attention is directed to various aspects of formulating product-market matching plans. In the third section, attention is directed to the fundamental matching strategies available to guide market planning. The fourth section reviews basic patterns of product diversity which a firm might select to employ in its overall strategy and to variations available within these patterns. The final section reviews five significant problems that are typically confronted in product planning.

ELEMENTS OF PRODUCT PLANNING RISK[1]

Because of the dynamic nature of business competition it is difficult to single out specific risks that are related to product development. How-

[1] This section draws extensively upon Thomas A. Staudt, "Higher Management Risks in Product Strategy," *Journal of Marketing,* 37 (January 1973), 4–9.

ever, from the many elements of risk that could be catalogued, this section presents nine that are universally confronted.

CAPITAL AND LABOR-INTENSIVE SYSTEMS

In many instances, United States enterprises are competing in world markets. Overseas labor costs are often lower than domestic costs, resulting in a total cost advantage to foreign producers. Because of the lower break-even points associated with labor-intensive systems, profitable operations are possible at a lower level of production. These considerations account for the seeming paradox of foreign firms operating profitably in markets that United States enterprises are slow to enter. When extensive capital must be deployed to support new product development, the associated risk is significantly greater in comparison to a labor-intensive system.

INVESTMENT REQUIREMENTS

The investment required for product additions is high. In some industries it has more than doubled in less than 10 years. This factor alone accounts for much of management's tardiness in entering potential growth markets. The magnitude and longevity of market opportunity must be well defined before making the final decision to enter a market.

Unfortunately, the state of the art in forecasting is barely able to bring investment uncertainty within tolerable limits for decision making. On the production side, most of the expenditures are concentrated in single purpose equipment and automated systems. Increasingly large expenditures are required on market development to shape positive consumer attitudes toward the firm's new offering. Such expenditures are most often not retrievable or redeployable.

If investment is not high, technological advantage at best is tenuous, in that differential competitive advantage can be expected to be short-lived. For example, within two years from the time General Electric introduced the automatic toothbrush, it had 52 competitors. Within one year from the time the electric carving knife was introduced, it was competing with seven others.[2]

The result of increased investment requirement is a high break-even point for new ventures and products. The existence of high break-even points often leads to operating losses during the pioneering stage of market

---

[2] Fred J. Borch, "Tomorrow's Customers." Speech before Sales Executive Club of New York, September 15, 1964.

development and requires courageous executives who are not prone to panic in the periods of early stress.

Investment requirements and the accompanying longer payback periods create pressure to carry products longer without change. There is tremendous pressure to be sure the product is right in the first place so that a satisfactory profit performance can be reached early. This was especially true with Chevrolet's pre-announcement on the Vega. "If you liked 1971, you'll like 1975."

EXTENDED PAYBACK PERIODS

The magnitude and character of investment requirements and the early operating losses resulting from high break-even points have lengthened the time period required for the firm to pay back its investment. These extended paybacks tend to encourage a more cautious product policy. Delays in the corporate decision-making structure of the enterprise grow longer as executives at each review level take more time to assess product proposals carefully.

ENVIRONMENTAL CONSIDERATIONS

Increasing environmental regulation and legislation will continue to specify and limit product change. In the automotive industry, for instance, legislation requiring substantial investments for improved safety and emission standards may not necessarily coincide directly with customer preferences in such areas as power plants, vehicle configuration, or economy. Product changes to meet environmental regulations are increasingly pervasive and important in the structuring of product programs.

PROLIFERATION OF TRIVIA

To avoid risk, a great deal of product adjustment has appeared in the form of minor change. Such trivia has created the risk of revenue division among a number of cost centers without any real growth in total sales. The proliferation of trivially different products has definite profit consequences and has created a form of product variation or depth that nobody really wants. Competitive performance measured exclusively on a market share basis fosters "me, too" product line expansions. In the process, engineering resources are drained that might otherwise be directed to making products that offer a diversity of real choice or products that work better and last longer.

EXTENDED LEAD TIMES

The consequence of a more careful total system analysis is that a longer lead time between product idea and market entry is now needed. This greatly increases management risk. As lead times increase and the dynamics of markets accelerate, the potential imprecision of product-market matches becomes serious. Longer lead times are often necessary for a variety of reasons—more detailed market research, sharpened forecasts, obtaining necessary approvals, or bringing on-stream capital-intensive automated production systems.

FAILURE PENALTIES

The penalties for failure are great because of investment requirements and the need for larger scale market entry to capitalize effectively on product innovation. We have just indicated General Electric's experiences with carving knives and electric toothbrushes. The capacity of rivals to duplicate new products successfully is one factor requiring larger scale entry. As

FIGURE 10-1
Break-even Points at Different Levels of Fixed Cost

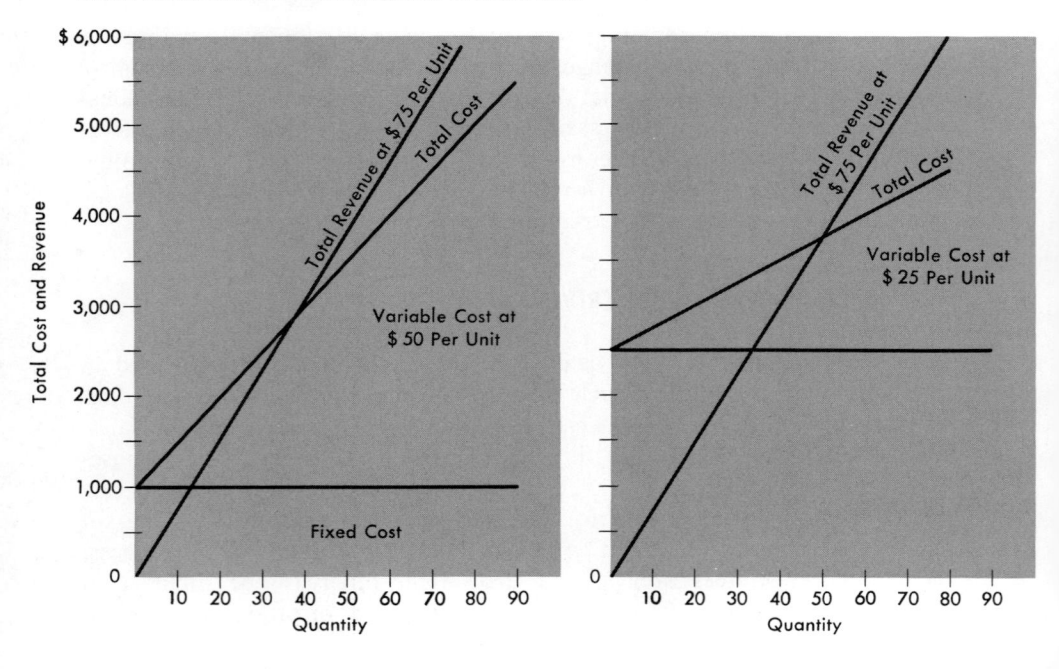

Fred Borch says, "The honeymoon cycle of a new product is becoming shorter and shorter."[3] This is in sharp contrast to the protected enclave that Gillette enjoyed for so many years with its safety razor blade.

The result of the need to make greater investments, coupled with increased competitive reaction time, is that production cost is tipped in the direction of a larger proportion of fixed cost in contrast to variable cost. This means that the break-even point in launching a new product is reached only with a larger sales volume. This is demonstrated in Figure 10-1. Notice the profit angles above the break-even point and the loss angles below the break-even point are wider than if the product could have been launched with a higher proportion of direct costs in relation to fixed charges. The result is that losses are greater or profits are sharply below expectation if the product fails to achieve the anticipated volume.

THE FURTHER PROJECTS GO, THE HARDER THEY ARE TO TERMINATE

The longer a project is sustained in the development process and the greater the amount of expenditures that have been made, the more difficult the decision for management to terminate. Frequently, the forlorn hope exists that just a little more time, money, or effort will produce the necessary breakthrough to success. This often is akin to "throwing good money after bad." Suffice it to say that the jeopardy of professional reputations, costs, and the uncertainty of success all lead to a decision. For this reason we have established definite kill points in the product planning framework discussed in Chapter 12. The terminology is deliberate and reflects the conviction that the burden of proof should be on keeping a project alive rather than terminating it and killing it earlier rather than later.

CONJUNCTION OF MARKET AFFAIRS AND TECHNOLOGY

The various stages and phases of the new product development process are ideally designed to bring technical and market research along parallel tracks in the hope that there can be a conjunction of technology and market affairs. Difficulties can be encountered if there is virtual preoccupation with one or the other. It is undesirable to have research and development personnel totally oriented to sitting back waiting for the marketing group to bring them a set of specifications for a new product in a defined area of market opportunity. It is equally bad to have the technical effort of a company going off in all directions that bear little or no relationship

[3] Ibid.

to the company's present market concerns and competitive problems. A conjunction of technology and market affairs is highly desirable.

The nine noted risks, plus others, have created an environment in which the pace of product innovation to which we are now accustomed may well be slowed unless the probability of product success can be improved. The objective of organized and systematic product-service adjustment is to reduce the risk of such innovation.

PRODUCT-MARKET MATCHING

The product offerings of a firm should result from matching product line as closely as is profitable to market opportunity. Such matching is an integral part of the firm's marketing strategy planning. As noted in Chapter 4, the basic marketing consideration evolves around the number of different market segments isolated as target markets. Given an overall rationale, the marketer must determine the number of different product lines and variations within any given product line to be offered. Such a determination is referred to as *product-market* matching.

The objectives of product-market matching were discussed in Part Two. At that time it was suggested that all firms should strive to develop a product-image compatible with the customer's self-image. However, consider the problem facing a manufacturer of women's shoes in deciding product-line composition. Imagine the number of styles, the variety of materials, the assortment of colors, the number of sizes, and the prices necessary to fulfill varied consumer expectations. Unfortunately, as noted in the previous section, there are economic penalties attached to excessive proliferation. Every enterprise has a problem of determining the optimum number of products and variations to offer.

An enterprise has the option of offering only a single product, or a variety of products. The number of products offered is sometimes called the assortment or *product mix*. The product assortment or mix can be further classified in terms of *width* and *depth*. A product mix is *wide* or *broad* if a large number of different product lines are contained within the assortment, and *limited* if the assortment is small. The mix composition is *deep* if a large number of variations are offered within a basic product line. The determination of the number of product lines is called *strategic product adjustment*. Determination of the variations to be offered within each line is identified as *tactical product adjustment*. Naturally, such measures as width and depth are relative when used to classify an assortment.

The objective in matching is to balance cost-revenue considerations so as to arrive at a highly profitable product assortment. Since the ideal can rarely be achieved, another dimension is added to the matching concept by developing a general characterization of any market as it appears to any firm.

A given market may be classified into three parts: (1) core, (2) fringe, and (3) zone of indifference. The core of the market for any product is the prime customer cluster. In the core, the product ideally matches customer needs, desires, preferences, motivations, and purchasing power. In other words, the product-image for customers in the core is fully compatible with their self-images. As we move away from the cluster toward the fringe of the market, a less exact fit exists in any one of a number of purchase variables. The product-image for this group of customers is only partially compatible with the self-image. Finally, at the zone of indifference, no compatibility exists, and it is almost by random chance alone that potential buyers will be attracted to the product.

FUNDAMENTAL MATCHING STRATEGIES

Among firms engaged in segmented marketing, two fundamental strategies are available. The difference between the two strategies rests primarily in the degree of width in product assortment. In their extreme the two strategies constitute significant differences in the nature of overall product strategy.

A LIMITED-LINE STRATEGY

The firm can cover a broad market with a limited product line, which is differentiated from the products of rivals both physically and also psychologically through promotion and advertising.[4] The essential assumption is that a single demand curve exists for the product. Existing variations in consumer desires are presumed capable of being modified to accept the product through large outlays for advertising and promotion. This limited-line strategy assumes that consumer choices may be partially molded around a given point on the demand schedule. A term that describes this notion is *plasticity of demand*.[5] Both price and the large promotional and

[4] For the basic work in development of matching strategy, see Wendell R. Smith, "Product Differentiation and Market Segmentation as Alternative Marketing Strategies," *Journal of Marketing,* 20 (July 1956), 3–8. The basis for differentiation is developed in greater detail in Chapter 19.

[5] Wroe Alderson, *Marketing Behavior and Executive Action* (Homewood, Ill.: Richard D. Irwin, Inc., 1957), p. 277.

advertising outlays determine the quantity to be demanded. It, of course, also assumes the possibility of expanding demand or a shift in the entire demand curve to the right.[6]

The results expected from a limited-line strategy tend to be diluted by a relative decrease of penetration that occurs as a larger market share is sought. Market expansion is limited by excessive and uneconomic outlays for persuasive propaganda required to offset the inexact match; by price concessions required to induce fringe and indifferent buyers to compromise their precise preferences; or by competitors' actions following essentially similar strategies that tend to cancel each other out. Usually, a combination of all factors sets an outer limit to the success of a limited-line strategy.

A BROAD-LINE STRATEGY

The broad-line strategy varies from the limited-line both in degree and in basic postulates. The marketer following this strategy visualizes a series of demand curves, each having peculiar and distinct characteristics. The objective is a more exact product fit and deeper penetration to each market segment. The result is the achievement of a sizable share of the total market rather than a broad but thin penetration across all segments. A broad-line strategy places high priority on precise product planning. A great deal of reliance is placed on the exactness of customer fit for effective product-market matching rather than relying heavily on promotional and advertising effectiveness.

The greater reliance on product matching does not mean that promotional expense can be drastically curtailed. The market must be informed and made aware of the available product assortment. Marketers following a broad-line strategy are less vulnerable to the promotional tactics of competitors (coupons, giveaways, special deals) and to consumer persuasion that can arise from comparative advertising claims and counterclaims. The strategy rests on a substantial foundation—a harmonious matching of product with customer preferences.

Consideration and selection of a broad-line strategy requires a precise measurement of demand variations and identification of the significant segments that derive from these differences. Such segmentation may be based on demographic or behavioral differences in market composition.[7] The need for careful product-market matching reemphasizes the impor-

---

[6] See Chapter 16, p. 353.
[7] Such foundations for segmentation were elaborated in Chapters 5–9 dealing with Market Opportunity Assessment.

tance of market delineation and purchase motivation analysis in the formulation of product strategy.

PATTERNS OF PRODUCT DIVERSITY

An understanding of product diversity patterns helps to clarify the strategic foundations of product planning for a particular enterprise. In total, four patterns of diversity are identified, based upon production and marketing similarities or differences. These patterns identify product opportunity structure by revealing some economic consequences of random product additions in contrast to the potential benefits of carefully controlled additions.

CONVERGENT PRODUCTION AND CONVERGENT MARKETING

The first basic pattern of product diversity is convergent production and marketing. The notion of convergence characterizes the way in which all products utilize common production and marketing facilities. That is, raw materials and purchased parts "converge" on the same production facilities, and finished products "converge" on common marketing facilities. This arrangement is diagrammed in Figure 10-2.[8]

In this illustration, three different products utilize the same production facilities. They may require slightly different finishing operations, but for the most part the same equipment, manufacturing methods, production skills, and labor force are used to produce all three. Because the products are similar in market characteristics, a single marketing organization sells them all.

An office equipment manufacturer, producing such products as metal desks, chairs, tables, filing equipment, bookcases, and wastepaper baskets, is an illustration of convergent production and marketing. Convergent production exists because each product is made from sheet metal and involves metal stamping, drawing, and finishing. Similarly, one marketing organization can distribute all the products because they are destined for sale in a common market. This is a preferred pattern of diversity because it combines the least risk with the greatest chance for success as new products are added that retain this basic pattern. Convergent production market-

---

[8] For what is believed to be the first exposition of this notion, see L. Lothrop, "What Our Firm Really Needs Is Something New," *Sales Management,* Part I, January 16, 1932, p. 82.

FIGURE 10-2
Convergent Production and Convergent Marketing

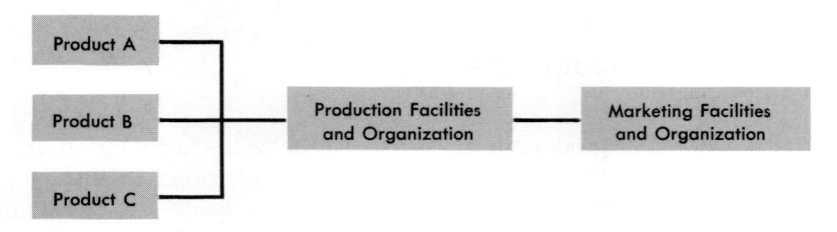

```
Product A ─┐
           │
Product B ─┼──── Production Facilities ──── Marketing Facilities
           │     and Organization           and Organization
Product C ─┘
```

ing minimizes risks because, with the same production and marketing facilities, the firm can capitalize on its existing management capabilities, engineering talents, production skills, facilities, methods, knowledge of markets and market behavior, brand image, and position among dealers and distributors. In short, it can bring all of its competitive capacity to bear in marketing the new product.

Another advantage of this pattern of diversity is greater efficiency of operation throughout the firm. Economies of scale may be realized from the additional volume of business that usually accompanies product expansion. A broader base is provided over which to spread fixed costs, resulting in lower unit cost for the product.

The spreading of fixed costs over a larger volume of business constitutes the major element in economies of scale, but other elements are not to be overlooked. Materials may sometimes be purchased in more economical lots; more stable employment may be achieved, reducing the costs of laying off and recalling help. Waste circulation in advertising may be reduced. For instance, a baby foods producer advertising in *The Ladies' Home Journal* reaches many women whose children are past baby food age. This is waste circulation, since these mothers are not potential buyers. If the manufacturer were to add a line of junior foods, he would broaden the age range of potential users, and his advertising would apply to more of the magazine's readers.

Finally, the convergent production-marketing pattern is advantageous because it helps to strengthen even an established market position. For instance, a machine-tool manufacturer successfully added planers, vertical boring mills, and planer-type milling machines to an existing line of horizontal boring, drilling, and milling machines. Because the convergent production-marketing pattern permits continuous operations in closely related fields, it is the simplest and least risky of the four patterns. Management should fully explore its possibilities before considering other patterns. Only when this pattern cannot achieve corporate objectives should managers consider other patterns.

CONVERGENT PRODUCTION AND DIVERGENT MARKETING

In the second pattern, all products utilize common production facilities but require separate marketing facilities and organization. Figure 10-3 illustrates this pattern.

Under this pattern products are manufactured with existing facilities, but because of selling requirements a variety of marketing organizations are necessary to achieve complete market coverage. For example, a portion of the Kimberly-Clark product line includes printing papers, industrial wadding, building insulation, wallpaper, industrial wipers, facial tissue, and barbers' neckbands. All these products are made on basically similar primary machines, although various specialized pieces of secondary equipment are required. Although production is essentially convergent, marketing requirements are divergent. No single marketing facility or organization covers the range of different markets. The differences in business practices between printers, contractors, barber- and beauty-supply houses, and interior decorators make it unlikely that the requisite understanding of user problems for effective marketing is within the competence and versatility of any particular sales force. Thus, for complete coverage market divergence is required.

Now that the concept of divergence has been introduced, it should be recognized as a relative term. There are all degrees of convergence and divergence. Notice that in the Kimberly-Clark illustration, equipment was utilized in production. Thus, to a degree, an element of equipment divergence existed. In anoher case, a manufacturer of hearing aids found his production skills adaptable to interoffice communications systems. This product expansion involved convergence of engineering, design, production skills, and quality control, but divergence in materials and equipment. A slightly greater divergence occurred in the case of a watch manufacturer who found his skills of production miniaturization adaptable to miniature scientific instruments. Here there was some, but not complete, convergence

FIGURE 10-3
Convergent Production and Divergent Marketing

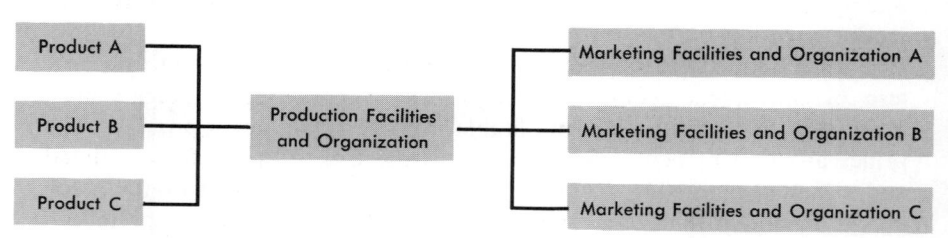

of production skills and technology. Thus, it is recognized that convergence and divergence are relative terms. The term *convergent production* is used, however, when on the balance there is a conjunctive in the major equipment, methods, and skills employed in the production process.

The same kind of limited convergence can exist on the marketing side, as illustrated by the appliance manufacturer who employs specialized salesmen in working with wholesalers in one part of his overall product line. In addition, some specialized dealers are used that sell only laundry equipment. Some degree of divergence could take place in ultimate consumers, type of dealers or outlets, type of salesmen, methods of promotion, placement of advertising media, shipping methods, pricing policies, and technical information required in the selling process. The term convergent marketing, however, is used when on balance the variations are limited enough to permit a single marketing facility and organization to accommodate all product lines with reasonable efficiency.

The convergent production-divergent marketing pattern of product diversity is the second most common of the four patterns. Two conditions seem to foster its use.

The first condition relates to high fixed-cost industries and the second to the need to diversify market risk. High overhead, decreasing cost industries have high break-even points and suffer adverse profit consequences from unused plant capacity. Thus, when production costs represent a large part of total costs, and fixed costs are a large proportion of production costs, management can be expected to exert every effort to maintain a high rate of plant utilization. This "machine orientation" helps to achieve low total and unit costs, allowing the firm to realize maximum profit advantages on all products once the break-even point is surpassed.

The second condition promoting this pattern of diversity is seasonal or cyclical fluctuations in sales, which firms try to offset and so reduce market risks. If all of a firm's products go to one market, its total sales will rise and fall as that market fluctuates. To avoid this condition necessarily means entering new markets—markets oftentimes different enough to bring about divergent marketing. Such conditions have prevailed in the machine tool industry, where extremely wide cyclical fluctuations in sales have been characteristic. Product expansion toward divergent marketing has been attempted in order to make such firms less vulnerable to this type of market volatility.

In all cases, when product diversity involves expansion into the pattern of convergent production and divergent marketing, managers must make sure that effective and profitable market cultivation is possible. The principal cause of new product failure is the lack of a carefully planned and executed marketing program. An established market position is much harder to obtain than either new machinery and equipment or specialized production knowledge. The competitive advantage from product diversity, capitalizing on plant facilities and production skills, may turn out to be relatively short-lived, in contrast to a pattern that draws on the market strength of the firm as the source of its competitive position and differential advantage.

DIVERGENT PRODUCTION AND CONVERGENT MARKETING

This pattern utilizes a company's basic marketing structure and trades on its established reputation, even though some products may require separate manufacturing facilities. It is diagrammed in Figure 10-4.

FIGURE 10-4
Divergent Production and Convergent Marketing

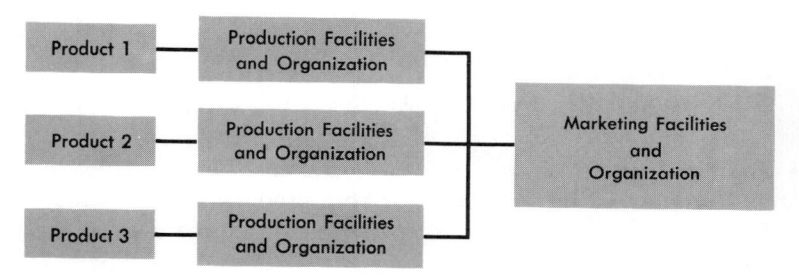

```
Product 1  ──▶  Production Facilities
                and Organization     ┐
                                     │
Product 2  ──▶  Production Facilities├──▶  Marketing Facilities
                and Organization     │        and Organization
                                     │
Product 3  ──▶  Production Facilities┘
                and Organization
```

The consumer appliance divisions of the larger appliance manufacturers, such as Whirlpool and General Electric, are excellent examples of this diversity pattern. They produce a full line of products—television sets, air conditioners, and electric ranges, among others—requiring different production facilities. All these products are sold to a common marketing organization. Depending on the product, there might be some variations among dealers, but on balance marketing is convergent. An excellent example is building materials manufacturers, who make a wide range of different products and materials that are marketed through one sales and dealer organization.

Product diversity of this type is most feasible when the firm has a clearly dominant market position and opportunities exist for additional products with interrelated demand. A well-organized and well-established marketing structure and organization constitute a particularly strong competitive weapon. Highly skilled sales personnel and a loyal dealer organization are difficult for competitors to duplicate. When a firm's line of products enjoys a priority position with dealers, a major barrier to market entry exists for other firms.

Product diversity involving complementary lines using the same institutional brand promotes wider awareness and helps to establish a reputation of more far-reaching importance than is possible with one product line or a number of unrelated lines. Promotional effort on any one product tends to benefit the total line. Also, a more sharply defined or clearer "corporate image" is likely to emerge in the marketplace under this pattern of diversity.

Under convergent marketing, as in any other pattern, management must be concerned with the net effects of product diversity. Of particular importance is the overall cost structure and the firm's capability to meet the requirements of effective completion throughout the whole production-marketing system. There is a limit as to how far diversity can be carried. Product lines may become too varied for effective assimilation by a single marketing organization. Once this point is reached, convergent marketing is no longer practical.

DIVERGENT PRODUCTION AND DIVERGENT MARKETING

The final pattern of diversity, as illustrated in Figure 10-5, involves separate facilities and organizations for both production and marketing.

This pattern of diversity is akin to separate business units. Products added are so different that they can neither be produced nor marketed through the same facilities. While such a pattern has many limitations, it has rather recently become increasingly common. Examples include the product expansion of Textron American, originally a woolen mill, into chain saws, outboard motors, and machine tools; a steamship company's entrance into the outdoor advertising business; and a food packer's entrance into the toy market.

With the extensive research and development expenditures in many industries, scientists working on a particular problem may make discoveries in an entirely different area. Such discoveries may provide the basis for product innovations entirely outside the existing company operations. The potential of the innovation may be such that management may undertake a whole new pattern of diversity in order to accommodate and capitalize on it.

In concluding the discussion of alternative patterns of product diversity, it is recognized that each has a degree of desirability in terms of a particular company's planning situations. Each firm is also limited with respect to potential patterns of diversity because of the existing nature of products, competitive factors, or the orientation and objectives of the enterprise. The basic pattern of product diversity to be followed is a stra-

FIGURE 10-5
Divergent Production and Divergent Marketing

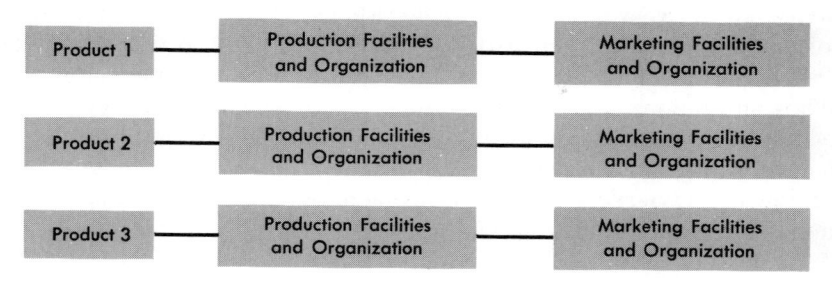

Product 1	—	Production Facilities and Organization	—	Marketing Facilities and Organization
Product 2	—	Production Facilities and Organization	—	Marketing Facilities and Organization
Product 3	—	Production Facilities and Organization	—	Marketing Facilities and Organization

tegic matter particular to the individual firm. Each pattern offers potential benefits and contains associated risks. The central orientation in the formulation of product strategy is to view the firm as a competitive and market entity and to arrive at a business rationale offering a basis for survival and growth.[9]

TYPICAL PRODUCT PLANNING PROBLEMS

In attempting to achieve effective product-market integration, certain common and recurring problems appear which are worthy of being highlighted. While no attempt will be made to catalogue the myriad of potential difficulties, five conceptually significant ones are singled out.

PRODUCT LINES— TOO BROAD AND TOO NARROW

That a product line could be both too broad and too narrow appears to be a contradiction. This occurs, however, where a marketer attempts to serve a number of distinctly identifiable markets with a broad assortment of products. The product line in such cases may be too broad, in the sense that the sales force cannot effectively spread its effort over so many different markets. That is, effort is diluted to the point where no market is cultivated sufficiently for a high degree of penetration. At the same time, the product line may be too narrow in one or several of the various segments to fulfill dealer and customer needs effectively. This kind of situation can be seen in the photographic equipment field. A manufacturer

[9] Elaboration of concept of *business rationale* is treated in Chapter 19 as an aspect of Marketing Strategy Planning.

might be offering 8mm movie cameras to the low-priced mass amateur market, with distribution through drugstores, department stores, and jewelry stores, as well as photographic shops; expensive movie cameras, projectors, and still cameras to the professional-like top of the amateur market through photographic dealers; professional equipment direct to studios, institutions, and industrial users; and photocopy machines through business machines dealers. Such a product line might be too broad for effective selling by a given sales organization, and yet too limited in the offerings in any particular area to provide adequately for dealer needs and competitive requirements.

DILUTION OF MASS PRODUCTION ECONOMIES

One of the most insidious dangers in attempting a high degree of segmentation with broad product lines is the dilution or even destruction of scale economies associated with mass production. This may tend to occur where an excessive preoccupation with customer orientation exists. That is, an imbalance takes place in manufacturing and marketing costs. The most enlightened marketing concept, however, recognizes the need for an optimum integration of cost centers throughout the system as a whole.

Marketing people must thus share a large part of the responsibility for the evolution of product lines that ultimately defeat the major economic advantages related to mass or "line" production. The danger is that there is generally a much stronger compulsion to add products than to drop them.

Production inventiveness has been sorely tested to maintain high levels of efficiency in the face of broad product assortments and customer choices. It is true that scientific advances in production scheduling, routing, and control have made possible versatile manufacturing within cost limits previously unattainable. There is a point, however, beyond which versatility cannot be accommodated without cost increases. The American automobile industry provides a case in point. An assembly plant appears to be a showplace of mass production efficiency because of the scientific procedures in scheduling, routing, and control. But the industry makes options available in thousands of combinations to buyers in the purchase of a car. It is estimated that Chevrolet could produce at full production for more than a year and never make exactly the same car twice. Many of these customer decisions would appear to be more intelligently made by an automotive engineer—types of springs, brakes, axles, steering mechanism, carburetor, exhaust system, and others. Some choices appear to be a needless waste of decision making for both seller and buyer—an extreme case being the choice of thickness of foam rubber in the seats that has been available in the past. Some of the success of foreign makes, such as Volkswagen and Renault, in the American market may well be related to the simplicity of product lines and customer choices. Cost savings are possible that go well beyond mere manufacturing economies. Think of the complexity of order handling, accounting systems, pricing, materials purchasing, checking and verification of the finished product, and billing that accompany the variety of customer choices offered in our automobile industry. The industry has come almost full circle, from the early custom building of each unit through the pioneering of mass production of a standard vehicle (the Model T) to today's custom building according to an individual order—either the dealer's or the ultimate consumer's.

THE TRAP OF THE FULL-LINE COMPETITOR

Evidence of recent years indicates that the full-line marketer on the whole has been more successful than his limited-line, more specialized rival. The result has been a trend toward so-called full-line product policies on the part of many retailers and manufacturers.

The overall market strength, customer recognition, dealer priority, promotional impact, and customer franchise that can derive from the full-line policies of such firms as General Electric are very real facets of competitive advantage. When the strategy is used too much, however, it can engender an empty management slogan devoid of meaning. Herein lies the trap: each product addition is defended completely by the argument, "We must be a full-line house."

To pinpoint the issue under consideration, reflect on product requirements in clock radios. First of all, is it necessary to produce radios to be considered a full-line appliance manufacturer? If so, is it then necessary to have a wide variety of various types and styles of radios? If so, is it necessary to have clock radios to be considered full-line? If so, must all of the following types be offered: 5-transistor single speaker set in six colors; 5-transistor dual speaker set in six colors; 5-transistor single speaker automatic shut-off and come-on in six colors; 5-transistor dual speaker automatic shut-off and come-on in six colors; 7-transistor, AM-FM band, single speaker in six colors—and so on? The tendency has been for this kind of evolution to take place under the presumed requirements and desirability of full-line competition. The number of models becomes so great, however, that it is unlikely that the market segments these products reach can be analyzed and quantified for meaningful revenue-cost calculations. Without such estimates it is impossible to arrive at an optimum assortment in product lines. Thus, the relevant questions regarding assortment decisions are obscured by the presumed complete rationale of full-line competition.

TRADING UP AND TRADING DOWN

One of the recurring problems of marketers attempting to stratify and segment markets by quality and price characteristics is the difficulty of marketing successfully products of both "high" and "low" quality in the same general class. When marketers known for marketing low-priced merchandise introduce products of higher price (and presumably higher quality), this is known as *trading up*. Conversely, marketers who introduce cheaper products than their original lines are regarded as *trading down*. Neither move is easy to assimilate without experiencing substantial imbalance between the sales of the two lines. The opposite effect tends to result, however, between trading up and trading down. When market segmentation is practiced that involves substantial trading down, a major risk is incurred in that the sales of the higher-priced line will be jeopardized. Sales increases gained by the new line are often at the expense of the older line. This result has occurred frequently in automobiles, major appliances, clothing, and jewelry, for example. The lower-priced Packard, for instance, enjoyed good market acceptance when introduced, but over a period of time the original price lines suffered continuous deterioration in market position. The sales success of newly introduced lower-priced lines can be accounted for partially by the tendency for the "quality image," market symbolism (prestige, status factors, and the like), and brand loyalty to be transferred or at least "slop over" from the old line to the new one. Product additions that do not add new business or succeed in holding old business that would otherwise be lost, but merely result in shifts of business from one product line to another, are generally unwelcome by management.

Several tactical approaches have been employed in trading down in an effort to minimize risks. Chances for success are likely to be greatest when at least several of the following conditions are present:

1. A distinctly different form accompanies the introduction of the new product and differentiates it from the older one.
2. Easily observable (for the purchaser) value differences exist between the higher- and lower-priced lines.
3. Different marketing channels, in whole or in part, are used for the sale of the new lines.
4. Brand identification clearly differentiates the products.
5. Promotional orientation accompanying the sale of the new product is distinctly different from that of previous lines.

In order to avoid possibly jeopardizing the sale of the higher-priced lines, some companies have gone so far as to disassociate the new product completely from existing lines, using different enterprises entirely to handle the two products. When this is done there is little or no opportunity for the market strength of the original product and enterprise to be of assistance in gaining consumer acceptance for the new line. This procedure is therefore regarded as an unduly limiting factor by many managements, and an excessive price to pay for compensating for the market risks incurred.

Trading up involves the opposite problem; that is, the difficulty of gaining acceptance for the substantially higher-priced new product line. There is difficulty in overcoming the market frictions of the lower-priced brand images and stereotyped corporate personality. The symbolism in markets and products is sufficiently strong to cause marketers commonly to fail in these attempts, even when new lines introduced have technological improvements. Numerous instances of this can be found in camera and watch markets, where low-priced-line marketers have been unable to penetrate the higher end of the market with any notable success. Successfully trading up to higher-priced brackets seems to require a number of intermediate moves of limited magnitude, so that over a period of time a new corporate personality emerges. Evolution seems more likely to succeed than revolution in these product-market integration attempts. A good example of trading up is Timex. Also, the conditions suggested for successful trading down are also relevant to tactical implementation of trading up. Finally, it should be noted that some marketers bring out new lines directed to substantially higher-priced markets, with the deliberate intentions of providing a "prestige line" designed to help the sale of lower-priced products through association rather than for a calculated profitable penetration of the upper levels of the market.

OVEREXTENSION OF PRODUCT-IMAGE

A final subtlety in achieving good product-market integration is the problem of disturbing a successful product that has developed a strong niche in the market with attempts to make the product-image fit another segment. Rather than add new products as psychologically oriented market segments are identified, many marketers seek access to these segments through promotional reorientation of existing products. This is sometimes thought of as "freshening" products to keep them abreast of the times, particularly when some physical change in the product accompanies the change in promotion. The danger in this policy, however, is that the product-image will be blurred in the process to the point that its once firm foundation of customer preference in the historic segment will be lost. The results can be, first, that little penetration of the new segment is achieved because the product has never been regarded as especially appropriate in the minds of buyers in the new segment, and at best is a substitute for other products psychologically more suitable; and second, the hold on the historic segment is weakened by the amalgamation of images to the point where competitors' inroads are facilitated.

For example, suppose a psychological market spectrum is identified that can be characterized at the extremes by two distinctly different purchaser profiles. At one end we have a tradition-oriented group that can be characterized as the conservative, stable, older age, middle- and lower-income working class who accept life as it is and look for "old, reliable" products. At the other end we have the "modern" group, going places, doing things, seeking the exciting life; the sophisticated white-collar and upper-income working class, oriented to the new and the different. Suppose that a marketer has a product which has gained entrenched acceptance among the former group. He has in some ways an envied position, in that a new product has great difficulty in penetrating the "traditional" market —one cannot manufacture a brand-new heirloom; only time can confer this title and image to a product. Conversely, by definition *modern* is the latest thing, and new products find fewer obstacles when directed to this segment. Should the marketer attempt to "freshen" the promotion and product-image that have so successfully held the "traditional" market, he does so at the grave risk that he may be giving up one of his most powerful sources of competitive differential advantage.

As this situation has been portrayed, it would seem to call for product-line expansion rather than adaptation of the old line to suit the newly identified segment. One of the difficult problems of product strategy is the choice between these two alternatives under dynamic conditions and circumstances. This problem, in varying forms, is observable in many companies seeking effective product-market integration.

SUMMARY

Reliance on new products for the achievement of corporate growth and profit objectives is increasing. High-growth companies place great emphasis on the development of new products, as well as on company acquisitions, as a part of their basic competitive strategy. Evidence seems to be mounting, however, that the failure rate for new products is increasing at a time when the economic penalties for failure are climbing higher. We can anticipate an even more hostile environment in the future for the launching of new products, owing, in part, to the relative increase in the youth market, the more rapid pace of market change in general, the phenomenon of more highly segmented markets, more rapid movement of products through stages of market development, the volume of new product development now taking place, and because more mature companies will exhaust opportunities in closely related fields and necessarily move into markets in which their previous experience is not as relevant.

In attempting to rationalize the process of new product development, it is noted that the effectiveness of a number of companies might be limited by having too many rather than too few developmental projects. Also, the further a project is carried through the total development process, the more difficult it is to terminate, which places a premium on decisiveness in the early stages. There is a particular need for getting a closer conjunction of market affairs and technological development.

Product policy and strategy are important means of market adjustment and should be designed to integrate corporate objectives and resources efficiently—by means of products—with markets in which these products are purchased and used. The marketer's objective is to balance cost-revenue considerations throughout the production-marketing system as a whole in arriving at a product assortment. In seeking effective product-market integration, two alternative strategies related to degree of differentiation are possible. These are a limited-line strategy or a broad-line strategy.

Four basic patterns of product diversity for an enterprise have been illustrated. These patterns are based on the degree of homogeneity or convergence of products in production and marketing. Each of the patterns is recognized as having special benefits and limitations. A preference has been shown, however, for patterns that involve more convergence than divergence.

In the variety of attempts used to achieve effective product-market integration, certain common and recurring problems in marketing enterprises are observable. The most pronounced of these are product lines that are simultaneously too broad and too narrow; product proliferation that dissipates economies of scale; excesses in product assortments attributable to importance of full-line competition; the imbalance of sales from trading up or trading down; and the weakening of product images in attempts to cover several market segments with a single product.

QUESTIONS AND PROBLEMS

1. Why is it important that a firm have a clear definition of the company business before beginning new product development?

2. What is the trend in the proportion of sales coming from new products? How has this trend been related to high growth companies and low growth companies?

3. What are the basic patterns of product diversity as outlined in this chapter?

4. "There would be very little difference in the degree of risk incurred in adding a new product that involved divergent production and divergent marketing as compared with convergent production and convergent marketing, since the failure rate for all new product introductions is high." Comment.

5. Are the terms *convergent* and *divergent* absolute or relative terms? Give examples to illustrate your reasoning.

6. "No one pattern of diversity is clearly superior to any other—it depends upon the circumstances surrounding the particular firm." Comment.

7. Discuss the concept of *product-market matching*. What is the fundamental difference between a *limited-* and *broad-line* product strategy?

8. What is the advantage in characterizing a company's business as "bulk materials handling" instead of "steam shovels"?

Chapter 11

Stages of Product-Market Development

The formulation of a product program cannot properly be completed without understanding market forces. The competitive environment in which products are sold influences potentialities of sale and the kind of marketing effort that must be used to capitalize on market opportunities.

The objective of this chapter is to introduce the concept of product life cycle as a model to assist in product-market matching and overall formulation of the marketing-mix strategy. The first section of the chapter develops the life cycle concept. Next, each stage of the cycle model is discussed in terms of the competitive conditions a marketer can expect to confront during a typical cycle. We then turn our attention to the importance of adjusting marketing-mix strategy in order to compete effectively in each stage of the cycle. The chapter concludes with a note of caution concerning the universal applicability of the life cycle model.

THE PRODUCT LIFE CYCLE CONCEPT

The purpose of product-market matching is to develop a product that satisfies a specific customer's need. As noted throughout the chapters on market opportunity assessment, customer needs are constantly changing. It logically follows that products will pass through a *cycle of perishable distinctiveness*. When a new product is introduced and accepted by a market segment it enjoys a degree of unique advantage. If the market segment has sufficient potential, it can be expected that the product will be copied by other producers.[1] As more firms market a similar product, its distinctiveness begins to perish in the eyes of customers. Thus, the initiator of the original product can be expected to lose some of the initial competitive

---

[1] Joel Dean, *Managerial Economics* (Englewood Cliffs, N.J.: Prentice-Hall, Inc., 1951), p. 410. For an interesting discussion of market share related to product life cycle, see Bernard Catry and Michel Chevalier, "Market Share Strategy and The Product Life Cycle," *Journal of Marketing,* 38 (October 1974), 29–34.

advantage. With the passage of additional time customer needs may change to an extent that the product is no longer demanded or a new product that satisfies the demand better may be introduced. Thus, we can conclude that all products will eventually die. The critical questions in product management are when and how will they die, who will better satisfy the market need, and what type of replacement product innovations will be necessary?

Marketers have identified the product life cycle which consists of well-defined stages through which a product normally passes during its competitive life. Five different stages are discerned: pioneering, market acceptance, turbulence, saturation, and obsolescence. Each stage represents a different competitive environment. Consequently, marketing effort must be adjusted to each new condition. The product life cycle is illustrated in Figure 11-1.

FIGURE 11-1
Stages of Market Development

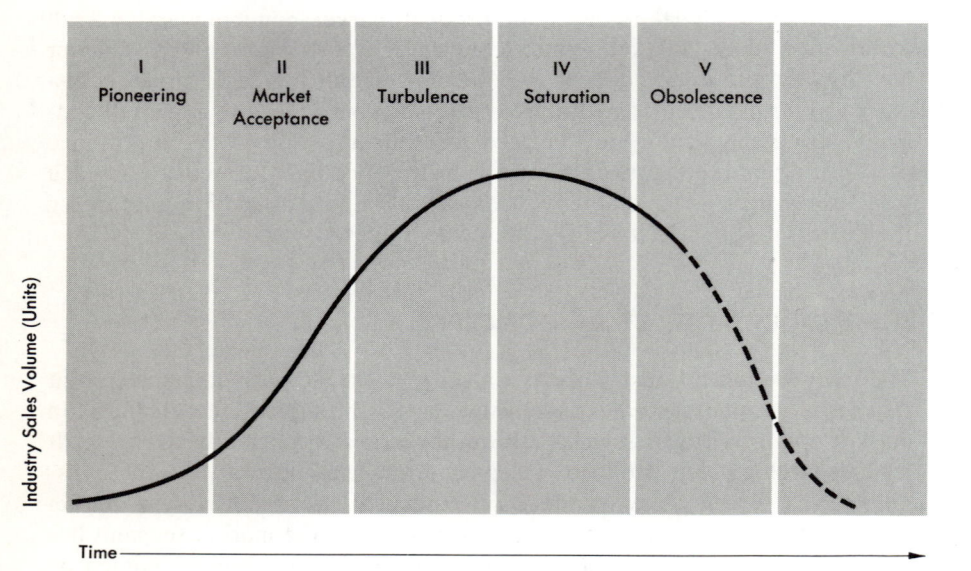

Not all products pass through each of the five stages. Moreover, there may be a great difference between how well a product is accepted in the market and how long it stays in any one stage. Some products are fads; their sales rise quickly at first and then decline almost as rapidly. Others retain small but profitable market positions for many years, claiming a rather small but durable niche in the marketplace. Although a wide variety of products have a tendency to go through the stages mentioned, these changes are more clearly discernible in consumer durable goods, such as washing machines, television sets, and refrigerators. For this reason, the following discussion is mainly concerned with such goods.

LIFE CYCLE STAGES AND COMPETITIVE CONDITIONS

The variations in competitive environment in each stage are important from the point of view of market investigation. We shall characterize the competitive environment in each stage by examining such factors as the size and character of the market, the competitive rivalry present, product changes, production and marketing costs, distribution outlets, and marketing effort. When certain characteristics are observed in an industry, the individual marketer can judge the current position of products in the various stages of market development and assess the future competitive environment more intelligently. In so doing, change can be anticipated in marketing effort that may be needed to keep the firm in a proper state of adjustment to the changing competitive environment.

PIONEERING

This is the stage in which a new class of product is introduced. A new product, in this sense, is one that generally performs an old task in a new way, or does something that was not possible before. For example, the electric refrigerator was a new class of product in that it provided for the preservation of perishable food in an entirely new way. The television set provides a service that had not been provided before its introduction. The most important characteristics of the pioneering stage are: a slow sales rise, few direct competitors, frequent changes in the product, high production and marketing costs, high prices, and marketing effort directed at primary demand. Let us examine each of these characteristics.

Slow Sales Rise

In the pioneering stage, sales generally rise slowly. The marketer of a new product must break down potential buyers' habitual purchase patterns before they can be expected to respond to a new product. For example, the sewing machine was invented long before the Singer Sewing Machine Company provided the marketing talent to gain a place for the product in the marketplace.

The market for a new product is generally concentrated among those buyers having the greatest need for the product and enough purchasing power to fulfill this need. In addition to this group there is a second market group who might be induced to purchase. They, however, feel less need or desire for the product and generally have restricted purchasing power resulting from the need to purchase other things. A third group might be considered the indifferent group. The people in this group see other ways of spending their money which are just as satisfying.

In the pioneering stage, sales are usually restricted to the "core" group, which is generally made up of higher-income purchasers. Over a period of time, the product will "filter down" to lower-income groups as it proceeds through various stages of market development.

Few Direct Competitors

When a new product manufactured by one firm exclusively is introduced, it, of course, faces no direct competition from similar products, because no similar products exist. For example, the first electric refrigerator did not face direct competition during its earliest days on the market. But it did face *indirect* competition from the ubiquitous icebox. As long as the old cold-storage unit continued to preserve food reasonably well, many potential buyers of electric refrigerators preferred to spend their money on other things. The later makers of electric refrigerators competing with Frigidaire in the pioneering stage competed for the consumer's purchasing power, and in a sense were competing indirectly with all other products.

The number of direct competitors will increase if the product gains market acceptance, but in the pioneering stage the number will be smaller than in any other, except for obsolescence. Usually the number can be counted on no more than one hand.

Frequent Product Changes

New products are usually not entirely free of technical imperfections that impair their performance. A soundly managed enterprise will make every effort to eliminate such difficulties as solutions are found for faulty performance that can prevent the product from gaining market acceptance. The firm usually will not wait for the introduction of a new model to correct these deficiencies, but will incorporate various minor improvements immediately. Even with elaborate quality control and testing devices, design and technical imperfections will often show up after a product is on the market. For this reason, frequent product modifications are not uncommon during the pioneering stage.

High Production Costs

Because of the great difficulty in forecasting demand for innovations, and the uncertainty of sales during this period, management is reluctant to make the heavy investments required in special equipment needed for efficient line-production methods. Management demands some assurance that sales will justify the expenditure. Job-shop methods using general purpose tools are more flexible, and are therefore better suited to a period of uncertain sales and frequent changes in the product. When sales are more certain and the product perfected, the initially more costly but ultimately more efficient production-line methods are usually introduced.

High Prices

Because of frequent product changes, the production methods used, and the limited quantities produced, production costs are higher during the pioneering stage than in later periods. These high costs present difficult marketing problems. Pricing is one. It is difficult to decide, for example, whether initial prices should be based on pioneering production costs or on the lower production costs anticipated after sales have increased.

High production costs also complicate decisions on the amount of advertising to use or the reliance that should be placed on personal selling, a high-cost method of cultivating the market. During this period, expenditures made to cultivate the market should be high. Yet high production costs do not leave a sufficient margin for advertising and personal selling expenditures. If the price is set high enough to absorb these expenditures, it limits the market. If the price is set to cover anticipated future production costs and large expenditures made to develop a market for the product, then generally management must plan on operating at a loss during this period. The decision to operate at a loss in anticipation of future profit is not an easy one, especially when future sales are unpredictable. Characteristically, prices will be higher in this period than in those that follow. Prices will typically show a downward movement in the advanced stages of market development, which helps to make possible the development of the mass market. You may recall the decline in television prices following its pioneering period.

High Marketing Costs

If management decides to make the necessary marketing erpenditures to alter established buying patterns, marketing costs per unit of product sold will be higher during the pioneering period than in later periods. If marketing costs are held to a ratio to sales found in a more developed market, expenditures will probably be too small to gain market acceptance for the product. Traditional marketing cost-to-sales ratios must be set aside during the pioneering stage. This is another contributing factor to the higher prices that generally prevail during this stage, in contrast to later ones.

Primary Demand Marketing Effort

The marketer's first job is to win buyers' approval of the new product type; that is, to stimulate *primary demand,* in contrast to stimulating demand for the product of a specific manufacturer, which is known as *selective demand* cultivation. Although the product may have little direct competition in this stage, it does compete indirectly with the traditional products used to provide the service or perform the task.

For example, when the first automatic washing machine was introduced by the Bendix Corporation, it competed with the older, manually controlled electric washers. Initial marketing effort stressed, therefore, the convenience of the automatic controls to the housewife. She didn't have to put her hands in hot water, and she didn't have to handle the clothes for rinsing and wringing. But after World War II a number of directly competing automatic washers were introduced, and marketing effort then emphasized the advantages of the Bendix. Bendix Corporation, for example, stressed the superiority of the tumble-action cylinder design over the competitors' agitator-type design.

In summary, the small market, the fewness of competitors, the frequent product changes, the high production and marketing costs, and the need to direct marketing effort toward primary demand all indicate why keen marketing judgment is called for in the pioneering stage. New product marketing is as complex a competitive problem as any because of pervasive uncertainty, which is reflected in the high rate of failures in new product introduction.

Characteristics of Pioneering

1. Sales rise slowly.
2. Competitors are few.
3. Sales to high-income groups (core markets).
4. Frequent product modifications.
5. Experimental production methods.
6. High production costs.
7. Product differentiation and limited lines.
8. High marketing costs.
9. Limited distribution.
10. High prices.
11. Primary demand cultivation.

MARKET ACCEPTANCE

In the second stage of market development, widespread buyer approval is secured for the product. The following are the more important characteristics of this stage: market size increases rapidly, the number of direct competitors sharply increases, efficient production methods are established, the number of distribution outlets increases, and selective demand marketing effort begins.

Rapid Increase in Market Size

In the acceptance stage of market development, sales rise rapidly, and often at an increasing rate of increase. What is sometimes called a take-off point is reached, from which industry sales turn up sharply, signifying a growth market. The product, in this stage, begins a process of filtering down from the high-income or core buyers toward the mass market of middle- and lower-income purchasers. Although in the early period of this stage upper-income groups continue to dominate total purchases, the middle-income group begins to become important. The rapid rise in sales is made possible partly because of the conjunction of factors characterizing the period, which are discussed in more detail following: softening prices, the appearance of the first major product improvements, greater product reliability, and increased competition.

Increase in Number of Direct Competitors

As the product becomes accepted in the market and a growth market seems assured, many more firms are likely to enter the market. As a result of the increase in the number of direct competitors, the first major product improvements (other than the modifications to perfect performance noted in the pioneering stages) are introduced. New producers often introduce refinements or innovations to make their own brands more attractive, and the pioneer firms are forced to follow with new models.

Continued increases in the number of competitors can be expected all the way through the period, with the total number likely to reach its highest level late in the period. Actually, the increase in the number of firms may even be characterized as an "explosion in the number of competitors." Larger firms in a hurry to enter the recognized growth market may do so by the acquisition of smaller firms; these acquisitions tend to be on extremely favorable terms to the seller (a high price-to-earnings ratio). In later stages, these same firms, under different competitive circumstances, may have difficulty in finding a buyer for the enterprise at any price, and may even be forced into bankruptcy.

Establishment of Production Methods

Changes in production methods take place. Continuing increases in sales and a more certain view of future sales encourage producers to shift from job-shop production methods to line or mass production. Risks are measurable enough to justify the large investment by management in single purpose tools and fixtures for mass production. Decrease in production costs materialize both from the more efficient production methods and the increased scale of operations.

Price Adjustments

Prices in the acceptance stage of market development typically have a generally downward trend from previous levels, or *soften,* as the term is sometimes used. This occurs as the product begins to filter down through various income groups toward the mass market. Four factors tend to account for the lower prices that usually prevail. First, the greater volume of sales produces some economies of scale. Second, fewer product modifications, with accompanying costs of shutdowns and longer production times, are being made during production runs. Third, the adoption of more efficient mass production methods (line production) enhances scale economies. Fourth, the increase in the number of firms increases competition with both a theoretical and an actual tendency toward lower prevailing levels in the price structure. If this stage is reached during an inflationary spiral in the economy, the reduction may not be so apparent, but may still materialize on a relative basis in comparison with other goods.

Scramble for Distribution Outlets

With the increase in the number of producers, more distribution outlets appear, and there is a scramble for the acquisition of outlets by these producing enterprises. The newer competitors want the product exposure necessary to establish their brands, and older producers often wish to expand distribution to increase their market share. Not all manufacturers increase their outlets, however. Those who make a full line of products and have well-established distribution organizations often limit sales of a new product to their established outlets. The rapid rise in sales, giving a profitable volume for the industry as a whole, encourages many distribution outlets to carry several brands of the same product. Manufacturers' efforts to secure more distribution outlets make it easy for the outlets to acquire new brands. Dealers, therefore, tend to adopt what can be called a multiple-lines policy in contrast to simplified lines in both prior and following stages.

Stimulation of Selective Demand Cultivation

In the pioneering stage, marketing effort emphasized the cultivation of primary demand. Now, however, with market acceptance of the product class and the increase in direct competitors, manufacturers begin to emphasize the stimulation of selective demand. Instead of promoting features and benefits of the product class, they emphasize the advantages of their own brands in comparison with competitors' brands. This does not mean that all primary demand stimulation stops, however.

The differences observed between this stage and the pioneering stage indicate the kinds of changes that must take place. In summary, the increase in sales and competitors brings about changes in products and production methods with accompanying lower costs and lower prices. The distribution outlets must be expanded, and marketing effort shifts to selective demand stimulation. Moreover, profits for the industry as a whole tend to be healthy during this period.

Impact of an Economic Recession

A final characteristic is important with respect to products in the market acceptance stage. This is the period when the product is in the best position to resist the adverse effect of a significant downturn in the general economy—a recession or depression. It is possible, with proper modifications, for market expansion to continue during this period. Whereas a product caught in the pioneering period may be killed, those in saturation will tend to rise and fall with changes in the general level of business activity because of the postponable nature of such products, and a recession may hasten the departure from the market of those entering an obsolescence stage. Modifications necessary for surviving a recession in the market acceptance stage involve adjustments in product form, price reductions (usually directly related to product adjustment) to keep the product within the prevailing level of purchasing power, and the sustaining of promotional expenditures on the product. During the depression of the 1930s, for example, electric refrigerator sales continued to rise even though sales of other kinds of appliances sharply declined. But these sales gains were made only because the marketing adjustments we have discussed were made. Manufacturers introduced very simplified standard models without deluxe features. The standard models were sold at material price reductions, and relatively intensive promotional expenditures were maintained.[2]

Characteristics of Market Acceptance

1. Sales increase at increasing rate.
2. Explosion in number of competitors.
3. First major product improvements.
4. Line-production methods.
5. High-income groups dominate purchases, but middle-income groups become important.

[2] Neil H. Borden, *Advertising In Our Economy* (Homewood, Ill.: Richard D. Irwin, Inc., 1945), p. 277.

6. Scramble for distribution outlets.
7. Dealers adopt multiple-lines policy.
8. Prices soften.
9. Profits healthy.
10. Selective demand cultivation.
11. Product capable of resisting a depression, with requisite:
    a. Product adjustments.
    b. Price adjustments.
    c. Promotion expenditures.

TURBULENCE

The stage known as the turbulence stage is so called because it represents a period of extreme competitive volatility. During this period competition is very intense, and there is a severe "shake-out" of marginal firms; only the most vigorous enterprises are capable of competing successfully. The most important characteristics of this stage are: the rate of market growth levels out; product policy changes; distribution outlets alter policies as a consequence of a profit squeeze; the number of competitors sharply decreases; and the general nature of marketing effort again shifts.

Leveling of Market Growth Rate

The first sign of a change in the stage of market development is usually seen in the volume of industry sales. Sales may continue to increase somewhat in this period, but the rate of increase typically declines. In this stage the product usually is sold to the mass market. That is, all income groups purchase, with the middle- and lower-income groups dominating. With this change in the type of buyer the motivating forces at work in purchasing change also. Price, for example, may be a much more important factor than it was in earlier stages. Likewise, changes in design of the product may be necessary to cater to the new groups of potential buyers.

Product and Service Adjustments

A number of changes take place during this period, the most important of which are: the introduction of annual models, with emphasis on styling; the handling of trade-ins; and the increased significance and complexity of product service and repair parts.

In the earlier stages, product modifications were made continuously, but now manufacturers introduce new models during each selling season. The introduction of annual models tends to be a response to the intense competition that prevails during this stage. Each manufacturer feels a more intense need to keep his product line up to date, hoping to achieve a competitive advantage through offering a distinctive product. After a time, model changes become more style and design oriented and somewhat less oriented to technical improvements, although the latter are still desired by manufacturers.

Although there may be a certain number of trade-ins in earlier periods, this period is the first in which trade-ins are frequent. The length of time the earlier products have been in service and the introduction of new models promotes an increased number of trade-ins. The proportion of total sales to previous owners of the product thus increases, and often exerts a downward pressure on prices. The effect of both price differences among competitive products and allowances made by dealers for older models is thus a twofold pressure toward a lower level of *effective* prices in the market.

Manufacturers not only introduce new models, but increasingly they tend to broaden their line of products to reach more effectively the differing segments of demand in the market.

As the product is in customer use for a longer period of time, the service and parts requirements increase. The broad-line policies of some manufacturers demand large quantities of parts, and the variety of brands handled by dealers results in parts inventories becoming increasingly more difficult to manage. Because of space requirements, labor costs, inventory carrying costs, and the added complexities of managing the greater varieties and numbers of parts, the cost of providing these services is likely to increase more than increases in revenues from them.

Dealer Margins and Profits Shrink

In this stage of market development, dealer gross margins and profits decline. The profit squeeze comes about because of pressures from both factors in the profit equation—cost and revenue. On the one hand, the effective price the dealer can obtain for the product declines. This reduction, as noted earlier, partly comes from the increasing price competition on new units and added price pressure from trade-in allowances. In addition, the introduction of annual models leads to carryovers of year-end inventories into the new model year. The sale of year-old models normally can be accomplished only with substantial price reductions, and in some cases at virtually liquidation levels. In these cases, distribution outlets are often caught in a position of being forced to reduce prices without any cost reductions. The result of all of these factors tends to be a reduction in the *effective* price level on a per unit basis over the entire selling season, and a consequent reduction in margin.

On the other hand, costs of doing business in the market have a tendency to increase as a result of the increased product services that must be provided and the increased inventories of spare parts that must be carried. The result of the two opposing forces is a cost-price-profit squeeze.

Brand Policy and Loyalty

To offset the pressure on profits, the distribution outlets try to reduce the amount of product service they provide and the number of parts they carry by reversing their earlier policies of carrying several competitive brands. Many will offer fewer brands, becoming more selective in how many manufacturers they will represent and how many products of any one manufacturer they will carry.

Partially as a consequence of dealer brand policy adjustments, institutional brand preferences among consumers strengthen during this period. When a consumer favors all or most of the products of a manufacturer's line (for example, General Electric appliances) over the lines of competing manufacturers, he is said to have an *institutional brand preference*. Thus, if he wants to buy a television set, General Electric has a preferred position because of this institutional loyalty.

In this period, institutional preference is strengthened because, as some smaller firms are forced from the market, the large manufacturers offer more assurance of good service and adequate supplies of spare parts. As dealers simplify lines it seems apparent that they will drop the products of smaller, specialized producers before they will drop those of manufacturers of complete lines of goods, such as General Electric. A consumer may, therefore, even ignore a relatively strong preference for a small manufacturer's product that is still available in the market, to gain assurance of future parts and service access, not knowing whether his preferred small manufacturer will survive. The strengthening of institutional brand preference, therefore, handicaps smaller firms while giving larger firms a competitive advantage.

Sharp Reduction in Number of Competitors

The increase in institutional brand preference, the need to provide product service and parts, the pressure to reduce prices during this stage, and the inability to get effective distribution of the product make it very difficult for the smaller firms to survive. Bigger firms with broad lines are in a much better position. Because of the breadth of their lines, they can induce distribution outlets to carry even those products that are not selling well. Many small firms go out of business during this period. The decline in the number of competitors is sudden rather than gradual. The position of the small firm thus shifts dramatically from one of strength during the acceptance stage to a struggle for survival during this stage. A small firm in the preceding stage may have been offered opportunities to sell out for forty to fifty times the amount of its annual earnings to a large firm anxious for rapid market entry during the acceptance stage; in the turbulence stage, it may have difficulty in making any reasonable sale of the business.

As this shake-out takes place, what might be called a "competition of desperation" emerges. In frantic attempts to survive, the smaller firms, rather than the dominant firms, tend to influence the basis upon which competition will be conducted. Price reductions and a bewildering assortment of promotional devices tend to accompany a "try anything" policy prior to imminent withdrawal, and the larger firms necessarily must formulate countering policies of their own.

Because this stage presents such a changed competitive environment, many changes in the character of marketing effort must occur. Only those firms that are willing and able to adjust to the new conditions can hope to survive.

Characteristics of Turbulence

1. Sales increase at decreasing rate.
2. Mass markets reached.
3. Annual model appears.
4. Product design oriented to style.
5. Trade-ins appear.
6. Parts and service requirements increase.
7. Prices soften further.
8. Dealer margins and profits shrink.
9. Dealers simplify product lines.
10. Market segmentation increases.
11. Institutional brand loyalty strengthens.
12. Great shake-out in number of competitors.
13. Competition of desperation.

SATURATION

The most important characteristic of this stage is that replacement sales dominate the total volume of industry sales. That is, the majority of sales are to purchasers who have previously purchased the product type and are now purchasing a new one. The proportion of replacement sales to sales to first-time buyers of the product type varies from product to product. For example, over 99 percent of the wired homes in the United States have radios, and practically all sales are replacement sales, or sales to homes desiring an additional radio. On the other hand, only a small fraction of wired homes have a permanently installed automatic dishwasher.

Still, it might be conceivable that, at the moment, the automatic dishwasher market is near saturation. The motivating forces at work in the desire for an automatic dishwasher, and use limitations, as well as the limits on capacity to purchase, make it unlikely that 99 percent of all wired homes will own an automatic dishwasher in the foreseeable future. For this reason the maturity of the market is measured by the ratio of replacement sales to first-time purchases of the product type. While it is difficult to determine precisely when maturity is reached, a number of characteristics dominate this stage of development.

Changes in Market Characteristics

During this period sales tend to rise and fall with changes in basic economic factors. Industries may reach this stage with either increases or decreases in sales. Some product types, such as automobiles, remain in this stage for long periods of time, with generally upward sales trends. However, this can only be done with skillful management, because the dominance of replacement sales creates conditions altogether different from those experienced in the previous stages.

For example, sales during this period are very sensitive to changes in business conditions. You will recall from our discussion in Chapter 5 that ability to postpone purchase in the durable goods field makes such goods much more sensitive to changes in business conditions. Since the consumer already has one unit of the product, he may postpone purchasing a replacement if his purchasing power is restricted in any way. He may decide to get by with his old refrigerator, power lawn mower, air conditioner, or television set in order to be sure he can meet pressing financial demands. The strategies of product modification, price reduction, and intensive marketing used in the acceptance stage to offset the impact of a recession effectively are not nearly so reliable in this stage.

First-time purchasers in the market are few, and reflect basic economic factors. The actual number may depend on such factors as the rates of marriages, births, and new housing starts. Chapter 5 showed that some of these factors change relatively slowly. Offsetting this factor in some cases is the ability of the marketer to promote the idea that more than one unit should be purchased, such as is now reflected in television, radios, and the "two-car family."

Frequency of Product Changes

Even during favorable business conditions, consumers have to be persuaded to replace old products. During these times they are more meticulous, or "choosey," in what they demand. As discussed in Chapters 6 and 7, the self-images that prevail in the marketplace are many and varied, and products must be adjusted if a satisfactory product-image is to be available. Since many consumers are quite content with their old products, an inducement to purchase requires the offering of a product that very closely satisfies the buyer's self-image. When a company offers many different varieties of the same product to cater to the many self-images in the market, it is said to be following a *segmentation strategy*. This stage is characterized not only by highly segmented markets, but also by a rather universal adoption of annual models to induce replacement purchase. This strategy is evident in such saturated markets as those for automobiles, television sets, refrigerators, and radios. Many different product varieties are produced, increasing the unit cost of production, unless engineering inventiveness is sufficient to keep costs low.

Necessity for Competitive Costs

It is more uncertain that a company can survive during this stage if its cost structure is not competitive. During pioneering and growth, firms with a somewhat higher cost structure could operate successfully because of the strength of the market. During the turbulent stage many of the higher-cost firms were weeded out, but now a comparable cost structure is almost a condition of any competition at all. Where fixed costs are a large part of total costs, such that significant economies of scale are present, there is inevitably a competition of the relatively few.

Changes in Distribution Outlets

With the need for a comparable cost structure also comes the need for distribution strength. Sales volume depends heavily on the strength of the distribution outlets handling a firm's products. During the pioneering and acceptance stages, manufacturers could obtain relatively good results in spite of a weak organization of distribution outlets. But in the mature period, having enough carefully selected, properly located, and sufficiently well-trained distribution outlets becomes almost indispensable to successful competition. It is generally conceded that an important part of Chevrolet's leadership in the auto industry is due to the superior size and strength of its dealerships.

The system of distribution outlets used may be a manufacturer's most prized asset. Related to this strength is the proportion of business the manufacturer accounts for in the dealer's total sales volume. If the manufacturer represents a small fraction of the dealer's total sales, he cannot normally expect the vigorous support that is likely to be present when large proportions are involved. This factor again tends to benefit the larger, more broadly based company handling full lines, and is a limiting factor confronting the smaller more specialized producing enterprise. If, then, the product normally moves through exclusively franchised dealerships, such as is characteristic in automobiles, the number and size of the dealership organization is important. If the product moves through outlets shared by more than one manufacturer, the proportion of the dealer's business accounted for by the single manufacturer is of special importance during this period.

It becomes difficult to induce replacement sales, and since the market for first-time users may be small, some manufacturers may seek product exposure in as many different kinds of outlets as possible. A departure from using traditional types of distribution outlets, and experimentation with different kinds of channels, may be attempted for this purpose. Television sets, for example, are now sold in channels broadened considerably from traditional outlets such as appliance stores and department stores.

Physical Distribution Complexity and Cost

During this stage the physical distribution aspects of marketing become especially complex and are often a high-cost component in marketing expenditures by manufacturers. This cost and complexity derives from the long period of product usage, the broad product lines directed toward highly segmented markets, the prevailing annual model practice, the large number of trade-ins, and the broadened distribution base of varied types of outlets. The physical distribution requirements for parts and products thereby become very sizable and costly, and the proper analysis of these requirements often holds significant potential economies for particular firms. In previous stages, the physical distribution aspect was not as significant in the total marketing effort. Not only is it a more substantial factor in this stage, but with the added necessity for competitive cost structures, its efficient management is virtually a paramount concern.

Stabilization of Number of Competitors and Erection of Entry Barriers

Market entry is now much more difficult than it was in the earlier stages. Established firms (now usually large) have already achieved the large sales volume and economies of scale that make low unit costs possible, whereas new entrants are not likely to achieve sufficient sales volume in a mature market to give them similar low costs. Other barriers are preferences for, and loyalties to, established brands; the difficulties in securing an efficient system of distribution outlets; the variety of products needed to provide a complete line; and the large initial investment required to match the production and marketing facilities of established firms. Consequently, few firms will enter a saturated or mature market.

The necessity for a reasonably competitive cost structure among rivals causes the departure of some firms from the industry during this stage, although it is marked by relative stability. The first two stages saw an increase in the number of firms, the third a rapid decline. Now for the first time, the number begins to stabilize. Few firms enter or leave the market.

The mature stage is a most difficult period in which to compete.

Characteristics of Saturation

1. Trade-ins dominate total market.
2. Sales rise and fall with basic economic forces.
3. Number of competitors stabilizes.
4. Markets highly segmented.
5. Annual model characteristic.
6. Competitive cost structure—a condition of survival.
7. Dealer strength critical.
8. Logistics complex and costly.
9. High entry barriers.

OBSOLESCENCE

In this period, innovations from competing industries make the product obsolete, and the market declines. There are many examples of products that have reached the obsolescence stage—for instance, horse-drawn carriages, Gramophones, coal stokers for household furnaces, and gaslights for indoor and outdoor lighting. As these products entered this stage, not all producers withdrew; some entered new business with different products, and some switched over to the innovations which had displaced their products.

An established product may also become obsolete as a result of change in consumers' purchase habits, attitudes, and values.

Market and Product Changes

There is an absolute drop in industry sales, and even more important, the decline will be gradual or abrupt, depending upon the speed with which the new substitute product goes through the earlier stages of market development. Generally, when obsolescence is caused by a change in consumers' habits, the change is more gradual.

When we discussed the pioneering stage we identified three groups of consumers on the basis of their need and desire for the product. During the obsolescence stage the decline begins among the third group—those who are somewhat indifferent. Successive erosions occur until only a small core of people who need and desire the product remains as customers. As these products gravitate back toward core markets, product lines tend to be greatly simplified from the very broad varieties that characterized earlier periods. Manufacturers rely more on product differentiation for capturing what little market remains than they do on broad product lines geared to different market segments.

Return to Cultivation of Primary Demand and Limited Market Exposure

Now again, as in the pioneering stage, the industry faces primarily indirect competition, although for a different reason, and marketing effort tends to return to the stimulation of primary demand in an effort to slow down the decline in the size of the market. However, companies have a tendency to spend less because of the decline in market opportunity. Industry-wide expenditures decline, and the expenditures of individual firms also decrease, partly because a smaller proportion of the sales dollar might be allocated to marketing and partly because even at the same allocation per sales dollar, lower sales mean lower expenditures.

The decline in marketing expenditures is accompanied by the use of more selective methods. In advertising, for example, narrower media are used, in contrast to the mass market media used in earlier stages. Major effort is directed toward the core market. Also, product exposure in the distribution network is not as important as previously, for the product tends to become a specialty good for the remaining core buyers, for which they can be expected to incur some inconvenience in purchasing. This tendency is a parallel movement, with the shift toward more selective promotional media and away from mass media.

Price Adjustments

Price also is used to preserve market position during this stage, and often follows a pattern of decline, then stabilization, and finally some upward movement. When a product moves into the obsolescence stage, producers attempt to maintain their sales by price concessions. Such price reductions are typically short-term defensive moves by which producers of the obsolete product hope to buy time to make the necessary technological changes in their product, to provide a more lasting solution to their problems.

Sometimes, however, price reductions are difficult to make. As sales decrease, per unit costs of production and marketing may increase, and a vicious circle may develop in which higher costs, if they result in higher prices, result in a further decline in sales. In the latter stages of obsolescence, however, demand may become more inelastic. This means that lowering prices becomes less effective in maintaining sales, or that firms could raise prices and pass on increases in cost to the consumer without sales decreasing. The best adjustment during this stage might call for either upward or downward price revisions, depending upon the consumers' reaction to the price change.

Decline in Number of Competitors

As total sales in the industry fall, the number of producers competing dwindles. It is possible that all firms might withdraw and the product no longer be produced regularly; but more commonly a sufficient market remains to enable a very small number of firms, or even only one, to continue operations profitably. There is a small demand even for such an obsolete product as gaslights, bought by those who value the charm and nostalgia associated with such lighting. For the surviving firms, profit opportunities can be quite attractive in the later phase of the period due to inelastic demand, few competitors, curtailments in market exposure that are possible, and the lack of need for broad product lines—assuming, of course, that sound management characterizes the enterprise. The surviving companies are often smaller specialized firms, because the limited market that exists is not attractive to the larger, more broadly based enterprises.

When this stage is reached, it is necessary for some companies to seek new products or make technological improvements in the old products, to slow down the continuous market decline. Unfortunately, many companies simply attempt to hold on by trying different marketing tactics until they are forced out of business.

Characteristics of Obsolescence

1. Sales declines permanent.
2. Number of firms declines.
3. Products gravitate back to core markets.
4. Products offerings narrow.
5. Prices soften, then stabilize, then increase.
6. Market exposure not as important.
7. Primary demand cultivation returns.
8. Profit opportunities can be good in late phase of stage.
9. Survivors tend to be specialists.

OPPORTUNITIES AND NEED FOR CHANGING MARKETING STRATEGIES FROM TIME TO TIME

Because markets, technology, and competition are dynamic, the means employed to achieve effective market penetration require adjustment from time to time. Flexibility that allows shifts in emphasis is desirable, and even basic changes in marketing strategy may be called for. The marketer whose

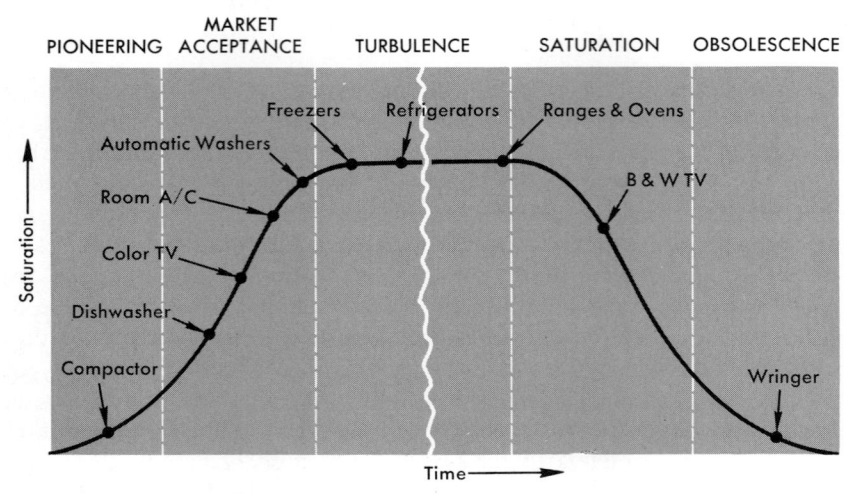

FIGURE 11-2
Life Cycle Stages of Various Products

[Figure: Product life cycle curve showing Saturation (y-axis) vs. Time (x-axis) across stages PIONEERING, MARKET ACCEPTANCE, TURBULENCE, SATURATION, OBSOLESCENCE. Products labeled along the curve: Compactor, Dishwasher, Color TV, Room A/C, Automatic Washers, Freezers, Refrigerators, Ranges & Ovens, B & W TV, Wringer.]

Source: John E. Smallwood, "The Product Life Cycle: A Key to Strategic Marketing Planning," p. 30, *MSU Business Topics,* Winter, 1973. Reprinted by permission of the publisher, Division of Research, Graduate School of Business Administration, Michigan State University.

strategic and tactical patterns are always predictable has lost something of value in the area of "competitive gamesmanship." Shifts in the scope of the product line to a broader or narrower base and related marketing-mix adjustments are necessary in both countering competitors' actions and in positioning products more effectively in the spectrum of varying customer demands.

From the viewpoint of overall product line management, the diversified firm will be engaged simultaneously in multiple product life cycles.[3] Figure 11-2 illustrates the characterization of selected household appliances. The overall process of product-market matching requires that all products which constitute a firm's line be positioned on a relative product life cycle scale for purposes of strategy formulation and cash flow management. The successful multiproduct firm must retain a degree of balance among all products with respect to their relative product life cycle position. The financial resources necessary for effective market competition vary greatly between different product life cycle stages. Likewise, a substantial risk differential exists between the different stages. The key to effective

[3] John E. Smallwood, "The Product Life Cycle: A Key to Strategic Market Planning," *MSU Business Topics* (Winter 1973), pp. 29–35.

growth is to maintain a balanced portfolio of products with respect to life cycle position.

The potentialities of varying market plans through time can be demonstrated by the actions of one of the largest radio marketers some years ago. The marketing manager responsible analyzed the complex and seemingly confused market for table radios. Competitors' lines had proliferated, as had his own, and extremely broad offerings were available to fulfill almost any specific demand. Particular. attention was paid in the analysis to volume of sales by price lines and the offerings available at these price breaks. A large peak in the purchase occurred at $49.95. A wide variety of 6- and 7-transistor radios were available at this price.

In analyzing sales trends it was seen that a definite shift had occurred favoring large numbers of transistors, particularly the 8-transistor radio, the cheapest of which at that time was about $72.50. In a study of customer preferences, the 8-transistor set appeared as a strongly preferred model by purchasers buying medium- and large-size table models. The marketing manager concluded after putting all parts of the analysis together that an 8-transistor radio that could sell for $49.95 would be extremely successful. Existing costs of manufacturing and marketing were such that this price target seemed impossible to achieve with existing models. The newly designed radio could meet cost requirements only with substantially more volume than any set then in the line had achieved. The marketing manager decided to withdraw all models within reasonable price limits on either side of the price and cluster all production on this single model.

The volume commitment given to manufacturing made possible specialized production methods and tools that increased economies of scale. The result of these actions was that this radio quickly became the largest-selling model in the entire industry. The demand converged on this price from both directions. Buyers who would normally have preferred to buy a radio in the $39 to $45 brackets were traded up because of the very superior value they could receive for just a few dollars more. Buyers previously above this price level also converged on this price because the higher-priced goods did not represent nearly as good a value, and any minor preferences in product features in other sets were not important enough in the light of the higher prices.

Rather quickly, the industry retaliated against this bold move to achieve a better competitive position by adopting the same price. As this happened, the marketing manager made a second strategy shift. He took the same chassis that was on the $49.95 model, removed one or two features, put on a cheaper cabinet, and introduced the set at $44.95. He also added several features to the basic chassis, put it in a more expensive cabinet, and sold it for $54.95. This enabled him to "bracket" competition and make available more variety as competition had narrowed offerings to achieve cost economies to compete with the first move. The second move resulted in the holding of the improved market position gained with the first change.

This illustration is not intended as a general solution to problems of product-market integration. It is given to demonstrate the value and oftentimes the necessity of varying basic approaches or emphases. The example also illustrates that one approach is not always better than another. There is not always one "best way."

A final point of product life cycle dynamics concerns critical decision points that management must not neglect in product market matching. Two basic decision points are fundamental to planning the degree of desired involvement in the life cycle. The first point is the decision whether or not to enter a product into the pioneering stage of market penetration.[4] As noted in Chapter 10, the longer product development projects continue, the more costly they are to terminate. Management must be decisive concerning the introduction of a product. It is far less expensive to kill a product project earlier than to proceed with an attempt to gain a market foothold in the pioneering stage, and then fail.

The second point of critical decision occurs at a point in the life cycle near the end of the turbulence stage or the early period of the saturation stage. The second critical decision concerns potential market exit of a firm based upon its appraisal of the odds of product-life regeneration extension or ultimate decline. The point of decision is typically characterized by sales increasing at a decreasing rate and by a stabilization or slight decline in unit profitability as a result of competitive conditions. At this point, management must make an appraisal of the product's future potential. This second critical point in the life cycle is illustrated in Figure 11-3.

If product innovations can be effected that will stimulate or regenerate growth, then the decision may be to reinvest in aspects of product development. Scotch Brand tape represents a perfect example of regeneration of a product by virtue of new use and new package development.

In other cases, the product may be such that the mature stage of market life may extend over a number of years. In such cases, the product may continue to fill customer needs until replaced by a major innovation or technological change. If the prospects for extension are encouraging, management may decide to make appropriate marketing mix adjustments to stick it out for the long run.

However, a third possibility exists that the product may be rapidly moving toward obsolescence. If this is the prediction of management, then

---

[4] The decision to "kill" a product prior to introduction is a difficult decision since a great deal of cost has been expended with no revenue return. The critical nature of this decision is more fully elaborated in Chapter 12, pp. 265–66.

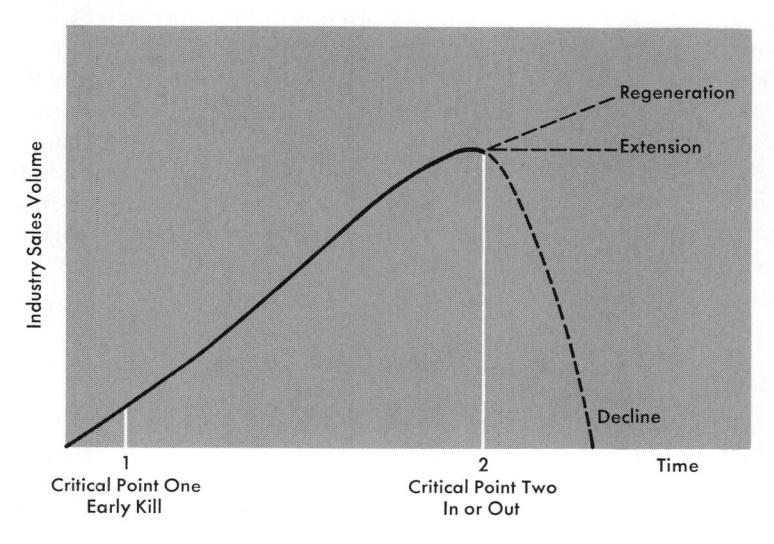

FIGURE 11-3
Critical Product Life Cycle Decision Points

[Graph showing Industry Sales Volume vs Time, with a curve rising to a peak at Critical Point Two, then branching into Regeneration, Extension, and Decline. Critical Point One (Early Kill) is marked on the rising portion; Critical Point Two (In or Out) is at the peak.]

a strategy of planned exit may be the most profitable and rewarding course of action. Exit by design rather than as a forced result of competition or desperation may not only protect against losses, but under selected conditions a properly executed exit strategy can be profitable.

The specifics of critical decision points will vary depending on product and competitive characteristics. Management should realize that the two critical points come at difficult times for "kill" decisions in the product life cycle. The initial point of potential kill comes at a time when development momentum is pushing for all-out introduction. The second point is characterized by a spirit of optimism. Sales are good, earning ratios are adequate; why pull out? At each point the marketer can be expected to face substantial resistance to an exit strategy. However, each point is sufficiently ahead of the potential crises to permit management by objectives rather than by desperation.

SOME LIMITATIONS AND BENEFITS OF THE PRODUCT LIFE CYCLE CONCEPT

The product life cycle is a concept and not by any means a pattern that will be followed by all products. As noted earlier, not all products pass through each of the five stages. In addition, the time duration that a given product stays in a specific stage will vary extensively between products. Finally, a manager should understand that the characteristics of competition associated with each stage of the product life cycle will also vary extensively between markets and industries, and between products.

The value of the product life cycle concept for the marketer is that it provides a planning framework to guide product management. The characteristics of competition associated with life cycle stages are sufficiently delineated to provide a foundation for formulating marketing mix strategy. Likewise, the life cycle provides a perspective to help structure the relative cost-benefit associated with critical decision points in product management. In total, the product life cycle concept is a useful tool for marketers, providing its inherent limitations are clearly understood.

SUMMARY

Most new products pass through a cycle of perishable distinctiveness. Beginning with its introduction and ending with its displacement, the product goes through rather well-defined stages of market development. Successive stages—pioneering, acceptance, turbulence, saturation, obsolescence—can be discerned, each with different competitive characteristics. The marketer, therefore, faces different problems in each stage, and must carefully adjust his strategy to meet each problem in turn.

We have seen how the stage of market development that a product is in affects product strategy, pricing, type of demand stimulation, distribution outlets, services, and production methods. Firms are in a less risky position when the product line as a whole has items spread through the various stages rather than clustered in one area. Marketing effort, however, must be geared to the specific requirements of individual products and competitive conditions faced by each. In view of the dynamics of the total competitive environment, variations in product strategy are an important part of "competitive gamesmanship." Profitable product management presumes precision in market measurement, cost analysis, careful planning, and competitive resourcefulness.

QUESTIONS AND PROBLEMS

1. Discuss the concept of *perishable distinctiveness* pertaining to products.

2. Do all products go through the *life cycle?* Do all products that pass through the cycle do so at the same speed? What would be the influencing factors?

3. Why do experimental, or job-shop, production methods tend to predominate during the pioneering stage of market development?

4. At what stage is the great shake-out in the number of competing firms likely to come? Why? What kind of firms are these likely to be?

5. "Profits are likely to decline before market size declines." Can you provide any plausible reasoning to support this statement?

6. "It is irrational for manufacturers and dealers to have limited product lines at one time, broader lines later, and then again narrow lines. Such variations only add to cost, and thereby limit profits." Comment.

7. What benefits can a marketing manager derive from being familiar with the various stages of market development?

8. What are the major limitations of the product life cycle concept?

Chapter 12

Framework for Product Planning

Thus far, it has been established that the composition of the product line ideally should: (1) derive from a business rationale that incorporates a pattern of product diversity; (2) result in effective matching of products with market opportunities; (3) accommodate different stages of competitive rivalry across the product life cycle; and (4) adjust over time. This chapter adds to and completes the treatment of product adjustment by presenting a process to guide product planning. A six-stage framework is presented and discussed.

The most successful product development programs are characterized by a close relation to principal corporate strengths and long-range company objectives. To achieve such results requires carefully formulated plans. It is common, however, for managers to presume that nothing need be done before proceeding with the search for profitable new diversification opportunities. When this type of approach is taken to diversification, available products, companies, or new fields are brought to the attention of management, and each is examined individually for its suitability. The decision-making process takes place on a diffused basis and without coordinated planning. While such an approach can be successful, it is not likely to be as productive as selective exploration of opportunities in light of the special character and problems of the particular enterprise. The following steps are regarded as constituting the basic elements of product planning:

1. A clear definition of objectives.
2. An analysis of the diversification situation in the light of present operations.
3. An audit of the tangible and intangible corporate resources to be capitalized on in diversification.
4. Establishment of specific criteria for new products in line with the three preceding points.

5. A comprehensive search for candidate products and areas and their evaluation against the criteria.
6. Choice of the means of market entry; that is, internal development, purchase of patent rights, merger, or company acquisition.
7. Careful implementation to ensure good product-market integration.
8. Prudent organizational planning for integrating the added product or enterprise into the existing operations of the firm.

The concept of *new product development* is used to connote something more fundamental than increases in sizes, models, colors, or qualities of existing products. Changes of this type are, as noted in Chapter 10, regarded as "tactical" adjustments in the product line. Planning for strategic diversification involves programming for the addition of entirely different products than those already offered.[1]

The planning framework for new product development and introduction is a six-stage process as presented in Figure 12-1. Each item appearing on Figure 12-1 is not discussed in the text since the items either require no elaboration or are treated elsewhere. The following treatment is therefore selective. The reader is urged to study Figure 12-1 in some detail so as to become familiar with the overall content.

STAGE I—CORPORATE RESEARCH

The underlying philosophy of Stage I builds on a goal-directed effort, with the careful setting of objectives and reasonable analysis of the prevailing competitive circumstance. It is an attempt to build on the existing basis for differential advantage or competitive strengths of the enterprise. Perhaps the most important point is the definition of the company business. Such a definition, if practical, provides a sense of direction for the company's technical efforts and tends to strengthen its overall posture in a problem-solving sense. The proper definition also helps to identify potential competitors and to clarify the nature of the total market opportunity.

The meaning of the above statement can be clarified with an example. One of the largest chemical companies in Great Britain has a major division which is the largest ammonia-producing enterprise in the country. If the division's business is defined as the ammonia business, then its competitors can be counted approximately on the fingers of one hand. As a competitor in the ammonia business the market offers that must be made to

---
[1] Strategic diversification is discussed in Chapters 4 and 19.

FIGURE 12-1
The Flow of New Product Development and Introduction

Phase	STAGE I CORPORATE RESEARCH	Kill Point
1.	Establishment of corporate objectives	
2.	Continuous surveillance of "marketing situation"	
3.	Analysis of corporate strengths and resources	
4.	Characterization of "the business of the corporation"	
5.	Specifications of criteria for new-product fields	
6.	Search for "pool of product ideas"	
7.	Screening, selection and preliminary validation of new-product idea	

PROJECT AUTHORIZATION — Kill Point

Phase	STAGE II FEASIBILITY RESEARCH	
1.	Experimental technical research a. Establishment of performance specifications b. Design studies of basic technical alternatives c. Feasibility of manufacturing d. Estimate of development time and costs	
2.	Market research a. Characteristics of market, its size and trends b. Nature of competition c. Specifications of product features to meet market requirements d. Strategy of product placement on form price–quality and psychological variables	
3.	Analysis and integration of findings a. Time b. Costs c. Manpower d. Commercial potentialities	

FIRST MANAGEMENT REVIEW
DEVELOPMENT PROJECT AUTHORIZATION — Kill Point

Phase	STAGE III DEVELOPMENT	
1.	Technical development a. Leading to product prototype b. Laboratory and use testing c. Preliminary design finalization	
2.	Production costing and planning a. Materials b. Labor c. Equipment d. Space	
3.	Market forecasting a. Demand analysis b. Cost analysis c. Price analysis	
4.	Marketing mix plans	
5.	Break-even analysis	

COMPREHENSIVE MANAGEMENT REVIEW
COST–PRICE–VOLUME–PROFIT ANALYSIS — Kill Point

Phase	STAGE IV TEST MARKETING	STAGE V MARKET INTRODUCTION	STAGE VI COMMERCIALIZATION
1.	Planning a. Selection of geographic area and accounts b. Complete schedules and budgets c. Establishment of standards to judge test performance	Buildup a. Production buildup b. Preliminary announcement to trade and sales force c. New-product program introduced to all sales personnel d. Training of salesmen, branches and dealers e. Distribution of product line to outlets f. Public showing and exhibits g. Distribution of promotional materials and advertising preprints h. Initial advertising and publicity	Program absorbed by established organization and operating system as a going enterprise
2.	Experimental production for market test	Launch a. First calls b. Filling of initial orders c. Field reports and information feedback	
3.	Final production planning	Follow-up and review a. Insure internal communication b. Prompt correction of "bugs" c. Measurement aginst controls	
4.	Execution of market test		
5.	Analysis and review a. Product modifications b. Package modifications c. Marketing modifications d. Price modifications e. General performance of test against forecasts and standards		
6.	Final plans for launch with gudgets and fixing of responsibilities		

FINAL MANAGEMENT—DECISION TO LAUNCH Kill Point

THE GO/NO-GO DECISION

249

meet the requirements of effective competition are reasonably straightforward. However, by far the largest proportion of the firm's ammonia production goes into fertilizer. The majority of the output is used in the division's own brand of fertilizer. If the division is characterized as being in the fertilizer business, then it has an altogether different set of competitors.

As a fertilizer producer an indirect group of competitors must be considered in new product development. For instance, if a farmer desires to raise the milk yield from his cow herd, he can do it either by fertilizing the pasture lands to increase grazing quality or by using feed supplements. Since both types of products are sold through common farm supply dealers, this has significant implications for the kind of market offers that must be made, including the types of sales personnel and their job definitions.

Finally, the division could conceive of itself as essentially in the business of increasing agricultural productivity through chemistry. In this event, its product line would quite likely require broadening to include chemically related agricultural inputs, such as fungicides, pesticides, and other chemical products. This definition would again materially alter the competitors, both direct and indirect, which the division would face.

The point of the above example is that the needs of the corporation will be quite different depending upon the selected business definition. Of particular relevance to our purposes here is that the definition has a major and direct bearing on the nature of the technical research effort to be undertaken by the division.

DEFINITION OF OBJECTIVES

A well-defined set of corporate objectives is the proper starting point for product development. Objectives, however, must be cast in a meaningful way. A large electric motor manufacturer insists, for example, that all new products should serve to increase sales of its basic line of fractional and small integral horsepower motors. But even this kind of objective fails to express specific needs. For example, the basic objective may be to even out cyclical demand or to make up for obsolescence of existing products. The underlying motivation must be crystallized and made explicit if it is to influence product decisions. Figure 12-2 provides a list of "reasons" for diversification that indicates how broad the range of motives can be.

THE SITUATIONAL ANALYSIS

Once objectives have been determined, they must be appraised against the specific circumstances surrounding the diversification problem. The

FIGURE 12-2
Why Companies Diversify

A. *Survival*
1. *To offset a declining or vanishing market*—A traditional example of this was Studebaker's move into the automobile field from its previous carriage manufacturing business.
2. *To compensate for technological obsolescence*—With the advance of technology, a producer of a part for battery sets found it necessary to manufacture electric radio sets in order to stay in business.
3. *To offset obsolete facilities*—Entering the industrial lubricants field was the response of a company engaged in filtering operations, when the methods of refining oil changed, making filtering plants obsolete.
4. *To offset declining profit margins*—Meat packers, for example, have made every effort to develop by-products in order to enhance profit margins.
5. *To offset an unfavorable geographic location brought about by changing economic factors*—Some northern nonintegrated[2] paper mills have found it necessary to add specialty paper lines and convert their operations in order to meet the competition of southern integrated rivals.

B. *Stability*
1. *To eliminate or offset seasonal slumps*—A mechanical toy producer, motivated by a desire to offset a seasonal slump, began making electric fans.
2. *To offset cyclical fluctuations*—"The average machine tool builder has over a period of years investigated and actually undertaken diversification projects, with the object of flattening out the peaks and valleys in the demand for regular machine tool products," says the president of a large machine tool company.
3. *To maintain employment of the labor force*—In 1943, when a substantial government parachute order was canceled with a request "to please stand by," one firm began the production of shower curtains, draperies, and negligees in order to maintain employment of 3,500 people.
4. *To provide balance between high-margin and low-margin products*—Housewares and soft goods have been added by supermarkets in part to achieve higher margins alongside low-margin food products.
5. *To provide balance between old and new products*—A food

---

[2] Here, *nonintegrated* means that pulp making and paper making are separate operations; in *integrated* mills they are one continuous process.

products manufacturer diversifies so that no product gets more than a third of company sales.
6. *To maintain market share*—A stove company, known for a low-price promotional line, purchased a company making a larger medium-price stove in order to capture a strategic share of the stove market.
7. *To maintain an assured source of supply*—Some companies have combined diversification with integration, aiming at independence from outside suppliers.

C. **Productive Utilization of Resources**
1. *To utilize waste or by-products*—A paper company added fiber-board to its line in order to make use of waste screenings and tailings.
2. *To maintain balance in vertical integration*—A canning company which had integrated backwards to manufacture cans for its own use decided to sell cans produced in excess of its requirements.
3. *To make use of basic raw material*—This is an important objective, for example, for rubber companies, who have become engaged in producing a wide variety of products from rubber.
4. *To utilize excess productive capacity*—In one instance the manufacturer of plastic light fixtures was able to convert idle equipment to the production of plastic dishes.
5. *To make use of product innovations from internal technical research*—The research department of a petroleum company developed a medicinal oil for its own use, then began to manufacture it commercially.
6. *To capitalize on distinctive know-how*—A company manufacturing hearing aids found its production skills adaptable to interoffice communication systems and subsequently diversified along these lines.

need for situational analysis, as well as what it involves, is demonstrated in the following illustration.

Company X decided it would be necessary to diversify to offset the serious inroads made by foreign competition. Preliminary analysis indicated that the market for the company's product consisted predominantly of young single men from the lower-income groups, without college education, and ranging in age from 17 to 23. One of the important objectives established for diversification was to utilize an increasing amount of excess productive capacity.

When the problem was studied in greater detail, it became evident that the sales decline in part resulted from the fact that a number of potential customers had diminished. This market shrinkage was primarily a natural consequence of the low birth rate of the 1930s. A forecast of sales for several years in advance showed that rather sizable sales increases could be expected as a larger number of potential customers became available from countering trends. Moreover, it was apparent that opportunities for additional sales were good as a result of slight but important modifications in the marketing program to counter foreign competitors. In view of this situation analysis, a substantially smaller percentage of productive capacity was committed to diversification than had initially been anticipated. The company was able to achieve its overall objectives with a limited diversification program tailored to the actual situation.

The principal purpose of the situation analysis is to quantify objectives so that specific goals can be established—for example, to utilize a given percentage of plant capacity; to consume a given quantity of waste product; or to establish specific economic characteristics for product additions.

THE RESOURCE APPRAISAL

Having carefully defined corporate objectives and having fully analyzed the situation surrounding the need for diversification, it is important to appraise in detail the tangible and intangible corporate assets or resources that can be capitalized on to greater advantage in entering new fields. The resource appraisal is designed to place the enterprise in the most favorable position to compete in the new field by most effectively using resources and distinctive competence. The principal diversification strengths (and limitations) of the several operating departments within the company should be evaluated individually and collectively, and compared to competition.

The appraisal should begin with an analysis of tangible factors. Examples of resources to be appraised are the financial strength, the nature of the manufacturing process, the type and quality of machinery and equipment used, the number and type of research personnel and facilities, the size and character of the marketing organization, and the nature and type of available staff services. Such tangible resources are usually much easier to appraise than are their intangible counterparts.

Appraisal of intangible resources involves value judgments that are largely subjective and open to controversy. Oftentimes, however, the intangible strengths of the enterprise are the most important competitive strengths to be used for diversification. Important intangible considerations include the quality of engineering skills, the resourcefulness of technical research personnel, the flexibility or adaptability of management, the interests of management members, the recognizable attributes by which the firm is known in the trade, and any unusual know-how or competence that provides distinctiveness and competitive superiority for the enterprise. The following example illustrates the importance of intangibles.

A large watch manufacturer chose for diversification a line of ladies' compacts that initially appeared ideally suited to the company's operations. The firm was known for the quality of its product, had a well-recognized brand name, and was the most preferred line among jewelers. Ladies' compacts, however, proved to be out of character with the distinctive know-how of the company. The frequent and substantial markdowns and the importance of style, which called for frequent design changes, proved to be incompatible with the firm's traditional operations. On the other hand, the company's long experience in the manufacture of high-quality precision watches had provided almost unique competency in the field of miniaturization. Even though the company had no previous experience in the industrial market, later events indicated that an unusual opportunity for successful diversification existed in the field of miniaturized scientific precision instruments.

Diversification appears most likely to be successful when it capitalizes on the unique know-how or special qualities that provide the firm with its basic strength and effectiveness. Final judgment should consider seriously the human capabilities that are available to support moves into new fields.

PRODUCT CRITERIA

The fourth step in corporate research involves establishing explicit criteria or specifications for products. The purpose is to set forth in detail the characteristics of an ideal opportunity. These specifications are then used to help direct the search and evaluation of product candidates.

The criteria can be classified as those items essential and those desirable. The essential characteristics derive from the primary strategic objectives that were established for diversification. These are criteria which must be met if the diversification is to accomplish the ends that were originally intended. The desirable characteristics of the ideal addition result from the analysis of the particular situation faced by the company.

For example, the actual criteria established for a manufacturer of internal-combustion engine equipment are illustrated in Figure 12-3.

Obviously, no individual product candidate could be expected to meet all the criteria. Nevertheless, once relative importance has been attached to the individual characteristics, a meaningful basis exists for evaluating alternatives.

SEARCH AND SELECTION

The search for products is a funneling process that starts off with many new product ideas and then narrows the field successively. The initial screening process is designed to eliminate product areas that do not com-

FIGURE 12-3
Characteristics of the Ideal Diversification Opportunity

Essential Characteristics

Must utilize existing excess production capacity.
Must require a minimum additional investment in production tools and equipment.
Must involve a minimum incremental investment for sales and distribution.

Desirable Characteristics

Would be harmonious with the present well-known brand name.
Would be similar to the internal-combustion engine in purchase and performance requirements.
Would reach a broader market than now served.
Would support the sale of present products.
Would use the existing service organization.
Would complement rather than magnify the existing seasonal sales pattern.
Would involve medium-precision manufacturing.
Would involve high value added by manufacture.
Would provide a sound basis for further diversification.

pare favorably, on the basis of readily distinguishable factors, with the essential and desirable characteristics. Thus, the products meeting the criteria previously set forth for the engine equipment manufacturer included: garden tractors, outboard motors, motor generator units, industrial trucks, materials handling equipment, refrigeration machinery, air conditioning equipment, engine accessories, compressed air drilling equipment, industrial engines, measuring and dispensing pumps, and blowers and ventilation equipment. The list of candidates surviving the primary screening can often be further narrowed by management judgment. A modest field investigation can usually provide the basis for quickly and convincingly discarding some products that at first appear to meet the desired criteria.

The final screening is characterized by thorough research of the limited number of products that have stood the test of preliminary research appraisal. A penetrating investigation includes an analysis of at least the following factors: industry growth and structure; competitive environment; important features and characteristics of existing products; potential technological obsolescence; characteristics of the market; purchase requirements and factors influencing the choice of suppliers; the effectiveness and costs of appropriate channels of distribution; methods and cost of demand cultivation; opportunity for market entry by a firm new to the field; competitive requirements for market entry; and the general suitability of the product field in the light of the specific criteria earlier established.

After screening has been completed and parameters established for new product exploration, a pool of product ideas should be generated. Hopefully, this is a continuing bank, systematically organized and categorized. Some may well remain dormant for a period until they can be formally reviewed. Ideas rejected once need not necessarily be totally discarded. For example, a cosmetic manufacturer rejected, on several occasions, the idea for an expensive line of men's toiletries, but recently launched such a line on the presumption of a more hospitable social environment.

The high attrition rate of new product ideas in Stage I should not necessarily be viewed with alarm. At this point little money has been spent and rejection conserves scarce technical resources. Criteria for project continuation will become increasingly rigorous in the later stages of development. It is desirable that only the most worthy ideas survive Stage I validation.

Those proposals that survive the first kill point should be moved directly to the stage of feasibility research. The technical director should have sufficient authority to do this. Management review at this point would not be justified because too little information is available. Furthermore, executive sponsorship of ideas at too early a stage can be undesirable because of emotional involvement that impairs objectivity and creates bias in the more critical decisions that eventually must be made. There is a time and place for deep executive involvement in the new product development process, but that is at a later stage.

STAGE II—FEASIBILITY RESEARCH

Feasibility research is a stage often ignored or omitted in planning structures. That is, once ideas have survived preliminary validation, they often jump directly into formal development. This bypassing is often regrettable because more detailed analysis of their potential commercial worth may well show them to be unworthy product candidates.[3]

The feasibility stage in most instances is not time-consuming. It is basically an attempt to reduce uncertainty to within tolerable limits for decision-making purposes. What is wanted is experimental research that considers basic technical alternatives, preliminary establishment of performance specifications, and an estimate of the developmental time and costs that can be anticipated if the company goes ahead with the program. When the con-

[3] For a review of techniques available to guide feasibility research, see David J. Luck, Hugh G. Wales, and Donald A. Taylor, *Marketing Research,* 4th ed. (Englewood Cliffs, N.J.: Prentice-Hall, Inc., 1974).

cept of the product is sufficiently structured so that its commercial worth can be assessed, an orderly market investigation should be undertaken. The market niches that the product is expected to occupy should be carefully considered, including the nature of the competition, both direct and indirect, that is anticipated. Size of the broader and narrower markets, and trends taking place in both, should be evaluated. If, for instance, a radically new powerboat design was being considered for development, trends in the leisure market in general might be evaluated. The size, composition, and growth of the broad boating market, the makeup of the powerboating sector, and its future must be considered. The most closely related indirect competition that the design would face in the powerboat sector should receive particular emphasis. This is what is meant by analysis of the broader as well as narrower markets that the product would occupy. At this point also, the earliest aspects of competitive strategy should be considered.

Much can be gained by testing a product concept in the very early stages of program definition. *Concept testing* permits the establishment of more precise parameters, a hierarchy of priorities, potential pockets of consumer resistance, and rough approximations of the demand structure. The concept testing that preceded the Vega's introduction, for example, provided an abundance of insights which influenced major product definition and broad outlines of marketing strategy. In retrospect, the predictive value of those concept studies was considerable when compared with post-introduction measures of buying motives, attitudes, and behavior.

Concept testing can save valuable time when compared to lengthy test market operation, and the old adage that time is money is nowhere more valid than when applied to product programs.[4] At best, the results of feasibility research provide a rough estimate of technical research and market investigation. At this stage, costs and potential revenues will not be precise. Nevertheless, they provide the best available estimates of the time, cost, and manpower required should a formal development program be carried out. Also, feasibility research gives an estimate of the commercial potentialities of such a venture. This material should then provide the basis for the first management involvement and review. Before specific developmental programs are launched, an important formal kill point must be passed. This gives management essential control of the bulk of its technical effort, serves vital means of information liaison planning, and provides additional insight into the potential competitive vitality of the enterprise in future periods.

---

[4] For an interesting discussion of measuring *needs* as well as interest, see Edward M. Tauber, "Reduce New Product Failures: Measure Needs as Well as Purchase Interest," *Journal of Marketing,* 37 (July 1973), 61–70.

STAGE III—DEVELOPMENT

The first task within the development stage is a technical effort sufficient to lead to a product prototype. In the majority of cases this consumes most of the expenditures committed to Stage III. The existence of a prototype makes possible a much higher degree of precision in planning and analysis.

With the existence of a product prototype further *laboratory testing* can be carried on and *use testing* undertaken. Use testing is important because products often perform differently in actual use than they do under laboratory conditions, where the operating variables can be closely controlled. These steps make it possible to arrive at a preliminary design finalization. The word *preliminary* is used because later customer preference studies or test marketing results might show the need for some design modification, which would be incorporated in the end product at the time of its formal launching.

With this degree of design certainty, production costing and planning can begin. This phase is essential in order that demand analysis can be sharpened from some estimates of product cost. Consequently, materials, labor, equipment, and space cost need to be considered, as well as the expected production rates and processes. Later, production planning will have to be carefully phased with market planning, and the foundation for that requirement can be provided through the information and analysis of the development stage.

With the existence of a particular configuration of product, a reasonable estimate of its costs under varying rates of output can now begin in addition to a vastly sharpened market analysis. The major objective here is to forecast the sales volume obtainable through various price alternatives and cost expenditures.

Demand analysis for a new product is a notoriously difficult analytical assignment. In some cases the demand variables are so complicated that it is, for all practical purposes, impossible to estimate with any reasonable accuracy the total potential demand for the product. In this instance, the procedure may need to be reversed and a "threshold of profitability" research procedure used. This approach uses a "cost out" rather than "market back" orientation. That is, reasonable cost estimates are made for the production and marketing of the product. The price is then established on the basis of cost and a calculation made of the volume that would be required to "sustain satisfactory commercial operations." This volume is the threshold of profitability. The analytical market assignment then becomes one of attempting to anaylze whether there appears to be sufficient pockets of demand to achieve this volume and where these pockets of demand are located. The analysis, however, is adequate to support a kill decision if the product does not lend itself reasonably to test marketing.

Ideally, demand should be estimated for various proportions and total amounts of marketing-mix expenditures. These estimates then make it possible to calculate profitability on the basis of the varying sales volumes that would be achieved under several alternate marketing mixes, and the costs of production at these varying rates of output. However, such precision is rarely possible in new product development.

STAGE IV—TEST MARKETING

The use of test marketing has increased greatly in recent years as a means of more precisely determining the potential success or failure of a new product prior to full-scale launching. The practice also enables marketers to anticipate the volume of sales expected in national distribution, with considerably higher confidence levels than in the absence of any prior testing in the real market on a localized basis. While the considerable advantages to be gained from test marketing account for its increasingly widespread use, numerous situations exist wherein its use is inappropriate.

WHAT A TEST MARKET CANNOT SHOW

While test marketing makes possible more precise estimates of expected sales results of full-scale marketing and can be designed so as to identify limitations of the planned overall marketing program, it cannot answer all questions of interest to the marketer of a new product. It will not necessarily show whether the basic product concept is good in contrast to potential problems in implementation. That is, some products fail in test marketing because of style or design factors in the particular product configuration, but this does not necessarily mean that the basic product concept lacks market acceptance. The test cannot show what will happen when competitive products that are close substitutes to the new product become available. That is, the product's capacity to resist competition generally remains unknown. Finally, tests do not of themselves indicate buildup in demand that can be expected over time because of the influence of unknown future environmental factors that cannot be built into the test at the time of its design.

COMPETITIVE REACTION TO TEST MARKET OPERATIONS

A firm can respond to a competitor's test market operations by allowing the test to proceed without interference, or it may engage in disruptive tactics. Rather than let the test proceed, the rival may engage in a variety of efforts to scramble the results and, indeed, may attempt to prevent the test from showing favorable results. The firm may elect to increase its own advertising expenditures, alter prices, use coupons and other promotional devices, and generally intensify its own efforts to counter the potential success of the product in the test market.

WHEN NOT TO MARKET TEST

Market testing is not appropriate for all new product situations. In fact, a number of factors can preclude its desirability. One of the major decision rules related to proceeding with market testing, or bypassing this stage and moving directly to the product introduction stage, has to do with the relationship between decision costs and revenues. What costs will be "born" with the decision? That is, forgetting costs that have already been "sunk" and are therefore irretrievable, what new costs will be incurred with a decision to launch, even though "all costs" will not necessarily be covered?

Another situation that militates against market testing occurs when the expenditures necessary for any level of customer purchase are a large proportion of total expenditures, regardless of the scale of operations. That means that there is an exceptionally high "startup" cost—which is why magazines and books do not lend themselves to test marketing. By the time an editorial staff is assembled, the copy for the magazine produced, type set, and plates purchased, the first unit of production is the most expensive by far, and additional copies of the magazine will be slightly more than the cost of paper and ink—a relatively insignificant part of the total expenditure involved.

Another situation that, for all practical purposes, precludes test marketing is where the time period required to change purchasing habits, attitudes, and preferences would be too long for any reasonable pilot operation. For instance, a new powdered dairy product was programmed for a forty-eight-month break-even period. A three-month or six-month test would not be sufficient to alter taste preferences, and little could be gained from such a test.

Other conditions that can militate against the feasibility of test marketing include the following: when the firm finds it essential to *match* a competitor's new product rapidly; when the firm is so thoroughly convinced that its new product is superior to existing products that success seems assured; when competitive security seems vital in getting a maximum jump on rivals; and, finally, when auxiliary installations or services would have to accompany the new product, such as in color telecasting.

PLANNING AND DESIGN OF TEST MARKET OPERATIONS

There are a number of phases in conducting a market test, the most important of which are the planning and the execution of the test, and the analysis and review of the results. While none of the phases shown in Figure 12-1 can be overlooked in an effectively designed test marketing program, our discussion will emphasize the selection of the test area, the establishment of standards by which to judge test performance, and the review procedures by which the significance of test results are considered in reaching a decision to proceed to full-scale market introduction.

Selecting a Test City

A number of factors must be considered in selecting a test city or cities for the pilot marketing program. Since marketers increasingly wish to test alternative elements of the market offer, such as variations in package design or prices for promotional campaigns, a few cities may need to be chosen. Several factors should be considered in making a selection. First, the city chosen should be representative of the broader market public. We will wish to project the results obtained in the test market to the national market, and, consequently, the test market must be a statistically reliable microcosm of the broader market universe. Primarily, population characteristics should be similar; that is, age groups, levels of education, existence of ethnic populations, and income levels should coincide with the national market into which the product will be launched. Special factors may need to be considered for the particular product, such as car ownership, proportion of home ownership, and occupational clusters. Purchasing power and discretionary spending levels are usually particularly important. If the product is intended to reach a highly specialized market, then we might not want the test city to be representative of the national market, but to have a composition similar to the demand variables for that product.

Second, one should be cautious about selecting what might be called an "overworked" test city. Because the number of cities that are indeed representative of the national market are relatively limited, there is a tendency for some of them to reflect a test fatigue factor. Consumers in these cities may become conditioned in such a way that results of the test may not be valid for projections into national marketing. If, for example, follow-up interviewing of purchasers is an important part of the test, interview-weary consumers may either refuse to be interviewed again or may give answers that quickly terminate the interviews. They may prefer to economize on time rather than tell their real feelings about the product. This fatigue factor may well become more important as the amount of test marketing of new products grows.

Third, the test city should have the same media alternatives as are anticipated in the national promotional campaign. The full range of market cultivation media is important in that, if a different promotional mix is necessary in the test city in contrast to plans for the national market, the results achieved in the test may not be a valid indication of what can be anticipated with full-scale operations.

Fourth, the market selected for testing should be a relatively self-contained one, insulated in part a least from other markets, and without too much waste circulation in promotional media. That is, the test marketer would not like to pay for a lot of television coverage going into areas not included in his test operations. The proportion of coverage not related to his operations would constitute wasteful expenditures, as could be the case with certain portions of newspaper advertising.

Fifth, the test city should be of an economical size. The area, on the one hand, should be small enough to be manageable and, on the other hand, large enough to be statistically reliable. Selecting one of the large metropolitan centers such as Chicago would constitute too big a job in getting the requisite distribution coverage, obtaining dealers' cooperation, having the necessary inventory backups and the like for a test of relatively short duration. Moreover, the cost would be excessive for the purposes of the test market. Too small a city, on the other hand, would not have the full range of promotional media required, nor would it be large enough to give good reliability in projecting from the sample test geographic unit to the total market universe. Cities like Grand Rapids, Michigan; Hartford, Connecticut; and Columbus, Ohio, are representative of the size of cities most frequently chosen for test marketing.

Sixth, the city should be one in which the marketer can gain good cooperation from distributors, dealers, and retailers. He needs the cooperation of marketing institutions in setting up displays, giving the product proper shelf space or exposure, pricing it at the suggested level for the test, handling coupons which might be used in conjunction with introduction of the product, having sufficient inventories, and reordering promptly when those inventories are depleted. Such kinds of assistance help provide the basis for reaching a valid judgment as to whether the product will have market acceptance in national or regional distribution. Characteristically, marketers want full cooperation in the test in order to assure themselves that, if the product does not go well, it did not fail for lack of knowledge of its existence on the part of the purchasing public or for lack of the requisite promotional effort. On the other hand, there are occasions on which marketers are willing to have the product face significant obstacles on the assumption that if the product can succeed in the test under reasonably adverse circumstances, they can have high confidence that it will be successful in national distribution with full-scale support.

Seventh, the city chosen should have representative competitive conditions. That is, the kind of competition reflected in the test ought to be reasonably typical of what might be expected on the broader scale. Some markets are notoriously price markets, others have a preponderance of manufacturers' own wholesale branches in contrast to independent distributors, while others lack the variety of types of retail outlets, such as discount stores, regional shopping centers, and the like. While no test city is a perfect replica of the national market, it should have a reasonable approximation of the basic competitive factors that are likely to exist on the broader scale.

Establishing Judgment Standards

It is extremely important to the test marketer that he carefully predetermine the criteria to be used in judging the success or failure of the market test. All too often the expected rate of sales during the period of test is not sufficient as a measure of future success. Many other considerations are important. For example, which product is the new product displacing? What is the rate of repurchase of the product? Is the product reaching the intended market? Is it being used for the intended purpose or for other purposes not anticipated? Is the level of satisfaction provided by the product what the marketer anticipated? These considerations and others may be very critical in terms of the longer-term market position the product can be expected to enjoy.

Analysis and Review of Test Operation

At the conclusion of the test, results should be analyzed to determine whether package, product, price, or marketing modifications are appropriate before launching the product into a roll-out leading to national distribution. In many instances, some variation of packaging or product will be tried in tests conducted simultaneously in several cities. As results come in, a complicated analytical problem is posed in determining the effect of the various approaches used. Did the variation in sales result from the difference in packages, for instance, or did it reflect better market coverage, better display, the absence of competitors' retaliation, or generally more favorable retail sales conditions in a particular market? In other words, in a direct comparison with results in other test cities, one cannot always ascribe a difference in sales to the effect of the distinctive marketing variable used in one market. One of the most successful cereal introductions reflected a rather significant package change resulting from experience in test markets. Several different packages were used in the test, and the one finally chosen for national distribution had a combination of the best features of those used in test marketing, on the basis of consumer preferences.

Reviewing the general performance of the test against sales forecasts and using the standards suggested above for judging performance should give the marketer the information needed for deciding whether to discontinue his plans for market introduction or to proceed with a full-scale launching of the product. It should be recognized that while the market test is being executed, final production planning is taking place. The last phase of the test market stage, therefore, reflects final plans for launch, with precise budgets and the fixing of responsibilities for market introduction. This is the point at which a final management review leads to a go/no-go decision.

STAGE V—MARKET INTRODUCTION

The stage of market introduction characteristically has a buildup phase, a launch phase, and a follow-up and review phase. There must often be a significant time interval between the conclusion of market testing and market introduction in order that the proper buildup can be made in all markets preliminary to market introduction. The buildup has both the production and physical distribution components.

The production buildup may require time for the purchase of special production equipment, the laying out of production or assembly lines, the recruiting and training of some new employees, and the smoothing out of production operations after start-up. This is, of course, preliminary to market introduction in order that the proper quantity of product can be in the distribution pipeline and in sufficient volume in all markets so that the initial demand generated by promotional expenditures can be capitalized on profitably by the marketer.

Simultaneously, there must be the proper introduction of the product to the company's own sales personnel, with sufficient training for them and assignment of responsibility. There must also be the training of dealers and distributors with respect to the program to be used in introducing the new product. A systems approach dictates that all elements in the total program be carefully coordinated and integrated. This includes, of course, distributor and retailer units as well as the manufacturer's own components.

The preparation of promotional materials, the purchase of space in magazines and newspapers and time on television, all require a buildup phase for market introduction in the promotional area. These efforts precede public showing of the product and the initial advertising and publicity. Characteristically, however, marketers like to have the benefit of some publicity prior to market introduction so that potential purchasers' interest can be stimulated and their anticipation heightened for the appearance of the product at the announced introductory date.

The days immediately following launch are some of the most critical and exciting of the whole new product development and introduction process. All previous effort has led to the climax in these days, and the first returns from the field are watched with special care in hopes that the program is moving according to projection. But occasionally the burst of enthusiasm and a failure to pay attention to minute details during the introductory period have jeopardized market success. An official connected with the introduction of the Edsel expressed to one of the authors his belief that failure to assign each dealer a quota during the week of the car's introduction proved to be a regrettable error. Caught up in the tremendous mass of people viewing the car during the first few days, the retail salesmen became so engaged in discussion and demonstration that they failed to recognize the need for taking individuals aside for the purpose of writing orders, even if it meant that a number of people had to view the car by themselves.

While the introductory approach suggested here reflects the value of having adequate inventories in the marketplace to capitalize on initial demand, it should be recognized that some marketers have successfully followed the practice of feeding a product onto the market relatively slowly and attempting to keep the supply just below the level of prevailing demand. This practice is used to create the impression that the product is enjoying heavy consumer demand; the underlying assumption is that what consumers find hard to buy may stimulate their interest to own, given widespread acceptance of the product.

COMMERCIALIZATION OR KILL?

A stage of commercialization is reached when the product is no longer subject to the special treatment extended to it during the introductory period, but rather is handled in a normal way within the established operating system as a part of the ongoing enterprise.

The difficult task of killing projects at appropriate points in the process requires further elaboration. The first hurdle is in the corporate research stage, and there is little objective data to make the decision at this point. On the other hand, product ideas at this stage are many and varied. The decision must be made on the basis of how well the proposed product fits the overall objectives of the company. Is it appropriate for the business the company considers itself to be in? Does it provide a potential differential advantage for future competitive strength? In the feasibility research stage survival is a matter of having sufficient market opportunity to proceed. Estimates made are admittedly rough, but obvious potential failures should be evident. Once the development stage is reached, and product prototypes are developed and perfected, more precise measurements of market opportunity and production cost requirements can be made. At this stage the decision to move to test marketing is based upon a matching of potential costs and revenues. Test marketing is an attempt to try the proposed product under actual conditions of sale. It not only provides a basis for checking market opportunity estimates made at earlier stages but also an opportunity to measure volume possibilities under differing marketing treatments. If shortcomings in the market performance of the new product become evident and cannot be remedied, this may still be the point at which the product candidate is dropped. If it survives the standards established for the test, it will move on to market introduction. The final decision to proceed with full-scale commercialization offers the last short-range kill point.

COMBINING THE ELEMENTS OF ANALYSIS

The following case demonstrates the application of elements of planned diversification outlined here.

The First Paper Company, a northern nonintegrated[5] mill, produced a variety of fine and coarse paper products. As was true with other similar northern mills, the company had suffered serious inroads from the competition of southern mills. Although a number of products were distributed through both fine- and coarse-paper merchants, the bulk of the sales were made to a relatively limited number of direct mill accounts which had been built up over a number of years through the personal efforts of company executives.

The mill's declining competitive position was abruptly magnified with the loss of one large and important customer, who accounted for approximately 25 percent of the gross sales of the company. In view of the critical condition of the mill, it was concluded by management that additional products were essential.

Several strategic objectives were established by management for new products. To improve the mill's position materially, they said, additions for the line should (1) be suitable for production on present equipment with no more than additions of accessory equipment; (2) be of a character precluding efficient production by southern mills; and (3) allow a minimum profit of $40 per machine hour.

The situation analysis indicated the characteristics of products that would be unsuitable for competitive southern mills, which enjoyed four

---

[5] See Footnote 2 for definition of *nonintegrated*.

principal advantages: (1) newer, bigger, faster equipment, (2) lower wage rates, (3) lower raw material costs, and (4) economies of operation from combining pulp and paper-mill operations. Hence, the new products of the First Paper Company should: have a high value added by the manufacturing process to offset or minimize the lower raw material costs and the cheaper labor of southern mills; require a type of pulp not readily accessible in the South; require relatively frequent, short production runs to offset or minimize the superior size and speed of southern equipment, which costs a great deal to shut down or leave idle; and also, if possible, be aimed at a market allowing a considerable potential sale within a relatively small radius of the company's plant, to take advantage of freight rate differentials (eliminating the expense of the long haul from southern mills).

When the resource audit was made, it revealed that the First Paper Company enjoyed a distinguished reputation in the trade as a quality mill, was known for its business integrity, and was particularly competent in the production of intricate grades of technical papers with close quality tolerances. This study also revealed a number of areas in the present marketing operations of the company that could be substantially improved. For example, inadequate market coverage existed and sales territories were of widely varying sizes. Some of these problems were amenable to short-term corrective action by management. Plans for diversification were then made which reflected the desired goals, the situation analysis, and the resource audit.

Next, a preliminary market audit was made of a wide range of market grades falling in the lightweight paper field. As a result, several particular grades were selected for comprehensive market appraisal. One of the products surviving the final screening and selected by management to be introduced to the market was a line of technical reproduction papers. The product dovetailed closely with the diversification plan and appeared to be an especially suitable competitive opportunity for these reasons:

1. The market for the product was growing at a rate appreciably more rapid than the field of lightweight papers as a whole.
2. A sufficient market potential existed for sales substantially in excess of the idle capacity on machines suitable for the production of this particular grade of paper.
3. The market was not dominated by the large, integrated pulp and paper mills; on the contrary, the smaller mills were capable of effective and aggressive competition. Buyers typically purchased in reasonably small lots, which precluded the long runs required by southern mills for efficient operations.
4. The product had a particularly high value added by manufacturing to minimize the raw material and labor advantages of southern rivals.

5. The number of potential customers provided a reasonably broad customer base to minimize the possibility of a large reduction in sales occurring through the loss of one account, as had happened in the past.

6. The majority of dominant buyers were located in close proximity to the mill, providing excellent opportunity for market penetration costs and the better service and quicker delivery that could be provided.

7. The product was particularly well suited to the technical knowledge and excellent quality characterizing the operations of the company. Precise manufacturing specifications had to be met in the new product.

8. The product was compatible with the present or contemplated production marketing facilities of the company. The grades to be offered were chosen after surveys of uses. Only modest operational changes were required prior to the introduction of the product. Finally, substantial evidence was available to indicate that adequate opportunity existed for market entry by a new firm.

The case described here indicates the feasibility of planned diversification as it applies to the solution of the peculiar problems of individual firms.

SUMMARY

Six integrated stages in the total new product development and introduction process were outlined beginning with the corporate research stage, which includes, among other things, a careful definition of the needs and resources within the company as it related to new products. In the feasibility research stage, an attempt is made, on a preliminary basis, to establish the technical and commercial feasibility of the product concept. The development stage follows, in which a product prototype is produced which makes possible sharpened cost revenue forecasts. A number of specific circumstances were explained to indicate that not all products should pass through the next stage of test marketing. Emphasis was given to the importance of decision costs and revenues and the potential value of higher-confidence levels in sales projections as a basis for deciding whether to test market or bypass this stage in favor of full-scale introduction. The planning, execution, and analysis phases of the test marketing stage were set forth, with particular attention given to the criteria for choosing the test market and for establishing standards by which to judge test performance. The last stage detailed was market introduction, with its accompanying buildup, launch, and follow-up phases. Emphasis here was given to the planning and monitoring requirements of introductory programs. Finally, the stage of commercialization for the new product would be reached when it was assimilated into the normal pattern of ongoing operations within the enterprise.

It was suggested that careful review be given each project before it passed to the succeeding stage and that top management attention be directed to the project neither too early nor too late in the total process. The view was expressed that the burden of proof ought to be placed on justification for moving the product to the next stage rather than on justification for the project's termination.

QUESTIONS AND PROBLEMS

1. What are the stages of the new product development and introduction process?
2. Why are the penalties for new product failure becoming higher as larger-scale market entry is required?
3. What are some advantages and disadvantages of test marketing a new product?
4. What factors must be considered in selecting a particular test market?
5. What environmental factors are likely to increase the already high new product failure rate?
6. Too many developmental projects may hinder a company's new product development program. Explain.
7. What is meant by feasibility research in new product development?
8. What is meant by "threshold of profitability" research? When is this procedure used in new product development analysis?

BIBLIOGRAPHY

ACHENBAUM, ALVIN A., "The Purpose of Test Marketing," in *The Marketing Concept in Action,* ed. Robert M. Kaplan. Chicago: American Marketing Association, 1964.

ALEXANDER, R. S., "The Death and Burial of Sick Products," *Journal of Marketing,* vol. 38 (April 1964).

BASS, FRANK M., "A New Product Growth Model for Consumer Durables," *Management Science* (January 1969), pp. 215–27.

COX, WILLIAM E., JR., "Product Life Cycles as Marketing Models," *Journal of Business* (October 1967), pp. 375–84.

HARDIN, DAVID K., "A New Approach to Test Marketing," *Journal of Marketing* (October 1966), pp. 28–31.

KOTLER, PHILIP, "Phasing Out Weak Products," *Harvard Business Review* (March–April 1965), pp. 107–18.
Management of New Products, 4th ed. New York: Booz, Allen & Hamilton, Inc., 1965.
PESSEMIER, EDGAR A., *New Product Decisions: An Analytical Approach*. New York: McGraw-Hill Book Company, 1966.
———, "New Product Ventures," *Business Horizons* (August 1968).
ROGERS, EVERETT M., *Diffusion of Innovations*. New York: The Free Press, 1962.
SMALLWOOD, JOHN E., "The Product Life Cycle: A Key to Strategic Market Planning," *Business Topics* (Winter 1973), pp. 29–35.
STAUDT, THOMAS A., "Higher Management Risks in Product Strategy," *Journal of Marketing*, 37 (January 1973), 4–9.
STILLSON, PAUL, and LEONARD ARNOFF, "Product Search and Evaluation," *Journal of Marketing* (July 1957), pp. 33–39.
TALLEY, WALTER J., *The Profitable Product: Its Planning, Launching, and Management*. Englewood Cliffs, N.J.: Prentice-Hall, Inc., 1965.
TAUBER, EDWARD M., "Reduce New Product Failures: Measure Needs as Well as Purchase Interest," *Journal of Marketing*, 37 (July 1973), 61–70.
URBAN, GLEN L., "A New Product Analysis and Decision Model," *Management Science* (April 1968), pp. 490–517.
ZARECOR, WILLIAM D., "High-Technology Product Planning," *Harvard Business Review* (January–February 1975), pp. 108–15.

Part IV

MARKETING PROGRAMMING

In Part One we emphasized that the enterprise seeks differential advantage —or competitive superiority—in markets to the end that corporate objectives are achieved. The firm must seek a total market posture that builds impact at the point of ultimate sale. Market action may then be precipitated to permit the fulfillment of the firm's objectives. We have emphasized in Part Two the need for the perceptive and comprehensive investigation of market opportunities through the performance of the market delineation and purchase motivation managerial functions of marketing. These investigations aid in identifying marketing objectives and selecting market targets. In Part Three the functions related to market opportunity assessment served as a foundation for performance of the product-service adjustment function. This function is concerned with determination of the manner in which the product mix is matched with market opportunities. In Part Four we turn our attention to the way in which the enterprise establishes linkages between the firm and the buyer, to the end that marketing objectives, market targets, and the marketing mix are coordinated.

Without some form of organized system, the task of matching supply and demand would be excessively costly and time-consuming. Many tasks must be performed to match a heterogeneous supply with a heterogeneous demand. The first is the task of assembling, from the conglomeration of products supplied, distinctive assortments to match the different segments of demand. The second is the job of physically moving goods to demand. The third task is to stimulate exchange. An elaborate organization of institutions has developed to aid in the performance of these tasks. In total, these institutions provide a network of retailers, wholesalers, and specialized agents.

The problems facing a single marketer will vary. It is the job of the marketer to select those institutions which will most efficiently contribute to the achievement of marketing goals. In Chapter 13 we examine the various combinations of institutions available to a marketer. The advantages and disadvantages of each institution is reviewed relative to the assembling of distinctive assortments to match the different segments of demand. In Chapter 14 the selection and management of the most efficient channels for transfer of ownership for a specific company are explored. The problems of overcoming time and space by achieving an efficient physical distribution flow are dealt with in Chapter 15. The combination of institutions selected constitutes the *distribution mix* of the firm.

The task of stimulating exchanges or market cultivation is primarily a matter of communication if the problems inherent in the separation of producer and consumer have been resolved reasonably well. It is the combination of communication means, or the *communications mix,* which energizes or activates the exchange process. In Chapter 16, the aspects of advertising are discussed, as well as the product, market, and customer characteristics that determine advertising performance. The management of advertising expenditures by the firm is also explored. Personal selling, an important element of market cultivation and a principal management consideration, is explored in Chapter 17. In addition to an employee sales force, attention is directed to the alternative use of agents and dealers. The overlap of the distribution mix and the communication mix serves to illustrate the highly integrative nature of marketing strategy.

Another important element of market cultivation is pricing. While this area could have been treated in Part Three, we have chosen to consider pricing policies here. Their placement in Chapter 18 reflects the following important considerations: (1) pricing is an important tool of market cultivation, as are advertising, sales promotion, and personal selling; (2) price adjustments are to some extent an alternative to communication expenditures; and (3) pricing should serve to integrate and bring into focus all aspects of markets, products, distribution, and communication. The pricing policies selected constitutes the *price mix* of the firm.

Finally, in Chapter 19 we discuss the formulation of a marketing strategy plan. The process of environmental monitoring to identify marketing objectives, selecting market targets, and establishing the marketing mix is illustrated to convey the way in which the managerial functions of marketing discussed throughout the text are combined into an integrated marketing plan.

Chapter 13

Marketing Channel Structure

The distribution channel provides the link between highly specialized and geographically dispersed producers of goods and the demand of millions of purchasing units. The treatment of marketing, thus far, has been oriented toward the management of a single business enterprise. It is now necessary to examine interorganizational relationships that develop as specialized firms jointly perform marketing functions.

Specialization in production creates problems of time and space between supply and demand. Such temporal-spatial separation must be overcome if goods are to be available when and where consumers or customers want them. The task of overcoming time and space through efficient exchange mechanisms is so important that a number of specialized firms have developed to deal with the problem. These firms, commonly referred to as *institutions, middlemen,* or *intermediaries,* combine to form a *distribution network* or *channel*.[1] This chapter is concerned with the fundamental channel structure and alternatives available to marketers.

The initial section of the chapter examines the nature of distribution channels. First, marketing intermediaries are classified and channel structure is defined. Appendix A to the text provides a statistical summary of the number and relative importance of each type of specialized institution in the United States economy. The next subject discussed is *sorting,* the primary purpose of channel systems. The initial section concludes with a review of the need or benefit gained by utilizing intermediaries in the marketing process. The second section of the chapter introduces functional specialization. The arrangement of channel organization to permit functional specialization is developed and discussed under the concept of separation. The result is a dual-structured channel system that provides specialization

[1] Throughout Chapters 13, 14, and 15, the terms *distribution channel* and *marketing channel* are used interchangeably.

opportunities in transaction creation and physical distribution. Complexities are introduced with respect to the dynamics of interorganizational behavior.

THE OVERALL NATURE OF MARKETING CHANNELS

Marketing can be described as an overall process in which no individual enterprise or institution is self-sufficient.[2] Even the most primitive of societies must resort to specialization in order to gain the greatest benefit from limited resources available. The moment specialization exists in an economy, some members have more of selected items and less of others. Exchange of the surpluses is essential in such a society, for it is the means by which individuals satisfy their economic wants.

In modern society goods are made available through a very complex distribution structure in which exist a variety of different forms of specialization. The channel of distribution is *a combination of institutions through which a seller markets his products to the user or ultimate consumer*. In total, the channel is not only instrumental in facilitating the physical flow of goods, but it is also the structure through which much marketing effort is channeled to buyers.

MARKETING INTERMEDIARIES CLASSIFIED

There are a large number of different types of specialized intermediaries available to participate in a distribution channel organization. The important thing to remember is that each of the intermediaries in the channel represents a composite of activities, the performance of which is essential to the efficient distribution of goods and services. Some alternative institutional arrangements are illustrated in Figure 13-1. An initial classification of intermediaries is important as an aid to understanding the many different types, the nature of their operation, and the integration of individual intermediaries into a channel structure.

While various intermediaries may perform services such as standardization and grading, as in the case of those middlemen handling fresh fruits and vegetables, or engage in minor processing, such as the roasting of coffee, these activities are incidental to facilitating exchange.[3] The broadest classification of middlemen distinguishes between those middlemen that purchase outright and actually take title to goods, and those that act in an

---

[2] Theodore N. Beckman and William R. Davidson, *Marketing* (New York: The Ronald Press Company, 1962).

[3] *Standardization* involves the determination of specifications to which goods must conform. *Grading* is the act of checking goods for conformity to specifi-

FIGURE 13-1
Alternative Distribution Channel Structures

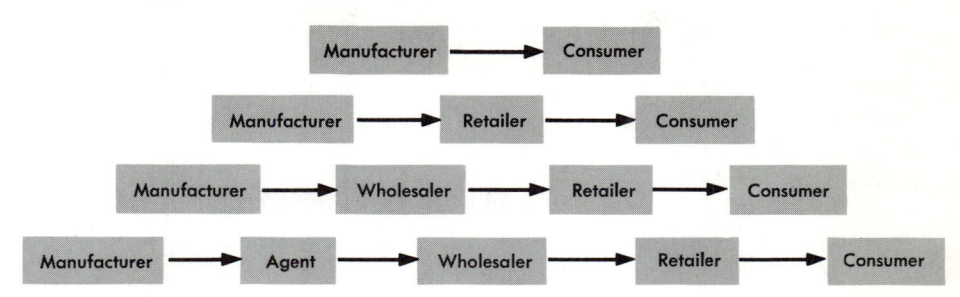

Manufacturer → Consumer

Manufacturer → Retailer → Consumer

Manufacturer → Wholesaler → Retailer → Consumer

Manufacturer → Agent → Wholesaler → Retailer → Consumer

agency capacity on behalf of clients. The former are called *merchant middlemen* and the latter *agents*. The classification by itself is too broad to be very useful; nevertheless, it is important, as the act of taking title to goods carries with it the risks of ownership.

Middlemen are classified in much more detail by the Bureau of the Census. Much data are published about different kinds of middlemen by this government agency. As these data are used extensively, it is important that we understand how the different classifications are used. They are used (1) in the interpretation of markets, (2) in the classification of middlemen for tax purposes, (3) in the administration of the Fair Labor Standards Act, and (4) in conjunction with a number of laws regulating commerce. Although court rulings deviate at times, the classifications used by the Bureau of the Census are almost uniformly accepted.

Appendix A presents a statistical review of data related to classification of intermediaries.

Merchant middlemen are of two types: retailers and wholesalers. *Retailers are middlemen primarily engaged in selling to ultimate consumers.* However, some manufacturers, such as Electrolux (vacuum cleaners), sell directly to ultimate consumers. For this reason, the Bureau of the Census has developed statistics on what is known as *retail* trade, which includes all establishments, whether they are middlemen or not, engaged in retailing. Retail trade is defined as including:

> All establishments engaged in selling merchandise for personal or household consumption and rendering services incident to the sale of such goods.[4]

---

cations. Generally, middlemen do not establish standards. Rather, they use trade or governmental standards and grade merchandise for conformity before offering it for sale.

[4] *Standard Industrial Classification Manual* (Washington, D.C.: Government Printing Office, 1957), p. 153.

Merchant wholesalers are merchant middlemen primarily engaged in selling to retailers; to industrial, commercial, institutional, or professional users; or to other wholesalers. Agents are engaged in the same kind of activity as wholesalers except that they do not take title to the goods in which they deal. Manufacturers engage in the same kind of activity as merchant wholesalers when they choose to own and operate manufacturers' sales branches with stocks. For this reason, the Bureau of Census has developed statistics on wholesale trade, which is defined as including:

> All establishments or places of business primarily engaged in selling merchandise to retailers; to industrial, commercial, institutional or professional users; or to other wholesalers; or acting as agents in buying merchandise for or selling merchandise to such persons or companies.[5]

In summary, the classification of intermediaries uses the degree of specialization in the distribution channel and legal responsibility or ownership of inventory as a grouping basis.

THE PROCESS OF SORTING

The problems of matching supply and demand in a timely manner constitute a barrier to efficient exchange. More specifically, three basic problems exist. The first problem results from the location of sources of supply and the centers of demand. Because the sources of supply are geographically concentrated and demand is comprised of millions of consuming units scattered over the entire world, there is the necessity for physical movement. The transport problem is aggravated by the fact that consuming units distant from producers desire only small quantities of any single product. The second problem results from the kinds of assortments demanded. From the conglomeration of products produced, unique assortments of different products in different quantities than those in which they are normally supplied must be assembled to match the millions of individual segments of demand. The third problem is providing the necessary stimulation for exchange. Even though the other two problems are effectively handled, there is no assurance that exchange will take place. The buyer must feel he wants different items in his assortment more than he wants the money he has to give up to purchase them.

Unless some means were found to overcome these obstacles, consumers would have to spend endless hours searching out producers of

[5] Ibid., p. 147.

items they wish to acquire. They would then have to move physically small quantities of these items to the locations where they are consumed. The inefficiency of searching for individual producers would reduce the variety of products consumers now enjoy. And producers would not be willing to offer a wide variety of products, as in all probability consumers would be ignorant of their existence. A solution to the first two problems of exchange requires some means of reducing the number of contacts consumers must make with sources of supply to acquire their unique assortments and to minimize the distance over which small quantities of goods must be moved. The activity designed to solve these problems is known as *sorting,* and a complete understanding of this process is essential.[6]

Sorting is a process of *concentration* and *dispersion.* Concentration is needed to reduce the cost of physically moving small quantities of goods from the sources of supply to the centers of demand, and to create some semblance of homogeneity of supply in locations close to consumers. Dispersion is needed to create assortments of goods which approximate the assortments buyers demand, and to make goods conveniently available to them.

Let us imagine a distance scale, at one end of which are almost 12 million producers of goods and services, and at the other end nearly 67 million consuming units. The first task is to concentrate like commodities at some point along the scale closer to the buyer. An example would be the centralization of agricultural products in the growing region. A large number of producers of wheat bring their supplies to the country elevator, where it is graded and stored until a sufficient quantity is accumulated to move it farther down the distance scale by means of economical shipments. In the case of wheat, it is moved to central markets closer to the buyer. This process of concentration is not limited to agricultural products. In the steel industry, producer installations are located in different parts of the country. The output of the different mills is shipped to warehouses closer to the buyers. The same is true of the processed food industry. Producing operations are usually located close to the agricultural regions that produce the base products. After processing, the finished goods are shipped in large quantities to warehouses farther down the distance scale.

We now have homogeneous suplies in a number of different locations closer to the buyer. It would be a laborious and expensive task if buyers had to visit even these centers of homogeneous supply. It is now necessary to disperse these homogeneous supplies and concentrate assortments that approximate the assortments buyers desire farther down the distance scale.

[6] For one of the original discussions of sorting, see Wroe Alderson, *Market Behavior and Executive Action* (Homewood, Ill.: Richard D. Irwin, Inc., 1957), pp. 201–10.

Goods that are associated in purchase and in use are shipped in large quantities from the concentrated supplies until an assortment of goods is located closer to the buyer. The distance from these supply centers to the buyer is still relatively great, and assortments in much smaller quantities are allocated to points located conveniently near the buyer. The assortments now assembled in any one location are not identical with those that buyers desire. However, the distance problem has been overcome, and the number of contacts that must be made is reduced. The buyer can now select from a relatively few assortments those items needed and, almost literally, carry them home.

The number of points at which goods are concentrated and dispersed in their movement from producer to buyer depends upon many things, including the weight of the product, location of supply, location of markets, competition, perishability, and a number of others.

In the sorting process we are dealing wtih a problem of transportation and storage. You will recall from economics that goods must, in addition to form utility, also have place and time utility before they accumulate value. That is, they cannot enter into exchange unless they are in the right place at the right time, or at least have the potentiality of being so. Since transportation and storage are costly, the way in which goods are concentrated and dispersed has an influence on the value these goods will command in exchange. Management of the physical distribution task is discussed in Chapter 15.

The sorting process also includes an aspect of marketing communication. First, exchanges are stimulated if goods are conveniently exposed to potential buyers. Exposure to purchase is very important for many types of goods and is dependent upon the particular sorting process used to move goods to the consumer. Second, the manner in which goods are offered is dependent in part upon the particular assortment in which they are offered. Let us consider the merchandise found in a hardware store as a specialized assortment. We can hardly conceive of a mattress within this setting as receiving any special stimulation. Likewise we can hardly conceive of a mattress kept in the storeroom of a furniture store as receiving any either. There is a qualitative aspect to the sorting process. Goods must not only be made conveniently available but must also be combined in the proper assortment and offered in a particular way before there is any stimulus to exchange.

THE ROLE OF MARKETING INTERMEDIARIES

The process of sorting is essential to the efficient distribution of goods in a specialized economy. It matters little whether this job is carried out by producers themselves or whether it is done by other linking entities. Since specialization usually results in efficiency, it is natural that a number of intermediaries have developed to aid in the sorting process. These intermediaries tend to specialize geographically and in terms of the assortments they carry. This is not to say that a single intermediary may not cover the entire country. However, if it does, it must specialize operations regionally, because to some degree all markets are local. The characteristics of different goods require different physical facilities, and the skills needed to stimulate their sales are so variable that specialization in assortment offers many efficiencies.

The economic justification for the existence of marketing intermediaries can be demonstrated by four principles: (1) the principle of minimum total transactions,[7] (2) the principle of massed reserves, (3) the principle of proximity, and (4) the principle of postponement.

THE PRINCIPLE OF MINIMUM TOTAL TRANSACTIONS

In Figure 13-2, a simplified distribution network is illustrated in which there are four producers and eight buyers. The left-hand side of the figure shows that 32 transactions would be necessary for all buyers to acquire an assortment of goods. The right-hand side introduces an intermediary, and the number of transactions is cut to 12. Transactions cost money, and anything that can be done to reduce them serves efficiency. Now let us examine the potential savings in transportation cost alone. On the left-hand side, goods are shipped to each of the buyers in very small quantities at a cost of $1 each, for a total transportation cost of $32. On the right-hand side goods are shipped from the producer to the intermediary in large quantities, at a cost of $4 for each producer. They are delivered by the intermediary to the buyer in smaller quantities over a shorter distance, at a cost of 50 cents each. The total transportation cost would be $16 ($4 × 4) + 4 (50 cents × 8), or $20, a saving of $12 in transportation

---

[7] For background development of these principles, see Wroe Alderson, "Factors Governing the Development of Marketing Channels," in Richard M. Clewett, *Marketing Channels in Manufactured Products* (Homewood, Ill.: Richard D. Irwin, Inc., 1954); George J. Stegler, "The Division of Labor Is Limited by the Extent of the Market," *The Journal of Political Economy,* 59 (June 1951), 185–93; Wroe Alderson, "Marketing Efficiency and the Principle of Postponement," *Cost and Profit Outlook,* No. 3 (September 1950); Louis P. Bucklin, "Postponement, Speculation, and the Structure of Distribution Channels," *Journal of Marketing Research,* vol. 2 (February 1965); and Margaret Hall, *Distributive Trading* (London: Hutchinson's University Library, 1961).

FIGURE 13-2
Principle of Minimum Total Transactions

——— $1.00 Transportation Cost

----- $4.00 Transportation Cost
——— $0.50 Transportation Cost

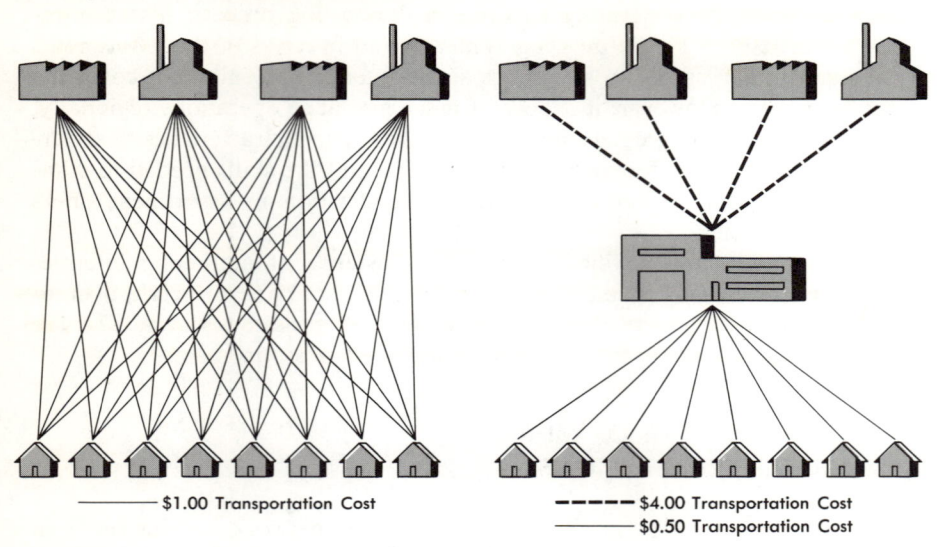

cost. Furthermore, we have not mentioned the convenience of having goods readily available.

It is possible—but unlikely—that the number of intermediaries might increase to the point where the transaction cost would equal that of the 32 transactions necessary if no intermediary existed. Moreover, as the number of intermediaries increases, the savings in transportation costs may more than compensate for the increase in transaction costs. In determining the number of intermediaries, transportation costs should be balanced against transaction costs, and the most economical balance used.

THE PRINCIPLE OF MASSED RESERVES

Storage, like transportation, is costly. Inventories must be held at each step in the concentration and dispersion of goods. Inventories exist at the producer level, at the accumulation level, at the assortment level, and in the household. The principle of massed reserves calls for storage of inventory to be located strategically throughout the total channel. In terms of the overall channel, the ready availability of inventory in the proper assortment reduces the amount or extent of stocks that households and retail firms are required to carry. Paradoxical as it may first appear, the extent of inventory in the overall channel when intermediaries are used may be lower than might otherwise be the case. Such an assumption rests on exacting inventory control and consistent product delivery. However, the basic point is that since final buying units are numerically much greater, the total quantity of goods in overall storage would be greater in the absense of intermediaries.

While the principle of massed reserves serves to improve the overall social efficiency of marketing, the consequences for any given channel member may be an increased responsibility to maintain larger inventories.[8] For example, a well-recognized trend in food marketing channels is for the manufacturer to take an increasing responsibility for holding a larger proportion of total channel inventory in return for large retailers agreeing to offer the manufacturers specific brands for sale. The tendency to "push" inventory holding responsibility "up" the channel is a form of functional transfer which results from countervailing power structures to be discussed later in this chapter. At this point it is sufficient to note that the principle of massed reserves relates to the aggregate channel commitment to inventories and not necessarily to the commitment of any single channel member.

THE PRINCIPLE OF PROXIMITY

Intermediaries are located closer to the buyer than are producers. In Parts One, Two, and Three, we discussed the importance of the manufacturers adjusting products and strategies to market forces. Intermediaries also contribute to this objective. Their proximity to the buyers makes possible more accurate investigation of buyer's desires. These establishments frequently are aware of forces in the market that producers, because of physical and institutional separation, would never observe. The intermediaries' interpretation of markets is reflected in the assortments they assemble and in the products they demand from producers. This does not mean that we can add intermediaries close to buyers at will. The costs involved in duplication in inventories would be prohibitive. The fact does remain, however, that there are intermediaries close to buyers and, as such, they interpret buyers' desires and transmit those desires to producers through their purchases.

THE PRINCIPLE OF POSTPONEMENT

The principle of postponement is an important feature to keep in mind with respect to channel structure. Alderson formalized the concept

[8] This aspect of functional transfer between intermediaries represents one of the major causes of conflict in channel relationships. The resolution of such conflict and the potential attainment of joint benefits represent one of the primary motivational forces behind the development of interorganizational programs. For an expanded discussion, see James L. Heskett, "Sweeping Changes in Distribution," *Harvard Business Review* (March–April 1973), pp. 123–32.

of postponement as an integral part of the sorting process performed by marketing intermediaries.[9] In essence, physical changes in product form and identity should be delayed as long as possible in the marketing process. Likewise, commitments to move specific inventory to specific market locations should be postponed as long as possible in the physical distribution process.

From the physical form and identification side, several outstanding examples of postponement are available. The fairly recently adopted practice of mixing paint colors at the retail store has the net effect of reducing stock units manyfold, while at the same time increasing the assortment of paint that can be offered within each market segment. The production of nonlabeled chemicals and frozen vegetables that are labeled only when customer orders are in hand permits products sold to broad market areas and assorted customers to be serviced from a single stockpile. The custom blending of gasoline at the pump by Sunoco represents the ultimate in postponement. The time and space aspects of postponement encourage the holding of inventories, as long as practical, in a single or homogeneous grouping so as to maintain flexibility.

The four principles discussed may at times offer contradictory advice in comparison to other principles concerning channel structure. At selected times, the principles may not be applicable, or firms may wish to speculate by not postponing product sorting. In other situations, excessive postponement could tend to dilute the advantages offered by proximity and the benefits of massed reserves. Thus, the principles are basic considerations in the formation of channel structure which are helpful but which can be violated when in the best interest of the channel membership. Each situation requires unique analysis.

In summary, marketing intermediaries exist to reduce barriers to exchange and to facilitate an orderly flow of physical products and ownership between suppliers and sources of demand. This orderly flow or sorting process is most efficiently performed by specialized intermediaries.

CHANNEL SEPARATION

In a broad sense, two types of specialized activities must be completed if the marketing channel is to satisfy its basic mission.[10] One is the physical distribution of the product. The other is the legal exchange of ownership title. While the two types of specialized activities are highly interdependent,

---

[9] Alderson, "Marketing Efficiency."

[10] The discussion that follows draws upon Donald J. Bowersox, *Logistical Management* (New York: Macmillan Publishing Co., Inc., 1974), pp. 48–51.

they are also somewhat unique. A given product may never move physically, while the ownership or title to the product may change hands numerous times. In contrast, a product may be transported across the nation and back within the distribution network without ever changing legal ownership. From the viewpoint of understanding marketing channels, it is important to realize that possession and ownership are not identical.

An opportunity for specialization exists when the activities of physical distribution can be separated from those of ownership transfer.[11] To accomplish a satisfactory marketing process, a series of transaction-creating efforts must be coordinated with a series of physical distribution activities. However, there is no logical reason why these two basic groupings of effort must sequentially transpire through the same network of channel intermediaries. The introduction of channel functional specialization is labeled *channel separation.*

The logic for separation is based on the independent economic factors engaged in transaction creation and physical distribution. Each form of activity is responsive to specialization factors unique to its own surrounding circumstances. Thus, based upon overall specialization the total distribution network is separated for structural analysis and choice as containing a transaction and a physical distribution subchannel.

The transaction channel consists of institutional arrangements between specialized intermediaries engaged in negotiation, contracting, and post-transaction administration of sales on a continuing basis. The physical distribution channel contains a network of intermediaries who are specialists in performing functions of physical product transfer.

Figure 13-3 illustrates potential separation of the overall distribution network or channel for color television. The reader should note that the only two times the transaction and physical distribution channels formally merge is at the manufacturer's factory and the consumer's home. Two separate sets of intermediaries are deployed in the overall channel, offering maximum opportunity for specialization.

The concept of separation should not be interpreted to suggest that either specialized subchannel can stand alone. Both must function to realize a profitable sale. Physical distribution performance must be controlled in accordance with specifications established during the negotiation phase of

---

[11] A number of authors have developed the flow concept and separation in relation to channel structure. See Roland Vaile, E. T. Grether, and Reavis Cox, *Marketing in the American Economy* (New York: The Ronald Press Company, 1952), and Ralph F. Breyer, "Some Observations on Structural Formation and Growth of Marketing Channels," in *Theory in Marketing,* eds. Reavis Cox, Wroe Alderson, and Stanley J. Shapiro (Homewood, Ill.: Richard D. Irwin, Inc., 1964).

FIGURE 13-3
Distribution Network Separation

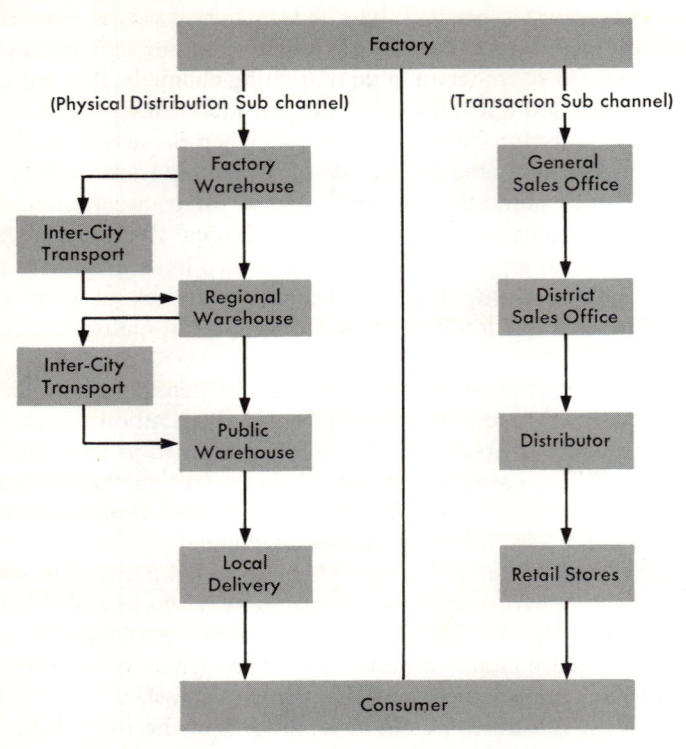

```
                                Factory
          (Physical Distribution Sub channel)    (Transaction Sub channel)
                                  │
              ┌───────────────────┤                    ┌──────────────┐
              │                   ▼                    ▼              │
              │              Factory              General             │
              │              Warehouse            Sales Office        │
         Inter-City               │                    │
         Transport                ▼                    ▼
              │              Regional             District
              └──────────▶   Warehouse            Sales Office
                                  │                    │
         Inter-City               ▼                    ▼
         Transport            Public               Distributor
              └──────────▶   Warehouse                 │
                                  │                    │
                                  ▼                    ▼
                              Local                Retail Stores
                              Delivery                 │
                                  │                    │
                                  ▼                    ▼
                                Consumer
```

Reprinted with permission of Macmillan Publishing Company, Inc. from *Logistical Management* by Donald J. Bowersox. Copyright 1974, Macmillan Publishing Co., Inc., p. 49.

transaction creation. Such specifications relate to time, terms, and location of physical product transfer.

Three fundamental points should be kept in mind concerning separation within the total distribution channel. First, both transaction-creating and physical distribution activities are essential to successful marketing. The marketing process requires the activities of each as integral to success. Separation is only engaged in to the extent that overall performance is enhanced as a result of an added dimension of specialization. Second, the specific tasks integral to each form of activity are subject to particular specialization benefits that are best achieved by independent organizational performance. These benefits are for the most part independent and enhanced by utilizing separate structural arrangements. Finally, separation is a managerial and not a legal concept. Thus, the same intermediary, as a legal enterprise, may be capable of performing both transaction-creating and physical distribution activities in a channel. The desirable degree of legal separation in enterprise ownership, in contrast to activity separation in channel structure, is based upon specialization opportunities, potential economies of scale, nature of product-market match, total available resources, and managerial capabilities, to name a few of the more important factors.

SUMMARY

Marketing intermediaries exist to aid in overcoming barriers to efficient buying and selling. These barriers are confined to problems of matching assortments, stimulating purchase activity, and physical distribution.

Middlemen, as the intermediaries are known, are classified as merchant middlemen or agents. The former take title to goods and must cope with the risk of ownership. Merchant middlemen are of two types: retailers and wholesalers. Retailers are merchant middlemen primarily engaged in selling to ultimate consumers. Wholesalers are merchant middlemen primarily engaged in selling to retailers; to industrial, commercial, institutional or professional users; or to other wholesalers. Agents are engaged in the same kind of activity as merchant wholesalers except that they act in an agency capacity. Retail trade and wholesale trade include all establishments, regardless of whether they are middlemen engaged in wholesaling or retailing transactions.

A channel structure is *a combination of institutions through which a seller markets his products to the user or ultimate consumer*. In total, marketing channels overcome barriers to efficient trading by *sorting*—the act of concentrating and dispersing goods as they move toward destination of final consumption. Specialization in the sorting process has resulted in the development of marketing intermediaries. Four principles—(1) the principle of minimum total transactions, (2) the principle of massed reserves, (3) the principle of proximity, and (4) the principle of postponement—exemplify their role in the marketing of goods.

The concept of functional separation in channel structure was introduced as a way to enhance the degree of obtainable specialization. Separation of the channel into a specialized grouping of activities related to transaction creation and physical distribution increases the number of options available for obtaining efficiency while at the same time maintaining maximum flexibility.

The next chapter is concerned with the design of the transaction creation aspects of the overall marketing channel. Thus, building on the concept of separation, attention is first directed to the design of the transaction channel. Chapter 15 is directed to physical distribution channel design.

QUESTIONS AND PROBLEMS

1. Define what is meant by the *channel of distribution*.
2. Explain and illustrate the concept of *channel separation*.
3. What is the distinguishing difference between a wholesale and a retail transaction? To what extent can a wholesaler retail, and a retailer wholesale?
4. Are the functions performed by marketing institutions eliminated when those institutions disappear from the distribution structure?
5. "Marketing institutions reconcile the heterogeneity of supply-and-demand forces." Comment.
6. What is meant by the process of sorting?
7. How does the principle of massed reserves influence distribution efficiency?
8. Comment on the notion that marketing intermediaries perform functions for hire on behalf of the manufacturer.

Chapter 14

Transaction Channel Design

The transaction channel structure represents a network of specialized marketing institutions that exist for the purpose of ownership transfer. The transaction channel consists of institutional arrangements between specialized intermediaries engaged in negotiation, contracting, and posttransaction administration of sales on a continuing basis.

Thus far, intermediaries within the transaction channel have been discussed on a functional as opposed to a behavioral basis. In addition, the complexities of the transaction channel have been oversimplified in the sense that relationships have been illustrated as simple step-like or straight-line progressions from manufacturer to customer. In this chapter the dynamics of transaction channel networks are introduced with respect to interorganizational behavior and conglomerate market competition. The chapter initially discusses interorganizational behavior. Next, we examine conglomerate market competition, which is presented as the prevailing state of behavior in contemporary transaction channel structure. To realize corporate objectives, it is necessary to effect transaction closure under conditions of conglomerate market competition. The last section reviews criteria for selection among alternative transaction channel structures.

INTERORGANIZATIONAL BEHAVIOR

A central issue in marketing centers around the question—who is the manufacturer's customer? One way to answer this question is to trace the flow of orders through the channel system. From this perspective, in a manufacturer-wholesaler-retailer-consumer distribution channel, the consumer is the retailer's customer, the retailer is the wholesaler's customer, and the wholesaler is the manufacturer's customer. This is so because a series of market transactions takes place in which there is a transfer of ownership at each stage of the distribution system. This approach has a further technical validity in that each of these participants is an independent legal business entity, rather than an agent acting in the place of his principal.

The wholesaler as a private business entrepreneur presumably cultivates his markets with his own resources in such a way as best to achieve his own goals. His functions traditionally include the development of retail outlets for products carried, and the "serving" of these accounts. His flow of orders, and the fact that the wholesaler is an independent legal entity, have caused manufacturers to regard the wholesaler as a customer, and to devote the bulk of their efforts to gaining a larger proportion of his business.

This traditional orientation has tended to obscure the more fundamental point that the ultimate consumer or buyer is in reality *the* customer of all participants in the system. Unless the ultimate consumer purchases, it is only a matter of time until purchases at intermediate points cease and the middlemen "customers" of the manufacturer become dormant accounts. This realization has led to a philosophy that recognizes the ultimate consumer as *the sole customer* of the manufacturer, and the distributors and dealers as providers of a group of functions for hire. According to this view, the manufacturer's job is either to assist the distributors and dealers in performing their functions as effectively as possible, or to perform them himself, if he can do so more efficiently. While this is a rather extreme view, the trend is in this direction.

In the early eras of marketing, most channels of distribution tended to be controlled by manufacturing organizations. In more recent years this historical position of authority has been reduced or weakened by the growth of powerful retail and wholesale intermediaries and to some extent by the formulation of trade associations and a modification of antitrust laws.[1] Thus, the channel of distribution can be described as a grouping of individual business organizations engaged in a confrontation between the desire to cooperate on the one hand and the motivation to undertake independent action leading to conflict on the other hand. The desire to cooperate stems from the potential economic rewards to be shared from such joint behavior. The temptation to act independently stems from the fact that divergent behavior may in many short-term situations bring greater immediate rewards than those realized by cooperative behavior. Thus, channel behavior is always a fine balance between conflict and cooperation.

---

[1] For an expanded discussion, see Bruce E. Mallen, "Conflict and Cooperation in Marketing Channels," in *Reflections on Progress in Marketing,* ed. L. George Smith (Chicago: American Marketing Association, 1964), pp. 65–68, or Robert W. Little, "The Marketing Channel: Who Should Lead This Extracorporate Organization," *Journal of Marketing,* 34 (January 1970), 31–38.

PRIMARY AND SECONDARY CHANNEL ROLES

In any dynamic system, there is some classification of participants according to role. Based upon the power to control performance, we can rank participants as performing primary or secondary roles in the overall channel.[2]

In a manufacturer-dealer system, the brand name generally plays a primary role. For example, in automotive marketing the manufacturer carries the most risk and stands to lose the most if the system malfunctions. As a result, the manufacturing enterprise tends to be the focus of leadership, authority, and decision. In other words, the manufacturer plays the primary role. All other participants exercise subordinate roles.

The category of wholesale intermediary has been less successful than the retailer in gaining power leverage in the distribution structure. This can be attributed, at least in part, to the inability of the wholesaler to enjoy a total perspective of channel opportunity and risk. It appears that the balance of countervailing power is today in favor of either the brand owner or the institution having achieved market integration by virtue of proximity to final customers of the overall channel. While few definitive studies exist, a reasonable judgment is that the higher the price of the item to the ultimate consumer and the greater the brand identification, the greater the balance of power in favor of the brand owner. Several large retail organizations, such as Sears, Roebuck and J C Penney, enjoy a powerful channel position as a result of their market proximity, the ability to control product-brand mix offered for sale, and the fact that they merchandise their own brand name products.

CHANNEL LEADERSHIP

The ultimate benefit of power within a channel structure is the authority to direct channel behavior.[3] Such power has a broader base than pure economic leverage. The channel members must have a willingness to comply with the direction or leadership provided by the primary role player.

[2] The ideas of primary and subordinate roles and a complex of mutual expectations were developed by Professor Valentine P. Ridgeway, "Administration of Manufacturer-Dealer Systems," *Administrative Science Quarterly*, I (March 1957).

[3] See Louis P. Bucklin, "The Locus of Channel Control," in *Marketing and the New Science of Planning*, ed. Robert L. King (Chicago: American Marketing Association, 1968), pp. 142–47. Also Louis P. Bucklin, "A Theory of Channel Control," *Journal of Marketing*, 37 (January 1973), 39–47.

Thus, a complex set of mutual expectations on the part of all channel participants must exist if coordinated interorganizational behavior is to result.[4]

The terms channel captain, channel leader, and even superorganization management have been applied to the channel member who enjoys sufficient power so as to spearhead the channel coordinating activity. It is possible for a firm to gain control by virtue of economic ownership. This is referred to as *vertical integration*. The term is applicable when a firm controls, by virtue of ownership, two or more consecutive levels in the distribution channel. In contrast to vertically owned channels, firms that dominate and direct channel activities by persuasion or coercion are referred to as *vertically controlled*.

At this point in the study of marketing, it is important to realize that channel systems are necessary to achieve marketing goals and that such interorganizational systems are dynamic in nature as a result of behavioral patterns. It is also important to realize that firms engaged in transaction channel arrangements are simultaneously cooperative and competitive. The reasons for these two conflicting behavioral states can be traced to the nature of conglomerate market competition.

CONGLOMERATE MARKET COMPETITION

The term *conglomerate market competition* refers to competition among different types of dealers and distributors selling the same commodity. Over a relatively long period of years there has been a trend for market outlets to "scramble" merchandise lines—that is, to diversify product assortments by adding different types of merchandise. Drugstores at one time handled only pharmaceuticals but then added fountains, drug sundries, and notions, and now carry cosmetics, toiletries, magazines, watches, jewelry, portable appliances, housewares, cameras, home shop tools, and many other items. Tire stores at first added only the closely related lines of batteries and automobile accessories but now handle appliances, sporting goods, toys and games, bicycles, outdoor furniture, and housewares. Food stores added meats to their staple, dry groceries, and eventually took on baked goods, drugs, toiletries, magazines, alcoholic beverages, flowers, and housewares. Some now stock clothing, portable appliances, portable electric tools, china, silverware, binoculars, and hardware items.

[4] Larry J. Rosenberg and Louis W. Stern, "Toward the Analysis of Conflict in Distribution Channels: A Descriptive Model," *Journal of Marketing*, 34 (October 1970), 40–46; and Bert Rosenbloom, "Conflict and Channel Efficiency: Some Conceptual Models for the Decision Maker," *Journal of Marketing*, 37 (July 1973), 26–30.

Transaction Channel Design

These few examples are only illustrative, for this trend has taken place in virtually every line of trade, to the point where we are now experiencing what can be called "conglomerate market competition." That is, there is a wide variety of different types of market outlets competing in selling the same commodities. Because of the extent of conglomerate market competition, we now turn our attention to the underlying causes and effects of this upon transaction channel behavior and structure.

THE CAUSES OF CONGLOMERATE MARKET COMPETITION

Many factors account for the increasing tendency toward scrambled merchandise lines. Some of these forces, having existed for many years, are basic and pervasive.[5] Others are more current in nature, deriving from dynamics in market forces and attempts by both producing and distributing enterprises to deal effectively with altered conditions. It is the combination of the two forces that is giving the trend its momentum and propelling markets toward an even more bewildering conglomeration of merchandise lines.

The Large Pool of Common Costs in Outlets

Perhaps the most basic force that has led to continuous attempts to expand product assortment is the large pool of common costs in distributive outlets. The vast majority of all costs incurred among retail establishments, for instance, are for the benefit of the total merchandise assortment handled, with only a small minority of costs traceable directly to any particular product. Not only is there a large pool of common costs, but the bulk of these common costs are of the fixed rather than variable variety. Specifically, the bulk of costs does not vary directly with unit sales volume over short and intermediate ranges of volume increases and contractions.

To demonstrate the impact that this pool of common costs has on product assortment, let us take the case of a jeweler in a downtown location of average size, who restricts his merchandise to jewelry items. In common with all merchants, he would like to find a way of increasing his profits without substantially increasing his costs. As he contemplates the various ways to do this, he cannot help but consider some variation in product

---

[5] For an excellent discussion of the basic forces leading to conglomerate competition, see Richard M. Alt, "Competition Among Types of Retailers in Selling the Same Commodities," *Journal of Marketing,* 24 (October 1949), 441. Also see Joseph Cornwall Palamountain, Jr., "Distribution: Its Economic Conflicts," in *The Marketing Channel,* ed. Bruce E. Mallen (New York: John Wiley & Sons, Inc., 1967), pp. 114–18.

assortment: he speculates over the feasibility of adding a limited line of luggage.

As the jeweler surveys the store's layout, he notices that by moving a few counters, he could free one corner for the display of a limited line of luggage. He recalls that a nearby luggage dealer is selling a rather attractive men's two-suiter for $39.95, and learns that, with the trade discount, he can purchase a similar piece for $24. As he thinks about adding this merchandise, he recognizes that he will have very little additional cost in the sale of the luggage item. That is, he will incur no additional rent for space, will need no additional heat, light, or power, and will experience no additional depreciation of equipment and fixtures, and no additioinal costs in his credit department. Additional wages for sales personnel would not have to be taken into account, since the sales clerks are already being paid a salary and have considerable idle selling time. In short, the jeweler fails to see where any significant increases in expenses will be incurred from the sale of luggage.

The thought occurs to the jeweler that he could sell a men's two-suiter, equivalent to the luggage dealer's $39.95 item, for $31.95, providing a substantial inducement to customers to buy from him because of the price differential of 20 percent, while still obtaining a gross margin of 25 percent on his retail selling price, or 33 percent on his cost of merchandise. This would contribute an incremental profit of approximately $8 on every item sold. He reasons that, at the end of the year, the profitability of the store will be $8 greater for every piece of luggage sold. This seems to be a powerful inducement to add the merchandise, which we will assume he does.

The luggage dealer down the street finds it difficult to match his new competitor's prices because, since luggage is the only merchandise he handles, all his costs must be reflected in his luggage prices. Since the jeweler's luggage constitutes a superior consumer value, his luggage volume begins to expand rapidly. Now he decides he will clear more floor space and add another sales employee. Also, because demand is great enough, he decides he could purchase in larger quantities at more advantageous prices by visiting the New York wholesale market. He begins a somewhat more aggressive advertising program to support the rather rapid increase in his luggage business. By this time, however, the sale of luggage has generated additional costs—and these must be covered from sales revenue.

So we see that there is a point beyond which the merchant cannot go in pursuing this particular business philosophy profitably. In fact, some merchants would argue that the jeweler misinterpreted his cost structure from the very beginning by failing to expect every item to bear its proportional share of operating expenses. While there is a controversy over the wisdom of varied markups of merchandise, it is nonetheless apparent that the existence of this large pool of common costs has led many merchants to expand their product assortments. Countermeasures taken by the affected merchants, who expand their own product assortments, have contributed significantly to the scrambled and conglomerate merchandise lines we observe today. Competition among various dealers in selling the same commodity has thereby been significantly intensified.

Changing Consumer Shopping Habits

Changing consumer shopping habits have had a pronounced effect on the increase in product assortments. The most significant trend in consumer shopping habits influencing product assortments has been the shift toward self-service. As other retail establishments have recognized that some of their merchandise lines are amenable to supermarket-like merchandising techniques, opportunities have arisen for broadening the product assortment traditionally handled by those establishments. Drugstores, for example, have found that many of their items can be handled on a self-service basis. Once this fact was established, it was then possible to broaden merchandise assortments without substantially increasing labor costs. Some additional display and shelf space could be installed without having to hire more help to handle the selection of newly stocked items.

The whole idea of open stock, together with freedom for the customer to deliberate for any desired period of time over his choice of purchases, was accelerated during World War II, when labor was in such short supply that it was impossible for many retailing establishments to continue doing business in the traditional full-service manner. Department stores, for example, found that it was necessary to put some items of men's furnishings on a self-service basis. Men's sweaters, for instance, which commonly had been kept in glass display cases, and shown only on request by sales clerks, had to be put on open counters and "islands" for easy inspection and selection by customers. To the surprise of many merchants, customers *preferred* to shop this way—to examine and contemplate the purchase of goods—and impulse purchases increased.

This new shopping pattern was particularly well suited to some departments, such as toys and games, but not so well suited to others, such as fashion apparel. The point is that as establishments such as department stores, drugstores, variety stores, tire, battery, and accessory stores, and surplus and supply outlets, among other institutions, learned of the attractiveness of self-service, many new possibilities were opened for the expansion of merchandise lines into nontraditional areas. Self-service has accentuated scrambled merchandise lines among a variety of types of dealers.

Interconnectedness of Demand

One of the early motives for broadening product assortments was to capitalize on the interconnectedness of demand for closely related items. Gasoline stations, for example, added cleaners and polish, repair parts and accessories, batteries and tires. Men's clothing stores added shoes and men's furnishings. More recently, women's shoe stores added handbags and millinery, to provide matched ensembles.

While the existence of interconnected demand has made attractive openings for some merchants, it has provided barriers for others. For instance, the men's clothing store could with relative ease clear space for a limited line of men's shoes, recognizing that the buyer of a new suit often purchases a complete outfit, including shoes. On the other hand, it is difficult for the shoe store to retaliate by going in the other direction. The purchase of a new pair of shoes does not usually precipitate the purchase of a new suit of clothes. Also, the relative investment and amount of skill required for the shoe merchant to add men's clothing is substantially greater than the other way around. Shoe stores have found it difficult to broaden product assortments beyond hosiery, shoe polishes, handbags, handkerchiefs, neckties, and millinery.

There is also a perplexing psychological dimension to consumer associations of demand. Customers of supermarkets, for instance, seem perfectly willing to purchase automobile waxes and polishes along with floor waxes and polishes, but gasoline stations have never been able to sell floor waxes and polishes successfully alongside automobile waxes and polishes. Where a natural interconnectedness of demand exists, however, it seems almost certain that merchants will attempt to capitalize on the opportunity for successful expansion of product assortments. But movements in this direction have tended to weaken the position of the traditional limited-line store in competition with its multiline rival.

Desire to Increase Traffic Flow

Both high- and low-traffic establishments exist in the retail structure. Food supermarkets and drugstores exemplify the high-traffic establishment. A relatively large number of buyers patronize these establishments each day, and quite a few are in the store at any given time. Furniture and appliance stores exemplify the low-traffic establishment. They normally have relatively few customers each day, and few in the store at any given time. Their overall volume of business does depend to some extent on the level of exposure to customer traffic. Consequently, some low-traffic establishments have added higher-volume merchandise lines (hardware) with appealing prices, in hope of attracting a higher-traffic count. By featuring such merchandise, an appliance store, for instance, hopes that the attractiveness of the major appliances and the abilities of a skilled sales force will succeed in converting a profitable proportion of the bargain hunters into purchasers of the major merchandise line. On the assumption that you cannot sell merchandise before attracting potential buyers to the establishment, merchants dealing in these categories of goods have attempted to stimulate the traffic count by this device, which of course intensifies competition throughout the market on the *added* category of goods.

Introduction of New and Improved Products

When a new product with substantial innovation is introduced, there is always a scramble among outlets to handle it. Over a period of time the product, if successful, may settle toward better-established and more orderly distribution. This progression can be observed, for instance, in the case of frozen foods. When frozen foods were first introduced, there was an attempt by many types of retail outlets, both old and new, to exploit the new category of goods profitably. Frozen-locker plants, home-delivery route salesmen, department stores, drug stores, delicatessens, ice cream dealers, and dairies, in addition to the traditional food store outlets, all were involved in distribution of the new type of product. The pattern of distribution which existed in the early days of frozen foods has now narrowed to a more limited number of outlet types. New product introduction can be expected to contribute to the additional scrambling of merchandise lines among different types of dealers as they persist in their attempts to find new profit centers for their enterprises.

The improvement of old products has been as important a factor as the introduction of new products in contributing to the scrambling of merchandise. Some products when first introduced are of such a technical nature that they require specialized distribution agencies. Frequently, however, they are simplified to the point where it becomes feasible to sell them through nonspecialized outlets.

One of the early examples of this situation was the introduction of pneumatic tires for automobiles. This product required the specialized equipment and facilities of a tire dealer. Product performance was such that frequent repairs were required, and the item did not lend itself to mass distribution. As a consequence, the tire dealer sold virtually all the tires marketed. But when manufacturers improved the product and simplified servicing requirements, product characteristics permitted distribution through such outlets as gas stations, department stores, auto accessory stores, mail-order houses, and such new outlets as surplus and supply outlets, military post exchange stores, and discount houses. The rubber manufacturers, when testifying in a Federal Trade Commission hearing on monopolistic practices in the industry, used this evolution as a major argument in explaining why the tire dealers' share of the market had diminished so much in recent years.[6]

More examples of the effect of product improvement on conglomerate

---

[6] Thomas A. Staudt, "Quantity Limits and Public Policy," in *Marketing: Current Problems and Theories* (Bloomington, Ind.: Indiana University School of Business, 1952), p. 72.

market competition are window air-conditioners and television sets. Initially, window air-conditioners required installation by a licensed plumber, and consequently had limited distribution. Today the window air-conditioner is an easy-to-handle, plug-in appliance with easy adaptation to any window opening; a much broader group of outlets are capable of handling the product and do. The same holds true for television. The complicated installation requirements of the early sets no longer exist, and there has therefore been a substantial broadening of the distribution base to discount stores, mail-order houses, furniture stores, tire stores, hardware stores, and even drugstores and supermarkets.

Emergence of New Types of Outlets

Because the market structure is in a constant state of flux, new types of outlets emerge periodically. Perhaps the most significant in recent years has been the discount house. The discount house began as a catalog establishment, with very limited space and without sales personnel, and obtained items on order from wholesaling establishments for delivery to customers. As it succeeded and developed, it expanded its base of operations, so that today it is handling a broad line of immediately available merchandise, and is offering additional service.

Initially, in attempts to protect established dealers, manufacturers refrained from selling to this type of establishment. But as the volume of business grew rapidly in the discount houses, manufacturers had to review their distribution practices: the new outlets were in some cases selling substantially greater volumes of merchandise than were the traditional dealers. In time, more and more manufacturers chose to provide the discount houses with merchandise, believing that these outlets would otherwise somehow secure it anyway from various obscure sources.

The discount house, however, is not the only new type of outlet. Others are cooperatives, initiated by labor unions and governmental employees; war surplus and supply outlets; catalog stores; and home-party merchandising plans. Obviously, as new types of dealers emerge, intertype competition intensifies with a conglomerate effect.

Consumer Credit

Many manufacturers have found it desirable to expand distribution through outlets with established credit customers and flexible credit availability. Cameras, for instance, were at one time marketed almost entirely through camera stores dealing primarily on a cash basis. Department stores and jewelry stores became important outlets because they made credit available and already had credit customers. Manufacturers presumed that sales volume would increase if installment credit was readily available, as well as desired outlets that could provide this service. Some furniture stores added limited lines of appliances, such as refrigerators and stoves, as a convenience to established customers who already had installment credit with the store. The purchaser of a refrigerator, for example, could easily be accommodated by simply lengthening the number of payments required by a customer from a previous credit purchase. Credit has been made available in some previously "cash only" establishments, such as the J C Penney Company, and this has made it possible to extend merchandise lines into higher price categories.

Manufacturers' Diversification Practices

Manufacturers' product diversification programs have sometimes involved the trading-up and trading-down of merchandise lines. When this happens, the manufacturer may attempt to move the newly added lines through market outlets distinct from those handling the traditional items of merchandise. When Bell and Howell, for example, added low-priced movie cameras to its traditional line of relatively high-priced camera equipment, it chose to distribute the new items through such outlets as drugstores. Manufacturers sometimes desire different outlets for different quality merchandise, so as to avoid damaging the existing volume of business done through traditional outlets. In the goods where trading-up and trading-down has been common (cameras, watches, radios, sporting goods) interdealer competition has been increased from the larger number of different types of dealers engaged in selling the same general class of commodity.

Manufacturers' Service Policy

In recent times, manufacturers have come to accept more responsibility than formerly for the performance of marketing activities connected with the ultimate sale of their products. One of the most troublesome areas, particularly relevant to consumers' durable goods, has involved product service.

The appliance manufacturer, for instance, must make sure that adequate servicing and parts facilities are available if he is to remain in a strong competitive position. To make product guarantees effective at the consumer level, he must back them with easily accessible service establishments. An illustration of the way the acceptance of this responsibility has led to scrambled merchandising is the decision of RCA to establish its own service branches throughout the country for various products. One of the earlier reasons for allowing only established radio and television dealers to handle its equipment was the essentiality of service and repair facilities that only these outlets could provide. With the RCA service branch readily available to all local customers, it became feasible for a variety of outlets to handle the product. Dealers without repair service merely explained to the customer that if he had any difficulty with the set, the RCA factory service branch would handle the matter and honor the manufacturer's guarantee. Such arrangements provided by the manufacturer have increased the number of outlets competent to handle the merchandise by adding those specializing in the selling function and without repair facilities.

Production Automation

The manner in which production automation has contributed to conglomerate market competition has been obscured by the emphasis on its manufacturing and labor implications. Automation has been one of the strongest of the current forces leading to accelerated scrambled merchandising. This pressure comes about because automation changes the character of the manufacturer's cost structure, creating a strong incentive for increased sales volume.

This incentive derives from two factors. First, automation increases the fixed-costs proportion of total costs, with an accompanying reduction in direct labor costs. That is, machinery is substituted for manpower; in a fully automated factory, there would be almost no labor cost. The result of heavy fixed charges is that: (1) the break-even point is increased, (2) the volume of sales that must be realized to maintain existing profits is increased, and (3) the volume required to maintain the same profit as a return on investments is a still higher figure. In cases such as this, profit leverage increases. That is, a modest increase or decrease has much more effect on profitability than it had prior to automation (the profit or loss angle is much wider). The second factor is that although a plant can be automated to the same level of capacity as before, almost inevitably the plant's capacity is increased through automation. This only serves to intensify the problems of the altered cost structure. The result of the combination of the two forces is a driving incentive for sales volume. As the marketer assesses opportunities to bring about increased volume, he cannot help but contemplate the potentialities of distribution through outlets additional to those being utilized.

The pronounced trend toward production automation in recent years has exerted a strong force for increases in sales volume because of the critical profit consequences of volume increments. This force has manifested itself in the seeking of additional outlets beyond traditional ones for the sale of the product, and the consequent further scrambling of retail merchandise lines and conglomerate market competition.

THE EFFECTS OF CONGLOMERATE MARKET COMPETITION

Given more intensified scrambled merchandising, what can be anticipated in the way of effects on marketing practices? The effects are likely to be: (1) reverberations in price competition and (2) various altered marketing policies on the part of manufacturers and dealers.

Price Competition

As the number of competitive enterprises of different types selling the same commodities increases, it will have a mixed effect on price competition and the retail price structure. In view of the fact that outlets of different types have different cost structures, we can expect price variations to be observable in the market offerings of the various outlets. This will intensify the pressures on the less efficient outlets. However, a second price reverberation may materialize. As the less efficient outlet finds its market position jeopardized because of vigorous price competition, it may rely more on nonprice competition. That is, it will compete more on the basis of service, quality selling, credit extension, and repair and maintenance effectiveness. Thus, there will be pressures on the price structure, with more aggressive pricing taking place in some quarters and emphasis on service in others. On balance, one cannot anticipate price competition to abate significantly in the foreseeable future.

Further Decline in the Market Share of Single-Line Stores

An increase in the degree of scrambled merchandising can only result in the further decline of the market share of single-line stores and limited-merchandise outlets. Stated another way, multiple-line and general merchandise outlets can be expected to improve their market share at the expense of their single-line rivals. Jewelry stores most likely will sell a smaller proportion of jewelry, shoe stores will sell a smaller proportion of shoes, and luggage dealers will sell proportionately less luggage, with some highly specialized types of single-line stores, such as bicycle shops, virtually fighting for their existence. This decline has been taking place over a period of time in several lines of trade, and unless a substantial change in consumer shopping habits and attitudes toward nonprice competition or service establishments takes place, it can be expected to continue.

Battle of Brands

Because of the conglomerate nature of competition, the battle of brands has intensified. One device that market outlets can be expected to employ in order to gain a monopolistic position is the further development of private-label lines. Because private-brand merchandise is not generally available, the distributor and/or dealer who can create a preference for his own brand of merchandise is in an advantageous defensive position for interagency competition. We have already seen the major chain stores develop private-label business to a substantial degree; this probably will spread to many lines of merchandise where little private-brand business exists. The prospect of decline in the number of brands in many lines of trade is not promising. The opposite is far more likely.

Manufacturer Responsibility for Demand Creation

The result of the effect of scrambled merchandising on private labels will be that manufacturers will exercise an increasing responsibility for the creation of demand for their established, nationally known products. This will be done to protect market shares in this conglomerate competitive structure—manufacturers will be reluctant to entrust their promotional effectiveness to dealers and distributors.

Many market outlets are caught in ambiguous market competition, to the point where their margins are inadequate to sustain promotional efforts. Manufacturers can be expected to rely on "pull"-type promotion, in which advertising, merchandising, and sales promotion are geared to the ultimate purchase level so as to draw the product through the various levels of distribution into consumption. This is in contrast to the "push"-type of promotion, in which the manufacturer expects each successive stage of the distributive network to forcefully promote the product to the next level, thereby finally winning a reasonable share of the market at the ultimate purchase level. This is one reason why we can expect aggregate advertising expenditures, which were running at an annual rate of $28 billion in 1975, to increase significantly.

Increased Emphasis on a Total System's Concept of Marketing

Directly related to the demand, creation effect will be an increased emphasis on the part of manufacturers to embrace a total system's concept of distribution. That is, the manufacturer will regard his total marketing system as being in competition with his rival manufacturer's total marketing system, and also the total systems of distributive rivals who have integrated backward to manufacturing. The manufacturer thus will seek to control all variables that make for effective marketing, and make every effort to integrate as carefully as possible all operations throughout the system, to the mutual advantage of the participants and his own enterprise.

Increased Pressure for Restrictive Legislation

As some manufacturers and dealers find it increasingly difficult to hold their share of the market in the face of intensified conglomerate market competition, they can be expected to turn to the government for help through restrictive legislation. We have already seen demands for reestablishing the Fair Trade Laws, Unfair Practices Acts, and local ordinances covering door-to-door selling; requests for licensing the number of distributive establishments; pressure for more vigorous enforcement of the Robinson-Patman Act; and increased trade association activities to develop more uniform cost control and marketing practices. While all of these pressures are certain to increase, it is doubtful if they will be effective, because it is difficult to legislate against the inherent economic advantages one type of market outlet has over another. Stated differently: It is hard to legislate against the dynamics of the marketplace in a free enterprise society.

CRITERIA FOR SELECTING TRANSACTION CHANNEL STRUCTURE

The purpose of this section is to provide a summary of factors that are relevant to the selection of a transaction channel structure. To select a channel structure requires extensive knowledge of the intermediaries available and their respective capacity to perform the desired functions. The ultimate decision or selection will rest on a combination of the market coverage and the market control needed.

MARKET COVERAGE NEEDED

The question of market coverage has primarily two facets. The first is the types of outlets which should handle the product, and the second is the intensity of distribution needed.

Type of Outlet Required

What types of institutions should carry the product? Should hardware stores carry camping equipment, and should variety stores carry outboard motors? The increase in scrambled merchandising represents a continuing problem to the manufacturer. The change in product assortments offered by different types of retailers is reflected in the assortments handled by different types of wholesalers.

Often the initiative for channel change comes from a retailer or wholesaler seeking to carry new lines—in a sense pursuing different product strategies by altering the usual assortments. Examples of this are the addition of building materials by hardware wholesalers, the handling of small appliances by drug and jewelry stores, and the inclusion of magazines, photographic equipment, ladies' hosiery, and housewares in the product assortments offered by food stores. In each case, the manufacturer must decide whether these outlets are appropriate for his products.

In other cases, the manufacturer may be seeking new ways to reach different markets and may take the initiative in attempting to alter traditional patterns. Such is the case with a large paper manufacturer placing stationery in a number of different kinds of outlets, or the manner in which book publishers have broadened their market for paperbacks by departing from the traditional book channels. More and more, the job of determining the proper type of outlet to handle a product is becoming a difficult one. As the character of retail stores changes, manufacturers must keep abreast, or find their products in the wrong channel.

In order for the manufacturer to determine the type of outlets best suited to sell his product, he must know the caliber of each of the potentially suitable outlets. If his product requires a substantial investment in inventory, the potential number of available outlets is immediately reduced. Where a particular environment for sale is needed, such as that required by expensive luxury items (for example, china and silverware), the number of outlets capable of providing this environment is limited. Other factors, such as need for consumer credit, availability of service facilities, or maintenance of repair parts inventories, may also restrict the number of available outlets.

Intensity of Distribution

The objectives of the company, the nature of the product, and the nature of the market determine the intensity of distribution required. The exposure to sale required by a manufacturer of toothpaste differs substantially from that required by a manufacturer of fine crystal. In general, more intense distribution calls for more indirect channels.[7] That is, more middlemen are used to fan out the distribution to make the product available to a large number of potential customers. Three degrees of intensity of distribution are discernible: (1) intensive distribution, (2) selective distribution, and (3) exclusive distribution.

Intensive distribution involves three different ideas. First, it can refer to the total marketing area over which distribution is desired. Using the

---

[7] The terms *direct channel* and *indirect channel* are often used in marketing. The directness of the channel refers to the number of channel members involved. The most direct channel is from manufacturer to ultimate consumer. For consumer goods, manufacturer-to-retailer-to-consumer is usually considered a direct channel. Indirect channels include either full-service or agent wholesale establishments.

term in this way makes a distinction between local or regional distribution and national distribution. Second, it can refer to the desire to gain exposure to sale in all outlets in which buyers are willing to purchase the product. That is, if drugstores are the proper type of outlet through which to offer the product, intensive distribution attempts to gain representation in every drugstore. Third, it may refer to the number of outlets, without regard to type. For example, chewing gum may be, and is, offered for sale in a number of different types of outlets. Distribution in this case is intensive because it is made available for sale in just about every kind of outlet that will handle it. Most low-unit-value high-frequency-of-purchase, staple products require intensive distribution. Representative of such products are foods, beverages, light hardware, and drug and sundries.

Selective distribution, as the name implies, involves a reduction in the number of outlets through which the product is made available. It is usually used in conjunction with products commonly referred to as "shopping goods." That is, the consumer rarely purchases the first product examined, but shops in many different outlets before coming to a final decision. By carefully selecting the outlets that handle the product, the manufacturer is assured that his product is represented as he desires. Restriction of the number of outlets handling a product, and selectivity within a type of outlet, are closely related problems. The number of outlets is restricted because the product requires an outlet that can provide specific services or environment in order to achieve desired sales volume. To place the product in just any outlet might damage the product's prestige. Such products as women's and men's clothing, ranges, and refrigerators and freezers, as well as many home furnishings, are selectively distributed.

Exclusive distribution may be considered a special type of selective distribution: a single outlet is given an exclusive franchise to handle the product in a prescribed territory. Products which have a high level of brand loyalty, which the customer will go out of his way to purchase, are distributed in this manner. If the product requires certain specialized efforts and heavy investment in facilities or inventories on the part of middlemen in the channel, they may be unwilling to handle it without assurance of exclusive representation. Wholesale paints, for instance, require a large investment in inventory and, consequently, paint distributors may insist upon exclusive representation for a given line. This, on the other hand, limits the manufacturer's market in the area. Consequently, multiple branding is sometimes used by the manufacturer to expand distribution through giving an "exclusive" on each brand to one dealer or distributor in the area.

Exclusive distribution at the wholesale level is more frequent than at the retail level. Wholesalers may insist upon exclusive representation in an area, but they, in turn, sell to retailers on an *intensive* or selective basis.

The decision of how intensive distribution is to be is most wisely made only after analyses of the market, the way in which the consumer buys, and the availability of channel members that can be induced to handle the product are complete.

THE DEGREE OF MARKET CONTROL

For many reasons, the task of selecting the channel of distribution is the responsibility of the manufacturer. The widespread branding of merchandise forces responsibility upon him. The act of identifying the source through a brand name, together with promoting the brand to achieve some level of customer loyalty, is public notice that responsibility is assumed. Likewise, the use of warranties has a similar effect. The increase in technically complex products, with a need for before- and after-sale service, is another factor forcing the manufacturer to assume responsibility. Perhaps the most pervasive influence is the fact that unless goods move through the channel, repeat orders will be at a minimum. The act of promoting a product line directly to the ultimate consumer in an effort to pull goods through the channel is evidence of the manufacturer's desire to control the channel. Through control, the manufacturer attempts to insure that his product will receive the required sales aggressiveness as well as all the other essential elements necessary to produce results that meet the objectives of the enterprise.

Different products require different degrees of control. Where close control is necessary, one of the ways of achieving it is through using relatively *direct* channels. By reducing the number of middlemen, it is easier to insure that all requirements are met. The use of direct house-to-house selling by manufacturers represents the ultimate in control—although it is quite costly. When *indirect* channels must be used—that is, when more middlemen are involved—attempts at control are made through establishing efficient dealer-manufacturer systems. As a rule of thumb, the degree of control achieved is directly proportionate to the directness of the channel.

There is a widespread belief that the more direct the channel, the less the cost of distribution; this belief is fostered by the familiar advertising slogan, "Direct from factory to you." In some cases, savings *are* achieved through direct sale. However, savings are achieved only if the manufacturer is able to perform the necessary activities at less expense than that incurred were independent middlemen to perform some of them. In most cases, direct sale is *more* costly, but it is the price paid to ensure that the product is properly presented in the market. In general, manufacturers desire the control provided by the more direct channels of distribution.

The decision of how intensive distribution is to be is most wisely made only after analyses of the market, the way in which the consumer buys, and the availability of channel members that can be induced to handle the product are complete.

THE DEGREE OF MARKET CONTROL

For many reasons, the task of selecting the channel of distribution is the responsibility of the manufacturer. The widespread branding of merchandise forces responsibility upon him. The act of identifying the source through a brand name, together with promoting the brand to achieve some level of customer loyalty, is public notice that responsibility is assumed. Likewise, the use of warranties has a similar effect. The increase in technically complex products, with a need for before- and after-sale service, is another factor forcing the manufacturer to assume responsibility. Perhaps the most pervasive influence is the fact that unless goods move through the channel, repeat orders will be at a minimum. The act of promoting a product line directly to the ultimate consumer in an effort to pull goods through the channel is evidence of the manufacturer's desire to control the channel. Through control, the manufacturer attempts to insure that his product will receive the required sales aggressiveness as well as all the other essential elements necessary to produce results that meet the objectives of the enterprise.

Different products require different degrees of control. Where close control is necessary, one of the ways of achieving it is through using relatively *direct* channels. By reducing the number of middlemen, it is easier to insure that all requirements are met. The use of direct house-to-house selling by manufacturers represents the ultimate in control—although it is quite costly. When *indirect* channels must be used—that is, when more middlemen are involved—attempts at control are made through establishing efficient dealer-manufacturer systems. As a rule of thumb, the degree of control achieved is directly proportionate to the directness of the channel.

There is a widespread belief that the more direct the channel, the less the cost of distribution; this belief is fostered by the familiar advertising slogan, "Direct from factory to you." In some cases, savings *are* achieved through direct sale. However, savings are achieved only if the manufacturer is able to perform the necessary activities at less expense than that incurred were independent middlemen to perform some of them. In most cases, direct sale is *more* costly, but it is the price paid to ensure that the product is properly presented in the market. In general, manufacturers desire the control provided by the more direct channels of distribution.

term in this way makes a distinction between local or regional distribution and national distribution. Second, it can refer to the desire to gain exposure to sale in all outlets in which buyers are willing to purchase the product. That is, if drugstores are the proper type of outlet through which to offer the product, intensive distribution attempts to gain representation in every drugstore. Third, it may refer to the number of outlets, without regard to type. For example, chewing gum may be, and is, offered for sale in a number of different types of outlets. Distribution in this case is intensive because it is made available for sale in just about every kind of outlet that will handle it. Most low-unit-value high-frequency-of-purchase, staple products require intensive distribution. Representative of such products are foods, beverages, light hardware, and drug and sundries.

Selective distribution, as the name implies, involves a reduction in the number of outlets through which the product is made available. It is usually used in conjunction with products commonly referred to as "shopping goods." That is, the consumer rarely purchases the first product examined, but shops in many different outlets before coming to a final decision. By carefully selecting the outlets that handle the product, the manufacturer is assured that his product is represented as he desires. Restriction of the number of outlets handling a product, and selectivity within a type of outlet, are closely related problems. The number of outlets is restricted because the product requires an outlet that can provide specific services or environment in order to achieve desired sales volume. To place the product in just any outlet might damage the product's prestige. Such products as women's and men's clothing, ranges, and refrigerators and freezers, as well as many home furnishings, are selectively distributed.

Exclusive distribution may be considered a special type of selective distribution: a single outlet is given an exclusive franchise to handle the product in a prescribed territory. Products which have a high level of brand loyalty, which the customer will go out of his way to purchase, are distributed in this manner. If the product requires certain specialized efforts and heavy investment in facilities or inventories on the part of middlemen in the channel, they may be unwilling to handle it without assurance of exclusive representation. Wholesale paints, for instance, require a large investment in inventory and, consequently, paint distributors may insist upon exclusive representation for a given line. This, on the other hand, limits the manufacturer's market in the area. Consequently, multiple branding is sometimes used by the manufacturer to expand distribution through giving an "exclusive" on each brand to one dealer or distributor in the area.

Exclusive distribution at the wholesale level is more frequent than at the retail level. Wholesalers may insist upon exclusive representation in an area, but they, in turn, sell to retailers on an intensive or selective basis.

DIRECT VERSUS INDIRECT CHANNELS

The activities that must be performed by the channels of distribution are a function of the needs and desires of buyers and the objectives of the manufacturer. Since the needs and desires of buyers vary with every product, it is difficult to explain in detail *all* the marketing factors which may be considered in selecting a channel of distribution. However, practitioners of marketing have been able to mark out definite areas of inquiry.

Approximately 97 percent of all goods sold for personal or household consumption pass through a retail store. Therefore, in consumer goods the question is how to get the goods into the retail stores. Should the manufacturer use an indirect channel, relying on various types of middlemen to sell to retailers, or should he go direct and assume responsibility for getting his goods into the retail stores? Likewise, in industrial goods a decision must be made on what reliance to place on industrial distributors versus going direct to the buyers with his own sales force. The approach is to analyze the characteristics of the product, the market, and the manufacturer, keeping in mind the types of institutions which, when combined as a channel of distribution, can most effectively perform the various activities so vital to the successful marketing of the product.

PRODUCT CHARACTERISTICS WHICH INFLUENCE THE CHOICE OF CHANNELS

The purpose of analyzing the product is to identify its characteristics to detect: (1) financial requirements, (2) any special handling needs, (3) storage requirements, and (4) requirements in sale. A discussion of some of the product characteristics and their relevance to channel selection follows.

Unit Value of the Product

The unit value of the product provides a clue to the funds available for distribution. In the case of high-unit-value products, more funds are available per unit of product sold than there are for low-unit-value products. Although a number of other influencing characteristics are generally associated with high-unit-value products (such as the need for servicing technical products), the general tendency is toward more costly, direct channels. Where the unit value is low, there is a tendency toward intensive distribution; channels are usually indirect just because of the need for intensive coverage. Direct channels for more market control are not generally used because there is not sufficient margin to cover the cost. However, low-unit-value products purchased in large quantities generate a favorable financial picture. That is, the absolute margin created in any single sale is large, and there is a large margin to absorb the cost of marketing.

Bulk

An important consideration is the value of the product relative to its weight. If it has a high value per pound, the extent of the market is not limited. If it is low, the cost of movement frequently restricts the entire market to an area reasonably close to the point of production. This has been true in the past in the brewing industry, wherein local brands play a major role. Some brewers have extended their markets by decentralization of producing facilities, along with attempts to build brand loyalty and to penetrate a larger geographic market at a premium price. The principle of *postponement,* whereby product adjustments are postponed to a point as close to the consumer as possible, is another means of overcoming this product characteristic. Coca-Cola is an excellent example. Bottled Coca-Cola, if distributed from a single plant over a wide area, would be considerably more expensive than it is under present methods of distribution. The shipment of the concentrated syrup to the bottling plant, and restriction of the market for each bottling plant to an area reasonably close to it, help to keep the cost down.

Perishability

Perishability may refer to physical deterioration, fashion perishability, or technological perishability. In each case, an element of risk is introduced. This risk is offset by the members of the channel purchasing on a hand-to-mouth basis, forcing a storage problem on the manufacturer. In physically perishable goods, the manufacturers or processors must find middlemen with the proper storage facilities. In the case of fashion perishability, the risk in inventory is enormous, and one that cannot easily be passed on to channel members. With technologically perishable goods, such as extremely complex machinery, leasing has become a prevalent policy, with the manufacturer assuming responsibility for all distribution factors. In general, perishable products tend to be handled through the shorter channels of distribution; with them, speed of movement through the channel is essential.

Technicality of the Product

When the product is technical, several requirements must be met. First, it may require a highly skilled technician to represent it to potential purchasers. Second, it may require more than just personal solicitation of customers; perhaps actual demonstration. Third, if the product must be adjusted to the customer's needs, the skills must be available to provide this before-sale service. Fourth, if there is a constant need for adjustment, after-sale service facilities must be provided. In this connection, it is often necessary to make sure that inventories of repair parts are conveniently available.

Width and Depth

A group of products associated in use and purchase usually is sold to a single market. In this sense, the broader the line, the higher the average-size sale, providing funds to take care of other requirements. Contrary to previous statements about the influence of the unit value of the product on the channel of distribution, a broad product line of low-unit-value products can be intensively distributed by direct methods. This is true because the average-size sale is relatively large. Many companies, such as the H. J. Heinz Company and the Campbell Soup Company, distribute broad lines directly to retail outlets from their own distribution centers. Care, however, should be exercised in combining products and attempting to sell them in the same channel.

Seasonality in Production or Consumption

Whenever production and consumption do not coincide, a storage problem is present. The middlemen within the channel are not usually willing to assume the out-of-season storage function, as it means an investment in inventory with no immediate return. Consequently, this activity is forced onto the manufacturer. Since storage is for many products an important activity, and since manufacturers have been forced to assume its responsibility, some have integrated vertically and assumed all of the activities that must be performed relative to it.

Degree of Market Acceptance

This characteristic is related to the aggressiveness needed to sell the product. Usually, for new products without a high degree of acceptance, very aggressive effort is required. Because many middlemen carry a wide range of competitive products, it often is not possible to achieve any special treatment for a given line. In these cases, the manufacturer must seek ways and means to control the channel of distribution. If the product is such that it lends itself to exclusive distribution, this may be the means used. When intensive exposure to sale is necessary, he may seek some more direct channel for distributing goods to a large number of outlets. If for any reason this is not possible, the use of independent middlemen, backed by the manufacturer's own salesmen (called "missionary salesmen" or "detail men") calling at various levels of distribution, may be used.

Missionary salesmen or detail men only incidentally take orders for merchandise. When they do, the order is turned over to the appropriate middleman servicing the account. Their purpose is to work with all middlemen to insure that the product is handled in the proper way. This may involve training wholesaler and retailer sales forces, building displays in retail outlets, and securing favorable shelf space in retail outlets, as well as seeking the proper use of advertising and promotional materials supplied by the manufacturer.

New products generally require a high level of aggressive selling, and to insure this the first channel used may be a more direct one. As a product achieves acceptance, a switch to more indirect channels may be possible.

Substitutability of Product

This is closely related to market acceptance. If there is little brand loyalty, and substitution is easy, maximum exposure to sale is essential. Not only must the product be conveniently available, but point-of-purchase communication is important. In many consumer goods, this means achieving favorable shelf space in self-service retail outlets, insuring effective display and aggressive personal selling at the retail level. These are not always easy to obtain. There is no particular reason why any of the middlemen carrying a wide range of products, including competing brands, should favor a given manufacturer. With exclusive or selective distribution, more than normal margins may be offered; or, to cite a more common occurrence, missionary salesmen, or detail men, may be used to gain the desired channel support.

MARKET CHARACTERISTICS WHICH AFFECT THE CHOICE OF CHANNELS

In part, analysis of a product identifies its users. However, precise analysis of the quantitative and qualitative aspects of the market is necessary to determine the size of the marketing job to be done and probable channel costs.

Users of the Product

The users must be identified, as the same product is often used by more than one type of consumer. For example, tractors are sold to farmers, manufacturing enterprises, county road commissions, municipal governments, and a number of other classes of customers. The activities necessary to sell to some classes differ from those necessary to sell to others; consequently, the channels used to reach these different classes vary. For example, the custom market is made up of a large number of individuals who purchase light tractors for commercial and residential landscaping and grading. They usually work part-time and use this as a source of extra income. The task of reaching these buyers and the method of selling to them differs substantially from reaching and selling to municipal governments. In the latter case, many buyers are large, buying in large quantities on a specification and bid basis. Frequently, demonstration is necessary, and technical service must be readily available.

Size of the Market

The size of the market gives an indication of the funds available for performing the activities needed. If the size of the market is large, even though the unit value of the product is small, the absolute dollar sales volume is large and provides considerable funds for allocation to the many activities which must be performed. Where the market is small, available funds are scarce, and the manufacturer might have to be content with a less elaborate program, relying more on the normal services that can be performed by middlemen without special incentives.

Geographic Concentration or Dispersion

When the market is geographically concentrated, ease of reaching all potential customers at low cost is greater. When it is thin and dispersed over a large area, the cost of solicitation is much higher. In the former case, there is reason to believe that direct channels will be feasible. In the latter, the product must be sold with others to increase the size of the average sale so that costs may be absorbed. This generally calls for indirect channels and the use of many middlemen.

Frequency of Purchase

When the consumer purchases frequently, this fact is reflected throughout each level of distribution, as each middleman will adjust to the rate of the flow of goods to the ultimate buyer. When purchase is frequent, the frequency of calls necessary is great. There is no sense in using a wholesaler who makes, on the average, four calls a year on an account, when proper service of the account requires eight calls a year. The selection of middlemen must take this into account. If the manufacturer deems it wise to go direct, the frequency of calls necessary gives some indication of the magnitude of the job. If twelve calls a year are necessary and there are 28,000 potential accounts, some 336,000 calls are required. If the salesman can make an average of 4,000 calls a year, approximately eighty-four salesmen are required. The cost of eighty-four salesmen can easily be determined, and some idea of expense arrived at.

Impulse Versus Deliberate Purchase

Some analysis must be made of buying behavior. This indicates the kind of product-image the manufacturer must provide. Since a part of this job is delegated to and performed by channel members, it is necessary to select only those members who will perform in the required way. If the product is purchased on impulse—that is, without preplanning—exposure to sale and effective point-of-purchase material are essential. If considerable deliberation is involved, then more reliance must be placed on personal representation. Some middlemen are able to provide this, but care must be exercised in the selection of the channel members to insure that the product is represented properly. The use of selective distribution serves this purpose.

Financial Capacity

It has already been demonstrated that some channels are more costly than others. A manufacturer may have a real need and desire to use a more costly channel, but not be able to, because he does not have funds sufficient to absorb the cost of all the activities usually performed by middlemen. He may perform them, or have reason to believe he can perform them, more efficiently, but the capital investments necessary to absorb the wholesaling activities will prove too great for him to afford.

Reputation of the Manufacturer

As we stated earlier, there are a number of middlemen within the distributive network from which the manufacturer selects. Sometimes the middlemen most likely to do the most effective marketing job for a manufacturer are tied up with competitive manufacturers, making proper entry into the channel impossible. In this case, the manufacturer may have to be satisfied with something less than optimum in terms of the middlemen he uses and assume the job himself, or set out to build an effective organization among those middlemen available to him. The reputation of the manufacturer has a good deal to do with the ease of entry into the channel. The better his reputation, the easier it is to attract the desired type of outlet.

A related aspect of this problem is found in those situations in which there is no appropriate middleman to do the job. An example will illustrate this situation. When mobile homes were introduced, there was no readymade terminal institution to handle this product. Eventually a new class of retailer developed, known as the mobile-homes dealer, but this took both time and the persistent efforts of the manufacturers.

Policies of the Manufacturer

Policies with respect to sales, service, price, and advertising influence the channels of distribution used. The manufacturers of the Kirby vacuum cleaner believe that demonstration within the home under actual operating conditions is the best way to sell the product. Since this task cannot very well be delegated to another institution, they use a direct house-to-house channel. Although this is costly, they prefer to compete on a quality basis. The price of the product reflects both the method of distribution and the quality of the product. Electrolux follows a similar policy. Most other vacuum cleaner manfacturers rely heavily on middlemen to perform the selling task.

Many pharmaceutical manufacturers state that service is the most important aspect of their marketing effort. By service, they mean service to the medical profession. This service is performed primarily by the detail man, whose costs account for 50 percent of marketing expenditures for purposes of providing information to the medical profession on the literally hundreds of new products appearing each year. Doctors could not possibly be fully acquainted with each drug on their own.

The cosmetic industry provides an example of contrast. The typical channel employed is indirect, using wholesalers to secure intense distribution in a large number of retail outlets. The manufacturer spends as high as 30 percent of sales in advertising to consumers to *pull* the product through the channel of distribution. Frequently, manufacturer demonstrators are used at the retail level to give the product a push at this point. Contrast this typical channel of distribution with that used by Avon. This company relies almost totally on a direct house-to-house selling force. Again the difference is attributed to a difference in policy, based upon the company's judgment as to the role of different marketing techniques.

Pricing policies often influence the channel of distribution. If the company follows a high-price, limited-market policy, which skims off the top of the market, the margins available to support different kinds of selling effort may be large. Consequently, expensive channels can be used. Usually, either selective or exclusive distribution is used, involving a minimum of middlemen. In contrast, if the company follows a low-price, mass market policy and attempts to penetrate every market in depth, intensive distribution is essential. Since the low-price policy reduces margins, lower-cost channels must be used. This is usually accomplished by mixing the product with those of other manufacturers in the assortments carried by wholesalers. In doing so, the selling cost is spread over many products, and the unit cost of the channel is low.

THE TENDENCY TOWARD DIRECT CHANNELS

Many manufacturers wish to circumvent wholesalers and sell directly to retailers, or in some cases directly to individual users and ultimate consumers. There are a number of reasons for this. Besides those associated with the characteristics of the product, such as technicality, perishability, and the need for aggressive sale, there are other forces at work contributing to this trend. Foremost is the desire of manufacturers to control the market. There has been a constant struggle between middlemen and manufacturers for market control. In general, wholesalers have been unwilling to give special attention to any particular manufacturer's product. When one considers the breadth of the line handled by the typical wholesaler, the manufacturer's expectation of special attention does not seem warranted. The lack of intensive cultivation of markets by wholesalers has caused manufacturers to establish brands wherever possible and promote their products directly to the consumer in an attempt to force middlemen to handle the product. This, in turn, has resulted in reductions in margins to wholesalers, which has only intensified the battle. Many middlemen have turned to their own private brands, coming into direct competition with the manufacturer's that were handled.

In the past, wholesalers, having experienced slight recessions in which large inventories were devaluated overnight, began buying on a hand-to-mouth basis. This, in turn, increased the warehousing burden on the manufacturer and he, having assumed this rather costly activity, found that the next logical step was to circumvent the wholesaler completely. Many manufacturers also found themselves under pressure from some large retailers who wished to buy direct at prices which reflected the performance of some wholesaling activities carried on by the retailer (purchase in large quantities). When the manufacturer did sell directly to retailers, charges of price discrimination were made by wholesalers handling the line.

The relationship between more direct channels and market control is clear. However, the ability to take advantage of it depends on a number of circumstances. Foremost is the financial capacity of the manufacturer. Can he afford to invest in the facilities necessary to assume the activities of the wholesaler? The ability to stand this cost depends upon the margins available and on the average-size sale. This means that it is possible only with high-unit-value products or a broad line of low-unit-value products. In the latter case, there must be some parallel between the line and the market in which the products in the line are sold. A broad line is of no value unless all products, or nearly all products, are sold to all customers. Also, the geographic dispersion of the market has a bearing on the economies of direct sale. Where the market is concentrated, direct sale is much more

...ere it is dispersed. The frequency of calls necessary, as ... the account, also has a bearing. If a very high frequency ...d with a large number of small accounts, the cost of direct ... prohibitive.

... of these limiting factors, one of three combinations is used. ...turers may sell directly to the larger accounts and use wholesalers. Second, they may use wholesalers completely and back ...salers' selling effort with their own sales force, usually called ...alesmen. Third, they may sell directly to retailers in the large ... there is a concentration of customers, but use wholesalers in ... parts of the market. Regardless of the desire to circumvent the ..., the capacity to do so is still determined by the characteristics ...duct, the market, and the manufacturer.

SUMMARY

While transaction channel systems appear to be flow diagram-type arrangements, in practice they are greatly influenced by interorganizational behavior and conglomerate market competition. Interorganizational behavior requires a careful study of the nature of confrontation within the channel structure. Leadership is essential for coordinated action. While conflict is bound to happen, the channel to obtain successful results must function in a cooperative and goal-directed manner.

One of the major elements of our dynamic market structure is the increasing intensity of conglomerate market competition, competition among different types of outlets selling the same commodity. Conglomerate market competition introduces an aspect of competition between members of the same transaction channel. Scrambled merchandising has undergone a long evolution, but has increased at an accelerated rate and shows no signs of abating in the immediate future. Some of the factors that account for this market condition derive from long-standing characteristics of distributive outlets; others are of more recent origin. Among the more influential factors are the large pool of common costs in distributive outlets; changing consumer shopping habits, particularly the preference for self-service; interconnectedness of demand among closely associated items; and the desire of low-traffic-count establishments to increase in-store buyer population. The introduction of new products and improvement of old ones, the emergence of new types of distributive outlets, manufacturers' diversification policies and service policies, and finally the strong shift to production automation in recent years are causes of more recent origin.

The effects of conglomerate competition have been felt for quite a few years. We can anticipate further reverberations in the price structure; a continued decline in the market share of single-line stores, in favor of their multiline rivals; a more aggressive battle of brands, with more outlets attempting to gain monopolistic position through private labels, manufacturers seeking to protect their own brand position, thus incurring added burdens of demand creation. Finally, the pressures for legislation are likely to be with us for some time to come.

From among the vast alternatives available, the marketing manager must structure the desired transaction channel arrangements. Such arrangements normally can be isolated by careful evaluation of market coverage needed and the degree of market control desired. The directness of the channel selected is determined in part by such product characteristics as unit value, bulk, perishability, technicality, width and depth of the line, seasonality, degree of market acceptance, and substitutability. Such market factors as users, size of market, geographic concentration, frequency of purchase, purchase behavior, financial capacity, and reputation and policies of the manufacturer also govern the transaction channel selected. In Chapter 15 we turn our attention to aspects of physical distribution channel design.

QUESTIONS AND PROBLEMS

1. Explain how one whole manufacturer-dealer system can be in competition with another. Give examples. What are the implications of this notion for competition? For antitrust policy?

2. "Whoever controls the market dominates the system." Explain and elaborate.

3. What accounts for the elements of both conflict and cooperation within the system?

4. What determines who performs the primary and who the subordinate roles within the system? Does the manufacturer always play the same role? Does the dealer? Explain. Is it always the same overtime in a single system?

5. What defenses does a small-scale retailer have against continuing pressure from scrambled merchandising?

6. What aspects of conglomerate market competition would lead in the direction of generally upward price levels? Which ones would tend toward lower price levels?

7. Would you expect a product that had high repetitive repurchase by consumers (high flow characteristics) to have direct, indirect, or split channel characteristics? Why?

8. What criteria for channel selection should the marketing manager employ?

Chapter 15

Physical Distribution Channel Design

The physical distribution channel structure represents a network of specialized institutions that exist for the purpose of physically delivering product assortments to purchasers. The physical distribution channel consists of institutional arrangements between specialized intermediaries engaged in the functions of distribution facility operation, transportation, inventory management, order processing, and material handling. These functions must be performed to support successful closure between producing enterprises and purchasing units. Whereas the primary function of the transaction channel was to stimulate demand and to execute ownership transfer, the primary function of the physical distribution channel is to perform product transfer in time and space.

In this chapter we will first discuss physical distribution within the broader concept of business logistics. Next, we will review the background of business competition that led to the development of the physical distribution concept. Included is a summary of competitive pressures and technological developments that underscored the emergence of integrated physical distribution. The next section will take an in depth look at the operating aspects of physical distribution systems. In the fourth section of the chapter attention is directed to the total cost concept, which has been the major integrating factor in the development of sophisticated physical distribution operating systems. In section five we discuss the aspects of customer service performance to which the operation of the physical distribution system is dedicated. In total, the chapter is designed to provide the introductory student with a feel of the importance of physical distribution to integrated marketing from the viewpoint of both performance and cost.

PHYSICAL DISTRIBUTION IN A LOGISTICAL PERSPECTIVE

Although most companies have for years given serious attention to the physical distribution process, it is only within a relatively short period that all the functions engaged in moving products to market have been viewed on an integrated system basis.[1] Physical distribution, as noted earlier, is concerned with the processing and physical delivery of finished inventories to satisfy customer orders. These orders might be placed by a consumer to a retailer or may be between specialized marketing intermediaries within the transaction channel, such as retailer orders to wholesalers or wholesalers ordering from manufacturers. The reader will recall that in Chapter 13 a distinction was made between merchant and agent middlemen.[2] By strict and formal definition, those intermediaries who perform the physical distribution function would be referred to as merchant middlemen.

The physical distribution process in any corporation is properly viewed as part of a larger management control system concerned with total expenditures within the corporation and within the overall channel of distribution for the movement of not only finished inventory but also raw materials, semifinished components, and parts. This broader context of movement is normally referred to as *business logistics*.[3]

The logistical system of an enterprise is seen as integrating all movement and associated costs from the point of initial commitment to procure a material until the final distribution of finished inventory. As such, logistical management encompasses the specialized areas of *material management* as well as *physical distribution*. In addition, it is common among large corporations to spend considerable effort within the enterprise to plan and control the movement of parts and materials as they pass through various stages of fabrication and assembly. This internal aspect is referred to as Material Requirement Planning (MRP). Its primary purpose is to reconcile the requirements of marketing and manufacturing in an orderly way by planning and controlling movement within the corporate structure.

The main activities involved in physical distribution are transportation, inventory management, order processing, storage, and material handling. It is important to recognize that within the logistical structure, operating systems concerned with material management, MRP, and physical distribution all may utilize identical trucks, warehouses, and computer control systems to perform the required activities. In operations, material management and physical distribution systems confront significant uncertainties.

---

[1] For an historical review of the development of the physical distribution concept, see Donald J. Bowersox, "Physical Distribution Development, Current Status and Potential," *Journal of Marketing,* 33 (January 1969), 63–70.

[2] See Chapter 13.

[3] Business logistics is defined as "The process of managing all activities required to strategically move raw materials, parts, and finished inventory from vendors, between enterprise facilities, and to customers" from Donald J. Bowersox, *Logistical Management* (New York: Macmillan Publishing Co., Inc., 1974), p. 1.

Material management, fundamentally concerned with procurement, must deal with the uncertainties of the supply environment as well as vendor performance in assuring an orderly flow of materials into the corporation. The physical distribution system, in contrast, must deal with the uncertainties that are characteristic of customer markets, wherein one is never sure concerning the what, when, and where of customer ordering. Again in contrast, the MRP system functions within controlled boundaries.

For efficient MRP, it is necessary to interpret uncertainty in the marketplace and to reconcile such uncertainty throughout the enterprise to guide resource commitment. First, it is necessary to reconcile the product forecasting area, which represents an interface between marketing and logistical management. Basically, marketing is concerned with forecasting in the sense of dollar and unit sales by region and marketing area. To support such forecasts logistically, it is necessary to develop a specific statement of expected individual stockkeeping unit sales in each specific market. For example, simply to know that one expects to sell 3,000 refrigerators in the Los Angeles market is not adequate. It is necessary to know precise specifications concerning the color, size, and features of each of these units. Second, it is necessary to reconcile a production schedule which is capable of supporting market forecast. Such scheduling clearly engages constraints with respect to manufacturing capacity, and therefore restricts marketing. The third stage of MRP is material planning. The material plan consists of breaking the production schedule into raw material and component part equivalents for purposes of procurement or fabrication. The widespread shortages in our economy during the past decade tend to offer an additional constraint on marketing in that shortages may interfere with plans and create final product shortages. Many firms have found it necessary to allocate output, mainly as a result of their inability to procure parts necessary to meet marketing requirements.

Throughout the remainder of this chapter we will concentrate on the physical distribution aspect of the overall logistical system. However, for an appreciation of the managerial responsibilities involved in integrated physical distribution within marketing, it is necessary that a manager maintain the proper perspective of total logistics in the corporation. Figure 15-1 provides a schematic of the relationships discussed in this chapter. It will be useful to view the total process as we look now at the details involved in the emergence and operations of physical distribution.

PRESSURES FOR IMPROVED PHYSICAL DISTRIBUTION PERFORMANCE

The operation of physical distribution within the firm has been referred to both as one of the oldest and one of the newest activities within commercial enterprise.[4] This dichotomy emerges from the fact that it has always been necessary to perform the functions of physical distribution in order to consummate a successful transaction. Thus, physical distribution is as old as the process of commercial trading. On the other hand, significantly new developments have occurred, both in terms of the competitive environment

FIGURE 15-1
Total Logistical Management Structure
Physical and Communication Flows

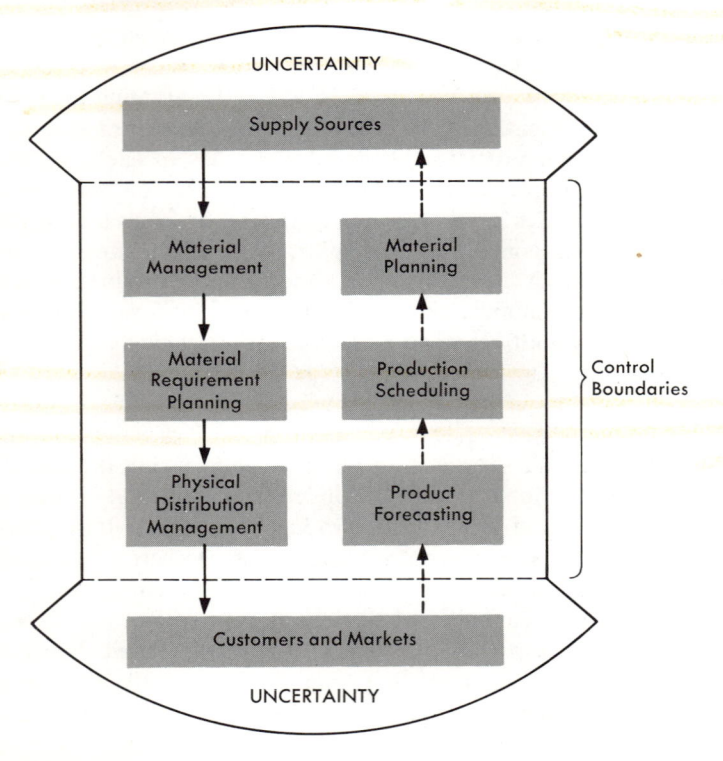

and with respect to technological developments, which have greatly enhanced an enterprise's capability to control and mold physical distribution operations to support marketing activities. In this section, we highlight the most significant developments that have led to the emergence of a sophisticated concept of physical distribution operations.

[4] For two examples of the traditional treatment of physical distribution, see Paul D. Converse, "The Other Half of Marketing," *Twenty-Sixth Boston Conference on Distribution,* Boston, 1954, and/or Peter Drucker, "The Economy's Dark Continent," *Fortune,* 72 (April 1962), 103–104.

COST EXPENDITURE

Perhaps the biggest pressure area for improved physical distribution performance was the recognition by management of the amount of revenue being expended to deliver products at the right time and to the right place. As early as 1954, experts were beginning to estimate that approximately one-half of the total cost of marketing was involved in physical distribution.[5] We are all aware that in the long run the price of the product must cover all costs, and it is clear that physical distribution is one of the highest costs of operation within the firm. It is not unusual for the cost of physical distribution to range from 10 to 35 percent of the final sales price.

In addition to being a high cost area, during periods of business slowdown and inflation it is necessary to view the improvement of physical distribution in a perspective of cost prevention. For example, a firm realizing a net profit of 2 percent on a sales dollar can realize significant profit gains by rather minimal prevention of physical distribution expenditure. A cost prevention of $20,000 in this example would provide the profit equivalent to a sales increase of $1 million.

In the broad logistical sense, it is difficult to pin down exactly how much American industry spends on the process of movement. The safe estimate is that 20 percent or greater of our gross national product is dedicated to the total cost of performing the logistical function. Transportation alone was estimated $62 billion in 1970 and is estimated to exceed $100 billion in 1980.[6] From the viewpoint of many firms the corralling and controlling of physical distribution cost is not only desirable but a necessity to remain an effective competitor. A firm does not exist for the purpose of cost reduction. However, one of the primary pressures for improved physical distribution performance clearly came from the fact that costs previously neglected could be controlled on an integrated basis by applying the systems approach to physical distribution.

INTENSE COMPETITION

A second aspect of the business situation characteristic of post-World War II is the intense competition which has prevailed throughout most industries. This competition, probably more than any other operating facet, tended to bring physical distribution planning into the formulation of mar-

---

[5] Converse, *Other Half*, p. 22.
[6] *1972 National Transportation Report,* Department of Transportation, and *Summary of National Transportation Statistics,* Department of Transportation, November 1972.

keting strategy. A great number of the meaningful differentiations possible in the marketplace evolved directly from physical distribution performance.

In the total marketplace, as more and more goods became available and consumers reached unprecedented levels of affluence, the overall buying public became much more meticulous with respect to buying behavior. Goods desired for purchase have to be available when and where they are wanted, as opposed to ordering for future delivery. For merchandising and promotion programs to be effective, it is clear that they have to be backed up with adequate inventories strategically located to provide rapid delivery.

For firms able to develop integrated systems capable of meeting these demands, their physical distribution systems offer a natural extension of total marketing efforts. Three aspects of intense competition are worthy of being singled out for brief review. These are: (1) the impact of new product proliferation, (2) the demands of conglomerate competition, and (3) the need for operational flexibility.

New Product Proliferation

Not so many years ago, item difference in a product assortment was related primarily to function and not to nonutilitarian aspects. For example, a line of typewriters would include different sizes and operational features. Today, typewriters are marketed in an assortment of colors to match any decor, as well as with a variety of special accessories. Such proliferation is also true of electrical appliances, plumbing fixtures, and even of such products as toilet tissue. The increase in variety means lower unit sales in each item, while at the same time it forces the physical distribution system to handle each and every stockkeeping unit as a unique product. Such proliferation often necessitates special handling, transportation, and packaging. For example, the widespread use of frozen foods has placed a great need upon the development of refrigerated and controlled environment distribution capability.

Conglomerate Competition

In Chapter 14, considerable time was spent in a discussion of the causes and effects of conglomerate competition upon the firm. As noted then, this phenomenon of selling in a wide variety of different types of marketing outlets is sometimes referred to as *scrambled merchandising* and *channel jumping*. In the physical distribution sense, conglomerate market competition requires a capability to supply a number of different channels of distribution simultaneously and efficiently with the same product.

This phenomenon is not limited to the retail level where it is most visible; for example, tires being sold in supermarkets. In addition to conglomerate competition at the retail level, quite often elaborate physical distribution arrangements are made to bypass wholesalers, jobbers, assemblers, and oftentimes even retailers, in the physical movement of products within the channel of distribution.

This changing pattern of physical distribution has forced a substantial alteration in the traditional concept of transportation and storage necessary to support a marketing program. In order to accommodate conglomerate competition, a firm must in fact develop multichanneled physical distribution systems capable of reaching a wide variety of different customers, each with unique purchase requirements. The simplicity of delivering manufacturing output to a limited number of wholesalers who assume responsibility for the remainder of the physical distribution process has substantially been replaced by complex multichannel systems. It is important to recognize that as a firm diffuses its output across a wide variety of different channels, the tendency is to lose the volume orientation in the flow to any specific channel. As will be illustrated later, physical distribution costs are to a degree subject to economies of scale. As volume flowing in any channel increases, unit costs of distribution decrease. Thus, one of the major impacts of conglomerate competition is increased cost which results from the diffusion of volume across a wide variety of different channels.

Operational Flexibility

Thus far, we have been stressing that the performance of managerial marketing requires constant appraisal of changing trends and the adaptation of resources to make maximum impact upon emerging opportunity. This need for constant adjustment requires flexibility in distribution performance. Namely, the firm must be able to adjust physical distribution operating capability rapidly, in order to provide required support in the marketplace.

This need for flexibility is clearly illustrated in the discussion of the product life cycle in Chapter 11. The form and reliability of physical distribution required during introductory stages are substantially different from those associated with later stages in the life cycle. During the introductory stage, it may be absolutely essential to have rapid delivery in order to assure minimum stockouts at the retail level. During this time, retailers may be reluctant to make major investments in inventory, whereas customers will have a high degree of intolerance for stockouts. Thus, a firm may require absolute premium on delivery reliability, almost regardless of cost, since failure could mean the loss of very costly market penetration. On the other hand, during periods of saturation and maturity, emphasis may shift toward the least-cost method of physical distribution, with the firm willing to suffer the penalties of controlled out-of-stocks in order to improve overall unit profitability. Operational flexibility is most clearly highlighted with respect to new product development. However, several other cases can be highlighted to illustrate the need not to become limited to one fixed way of conducting physical distribution operations.

A common example is found in the food industry, where manufacturers and retailers cooperate in massive promotions of a particular product assortment. Oftentimes such promotions are referred to as "truckload sales," the notion being that manufacturers ship directly to the retail store, bypassing all intermediate handling. The cost saved by this form of direct distribution is promoted as being passed on to the consumer in the form of lower prices. Under such conditions, a firm must have the flexibility to, in fact, bypass manufacturers' regional warehouses, wholesalers' warehouses, and chain warehouses, in order to bring the product directly from the manufacturing plant to the retail store. This form of flexibility is integral to effective local promotion.[7]

In total, the job of maintaining flexibility becomes more difficult in relation to the degree of product proliferation and conglomerate competition. All three of these aspects of intense competition in turn have profound impacts upon the cost structure of the firm. Thus, the job of physical distribution is becoming more complex and more expensive as marketing becomes more sophisticated. In the final part of this section, we turn attention briefly to the emergence of a few factors from a technological viewpoint that have helped managers to cope with these increased pressures of cost and complexity.

TECHNOLOGICAL DEVELOPMENTS

Extending from World War II into the 1950s, four technological developments were directly applicable to a new and revitalized approach to improving physical distribution performance.[8] In total, these four developments offer reasons why the contemporary physical distribution manager can be expected to perform more efficiently than his predecessor, and to play a more vital role in the formulation of marketing strategy. Each is briefly summarized in the following subsections.

Time Compression

A major technological development to impact on physical distribution operating efficiency results from the combination of high-speed digital computers and high-speed data transmission. We call the combination of

---

[7] For discussions pertaining to shared responsibilities in distribution, see Walter F. Friedman, "Physical Distribution: The Concept of Shared Services," *Harvard Business Review*, 53 (March/April 1975), and Donald J. Bowersox, "Showdown in the Magic Pipeline," *Handling & Shipping Presidential Issue* (Fall 1973).

[8] For an expanded discussion, see Bowersox, *Logistical Management*, pp. 1–32.

these two hardware innovations *time compression* in order to emphasize their impact upon the marketing process. Time compression, placed at the disposal of physical distribution managers, provides a capability of maintaining continuous inventory status throughout the network of facilities used to support marketing programs. The capability of high-speed data transmission allows information to be processed rapidly and accurately from the point of customer ordering to a central control for purposes of order allocation to a specific servicing facility. This transmission and processing capability reduces the elapsed time of order cycles and increases the operational flexibility of the firm at hand.

The case of the grocery manufacturer who was shipping all products twenty-four hours after paper work was received at the warehouse level provides an excellent illustration of the way in which time compression can benefit a marketing system. Despite the fact that delivery was dispatched no later than within twenty-four hours after order receipt, the company confronted serious customer complaints and competitive deficiencies with respect to the speed and consistency of delivery. Diagnostic review of the situation discovered the fact that, from the time orders were given to a salesman until the time they were received at the warehouse, it could take from as few as five to as many as twenty-five days to transverse the total system. Reorganization to place data transmission terminals at sales offices, combined with computerized order processing and credit checking, permitted the same orders constantly to be available at the shipping warehouse within twenty-four hours of the time that the customer committed to the salesman.

As a result of the revamped system, the firm benefited from the availability of additional time for purposes of performing the physical distribution function. Rapid availability of orders permitted the development of a scheduled delivery program to specified areas and customers in combination with shipment consolidation. Both of these features, as will become clearer throughout the development of this chapter, not only reduced *total cost* for the grocery manufacturer, but also guaranteed regular delivery on a consistent basis to the customers. For the firm, the advent of time compression allowed the manufacturer to improve customer service and at the same time reduce cost.

In the above example, time previously wasted was utilized in the system to assure more efficient performance. Time is management's most crucial asset. Whenever time utilization can be improved, the net result is the easing of pressures throughout other phases of the physical distribution operation.

Quantitative Developments

The second technological development of direct benefit was the emergence of quantitative tools capable of planning and controlling physical distribution operations. This specific category of tools represents the application of techniques not necessarily designed to optimize solutions to operating problems. Mathematics, by definition, is a precise science. However, business decision making and planning is not precise in that it must constantly select a satisfactory course from among an enormously complex set of variables. In addition, such plans must be implemented by imperfect human beings and within a structure of fixed commitments, which permit only gradual change during any short-term period. The modern orientation toward utilizing mathematical and statistical concepts to assist planning offers management a better solution without being preoccupied with seeking the optimum solution.

The advent of a realistic orientation to the development of mathematical models has opened the door for applications which are useful both in designing and operating physical distribution systems. Such tools as dynamic simulation, which replicates operations across time under different operating assumptions, have become commonplace items.[9] Locational structure models now exist that are capable of studying locations in a multiechelon setting throughout the full channel of distribution. Suffice to point out that today's manager has a far more powerful arsenal of planning tools available than did any of his predecessors. Since the field of physical distribution deals with many measurable attributes, namely, time, space, demand, and cost, it has been a prime choice as a candidate to be utilized in the development of new quantitative measures.

Systems Concept

The third technological development which has improved physical distribution performance is that the operation is a natural application of the systems concept. Elements of the systems concept were introduced in Chapter 3 as a method wherein many managerial marketing functions are integrated into a single effort. At that point, it was stressed that the systems approach is basically simple in concept. It emphasizes total performance without concentration on any specific part. Thus, the marketing system in total constitutes a subsystem of the corporation. Conversely, within the marketing system, physical distribution constitutes a subsystem.

It is important to stress that the components or parts of a system exist only to the extent that they contribute to the performance of the total sys-

[9] For example, see Donald J. Bowersox, "Planning Physical Distribution Operations with Dynamic Simulation," *Journal of Marketing,* 36 (January 1972), 17–25; Robert E. Markland, "Analyzing Geographically Discrete Warehousing Networks by Computer Simulation," *The Journal for the American Institute of Decision Sciences,* vol. 4 (April 1973); and Michael M. Conners, *et al.,* "The Distribution System Simulator," *Management Science,* vol. 8 (April 1972).

tem. Total system performance is singularly important. The design of the parts is not crucial. What is crucial is the relationship between the parts as they interact toward the accomplishment of the system's target objective. This interaction is technically referred to as component *tradeoff*. In any system, tradeoffs can either jeopardize or enhance system performance. In a physical distribution system, tradeoffs can be positive or negative with respect to the accomplishment of overall mission.

Tradeoffs normally confronted in physical distribution planning are of two general types. First, cost-to-cost tradeoffs exist between individual components of the physical distribution system. For example, high-speed transportation is faster and more costly than slow-speed transportation. However, the increased speed may result in reduced inventory investment and perhaps the need for fewer warehouses. The net result is that additional expenditures on transportation may result in more than a comparative reduction in inventory and warehousing costs. Such an illustration represents a form of cost-to-cost tradeoff that operates to the benefit of the total system.

A second category of tradeoff within the physical distribution system deals with the degree of service that the system is able to provide with respect to level, speed, and consistency of performance. *Level* of performance means the percentage of times that a product is available when ordered. *Speed* of service deals with the length of time required to receive delivery of an available product once an order is placed. *Consistency* of performance deals with the measurement over time of the degree to which a firm is able to maintain its level and speed of service. It is important to stress that cost-of-service tradeoffs deal with the output or support capability of the physical distribution system in perspective to overall marketing strategy. Whereas cost-to-cost tradeoff purely concerns efficiency, cost-to-service tradeoffs deal with a combination of effectiveness and related efficiencies.

The systems approach provides an analytical framework within which the design and administration of physical distribution can be quantified. In short, it is an enabling logic borrowed from science in general and applied specifically to cope with the complex pressures of contemporary physical distribution.

Total Cost Measurement

The fourth technological development important to physical distribution was the emergence of a measurement system that challenged the supremacy of purely natural cost accouning.[10] In the early evolution of busi-

---

[10] For an excellent example of cost/revenue analysis, see Michael Schiff, *Accounting and Cost in Physical Distribution Management* (Chicago: National

ness, as resources became increasingly scarce, management was forced to improve techniques for cost control and reduction. It was quite natural that in order to rationalize operations, a formal method of accounting and control was developed which received approval of governmental taxation units. With the advent of standard accounting procedure, business became both the benefactor and the victim of a routinized way of accounting for operations. The traditional accounting approach helps to control cash expenditures and to correlate them to natural accounts and charts. However, it fails to place emphasis on the interrelationship of costs between operating activities in a specific system. To counteract this, manfacturing was forced to develop cost accounting procedures in order to measure and control the manufacturing process. This same form of functional measurement has also developed in the area of physical distribution and is commonly referred to as *total cost* analysis.[11]

The word *total* evolved from the objective to accumulate all costs associated with a specified activity as opposed to just those costs normally identified on a profit and loss statement. The cost of carrying inventory, for example, is not that readily identified on typical corporate profit and loss statements. Direct expenditures related to the procurement and maintenance of inventory are scattered throughout the statement of conventional accounts. Oftentimes the interest charges for assets deployed do not appear on operating statements. In certain categories of business, such as retailing, it is standard practice to include transportation as part of the cost of procurement of goods to be sold, and, thus, by definition it is placed outside the control of retail management.

Total cost analysis is concerned with the functional costing of performing the overall physical distribution activity. As such, attention is placed on cash as well as noncash expenses associated with the deployment of assets in the achievement of physical distribution operating objectives. The total cost approach provides a measurement base for operationalizing systems analysis. Thus, the manager gains a handle on costing cost-to-cost and cost-to-service tradeoffs.

Council of Physical Distribution Management, 1972), pp. 1–10, and Frank H. Mossman, Paul M. Fischer, and W.J.E. Crissy, "New Approaches to Analyzing Marketing Profitability," *Journal of Marketing,* 38 (April, 1974), 43–48.

[11] For early development of this concept, see Howard T. Lewis, James W. Culliton, and Jack D. Steel, *The Role of Air Freight in Physical Distribution* (Boston: Division of Research, Graduate School of Business Administration, Harvard University, 1956); Marvin Flaks, "Total Cost Approach to Physical Distribution," *Business Management,* 24 (August 1963), 55–61; and Raymond LeKashman and John F. Stolle, "The Total Cost Approach to Distribution," *Business Horizons,* 8 (Winter 1965), 33–46.

The above noted technological developments provide the contemporary physical distribution manager with a powerful combination of tools for attacking the problem of design and administration of a physical distribution system.

OPERATING AREAS OF PHYSICAL DISTRIBUTION

There are five major components in a firm's physical distribution system. As noted earlier, these components also function to a significant degree as part of the company's overall logistical effort. Thus, a firm must maintain a high degree of congruency with respect to the material management and MRP activities in conjunction with its physical distribution performance. These components are each discussed in this section in order to provide a brief insight into the nature of physical distribution planning within the formulation of a marketing strategy. The final section briefly summarizes essential characteristics of physical distribution operating systems.

DISTRIBUTION FACILITIES

One of the essential questions in the design of a physical distribution system is to determine the number and location of facilities at which inventories will be staged and processed. Historically, the tendency was to decentralize vast numbers of inventories, since it was difficult if not impossible to assure rapid and consistent delivery from locations distant to the marketplace. Advancements in transportation and order processing have radically altered this restriction. Today's physical distribution manager has substantially more latitude in selection of the number of facilities than did his historical counterparts. Concentration of business into geographical areas was highlighted in Chapters 5, 8, and 9 dealing with consumer intermediate and international market delineation. It is a fact of business life that considerable differences exist between the purchasing potential of different geographical areas. For example, the top ten trading markets in the United States account for over 42 percent of the potential sale of any product or service.

From the viewpoint of market planning, one of the primary considerations is to select the number of warehouse locations that will be used for servicing market areas. These locations become the fixed points around which the entire physical distribution system is structured. While in part the appropriate number of distribution facilities is a function of the total cost and service requirements placed upon the system, these same facilities place restrictions on the operating capability and flexibility of the finalized distribution system. Therefore, it is appropriate to view total cost associated with transportation, inventory, order processing, and material movement as combining to determine the appropriate number and location of distribution facilities. The total cost must be evaluated in terms of attainment of a specified service.

The specific type of facilities that we are concerned with in the design of a physical distribution system are often referred to as *distribution centers*. While traditionally the word *warehouse* has been utilized, it tends to convey the thought of a repository for the more or less lengthy storage of goods. In essence, a static quality is associated with warehouse, which is not the essential idea in modern distribution planning. Therefore, the modern term *distribution center* is often used because it conveys the dynamic aspect of the underlying flow of goods.

The principal purpose of a distribution center is to provide an economical means to facilitate sorting in the channel structure. Furthermore, the principles of minimum total transaction, mass reserves, proximity, and postponement all are integral to the determination of the appropriate number and location of distribution centers within the physical distribution system.[12] The objectives are to hold transactions to a minimum, optimize inventories that are massed in anticipation of transactions, and maintain reasonable proximity to assure consistency in speed of delivery, while simultaneously postponing time and space commitments to as late as possible in the transaction creating process.

A firm may select either to utilize its own facilities or to hire the services of a public warehouseman. Somewhat analagous to a common carrier transportation company, a public warehouseman will provide the storage and materials handling function for an individual firm. The entire field of public warehousing is one of the most rapidly growing areas of specialization within the physical distribution structure. In addition to storage, many modern warehousemen provide a combination of special services and special protective environments that might otherwise not be possible for a firm to develop over a short period of time. For example, it is common for public warehousemen to consolidate shipments, to break down large volume transport shipments for redistribution to local markets, and to provide other distribution services. In addition, if a firm would desire to enter into a new market, such as frozen food distribution, readily available networks of frozen food distribution warehouses exist to provide national distribution on nearly an overnight basis. The hub around which the achievement of these objectives is met is a distribution facility structure from which the firm conducts its physical distribution operation.

---

[12] See Chapter 13.

TRANSPORTATION

Transportation provides the means by which goods are moved from production plants to the marketplace. To the extent that field inventory is deployed, transportation provides the link that connects manufacturing plants to distribution centers and then forward from those facilities to the

FIGURE 15-2
Distribution of Intercity Freight Movement by Modes, 1947–70

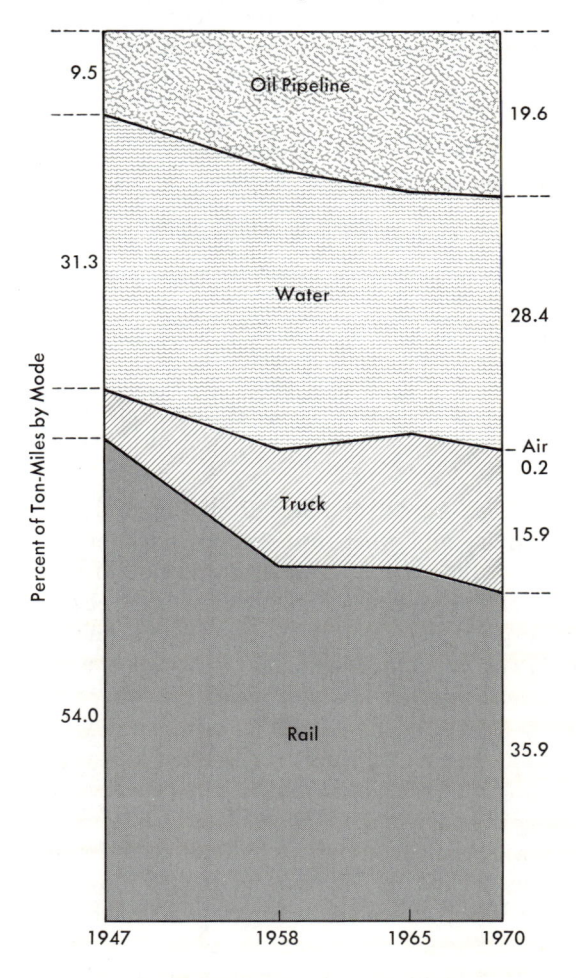

Mode	1947	1970
Oil Pipeline	9.5	19.6
Water	31.3	28.4
Air	—	0.2
Truck	—	15.9
Rail	54.0	35.9

Y-axis: Percent of Ton-Miles by Mode
X-axis: 1947, 1958, 1965, 1970

Source: Chart III–9, *1972 National Transportation Report,* U.S. Department of Transportation, pp. 2–55.

marketplace. The United States is fortunate to have one of the most sophisticated transportation infrastructures of any nation in the world. While fraught with current problems, this system is capable of providing substantial service at reasonable expenditure.

The United States transport system consists of five basic modes, each of which has its own essential economic characteristics. The five modes of transportation are air, truck, rail, pipeline, and water. Figure 15-2 provides a distribution of intercity freight movement by mode, measured in percentage of ton miles for the period of 1947 through 1970. Table 15-1 gives a ranking of the same modes on the basis of revenue per ton mile. Clearly, the modes of transportation that carry the smallest percentage of ton miles are the same that receive the highest price per ton mile.

TABLE 15-1
Comparative Average Revenue in Cents Per Ton Mile:
Five Basic Transportation Modes

Air	21.88
Truck	7.70
Rail	1.43
Pipeline	0.27
Water	0.30

Reprinted with permission of Macmillan Publishing Company, Inc., from *Logistical Management* by Donald J. Bowersox. Copyright 1974, Macmillan Publishing Co., Inc., p. 146.

A great deal can be extrapolated from Figure 15-2 and Table 15-1 with respect to where and when firms might select to use the individual modes of transport. In order of comparative value, Table 15-2 ranks the capabilities and relative operating characteristics of each of the basic five modes. In this respect, *speed* refers to the elapsed time of intercity movement. *Availability* is concerned with the ability of a mode to service any given pair of locations. *Dependability* relates to the average variance of expected delivery schedules. *Capability* is concerned with the ability of a mode to handle any and all transport requirements. And, finally, *frequency* relates to the quantity of scheduled movements between two points.

The trucking industry in the United States, while transporting less than 20 percent of total intercity ton miles, shares in over 75 percent of the total revenue. With the decline of railroads in the 1960s and 1970s, the percentage of traffic being allocated to highway has substantially increased, making this transport system the primary method of physical distribution movement in support of marketing programs. The widespread dependence on trucks has caused considerable concern in terms of energy utilization

Physical Distribution Channel Design

and ecological problems related to emissions. Nevertheless, today and for the foreseeable future, the physical distribution of the United States seems to be dependent upon our capability of maintaining a viable motor carrier system operating across more than 3 million miles of improved highways.

TABLE 15-2
Relative Operating Characteristics:
Five Basic Transportation Modes

Operating Characteristic	Transportation Mode				
	Rail	Highway	Water	Pipeline	Air
Speed	3	2	4	5	1
Availability	2	1	4	5	3
Dependability	3	2	4	1	5
Capability	2	3	1	5	4
Frequency	4	2	5	1	3

Reprinted with permission of Macmillan Publishing Company, Inc., from *Logistical Management* by Donald J. Bowersox. Copyright 1974, Macmillan Publishing Co., Inc., p. 149.

The transportation infrastructure can be further classified with respect to the legal forms of transportation that are authorized in the United States. Four basic legal types of carriers which can perform transportation services are *private, contract, common,* and *exempt.* A private transport alternative is characterized by the fact that a firm may operate its own transportation as long as it restricts operation to the transportation of its own inventories.

Contract carrier is a "for-hire" carrier authorized to transport for a fee the products of one or a limited number of shippers. Such contracts normally extend over a certain number of months and must be authorized and approved by the Interstate Commerce Commission if the firm engages in movement across state lines.

The largest category of available transportation service is provided by common carriers. Common carrier truckers are firms authorized by the government to provide transportation services for a regulated fee. The complexities that underline the common carrier network are numerous in that a wide variety of different rates, combination of operating authorities, and different services are available. It is important to stress that the common carrier is, in fact, a specialized intermediary available for hire for utilization in the physical distribution structure. As such, the common carrier acts in many ways similar to a retailer or wholesaler in the transaction channel.

The fourth category of legal transportation is referred to as an exempt carrier. The exempt carriers need not conform to direct regulations beyond those of licensing and safety laws of the states within which they operate.

The origin of exempt stems mainly from the support of the agricultural sector, wherein unprocessed farm products are authorized to be hauled without regulation to processing centers. Today this concept is extended somewhat to include local cartage within metropolitan areas and other specialized services in the backhaul of selected commodities.

Beyond the five basic modes and related legal types of operation, other transportation services are available in the United States. All of us are familiar with certain combinations of the modes referred to as piggyback or Trailer-On-Flat-Car (TOFC) operations. TOFC is a combination of truck trailer movement over-the-road and over-the-rail to capitalize on the inherent advantages of both modes. There are several other forms of coordinated transportation: trailers on barges, rail cars on barges, containers in air, and various others for combining the efficiency of multimodal transportation.

In addition, several package services specialize in the handling of small shipments, which are of critical importance to many firms' marketing programs. United Parcel Service (UPS) is the best known of the carriers that provide distribution of individual packages. The UPS service distributes packages conforming to specific size and weight restrictions on an overnight basis between most United States cities within 150 miles of each other. In addition to UPS, REA Express and the post office provide distribution of small shipments.

It is difficult to explain the complex United States transportation system in a few short paragraphs. This discussion has tended to neglect the important role of certain consolidators and freight forwarders, and the availability of other services important to distribution provided by transportation companies. For example, many transportation firms offer services that permit shipments to be reconsigned between customers while enroute and in some cases to be stored and processed in-transit. In addition, many companies provide protective services such as refrigeration and security for a specified fee.

It is important to recognize that the transportation infrastructure available to the physical distribution planner in the United States offers a vast capability which can be efficiently deployed to guarantee achievement of operating objectives. Within the complex structure of transportation, the firm must select a combination of modes and carriers which can perform the desired service within the cost structure that can be allocated to the transportation portion of logistics. Always keep in mind that total cost analysis stresses the fact that the freight cost associated with a specified movement is not necessarily the most important cost. Rather, it is essential to remember that transportation is one of many costs involved in physical distribution. The ultimate objective is to regulate and integrate the capability of transportation into the total system perspective and avoid sporadic and inconsistent transportation delivery.

INVENTORY

The requirements for transportation, and to a degree the number of distribution centers desirable in a physical distribution system, are based on the inventory policy specified by the enterprise. In a broad sense, a firm could stock every product at every distribution center at a level that would assure 100 percent availability when ordered by the customer. Such a luxurious program would result in extremely high levels of customer service, but at a prohibitive total cost. The objective in inventory management is to integrate and deploy within the logistical system the minimum amount of inventory consistent with desired delivery capability and total cost expenditures.

Excessive field inventory violates the principle of postponement and creates the potential risk of obsolescence and excessive deployment to the wrong markets of inventory subsequently needed to support marketing in other geographical areas. Thus, the ideal inventory program should be initiated around a policy of minimum asset commitment.

The answer to a sound inventory program is found in the selective deployment of stocks in consideration of four essential factors: (1) customer requirements, (2) product critical nature, (3) transportation integration, and (4) competition. Each is briefly noted.

In terms of *customer requirements,* it is essential to point out that not all customers are of equal importance to the marketing activities of a firm. Therefore, the products that are most frequently purchased by a firm's core customers must be given selective consideration in the stocking of inventories. The typical firm experiences what is referred to as a 20–80 rule; 20 percent of the products do 80 percent of the business, and 20 percent of the customers do 80 percent of the business. The essential point is to make sure that the products purchased by the critical 20 percent of the customers are maintained as high priority items in inventory stocking policy.

In terms of *product critical nature,* it is important to keep in mind that different products have essentially different cost and service requirements. A product that is crucial to the operation of a tractor or a bulldozer in the field is much more important in terms of inventory control than is a sun visor or a seat cushion. Remember that the cost and critical value of an item to the user and supplier should be one of the important elements in the determination of inventory policy.

Transportation integration deals with the capability of combining different products in a single shipment. To a degree, transportation cost can be minimized to the extent that the size of the average shipment is increased. It is essential that products which move together be stocked together. Consideration must therefore be given to the formlulation of family lines in inventory assortment to help achieve consolidated processing.

Finally, the latitude available in inventory deployment is directly related to *competitive action*. It goes without saying that one must either be equal or superior to competition if one expects to gain a differential advantage by virtue of the physical distribution activity. The competitive strategic placement of inventory is a direct determinant of what degree of customer delivery service is available from a given enterprise.

In summary, it is important to realize that inventory planning constitutes a major cost in the physical distribution system but also is one of the prime ingredients of the system's capability of providing service. The formulation of inventory strategy is highly related to sales forecasting, and consequently represents the firm's attempts to cope with uncertainty. While the detail of establishing base and safety stocks is substantial, a firm's physical distribution capability is highly integrated to its inventory strategy. To be everything to everybody is an expensive process; therefore, the underlying philosophy of good inventory management is centered on the application of creative selectivity in stocking policies.

ORDER PROCESSING

Order processing constitutes the communication linkage that stimulates a physical distribution system into action. Basically, if one can envision a series of distribution systems linked together by a transportation capability with each maintaining a level of inventory, it is the order processing that makes the system dynamic. Earlier in the chapter, the importance of compressing time by rapidly transmitting orders was illustrated by a short example. It is important to realize that order processing is the igniter of the system. When the processing of an order begins, the customer has made a commitment; and when a physical delivery is completed, the system has met its objective. Order processing then becomes a communication linkage for the overall system.

Alternate speeds of processing are available and each has its associated degree of reliability. For example, telephone orders are rapid and highly reliable, whereas the mailing of orders may be erratic and slow. With each speed of communication comes a cost that must be integrated in a total cost structure of a physical distribution system. To the extent that erroneous orders are processed or that the orders are not handled in an efficient manner, total capability of the logistical system may be diluted. It also should be pointed out that the speed of processing is integral to determining the combination of distribution centers, transportation, and inventory engaged in the logistical system design.

MATERIAL HANDLING

The final cost area of the logistical system that is interrelated to the previous four is material handling. Handling takes place within distribution facilities and throughout the transportation infrastructure. Every effort must be made within a physical distribution system to protect products through packaging to assure that they will arrive at the customer's location in usable condition. In addition, every effort should be made through master cartons, containers, and unit loads to reduce the number of individual products that must be handled in a distribution system, thereby increasing efficiency of operation.

The area of material handling is particularly integral to the internal operations of distribution center facilities. In this sense, a great deal of effort has resulted in the development of computerized and semiautomatic handling facilities to improve the productivity of sorting in the channel of distribution.

Thus, material handling is an integral part of total physical distribution as well as a special aspect of obtaining high degrees of efficiency. It is important to recognize that while handling does not stand out as vividly as the number of distribution facility locations, transportation expenditures, inventory deployments, or order processing, its cost can be extreme and its impact on physical distribution performance detrimental if not properly coordinated.

THE INTEGRATED SYSTEM

The hallmark of the physical distribution concept is that the activity areas described can be integrated into one operating system. This system exists to provide specific customer service at the lowest associated total cost.

The synergistic effect of tradeoffs between these five activity areas will limit what can be achieved both in terms of quality of service and cost. Several different forms of distribution have evolved in the United States for purposes of supporting different marketing programs. Many systems could be characterized as *echelon* structured, in which goods flow from manufacturing through a series of distribution centers for purposes of sorting until ultimately arriving at a retail store. Other systems are characterized as *direct,* in that movements generally flow from point of manufacture directly to retail stores or consumer units. Some mail order systems best reflect this type of distribution.

The essential quality that all distribution systems should maintain is the flexibility of *dual performance.* That is, the system should not be structured in such a way that all orders *must* be processed within the same operational structure. Flexibility is necessary to accommodate competitive requirements of conglomerate competition and to facilitate new product and venture expansions.

It is beneficial to distinguish between systems with respect to where the impetus for movement originates. Many systems of distribution in the United States are *pull systems*. In a pull system, products tend to be "pulled" toward the marketplace by the advent of customer orders. To the extent necessary, products are moved in anticipation of orders to stock individual distribution centers, but no effort is made to move them further until the customer order is received. This type of system is typical of grocery manufacturers who engage in the distribution of such products as cereals and canned foods.

In contrast, systems can also be characterized as *push systems*. In a push system, products are "pushed" to the retail level by virtue of substantial volume in anticipation of purchase by the consuming public. Systems that are characterized by push distribution strategy are typical of bakery products, milk and dairy, and meat products. It is essential to characterize in the early stage of physical distribution analysis whether a system has predominantly a push or pull mission. The mission will limit the range of capabilities that can be deployed in the system design. In consecutive sections, this chapter concludes with a look in depth at total cost and customer service performance.

TOTAL COST—THE INTEGRATING CONCEPT

The fundamental concept of total cost was discussed under technological developments leading to improved physical distribution performance. To a large degree, total cost measurement evolved from the general neglect of functional costing in the accumulation of traditional accounting costs. Like many essential concepts, total cost is not difficult to understand but is somewhat difficult to operationalize within the structure of accounts available in a typical corporation. The objective is clear: *what we wish to obtain is some reflection of the way that we would expect total cost to react in the design of a distribution system.* In other words, as we increase the number of distribution center locations, how would the costs associated with transportation, inventory, order processing, and material handling react? Is there a specific combination of facilities that would offer the lowest total cost? We are sure that such a relationship exists and the principles of systems analysis tell us that it is quite likely that the lowest system total cost will not be at the minimum cost of any of the individual functions.

In terms of transportation cost, we can generally expect that as the number of warehouse locations is increased, the cost of transportation will initially decrease and then, as more and more warehouses are added, will begin to increase. This function is illustrated in Figure 15-3 by the U-shaped transportation cost curve. The logic is that, in terms of transporta-

FIGURE 15-3
Total-Cost Logistical Network

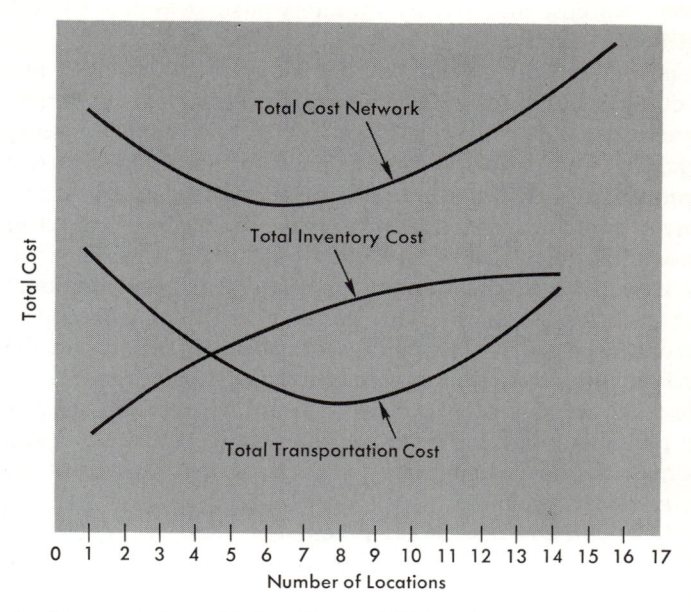

Reprinted with permission of Macmillan Publishing Company, Inc., from *Logistical Management* by Donald J. Bowersox. Copyright 1974, Macmillan Publishing Co., Inc., p. 325.

tion expenses, small shipments on a per unit basis are more expensive than large shipments. Therefore, as we operate a system with no or few warehouses, it is necessary to make small shipments directly to customers, and the only transportation savings that we can enjoy is when we can combine more than one customer's shipments in a single transportation movement. The addition of a warehouse will allow us to ship in large volumes, long distances to the warehouse, and then make very short individual customer deliveries, thereby enjoying the benefits of lower line-haul transportation rates in combination with short high-cost delivery rates. Warehouses can be sequentially added, as long as the savings in inbound transportation, combined with the outbound transportation, is cheaper than direct movement from the plant to the customer. In a given period, as more warehouses are added, our ability to make consolidated shipments into the warehouse will be diminished as volume is more and more segmented. Consequently, if we continue to add warehouses we would expect that transportation cost will a some point begin to go up.

Also in Figure 15-3, notice that the total cost of inventory increased as we added more facility locations. In this illustration, the cost of inventory is defined to include all of its aspects. Included in inventory costs are material handling within the warehouse and order processing, as well as the maintenance cost incurred by inventory taxes, storage, capital, insurance, and obsolescence.

Inventories can be basically divided into two categories or groupings. The first consists of the *base stock*, which is necessary to support the average level of demand placed upon the system. The second is the *safety stock*, which is added over and above base demand for purposes of providing additional protection to cover uncertainty of sales and delivery. As a general rule, safety stock increases in a system as the average number of locations increases, whereas base stocks essentially remain the same. The pattern of inventory expansion results from the need to establish additional safety stocks for each new location. The statistical base for estimating market sales is reduced in geographical size with each new facility location without a corresponding reduction in variability. The result is that larger safety stocks are required to service a demand from two locations or more than would be required from one location. Thus, the general rule is that safety stocks increase at a decreasing rate as more and more locations are added to the distribution system.

Total cost, in contrast, is the function of these two categories: total inventory cost and total transportation cost. It should be noted that total cost for the system, as expected in terms of the tradeoffs discussed earlier, will not necessarily be at the point of lowest cost for either inventory or transportation commitments. This point is illustrated in Figure 15-3 and represents the hallmark of the total cost concept.

CUSTOMER SERVICE PERFORMANCE

Determining the total cost of a system is critical to physical distribution planning, but it does not provide the total answer to system design. The essential aspect of physical distribution as an integral part of marketing is that it is oriented to providing a tangible means wherein the offerings of one firm can be differentiated from its competitors. This is accomplished by the essential ingredient of *customer service*, namely, level of service, speed of service, and consistency of service.

For purposes of viewing customer service capability, it is important to distinguish between physical delivery customer service and the human aspects of customer relations often referred to as customer sales-service in the business enterprise. Physical delivery service relates purely to the way in which the physical distribution system reacts to the receipt of a customer order and its ability to maintain level of performance over time. Beyond physical delivery, a vast amount of human relationships exists within the transaction and posttransaction activities of marketing that are appropriately forms of overall customer service.

Both transaction and posttransaction activities of marketing administration represent significant aspects of customer service. They should be identified and effectively managed in all marketing programs. Likewise, they should be differentiated from the base capability of the physical distribution system to provide a quality of delivery service that makes physical distribution an integral part of the overall marketing strategy. In this section we are dealing with the mechanical or structural customer service capabilities of the physical distribution system.

The essential structure for viewing customer service performance centers around the order cycle. In essence, the physical distribution structure of a company consists of a number of different order cycles which link together through order processing and transportation, servicing distribution facility and customers. At each distribution facility within the order cycle structure, inventory levels are held for the purpose of anticipating customer requirements. Essentially, this system in its nodal structure is multiechelon, and is illustrated in Figure 15-4.

Note that the capabilities of flexibility are included in this structural diagram by virtue of the fact that any particular distribution center customer assignment may be varied, depending on the nature of the physical movement requirement. Customer service measurement begins when the customer makes a commitment and ends when the product is delivered at his location available for use. Appropriate measurement of customer service must include the total order cycle and not the time required to perform any specific link such as transport or order processing.

It is also important to realize that the speed with which a cycle is performed is not in most situations as important as the consistency of performance over a wide number of situations. For example, continuous orders placed against a particular supplier over time offer a measure of his capabilities as opposed to the speed with which the service is accomplished on any one particular order cycle. Consistency results not only from control over the order processing and transportation segments, but also from control over the inventory levels. All of these possible factors of decay, that is, erratic transportation, order processing, or inconsistent levels of inventory, can result if the firm is not able to cope properly with the uncertainties of competition. A firm, in contrast, which gains a high degree of consistency in both level of availability and in consistent speed of delivery is considered to have a high degree of structural physical distribution customer service performance.

FIGURE 15-4
Structure of the Physical Distribution Network

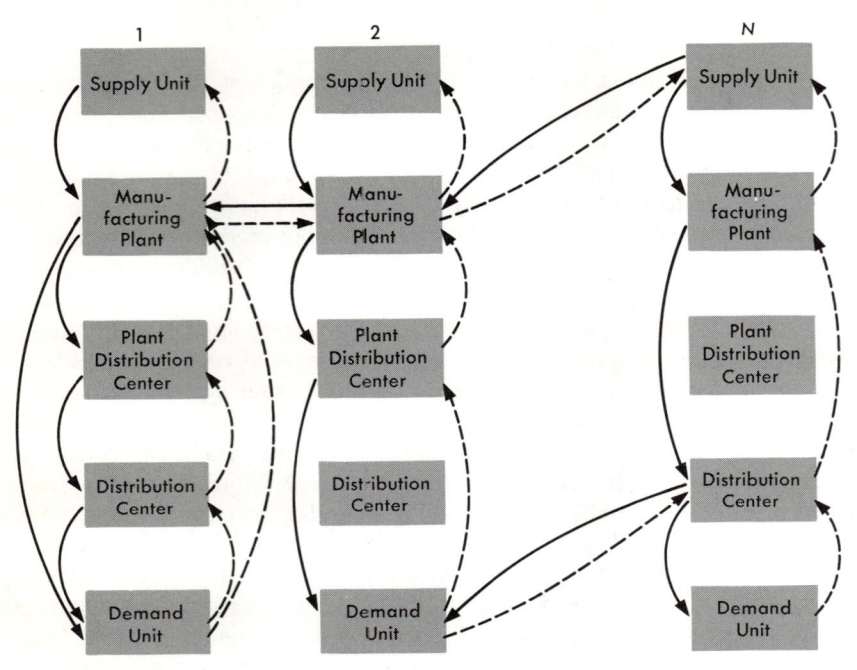

Reprinted with permission of Macmillan Publishing Company, Inc., from *Logistical Management* by Donald J. Bowersox. Copyright 1974, Macmillan Publishing Co., Inc., p. 396.

From the viewpoint of the total cost structure, it is increasingly expensive either to expand the level of inventory protection or consistently speed up the process of order processing or transportation. If a firm wishes to improve customer service offering to an extremely high degree of consistency in level of availability and speed of service, the cost per unit of the distribution system can be expected to increase. As a general rule, the higher the performance, the higher the unit cost, with costs increasing at an increasing rate. Therefore, the ultimate tradeoff is between the total cost of the system from its least cost perspective, as illustrated in Figure 15-4, and the degree of customer service desired to support the marketing program. Any increase in service over and above the lowest total cost system should ideally return revenues greater than corresponding costs of performing the service. This form of marginal tradeoff is discussed both within the physical distribution system and in relation to the total formulation of a marketing strategy in Chapter 19.

SUMMARY

In this chapter, physical distribution has been developed in terms of its role in a dual channel system. Because of the high cost and increased difficulty in physical distribution performance, it is desirable to separate this form of activity from the remainder of the channel in order to provide maximum opportunity for specialization. Physical distribution in the total corporation extends into operating areas much broader than purely marketing. A typical firm today finds it necessary to look at total movement from both the procurement and the selling side of the corporation, as well as the internal, in order to manage adequately total resources committed to this process.

Physical distribution is concerned with delivery of customer orders. The quality of physical distribution performance is a critical concern of managerial marketing. In contemporary business the pressures for improved physical distribution performance have been paramount. Relative cost of physical distribution performance has gone up as a result of inflation and increased cost of labor. Another factor leading to increased complexity in physical distribution has been intensive competition as reflected in new product proliferation, conglomerate competition, and the need to maintain operational flexibility.

To offset this increase in cost and complexity, contemporary management has benefited by several technological developments. Singled out in this chapter were time compression, quantitative techniques, the system concept, and total cost measurement as four developments that encourage improved efficiency in the physical distribution mission.

The overall physical distribution system was illustrated as an integrated operation combining a network of distribution facility locations linked together by transportation, inventory, order processing, and material handling operations. The essential ingredient of physical distribution planning is to view the system in its totality, understanding that the interrelationships exist between the parts and that these interrelationships must be managed for maximum benefit. As such, we identified two types of trade-offs that can exist in the system—cost-to-cost and cost-to-service. Systems can be characterized as being structured in an echelon manner or as being direct. The ideal physical distribution system maintains a flexibility to combine the virtues of these two distributive patterns. In addition, it is useful to describe systems as basically having a push or pull mission for purposes of planning.

The integrating concept for the physical distribution system is total cost. Total cost essentially centers around the two prime cost areas—transportation and inventory. Both are combined to determine the number of locations that are ideally needed to minimize total cost and servicing of market areas. As locations in the form of distribution centers are added to the system, it is expected that transportation costs will go down as a function of consolidation economies. However, inventories will go up with the addition of locations as larger safety stocks are required to support customer service levels. Least total cost for the system can be expected at some point that is neither the minimization of transportation or inventory cost.

It is important to realize that physical distribution is much more than a cost center in the marketing effort. Its primary benefit is to function in terms of a distinguished service that can be integral to the differentiation in the firm's total offering. As such, therefore, on a marginal basis, additional service will be desired if, at least in theory, it is offset by corresponding revenues. Customer service capability must be integrated in comparison to total cost requirements. The customer service of concern here is structural in nature and not behavioral, such as sales servicing.

In a structural sense, customer service is measured by the performance around an order cycle measured from the time of customer commitment to the time of product delivery. Such measurements as level of service and speed of service are important in determining the basic capabilities of the system. However, consistency of service, which is a measure of how frequently the objectives of speed and level are accomplished, is the critical measure over time.

In total, this section has thus far presented three chapters dealing with channels of distribution. Proceeding from the broad concept we have singled out, based on the justification of separation for increased specialization, the transaction-creating and the physical distribution channels. The two must combine to form the linkage between the production capability and the purchasing units for effective physical distribution. Attention is now directed to managerial functions related to the communication mix.

QUESTIONS AND PROBLEMS

1. List the parts of a manufacturing enterprise that have a participating role in a *total logistics system*. Relate *logistics* and *physical distribution*.

2. Should a physical distribution system be *designed to meet* a specific level of marketing service, or should the highly efficient physical distribution system *lead to and produce* a certain level of service? Comment and elaborate.

3. Should a manufacturer be especially concerned to maintain ex-

tremely close control over his fast-moving items, or his slow-moving items that enjoy only very sporadic purchase? Why?

4. Under what conditions would private carriers most likely dominate transport volume?

5. Under what conditions might a maximum service orientation to physical distribution be followed by a company?

6. What is the impact of conglomerate competition on the design of a physical distribution system?

7. Explain and illustrate a *cost-to-cost* tradeoff. In terms of system planning relate *cost-to-cost* tradeoffs to *cost-to-service* tradeoffs.

8. Explain: "In terms of transportation cost, we can generally expect that as the number of warehouse locations are increased, the cost of transportation will initially decrease and then as more and more warehouses are added, will begin to increase."

Chapter 16

Advertising

Thus far in our discussion of programming, we have tried to establish a proper setting for dealing with the individual components of a total program. Most importantly, a communication orientation is required, for all market cultivation in one way or another involves information transfer with the market. The exchange process is actuated essentially through communication. That is, demand is triggered, or purchase precipitated, through information flows of all kinds between buyer and seller. Some understanding of the essential elements of the communication process is regarded as a prerequisite to programming considerations in the individual components of market cultivation.

In this chapter, we turn our attention to that part of the communication process which is usually the first stage of market cultivation. Advertising has as its purpose the informing and persuasion of others to act favorably upon an idea, product, or service. The word advertising has its roots in a word that means "to turn." In terms of overall communication advertising and selling are not synonymous. For successful marketing one must ordinarily have a combination of personal selling and advertising.

The purpose of this chapter is to examine the basic concepts of advertising. The first section develops a basic model of the communication process. Next, the terminology of advertising is reviewed. The third section develops alternative objectives that may underlie the deployment of advertising expenditure. The fourth section reviews factors that influence the use of advertising for both primary and selective demand stimulation. The final two sections deal with media selection and budget determination. In total, the chapter examines the informational background of advertising that is necessary for the marketing manager to employ advertising in his marketing mix effectively.

A COMMUNICATION MODEL

The word *communication* is derived from the Latin *communis,* "common." Communication may be regarded as a process by which a verbal or non-verbal effort is made by a source to send a message through a channel to establish a "commonness" with a receiver. All human communication has a source—a person, group, or institution—and a purpose—usually to arouse, inform, or elicit some sort of response. Given a source with ideas, needs, intentions, information, and a purpose, an encoding process must take place which translates these ideas into a systematic set of symbols—into a language, expressing the source's purpose. The function of encoding is thus the provision of a form in which ideas can be expressed as a coded message. Next, a channel, medium, or carrier of messages is required. The appropriate choice of medium is a critical variable in effective communication.

Obviously a transmitted message is intended to reach some receiver. Before a receiver can respond to a message, it must be decoded in terms of relevance to the receiver. In person-to-person communication, encoding and decoding are performed by the source and receiver via their motor skills and sensory capacities. In more complex communication situations, the source is often separated from the encoder, as often are the decoder and receiver. For example, the advertising manager may be the source, and a copywriter, the encoder. These five elements are inherent in the communication process and are diagrammed in Figure 16-1.[1]

FIGURE 16-1
Basic Communication Model

Source → Encoder → Message Channel → Decoder → Receiver

A breakdown, an interference, a distortion, or a *noise* can occur anywhere within the communication process. *Noise* is used in this context not only as representing an audible sound, but as anything that will interfere with the communication process—a distraction, a misinterpretation, different meanings assigned to the same words by different people, mind wandering and the likes. All these factors serve to distort a message or reduce fidelity, and can be termed noise. Because message fidelity is rarely, if ever,

[1] David K. Berlo, *The Process of Communication* (New York: Holt, Rinehart & Winston, Inc., 1960), pp. 30–32.

100 percent perfect, provision for feedback in the communication process is desirable. Feedback provides a channel for audience or receiver response; it permits the source to determine whether the message has been received and has produced the intended response. Feedback of information may be carried through the same channel as the original message or through an entirely different channel. With the addition of the elements of noise and feedback, the model is as illustrated in Figure 16-2.

FIGURE 16-2
Communication Dynamics

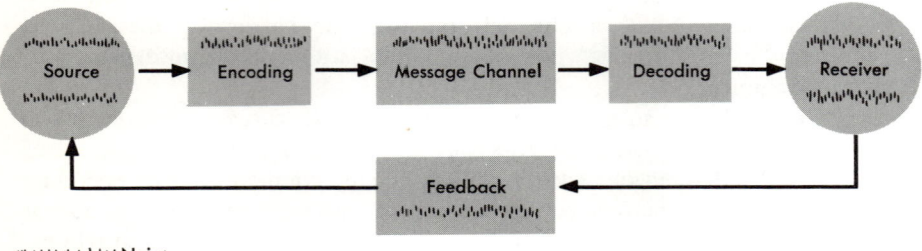

Source → Encoding → Message Channel → Decoding → Receiver

Feedback

Noise

The system as a whole has great interdependency and is no stronger than its weakest component. Distortion can come about through malfunction in any of the parts. If the source does not have adequate or valid information or his purpose is unclear; if the message is not encoded accurately, fully, and in transmittable signs of relevance to the receiver; if the message is not transmitted fast enough or accurately enough despite interference; if the message is not decoded in precisely the way it was encoded; or if the receiver is unable to accept the decoded message in such a way as to produce the desired response—then the communication process lacks perfection.

One hundred percent efficiency, however, is an unattainable goal. For example, the efficiency rating of an electric motor measures the ratio of output to input. It must always be below 100 percent because of the slight loss which must occur in the conversion of one form of energy to another. So it is in communication. The conversion of abstractions through encoding into messages and the conversion back through decoding into precisely the same abstractions is unattainable. The objective of the communicator is to attain as closely as possible perfect fidelity in producing the desired response.

Perhaps the most important factor that breaks down the desired "commonness" in communication between the source and the receiver is the variation that takes place in encoding and decoding. Some of the most effective communication, in this respect, takes place among a neighborhood gang of youngsters of similar age. Chances are they have all come from a common environment—the same neighborhood, school, drugstore, playground, and type of living quarters. They have all shared a majority of common experiences. Frequently, they will have a large number of common interests. They may speak in a slang language (that exists without anyone ever carefully defining terms) that seems incomprehensible to adults. The encoding and decoding, however, are almost precisely identical—they communicate most effectively even with a limited vocabulary. But over a period of time the homogeneous nature of these conditions tends to break down. Environments, experience, vocabulary, knowledge, interests, attitudes, values, personalities, and goals vary increasingly with age; that is, they grow further apart. Norbert Weiner refers to this condition as "entropy," or the inherent nature of human processes to break down rather than come closer together as a civilization advances.[2] The result is that great barriers to effective communication are erected, which reflect themselves in inexact encoding and decoding.

Schramm diagrams the nature of this problem as illustrated in Figure 16-3.[3]

The circles represent the accumulated experience of the two participants in the communication process. If the circles have a large area in common, then communication is facilitated. If the circles do not meet—if there has been no common experience—then communication is impossible. The task is to achieve via advertising effective mass communication as an integral aspect of the overall marketing mix.

FIGURE 16-3
Barriers to Communication

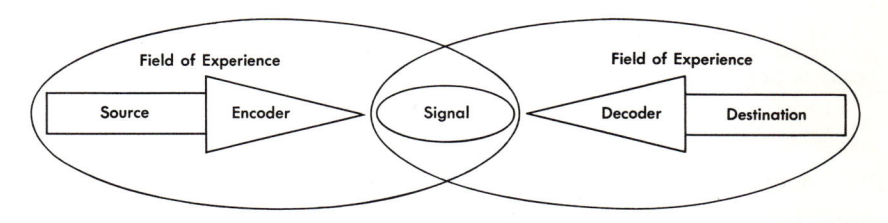

[2] Norbert Weiner, *Cybernetics, or Control and Communication in the Animal and the Machine* (New York: John Wiley & Sons, Inc., 1948).

[3] Wilbur Schramm, "How Communications Work," in *The Process and Effects of Mass Communication* (Urbana, Ill.: University of Illinois Press, 1954), p. 6.

THE TERMINOLOGY OF ADVERTISING

Advertising is any paid form of nonpersonal presentation and promotion of ideas, goods, or services by an identified sponsor.[4] Two characteristics are important in this definition: first is the requirement of payment, and second is the need for authorship. Many times, a company is successful in communicating messages about itself or its products through the usual advertising media such as newspapers or magazines but does not pay for the message. This comes about through editorial comment by newspapers on new products or new policies of the company. This information reaching the market is generally referred to as publicity and is not therefore advertising. One of the reasons for excluding publicity from advertising is that the frequency of such messages cannot be planned and managed.

The question arises, What activities are included under *nonpersonal presentation and promotion of ideas, goods, or services?* A distinction is made between advertising and sales promotion. Messages conveyed through the usual communications media, such as newspapers, magazines, radio, television, outdoor signs, car cards, and direct mail, are considered advertising. Messages conveyed through labels, tags, store signs, point-of-purchase display material, calendars, blotters, catalogs, and circulars are technically advertising but are more often called sales promotion. Other activities, such as the use of demonstrations, displays, and exhibits at fairs and conventions, and the giving of premiums to consumers, are also considered sales promotion. The distinction between advertising and sales promotion is made because of the differences in objectives sought and skills needed to manage these two types of activities.

TYPES OF ADVERTISING

Figure 16-4 illustrates the variety of advertising used in modern business. A brief explanation of each follows.

Advertiser

Advertising is both planned and paid for by the manufacturer, the middlemen, and service establishments such as banks and insurance companies. A glance at any newspaper reveals the huge amount of advertising placed by retailers. In fact, the greatest share of the advertising dollar—approximately 30 percent—is spent on newspaper advertising.[5] Some of

---

[4] R. S. Alexander, *Marketing Definitions* (Chicago: American Marketing Association, 1960), p. 9.
[5] See *Advertising Age,* December 16, 1974, p. 23.

FIGURE 16-4
Types of Advertising

THE ADVERTISER

Manufacturer
Middlemen
Service Establishments

TARGET	PURPOSE	THEME	COPY	PAYMENT
Consumer	Primary demand	Indirect action	Product	Individual
Trade	Selective demand	Direct action	Institutional	Cooperative
Producers				

this is of course placed by manufacturers and service establishments, but the bulk is by retailers. Wholesalers also advertise to their customers—retailers, manufacturers, and other wholesalers.

Targets

All advertising is directed to either (1) consumers, who purchase for ultimate household consumption; (2) middlemen, who purchase for resale; or (3) producers (industrial and public sector users), who purchase for further processing or fabrication. The advertising directed to producers or middlemen is known as trade advertising. Advertising directed to consumers—the kind with which we are all familiar—is called consumer advertising.

Purpose

Another dichotomy in advertising types is between primary and selective demand stimulation. The stimulation of primary demand attempts to increase the demand for a product type rather than for the specific brand of any particular manufacturer. In the initial stages of television, much advertising was directed toward the enjoyment to be received from television in contrast to the virtues of a particular advertiser's brand, which was of secondary importance.

Primary-demand advertising is particularly important in new products which are truly innovations. It is also widely used where one firm dominates an industry. For instance, Kodak, by promoting home photography on a primary-demand basis, seeks to expand the film market, recognizing that it will receive by far the greatest share of any expansion in the sale of film that the advertising produces.

Selective-demand advertising emphasizes the advertiser's own brands. Rather than primarily trying to expand existing demand for the class of product, it attempts to redivide existing demand in favor of the advertiser. There is always an element of primary-demand stimulation in selective-demand advertising. However, the emphasis favors either one or the other. There is little sense in emphasizing primary-demand stimulation in the advertising of salt. The only expansibility of demand comes from an increase in the size of the population. Consequently, most salt advertising is highly selective.

Theme

Advertising themes may seek either indirect or direct action. Indirect action is for the purpose of building broad recognition and acceptance. It tries to create a favorable attitude toward a brand. Indirect-action advertising also features appeals, such as service policies, that will indirectly influence the sale of the product. A good example of indirect-action advertising is Boeing Aircraft's announcing the names of all airlines using 707, 727, and 747 jetliners.

Direct-action advertising, in addition to developing brand recognition and acceptance, tries to stimulate the recipient of the message to immediate purchase action. It attempts to motivate purchase of the product immediately, to request further information, or to undertake some other direct action desired by the advertiser, such as requesting a salesman to call. Most retailer-sponsored newspaper, radio, or television advertising is of the direct-action type. The direct purpose of placing an advertisement in the food section of a newspaper is to stimulate weekend purchases.

Both types of action can be combined in the same advertisement. When a department store advertises specific merchandise and at the same time stresses some of its policies, such as credit or adjustments, or some of its store characteristics, such as air-conditioning and courteous employees, it is combining these two types.

Copy

Advertising either emphasizes the products or services of the advertiser or attempts to convey a favorable impression of the advertiser. The latter is called institutional advertising; the former, product advertising. A glance through any magazine will reveal examples of institutional advertising. Most of the advertising of the ethical pharmaceutical houses is institutional. In such ads, they are trying to convey an image of a competent research-oriented institution with the skills and technology necessary to bring the latest findings of science to the medical profession. Confidence in medical preparations by the consuming public is essential in building sales patronage.

Payment

Payment may be made by the individual manufacturer or middleman, or it may be on a cooperative basis. There are two types of cooperative arrangements for the payment of advertising. One is called *horizontal cooperative advertising*. In this, payment is shared by a group of firms. The largest campaigns of this sort are by manufacturers or producers. Some of the more common campaigns are those sponsored by the American Meat Institute, the American Trucking Association, and the brewing industry. A number of regional campaigns have been conducted by producers' cooperatives in the agricultural field. Most horizontal cooperative advertising is an attempt at primary-demand stimulation.

The other cooperative form, which is much the more important in terms of advertising expenditures, is *vertical cooperative advertising*. The cost of advertising in this setup is shared by firms on different levels of manufacturing or distribution, most often by manufacturers and retailers of consumer goods. You will recall, in Chapter 14, the use of selective and exclusive distribution to achieve aggressive selling throughout the channel. When selective distribution is used and care is given to choosing the middlemen allowed to handle the product, a number of cooperative services usually are included in the arrangement. Vertical cooperative advertising is one. It spreads the cost of advertising and can result in a wholly integrated advertising campaign, from the manufacturer throughout the entire channel to the ultimate consumer.

It is clear that any number of combinations of advertising types can exist. For example, it is possible to have manufacturer-product, indirect-action, primary-demand, horizontal cooperative advertising directed to all consumers. Some combinations, however, are unlikely. In terms of the explanations given, a combination of direct-action, institutional advertising would be highly unlikely.

THE ADVERTISING AGENCY

Advertising is highly technical and it is common practice for large advertisers to work through an advertising agency. The first advertising agencies in the United States were organized in the early part of the nineteenth century. Their principal function was to act as agents in buying space from publishers and selling it to advertisers. In fact, the agencies were called "space merchants" at that time. Today, the advertising agency aids the advertiser in planning the media communication program, and may even provide counsel on the total marketing program.

The major function of the advertising department of the manufacturer or producer is to provide a broad policy framework that the company wishes to follow, and to make final decisions. In some of the largest corporations, the advertising departments perform many of the activities available through an agency. Many companies prefer to conduct their own market research, evaluation of advertising, and independent analysis of media.

However, an agency is normally retained because the payment rarely raises the overall cost to the client. Compensation to the agency is on a commission basis. The media cost of any advertisement placed by an agency is billed to the agency by the media at a percent discount from its published prices. The agency in turn bills the client for the total amount (if the advertiser were to buy the space directly from the media, he would also be charged the total amount). The percent commission usually covers the agency functions of planning, creating the advertising campaign, producing the particular advertisements to run, and analyzing and buying the desired media time or space. If the advertiser's campaign is a large one, the percent media discount may be a large enough fee to cover the cost of market research done by the agency to provide the basis for planning the campaign. Charges for special services performed by the agency are normally billed separately to the client.

The inherent danger in the commission method of payment is related to the three-party arrangement which exists. The advertiser, the agency, and the media are all attempting to look after their own self-interests. The agency's revenue is provided by the media and depends on the amount of advertising done. This structure could cause the agency to favor certain media and advertising expenditures which would be contrary to the best interests of the advertiser.

THE OBJECTIVES OF ADVERTISING

The overall objective of advertising is to increase the profits of the advertiser or to prevent their reduction by influencing the level of product sales. Many times, a firm is forced to advertise because of the actions of competitors. Under such circumstances, there may be little chance to increase profits, but failure to advertise could result in sales and profit losses. The ability to increase profits or to prevent loss depends on how successfully this communication instrument achieves three other objectives. The specific objectives of advertising are: (1) to expand demand, (2) to create inelasticity of demand, and (3) to aid the salesman in the performance of his duties.

DEMAND EXPANSION

In a technical sense demand is expanded if the demand curve is shifted to the right, as illustrated in Figure 16-5. Demand expansion may

FIGURE 16-5
Demand With and Without Advertising

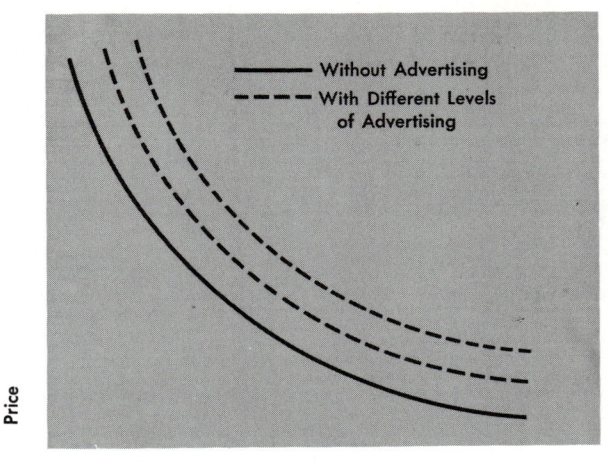

―――― Without Advertising
― ― ― With Different Levels of Advertising

Price

Unit Sales

be viewed from the standpoint of the industry or the firm. Since the total demand is the combination of the demand curves facing all firms in the industry, it is possible for a single firm to shift its demand curves without any expansibility of demand for the industry. Such represents a redivision of existing demand.

In quantity sold, a distinction must be made between increases resulting from a shift in demand, and those resulting from moving along or down through a demand curve. The firm may have the alternative of increasing the quantity it can sell by moving down the demand curve by price adjustments. The decision to favor price changes depends on how profitable the increased volume is at the same price with advertising versus the increased volume at a lower price without advertising. This depends on: (1) the amount of the increase and (2) the relative costs of production and marketing at the different volume levels.

Figure 16-6 is a highly simplified explanation of the use of price adjustments versus advertising. In Chart A, point O_1 on the price line P_1 represents the quantity sold at P_1, and O_1A_1 is the profit. Point O_2 on price line P_2 represents the quantity that may be sold with the lower price P_2. Profit is O_2A_2, and the difference between this and O_1A_1 is the increase in profit.

In Chart B, point O_1 on the price line P_1 represents the quantity that will be taken, and O_1A_1 is the profit. Through making an expenditure for advertising at quantity O_1, an increase in the fixed-cost curve results, and the total-cost curve is no longer a continuous function. If the quantity sold is increased to O_2, the new profit is O_2A_2, representing an increase over the

FIGURE 16-6
Comparison of Profit Effect from Price Reduction Versus Use of Advertising

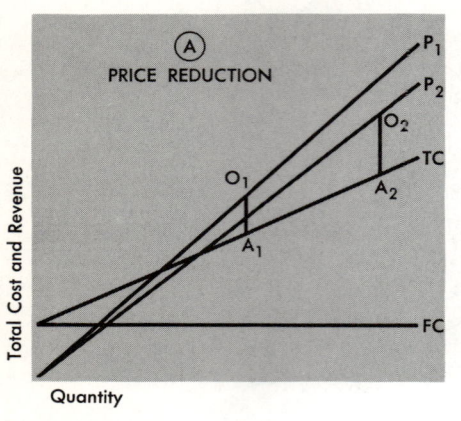

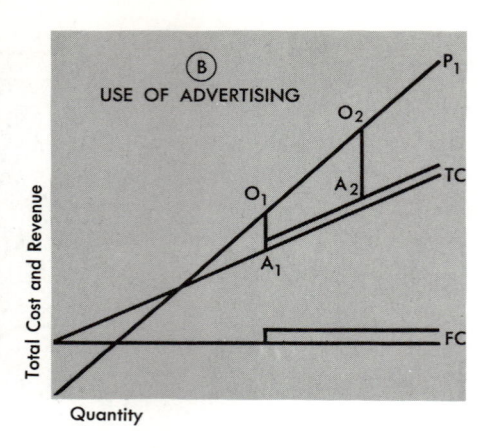

TC = Total Cost   FC = Fixed Cost

previous quantity level. If the profit is greater than that achieved through the price reduction in Chart A, advertising should be favored. If not, price reductions should be favored. It is quite possible that neither procedure will leave the firm better off in its profit returns. Conceivably, neither the price reduction nor the advertising expenditure would have an effect on the quantity sold.

The above analysis applies to any form of demand cultivation effort. Price reduction is always an alternative to promotional expenditures. Expenditures to expand demand must be compared with the possible effect of price adjustment. This analysis is greatly simplified and omits four complicating factors.

First, to carry out such an analysis requires a determination of quantities that will be sold at different prices and at different expenditures for advertising. This is a measurement problem which almost defies analysis. Nevertheless, such attempts are made.

Second, the increased quantities cannot be moved without increases in cost. The straight-line cost function is used, and the break-even charts are not wholly realistic. Determination of the decreases and increases in cost which result from increased volume is necessary.

Third, the firm may be in a very competitive situation, and it is not known what reductions in volume take place without advertising or with failure to increase advertising. It is quite possible that the end result of an advertising expenditure is no change in profit from previous periods. However, if this expenditure were not made, it certainly could result in losses from the level of the previous period.

Fourth, the firm very rarely has the simple choice of electing one alternative or the other. Usually, a combination of price, advertising, sales promotion, and personal selling is used. To determine the effect of the total communications mix beforehand is a multivariable problem reserved for Chapter 19.

INELASTICITY OF DEMAND

If demand becomes more inelastic through advertising, the firm can sell the same quantity at higher prices. And if successful at demand expansion too, it may even increase the quantity. In direct-price competition, it may maintain the same quantity at the same price if it has achieved inelasticity of price demand. How does this come about? The effect is generated through selective-demand advertising. If the firm can develop a loyalty among consumers through establishing brand preference, a distinction is made in the consumer's mind between that firm's products and competitors' products. A firm with a highly differentiated product may even extract a price premium because of the customer loyalty it enjoys. In doing so, it may reduce volume slightly but still enjoy greater profits than if it sought an expansion of demand through price reduction.

These two objectives, demand expansion and inelasticity of demand, may be sought independently of each other or together. Most primary-demand advertising, as well as horizontal cooperative advertising, reflects the desire to expand demand and rarely seeks inelasticity of demand. Much advertising by middlemen, especially to consumers, seeks to expand demand and may even, at the same time, use price as the major competitive weapon. Most manufacturer advertising seeks a combination of each. It first tries to build brand preference and achieve inelasticity of demand, and, in so doing, expand the demand curve it faces.

SALES ASSISTANCE

Advertising is rarely used alone to communicate the firm's offer to the market. Almost always, some form of personal selling is used, and the advertising may be used to pave the way for the salesman or even to develop leads of interested prospects. In paving the way for the salesman, the advertising is of an institutional or indirect-action nature. It maintains the name of the company in the market, making the task of the salesman somewhat easier when he approaches potential customers. Or, it may seek inquiries from potential users of the product, thus providing a prospect list for the sales force. This objective is particularly relevant in the industrial goods market, where actual sale of the product depends on some form of personal solicitation.

FACTORS AFFECTING THE SUCCESSFUL USE OF ADVERTISING

Most companies allocate a part of their total communications budget to advertising. Although the value is not completely measurable, it perhaps is a safe assumption that funds spent in this way will have a desirable effect. The problem, however, is to spend money in a manner which will produce the *most* desirable effect. Fortunately, there are identifiable circumstances which indicate that advertising, more than other instruments of communication, will be effective. Similarly, there are circumstances which act as a deterrent to its successful use and which indicate the need for alternative means of market cultivation. Since the factors affecting the use of advertising differ somewhat according to whether it is used for primary-demand stimulation or selective-demand stimulation, we will deal with each of these areas independently. Since the primary purpose of advertising is to expand demand and/or create some degree of inelasticity of demand for the advertised product, our discussion will deal with these objectives.

PRIMARY-DEMAND STIMULATION

As stated earlier, primary demand relates to a particular product class and not to the product of a single supplier. The use of advertising for this purpose is necessitated by several conditions. First, new products require an introduction to the market and an explanation of their value. Second, advertising may be necessary when the consumption of old products declines. Third, advertising may be used when one firm strongly dominates a market and stands to gain from its overall expansion. Before any expenditures are made to expand primary demand through advertising, the following aspects should be investigated.

Extent of Use

An investigation of potential users and the way their needs are being met reveals both the market opportunity available for many new products, and the product that must be displaced. For old products which have enjoyed widespread use, an investigation of current usage is necessary. Comparing existing markets with those of previous periods shows the substitutions which have taken place, and the changes necessary to regain previous position.

Demand Trends

What social forces are at work affecting demand? Many new products have come on the market which have run counter to deep-seated social forces. Some examples will illustrate. Attempts by manufacturers to promote the use of self-service dry cleaning establishments were made at least in the early 1950s. The venture was unsuccessful. It appears that present efforts in the same area are more successful. The reasons for failure are unknown, but outdoor living, suburbia, self-service, and drive-in establishments in general had not yet reached their present levels, and the social environment prevented the public's acceptance of this service. In another case a manufacturer of teaching machines was until recent years faced with considerable resistance, rooted in years of tradition.

The covering of entire fields of crops with paper or polyethylene for mulching purposes has been advocated for over thirty years without success. High-protein foods were introduced in the early 1950s without success. The strikingly streamlined automobile was introduced in the 1930s and was not accepted. The point is that change is relative. Consumers seem willing to accept rather sizable amounts of absolute change as long as relative change is limited.

Under proper circumstances, primary-demand advertising may change habits. The forces underlying demand must be carefully analyzed to assess the ability of advertising to overcome or change them.

Price Income Relationships

Often the consumption of old products declines because of the failure of manufacturers to adjust prices to new income levels. This is particularly true in recession periods. The composition of products that the family purchases changes throughout the economic cycle. This is a reflection of the consumer's desire to adjust to new price-income relationships. If the price of a product is not in accord with the new income levels, advertising can do little to reverse the demand trend. Frequently, the situation calls for product adjustments to make it possible to bring the price of the product more in line with economic conditions.

Extent of the Market

Through analysis of use, social trends, and price-income relationships, the advertiser should be able to make some judgment on the potential size of the market. Most primary-demand advertising failures result from overoptimism in this area. The qualitative side of market investigation is not given sufficient attention, and all consuming units are regarded as potential customers. Generally, primary-demand advertising will affect some consumers, but not all, and the number it will affect is crucial. The advertiser must calculate market size, the cost of reaching the market, the number of potential buyers that will be influenced, and potential profitability if successful. If the market is small, it may be impossible for advertising to generate a profitable sales volume. If the market is large, the risks and dollar value of the investment must be projected.

Funds Available

The extent of the market, along with the price of the product, the frequency of purchase, and the other costs of marketing, gives some idea of the margin available and the size of the revenue pool for advertising. If the product is of high unit value and can look forward to a large potential market, there may be substantial funds available. If it is of low unit value and high frequency of sale, the total number of units sold will produce considerable funds for advertising. If, however, the market is small, the unit value low, and the purchase infrequent, funds available are not large. The advertiser should be familiar with some of the costs of reaching different markets and should determine the amount of advertising one can purchase with the funds available. It generally is not wise to spend only token sums in advertising. A certain level of expenditure is needed to achieve impact, and unless enough funds can be allocated to reach this minimum point, probably the money can be spent in more productive alternative ways.

Appeals

Conditions may seem to favor the use of primary advertising, but unless a satisfactory appeal can be made, little return can be expected. What can the advertiser say about his product? Among new products, the innovation that makes possible substantial product differentiation usually provides a wealth of material for advertising appeals. The problem of course is to be sure the most effective ones are used and that they will, in fact, have customer impact. In trying to recapture market position for old products, the question of appeal poses more problems. Unless an appeal can be made which will be effective against products currently used to fill the need, advertising can be of little help. As a rule, this condition will become apparent early in the analysis.

SELECTIVE-DEMAND STIMULATION

This type of advertising, which emphasizes the advertiser's own products in an attempt to redivide existing demand in his favor, may or may not seek to create inelasticity of price demand. As with primary-demand stimulation, a number of factors determine the feasibility of using advertising for this purpose. There are differences in the ways in which certain factors affect the use of advertising by manufacturers and by the trade. Whenever these differences are significant, their relevance is indicated. There are certain similarities between selective-demand and primary-demand advertising in the area of market factors, but these will not be repeated here.

Ability to Brand

Identification of a manufacturer's products is necessary before selective demand may be stimulated. Without identification, the benefits of advertising do not necessarily accrue to the advertiser. Although there are many objectives sought through branding, its promotional value is one of the more important. Since there is considerable confusion in terminology in this area, a brief discussion of the different terms used is necessary.

The term *brand* is a broad term, used to refer to a company name, trade name, trademark, or brand name. A brand is *any letter, word, name, symbol, or device, or any combination thereof which is adopted and used by a manufacturer or merchant to identify his goods and services and to distinguish them from those manufactured and sold by others.*[6] The term *brand name* simply refers to the oral expression of the brand. A *trademark* is the legal term for a brand name. Since there are certain restrictions on the registration of brands, all brands are not trademarks, but it is a safe assumption that all trademarks are brands. A brand name may be a company name, if the name of the company is used to identify its products. Such is the case with Cannon towels. To avoid becoming entangled in legal implications, we shall use the term *brand*.

Although it is difficult enough to establish identity of source through a brand name, to signify a tradition of uniformity of quality through a brand name is often far more difficult. The purpose of advertising brands is to build customer loyalty to the point where the purchaser will buy by brand rather than by inspection. Brand preference by customers can be achieved only if they feel that every time they purchase the brand, they will receive similar merchandise. If wide ranges in quality are experienced by a customer, he will no longer insist upon the brand.

[6] Public Law 489 (Lanham Act, H.R. 154), U.S. Statutes, 1946 (79th Congress, 2nd Session) (Washington, D.C.: Government Printing Office), p. 19.

The Product

A differentiated product favors the use of advertising to stimulate selective demand. Creating customer loyalty through the development of brand preference is much easier to accomplish if substitution of brands by the customer is difficult. If the product has hidden qualities which are not readily apparent, the complexities of developing brand preferences are greatly increased. The customer must rely on the advertiser's message regarding the characteristics of the product. Such is the case with watches, paints, and proprietary medicines. It is no accident that the advertising of nonprescription medicines receives a larger share of the sales dollar than any other product. In addition to the appeal to better health that can be made, qualities of the product beyond the buyer's observation can be extolled, and the buyer must rely on the reputation of the advertiser and on the veracity of the claims made.

Although product differentiation usually contributes to the successful use of advertising to stimulate demand, there are exceptions. When the advertiser is attempting to develop the gift market, he can be successful without a high degree of differentiation from competitors' products. Through very extensive advertising, the product name may become well known and the general price level established. Often, when the value of the product is known, the giver of a gift will prefer to give well-known merchandise, to assure that the recipient is familiar with its value. Another exception is found in the way in which the customer purchases the product. A discussion of this follows.

The Customer

The prospective advertiser must analyze the way in which the customer purchases. The major forces operative in the purchase decision must be analyzed and the capacity of advertising to stimulate these forces assessed.

Habitual, routine purchases are generally limited to goods with little visual product differentiation; yet, they are heavily advertised. Such products as cigarettes, razor blades, soft drinks, and many food products fall into this category. Since the unit value of these products is low and the frequency of purchase high, once a satisfactory brand is found, the buyer will continue to purchase without the exercise of care in the purchase decision. Under these circumstances, "reminder advertising," which constantly keeps the brand name in the market, can be successful in diverting demand to the advertiser.

Another variation is the use of trial and error in purchasing such products. Since it matters little to the buyer if an unwise selection is made on any one occasion in view of the frequency of purchase, there is a very good chance that those brands which are most heavily advertised will be foremost in his mind and will be favored in trial-and-error purchasing. Purchases calling for more skill in decision making usually involve higher-unit-value products, purchased less frequently and, on the whole, more complex technically. Here, the buyer must have considerably more information, and some basis for comparing the value of the various brands available.

Advertising can emphasize the differentiated characteristics of the brand and stimulate selective demand for the advertiser. The major problem in advertising products purchased in this way is the funds available.

The Market

Analysis of the market is an extension of customer analysis but emphasizes the quantitative aspects of the market. One of the first characteristics to be analyzed is the location of potential customers. Can they be reached by the available media without considerable waste in circulation? If buyers cannot be identified and a broadcast form of advertising through many media is used, this can be very costly.

Size of market, frequency of purchase, and probability of repeat sales are, of course, important to the determination of funds available for advertising. The channel of distribution used also has a bearing on the ability to advertise.

When goods are distributed on a selective or exclusive basis, advertising becomes rather costly. For example, manufacturers of furniture find it difficult to advertise, since their products are available to consumers only in selected outlets. This means that identification of the outlet for the consumer must be provided in some way. Advertising over the retailer's name by the manufacturer, or some form of vertical cooperative advertising, is used to accomplish this. On the other hand, selective or exclusive distribution is used when the product requires aggressive effort. The very use of this form of distribution means that advertising is not relied upon as the major communications instrument. That is, its role is secondary to other instruments of demand cultivation, such as store prestige, product availability, display, and personal selling.

Vertical Cooperative Advertising

As we have already seen, the channel of distribution used may require that the manufacturer use some form of vertical cooperative advertising. Other factors favor its use. Where dealer interest is important in the sale of the product, using cooperative advertising forces an investment on the part of the dealer. With money invested, the attention given to the product by the dealer is thought to be greater. Sometimes this is useful to the manufacturer, as it enables him to trade on the prestige of the dealer. This is true when large, well-known department stores cooperate.

There are a number of factors which must be taken into consideration before embarking upon a cooperative campaign. First, some means must be found to insure participation by the trade. If it is purely on a voluntary basis, limited participation is the result. Incentives in the form of tie-ins with manufacturer advertising can be useful; or, the supplying of mats for newspaper advertising and of examples of advertising copy, along with follow-up by the personal sales force, can do much to stimulate participation. Many manufacturers publicize their cooperative campaigns to local newspaper-space salesmen, hoping that space salesmen will persuade local retailers to take advantage of the manufacturer's cooperative arrangements.

Second, administration of the program is difficult. Evidence of funds spent for advertising by the trade is essential to the manufacturer in his effort to maintain control of the program. Also, if the manufacturer pays for advertising which was not placed, the payment is a price reduction and can, under the Robinson-Patman Act, result in prosecution for illegal price discrimination.

Third, the Robinson-Patman Act requires that if a cooperative advertising allowance is offered to the trade, it must be made available to all buyers on proportionately equal terms. Obviously, it may be more useful to make the offer to large dealers and exclude small ones. That is, there are many cases where the manufacturer would prefer to concentrate his funds on a few large, prestigious dealers, rather than dissipate them in small amounts over many different accounts.

Fourth, a conflict in objectives frequently arises. The manufacturer is more interested in indirect-action, selective-demand advertising. The trade is more interested in direct-action advertising. That is, the dealer is concerned about bringing traffic to the store and selling merchandise, rather than selling a *specific brand* of merchandise. The manufacturer, on the other hand, is not nearly so concerned about the dealer's level of sale of general merchandise as he is with the sale of his brand. This conflict is usually at the root of dealer's refusals to use manufacturers' advertising suggestions.

Fifth, the budgeting of expenditures for cooperative programs is difficult for manufacturers. The advertiser never knows what level of participation will be forthcoming.

In spite of all these difficulties, however, vertical cooperative advertising is widely used today. One of the greatest stimuli to its use is financial. The retailer purchases space at local rates, which are lower than those offered to the manufacturer, who must pay the higher national rate for the same space and advertising. For a given sum of money, therefore, more space can be purchased through vertical cooperative advertising than if the entire campaign is undertaken by the manufacturer.

THE SELECTION OF MEDIA

Although the management of media is only one phase of overall advertising, it is a complex business. In 1974, for example, media advertising exceeded $22 billion. In order to understand selection, it is necessary to examine media requirements and characteristics.

MEDIA REQUIREMENTS

The selection of a specific advertising media should be based on a number of variables which are reviewed in this section.

Selective or Mass Coverage

What is the purpose of the advertising? Is it the desire of the advertiser to rifle the message directly to a well-delineated market? Or is it to convey a message to a mass market at low cost? Some media, such as radio or television, are known as mass media. Direct mail, on the other hand, is a more selective medium. The term *impact* refers to the capacity of the medium to transmit a real selling message to the market. For example, reminder advertising may not be high-impact advertising. On the other hand, most direct-mail advertising concentrates on impact in the selling message.

Audio or Visual

All of the printed media can convey only a visual message, whereas radio conveys an audio message and television both audio and visual messages. Consider the case of selecting a medium to advertise combination storm windows. In an audio medium, such as radio, it would be difficult to convey a clear explanation of the way these windows work. Radio may be useful for a selling message that simply states that windows are available at a given location, but it is not very useful for explanation purposes. Newspapers may illustrate the window, but it is difficult in printed copy to convey the window's mechanical operation. Television, with its combination of audio and visual messages, is ideal—the major limiting factor being its relatively high cost compared with other media.

Frequency of Insertion

Some types of advertising require very frequent insertion if they are to be successful. For example, reminder advertising, or advertising aimed primarily at brand recognition, requires a medium which can communicate the message a great number of times. Newspapers, radio, television "spots" (brief commercial announcements), and direct mail are all media which offer opportunity for frequent insertion. Weekly or monthly magazines are less acceptable for this purpose.

Type Selectivity

The type selectivity of a medium refers to its ability to reach a specific type of person. If the medium reaches a large number of different types, it must offer the advertiser some means to assure that the specific market is reached without excessive waste in circulation. For example, professional trade journals reach specific types of individuals. To try to reach these people through a national household magazine would result in too much waste circulation. Direct mail is highly selective in this respect, if adequate mailing lists are available. Newspapers, radio, and television offer little type selectivity. An attempt is made in these media, however, to achieve type selectivity in the following ways: (1) Position in newspapers affords some type selectivity; an advertisement in the sports section will be exposed to a different type of reader than an advertisement on the social pages. (2) Radio and television attempt the same thing by varying the time at which the advertising is broadcast and the programming in connection with which it is used.

Geographic Selectivity

Geographic selectivity refers to the capacity of the medium to reach only certain geographic areas and not others. There are three major reasons why the advertiser prefers geographic selectivity. First, if he does not market the product nationally, there is little value in using a national medium. Second, competitive conditions may vary, and the advertiser may wish to allocate more advertising to some areas than to others. Third, because of ethnic variations or different habit patterns in different parts of the country, different appeals may be necessary.

Some national magazines vary their content for different parts of the country, and thus provide geographic selectivity. Local newspapers inherently provide geographic selectivity; many provide quite precise selectivity through the practice of publishing both a home edition and a rural edition. In the large cities, such as New York, some of the newspapers even vary the content going to different sections of the city.

An advertiser may have several specific objectives in mind and have

Advertising

to use a combination of media to do the job. The important thing to remember is that some media are better than others for doing certain things.

MEDIA CHARACTERISTICS

Table 16-1 ranks available media on the basis of the characteristics discussed. A rating of 1 means that the media offers the maximum in that characteristic, 2 means it is average, and 3 means it is poor or does not offer the characteristic at all.

Magazines, radio, and television have been subdivided for this comparison, since there are variations in these media, depending upon the specific type of magazine used or on the way radio or television is used. Trade magazines are specialized magazines, read by specialized people. There are a large number of these going to just about every occupational and professional class. Household magazines are more general in content and, as the name implies, are aimed at a broader group of readers. Three trade magazines are *Chain Store Age, Engineering News,* and *Chemical Week.*

Spot (or *local*) radio and television stations, concentrating on advertising, broadcast many one- or two-minute advertisements of certain products or services of only local importance. *Network* radio and television, on the other hand, emanate from the network studios and concentrate on programming, giving advertisers the opportunity to be part- or full-sponsor of entire half-hour or hour-long programs, which are usually broadcast to the entire network area.

Direct mail is perhaps the most versatile of all media. It receives a rating of 1 on every characteristic except audio and coverage. But even coverage can be achieved if the advertiser is willing to absorb the cost. Generally, it does not seek wide coverage but relies on type selectivity to

TABLE 16-1
Ranking of Advertising Media on Specific Characteristics

		Magazines		Radio		Television				
Characteristic	News-papers	Trade	House-hold	Spot	Network	Spot	Network	Outdoor Signs	Car Cards	Direct Mail
Impact	2	1	1	2	1	1	1	3	3	1
Coverage	1	2	1	1	1	1	1	2	2	2
Audio	3	3	3	1	1	1	1	3	3	3
Visual	1	1	1	3	3	1	1	2	2	1
Frequency of insertion	1	3	3	1	3	1	3	3	3	1
Type selectivity	2	1	2	2	2	2	2	3	3	1
Geographic selectivity	1	2	3	1	3	1	3	1	1	1

reach a specific market. Outdoor signs and car cards are very low in impact. The time period of exposure is so short that they are used primarily for reminder advertising.

The selection of media is not solely a matter of the user's matching his requirements with media characteristics. There is still the question of the relative cost of each medium. Cost may be a deterrent to the media type desired and is of course a critical variable.

SELECTION OF THE SPECIFIC MEDIUM

Since most media within a type have many common characteristics, the selection of the specific medium to carry the advertising is importantly related to cost. Cost, however, has little meaning unless it is related to circulation. The *milline rate* has been developed to make cost-related-to-circulation comparisons among newspapers. It is computed as follows:

$$\text{Milline Rate} = \frac{\text{Line Rate} \times 1{,}000{,}000}{\text{Circulation}}$$

Examination of the formula indicates that it converts the cost line to a ratio of the cost per line per million of circulation to the actual circulation of the newspaper. In this way, the milline rate takes into consideration the differences in circulation among newspapers.

Magazine space is usually sold on a page or fraction-of-page basis. A measurement similar to the milline rate, called the *cost per thousand,* has been developed to make comparisons among magazines with different circulations. The calculation is as follows:

$$\text{Cost Per Thousand} = \frac{\text{Page Rate} \times 1{,}000}{\text{Circulation}}$$

Comparison of radio or television stations is based upon measurements of the listening or viewing audience. There are a number of syndicated data organizations supplying this information. Some of the largest raters of radio and television audiences are the A. C. Nielsen Company, *Trendex,* The American Research Bureau, *Pulse,* and Television Impact Service. Many methods are used for measuring radio and television audiences, and consequently, the results are not always consistent. The advertiser should be familiar with these techniques.[7]

The audiences of outdoor advertising are measured by the number of cars passing the billboards. The Traffic Audit Bureau supplies this informa-

---

[7] For a more detailed discussion of broadcast media research, see David J. Luck, Hugh G. Wales, and Donald A. Taylor, *Marketing Research,* 4th ed. (Englewood Cliffs, N.J.: Prentice-Hall, Inc., 1974), Chapter 16.

tion by stationing observers at outdoor advertising locations to observe the number of people and vehicles passing the point at different times of the day.

The Advertising Research Foundation has been conducting studies of transportation car-card advertising. These studies measure the number of persons who read car cards in the different transportation systems in which they are used.

Although the number of potential consumers reached is an important criterion in selecting a specific medium, the quality of the audience must not be overlooked. Practically all media do market research on those exposed to the medium to try to provide for advertisers a detailed profile of their audience. Many magazines and radio and television stations can supply detailed information, such as age groups, occupational classes, and income groups. This information is also important in selecting a specific medium, because it does little good to reach a large audience that is not particularly suited to the purchase of the product. For this reason, advertisers have attempted to develop more accurate measurement of media effectiveness—especially media related to their own markets.

The cost per reader, listener, or viewer reached has been indicated as a starting point in media evaluation and selection. A second, more precise, measure figures the cost per potential customer reached, which requires that a knowledge of the composition of the medium's audience be matched with the company's own market definition. Next, measures of effectiveness may be related to the effectiveness of the media in serving the advertiser's purpose and desire for impact. For instance, he may wish to compute the cost of inquiries received from two different media in the past in making current choices of expenditures. Or even more significantly, the advertiser may try to develop by various purchase-tracing procedures the cost-of-customer-generated by alternative media. For instance, a retail store will run an advertisement on men's shirts of a particular make at a specific sales price in one newspaper. The next week it will run the same advertisement in another paper and attempt to determine the cost of the space on a per-customer-generated basis. National advertisers make similar kinds of evaluations by offering merchandise, or free home trials, or by including redeemable coupons of various sorts in the advertisement. The point is that one medium could have a lower cost per reader, while another has a higher cost per reader but a lower cost-per-inquiry-generated; the latter could thereby be a more economical purchase of space by the advertiser. The problem is thus essentially one of matching *effective audience* with *potential purchasers* on a cost basis.

It should be clear that the task of selecting a specific medium cannot be done on a completely scientific basis. The data available to the advertiser may be sketchy, and there is frequently conflicting evidence as to the circulation of any given medium. Nevertheless, cost comparisons, along with more qualitative appraisals which take account of the composition of the audience, should enable the advertiser to select the medium which most likely will meet his requirements.

DETERMINATION OF THE ADVERTISING APPROPRIATION

A discussion of the advertising appropriation is presented at this point because it is the next logical step in the management of advertising. However, it is unwise to consider the sums to be allocated to advertising as a separate and distinct problem. Advertising is only one of many activities which may be used in the communication mix. The amount that should be allocated cannot be determined without reference to the other means, such as personal selling, and sales promotion, which may be used. Rarely is advertising used alone, and its success as a part of the communication mix is dependent on the amounts allocated to the other parts and how well they are executed. Depending upon the sums allocated for other purposes, the amounts allocated to advertising can vary. The objective is to find the optimum allocation of each means used. Some of the problems inherent in this kind of analysis are discussed in Chapter 19.

COST OF ADVERTISING TO THE CUSTOMER

Much controversy has taken place over the cost of advertising to the customer. Some advertising is wasteful from the customer's point of view, some is not. The issue is directly related to the previous discussion—namely, advertising's effect on demand and the cost of production and distribution at various levels of output, both for the industry as a whole and for the individual firm.

A simplified explanation and conclusion related to this issue are that if advertising expands demand over what it otherwise would be, and if there are economies of scale in production and marketing such that the lower costs on the greater volume meet or exceed the cost of advertising, then such advertising is in the customer's interest. If, on the other hand, expenditures for advertising do not expand demand, but merely result in the shifting of competitors' shares of market in an existing demand, then the case is much more doubtful as to its customer value. It is this kind of situation that raises the question about wasteful advertising from a customer welfare point of view. There is some evidence that advertising does have an effect on demand. For example, three products with very high advertising expenses are toilet preparations (14.7 percent of sales), cleaning and polishing preparations (12.6 percent of sales), and drugs (9.4 percent of sales). To what extent these industries have experienced decreasing costs is not known. It is probably true, however, that the bulk of our major industries are decreasing-cost industries and will become more so in the future as automation increases. Advertising in most cases does influence the level of demand and, therefore, does not adversely affect customer value. The bulk of our mass production industries rests upon mass consumption, and advertising is usually a major means of high-level demand cultivation.

The case is complicated by the fact that some amount of market information is essential to consumers. This information has to be communicated in some way or another—possibly through salesmen, or expensive training meetings of personnel in distributive organizations in order for them to pass the necessary product and market information through the various channels. It may be in such cases that advertising is a more economic means of transmitting this information than any other device. In this instance, then, advertising would not be a wasteful expenditure from the customer's viewpoint. When the level of advertising, however, is substantially above the level of "necessary information," it may be wasteful. The controversy is over the issue of when this point is reached.

From the individual firm's standpoint, several factors bear on the cost of advertising to the customer. Charges are frequently made among the lay public that the customer pays for a great deal of advertising in heavily promoted brands as contrasted to less heavily advertised brands, and that therefore superior value may be offered to the customer in the latter case, particularly when price differentials exist between the two. This issue is related to other categories of cost in market cultivation and needs careful consideration by would-be customers. Frequently, the heaviest-advertised brand has a lower per unit advertising cost than less heavily promoted rival brands. Chevrolet does the greatest amount of advertising among car makers, yet its cost of advertising per vehicle is among the lowest. If brand "X" has advertising expenditures of $1 million and sells one million units, then its per unit cost is less than that of brand "Y," which sells only 500,000 units but has an advertising expenditure of $700,000.

This point is often confused. Consumers hear a great deal about the "savings" that can be made by buying clothing from "low-overhead stores out of the high-rent district." If a store in a prime downtown location sells 1,000 suits of men's clothing per month from a location costing $1,000 per month in rent, the cost of rent in a suit of clothes is less than that from a store in an outlying location out of the "high-rent district" that sells 300 suits per month from a $500 per month location. Customers need to be wary of all such promotional claims, and managements need to be prepared to deal with this issue in their customer relations.

There is no reason to believe that a decrease in cost equal to advertising expenditures would be reflected in a price decline. The amount of advertising cost is a very small proportion of total sales price.

In fact, the national expenditure for logistical support of business is ten times greater than the combined all-media advertising expenditure. It is only in a very few categories, such as toilet articles and preparations and cleaning and polishing preparations, that the ratio is over 10 percent. These, on the other hand, amount to less than 1.0 percent of total personal consumption expenditures. Price is determined by many factors other than advertising costs.

Finally, customers normally should be more interested in which competitor can provide them a superior value than with what part of the price they pay is accounted for by research, engineering, material, administrative, or advertising expense, and the like. Manufacturers in all cases are trying to adjust their cost centers in an optimum way from a profitability standpoint.

SUMMARY

Advertising is defined as *any paid form of nonpersonal presentation and promotion of ideas, goods, or services by an identified sponsor.* The distinction between advertising and publicity is that advertising is paid for by the advertiser, and he is identified as the sponsor, whereas the advertiser does not pay for publicity, nor does he identify himself as the sponsor. Advertising includes all types of messages, including those usually considered as sales promotion, such as point-of-purchase display material, labels, tags, store signs, calendars, blotters, and circulars. Because of the difference in managing these types of advertising, we have considered these sales promotion, along with such usual sales promotion activities as demonstrations, displays and exhibits at fairs, and consumer premiums and contests.

A simple communication model includes a source; the process of encoding the abstract ideas of the source into a message or signal, which is transmitted through a channel; and message decoding at the destination by receivers.

There are many different types of advertising, and they are divided into manufacturer, middleman, or service establishment advertising; advertising directed to consumers, the trade, or industrial users; and advertising stressing the product or the institution for the purpose of stimulating direct action or indirect action by the receiver. Advertising seeks to stimulate either primary demand or selective demand. Payment may be made by the individual advertiser or on a cooperative basis.

The factors affecting the use of advertising for purposes of stimulating primary demand are the extent of use of the product, demand trends, price-income relationships, extent of the market, funds available, and appeals. The factors affecting the use of advertising to stimulate selective demand are grouped into ability to brand, the characteristics of the product, the customer, and the market. The task of determining the advertising appropriation must include consideration of the other forms of communication used.

The selection of media involves two problems: (1) determining the media type, and (2) selecting the specific medium within a type. The first problem may be solved by matching such media requirements as impact, coverage, audio or visual, frequency of insertion, and geographic and type selectivity, with the capacity of different media to meet these requirements. The selection of a specific medium within a type primarily reflects selective cost comparisons.

The objective of advertising is to increase the profits of the advertiser or prevent their reduction. This is achieved if the advertising is successful in expanding demand and/or creating some degree of inelasticity of price demand. Since price may be used as an alternative to advertising for demand stimulation, estimates should be made of profits accruing from a price reduction versus those accruing from an advertising expenditure.

The cost to the consumer of advertising depends upon its ability to expand demand, and the nature of economies of scale in production and marketing it produces. Customers need to be wary of making overall value judgments on the basis of individual cost components in price, and advertisers and their management need to be prepared to deal with this issue in the marketplace.

QUESTIONS AND PROBLEMS

1. Diagram and explain a simple communications model.
2. Define horizontal cooperative advertising. Give examples. Under what conditions is this type of advertising used? How is it different from vertical cooperative advertising?
3. For the usual kinds of service provided by an advertising agency, how is the advertiser charged? Do you agree with this form of payment? Why?
4. What are the principal functions of an advertising agency?
5. Technically distinguish how advertising and price adjustments can be substitutes for each other.
6. Select four brands of a single product and examine the advertising of each. Are there differences in the product-images the advertisers are

trying to create? If differences are observed, characterize the desired self-image of the purchaser with which each might be compatible.

7. What are the various factors that the advertiser should consider in choosing media?

8. "Advertising is a business expense and is therefore a cost that is paid for by the consumer." Comment.

Chapter 17

Personal Selling

The enterprise seeks a total market posture that builds impact at the point of ultimate sale. Market cultivation is to a great extent a matter of communication with potential customers. In Chapter 16 we discussed advertising and the vital role it plays toward energizing or activating the exchange process. In this chapter we turn our attention to another component of the communication mix—personal selling.

Modern business enterprise has reached a point wherein market requirements preclude using inept selling efforts. Rapid product diversification, expanded markets, changing channels of distribution, and more exacting purchase requirements all demand in today's marketplace a sales representative keenly sensitive to customer needs. An effective salesperson must be equipped with the technical knowledge and skill necessary for effective communication to the mutual advantage and profit of both parties to a transaction. Similar to advertising, decisions must be made on the specific role personal selling is to have in the total marketing mix.

Our approach in this chapter is first to examine the development of a personal selling strategy. The initial section is directed to a detailed review of personal selling in integrated marketing. We then turn to managerial aspects related to an *employee sales force.* Given the decision on personal selling objectives, personnel requirements must be specified and the task of molding an effective selling structure must be addressed. The term *employee sales force* is used to distinguish the use of a firm's own personnel for selling as opposed to specialized selling intermediaries. In meeting sales objectives, a firm may elect to use *agents* or may establish a *dealer structure* to perform the personal selling function. In selected situations, two or more alternatives might jointly be deployed. The decision to use specialized selling intermediaries rather than an employee sales force introduces a different set of managerial considerations when formulating the communication mix. In the final two sections of this chapter, we examine the use of manufacturer's agents and dealer arrangements in terms of comparative features and managerial considerations.

NATURE AND IMPORTANCE OF PERSONAL SELLING

Selling has traditionally played a vital role in the development of modern enterprise. In fact, aggressive selling is one of the essential and distinguishing features of a free market system. However, despite the central importance of personal selling, the field as a profession has long carried a stigma. In terms of other employees of an enterprise, the sales representative has traditionally been viewed as a flamboyant, diamond-studded, overpaid, obnoxious heavy, who by virtue of a lavish expense account is constantly immersed in wine, women (or men), and song.[1] From the perspective of potential buyers, the warning of *caveat emptor* ("Let the buyer beware") has created an image of distrust and suspicion of fraudulent behavior with respect to selling. Consumer protection has concentrated more on selling and selling practices than on any other single aspect of modern marketing.[2]

Unquestionably, the bad image of selling was and is still justified in a great many cases. On the other side of the coin, the personal selling profession in a broad sense employs a significant share of the United States work force. The scope of personal selling activities range from the typical activities of a retail clerk in a department store to those of a computer sales representative. Without the performance of vital sales activities, the ultimate purpose of the marketing mission would be aborted. Among entry level jobs, selling offers one of the fastest ways for a young recruit to be noticed and rewarded in a large enterprise. In terms of modern marketing, personal selling is viewed as a vital aspect of the total effort to gain a differential competitive advantage. The range of selling effort can vary from order taking to creative solving of customer problems. Each may be vital depending upon the product-service offering of a firm. In this section, we will examine the role of personal selling by looking in greater depth at objectives, followed by a classification of selling missions, and a review of basic objectives in formulating a sales development program.

---

[1] For a detailed discussion of the role of selling in modern marketing, see Joseph W. Thompson, *Selling: A Managerial and Behavioral Science Analysis*, 2nd ed. (New York: McGraw-Hill Book Company, 1973).

[2] Ibid., Chapter 3.

THE OBJECTIVES OF PERSONAL SELLING

The basic objective of personal selling is to facilitate ownership transfer by face-to-face contact with potential customers. To this extent, the sales effort is the last step in the marketing process. In modern marketing, performance of the selling function is, for most businesses, much more than merely signing an order. Effective selling is the establishment of a buyer-seller relationship that encourages two-way communication before, during, and after the transaction. In this sense, sales personnel in a marketing organization are primary employees involved in the performance of *pretransaction, transaction,* and *posttransaction feedback*.

In Chapter 3, the importance of pretransaction, transaction, and posttransaction was discussed as a vital part of the managerial function of administration. While the control and analysis of marketing administration are reserved for Chapter 21, brief comments concerning the role of selling in the performance of these subfunctions is necessary for a comprehensive treatment of personal selling.

The pretransaction aspect of marketing concerns all activities necessary to *create* a meeting of the minds among parties favorable to ownership transfer. The transaction aspect of marketing engages all activities once agreement to exchange ownership occurs between parties to the transaction. In selected marketing situations, the potential purchaser has predetermined to purchase a product prior to the time personal contact is made with a sales representative. In some cases, such as mail order, the transaction is culminated without personal contact. Cases where little, if any, persuasion and personal contact are needed to create a pretransaction meeting of minds between buyer and seller are known as *sales-service situations*. A vast majority of selling situations in the retail field and among service industries are of the sales-service variety. It is important to keep in mind that while a representative need not provide extensive information or persuasion to perpetuate the transaction in a sales-service situation, failure to perform the perquisite service activities could result in failure to make the sale, and even in the permanent loss of the customer's patronage.

In contrast to a sales-service situation is a selling environment wherein the sales representative plays a vital role in assisting the potential buyer during the pretransaction period. Such cases, requiring informative and persuasive selling effort, are referred to as *creative selling*. The objective in creative selling is to bring about an enabling foundation for transaction. In many cases of industrial selling, the sales representative is viewed as a vital source of expert information and product modification ideas. For example, firms desiring to purchase trucks were found in one survey to depend upon leasing company sales representatives as one of the most respected sources of information.[3] Similar situations exist in the automotive and retail industries, where supplier sales personnel are traditionally expected to assist in new model ideas and the assortment of products to be considered for retail sales.

The essential distinction between sales-service and creative selling is the *degree* of effort and expertise required to bring about a transaction agreement that is mutually acceptable to buyer and seller. Once such agreement is reached, each category of selling effort must perform order taking and coordinate other activities necessary for successful completion of the transaction. At this point, the sales representative becomes engaged in posttransaction relations with the customer.

Posttransaction is concerned with the continued state of affairs that exists between a buyer and seller after the ownership transfer is completed. The sales representative is of critical importance to this aspect of marketing administration in at least three ways. First, it is important to assure that the products sold give satisfactory performance in use in order to maintain customer loyalty and brand franchise. Second, many sales are replacement or repeat purchases, which make posttransaction satisfaction essential to survival. Third, the sales representative, by virtue of his customer proximity, is in an ideal position to provide informational feedback as a "frontline intelligence" concerning such things as competition, sales forecasting, new product ideas, and necessary product modifications.

The above discussion highlights the role of personal selling in integrated marketing. A salesperson is first and foremost a source of product orders. However, many other vital marketing functions can be performed by a well-structured and well-managed sales force. To assure proper planning of sales force objectives, it is desirable to distinguish between selling missions.

CLASSIFICATION OF SELLING MISSIONS

A variety of different schemes have been offered for segregating and classifying selling missions. The most common classifications group missions on two interactive variables—classification of sales representatives in terms of whom they are working for, and classification based upon whom they are selling to.[4] For present purposes, we will concentrate our effort on a discussion of to whom the salesman is selling. Sales representatives are engaged in selling at every level of the channel of distribution. Thus,

---

[3] *Special Study on Competitive Transportation,* Regular Route Common Carrier Conference, Washington, D.C., 1975.

[4] See James H. Donnelly, Jr., and John M. Ivancevich, "Role Clarity and the Salesman," *Journal of Marketing,* 39 (January 1975), 71–74.

selling effort takes place to consumers, to retailers, to wholesalers, and to manufacturers.

Sales to Consumers

Consumers normally purchase products in one of four ways. First, they may go to a retail store and purchase the product either on a self-service or a clerk-attended basis. Second, the consumer may purchase a product through a vending machine, which is one of the fastest-growing channels of distribution in the United States. Third, a consumer may purchase by mail order from a catalogue, newspaper ad, or an advertisement seen on television or heard on radio. Fourth, a consumer may purchase directly from a sales representative who is involved in door-to-door canvassing. Direct selling is frequently used for women's cosmetics, household brushes, and vacuum cleaner distribution. You can see from the broad range of ways in which a consumer may purchase that some extensively involve the services of personal selling while others do not. In addition, we can make a distinction between those items purchased by the consumer wherein the transaction is predominantly sales-service in comparison to situations wherein considerable creative selling is required. By and large, consumer selling is preceded by a large degree of advanced purchase behavior influence. As we studied in the chapters dealing with purchase behavior motivation, a substantial amount of pretransaction influence is cast by the product purchase decisions of a consumer's peer group. When creative selling is required, it usually is associated with such items as automobiles, recreation vehicles, large appliances, and similar "big ticket" items, which require explanation and consumer reassurance during purchasing. This first category of selling represents the apex of marketing in that no channel of distribution can long exist unless numerous repetitive sales are made to consumers. However, the opportunities for creative selling at the consumer level is limited to specific categories of goods and to limited selling situations. Thus, the predominant situation in consumer selling is a sales-service relationship.

Sales to Retailers

One of the major areas of selling is to retailers. This form of sales activity is normally carried on by wholesalers or manufacturers, employee sales force, or their designated selling agents. As indicated earlier, selling to retailers is an extremely important part of overall marketing because it is essential that retailers be exposed to the broad line of merchandise available from manufacturing. In many situations, as will be discussed later under dealer structures, retailers are an integral part of the selling and marketing mechanism of the manufacturing firm. Appliance dealers, automobile dealers, and airplane dealers represent retailers who have a close working relationship with the manufacturing firm. Many wholesalers, such as hardware organizations and cooperatives, also formulate close working relationships with a select group of retailers. Finally, many consumer outlets are franchised by manufacturers for the purposes of marketing specific brand-name products or services. Such franchise relationships are prevalent in the fast food and home service industries such as carpet cleaning and water softeners. Under these specialized arrangements, the retailer receives a substantial amount of guidance from the sales force of either the manufacturer, wholesaler, or franchiser involved. Thus, the selling mission requires a degree of training and high-caliber managerial effort in order to carry out the designated function.

While it is impossible to categorize all types of sales made to retailers, two are of particular importance. First is a category of selling effort wherein the primary activity of the sales representative is to work with the retailer in order to build goodwill and to assist in the point-of-sale merchandising and marketing of products. This type of selling activity is often referred to as *missionary selling* and is found frequently in the food and housewares industries. The primary purpose of the missionary sales force is to work with the retailer to help form a favorable transaction situation. The second type of specialized retail selling is sometimes referred to as *technical sales,* wherein the manufacturer or wholesaler sales representative works with the retailer to assure the proper installation of products which the retailer sells to consumers. This type of situation is quite often found in home heating and air conditioning systems.

The question always remains: To what degree are retailers sold in comparison to professional purchasing on their part? It is common practice for retailers to attend trade shows, where they are able to observe a wide variety of products offered by different manufacturers and wholesalers. For example, the annual houseware show normally has in excess of 2,000 different exhibitors displaying products available for sale to retailers. Similar shows are held in the fields of gifts, novelties, boats, recreation vehicles, and sportswear, to name but a few. To be sure, retailers do purchase professionally. On the other hand, selling to retail organizations on a continuous basis and helping the retailer promote and resell products to consumers are the primary missions of a large number of manufacturing/wholesaling sales forces.

Sales to Wholesalers

Selling at the wholesale level of the channel of distribution usually means that the middleman in question would be classified as a *merchant middleman.*[5] The merchant middleman, you will recall from Chapter 13,

---
[5] See Chapter 13 and Appendix A.

performs a resale activity and also maintains an inventory and normally provides the physical distribution of products to retailers or dealers. Generally, a manufacturer will work with a limited number of wholesalers in the marketing of his products. For example, one major appliance firm maintains less than 50 distributors to service over 3,000 dealers. In situations where manufacturers are selling to wholesalers, the selling mission becomes much broader than sales-service or even what was previously described as creative selling. It is essential that the sales representative calling on a wholesaler or distributor be a relatively high-level manager in his firm. This sales job could well range from total marketing guidance with the wholesaler to field training of the wholesaler's sales representatives. Perhaps the least demanding function of the sales representative calling on a wholesaler is the actual writing of orders. In many cases, the situation confronted is a reorder process, and under such circumstances many systems are highly automated and linked together by data transmission and computer processing. In working with wholesalers, a manufacturer has the sole objective of gaining retail market exposure by virtue of the wholesaler's organization. While such situations do have elements of conflict, by and large the selling mission of the manufacturer's sales representatives is to motivate wholesalers and to assist them in every way possible to gain the deepest market penetration possible for the manufacturer's product line. This will require working with the wholesaler in every possible way and at levels demanding broad skills and business understanding. For this reason, sales representatives calling on wholesalers are normally high caliber and reasonably professional.

Sales to Manufacturers

Selling to manufacturers is quite often labeled *industrial marketing*. The main reason is that component parts and materials purchased by manufacturers are normally obtained to serve as inputs in the formulation of a finished product. Therefore, manufacturers are not purchasing for purposes of resale but rather for purposes of performing the manufacturing function. The variety of personal selling to manufacturers ranges from representatives of other manufacturing organizations to those who represent extractors of raw materials, in some cases, wholesalers, and in limited cases, retail organizations. A distinction can be made between those who sell manufacturers' basic materials, partially fabricated components, supplies, and services. While such distinctions are not elaborated here, it is important to recognize that not all those who sell to manufacturers are representatives of materials or semifabricated marketers. This form of selling requires technical knowledge of the customer's requirements and in many industries must include an expertise that allows the selling firm to assist the manufacturer in solving technical problems. In comparison to other levels of sales activity, a relationship at the manufacturing level normally involves large dollar transactions and, providing all aspects of the required service are satisfied, a long-term relationship.

SALES FORCE DEVELOPMENT OBJECTIVES

The specific selling mission involved will determine the precise activities that representatives should be required to perform. However, a number of broad objectives can be stated which are important to the development of any effective selling program.

1. To obtain personnel with the proper qualifications to meet the requirements of job performance.
2. To develop in each individual, through training, a proper personal adjustment to the job and essential market and product knowledge and sales skills in order to accomplish maximum job performance.
3. To provide the proper environment which develops a sense of loyalty to the company and encourages each person to assume responsibility to the limit of their capacity.
4. To assure an adequate supply of trained personnel to fill job openings created by promotion, expansion, retirement, transfer, resignation, or termination.

We now turn our attention to the managerial aspects of employee sales force organizations.

MANAGEMENT OF EMPLOYEE SALES FORCE

The effective management of a sales force requires attention to many specified areas. In particular, it is necessary for management to select a territory structure, to develop a program for personnel selection and training, to develop a motivational program that includes both monetary and nonmonetary compensation, and to formulate a program for evaluation and supervision. While it is beyond the objective of this chapter to present an in depth discussion of sales management, each of these major areas of managerial concern are briefly discussed.

DETERMINATION OF TERRITORY STRUCTURE

Given a clear statement of the desired selling mission and an understanding of the general sales force development objectives, the next step is to decide upon the control units to be used in assigning and evaluating personal selling effort. In most situations, the basic unit used for control purposes is oriented to geography, such as county, state, or regional areas. However, the sales force organization can be structured around product groupings, channels of distribution, or classes of customers. It is common for organizations to use more than one form of territory structure simultaneously. For example, while local sales representatives may be assigned customers on a county territorial basis, it may also be desirable to maintain a select group of executive level sales representatives to handle large customers on a national basis. Given the territorial control structure, it is possible to address the question of the desired sales force size. The amount of coverage a sales representative can provide is directly related to a specified job description and the sales potential of the territory. The objective is to arrive at a territorial structure that will provide maximum cultivation of market opportunity in concert with the remainder of the marketing-mix activity. It is on a balanced consideration of potential and mission that territorial assignments should be made to the sales force.

The determination of sales assignments usually involves assigning responsibility for a geographic area or territory. There are a number of reasons for making each sales representative responsible for the company's sales activities in a specific area. First, it establishes the sales task and clearly defines an area of responsibility. When the extent and limits of the job are known, it is possible to program activities to accomplish the goals set forth. Second, it insures effective market coverage of the designated area or customer group. Without definite territories there is a tendency for the sales representative to skim off the cream and sell only the easier accounts over a large area. Third, more intensive market coverage may give a competitive advantage, as it will become more difficult for competitors to make inroads into the company's total marketing area. Fourth, the territory is a managerial unit. The total marketing effort may be evaluated territory by territory, and appropriate remedies taken to correct poor situations. Fifth, territorial responsibility by the sales representative prevents crisscrossing of selling effort, which inevitably results in high cost of solicitation. Sixth, it minimizes disputes over commission payments on sales made where joint effort was involved.

The determination of territories is an extension of quantitative market delineation. The objective is to determine areas of equal sales opportunity. This can never be completely realized, since the size of customers, the frequency of calls necessary, and the accessibility of customers varies geographically. The steps in approaching the ideal follow: (1) divide the total market area into areas of approximately equal sales opportunity; (2) identify the accounts; (3) calculate the length of time for an average call, including travel time, waiting time, and interview time; (4) determine the number of calls that can be made per day; (5) calculate the frequency of calls for various accounts; (6) determine how many accounts can be serviced in a month; and (7) put together areas with a number of customers the representative can be expected to service. This kind of analysis provides a beginning for the establishment of sales territories.

A number of other factors must be considered. For example, the volume of business necessary to operate the territory profitably must be taken into consideration. There might be some areas where the accessibility of customers is such that the number of accounts that could be adequately serviced by one representative would not produce profitable sales volume. It may be necessary to give parts of this area to adjacent territories. The state of sales development may be a consideration. A territory may be smaller than usual simply because the company is trying to enter the area and much development work must be done. Ability of the sales representative may also be a variable which has to be taken into consideration. Geographic variations in economic conditions may call for frequent realignment of territories. Also, the basis upon which market information is available from published sources must be taken into account for purposes of evaluating territorial performance. The determination of territories and the assignment of responsibility for territory management is necessary for effective use of personal selling in the total communication mix.

A continuing function is constant solicitation of each account in the territory. Based upon market information about each account in the control unit, call strategies should be developed. As competitive and market conditions are constantly changing, careful planning of the strategy to be used on each call is important if personal selling is to produce maximum results. A final step is monitoring sales force performance so that adjustments can be made when results depart from expectations.

SELECTION AND TRAINING OF SALES PERSONNEL

The tasks to be accomplished have been identified through the establishment of a personal selling strategy. Accomplishment depends upon careful selection of manpower, continuous attention to training for the job, and provision for motivating desired performance. These areas are usually referred to as the major aspects of sales management.

The same job description useful in establishing a personal selling strategy is absolutely essential in selecting, training, and motivating the sales force. Unless this is done it is impossible to determine the kind of individual capable of performing the job. After potential sales representatives are selected, the areas in which they need specific training cannot be identified without comparing the characteristics of each with the job requirements.

How should the job description be formulated? A basic understanding of the nature and scope of markets and of the forces influencing these markets is, of course, the foundation for the formulation. Management will have some ideas about the activities that must be performed as a result of having determined the role of personal selling in the communication mix. However, to achieve unanimity of opinion about the job between management and the field sales force is most difficult. The development of a job description requires extended discussion between management, the sales supervisors, and the sales representative. The purpose of these discussions is to establish the views of each group concerning desired duties, and to resolve differences in points of view. Likewise, discussions with customers and prospects should be used to determine the buyers' opinions of what activities the sales representative should engage in to be of maximum service and influence in the purchase decision. Such discussions should serve as a basis for developing precise job descriptions, which take into consideration potential selling problems and the objectives of management in using personal selling as a part of the total communication mix.

A more analytical approach to the development of job descriptions uses time-and-duty analysis. Time-and-duty analysis of selling is analogous to time-and-motion study of production employees. Its purpose is basically the same. Time-and-duty analysis involves stating precisely what the sales representative does every minute of the working day. Information is collected either by having the sales representative keep a detailed diary of his day's activities or by having skilled analysts observe selling effort over a period of several days. Both methods run the risk of incurring the ill will of the field sales force unless the sales representative is apprised of the purpose and can be made to recognize the value to him of such studies. After the activities of the entire sales force or a large sample have been recorded, the salesmen are divided into most productive and least productive groups. This division is usually based on such standards as sales volume, gross margin, and profitability. The activity data are then analyzed to determine if there are differences in the activities of good and poor representatives. Those activities performed by the good, and not by the poor, are determined to be essential in the job description. Of course, activities common to both groups are also included. In this way job descriptions which have some relationship to success are developed. When precise job descriptions are available it is possible to proceed to the major tasks of selection and training.

Selecting Sales Representatives

With an understanding of the tasks to be performed, specifications are developed, which state the characteristics needed in the sales representative.

By studying the job description carefully, it is possible to establish deductively a reasonably accurate specification. This is particularly true if the person developing it has had experience on the job.

There is much controversy over which characteristics of temperament and aptitude are necessary for selling success. One approach is to recognize that the characteristics needed for any job may be grouped under a number of categories. One such grouping includes: (1) previous experience, (2) sociability, (3) maturity, (4) leadership capacity, (5) manner and appearance, and (6) training. The problem then is to determine what is needed in each category for a particular selling job.

Not all selling jobs require the same requirements in each category. Some decisions must be made regarding the kind of previous experience one should have to perform well on the job. Variations in previous experience requirements exist from industry to industry. For example, the selling requirements for many industrial goods require familiarity with buyers' needs, and with technical terminology in their business. In the case of house-to-house direct selling of household items, previous experience may not be necessary. There are also variations between companies in the same industry. Some companies have elaborate training programs and are not concerned with the previous experience of the applicant. Others, to minimize the sales training job, seek only those with experience in the same industry.

It is fair to assume that all sales representatives must be socially acceptable. Different types of selling, however, require this trait in different degrees. The representative selling agricultural chemicals to farm supply houses, and sometimes direct to farmers, generally needs different personality traits to achieve social acceptability than one representing pharmaceutical companies to the medical profession.

Likewise, maturity requirements vary. The investment banking house representative is usually an older, dignified individual, in whom the client can place confidence. In fact, in this business, younger people are given extensive training in the head office until they acquire the maturity necessary for this kind of selling. On the other hand, representatives of food processors, calling on the retail trade, do not need the same level of maturity.

Leadership capacity is important in different types of selling jobs. Some companies give sales representatives considerable latitude in negotiating terms of sale, adjusting complaints, and adjusting the product to the buyer's needs. Other selling jobs are more routine, and do not require a representative to exercise judgment beyond a minimum amount spelled out in company operating procedures. In the former case, the traits required are initiative and ability to make decisions. These are leadership qualities. In the latter case, leadership is not so important. But, as it is almost universal practice to use field selling experience as a steppingstone to managerial positions, leadership potential should be considered in selection. The sales force is viewed by many companies as a pool of managerial talent.

Acceptable manner and appearance are important in selling. Beyond the basic requirements, such as cleanliness and capacity for expression, these traits must be tailored to the buying group. The manner and appearance needed in the investment banking house representative differ greatly from these requirements in the agricultural chemical sales representative.

Training requirements also vary. Different levels of formal education are required for different types of selling. For example, whereas a seller of chemicals in the industrial market generally must have an engineering or chemistry degree, or at least substantial specialized education, the formal educational requirements of selling in most consumer goods manufacturers can be set at a lower level.

Although the main requirements can be grouped under the six categories mentioned above, some decisions must be made about the requirements needed in each category to perform satisfactorily on the job. This may be done deductively by those having had experience on the job, or a search may be made to demonstrate empirically the relationship between objective identifying characteristics of the person and success on the job. To develop sales profiles for a specific job, a number of objective characteristics are recorded. Such illustrative items as age at time of employment, home ownership, marital status, amount of insurance carried, and formal education can be used.

These various means may be used to establish the main specifications necessary to perform the activities detailed in the job description. The next step is to determine whether the applicant possesses the characteristics in the desired degrees and combination.

Some writers have suggested that more attention should be given to the emotional and interactional demands of the sales job. That is, job descriptions and specifications should reflect a recognition of the many roles the sales representative plays, such as persuader, customer service, and information gatherer. Each has slightly different emotional demands. The numerous personality types with which the sales representative must interact require flexibility in adaptive behavior. Selection procedures should seek to specify these demands and identify capacity to deal with them in potential candidates.[6]

The four methods most widely used for determining whether the applicant has the characteristics stated in the specification are: (1) application blanks, (2) references, (3) interviews, and (4) tests. All four

---

[6] James A. Belasco, "The Salesman's Role Revisited," *Journal of Marketing,* 30 (April 1966), 6–8.

methods can be used successfully only if the preceding step of preparing a detailed specification has been carefully executed. All methods must be used in combination before a composite picture of the applicant can be assembled.

The *application blank* serves as a means for gathering factual information about the candidate. It can be as extensive and detailed as is necessary to acquire the desired information. The important requirement is that the information that is acquired be used. Unless the information asked for has some relevance to the specification and will be used to assess the applicant's potential ability to perform well, it should not be sought.

The application blank also aids in identifying obviously unqualified candidates. If formal educational background is not sufficient or age and previous experience is unsatisfactory, there is no need to pursue the selection procedure further. If ability to write legibly is a requirement of the job, the application blank is a ready test of this quality. Lastly, it provides cues from the applicant which can be used in planning the interview.

References are an evaluation technique which has been subject to much controversy. There are those who believe that they have little or no value. Perhaps the greatest value of references is to help identify very risky applicants who have not performed well on past jobs. It is rather rare, however, for a previous employer to affect an applicant's employment opportunity adversely in writing. As a rule, statements are generalized and vague. This tendency, along with the fact that replies are often slow in coming, has caused many employers to put little confidence in this technique. Some have found that telephone discussions have some advantages over the written reference. Form letters with evaluation scales have been used to overcome the vagueness of reply, but even here it is difficult to check an evaluation scale with accuracy. Often references are of the verification type and ask for verification of statements made in the application blank about the applicant's work history. When they are used in conjunction with the other methods, they may aid in developing a total picture of the applicant.

The *interview* is the most widely used selection technique. Often it is the only means used. A variety of interviewing techniques, such as the patterned employment interview, or interview guide and rating sheet, as well as multiple interviews and interview reports, are utilized in selection today. All of these have proved to be valuable variations in interview procedures. Regardless of the particular kind of interview used, certain requirements should be met.

It is desirable for the interviewer to get as much information as possible about the candidate ahead of time (the application blank serves a useful purpose in this respect). By so doing, the interviewer is able to plan the course of the interview and guide it along the lines necessary to evaluate the candidate in terms of specifications. Too frequently interviews are conducted without plan. A pleasant exchange of viewpoints is the result, but little is gained from the point of view of evaluation of the applicant. Without a plan, the interviewer often talks too much and the applicant learns a great deal, but the objectives of the interview are not achieved. The interviewer must draw out the applicant and encourage discussion along lines useful to the evaluation process, while at the same time remaining sufficiently flexible to go down potentially useful avenues of investigation not called for in the plan. Without a plan, many topics which should be covered are overlooked. In final analysis of the applicant this deficiency often becomes apparent. A plan, along with providing sufficient time to cover all topics, enhances the prospect of an effective interview.

Tests are used to acquire information on those facets of the applicant's total personality which are not revealed through the other methods. Using tests has been stimulated by a desire to reduce the task of selection to a numerical process. Although employing tests in this manner is not desirable, they do permit an apparently objective evaluation and lend a scientific "halo" to the selection process when they are used. It may be argued that numerical rating through the use of tests is no more conclusive than subjective rating without their use, since subjectivity must be introduced in developing any numerical standard evaluation. On the other hand, if those administering the tests are fully aware of their limitations, they can be a valuable technique when used with the other means.

For the most part, tests for sales representative selection measure mental ability, aptitude, and personality. One source of difficulty with tests is the way in which they are interpreted. Most companies rely on standard tests, which may be purchased from companies which provide testing services. Results must be interpreted in the light of the job for which the applicant is to be selected. To use tests of any kind effectively, standards of test performance must be established. This can be done only by administering the test to both good and poor sales representatives. Once a significant variation in test results is demonstrated, the test may be used to evaluate the presence or absence of certain characteristics detailed in the job specifications. This is called *validation of the test.*

Validation of tests for a specific purpose complicates their use, but unless this is done they may do more harm than good. They become a means of shifting responsibility for the selection of capable personnel. Responsibility is shifted to the test, and it becomes a substitute for the exercise of sound judgment by management.

When the time comes to make a final decision on an applicant, the person or persons responsible for making the decision ordinarily have at their disposal a wealth of information about the applicant. If the selection program has been soundly conceived, they also have a detailed statement of the requirements necessary to perform on the job. Through the exercise of careful judgment, the characteristics of the applicant and the specification must be matched and a final decision made. There is no way of evading the exercise of judgment in this procedure.

Training Sales Representatives

With the sales force selected, the next task is to provide the kind of training necessary to insure performance on the job. It is not often that a company can escape the need to provide some training for the sales force. Even if in the selection process standards are high, there will always be some aspects of the job description that require knowledge that a new employee is not likely to have. If some training is necessary, the major questions are: How much? and How should it be conducted?

Many factors influence the amount of training necessary. First is the experience of the new sales representative. If they have had considerable selling experience, this may be one aspect of training that can be minimized. However, some training must be given because of variations in company practice. If they are "green," so to speak, considerable training in selling may be necessary. The second factor is the product lines they are to sell. If the products are complex, technical familiarity with them might require extensive training. The ease with which familiarity with the product may be accomplished will depend on the levels of knowledge required in the job specification. Third is the customer group. A representative selling processed foods to a divisional food chain-store buyer needs an altogether different kind of understanding of the buyer's problems than one selling to the small independent retail store. Both customers talk an entirely different language.

The task of determining how much training is needed cannot be separated from the knowledge and skills in which training is needed. The job description again provides the basis for establishing the content of the training program. In the job description all duties are described. Experienced personnel must then determine what kinds of knowledge and skills are necessary to perform these duties. As soon as a list of knowledge and skills and levels of accomplishment in each is established, these can be compared with the characteristics of the person. The specification used for selection purposes dealt with requirements that would *potentially* enable the representative to perform the job. There may be wide differences between the knowledge and skills necessary to perform on the job and those necessary for selection. Matching the list of knowledge and skills needed with the characteristics of the individual will give some indication of the content and extent of desired training. By approaching training in this way there is some assurance that the sales force will be provided with the skills and knowledge necessary for effective performance on the job.

Although variations in training programs are found between different companies, the National Society of Sales Training Executives has found that the content of most sales training programs covers: (1) company organization, (2) sales policies and procedures, (3) selling techniques, and (4) technical knowledge or information. The specific content in each of these areas will vary by individual situation.

MOTIVATION

With the sales force selected, trained, and assigned to their respective territories, the remainder of the task of sales management is to insure that performance is as planned. If one could be certain that sales representatives properly selected and adequately trained would perform as expected, the only task left would be that of providing a system of rewards for effort expended. Unfortunately such utopian performance cannot be expected, and a number of activities must be undertaken to prevent deviations from expected performance.

The word *motivation,* as used here, is not meant to convey only the development of enthusiasm. It is used in a broader sense to connote the direction of selling activities in conformance with plans. A number of different elements such as personal supervision, reporting, sales meetings, sales contests, sales correspondence, job rotation, promotion, salary administration, and compensation all influence motivation. We shall examine only two of these: supervision and compensation.

Supervision

The sales representative in the field is somewhat removed from personal contact with superiors. They work alone most of the time, representing the company to prospective and actual customers. Direction is often needed when dealing with unusual problems, and enthusiasm must be stimulated from time to time. This is the job of supervision.

Personal supervision means the use of supervisors or managers who are periodically in touch with sales representatives. Their job is to insure performance in accordance with the job description. They identify weak spots in territory management, and take the necessary steps to remedy the situation. Sales reports are frequently an integral part of the supervision process. Reports are used principally for two reasons. First, they are an evaluation device, and through analysis of them management is able to determine those situations calling for corrective action. Second, they force certain activities deemed desirable by the company simply because these activities must be reported.

In supervision systems there is a problem of balancing the positive benefits to be derived against the possibility of negative results. All forms of supervision run the risk of negative results in the form of high cost and a loss of individual initiative. There is always the irate salesperson who believes management does not understand the problems in the territory. Personal supervision which aims at excessive control can stifle initiative.

The important question to answer is, How much supervision—and what kind—is needed? This will vary from company to company. Although no specific answer can be given, the type of product, capacity of the sales representative, and size of the organization are influencing factors.

Complete reporting systems in some cases have been used as a partial substitute for close personal supervision. Analysis of the reports by management may take the place of the personal supervisor's evaluation of conditions in the territory. However, the identification of problems does not solve them, and a reporting system should be accompanied with some form of personal supervision in order to bring about solutions to problems, as well as to serve other motivational purposes.

Monetary Compensation

The plan for sales compensation should accomplish two objectives: (1) reward effort, and (2) direct effort along certain lines of endeavor. When developing a plan of sales compensation, the developer is faced with two questions: How much should the representative receive? and How should this amount be given? The answer to the first question achieves the first objective—to reward effort. The way in which compensation is earned achieves the second objective—to direct effort along certain lines of endeavor.[7]

The company must decide upon the level of compensation. This will be dependent upon the caliber of person desired and the state of the labor market, as well as specific policies of the company regarding its own wage structure. Once the level or range of income is established, a return to the job description is necessary to identify those things that must be done to earn the income. The next step is to select a means of payment which will induce activities specified in the job description and avoid behavior contrary to company policy.

There are three methods of payment available: *salary, commission,* and *bonus*. They may be used singly or in any combination. The point to remember is that these methods direct activity along certain lines. For example, the *salary* method offers greatest opportunity for control, in that control may be exercised through other means, such as personal supervision. Also, since sales representatives receive income regardless of pro-

---

[7] Frederick E. Webster, Jr., "Rationalizing Salesmen's Compensation Plans," *Journal of Marketing,* 30 (January 1966), 55–58.

ductivity, they are more willing to follow directions given by management. *Commission* reduces the opportunity for close control and encourages selling of the easiest products in the line, potential neglect of new account development, and generally skimming of the territory. Since commission income is based solely on results, it is difficult to control activity. These potential malpractices can be overcome to some extent by separate commission rates on different products, payments for opening new accounts, and bonuses for achieving sales quotas in the territory. *Bonuses* can be used with both salary and commission payments to induce the performance of desired activities.

Once a method of payment is selected, the rate of payment must be established. If salary alone is used, there is no problem. If commissions are used, the rate of pay must be adjusted to the sales opportunity in the territory to insure fair compensation.

Prevailing practice is to use a combination of salary and commission and/or bonus. The salary provides the major part of the income, and commissions and bonuses are used to provide incentives up to approximately 20 percent of the base figure established as the income level.

In many sales situations, commissions and bonuses are provided for the performance of specialized activities determined critical for a firm's continued market growth. For example, special bonuses may be paid for new account selling. The important point in the establishment of a commission or bonus structure is to determine a fair range of compensation in advance of introducing the program to the field sales force.

Nonmonetary Compensation

It is a well-proven principle that sales representatives can only be encouraged to work so hard for the prospect of additional income. While it is not true for all individuals, many seem willing only to work hard enough to assure a comfortable life. In an attempt to motivate higher levels of achievement, it is common practice in industry to engage in nonmonetary compensation in the form of merchandise, rewards, and travel in return for outstanding performance. Several companies specialize in this form of sales incentive and motivational programming. The basic principle is that a merchandise reward or the experience of a trip involves the salesperson's self-concept in relation to his or her family. The awarding of points, for example, to an automotive sales representative for outstanding unit sales may result in a new dining room suite or a grandfather clock that will stand in a home for many years to come. The principle is essentially the same as recognition given an outstanding athlete in the form of a plaque or cup for his or her accomplishment. In a similar way, with the increased mobility of society, trips to exotic places to experience the good life as a reward for outstanding performance have proven to be very powerful motivating forces. The overall path of motivation has come a long way from early days of simply discharging nonproductive representatives. Most salespeople, when equipped with the basic skills and a verified mission, can be productive if properly motivated. A modern approach to sales management utilizes a fine blend of monetary and nonmonetary compensation to reach this goal.

EVALUATION

A final aspect of sales management will be briefly noted at this point because it is one of the major subjects of Chapter 21 dealing with market administration. In order to assure continued relevancy of the sales force structure, it is necessary to evaluate constantly how well a specified organization is achieving its mission. To a degree, evaluation in this respect is concerned with organization. In addition, it is necessary to evaluate and monitor sales force performance so that appropriate adjustments can be made when results depart from expectations. This element of control requires measurement of potential within the sales territory definition, and then the comparison of accomplishment to potential. It is important in the evaluation of a sales force not to set goals that are above and beyond the realm of practicality. While these may be psychologically satisfying to top management, they will in most cases become deterrents to progress in the field. Additional discussion of the evaluative procedures appropriate for marketing control are discussed in Chapter 21.

THE USE OF MANUFACTURERS' AGENTS

In preceding chapters dealing with the distribution mix, we examined the requirements for efficient physical flow of goods from production to consumption. In Chapter 13, the concept of separation in channel structure illustrated that the route of ownership transfer may or may not parallel the physical distribution flow.[8] In this section attention is directed to a further discussion of the role of manufacturer agents. The agent is part of the transaction channel structure who represents a specialized intermediary which is extraorganizational to the producing firm. In this sense, agents represent a vital aspect of the distribution mix. Agents can also be treated as an integral part of the communication mix in that they offer a partial or complete substitute for the use of a manufacturer's employee sales force. Agents, such as brokers, commission merchants, selling agents, and manufacturers'

---

[8] See Chapter 13, pp. 282–83.

agents, provide a variety of services for hire. Management must decide whether to have its own sales force or use the services of such specialized agents. Management considerations in making the decision are many.

SELECTING MANUFACTURERS' AGENTS

Selecting manufacturers' agents is very similar to selecting any distributor that will represent the manufacturer in the marketplace. Agent selection will be improved when attention is directed to the following practices:

1. Comprehensive knowledge of the agent and lines and operations should be obtained. Inquiries should be made of some of the manufacturers the agent is already representing and some of the customers the agent is selling to, or should be selling to. Personal interviews should be conducted with the prospective agent in all cases.

2. The agent should select lines with the objectives of: each line being closely related to the others; each customer called on as a potential buyer of all lines handled; the price and quality of each line is compatible; lines limited to the extent that aggressive representation may be afforded all.

3. Similar or identical territories should exist for all products sold by the agent so that maximum trade cultivation and continuous representation of all client-manufacturers is possible.

4. The agent-principal relationship should be surrounded with an environment of mutual confidence, cooperation, and integrity. The manufacturer should declare intentions of permanent agent representation and thus alleviate the agent's fear of loss of the line. The representative should accept the line only if the intention is to devote sufficient time and effort so that sales results will be forthcoming.

5. The rate of commission should be carefully determined. Adequate commissions should be established to entice high-caliber agents as well as to promote aggressive representation. In other words, compensation should be lucrative enough to command the quality of representation capable of supplying gratifying sales volume.

6. The manufacturers' agent should be supplied with adequate tools to operate effectively in the field. Promotional aids and engineering and sales assistance should be made available to the representative. Agent suggestions should be freely solicited.

7. A comprehensive contractual agreement should be formulated in writing. Such contracts normally have termination clauses, but many techniques can be applied to free either party from such an agreement. The purpose of the contract is not primarily to supply legal protection. Rather, its major benefit is that the agent and principal are forced to consider and

come to a definite understanding about numerous policies and procedures at the outset of the relationship. Even in good faith, misunderstandings may develop without such an explicit agreement. For example, the division of split commissions may cause friction unless the division of the shares is clear in advance.

The major competition of the manufacturers' agent is limited to a few types of operation. As a marketing institution, the agent faces greatest competition from manufacturers who choose to use their own sales force. Sporadic or limited competition is provided by other types of wholesale establishments. Auction companies, brokers, selling agents, commission merchants, and the like are generally used under somewhat different circumstances than the manufacturers' agent, a fact which tends to limit competitive overlapping among the various agents. When a manufacturers' agent operates in packaged foods, he is called a food broker—a confusing term from a technical definition point of view, but a fact of the trade.

COMPETITIVE ADVANTAGES OF THE MANUFACTURERS' AGENT

The nature of the agent operation provides special advantages in competition with a manufacturer's own sales force. Some of these advantages are inherent in agent operation; others may relate to, or depend upon, the capabilities of the individual agent. The capability factor suggests that competitive advantage depends upon the ability of the manufacturer to obtain high-caliber representatives. This same limitation, however, appears when the manufacturer uses his own sales force. The advantages of selling by means of representatives include the following:

Predetermined Selling Expenses

When an agent sales force is used, the manufacturer can maintain comparatively rigid control of selling costs. Personal selling expenses as a percentage of sales are fixed. Other sales costs, such as advertising, research, and related expenditures, can be controlled in dollar amounts, but their ratio to sales depends on the volume of sales. The major selling cost of cultivating customers by means of personal selling to customers, however, varies with sales volume. When manufacturers' agents are used, this cost automatically stabilizes, inasmuch as the compensation rate is absolute. Selling expense as a percentage of sales can thus be predetermined regardless of volume of trade. Control of costs may be of special importance to the manufacturer of small size or one whose sales are characteristically vulnerable to seasonal or cyclical fluctuations. As sales decline in periods of restricted business activity, commission compensation automatically curtails dollar costs. The ability to predetermine selling costs with some exactness facilitates better planning and control of the marketing program.

Little or No Cost Until Sales are Forthcoming

When an agent sales force is used, direct selling costs may be minimized by the manufacturer until sales have been made. This factor is particularly advantageous to the new, small, or weakly financed manufacturer. Were such a manufacturer to use an employee sales force, a substantial investment would be necessary prior to obtaining any volume of trade. Expenditures for recruiting, selecting, training, and maintaining sales representatives would be necessary in advance of any income obtained from sales. For the type of manufacturer noted, these expenditures may be impossible. The avoidance of such advance expenses may be the dominant consideration in making the decision to sell through manufacturers' agents. When this advantage is considered in conjunction with the ability to predetermine sales costs, an agent sales force has some inherent advantages over an employee sales force.

Economy

The use of an agent sales force may provide marked sales economies. Sales economies are most pronounced when the manufacturer produces a narrow line or sells in a market of limited sales potential. Revenue received from a limited volume of trade, as a result of such conditions, may not cover the cost of sustaining a company sales force. When the manufacturers' agent is used, costs are spread among several producers. Agents can thus provide the manufacturer with a low sales-expense ratio by virtue of their ability to spread costs over the merchandise of several producers.

Intensity of Territory Coverage

An agent sales force may provide more intensive coverage of the territory than manufacturers' sales representatives. To obtain sufficient volume to offset the cost of a representative, the territory may need to be large, implying extensive sales coverage. Under these circumstances, company personnel tend to "skim the cream" off the market by calling on only those accounts that can provide sizable sales. From necessity, the smaller and less profitable accounts may be overlooked or avoided. On the other hand, the manufacturers' agent may be able to obtain a profitable volume from a more restricted territory because of his multiple lines. An adequate all-product volume from an individual account may justify regular customer calls on all sizes of customers. More intensive coverage of the territory may thus result from an agent sales force.

Accessibility to the Trade

The manufacturers' agent may have greater access to markets which results from several factors. First, entry to otherwise difficult prospects may be aided because of the agent's multiple lines. For example, a plumbing supplies agent may be able to sell a new client's product to a particular buyer who is already a customer. Multiplicity of lines also increases trade accessibility because the agent usually can secure the audience of a regular customer to present adequately a new client's line. Certain groups of large customers are also sometimes relatively inaccessible to salesmen of new or small manufacturers. The agent who has been calling on this type of customer for a long period of years can more easily introduce products in such a market.

Ease of Sales Administration

The manufacturer who uses an agent sales force minimizes the problem of recruiting, selecting, and training. The management problems incident to maintaining a sales force are, in a large measure, shifted from the manufacturer to a more specialized marketing institution. Although the sales administration burden cannot be eliminated, the magnitude of the problem is substantially reduced. Once representation has been established in the various territories, the marketing program can be carried out with a minimum of management control. Responsibility for maintaining offices, employing capable personnel, keeping records, routing, and meeting payrolls is substantially curtailed. Such a shift of administrative responsibility may be most desirable for the manufacturer who lacks marketing experience or possesses a limited staff. By using agents, the manufacturer has the benefit of numerous "sales offices" maintained throughout the territories. This advantage is inherent in the use of manufacturers' agents.

Quality of Sales Representation

The manufacturer can sometimes acquire more capable and experienced sales representation from agents than a captive sales force. The client may be able to obtain agents having long years of experience in a given trade and possessing a comprehensive knowledge of the market for a particular line. The manufacturer may have difficulty in recruiting this type of representation.

Aggressive Selling

Aggressive selling is not an inherent competitive advantage of the manufacturers' agent, nor is it impossible to obtain aggressive selling through other channels of distribution. Obviously the degree of aggressiveness depends upon the individual agent. The point to be made, however, is that the agent's remuneration is entirely dependent upon productivity because of commission compensation. This advantage is primarily contrasted to manufacturers' salaried sales representatives. A commission plan can be used for manufacturers, but such an arrangement does not eliminate the need to maintain offices and to carry the attendant administrative burden. The aggressive selling promoted by commission compensation can be obtained without facing these limitations by using agents.

Immediate Entry to the Market

Sales may be forthcoming almost immediately when the manufacturers' agents are appointed. By electing to sell through representatives, a new manufacturer or an old one entering a new field taps experienced and established sales organizations with a definite clientele of relatively permanent customers. Were the manufacturer to organize a sales force, a substantial lapse of time might pass between the initiation of action and the receiving of any significant volume of orders. Management that is impatient for sales results may thus find an agent sales force attractive.

Rapidity with Which Regional or National Distribution Can Be Obtained

Closely related to immediate market entry is the opportunity for rapid nationwide distribution. One manufacturer, for example, obtained national market coverage by means of an agent-type sales force in five weeks. Several years may be saved in attaining complete market coverage by the manufacturer who elects to distribute through agents.

AGENT LIMITATIONS

From the manufacturers' point of view, an agent sales force involves some limitations. Several are as follows:

Cost

Although the suggestion has been made that the use of an agent sales force may be less expensive than the use of a company sales force, the comparative economy of the types of sales representation depends upon the volume of business that can be obtained from a given trading area. Manufacturers with a wide line of established products which are in an advanced stage of sales development may find the cost of manufacturers' agents excessive. After a given volume of trade has been attained, manufacturers' salaried sales representatives may be employed at less cost as a percentage of sales.

Lack of Control

The manufacturer does not have the same control over an agent that he has over his own sales force. The manufacturer can control the major policies and procedures of the agent, but has trouble in controlling the agent's detailed activities. This lack of control is an inherent limitation. The agent is in business, and thus is responsible for guiding the daily operations of a selling organization. As a result, the client manufacturer cannot route sales representatives, control sales demonstrations, the length of the work day and work week, the frequency of calls, the amount of services rendered, the selection of subagents, or similar matters.

Partial Representation

The manufacturer who uses an agent sales force obtains only a portion of the agent's time. Obviously, each client must share the selling efforts of the agent with other manufacturers. This limitation may prohibit maximum coverage of a given territory and the continuous promotion of the one line. The sales manager of one firm believed the company received no more than fifteen minutes of active selling time per day from each agent. This company, in the process of transition from agents to its own sales representatives, felt that the amount of time devoted to selling the company's product in each territory would be quadrupled merely by eliminating agents. The manufacturer, in addition, cannot always control the number of lines agents carry. If the manufacturer is interested in increasing the amount of selling effort then a captive sales force can better provide this result.

Obtaining Maximum Market Potential

Opportunities to obtain maximum market potential may be jeopardized. Partly as a result of multiple lines previously noted, the manufacturer may be unable to obtain maximum sales from a given territory. But in addition the agent, fearing replacement by a manufacturer's own sales representative if commissions get too high, may deliberately limit effort when this point of cost equilibrium is reached. (Agents' commissions are equal to salary plus field sales expense.) Proper selection of agents, complete understanding, and explicitly stated objectives may minimize the likelihood of such a possibility. Yet, this risk must be faced when agent representation is used.

Less Market Stability

Should the agent choose to discontinue his relationship with the principal, the manufacturer may find that the agent is able to shift a substantial sales volume to another manufacturer. While this may not always be a significant factor, the manufacturer is unlikely to retain the same volume of trade immediately after the loss of a competent agent. Such an issue is less significant with a company sales force because they must, of necessity, primarily promote their company and its products. Sales volume gained by the manufacturers' agent, however, may have been inspired more by the agent's prestige and acceptance than by the manufacturer's acceptance.

Direct Contact with Buyers More Difficult

The manufacturer normally desires to be as closely associated with buyers as possible. As has been indicated, a sound marketing plan begins with a consumer or user and is based upon needs and desires. When a manufacturer uses an agent sales force, the degree of direct contact with customers is reduced. More difficulty is thus experienced in closely observing marketing conditions, buying habits, and customer needs or preferences.

MANUFACTURER-DEALER ARRANGEMENTS

A specialized selling arrangement exists when manufacturers select to use a dealer structure for purposes of performing the selling function. Such dealers are independent in that they own and operate their own establishments. However, because of the exclusive arrangement, a special set of expectations and dependencies exists between manufacturers and dealers. The producer-marketer must be concerned with the roles and effectiveness of dealers because the total manufacturer-dealer system must compete effectively with other marketing systems. Similar to the previous discussion of manufacturers' agents, dealer arrangements influence formulation of both the distribution and communication mix. The primary reason for coverage of dealer arrangements in this chapter is that dealers offer an important source of selling at the point of ultimate sale. A dealer-management concern exists from the manufacturers' viewpoint because of the risk involved in gaining market penetration. This section reviews the manner by which manufacturers exercise their prerogatives and responsibilities in a dealer arrangement.

THE DEALER STRUCTURE

A dealer structure represents a specialized marketing organization in that it is a more or less permanent arrangement between independent businesses. However, each link of the channel cannot be treated as having independent identity if a coordinated marketing program is to materialize. In this section the inherent nature of a manufacturer-dealer system is analyzed.

A Complex of Mutual Expectations

In any manufacturer-dealer system there is a set of expectations from the system on the part of all participants. An understanding of these expectations makes it possible to perceive more clearly the nature of administrative actions which must be taken to sustain the system under vigorously competitive circumstances. Let us first consider the nature of the manufacturer's expectations.

While some variations in expectations result from differences in products, markets, and firms, manufacturers commonly expect the following supporting roles from their dealers: first, and usually most important, the manufacturer expects the dealer to provide continuously aggressive selling effort. This facet of the dealer's role is the manufacturer's principal concern. In fact, the bulk of the manufacturer's efforts with dealers is directed toward developing the highest possible level of performance in this area.

Second, the manufacturer expects dealers to conduct promotional programs from time to time to tie in with the manufacturer's own promotional effort. Dealers are expected to use merchandising aids, promotional materials, point-of-purchase displays, and cooperative advertising allowances in such a way as to effect a totally integrated promotional system.

Third, a manufacturer desires full-line coverage by the dealer. Manufacturers do not always market the full range of products through all dealers. In some instances, they provide particular classes of accounts with a special grouping of products. Whatever the grouping or line of products made available to the dealer, the manufacturer desires full coverage of the assortment. Opposed to this desire, dealers frequently promote only the best-selling products selected from a number of manufacturers. This practice, frequently referred to in the trade as "cherry picking a line," generally is condemned by the manufacturer, who feels that promotion of the entire line is essential to a balanced position in the marketplace.

Fourth, the manufacturer expects adequate product exposure supported by adequate inventory levels on the part of the dealer. In recent years, the tendency of numerous dealers to minimize their inventory holdings has created friction in manufacturer-dealer systems. In such cases, dealers carry only display models, and order merchandise only after a sale has been made. Some volume of business is bound to be lost from this practice; in certain product categories, the loss can be substantial. For example, demand for window air-conditioners reaches a peak after four or five successive days of temperatures over 90 degrees. When inventories are not immediately available at the retail level, the manufacturer permanently loses many sales.

Fifth, the manufacturer expects dealers to practice responsible pricing. While difficult to define exactly, responsible pricing, in general, means maintaining a price level that is neither so high as to curtail the potential volume of business nor so low as to disrupt prices in the market to the degree that dealers can earn only minimum profits from the manufacturer's line. When a manufacturer's line is unprofitable to a significant number of dealers over any period of time, the manufacturer faces considerable difficulty in obtaining the kind of support needed from dealers.

Sixth, manufacturers expect adequate parts service to be provided by dealers when that is an important part of the sale of the product. Adequate parts service presents one of the more difficult problems manufacturers must solve. Here again, friction develops in the system when dealers fail to meet manufacturers' expectations.

Seventh, the manufacturer requires an adequate flow of market information from dealers in order to conduct business intelligently. Since in this type of system the manufacturer is physically removed from the ultimate customer, information is needed regarding what is happening at the point of ultimate sale. This information usually takes the form of sales reports, inventory levels, competitors' activities, price movements, and the like.

The dealer, on the other hand, has a number of expectations from the manufacturer, which tend to counterbalance those of the manufacturer and provide the basis for a mutuality of interest and a harmonious relationship. First, and usually most important, the dealer expects the manufacturer to provide an attractive, salable, and competitive line of products. That is, the dealer expects the manufacturer to maintain a line, usually through research and development, fully competitive with the lines handled by the dealer's rivals. Dealer grumblings and dissatisfactions are almost sure to occur when the product line is not competitive in terms of price, quality, features, or design.

Second, the dealer expects the manufacturer to develop a high level of consumer brand acceptance for his product. That is, the manufacturer, through advertising and promotion, is expected to create a favorable climate for dealer selling effort. The dealer believes that preselling is necessary to compete effectively with competitive dealers handling products that enjoy such preselling. In consumer goods particularly, this factor has become almost crucial in obtaining strong dealers. Strong dealers are almost in a position to elect the product line they wish to carry, and they strongly favor those that have customer acceptance.

Third, the dealer expects fair margins and equitable price treatment.

Frictions develop from such pricing arrangements as a manufacturer's selling both through wholesalers to smaller dealers, and direct to large retail accounts. Prices may vary, depending upon the class of customer, and the dealer expects the manufacturer to maintain a price schedule that enables all dealers to compete effectively and profitably.

The fourth expectation relates to territorial trade protection. The dealer, in other words, presumes what is called orderly distribution. Trade protection is expected when handling the product entails a considerable investment in inventory, spare parts, service facilities, and the like. The dealer expects the manufacturer to respect the dealer's franchise and not give the line to a directly competing dealer.

Fifth, the dealer expects merchandising assistance in the form of dealer aids and promotion materials. The tools needed to do an effective job are regarded as a manufacturer's responsibility. Additionally, the expectation is that the manufacturer will provide prompt delivery, fair treatment on returns and allowances, regular calls from sales personnel, and, in general, businesslike servicing of the dealer.

Figure 17-1 shows a statement of policy concerning the expectations of both the manufacturer and distributors. You will notice that each of the expectations mentioned above is stated.

A System of Rewards and Penalties

Any manufacturer-dealer system operates essentially through a system of rewards and penalties. Rewards relate primarily to profits. The rewards for both the dealer and the manufacturer essentially reflect increased profitability to both parties. Such profitability comes from coordinated and integrated action on the part of both parties. However, special incentives of a financial nature emerge for dealers from time to time in the form of special promotion of merchandise, movement of accumulated inventories, year-end closeout of lines, and so on.

Penalties involve foregoing profits, threats of disciplinary action, loss of the line, and, possibly, legal prosecution as, for example, under Fair Trade price violations by the dealer. Penalties relevant to the manufacturer involve emphasis by the dealer on other lines, inadequate inventories, inadequate promotion, or, finally, dropping of the line by the dealer.

A Structure of Authority

A manufacturer-dealer system involves a structure of authority which circumscribes the decision and action areas. The relationships among the participants in a system should be clearly defined by specifying the rights, privileges, and obligations of all parties. Definitions of this type frequently take the form of a written contract, but the main purpose of such explicit

Courtesy: The Conference Board.

A STATEMENT OF POLICY

INDUSTRIAL DIVISION

It is our firm belief that Black & Decker and its duly Authorized Distributors have fundamental obligations to each other. We believe that mutually profitable operations depend upon mutual acceptance of those obligations as outlined.

WHAT DISTRIBUTORS CAN EXPECT FROM BLACK & DECKER

1. Selective Distribution:
   - Appointed on the basis of power tool potential in each marketing area.
   - Adequate to insure penetration of all markets for our products.
   - Selected in accordance with the terms of this "Statement of Policy."

2. Specialized Field Sales Assistance Through:
   - The largest, best-trained field sales organization in the industry.
   - Product and market training for Distributor's sales organization by means of effective sales meetings, power tool clinic sessions and joint sales calls in the field.
   - Availability of market potential information to assist Distributor's sales planning.
   - Assistance in the maintenance of a well balanced and current power tool and accessory inventory.

3. Healthy Profit Opportunities Through:
   - Equitable profit margins on power tools and accessories.
   - Assured inventory turnover.
   - Maintaining an orderly market.
   - Refusal to deal with Distributors who do not feel that the sales policies we suggest are based upon sound business judgment.

4. Aggressive Advertising and Sales Promotion Through:
   - The best known brand name in the industry.
   - The largest and best program of national advertising, direct mail assistance and display materials in the power tool field.

5. Leadership in Research and Development Through:
   - The broadest, most complete line in the industry.
   - Continued leadership in product performance, value, styling and innovation.

6. Leadership in Manufacturing From:
   - The largest, most modern plants in the industry.
   - Unparalleled quality control standards.
   - Thorough testing of all products before shipment.

7. Nation-wide Network of Factory-operated Service Facilities Which:
   - Offer prompt, expert repair service at reasonable cost.
   - Stock genuine Black & Decker replacement parts.

8. The Famous Black & Decker Guarantee Which:
   - Protects the purchaser against defective material or workmanship for the life of the product.

WHAT BLACK & DECKER EXPECTS FROM DISTRIBUTORS

1. Effective Sales Results Through:
   - An aggressive sales organization, knowledgeable in the application and selling of Black & Decker products.
   - Effective sales management focus on our line.
   - Adequate penetration of the potential market for our products in the Distributor's normal trading area.
   - Cooperation with Black & Decker's field sales personnel in developing sales programs, meetings and work schedules designed to build sales performance.

2. Vigorous Promotional Activity Through:
   - Imaginative advertising, direct mail activity, displays and catalog coverage of the Black & Decker line.

3. Protection of Black & Decker's Brand Name and Reputation By:
   - Following the sales policies recommended by the company.
   - Restricting sales to the Distributor's normal trading area.
   - Discouraging the sale of Black & Decker products through non-authorized sales organizations, so that the customer will receive maximum service after purchase.
   - Abstaining from marketing practices that, in any way, damage the reputation of the company or its products.

4. Maintenance of an Adequate Inventory By:
   - Stocking tools and accessories of a variety and quantity commensurate with markets served and the highest standards of customer service. ("Adequate Inventory" shall be a matter of agreement between each Distributor and the appropriate Black & Decker sales representative.)

5. Provision of Those Other Services and Functions Which Characterize a Good Distributor, Such As:
   - Extending credit to the user.
   - Following up customer inquiries.
   - Rendering prompt delivery from local stocks.
   - Making available prompt technical services to customers.
   - Keeping informed on market conditions.

With this STATEMENT OF POLICY, we reaffirm our belief in the economic soundness of the Distributor, our resolve continually to improve and diversify the products we offer and, through Distributor channels, to cultivate an ever-widening market for Black & Decker products.

THE BLACK & DECKER MANUFACTURING COMPANY

_____ _____
President   Chairman of the Board

statement of relationships is to alleviate future misunderstandings. These contracts are known as *franchise agreements*. Some of the legal questions involved in them follow shortly, under "Franchise Agreements and the Law."

A Communication Structure

A particularly important feature of manufacturer-dealer systems is communications. Essentially, channels must be available for the orderly flow of information back and forth through the system. The system fails to work effectively when information is either overabundant or inadequate. That is, manufacturers can so bombard dealers with promotional aids, training materials, sales correspondence, and personal contact that the dealer is unable to absorb or use intelligently all the information provided. Consequently, the tendency may be to discard or ignore important as well as unimportant bits of information. Conversely, the dealer may fail to provide the manufacturer with information adequate to the performance.

Channels of communication must be known. In one particular situation, a dealer was found to have received information from seventeen different sources, including both manufacturer and wholesaler personnel.[9] Under such circumstances, the dealer hardly knew with whom to communicate when difficulties arose or when important available information should have been relayed to the manufacturer. Almost invariably, an inefficient and ineffective manufacturer-dealer system has an ineffective information flow.

When we consider the features of the manufacturer-dealer system, it is apparent that any manufacturer will seek and strongly desire a highly responsive dealer organization. Given this primary systems role, manufacturers have developed a great variety of programs to secure responsiveness and a measure of control over the system.

RESPONSIVENESS AND DEPENDENCY

When we speak of responsive and nonresponsive areas of administration in the system, to what are we really referring? Visualize a manufacturer-dealer system as diagrammed in Figure 17-2. Here is shown the entire system: from the manufacturer's marketing personnel, to the sales representatives, on to the distributor's (wholesaler's) management and sales personnel, continuing to dealer management and sales personnel, and finally to prospects and customers in the marketplace. We can regard the upper half of the figure as a responsive area of administration because the

[9] From a *Census of Appliance Retailing in the Saginaw (Michigan) Market*, conducted by the author for a major manufacturer for private use.

Personal Selling

manufacturer has recruited, selected, trained, and compensated these people. Presuming this job has been done reasonably well, we can expect these line personnel to be highly responsive to programs formulated for field operation simply because they are the manufacturer's own employees.

An effective degree of control can be reasonably expected over field marketing operations up to that point in the total system. Beyond it, however, we encounter independent businesses who are neither employed nor paid by the manufacturer, who generally carry other product lines, and who have other commitments and demands upon their time and resources. As a consequence, we cannot expect the same degree of responsiveness in this part of the system. The manufacturer's objective, however, is to have this part of the system respond. Many devices are employed to bring this situation about, with the objective of making what otherwise would be a nonresponsive area of administration more like the responsive area. The manufacturer cannot command this condition; it is not a right, it must be earned. Much depends on the degree of dependence between the subordinate and primary participants in the system.

FIGURE 17-2
The Total "Line" Organization of a Common Manufacturer-Dealer System (Objective: To Develop a Mutual "Responsiveness" Throughout the Total System.)

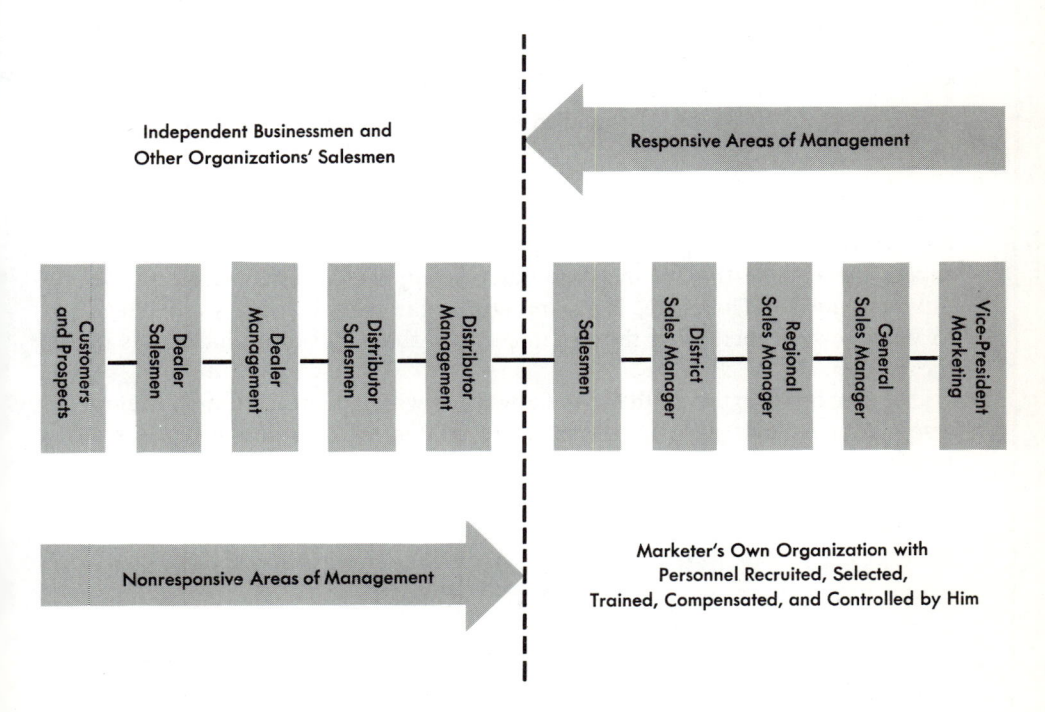

Dependency Level

The dealer has a high level of dependence on the primary participant when the bulk of the dealer's sales volume is derived from a particular manufacturer's line. If the dealer derives 80 percent of sales volume from one manufacturer, chances are the dealer will respond fully to the manufacturer's promotional and distribution programs. In effect, the dealer behaves as one of the manufacturer's employees. But if the dealer derives only 2 or 3 percent of sales from the particular manufacturer's line, it is difficult to arouse the same level of responsiveness. A dealer may legitimately conclude that, if time and resources are devoted to a full implementation of the manufacturer's promotional program, the incremental revenue derived from that will be much less beneficial than the same amount of time allocated to another manufacturer's product line, which accounts for substantially greater sales volume.

Suppose, for instance, that a particular dealer covers the full line of General Electric appliances and also carries a line of electric fans produced by a small electrical goods manufacturer. If the fan line accounts for only 2 to 3 percent of the dealer's total sales volume, it is difficult to justify implementing a promotional program of the fan manufacturer (even presuming it would be an effective stimulant to sales) when a more substantial gain in sales volume could be derived from devoting the same amount of effort to the more complete line promotion of General Electric (even if it was not as well conceived as the smaller manufacturer's plan). This illustrates a rather extreme case of a dependency, but indicates the difficulties that might be expected in developing a highly responsive dealer organization.

On the other hand, visualize the level of dependency between the Coca-Cola Company and its franchised bottling plants. Since in many cases the bottling plants depend entirely upon Coca-Cola for profits, we can expect them, even though they are independently owned businesses, to be fully responsive. Therefore, it is generally to the manufacturer's advantage to work toward increasing the dependency of those in subordinate roles in the system.

Let us now examine the specific ways in which manufacturers develop responsiveness and an effective measure of control over the system as a whole.

Means for Developing Dealer Responsiveness

A number of techniques are used by manufacturers to induce independent dealers to respond to the manufacturers' wishes. The means used vary, depending upon the product and its marketing requirements. Some of the more common methods may be classified as monetary, advertising, dealer sales training, inventory protection, and other operational aids.

Monetary inducements are given in the form of discounts larger than those of competitive manufacturers. By making possible a large gross margin to the dealer, it is assumed that the dealer will give special attention to the manufacturer's line. But there are certain limitations to the use of this means to gain responsiveness. First, if the product is faced with intense price competition, the dealer may not be able to benefit from the wider margin, as the selling price must be reduced to meet competition. The discount given must be adjusted to the resale of the dealer if it is to be effective. Second, the granting of larger discounts can be easily copied by competitors. If this is a useful device for securing dealer cooperation, it is almost a certainty that competitors will do likewise. Third, even though the product is not facing intense price competition, some dealers may use the discount to compete on a price basis. The wider the gross margin, the more opportunity there is to do this. This generally causes some dissatisfaction on the part of other dealers, thus weakening the entire system.

Manufacturers selling through dealers try to get the dealers to coordinate *advertising efforts* with their own. Thus, an integrated advertising message is communicated to potential buyers with the possibility of greater impact than if each advertises in his own way. To achieve this integration the manufacturer must induce the dealer to advertise in a manner consistent with the manufacturer's program. If the dealer is not prone to spend much on advertising, the manufacturer may enter into an agreement with him to share the cost. This is known as *vertical cooperation advertising* and was discussed in Chapter 16. Sometimes the manufacturer pays for the total cost of advertising but advertises over the dealer's name in media serving the dealer's trading area. If the dealer does advertise, the manufacturer places large advertisements in media serving the dealer's area, and through cooperation with the media tries to get the dealers to place smaller advertisements, featuring similar copy, at the same time. The manufacturer's large investment increases the impact of the dealer's smaller advertisement.

The manufacturer views the dealer's sales force as an extension of his own sales organization and strives for efficient represntation of the product at the dealer level. Many manufacturers conduct *dealer training programs* for sales representatives to insure that the product receives the proper kind of representation. Much of the training program emphasizes improving product knowledge and providing the dealer with information of the product's points of superiority over competitive products. It is hoped that by providing more knowledge, the natural inclination will be to stress most familiar products. If the dealer is an exclusive agency not handling competitive products, the dealer training is useful in aiding the dealer's sales representatives to compete with competitive dealers.

The maintenance of adequate stocks at the dealer level is of vital importance to the manufacturer. Dealers, because of limited funds, perishability of merchandise, or desire for rapid turnover and cost reduction, have a tendency to carry thinner stocks than are desirable from the manufacturer's point of view. The manufacturer wishes a sufficient assortment to protect against lost sales arising from the dealer's being out of stock when consumer demand is strong and thus may select to provide inventory protection. If a dealer is not financially strong, special terms of sale may be given to provide time to sell some merchandise before payment must be made. In product lines with a marked seasonal demand, such as toys, payment is often deferred until the selling season begins. If the product is perishable, the dealer may tend to minimize inventory unless permitted to return stock after a certain period of time. The returned-goods privilege is a practice in the chocolate candy industry. Dealers may also hesitate to carry adequate inventories if prices are not stable. To compensate for this reluctance to carry adequate inventories, some manufacturers give guarantees against price declines by making rebates on stock on hand when prices drop.

FRANCHISE AGREEMENTS AND THE LAW

As we have seen, there are certain advantages both to the dealer and the manufacturer in operating together in a system. Since such a system involves independent legal entities, the responsibilities of the parties are often negotiated and given legal sanction through contractual *franchise agreements*.

Two provisions frequently found in franchise agreements have been the source of much litigation. They are: (1) cancellation without cause, and (2) the one-year franchise. Many dealers have taken legal action against manufacturers for damages suffered because of cancellation. After spending considerable sums to develop a market in an area, cancellation results in a substantial loss of investment. The use of the one-year franchise, with the manufacturer holding the option to renew, causes a similar uncertainty and a potential loss to the dealer.

In the past, dealers have not been able to collect damages under these agreements. The courts have held closely to the concept of freedom of contract. They have viewed the relationship as one of vendor-vendee, and recognized the right of each party to stipulate conditions, even "improvident" conditions. The dealer has not been able to claim damages for actions by the manufacturer specifically covered by the contract.

There is, however, a belief that a mutuality of obligation does not exist, and that the manufacturer exercises considerably more control than would be normal in a vendor-vendee relationship. This is particularly true in one-year franchises or those with "cancellation without cause" clauses. The "freedom of contract" concept is still very influential in manufacturer-dealer litigation, but there is evidence that the courts have been following a more limiting approach. In some cases the dealer has been able to collect damages; however, these have been special-fact situations. In the automobile industry an attempt was made to solve the problem of unjust cancellation through the passage of the Automobile Dealers Franchise Act in 1956. The Act gives the dealer the right to contest a cancellation in court if one feels the manufacturer has not acted in good faith. Most interpretations have been special-fact situations and it does not appear that the Act has materially changed the law in the area of cancellations.

A much more limiting factor in the writing of franchise agreements is found in antitrust legislation. An exclusive-dealing franchise agreement generally states that the dealer will refrain from handling competing lines and that the manufacturer, in consideration for his products' being stocked by the dealer, agrees not to sell to competing dealers in a prescribed territory.

Exclusive-dealing arrangements are not illegal per se. However, under Section 3 of the Clayton Act, and under the Federal Trade Commission Act, they may be illegal "where the effect . . . may be to lessen competition substantially or tend to create a monopoly in any line of commerce." A rule of reason has been applied in most cases. However, in 1949 the Supreme Court ruled against Standard Oil of California, stating that its exclusive supply contracts were in violation of the antitrust law. Standard Oil entered into exclusive supply contracts with 5,937 independent stations, or 16 percent of their retail outlets, in the West. Dealers agreed to purchase from Standard Oil all of their requirements of one or more products. The court held that the contracts restricted distribution to competitors, thereby substantially lessening competition, and tended towards the establishment of a monopoly. The legality of the contract has a relationship to the seller's size and share of market enjoyed. In 1959 the Supreme Court declared Sun Oil Company's exclusive dealing practices illegal. In this case the company had no written agreements prohibiting dealers from carrying competitive products or requiring exclusive handling of Sun's products. They did, however, enforce this through minimum quantity purchase requirements, refunds to dealers on a progressive percentage scale based upon quantity of products purchased, and right of cancellation unless minimum sales requirements were met. Restriction of dealers to only the products of the manufacturer may be illegal regardless of whether it is expressed or implicit.

Territorial security provisions—or giving, as an exclusive privilege, to a single distributor the right to sell the product in a defined geographic area—are not illegal, per se. Most cases have been handled on a special-fact basis. However, in 1967, the Supreme Court did stipulate circumstances under which exclusive territorial arrangements are legal. Arnold Schwinn & Co. sold bicycles to dealers on the Schwinn-Plan, whereby

Schwinn sold on consignment to Schwinn-Plan dealers. As Schwinn retained title and assumed all of the risks pertaining to ownership, the dealers were agents, and the restrictions imposed would be illegal only if they were "unreasonably restrictive of competition." In 1975 the Supreme Court ruled that the Coors Brewery Company could not restrict the sales area of their distributors thereby adding more doubt concerning the legality of exclusive territorial arrangements.[10]

SUMMARY

In almost all markets, an aggressive, well-trained sales force is a necessary condition to surviving competition. Failure to establish a personal selling strategy and to make the necessary investment in the proper development of the sales force is to turn one's back on market opportunity.

The establishment of a personal selling strategy involves a thorough understanding of the objectives to be obtained from the selling effort and a clear understanding of the sales mission. Several aspects of the management of employee sales forces are crucial to the formulation of an effective marketing mix. These are: (1) determination of territory structure, (2) selection and training of personnel, (3) motivation from a supervisory, monetary, and nonmonetary perspective, and (4) evaluation and control of the sales force.

Any marketer has alternatives for performing personal selling other than the establishment of management of an employee sales force. While all intermediaries in the transaction channel perform selling activities, there are two particular categories that were treated in this chapter as logical alternatives to an employee sales force: (1) manufacturers' agents, and (2) dealer arrangements.

The selection of manufacturers' agents requires a careful matching of the competency of the agent to the sales objective of the firm. Several competitive advantages favor the selection of manufacturers' agents. In turn, these advantages are offset by selected limitations which the management of a manufacturing firm must consider in making a final determination.

The effectiveness of the channel of distribution depends not only on the channel decided upon, but also on the implementation of the decision. That is, the participating enterprises that make up the channel must be

[10] For an updated review of the legal environment surrounding dealer-manufacturer relations, see James Robert Burley, "The Legal Environment for Strategic Vertical Marketing System Design" (unpublished dissertation, Michigan State University, 1974).

carefully chosen, and directed in such a way that the whole becomes a coordinated and integrated total system of action.

Within any manufacturer-dealer system there are present elements of both cooperation and conflict. Also, there are primary and subordinate roles played by participants. The primary role normally is performed by the brand owner; this tends to establish the focus of power, authority, and decision within the system. Also, the system functions on the basis of a complex of rewards and penalties, and on a set of mutual expectations.

QUESTIONS AND PROBLEMS

1. What is the distinction between sales-service and creative selling?
2. How does selling to consumers differ from selling to wholesalers?
3. Why should management be especially concerned about the effective development of the sales force?
4. What are the elements involved in determining territories? Should territories ideally be of equal sales opportunity or geographic size? Why?
5. What are the various devices that can be used to determine whether a particular candidate or sales applicant meets desired specifications? What is the particular purpose or special feature of each device?
6. Distinguish between a manufacturers' agent and a merchant wholesaler.
7. What are the expectations manufacturers commonly hold with regard to the dealer component in a manufacturer-dealer system?
8. What is meant by the dependency level in a manufacturer-dealer system?

Chapter 18

Price

There are no more important decisions in market affairs than those connected with pricing. No matter how intelligently the product, distribution, and communications mixes are conceived, improper pricing of a product may nullify the effect of all other actions. But in spite of the importance of pricing decisions, the skills and analyses which are often used in practice do not approach the professional orientation used in the management of advertising, sales promotion, or personal selling. Perhaps one of the reasons is that price decisions cut across all areas of business operation, and are not centered in any of the functional divisions of the firm's organization. Nevertheless, there are some fundamental theories and principles underlying pricing decisions, and it is the purpose of this chapter to examine them.

In this chapter much reliance is placed on economic theory in developing concepts useful in the determination of price. The role of price as a means of relating the firm to the market is examined first. The role of the price system, the aggregate of all prices, is then explored, with special attention given to interpretation of price behavior within an industry. Theoretical models relating to price determination are developed and applications of the fundamental concepts are made. Next, procedures available to guide new product pricing are discussed with comments concerning limitation and variations in pricing practices. The final section deals with the legal and administrative aspects of pricing.

THE ROLE OF PRICING

It would be presumptuous to attempt to develop the comprehensive role of prices in a free enterprise economy in a part of one chapter. In a limited way, however, we can present some concepts which will aid our understanding of prices and how they operate (and influence operations) in the marketplace.

A natural consequence of freedom is specialization in productive effort. The point is developed thus far that whenever specialization exists, exchanges are essential to enable the members of society to satisfy their wants in varying degrees. It is within the process of exchange that value is created. Value is the result of the capacity of the participants in the exchange to resolve conflicts through a process of negotiation. Price is a monetary expression of value and is the focal point of the entire exchange process. The customer's evaluation of the compatibility of the product-image with the self-image, discussed in Chapter 6, is expressed in the price he is willing to pay. Price quantitatively expresses a large number of subjective evaluations made by the consumer and by the supplier concerning the value of the money exchanged for goods sold. Any change in these evaluations will result in a change in the quantity exchanged or a change in price.

The price system, the aggregate of all prices, is a very delicate mechanism which conveys the present state of evaluations of buyers and sellers. Another characteristic of the price system is the way in which it operates to balance conflicts between exchange participants. The price will adjust until the quantities demanded and the quantities supplied are equal and a state of equilibrium is achieved. An *equilibrium price* is one that prevails when the quantity of product that suppliers are willing to offer and that consumers are willing to purchase is equal. Consequently, one of the roles of price is to allocate scarce resources in a manner most satisfactory to both consumer and supplier. How does this theory work today?

In Chapter 2 the idea of competition for differential advantage was developed. The objective of competition on this basis is to isolate the competitor from the price of his rival. One of the objectives of advertising as expressed in Chapter 16 was to achieve some degree of inelasticity of demand for purposes of removing the competitor from direct price competition. It is true that much competition today is implemented through marketing action and prevents the price system from allocating resources according to the theoretical model. In fact, firms are faced with the problem of determining price precisely because they have differentiated their product sufficiently to remove them from total reliance on prevailing market prices for similar goods. On the other hand, the effect has not been to nullify completely the role of price in allocating resources. Rather, it has been to slow up the rate of adjustment to new evaluations of consumers and suppliers. Price movements are more sticky, but prices in the long run still exert an influence in the allocation of resources. Discount battles are one indication that price is a potent competitive weapon.

At times it is necessary for the price system also to direct the allocation of scarce resources. This type of condition prevailed during the energy crisis in 1974. However, given the inflationary condition, the government was not willing to allow free market price to determine allocation for such products as heating fuel oil.

The rapid rate of technological development and the commercial implementation of these developments have not waited for the price system to force efforts in other directions. The initiative has been seized by the manufacturer and intermediaries. Developments are taking place at such a rapid rate that the function of the price system is in large measure relegated to providing a means whereby the consumer can register his evaluation of the new goods that are offered to him. If products and the price at which they are offered are not to his liking, purchase is postponed until either product or price is modified.

From the manager's point of view, it is important to recognize that price functions to some extent in its theoretical role. The prices set by the firm must reflect its best judgment of consumers' evaluations of the offer. They must also reflect the firm's judgment of its capacity to achieve its objectives within the prices established. Since both are in a state of flux, prices do change or, more technically, are volatile. The alert competitor will assess what these price changes mean and adjust his own prices accordingly.

Much concern has been manifested over near identical prices across total industries. The prevalence of uniform prices among suppliers with little variation in price through time is sometimes interpreted as evidence of undesirable competitive practices. In situations, this might be a valid interpretation. However, such price behavior may be the result of economic forces.

In mature industries, where there is less opportunity for any single supplier to gain production economies from scale or more efficient methods, it is logical that there would be some uniformity of price between suppliers. This is particularly true in the case of standardized or homogeneous products in which no supplier has an opportunity to gain a differential product advantage. In fact, there is little reason for any competitor to compete on a price basis, since all would follow, and existing demand is redivided at lower prices and lower revenues to each supplier. Consequently, there is a tendency for all suppliers to move prices upward together, and little tendency for suppliers to move prices downward, particularly if demand is relatively inelastic.

The relative stability of prices through time may well reflect these basic economic forces. Wide variations in price through time may simply be an indication of changing conditions of supply, such as in the case of agriculture. Excess supply, with no change in demand, can be moved only through price reductions.

For the most part, the arguments concerning the relationship of price behavior to desirable competitive practices are not concerned with the price itself. Rather, they are concerned with the profits which the maintenance of certain prices generates. The moral and ethical considerations here do not rest entirely on economic matters. The question of a "fair" or "just" price cannot be easily resolved. As long as we maintain convictions about the essential value or worth of a free enterprise economy, we are relying on a price system to allocate resources in the most efficient manner. If prices are not freely determined or if there are barriers to entry into a particular industry, price behavior may reflect these rigidities. It is equally possible, however, that in the absence of restrictions on price movement or barriers to entry, profits may still be high or low, with identical price behavior. Care must be exercised in making judgments concerning price behavior and the degree of competition existing.

THEORETICAL CONCEPTS OF PRICE DETERMINATION

A point of primary importance is to recognize that management is not confronted with a single pricing problem, but with many. Since the forces which determine the efficacy of pricing decisions vary depending on the problem faced, it is important to realize the kind of pricing problems confronting management. A major distinction divides pricing problems into those dealing with: (1) the determination of price and (2) the administration of price.

THE ROLE OF PRICES IN THE FIRM

Pricing may be considered by management as just another element in the mix of market cultivation. Just as advertising, sales promotion, and personal selling are forms of market cultivation, so is price. It is possible, as discussed in Chapter 4, to vary prices and other forms of cultivation to achieve that combination which best meets the firm's objectives. On the other hand, price is something more than just another cultivation device. Price is a reflection of all of the actions of the firm. It brings into focus the kind of product strategy followed, of the system of intermediaries used to make the product available, and of the communications instruments used to persuade the market to purchase. Price is related to product strategy in that interpretations of markets and the development of products to cultivate these markets are expressed in the price placed on the products.

The specific problem in price determination is to establish the price for a specific product. A part of this problem is to determine relative prices for variations in a product type as well as relative prices of different products in a line which are associated in purchase and in use. For example, a manufacturer of fishing equipment may be faced with the need to determine a price for a fishing rod, then a price for different rods, and a price for fishing reels and other equipment within the line. Since the subsidiary problems of determining relative prices of products within the line are secondary to determining the price of a specific product, this chapter deals basically with the primary problem.

Price is related to the system of intermediaries used. In Chapter 14 the need for the performance of a number of activities in a manner which meets the objectives of all concerned was emphasized. To price a product at any stage of distribution without giving consideration to the needs of the manufacturer, channel members, and the consumer, materially increases the prospects of market failure. Prices are also related to the entire communications mix, in that the price selected reflects the reliance placed on other communications instruments. Rarely can large sums be spent on various communications instruments concurrent with low prices. Usually, if a company's pricing policy is one of using low prices to increase quantities sold, some sacrifice in other means of demand cultivation must be made.

In the final analysis, price is a major determiner of profits or losses. The conventional accounting identity of price-cost-revenue relationships gives price a significant role to play in determining profit. The size of revenues from which costs are deducted is dependent on price in two ways: (1) revenues are a function of *unit prices* times *quantity* and (2) price as a means of market cultivation is a determinant of quantity. Since quantity has a major bearing on the level of production costs and marketing costs, price again influences the profit equation. This series of relationships must be evaluated by those charged with responsibility for determining prices. Although the basic relationships are shown in accounting statements, a more refined discussion of these relationships is found in economic theory.

CONTRIBUTIONS OF ECONOMIC THEORY

Frequently the allegation is made that economic theory has little relevance to the real world and is of little value to the practitioner. However, there is value in theoretical economic models if they are accepted for what they are. The theoretical model describes the way in which competitive forces interact to create profits or losses. It is well to have some technical comprehension of these forces, although they are explained in simpler managerial terms later.

Economists have established four market structures to explain how

Price 417

prices are determined in a free economy. Each is examined separately as an elaboration upon coverage in Chapter 1.

Pure Competition

In this structure the number of sellers is large. The output of each is so small that no single firm can influence the price. Products are completely homogeneous, and each buyer and seller has complete knowledge of conditions in the marketplace. In such a structure the demand curve is a horizontal straight line; it is perfectly elastic. That is, if a firm raised its price over the market price, it would sell nothing; and as it can sell all it makes at the market price, there is no tendency to lower price. Under these circumstances the firm has no pricing problem. It simply makes a quantity adjustment to the market price in a manner that maximizes profits. Prices in this kind of structure are referred to as market prices.

Pure Monopoly

This market structure is the reverse of pure competition and is characterized by the dominance of one firm. Since there are no substitutes, the demand curve is the same as the industry curve and slopes to the right. Any increase in price decreases the volume that will be purchased, and any decrease in price may increase the volume a little. The pricing problem in this kind of market structure is to determine the best combination of price and quantity to achieve the goals of the company. These prices are often called business-controlled prices because the firm does control the price it will ask. Sometimes, as in the case of public utilities, the price is set by a governmental agency and is called a government-controlled price. It is doubtful whether there is such a thing as a pure monopoly, as the firm must still compete for a share of the consumers' disposable income. From a theoretical point of vieiw, it does, however, represent a polar extreme.

Monopolistic Competition

In this market structure there are a large number of buyers and sellers, but each seller differentiates his product slightly. In effect each firm becomes a small monopolist. On the other hand, the offerings of rivals are substitutes, and the demand curve slopes to the right but is not nearly so steep as in the case of the pure monopoly. This is so because of the number of close substitutes.

Since this is the most typical market structure in which corporate enterprise functions today, we shall examine it in more detail. The most common geometric description of the way a firm will price in this kind of market structure is shown in Figure 18-1. Let us examine it and determine what relationships are implied. Figure 18-1A describes the relationship between input and output and is sometimes referred to as *the production function*. The total output curve is divided into four stages. In Stage I, output is increasing at an accelerating rate until the rate of increase reaches a maximum at point A. In Stage II, output increases at a slower rate until the rate of increase is equal to average output at point B. In Stage III, output continues to increase at a slower rate until maximum output is reached at point C, at which point output begins to decline in Stage IV. Marginal output and average output are derived from the total output curve.

Marginal output—the increase in total output resulting from an additional unit of input—reaches a maximum when the rate of increase in total output is at a maximum, and will decline to zero when the total output is at a maximum. Average output—the number of units of output per unit of input—reaches a maximum when the rate of increase in total output is equal to average output, and declines thereafter. Another relationship of interest is that marginal output equals average output when the latter is at a maximum.

In Figure 18-1B, the costs connected with the output characteristics described in 18-1A are portrayed. The behavior of both fixed and variable costs are shown. *Fixed costs* are those costs that do not vary with output. They are fixed in total and vary per unit and, consequently, influence the average total cost curve. Fixed costs do not influence the marginal cost curve because by definition *marginal cost* is the increase in total cost necessary to produce an additional unit of output. *Variable costs* are those that vary with output. These costs are fixed per unit of output but vary in total cost. The average fixed-cost curve declines over the entire output range. Marginal cost is at a minimum where marginal output is at a maximum. Average variable cost is at a minimum where average output is at a maximum. Marginal cost is equal to average cost where average cost is at a minimum. Average total cost, the combination of average fixed cost and average variable cost, is at a minimum to the right of the point where the average variable-cost curve is at a minimum, as it must reflect the constantly decreasing influence of the average fixed cost.

In Figure 18-1C the demand curve is added to the cost curve. The curve DD represents the average revenues associated with each unit sold. The average revenue is simply the price charged. As price declines, the quantity which will be demanded increases. The curve dd is the marginal revenue curve and depicts the increases in total revenue from the sale of the last unit sold. Marginal revenue must fall faster than the average-revenue curve as output increases. Any increase in units sold can only come about at a lower price, and consequently the decrease in average revenue is equal to the reduction of selling price, but the decrease in marginal revenue is affected by the lower selling price averaged over all units sold.

FIGURE 18-1
Output, Cost, and Demand Curves

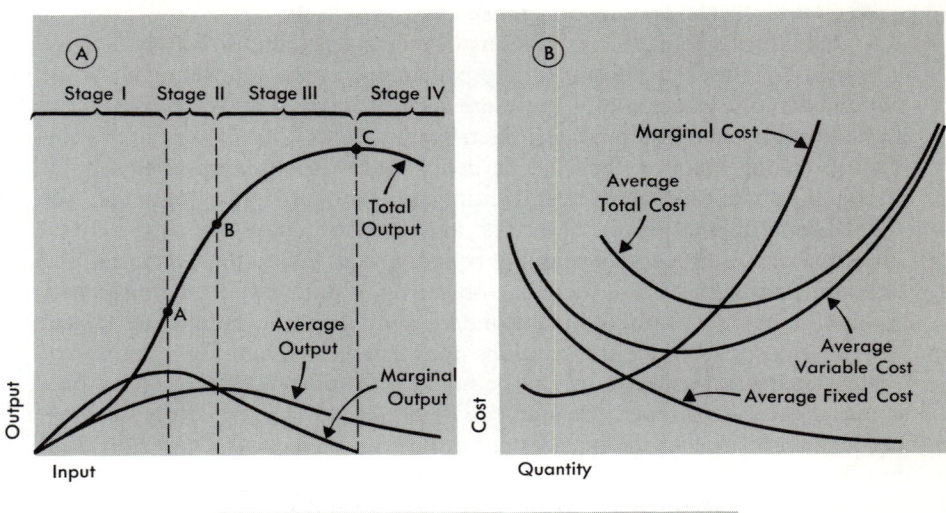

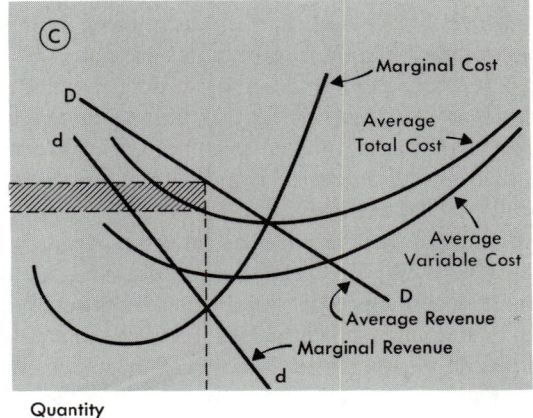

In simpler managerial terms, under the conditions set forth in Figure 18-1, the firm will make a price and quantity adjustment which will maximize profits. It will sell that quantity at which marginal cost equals marginal revenue and set the price at the average revenue for that quantity. To offer less than this amount would be foregoing the opportunity to reap additional profits on additional units sold. To offer a greater quantity would incur loss on each unit sold beyond the point at which marginal cost equals marginal revenues. Conceptually, this matter shows that two sets of forces have a bearing on the determination of profitable prices. The first set of forces is costs. They are internal to the firm and, for the most part, are controllable. The second set of forces are those included in the demand schedule. They are external to the firm and, although not controllable, are subject to influence by different marketing actions.

Circularity between the two sets of forces exists in the following way. The costs of the firm are not totally production costs. Marketing costs are also included. Since some of these are incurred as a result of activities designed to persuade potential customers to buy the product, they have an influence on the quantity that will be demanded. Likewise, price itself influences the quantity demanded. Quantity, on the other hand, influences the unit costs at different levels of output, as shown in Figure 18-1. The general objective of the firm in determining prices is to combine these internal and external forces in such a way that objectives are achieved. A satisfactory level of long-run profit is an absolute essential to the maintenance of a healthy enterprise. Once the relationship is established between both sets of forces, final pricing decisions can be made with full recognition of the outcome, if precision in measurement can be presumed. The prices in this market structure are called business-controlled prices because the individual firm has some control over the price it will charge.

Practitioners often complain that costs do not behave as depicted by the theoretical model. To be sure, current accounting systems do not allow the measurement of cost with the precision assumed, nor do they isolate decision costs. It matters little whether costs do behave as assumed, since some cost structure is prevalent in every combination of the factors of production. Regardless of the nature of cost behavior, it does influence the profit outcome of different prices in some way.

The difficulty of determining the demand schedule presents serious problems. The demand schedule assumes rational, economic behavior. The "diminishing marginal utility" explanation of demand does imply a highly simplified mechanism of the way in which consumers satisfy their wants. On the other hand, a demand schedule is a combination of monetary, real, and psychic forces. It is psychic in that it really depicts a balancing of the utility expected against the disutility required to earn the income necessary to purchase the product. This disutility is expressed in terms of price, a monetary expression. The utility is expressed in terms of the quantity that will be taken at a series of prices, a real expression. The important thing to keep in mind is that utility represents a host of psychological forces bearing upon the individual's desire for goods and his assessment of the value of different quantities of goods to him. The explanation for purchase behavior developed in Chapters 6 and 7 is treated here in this simplified way for the purpose of geometric description. Obviously, we cannot draw a highly precise demand curve for a given product, but since we know that price does influence the quantities that will be demanded, we must make some approximation of the demand schedule in making price decisions.

Although the theory of the firm does present some difficult measurement problems, it is a valid point of departure in price determination. Its most valuable contribution is to depict the way cost, demand, and price interact to create profits or losses. The most significant lesson of all to be learned from the model is that a profitable price cannot be determined from demand alone or cost alone, but only from a combination of both. While the practical measurement problem is a severe one, we must deal with it as best we can with currently available tools of sales-cost-profit forecasting.

Oligopoly

A few large sellers characterize the oligopolistic market structure. Because of the fewness of sellers, the actions of any one has an effect on the others, and so in pricing each will carefully consider retaliatory actions. If the product is homogeneous, there will be a tendency for price uniformity. If the products are differentiated, there may be different prices with the degree of difference dependent upon the extent of differentiation in product. The demand curve in this kind of market structure is depicted in Figure 18-2, and is known as a "kinked" demand curve. In this case, the prevailing price is OB. There is little tendency to decrease price below OB, as all sellers would follow suit and they might end up sharing the market as before, but at lower total revenues. If a firm were to increase price to OE, the other firms will not likely do so, and the firm increasing its price will lose a considerable share of the market. Consequently, the demand curve faced by the individual firm is much more elastic above the prevailing price OB than below it. In oligopolistic industries the price does change over time. All firms increase the price together, establishing a new price from which there is not likely to be any departure for some time.

PRICING TO ACHIEVE CORPORATE OBJECTIVES

The objectives of the price established should parallel the objectives of the firm. The objectives of the firm, however, are not always internally consistent, and close inspection may show them to be very much in conflict. For example, there may be a conflict between the desire for short-run profitability and a desire to gain prestige by being the biggest firm in the industry. It is through a review of corporate objectives that specific pricing policies are developed. To state that the only objective of price determination is to maximize profits is to oversimplify the problem. Obviously, profits are a measure of success and are important for survival. The refinements introduced by stating long-run profitability as a goal may be a very logical and meritorious objective, but it is of limited value in guiding

FIGURE 18-2
Demand Curve Under Conditions of Oligopoly

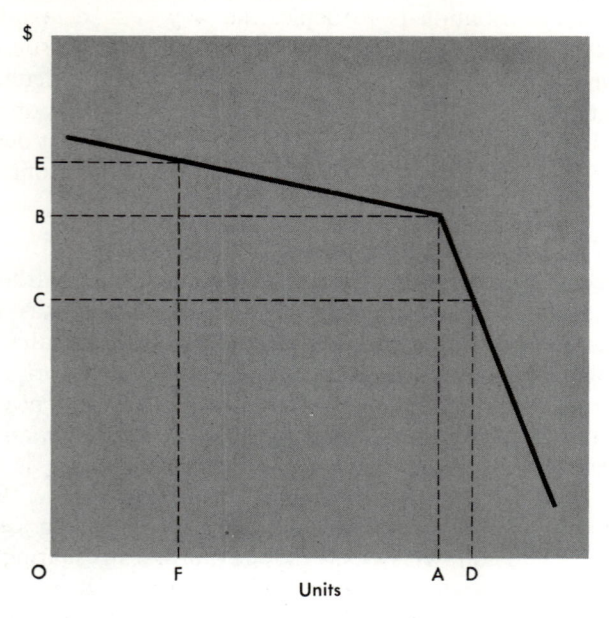

the determiner of prices. Pricing policies must be more specific and give direction to decision making.

Some of the most common policies related to price determination are: (1) return-on investment pricing; (2) penetration pricing; (3) skimming pricing; (4) ethical pricing; (5) full-line pricing, and (6) minimization-of-loss pricing. *Return-on-investment pricing* requires that the price determiner calculate the returns available at the different prices and quantities assumed in the analysis of the preceding section. He will select that price which most nearly approximates the return desired. *Penetration pricing* is closely related to the overall corporate objective of growth. Under such a policy the price which maximizes profits would not be selected. Rather, a price which maximizes quantity at a satisfactory profit level would be chosen. It is selected on the assumption that it would enable the company to penetrate certain markets, win customer loyalty, limit new firm entrants, and generate long-run profitability for the firm. A penetration policy is generally analogous to a low-price policy.

Skimming pricing, on the other hand, involves pricing in such a way as to "skim off the cream" of the market. Those potential customers that are not adversely influenced by high price are the target of this pricing policy. It is generally followed where no entrants are expected to follow, and to enable a recoupment of investment as fast as possible. It results in a price at which profits are maximized and contributes to short-run profitability. *Ethical pricing* involves concern over questions of public welfare, as in the case of immunization drugs. In these cases, the firm is faced with a responsibility to the public. In such cases, the price which produces satisfactory profits may be unacceptable to the market. It is unacceptable in the sense that only a small number can take advantage of the product, or that the price would bring a deluge of public criticism. Under such circumstances, a price much lower than that necessary to maximize profits or satisfactory return on investment may be used. The multiproduct firm is in a much better position to follow such practices than a single-product firm, as it can cover small losses on (spread their cost over) some products in the remainder of the line.

Full-line pricing is also similar to ethical pricing, but for a different reason. The offering of a full line may be predicated on the assumption that one product aids the sale of others. Because of cost-quantity relationships, it may be necessary to price some products at very high prices to satisfactorily insure a profit. The price in itself may defeat the purpose of the full line. Consequently, products may even be sold at below profitable price levels, with the result that the loss is absorbed by other products in the line. *Minimization-of-loss pricing* is another case of pricing below cost. In high-fixed-cost industries, idle plants are excessively costly. If by reducing prices the plant can be utilized, any contribution to fixed cost reduces losses. The firm may set prices which are below total cost but not below average variable costs.

Regardless of the pricing policy pursued, it is important to make the decision with some knowledge of the possible outcome. Only through measurement of the quantities expected at different prices and the effect of different quantities on production and marketing costs can intelligent price decisions be made.

NEW PRODUCT PRICING

In terms of pricing new products it is important to recall that most all products go through a cycle of perishable distinctiveness. The characteristics of competition associated with each stage were reviewed in Chapter 11. This section is concerned solely with the pricing problems associated with the initial or pioneering stage of the product life cycle. In this situation the marketer has no past experience with the specific product to be priced. The problem is to determine a price and a statement of terms of sale that he plans to follow during the initial offering or introduction of the product.

FORMULA PRICING FROM COST BUILDUPS

Extensive study of a number of companies shows that most companies initially develop a pioneering price from cost buildups. Often the formula price is modified slightly to adjust to competitive realities in the marketplace. The strength of the marketing department within the organization of the company is also influential in determining the amount of variance existing between the formula price and the market price actually charged. Where the firm is market oriented, more deviation occurs between the formula price developed initially and the actual price established in the marketplace. Nevertheless, the formula price is the starting point, and the different formulas used are explained first.

Table 18-1 illustrates the types of formulas used by companies in the initial stages of price determination. On the surface, these formulas appear to be quite simple, and one might easily conclude that they reflect unusually haphazard price determination. However, these formulas are the result of

TABLE 18-1
Formulas for Pricing New Products

Example I		Example II	
Direct labor	$ × 5.	Materials	$ × 1.75
Subassemblies from outside suppliers	$ × 3.	Subassemblies from outside suppliers	$ × 1.75
Materials	$ × 2.	Direct labor	$ × 6.
Royalty payments	$ × 1.	Total (+ 10% for development) = Price	
Total = Price			
Example III		Example IV	
Director labor	$ × 8.	Materials	$ × 1.
Materials	$ × 2.	Direct labor	$ × 1.
Total = Price		Factory overhead at 185% of direct labor	$ × 1.
		Total ×2 = Price	

a more penetrating analysis than at first appears. The formula shown in Example IV was derived from an historical analysis of operating statements. This company had as its dominant goal a profit of 10 to 15 percent on sales before taxes. Selling expenses were known to have averaged, over a period of years, approximately 17 percent; general and administrative expenses, 15 percent; amortization of development expense, 5 percent. With an expected profit of 10 percent, cost of goods sold averaged 53 percent of sales revenue. When manufacturing costs were analyzed, it was found that factory overhead expenses approximated 185 percent of direct labor costs.

Consequently, the cost of direct labor plus material plus overhead at 185 percent of direct labor should equal the cost of goods sold and be approximately 50 percent of sales revenue. Doubling this figure should then give a price which would provide sufficient gross margin for the other expenditures as well as a profit of 10 percent on sales revenue. The limitations of this kind of cost buildup pricing are reviewed later.

The more detailed illustration of pricing from cost buildups shown in Table 18-2 is taken from a well-known company. This company is an integrated manufacturing-marketing concern in that it owns its own retail outlets. Management is decentralized, and an attempt is made to isolate operating profits in every segment of the company's business, primarily for the purposes of evaluating managerial personnel and profit-sharing participation. It should be noted that each manager of the company-owned retail stores is free to price the product at the level he pleases. Normally, however, the store manager follows the judgment of merchandise managers in these matters, for he relies on the judgment and analysis of the headquarters planning staff with respect to the suggested price that is expected best to meet merchandising needs at the retail level.

In this example all factory costs except tools are totaled and 10 percent added to cover manufacturing profit. The cost of tools and outbound

TABLE 18-2
Pricing Procedure for a New Product by a Major Integrated Consumer Goods Producer (factories and retail stores)

Materials (62 parts, at actual purchase price)	$18.99
Labor charges (7 depts.—no. hrs. × avge. hrly. wage rate)	4.35
Factory burden (at 201 percent of direct labor)	8.74
Total	32.08
Variations contingency (at 2 percent)	.64
Administrative expenses (at 6.5 percent)	2.08
Subtotal—Manufacturing cost (less tools)	34.80
Factory profit (at 10 percent of manufacturing cost)	3.48
Total	38.28
Tools and tool tryout	4.00*
Freight factor	1.55**
Price to retail store	43.83
Retail markup (at 38 percent)	26.86
Awkward retail price	70.69
Psychologically adjusted price	69.95

* Based on expected production over a two-year period or computed by cost of special tools and fixtures divided by number of units forecast in first two years of production.
** Average expectancy.

freight are added to determine the cost to the company-owned retail stores. The markup of 38 percent on selling price is added on to the cost to the retail store, and the price is adjusted to one that is psychologically acceptable to the market.

LIMITATIONS TO FORMULA PRICING

The limitations to formula pricing vary, depending on the extent to which the prices are adjusted for competitive factors. In Table 18-2 the limitations are not as pronounced as they might be. This company made an analysis of the demand factors which enabled it to set a target price. That is, the merchandise manager proposed a product development program that would lead to a product that would sell at a retail price of $75. However, when formula pricing from cost buildups is relied upon without concern for market forces, the procedure suffers from the following limitations.

1. Demand analysis is cursory. Adequate attention is not given to buyers' needs and willingness to pay. Possible cross-elasticities of demand between products are ignored. The relationships of price among products sometimes acts as a stimulus or deterrent to sales. If two products are substitutes for one another, an increase in the price of one may increase the sales of the other. No projection is made of the number of buyers that can be expected to purchase at various price levels. No possibility exists, then, except by accident, for profit maximization to be reached.

2. Competition is not reflected adequately. Not only does immediate competition tend to be ignored but also potential competitors' reactions to the initial price are not adequately reflected in this kind of procedure. Consideration of whether market entry is invited by the price or whether it acts as a barrier to market entry is pertinent. Firms have a strategy choice here.

3. In general, formulas do not serve marketing strategy adequately. Price should be recognized as but one part of a total marketing mix designed to precipitate purchase of the product. It must be considered in the context of communications expenditures to be made, type of consumer to be reached, purchase motivation factors, consumers' habits in purchasing the product to be displaced, and the like. Also, the strategy choice exists as to whether price is to reflect current costs or is to be set at a level which will generate sufficient volume to produce a future cost structure justifying the price.

4. Formulas tend to overplay the precision with which costs are allocated. The most common basis for allocating overhead costs is to prorate them to products according to direct labor hours. At best, these procedures are arbitrary, and should be recognized as such. Many executives

have unwarranted faith in the precision of their cost buildups. Other accepted accounting treatments could be used that would produce quite different results, yet the executive tends to accept the *cost* as an exact or precise measure.

5. Rigid application of formulas may result in uneconomic procedures. Managers may undertake uneconomic courses of action, depending upon the particular formula used. Product managers may find, for example, that they are better off to subcontract a large number of parts so as to reduce direct labor hours, because overhead is usually allocated as a percentage of direct labor cost. By so doing, the total cost may be reduced for pricing purposes. This was found to exist in one case even when the factory had unused plant capacity.

6. The procedure involves (to some extent) circular reasoning. This is true because price will in part determine the quantity of sales, which determines output, which influences cost, which in turn is used for determining price.

Since companies are often familiar with the limitations to formula pricing from cost buildups or variations thereof, why then do they prefer to follow it nonetheless? This can be explained in part by the great uncertainty that tends to pervade pioneering pricing when a product is new to the market. Such factors as resistance to change on the part of potential buyers, limited data with respect to the potential size of the market, and the uncertainty of future competition and business conditions, lead firms to seek procedures which are relatively simple and which will provide reasonably gratifying results if all goes well. Therefore, a trial price is used which, if accepted by the market, will provide a desirable ratio of profits to sales or investment with full allocation of overhead costs. While this may not be the price that is most profitable, it is considered by management to be a fair price, one characterized as producing profitable business. Moreover, prices are presumed to be more easily lowered than raised. If it is learned later that market conditions preclude a high price which may result from full-cost-plus formulas, downward adjustments can be accomplished with relative ease. In a sense, then, this is a trial-and-error approach to price determination in the marketplace, and selective trial and error is an experimental method which does have some commendable attributes.

VARIATIONS FROM FORMULA PRICING

While most firms profess cost-plus formula pricing in the pioneering period of market development, closer scrutiny shows that such is not strictly the case. A number of procedures are employed that in one way or another either directly or indirectly affect the introductory price. Most of these take the form of making some adjustment for the competitive conditions which exist, or providing built-in flexibility for a rapid retreat from formula prices if initial market reaction is not completely satisfactory. Some of the more important variations follow.

1. *Initial selection of target prices.* In the example of the integrated producer-marketer cited earlier, the company was seeking a product in the design stage that could be sold profitably at retail in the vicinity of $75. Initial market considerations convinced management that this was the vicinity of greatest competitive opportunity. However, once this target area was established and the design frozen, final pricing followed the cost build-ups as demonstrated.

2. *Introductory offers.* Introductory offers can be made in such a way as to make possible any needed subsequent adjustments to the formula price, depending upon the market response received. This sort of initial demand probing provides an opportunity to measure the potential response of the market to the formula price level without placing psychological market barriers in the way of a price adjustment. This procedure is often used in the pricing of consumer goods innovations.

3. *Adjustments for psychological barriers.* Often adjustments are made from the formula price to better adapt the product to its competitive environment. In a case involving a piece of medical diagnostic equipment, a price of $1,985 was placed on the product, instead of the formula figure of just under $2,100, when it was recognized that many institutions that were potential buyers had purchasing policies requiring approval from the hospital board of directors for any expenditure in excess of $2,000. In another instance in the same industry, application of the formula produced a price that appeared to be high in relation to other equipment previously sold. The new product involved considerable miniaturization and did not look as expensive as other equipment sold by the firm. This obstacle was overcome by placing the equipment in a larger case (or housing) than was required and restyling the outside shell to give it a more expensive-looking appearance. This is a type of allowance, for competitive facets of the price problem, that is not immediately apparent in a firm professing formula pricing.

4. *Adjustments for meeting payout policies of purchasers.* In the industrial market, purchasers frequently have policies regarding the length of time allowed for a machine to pay for itself out of cost savings. These policies vary, but a usual range appears to be from one to four years, with twenty-four or thirty-six months common. Several detailed case studies were made by one company to determine the cost reductions possible to the buyer in the utilization of a new piece of textile-making machinery. Analysis of these data resulted in a downward price adjustment from the prelimi-

nary level to bring it within a three-year payout for the average user. This is a type of "demand analysis" that is somewhat different from the conventional form envisaged for price determination. Nevertheless, it reflects adjustment to demand forces within a competitive market.

5. *Trial prices and cost modifications.* A popular time for introducing new industrial equipment is during trade shows and exhibits. The immense national machine tool show is an occasion for the announcement of new equipment by many producers. It also provides an opportunity to probe users' reactions to anticipated prices. Several companies introduced products at one show, with exhibit personnel instructed to inform prospects that the price for the equipment had not been set, and to announce the formula price as the approximate price. In two instances, one involving an automatic boring machine and the other an electronic data processing machine, this trial-balloon approach resulted in a post-show general management conference in which an all-out attempt was made to cut costs of the equipment because of market resistance. For both products, cost-reduction programs took the form of a reevaluation of material costs, tooling expenses, production layouts, time study of labor, design changes, and burden or overhead rates, to achieve costs which would permit a considerably lower price within the formula framework. This forcing of the formula tends to conceal important aspects of the total price-making process.

6. *Research and development cost write-offs and amortization.* Cost-plus pricing from a formula base can be illusory unless care is taken to inspect the costs included in the formula. Several procedures can be used which have the effect of lowering costs and, therefore, prices. One area for management manipulation has to do with government research and development contracts where commercial applications are feasible. Business firms holding sizable contracts of this type frequently maintain large engineering and development staffs for this primary purpose, but their work, either on a planned or unplanned basis, often leads to commercially useful products. Questions are then in order as to how the costs of these departments and common production facilities are to be allocated. In one case, commercial products were withheld until research and facilities costs had been largely covered with governmental charges. Even though government practices involve the prorating of costs, new commercial products can sometimes get a sizable cost advantage in the formula-pricing procedure under these circumstances.

7. *"Scooping out the demand curve" prior to the application of formula pricing.* Formula pricing can be an integral part of the pricing procedure, but it may be withheld until initial advantage has been taken of the innovation. This variation may take the form of selecting for initial cultivation those potential buyers who are not especially cost conscious and covering sizable fixed or sunk costs from initially high prices to these cus-

tomers prior to an attempt at a major market penetration with a formula or "adjusted formula" price. In the case of a wholly new type of blood-fractionating equipment, for example, initial sales effort was to be directed at military or government hospitals, principal Red Cross centers, and foundation-supported experimental facilities where large quantities of blood are separated and where equipment costs, in the light of these quantities, are relatively unimportant. After these purchases were accounted for (with the recapture of sizable fixed costs), a broader market-cultivation program could be launched on a formula-price basis to reach such buyers as the average- to large-sized hospitals. This approach then might be called "scooping out the demand curve," but without the demand schedule being recognized as a curved line. Only two points in the curve are recognized and, within this framework, the cost-plus formula is an integral part of the price-making process.

8. *Tooling amortization.* Tooling decisions affect price levels in several ways. The first important way in which tooling decisions affect costs, and therefore prices, of manufactured product innovations, is the extent of tooling to be used in the production process. If extensive tooling is employed to make possible "line" or "mass" production for the new item, it oftentimes reduces the direct labor costs in manufacturing and assembly. This is in contrast to employing "job-shop" procedures in the initial production process. If factory overhead charges are allocated to products on the basis of direct labor costs, then extensive tooling can have the effect of lowering these overhead burdens in absolute dollar amounts. Limited tooling resulting from job-shop procedures has the effect of increasing direct labor costs.

A second way in which tooling policy affects prices is the procedure used for charging tooling costs to products. Two predominant policies are observed. One approach is to carry tooling costs as a part of general overhead expense, as in the case of a large machine tool manufacturer. Tooling is thus carried in the same way as management salaries. This, incidentally, results in buyers of products in the line with the most tooling involved paying the least proportionate share of this expense (because direct labor hours are reduced from what they would be with less tooling, and a smaller allocation of overhead is made). The second approach is to charge special tooling costs directly to the product; this has a pronounced effect on "costs" and, thereby, prices.

A third way in which tooling costs can affect prices has to do with the length of time or quantity of production over which tooling costs charged directly to the product are amortized. There are cases where tooling has been amortized over the first year's production, two years' production, the first twenty units, and the first production order. The effect on prices is obvious, particularly if tooling costs are large. In one case, to get a cost reduction, tooling costs were arbitrarily spread over two years of output instead of the normal first year's output, principally because of the competitive facets of the price problem. In another case, having to do with the pricing of a new piece of argicultural equipment, management decided to absorb all tooling costs into overhead (normally it was charged directly to the product) to give the product a better break in the introductory marketing program. This adjustment was made quickly after initial market response was sluggish when the price included tooling cost.

9. *Safety costing through subcontracting.* In introducing new products, some firms prefer to minimize risk by relying heavily on subcontractors for a large portion of the initial production of the product. Where opportunities exist for procuring subassemblies and fabricated parts on this basis, some managements feel there are important advantages to doing so. Needed capital is not committed on an unproven product in advance of a measure of potential market acceptance. Also, job-shop production methods may be bypassed by moving directly into line production when the firm decides to make the entire product with its own facilities. Costs are more definite at the initial stage of production as a result of fixed-price quotations on subassemblies, and profitability during introductory marketing is therefore easier to measure.

Moreover, there is believed to be a safety factor in this cost picture, in that managements often feel costs can be reduced when they assume manufacturing operations and absorb suppliers' profit margins. This is believed to provide a cushion for formula cost pricing until the exact nature of competition is more certain and the ultimate success of the new product is easier to judge.

10. *Choice of alternate production lines.* One very vivid case may show how the use of alternative production lines could have a pronounced effect on formula prices. The particular firm involved had three separate production lines, which to a large degree were interchangeable in terms of products. Line A was a low-speed line, principally because of older equipment and the necessity for more hand operations. Line C was a new high-speed line with modern, efficient equipment and many more automated operations. Line B was between the two in terms of efficiency and cost. In making a new product apparently headed for rather severe price resistance, management wanted the lowest price that costs would justify. The product was produced on line C. This produced a lower formula price because the costs were less on this line. This procedure, of course, raises the whole question of costs to a firm in such instances. Production of items originally on line C was moved to another line to make the facilities available for the new product. From a profitability point of view for the firm as a whole,

was this move really necessary? At any rate, this choice of production lines is a facet of competitive flexibility that is not readily apparent in firms professing formula-pricing procedures.

11. **Multiple-formula comparisons.** Another approach to modifying prices derived from cost formulas was uncovered in the scientific instrument field. The formulas used by several competitors were compared by one firm which anticipated that competitors' models would be introduced shortly after the appearance of its product. In this instance, the price chosen was the lowest yielded by a comparison of three formulas. Management presumed that the price selected was unlikely to be too far out of line with what competition might be expected to charge. Here again is an allowance for the competitive aspects of pioneering pricing that is somewhat clouded by the umbrella of cost-plus formula pricing.

In view of all these factors, we may conclude that while studies have shown the predominance of cost formulas for pricing new products, many of the practices used actually take some account of demand and competitive factors, even though the firm may rely in general on a formula approach to price determination.

ALTERNATIVE PRICE STRUCTURES

Variations in price to reflect transactions made under different market or firm conditions are achieved in a number of ways. These variations are generally referred to as price administration. Reasons for the use of varying prices will be discussed as each of several such conditions is developed.

NEGOTIATIONS

The strength of the buyer's position often results in his ability to negotiate a variation from the base price. His ability to do so may come from the alternative sources of supply available. The intensity of price competition among sources of supply is another factor influencing the negotiating ability of the buyer. The buyer's bargaining ability may also be strengthened by the fact that the seller may wish to expand his market. If the buyer is a new class of purchaser or in a new market area the seller is developing, the motivation to give special consideration is great.

Marketing enterprises that are willing to negotiate are said to be following a *variable-price policy,* or one in which prices may be varied on the basis of the bargaining strength of the participants. The program of rebates offered by automobile manufacturers in 1975 is an example of a variable price policy assumed by the manufacturer rather than the dealer.

This practice can hardly be called a system of price administration; however, it is prevalent and should be identified.

To avoid the negotiating demands of purchasers, many companies follow what is known as a *nonvariable-price policy*. This does not mean that prices to different buyers do not vary, but they vary only under certain conditions, such as different prices for different quantities, different kinds of intermediaries, or variations in location of the purchasers. Although a firm may follow a nonvariable policy and administer it well, there are instances in which variations will occur which are, to some extent, beyond the firm's control. Whenever advertising allowances are made or payments for special services, these amount to a variation in price, if in fact they are not used specifically for the purpose stated.

A related policy is that of the *single-price policy*. This means that the seller deals only in a single-price line, such as shoes at $9.95. Such a policy is even more restrictive than a nonvariable-price policy. No variations in price are made regardless of the circumstances under which the sale is made. This policy is not, however, a satisfactory one for large buyers whose negotiating strength could extract lower prices which reflect economies in larger order sizes.

QUANTITY DISCOUNTS

These are discounts given theoretically to reflect differences in costs in selling different quantities. Cost is reduced when buyers can be induced to order in large quantities. Personal selling costs are reduced, as are costs of credit investigation, order filling, packing, and transportation. When the discount is determined on the quantity purchased at a given time, it is known as a *noncumulative quantity discount*. *Cumulative quantity discounts* are calculated on the total orders placed during a time period, and are not restricted to a single purchase. Except on continuity of buyer-seller relations, they are difficult to justify on the basis of reduced costs of selling, because the buyer may still place many orders. Cumulative discounts are promotional in nature, and have several purposes: (1) to tie a purchaser to a single supplier. There is a tendency for buyers to place succeeding orders with a seller because of the larger discount involved on his total purchase; (2) to increase sales in slow periods; and (3) in the case of perishable items, to encourage the buyer to purchase in large total quantities by placing frequent small orders without risking physical deterioration of the product. Cumulative quantity discounts have a tendency to increase peaks and valleys in the production schedule. At the end of a discount period, buyers frequently place large orders so as to qualify for the larger discount. These customers subsequently place smaller orders at the beginning of the next discount period.

TRADE DISCOUNTS

These discounts are reductions in price given to different classes of buyers to compensate them for the performance of certain activities in the movement of goods to ultimate consumers. For example, wholesalers perform certain activities for manufacturers, which in their absence might have to be assumed by the manufacturer if he sold directly to consumers. It is common practice to give wholesalers a larger discount off the base price than that given to retailers. The justification for the discount is payment for the activities performed. The blending of wholesale and retail activities through the operation of retailer cooperative chains and the operation of retail stores by wholesalers and manufacturers make this justification somewhat weak. Some large retailers also operate their own wholesale establishments. They purchase directly from the manufacturer and perform all wholesaling activities.

If not justifiable on a "payment for services rendered" basis, trade discounts are sometimes justified as a means of maintaining distribution. If, because of variations in efficiency among different classes of intermediaries, one is able to undersell the other, the abolition of trade discounts would seriously hamper some, perhaps to the extent that they could not continue to distribute the product for the manufacturer. This defense hardly seems justifiable, for it frequently subsidizes the less efficient outlets.

LEASING ARRANGEMENTS

Leasing is more than a variation from a base price; it really amounts to another form of payment. When a buyer purchases a product outright he is prepaying for the services to be rendered by the product over its life. In a leasing arrangement the buyer pays a predetermined rental fee for the services rendered by the product for a specified period of time or output.

There are many reasons for the use of leasing rather than outright sale.[1] This pricing arrangement is perhaps most frequently used as a means of expanding the market that would prevail under outright sale. The product may be useful to all size classes in the customer group; however, it may be so expensive that smaller companies cannot afford to purchase it outright. Leasing is also a useful means for increasing the total revenue from each buyer. For example, the savings from the use of some industrial products are dependent upon the output of the user. The greater the usage

---

[1] For a classic discussion of leasing, see W. J. Eiteman and C. M. Davisson, *The Lease as a Financial and Selling Device,* Report No. 20, Bureau of Business Research (Ann Arbor, Mich.: University of Michigan Press 1951).

the greater the savings. Consequently, the larger buyer is willing to pay more than is the smaller buyer. To capture both markets by means of outright sale would involve setting a price much lower than the one the larger buyer would be willing to pay. By leasing and establishing a fee on the basis of unit output, total revenues are greatly increased.

Another reason for leasing on the part of the lessor is that equipment frequently is highly technical, and unless the lessor is able to control maintenance and service completely, it may not perform as intended. In using leased equipment, the user can be absolved of all responsibility for maintenance and service, and thus be relatively certain of its almost continuous operation.

Leasing also allows the user to avoid most risks present in the ownership of equipment. In products for which there is a rapid rate of technological advancement, such as electronic computers, buyers are hesitant to purchase outright because the equipment is likely to become technically obsolete in a reasonably short period of time. Through leasing, users are able to maintain the most up-to-date equipment without running the risk of obsolescence. The major advantage to the lessee is the maintenance of capital which can be used for other purposes, since the capital burden is assumed by the lessor. In addition to the savings in capital to the lessee, a tax advantage may be available. The lease rental, which is fully tax deductible as an operating expense, often is greater than the allowable depreciation rate if equipment is purchased outright. Consequently, the actual total cost of leasing equipment is sometimes less than the cost of outright purchase.

Leasing was formerly a devise used primarily by manufacturers of highly technical, expensive industrial equipment. For years, the International Business Machines Corporation leased most of its equipment. Today the lease has spread to a large number of products. A number of leasing companies have developed which lease to industrial buyers just about every product imaginable.

UNIFORM DELIVERED PRICES

Uniform delivered prices are those in which the same prices are charged to buyers irrespective of location. The opposite of uniform delivered prices is F.O.B. (free on board) factory prices. Buyers pay the same price to the seller, but the actual cost of merchandise to them must include the cost of transportation. Uniform delivered prices are a form of price variation, since the buyer located some distance from the supplier is not penalized in price. There are three types of uniform delivered prices: (1) freight absorption, (2) basing-point pricing, and (3) zone pricing.

Freight Absorption

This is a method whereby the seller is able to offer all buyers a uniform price, regardless of location, by absorbing freight charges for those located some distance from him. In Figure 18-3, A and B represent two producing points. The price is set at A and at B. The lines OA and OB represent the cost of merchandise to any buyer located between A and B. These lines represent the cost to the purchaser if he were to buy from either A or B on an F.O.B. factory price basis. The total market is divided between A and B where lines OA and OB cross. Neither A nor B will cut the price to extend the market area, since retaliation by the other is almost certain. With a price cut, the two sellers would share the market in the same way at the higher price, but at lower revenues to each. However, a customer located at X could be induced to purchase from A, if A would charge the same price as B, and absorb the freight cost represented by the line YZ. By absorbing the freight costs both seek to expand their markets, and competition on some basis other than price is used in the respective market cultivation by the rival firms.

FIGURE 18-3
Pricing with Freight Absorption

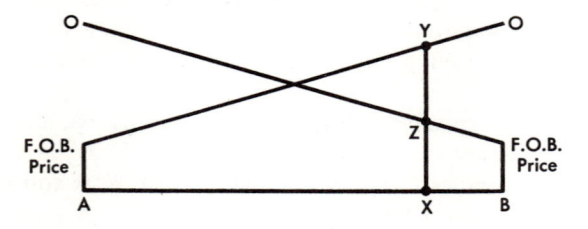

Basing-Point Pricing

This pricing system is an outgrowth of nonsystematic schemes of freight absorption. Freight absorption reduces the net price to the buyer; and originally, basing-point systems were a means whereby freight absorption was wholly or partially offset by charging "phantom freight" to those located close to the buyer. Buyers paid the mill price plus rail freight from the nearest basing point, whether the actual freight was subject to more than or less than this charge. When actual freight costs were less than that charged, the differential was termed "phantom freight."

In Figure 18-4, a simplified basing-point pricing system is diagrammed. Points $B_{1,2,3}$ are buyers' locations, and $S_{1,2}$ are sellers' locations. The lines between the points represent the distance between them. The cost of

Price

FIGURE 18-4
Simplified Basing-Point Price System

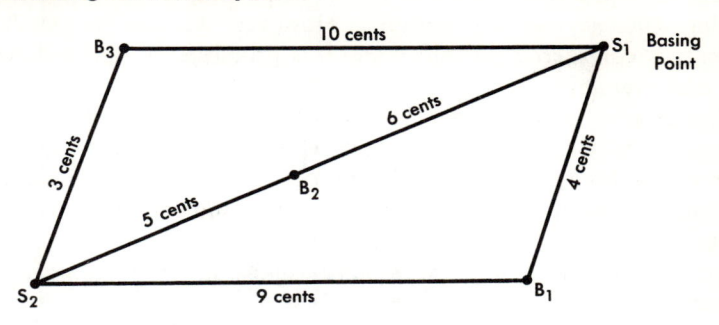

moving a unit of merchandise along the line is designated by the price on the line. S_1 is a basing point. The price charged any buyer by the seller is the base price plus rail transportation from the basing point to the buyer's location. Under these circumstances the net to seller S_2, the cost to the buyer, the freight absorbed, phantom freight paid, and the actual freight charges are as follows:

Buyer	Cost to Buyer	Freight Absorbed	Phantom Freight	Actual Freight	Net to Seller
B_1	$1.04	$ .05	$ —	$ .09	$ .95
B_2	1.06	—	.01	.05	1.01
B_3	1.10	—	.07	.03	1.07

LEGAL IMPLICATIONS OF PRICE DETERMINATION AND ADMINISTRATION

In addition to consideration of the relationship between cost and demand, the price maker is confronted with another external variable, the legal framework. The legal influences are of two types: (1) statutory law and (2) governmental intervention.

With respect to statutory law, there is only one law which is of concern, and it does not apply to the price determination practices of manufacturers. Rather, it governs the pricing practices of intermediaries. Unfair Sales Acts or Unfair Practices Acts have been passed in thirty states, and twenty-five of the acts are still in existence. These acts are designed to prevent predatory price cutting. Price cutting at any level of distribution cannot be prevented if it is based upon low-cost merchandise and efficient operating methods. It is the major means of passing on improvements and marketing efficiency to the consumer. However, the sale of merchandise below cost is considered predatory and it is prohibited in those states with unfair sales statutes.

The general effect of such laws has been negligible because of poor enforcement. Most laws require that a wholesaler add 2 percent at least and a retailer about 6 percent to the merchandise cost to cover the cost of doing business. In a retail or wholesale establishment the broad line of products carried does not permit the calculation of the cost of selling any single product. Consequently, the statutes usually state a percentage-above-invoice cost, which sets the floor below which prices cannot be set except under special conditions such as with damaged merchandise.

The effect of governmental intervention, although not so formal, is perhaps a much more difficult variable to deal with. In the last few years a number of governmental investigating committees have been inquiring into the pricing practices of certain industries. Their concern is not totally to establish unfair trade practices or collusive pricing arrangements, but rather to assess the fairness of pricing policies in a given industry. There is a tinge of exploitation of the public when high prices at large profits are demonstrated. It is a basic principle of law that the seller has the right to set his price as he pleases (except in regulated industries). As yet no laws have been passed regulating levels at which prices may be set. However, during the early 1970s the administration did institute price controls in an effort to curb inflation.

Legal restraints also exist on the price administration practices employed in the absence of any collusive actions on the part of competitors in a single industry. The remainder of this section identifies selected legal aspects of price administration. The discussion is in no way intended to enable the manager to competently interpret the law. This task requires competent legal counsel. However, some general familiarity with the laws concerning certain price administration practices is essential. To that end, we shall discuss the two major acts governing price administration: the Robinson-Patman Act and the Federal Trade Commission Act.

THE ROBINSON-PATMAN ACT

The Robinson-Patman Act, passed in 1936, was an amendment to the Clayton Act. The general purpose of the act was and is . . . "to prevent large buyers from using their economic power to extract favorable prices which are not granted to others less powerful and are not justified by savings to the seller resulting from differences in cost of manufacture, sale, or delivery."[2] In essence the law is designed to preserve competition by curbing the ability of buyers to extract discriminating prices and the willingness of sellers to offer them.

Section 2 details the kinds of action which are likely to result in illegal discriminations in price. The pricing practices prohibited by the act are reproduced here in summary form.

Section 2(a) makes unlawful any discrimination in price which lessens competition or tends to create a monopoly. It is aimed at such discriminations in price which may be prevalent in the use of variable price policies of manufacturers or those present in the offering of quantity and trade discounts. Even uniform delivered pricing practices may be declared illegal, since there may be a lessening of competition among buyers as those buyers close to the source of supply are not given the benefit of their proximity.

Section 2(c) is designed to prevent discrimination in price through the payment of brokerage fees to large buyers who perform their own brokerage services, or payment of brokerage fees to agents under the direct control of the buyer. Brokerage fees may not be paid to the buyer, except for services rendered, or to any agent of the buyer who is under the control of the buyer.

Sections 2(d) and (e) are designed to prevent indirect discrimination in price through the use of advertising allowances and the provision of certain services such as window displays, demonstrations, and the like. The only way in which these devices may be used is through offering to provide them to all buyers on equally proportionate terms.

Upon proof that a discrimination in price has been made, the burden of rebutting the case falls upon the giver of the discriminatory price. The bases for rebuttal are found in the defenses written into the act. These are as follows:

1. Goods are not of "like grade and quality."
2. No injury to competition.
3. Price differentials based on savings in cost associated with different quantities purchased.
4. Differences in price made in good faith to meet the equally low price of a competitor.
5. Differentials in price to reflect changing market conditions or the marketability of goods concerned.

---

[2] From an unpublished address entitled "Self-Regulation Through Business Education: A Key to the Preservation of Our Competitive System," by Earl W. Kintner, former Chief of the Federal Trade Commission, delivered at Michigan State University, East Lansing, Michigan, March 31, 1961, p. 5.

Illegal price discrimination is confined to differences in price given to competing buyers purchasing "like grade and quality." The commission and the courts have not always been consistent in their interpretation of "like grade and quality." In *Federal Trade Commission* v. *The Borden Company,* the commission ruled that the private label brand of condensed milk sold to a large food chain at a lower price was equal in grade and quality to Borden's national brand sold to other retailers at a higher price. The products were chemically identical, but the national brand was highly advertised and sold under a different brand name. The Court of Appeals reversed the commission, upholding that the consumer preference for the advertised national brand makes the national brand different in grade, although chemically identical with the private label. The United States Supreme Court reversed the Court of Appeals and upheld the commission's ruling.[3]

No injury to competition is, for all practical purposes, only a theoretical defense. In 1948 the United States Supreme Court ruled that it was not necessary for the commission to prove any injury to competition, but only to show that there is a "reasonable possibility" that this may be the effect. In *Federal Trade Commission* v. *Morton Salt Company,* the Court ruled that although the quantity discount structure was offered to all buyers by Morton, only a few were large enough to take advantage of it. The result was a "possible" injury to competition among buyers.[4] If the giver of discriminatory prices is charged with illegal price discrimination, he can be sure that injury to competition is involved in a prima facie way.

The cost defense is the most widely used defense but perhaps one of the least effective. A major source of differences in prices to buyers is the quantity discount structure used. To the extent the differences in prices can be justified on the basis of differences in costs, they are legal discriminations. The commission has not been willing in most cases to accept cost accounting designed to justify cost differences. Prior to 1962 there were only ten cases in which cost justification was a valid defense.[5] A part of the difficulty stems from the problem of allocating joint marketing costs to individual buyers. Computerized accounting may make this task somewhat easier in the future.[6]

The good faith defense has been subject to only a few special-fact cases. Two decisions are significant. In *Standard Oil Company* v. *Federal*

---

[3] *Federal Trade Commission* v. *The Borden Company,* 86 S.CT 1092 (March 1966).

[4] 334 U.S. 37, 68 S.CT 882, L. Ed. 1196.

[5] Frederick M. Rowe, *Price Discrimination under the Robinson-Patman Act* (Boston: Little, Brown and Company, 1962), p. 296.

[6] See Charles C. Slater and Frank H. Mossman, "Positive Robinson-Patman Pricing," *Journal of Marketing,* XXXI (April 1967), 8–14.

Trade Commission, the commission had charged illegal price discrimination when Standard gave lower prices to four jobbers in the Detroit area than it gave to smaller service station customers in the same area. The Court of Appeals supported the commission, but the United States Supreme Court reversed the commission ruling. The Supreme Court reasoned that failure to allow Standard to meet the lower price offered to the jobbers by a competitor could result in a higher unit cost and a higher selling price to Standard's other customers if the jobbers did take a substantial portion of Standard's output.[7]

In 1963 the United States Supreme Court ruled against the Sun Oil Company. In *Federal Trade Commission* v. *Sun Oil Company,* the Court ruled that Sun could not give a lower price to one of its service station customers to allow that service station to compete with an adjacent service station selling another brand. It held that the equally low price being met by Sun was the price of a customer's competitor and not its own competitor. The defense can only be used among competitors at the same level of competition.[8]

Although the Robinson-Patman Act has existed for more than twenty-five years, it is still undergoing interpretation by the courts. The major issues in interpretation center around the language used—what is meant by such phrases as "made available," "proportionally equal," "substantially to lessen," "tend to create a monopoly," "like grade," "services rendered," "competing buyers," and finally, and perhaps most important, what is legally meant by "competition" itself.

The effects of the law, however, have been to simplify discount structures in many firms; to diminish the use of cumulative quantity discounts; to do away with brokerage houses wholly owned by retailers; to change materially some prices placed on private brands by supplying manufacturers, by requiring similar cost treatment between their own brands and the private labels; and most important, to greatly increase the use of distribution cost analysis, since manufacturers must justify prices on the basis of provable cost savings.

THE FEDERAL TRADE COMMISSION ACT

This act was passed back in 1914. It proclaimed: ". . . unfair methods in commerce are hereby declared unlawful." In 1938, the act was amended to include unfair or deceptive acts or practices as illegal. The determination of when an act is unfair or deceptive is left to the Federal

[7] *Standard Oil Company* v. *Federal Trade Commission,* 340 U.S. 849.
[8] *Federal Trade Commission* v. *Sun Oil Company,* 371 U.S. 505 (1963).

Trade Commission, an agency established at the same time as the passage of the act.

With respect to price administration, the Federal Trade Commission Act has been used in connection with uniform delivered pricing systems. The rigid adherence to a uniform delivered pricing system is considered to be an indication of price fixing among the members of an industry. Collusion need not be proved. The presence of price fixing is sufficient to constitute a lessening of competition among sellers and a violation of Section 5 of the Federal Trade Commission Act. There is no question concerning the legality of uniform delivered pricing systems under the Federal Trade Commission Act, if practiced only by a single seller. They, however, possibly may be unlawful under the Robinson-Patman Act.

The Federal Trade Commission has broad control over the almost boundary-defying area of trade practices. It is charged with the responsibility of preventing unfair methods of competition, without any attempt by the Congress in passing the legislation to spell out what is to be included under "unfair practices." The commission continuously undertakes a large number of investigations in an attempt to insure the preservation of "fair" competition. It has important jurisdiction over a number of areas beyond pricing, including: false and misleading advertising practices, promotional devices, packages, labeling, franchise agreements, and virtually every other means of market cultivation used by marketers in attempts to gain competitive advantage. Almost all observers would agree that the legislation creating the commission was desirable, and that the commission has performed an important and necessary function in the regulation of competition. Fewer would agree on the propriety of the commission's procedures, and, as would be expected, many of the commission's rulings have been the subject of great controversy.

RESALE PRICE MAINTENANCE

Resale price maintenance is not a variation of price from a base price, but is a means of controlling prices at which goods are resold at the retail level. Some of the principal reasons why manufacturers are interested in controlling prices at this level follow.

Advantages to Manufacturers

If the product is such that intensive distribution is necessary, volatile prices at the retail level may place a limit on the number of outlets willing to stock the item. If a low-operating-cost retailer offers the product at especially low prices, the high-operating-cost retailer will find it difficult to compete. The higher-cost outlet under these conditions is likely to seek a price reduction from the manufacturer, or refuse to handle the item and seek a different source of supply providing a comparable item. Neither is satisfactory to the manufacturer that needs intensive distribution.

Manufacturers spend large sums of money over a period of time to establish brand preference and some measure of consumer loyalty. This objective can be achieved only if the product develops significant prestige in the eyes of the consumer. When the product is offered at a number of different prices in the same market, it is thought that its prestige is weakened. This is a valid justification for maintained prices, in that the trademark to which all prestige attaches is a property right recognized in law. If the actions of some retailers are such that the property right is damaged, restrictive measures seem legally justified. The problem, however, is to prove damage to prestige.

Throughout this text, emphasis has been given to the desire of the manufacturer to compete on a basis of differential advantage. By so doing, the seller removes himself from direct price competition and makes it possible to achieve a more profitable price for his goods. The ability to support a price premium is not necessarily assured simply by using resale price maintenance, but the act of trying to maintain the price at which goods are sold at the retail level is a means to this end.

A sound dealer organization is essential in the distribution of most products. When some dealers in the system compete with others on a price basis, the system may be weakened. Often the selling of merchandise at excessively low prices requires a reduction in other services thought appropriate for the effective distribution of the product. The harmed dealers insist that the manufacturer exert the control necessary to prevent this form of competition or else that he remove the price competition from the system.

Advantages to Retailers and Wholesalers

From the retailer's point of view, devices used to maintain resale prices protect some retailers from low prices and more efficient retail operators. In general, the low-price operators are the large chain organizations. To the extent that they gain large shares of the total market for certain kinds of goods, they weaken the competitive and profit position of the smaller independent retailers. Since the large chains usually perform their own wholesaling activities, the weakening of the small independent retailers means a substantial loss in the markets of the wholesaler. Some wholesalers, therefore, vigorously support resale price maintenance.

These reasons for resale price maintenance all have a certain degree of validity. Most manufacturers and retailers seek the enviable position of being totally removed from price competition. The controversial question is whether or not they should receive the benefit of law to achieve and maintain this position.

Legal Background

The initial fair trade acts were passed in the early 1930s, with California passing the first in 1931. All states except Alaska, Missouri, Texas, and Vermont, and the District of Columbia passed fair trade laws. These laws permit manufacturers to enter into contractual agreements with retailers handling their trademarked merchandise, to maintain the prices at which their goods are sold. Because of the difficulty in entering into an independent agreement with each retailer, practically all state fair trade laws have a "nonsigners" clause. This means that when the manufacturer enters into an agreement with one retailer in the state, this agreement, with proper notification, binds all other retailers handling the product in the state.

Since these state laws legalized intrastate vertical price-fixing agreements, they were legally valid as long as the goods did not enter interstate trade. If the goods were involved in interstate trade, such laws were a violation of the Sherman Act. In 1937, Congress passed the Miller-Tydings Act, which in effect removed such practices from violation of the Sherman Act.

In a celebrated case, the Calvert Distillers Corporation charged Schwegmann Brothers, a large retailer, with breach of contract when the latter sold at less than the maintained price.[9] The case was tried on the basis of the constitutionality of the "nonsigners" clause. In 1950, the Supreme Court held that it was not the intent of the Congress in passing the Miller-Tydings Act also to legalize the "nonsigners" clause. In 1952, the McGuire amendment to the Federal Trade Commission Act was passed, making the "nonsigners" clause legal in interstate trade.

Since 1952, a number of cases have been tried in state courts, testing the constitutionality of the state laws. The number of states now having fair trade laws has been reduced to thirty-one. Regardless of the legal status of fair trade acts, use of them by manufacturers is purely voluntary. The rash of discounting experienced during the decades of the 1950s and 1960s is evidence that, economically speaking, they are breaking down. A manufacturer cannot afford to refuse to sell to some of the large retailers who compete primarily on a price basis. Enforcement is costly and difficult for the manufacturer, and during periods of intense price competition, enforcement is only token.

Present Scope of Resale Price Maintenance

As we have pointed out, although legally supported in 35 states, the economic force of competition has diminished the use of fair trade laws by manufacturers. Although these laws are operative in such fields as drugs

---

[9] *Schegmann Brothers, et al.,* v. *Calvert Distillers Corp.,* 341, U.S. 384.

and cosmetics, appliances, sporting goods, liquor, and photographic equipment, it is not likely that more than 5 to 10 percent of all goods sold at retail is subject to them.

In summary, there are undoubtedly sound managerial reasons for the maintenance of resale prices. It is, however, doubtful whether a manufacturer should receive the benefit of law to achieve this position. To do so deprives the customer of the right to purchase at lower prices if he wishes to forego certain services. Further, forced maintenance all too frequently subsidizes the inefficient retailers. Therefore, these laws raise controversial issues of public policy and involve questionable elements of economic welfare. While their present status provides a materially weakened position for effective control, they could be reinstated at any time with more effective legislation. There are recurring attempts to bring this about, and the prevailing legislation and court interpretations could change at any time.[10]

SUMMARY

Pricing is one of the most important decision areas in the market affairs of the firm. Price is the focal point of all other actions the firm has taken. In this chapter some concepts regarding the role of prices in the economy and in the firm have been developed.

Price is a monetary expression of value and quantitatively expresses the subjective evaluation of consumers and suppliers regarding potential benefits from exchange. The price system, the aggregate of all prices, may be viewed as a system which communicates the present state of evaluations of buyers and sellers. Whenever these evaluations change, either the price or the quantity exchanged will change. In this way the price system theoretically directs the allocation of resources. Although prices do not direct resources with the rapidity theoretically assumed, they still are influential in this respect. Prices do change, and the alert competitor must assess the reasons for change, and adjust accordingly.

Although price behavior within an industry may be indicative of unfair competitive practices, caution must be exercised in making such assumptions. Uniformity of price among all suppliers in an industry, as well as stability of price over time, may be the result of the interaction of economic forces.

From the point of view of the firm, the price established is a reflection

[10] See Jerome C. Darnell, "The Impact of Quality Stabilization," *Journal of Marketing Research* (August 1965), pp. 274–82. See also "Congress May Retire Depression Era's Fair Trade Laws," *Marketing News,* February 28, 1975, p. 5.

of all other actions taken by the firm. Theoretically, the firm should price at that point at which marginal revenue is equal to marginal cost. Although the economic model depicting cost and demand is useful for portraying the internal and external forces which interact to create profits or losses, it is only of limited value to the marketing practitioner. The task of measuring cost and demand makes the model's use extremely difficult.

The exact prices selected depend on the objectives of the firm. A number of pricing policies have been used, such as: (1) return-on-investment pricing, (2) ethical pricing, (3) penetration pricing, (4) skimming pricing, (5) full-line pricing, and (6) minimization-of-loss pricing. In each case different objectives are sought.

Because of the uncertainty that pervades pioneering pricing, executives seek procedures which are relatively simple. The resulting price may not be one that provides the greatest profit, but is considered by management to be a fair price and one characterized as producing profitable business. The formula-pricing practices employing cost buildups used by businessmen have the following limitations: (1) demand analysis is cursory, (2) competition is not reflected adequately, (3) in general, formulas do not serve marketing strategy adequately, (4) formulas tend to overplay the precision with which costs are allocated, (5) rigid application of the formula may result in uneconomic procedures, and (6) the practice involves circular reasoning. While most managers profess formula pricing from cost buildups for new products, this is not strictly the case. The following practices may actually take account of competitive conditions: (1) initial selection of target prices, (2) introductory offers, (3) adjustments for psychological barriers, (4) adjustments for meeting payout policies of purchasers, (5) trial prices and cost modifications, (6) research and development cost write-offs and amortization, (7) "scooping out the demand curve" prior to the application of formula pricing, (8) tooling amortization, (9) safety costing through subcontracting, (10) choice of alternate production lines, and (11) multiple-formula comparisons.

Variations from base prices are necessary because of sales made in different quantities, differences in conditions of sale, and sales made to different kinds of intermediaries and to purchasers in different locations. Other facets of the price administration problem are uniform delivered prices to overcome geographic limitations of markets, and control exercised by manufacturers over the price at which goods are resold at distributive levels.

Leasing arrangements constitute an entirely different means of price administration. The buyer pays a rental fee for the services of the product for a specified period of time or output. The major reason for leasing, on the part of the seller, is to expand the market for his products over what it would be with a policy of outright sale.

The legal restrictions in price determination are of two types. The

Unfair Sales Acts govern pricing practices of intermediaries, and are an attempt to prevent predatory price cutting, or sale below cost. The second type is less formal and involves governmental investigations into the pricing practices of certain industries. To date, no laws have been passed which in any way would set an upper limit on prices in nonregulated industries.

Any variations in prices to different buyers of like merchandise is a discriminating price. Some discriminatory prices are legal, and some are illegal. They are illegal if they are in violation of the Robinson-Patman Act, that is, if their effect is substantially to lessen competition or to tend to create a monopoly or to injure, destroy, or prevent competition. The Robinson-Patman Act, passed in 1936, is designed to prevent large buyers from negotiating favorable prices not granted to other competing buyers and not justified by savings resulting from differences in cost of manufacture, sale, or delivery. A number of specific practices are detailed in the act, as well as the defenses available to those charged with illegal discriminatory prices.

The Federal Trade Commission Act, passed in 1914, declares illegal all unfair methods of competition in commerce. The commission has a broad responsibility for maintaining competition and for surveillance over the market cultivation practices of rival enterprises.

Retail price maintenance is an important part of selected marketing programs. The advantages and disadvantages vary by channel level and geographic area of operation.

QUESTIONS AND PROBLEMS

1. What is the role of price in a free enterprise economy?
2. Under what conditions might price uniformity among rivals be evidence of competition or economic force rather than of undesirable business practices?
3. What is penetration pricing? How does it differ from a skimming price policy?
4. What is meant by formula pricing? How does it differ from theoretical price determination?
5. Since many companies are aware of the limitations of formula pricing, why is its use so prevalent?
6. Explain the various types of uniform delivered prices.
7. What was the general purpose of the Robinson-Patman Act? In laymen's language, what are the major provisions of the act?
8. What are the major reasons for leasing rather than outright sale?

Chapter 19

Marketing Strategy Planning

In Chapter 4 we introduced the concept of marketing strategy as *a predetermined plan to guide the deployment of resources in an effort to generate growth.* Given the large number of variables and combinations that strategic marketing must consider, it is impossible to treat all aspects of planning in a single chapter. Throughout Chapters 5 to 18 the managerial functions of market delineation, purchase behavior motivation, product-service adjustment, channel selection, physical distribution, communications, and price have been examined separately and for the most part independent of each other. It is now time to consider these functions on a combined basis and in relationship to strategic planning.

In this chapter we will examine the formulation of marketing strategy as an integrated plan. The chapter begins with a review of the planning sequence which a manager should go through in devising a strategy. Next, the formulation of specific marketing objectives is reviewed. The third section discusses the selection of target markets in perspective of formulation of the product mix. Decision making is discussed in the fourth section of the chapter from the viewpoint of tradeoffs between alternatives. Attention is then directed in the same section to an analysis of tradeoffs between individual mixes as they formulate a total marketing mix. In total, this chapter treats the first three steps in strategic planning. The resultant plan guides the allocation and mobilization of resources, which is the sole subject of Part Five. We suggest you review Chapter 4 as background for this chapter. Given the intervening materials, we are now ready to operationalize the concepts initially presented in Chapter 4.

THE PLANNING FORMAT

The following five interrelated planning steps were suggested in Chapter 4 to guide strategic formulation.

1. Environmental monitoring.
2. Identification of objectives.
3. Selection of target markets.
4. Formulation of the marketing mix.
5. Resource allocation and mobilization.

Because the planning sequence is critical to this chapter, it will be briefly reviewed. The process begins with *environmental monitoring,* which results in the establishment of objectives, which are to be achieved through purposeful or instrumental action in specific markets. These markets must be carefully evaluated and analyzed to determine their nature and scope and the forces that influence market behavior. Then *target markets* must be selected and all effort must be directed toward achieving objectives through action in these markets. Depending upon the objectives and target markets selected, the manager must develop the correct combination of marketing activities to serve them effectively. This combination is frequently called the *marketing mix,* and is composed of four subcombinations called a *product mix,* a *distribution mix,* a *communication mix,* and a *price mix.* The marketing mix to be executed governs *the resources allocated to meet the requirements of effective competition.* Facilities and personnel requirements are of primary concern in this respect. The *mobilization of resources,* through the establishment of a workable organization and effective operations, completes the planning process. The overall formulation of strategy is referred to as *marketing strategy.* The sequence of decisions involved is illustrated in Figure 19-1. It should be noted that these steps cannot be performed in the neat chronological order portrayed. As will be illustrated, considerable moving back and forth between adjacent steps is required before decisions can be formulated concerning each stage. When these planning elements are aligned and properly balanced, performance should lead to the achievement of specified corporate objectives. Stated somewhat differently, it should lead to a matching of effort with market opportunity.

FORMULATING SPECIFIC MARKETING OBJECTIVES

As noted in Chapter 4, two broad categories of objectives exist in all firms—financial and operational. To formulate a marketing strategy a firm must arrive at a central notion of its business rationale in order to select target markets and develop an effective marketing mix.

The product mix the firm elects to market is a major indicator of the "business" that firm is in. In a dynamic competitive environment, the need for continuous additions to and deletions from the offerings of the enterprise can create a wide diversity of marketing objectives through time. In

FIGURE 19-1
Marketing Planning Sequence

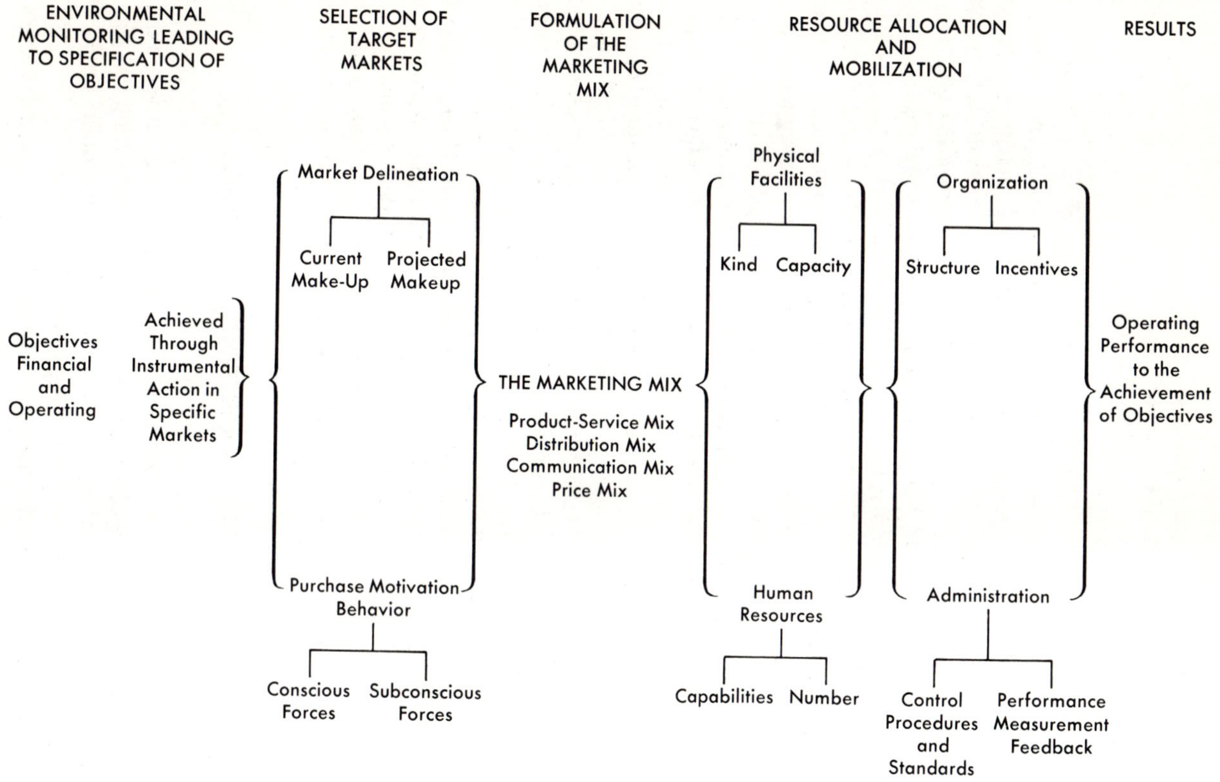

| ENVIRONMENTAL MONITORING LEADING TO SPECIFICATION OF OBJECTIVES | SELECTION OF TARGET MARKETS | FORMULATION OF THE MARKETING MIX | RESOURCE ALLOCATION AND MOBILIZATION | RESULTS |

Objectives Financial and Operating
— Achieved Through Instrumental Action in Specific Markets

Market Delineation
— Current Make-Up
— Projected Makeup

Purchase Motivation Behavior
— Conscious Forces
— Subconscious Forces

THE MARKETING MIX
Product-Service Mix
Distribution Mix
Communication Mix
Price Mix

Physical Facilities
— Kind
— Capacity

Human Resources
— Capabilities
— Number

Organization
— Structure
— Incentives

Administration
— Control Procedures and Standards
— Performance Measurement Feedback

Operating Performance to the Achievement of Objectives

450

Chapter 10 we reviewed, through an examination of product diversity patterns, how the composition of the product mix results in convergent and divergent production and marketing requirements. It is desirable, therefore, to seek a *business rationale* to help management clarify feasible market opportunities. Three such rationales are reviewed in this section to define more sharply corporate objectives and to help formulate marketing strategy.

A MARKET RATIONALE

A basic market rationale provides an enduring focal point of competitive purpose. For instance, suppose a company characterizes itself as a producer of commercial refrigeration equipment. If the company directs all of its effort to this product orientation, it may at some point face a vanishing market, because it is conceivable that foods may be preserved without refrigeration.[1] Or a furnace manufacturer may find that temperature control may be maintained in the home by devices other than the current gas or oil furnaces, for example, either with heat pumps or solar energy. If the business had been characterized as "home climate control," it might have a more enduring and relevant focus of competitive purpose. This is what is meant by the term *market province*—a statement of application of corporate resources and effort that are relatively permanent in nature within a dynamic or rapidly changing market environment.

Railroad companies, with some minor exceptions, offer a classical example of failure to develop a market province. If United States railroads had not considered themselves engaged in railroading, but rather as transportation or distribution companies, their managements might have forced legal modification to allow participation within other modes of transport, servicing a broader spectrum of market needs.[2] The Canadian Pacific Railway is a prime example of an organization that was able to embody a market rationale within a similar industry.

In contrast, the American Telephone and Telegraph Company increasingly regards its business as "communications" rather than telephones. Oil firms see themselves as "energy companies." In each case, very different production and marketing are involved, but an integrating rationale for the business of the particular enterprise also exists.

The Gerber Products Company, whose well-known slogan is "Babies are our business—our only business," has long been a producer of baby foods. Perhaps the use of this slogan over the years is what accounts for the

---

[1] For an excellent treatment of problems of this sort, see Theodore Levitt, "Marketing Myopia," *Harvard Business Review* (July–August 1960).

[2] Ibid.

very strong image that Gerber enjoys among mothers. Researching the nature and depth of this image among mothers might show, however, that they unconsciously insert the word food in the slogan; thus: "Baby *foods* are our buisness—our only business." If the company then decided not to change this image, perhaps not wishing to "break faith" with mothers, the result would be a pattern of product offerings, almost the pure case of convergent production and convergent marketing. If, however, the image proved to be very much in line with the actual slogan, then this characterization of corporate purpose could provide an overall market rationale for what would be in reality a rather wide range of product-service offerings. For instance, lines of baby toys, clothing, and furniture might be added. This pattern is shown in Figure 19-2, and would lead to considerable diversity in production and marketing.

FIGURE 19-2
Market Rationale Leading to Divergent Production and Marketing

```
Baby Foods ——— Production Facilities ——— Marketing Facilities
                                           and Organization      ┐
Baby Toys  ——— Production Facilities ——— Marketing Facilities    │   Babies
                                           and Organization      │   Are
                                                                 ├   Our
Baby Clothing ——— Production Facilities ——— Marketing Facilities │   Business
                                             and Organization    │
Baby Furniture ——— Production Facilities ——— Marketing Facilities┘
                                              and Organization
```

In these instances, very substantial differences would exist among the product lines. Food, clothing, furniture, and toys have virtually no production similarity—either in research, design, materials, production methods, equipment, or skilled labor. The marketing of each is actually very different from the others. Baby foods involve many stable items, whereas toys have significant fad characteristics, with virtually a whole new product line for each Christmas season. The types of retailers are very different, ranging from apparel stores to furniture stores, department stores, supermarkets, and a bewildering range of outlets for the distribution of toys. The competitive strategy would be to associate all products with the Gerber customer image. Such a market rationale could serve to integrate the various areas of corporate activity into a meaningful pattern.

Another way in which Gerber might view itself is only incidentally in the "baby business" and essentially as a specialty foods packer. This characterization would presuppose that the company's basic knowledge, skill,

Marketing Strategy Planning

and organizational competence were centered in an unusual capacity for the successful movement of food products through supermarkets, backed by vigorous promotional effort at the store level. Characterizing the firm in this way could lead to the addition of specialty lines, for instance, geriatric and health foods. On this basis, the business would look very different, as is shown in Figure 19-3. All products are produced with essentially the same production facilities, but distributed through supermarkets. Thus, this view of Gerber's "business" could result in a significantly greater convergence in the firm's production and marketing. A very different enterprise would emerge through time, with quite different future patterns of the business it is in.

FIGURE 19-3
Market Rationale Leading to Convergent Production and Marketing

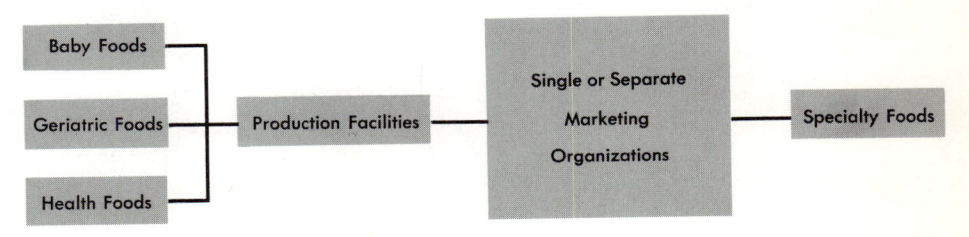

Baby Foods ─┐
Geriatric Foods ─┼─ Production Facilities ─ Single or Separate Marketing Organizations ─ Specialty Foods
Health Foods ─┘

A SUPPLY RATIONALE

A supply rationale can likewise provide a persistent integrating logic for strategic planning. This focus is more likely to prevail where the firm has a substantial proportion of its total investment in its source of supply. Some paper mills, for example, have many millions of dollars invested in timber lands, and might thereby see themselves essentially in the business of growing trees and using them commercially. They might consider the marketing of all products that derive essentially from their timber lands base. Another approach would involve a shift in terminology, but would change the nature of operations more significantly. The term *wood fiber utilization* would construe more of a technological orientation to business purpose, and this could be broadened still further by the term *fiber utilization,* which would allow for accommodation of the newer synthetic fibers. This latter characterization could lead to a strikingly different line of products. Finally, one might emphasize the production process more, and characterize the firm as simply a member of an important segment of the chemical processing industry whose business was essentially tied to this process foundation. Using the wood fiber utilization notion, however, a somewhat more elaborate view of convergence and divergence is illustrated in Figure 19-4.

FIGURE 19-4
Supply Rationale Leading to Convergent Production and Divergent Marketing

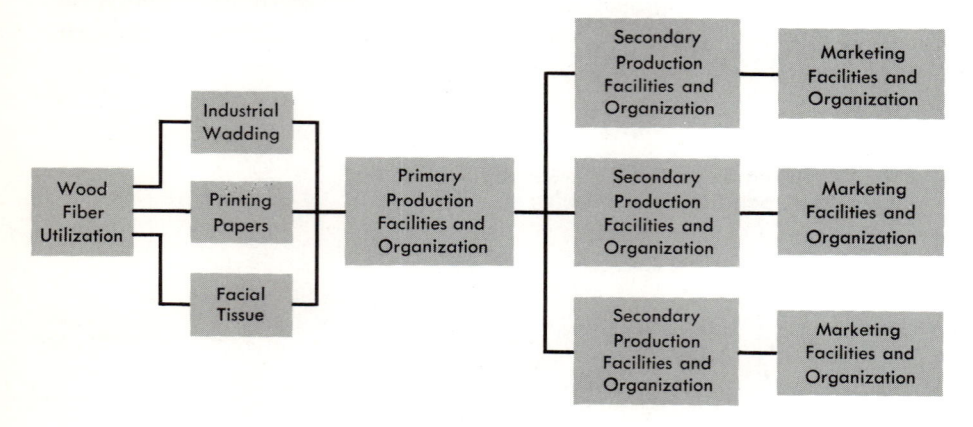

A FINANCIAL RATIONALE

The third and final integrating rationale is financial in orientation. In a complex marketing-competitive environment a great deal of cash flow is required to support continuous introduction of new products. Thus, at any time a portfolio of products offered by a firm must constitute a balance between those consuming cash and those capable of generating cash flow.[3] While a financial rationale overlaps both a market and supply rationale, introduction of return-on-net assets deployed and the degree to which products generate or consume cash introduce another managerial perspective to formulating strategy.

A measure of return-on-net assets deployed to support a specific product offering provides a clear indication of the vitality of that specific business unit. At any given time the balance across the line must support a positive return-on-net assets and a positive aggregate cash flow. The illus-

---
[3] See Patrick Conley, "Experience Curves as a Planning Tool," *Spectrum* (June 1970), pp. 63–68.

Marketing Strategy Planning

tration in Figure 19-5 classifies a representative grouping of products into a matrix based upon cash-flow characteristics.[4]

Products may be classified as cash consumers (negative cash flow) or cash generators (positive cash flow). In the matrix, the cash consumers are labeled as "innovative" and "good potential," with respect to immediate cash needs and apparent short-term capability to reverse a negative cash flow. The innovative product is a substantial cash consumer. While its long-range potential is worthy of investment, given fatality rates for new products, the innovative newcomer is a "long shot." Those products having "good potential" appear to be making it in the marketplace. While still cash consumers, the net drain is less than that of their innovative counterpart.

FIGURE 19-5
Product Classification of Cash Flow Characteristics

	Innovative	Good Potential
Negative Cash Flow	− − Needs Cash (Long Shot)	− + Needs Cash (Young Filly)
Positive Cash Flow	Prime Time + + Provides Much Cash (Mature Winner)	Good Record + − Provides Some Cash (Getting Old)

Among the cash generators, "prime time" is the "mature winner" or "blue chip" category. Prime timers have a substantial positive cash throw-off due to the degree of sales and a favorable cost structure. In short, prime timers enjoy a significant market share and a cost effective production-distribution support network. While less positive in cash generation, "good record" provides cash; however, the throwoff is declining with time.

Two factors are important concerning a financial rationale as an overall corporate objective. First, a steady stream of innovative and good potential products must be developed and acquired as investments if the firm is to endure over time. Second, competitive and changing market preferences will, with passing time, force most prime time products to become less productive, have a declining net cash contribution, and finally reach a zero cash throwoff.

The key to an effective financial rationale as a focal orientation to an overall rationale is to maintain a balanced portfolio of products that generate sufficient positive cash flow to endure through reinvestment over the long run, while maintaining an aggregate positive return on net assets to

[4] Ibid., p. 67.

assure short-run operative profits. This is essentially the strategy followed by conglomerate firms.

CONCLUSION BUSINESS RATIONALE DETERMINATION

In concluding the above discussion concerning alternative business rationales, it is important to make two basic overall comments. First, no single rationale is dominant or more right than any other. Each provides an orientation to be incorporated into an enduring and flexible strategy. In most complex organizations, the best rationale will incorporate features of market, supply, and financial orientations.

Second, business rationale as developed here relates to a focus or orientation for selection among product offerings and the subsequent integration of an overall product portfolio. All rationales are market oriented in the sense that the selection of specific product is based upon market opportunity. Regardless of the rationale that prevails within the firm, the final verdict and veto power over product success or failure rests in the marketplace.

Once an overall business rationale is decided upon, it provides specific marketing objectives. For example, a major producer of electric power generating equipment may elect to consider its market province the energy needs of society. In this case, it is appropriate that the company would conduct a continuous technological search for new energy sources, as well as market evaluations when appropriate, to specify marketing objectives for these new sources. The market delineation and purchase behavior motivation managerial functions are performed to specify marketing objectives for product-candidates selected within the business rationale elected.

SELECTION OF TARGET MARKETS

The task of selecting target markets amounts to identifying the various segments on the basis of physical or behavioral attributes of the market for a specific product-service offering. For purposes of marketing strategy planning, the selection of the target markets to which effort will be directed is dependent upon two considerations. First, a determination is made based on an overall opportunity assessment of the different segments. This can be based on competitive strengths and weaknesses which determine ability to enter a market and operate profitably. Second, a decision is made on whether to follow a non-segmented or a segmented strategy. This, in turn, is based upon the competitive superiority and relative profitability of one in comparison to the other. In a consideration of whether to use a broad-line or limited-line segmentation strategy, there is considerable difference in the various mixes constituting the marketing mix. The costs of these variations must be weighed against the revenue-generating capability of each strategy. Thus, the selection of target markets involves the third managerial function of marketing—*product-service adjustment.* Product offerings must be matched with market opportunities. This section is developed on the assumption that a firm has selected to follow a segmented strategy.[5]

BROAD-LINE SEGMENTATION STRATEGY

Within this strategy, the product mix is substantially altered to accommodate different market segments. Two bases for broad-line segmentation exist. The first is segmentation by product form and the second is segmentation by price and quality.

Segmentation Based on Product Form

The most common application of a broad-line strategy is to direct products of different physical characteristics to identifiable market segments which have different needs. For example, a best-selling major appliance at one time was the freezerless refrigerator, which was a manufacturer's response to the refrigerator needs of owners of home freezers. It is interesting to note, however, that this product was introduced as an unexpected by-product of a consumer preference study on freezer space in refrigerators. This study showed a conflict of opinion among potential purchasers, with the majority wanting more freezer space. A very small size group, however, preferred less freezer space than in existing models. Since the whole trend of design had been toward increasing freezer space, a more detailed analysis was conducted of those preferring less freezer space. The investigation indicated that these people were predominantly home freezer owners, hence the differing needs that could be capitalized on with the new model.

Other examples of demand varying according to product form are: large refrigerators for families with several children, compared with

---

[5] For a discussion of segmentation strategy, see R. C. Blattbey and S. K. Sen, "Market Segmentation Using Models of Multidimensional Purchasing Behavior," *Journal of Marketing,* 38 (October 1974), 17–28; J. T. Plummer, "The Concept and Application of Life Style Segmentation," *Journal of Marketing,* 38 (January 1974), 33–37; and R. D. Hisrich and M. P. Peters, "Selecting the Superior Segmentation Correlate," *Journal of Marketing,* 38 (July 1974), 60–63.

smaller sizes for apartment dwellers; portable dishwashers for transient families, compared with custom installations in permanent residences; and a line of outboard motors that includes models for a trolling fisherman, for water skiing, and for the cruising yacht. While quality, price, and motivational factors may all be involved to some extent in these segmentation attempts, the dominant need is for physical product adjustment.

Segmentation Based on Price and Quality

Another frequently observed pattern of achieving a broad segmentation strategy is adjustment in price and quality. Quality levels, however, have market complexity that is not always clearly perceived when related to consumer use. "High quality" is usually taken to mean obvious superior physical quality as well as quality perceivable to consumers in the use of the product. We might think of professional carpenters' tools, refrigerators built to an extended thirteen-year quality base (a thirteen-year expected life-span) or only the finest overall quality of men's Oxford-cloth cotton shirts.

Below this superior quality level many other levels are possible, but in two different quality concepts. The first quality concept is to reduce actual quality, but maintain the level of user quality. For example, the shirt marketer might continue to use the finest quality material in the cuffs and collars of the shirt but reduce slightly the quality in the body of the shirt. Inasmuch as the cuffs and collars are the first to show wear in a shirt and in view of the fact that the tendency is to discard the shirt when such wear appears, the consumer quality in use would be the same as in the higher actual quality product.

The second quality concept is to produce products with lower-quality levels of performance and physical criteria. Such products would be directed to buyers whose needs, preferences, or purchasing power do not warrant the higher-quality product. The typical "do-it-yourself" fan does not want or require the quality levels in tools appropriate for a professional carpenter, because of both skill differences and intermittent use. Consider a slightly more complex situation. The best-quality home refrigerator might be built to a thirteen-year length of life quality base and sell at retail for $429.95. A similar model in size, features, and design might be built to a seven-year quality base and sell for $329.95. If one were to "use up" all of the "quality," the yearly depreciation cost on the "more expensive" model would be approximately $33 per year, whereas the "cheaper" product would require approximately $47 per year. But even so, the lower-priced model might appeal to young married couples whose purchasing power had to be spread over many items in furnishing a house or apartment, and whose needs therefore are better served by a lower-priced offering. The same low-priced refrigerator, however, might also appeal to consumers with much higher income and purchasing power. These buyers might not expect to keep the refrigerator long enough to "use up" the quality, either because of expected job mobility and the practice of sale and replacement on intercity moves, or because they forecast that many new features will appear in new models during the life-span of the purchased item which will bring about the trading-in of the old model on a new one after it suffers style obsolescence. Here again there is an overtone of "customer use" quality.

Segmentation based on price and quality levels does directly affect product form. However, this form of broad-line segmentation generally results in a narrower product line than a segmentation based totally on diversity in product form. More importantly, the costs of this strategy are generally not as high.

LIMITED-LINE SEGMENTATION STRATEGY

The most difficult type of segmentation strategy is through matching product images, communication mix, or products with psychological and motivational forces that are often hidden, perhaps even below the threshold of conscious awareness among purchasers. In the case of a limited-line strategy, product form is modified only as absolutely necessary to accommodate specific segment requirements. In most cases, there is no or very limited variation in product form. However, there is normally considerable variation in other parts of the marketing mix.

Segmentation Based on Product Image

Consider the motivational forces in the already large and growing geriatrics market. The older portion of our population is increasing considerably more rapidly than the population as a whole. Attempts to market geriatric foods successfully on a broad scale have met with little general success. Products identified as such present an image to the older person that is displeasing. These people find unpleasant the subliminal suggestion that their teeth and digestive systems may not be as hearty as they once were. At least they do not like to announce this fact to others through the purchase of such foods in the marketplace and through conspicuous use. The image of a robust, virile, and active life is a more treasured self-image. Packers of baby foods find that a significant volume of their business comes from such older people who ostensibly may be "purchasing for the grandchildren." These purchases can take place without "conspicuous involvement of self-images" on the part of the buyer.

FIGURE 19-6
Psychological Segmentation of Farm Buyers

	INNOVATOR	EXPERIENCED	NOVICE	BACKWARD
Outlook	Optimistic Future Oriented	Pessimistic Looks Back	Insecure	Fear Mentality
Learner Type	Conceptualizer	Concrete Learner Result Oriented	Static Doesn't Know Which Way to Turn	Pseudo Scientific Religious Overtones
Status	Individual Respected But Resented	Group Oriented Afraid to Make Mistakes	Sensitive to Community Opinion	Individualistic Often Religious Conformity
Local Relationships	Transcend Local Organizations	Community Leader (Formal)	None	None Bitter in Relations With Farm Community
Self Image	Businessman and Professional	Business Manager	Laborer	Not a Full-Time Farmer
Information Needs	Aggressive in Seeking Information	Lets Information Flow to Him	Lets Information Flow to Him	Rejects Information Which Conflicts With Beliefs
Decision Time	Swift	Moderate Speed	Slow	Slow
Education	High	High	High	Low

Courtesy: Agricultural Division of Ciba-Geigy Corporation.

Another illustration of problems involved in this type of product-market integration can be drawn from products directed to the teen-age market. Here again is a rapidly expanding market that many merchandisers have isolated as an important segment of the overall market for their products. A feminine-hygiene product was directed to this market segment, identified in its brand name as a teen-age product, and introduced with very sizable promotional outlays. After a period of time the product was found to be not as successful as the merchandiser had expected. An important factor here was that teen-age girls' desired self-image was not one of an adolescent. More commonly, they preferred to think of themselves

Marketing Strategy Planning

FIGURE 19-7
Promotional Appeals

APPEAL VEHICLES	INNOVATOR	EXPERIENCED	NOVICE	BACKWARD
Personal Contact	New Ideas	Future Developments	Reinforce Actions Taken	Announce Availability and Terms of Sale in Mass Media
Supplier and Retailer Advertising	Future Problems and Solutions in Abstract	Reinforce Actions Taken	Provide Concrete Alternative	
	Seek Information on Experiments	Concrete Examples of Product Use	Give Him Status as Farm Manager	
Farmer Clinics	Avoid Aggressiveness in Communication	Aggressive in Communicating	Aggressive in Communicating	

Courtesy: Agricultural Division of Ciba-Geigy Corporation.

as attractive, desirable, mature young women of sophistication and poise. This self-image is not compatible with a personal product identified as teen-age.

Where purchasing patterns reflect different stations in life, product policy must be geared to these differences. Actually, a persuasive argument can be made for the theory that all consumer purchasing, either directly or indirectly, consciously or subconsciously, reflects a person's preferred station in life and his desired self-image.

Segmentation Based on Communication

In these cases, the product is unchanged but the selling effort via communications is varied to fit the psychological needs of different groups of purchasers. A market study conducted for Ciba-Geigy Corporation's Agricultural Chemicals Division revealed that farmer buyers of agricultural chemicals are divided into four distinct psychological segments.[6] Figure 19-6 shows some characteristics of the four groups and how each group reacts throughout the crop cycle. After reviewing the findings it became clear that to approach the market with a single communication mix would not be as effective as tailoring, wherever possible, the different messages to each group. Figure 19-7 was designed to show the different kinds of

---

[6] Adapted from Donald A. Taylor, "Development of Marketing and Promotional Programs." Courtesy of Agricultural Chemicals Division, Ciba-Geigy Corporation, U.S.A.

appeals to be used with each group. As the decision-making calendar for each group was different, Figure 19-8 was developed to show when **three** basic tools—personal contact, supplier and retailer advertising, and **farmer clinics**—should be used with each group. In this illustration, segments **were** recognized and the communication mix adjusted to each segment.

FIGURE 19-8
Promotional Calendar

	INNOVATOR	EXPERIENCED	NOVICE	BACKWARD
Fall/After Harvest	Provide Literature, Limited Personal Contact	Minimum Literature	Personal Contact	Mass Media Announcements

Personal Contact on a Selective Basis |
Winter	Personal Contact, Limit Literature, Close Sale	Increase Literature, Minimum Personal Contact	Limited Literature, Personal Contact Limited	
Late Winter Early Spring	Limited Personal Contact as Resource	Personal Contact, Limited Literature, Close Sale	Increase Literature, Personal Contact	
Planting Time	Avoid	Limited Personal Contact	Limited Personal Contact	
Growing Period	Limited Personal Contact	Limited Personal Contact, Check for Adjustments	Limited Personal Contact Reinforcement	
Harvest	Limited Personal Contact, Check Results	Limited Personal Contact, Check Results	Limited Personal Contact, Check Results	

Courtesy: Agricultural Division of Ciba-Geigy Corporation.

Segmentation Based on Cosmetic Change in Product Form

In many cases, the product form may change but the cost and real effect is minimal. Imagine the market for vacuum bottles, segmented wholly or partly on motivational forces.[7] The performance requirements for keeping liquids warm is approximately the same for the construction worker's

---

[7] Vacuum bottles are often referred to as "thermos" bottles, although this is a brand name rather than a generic term.

lunch pail and the sporting gentleman's needs in attending a football game on a chilly November Saturday. The product images must be decidedly different if psychologically segmented demand components are to be cultivated effectively. The vacuum bottle for the lunch pail needs a "rugged, workmanlike, unpretentious, functional, 'he-man-like' " image. It would perhaps be black or of a plain color, with a cork stopper, and have an unpretentious metal or plastic drinking cup. The same performance requirement in the model for the typically well-equipped football fan cheering on his dear old Alma Mater would be implemented in quite a different way. It would be perhaps a colorful plaid, with a plastic cap or rubber closure, a gaily matched thermal drinking cup, and a color-keyed carrying case. Purchasers expressing different self-images in these two situations call for product-images that are quite different if the marketer's strategy is to be based on psychologically differentiated market segments.

COMBINATION APPROACHES

The most fruitful solutions to effective segmentation often employ a combination of approaches worked in combination. Various market segments that call for differences in product form, quality levels, price difference, and motivational orientation are identified and quantified. Product offerings that are designed to match these multiple variables are then arranged.

An illustration of this may be drawn from the approach employed by a large national brewery in attempting to increase its share of the beer market in the large metropolitan markets. The brewery marketed a well-known single brand, with very sizable promotional and advertising outlays directed at product differentiation, and sold the product in large volume at a premium price level. Ultimately, however, diminishing returns from promotional expenditures were perceivable, and more and more difficulty was encountered in increasing the share of the market obtainable by this brand. Detailed investigation and analysis indicated that the overall market had relatively distinct segments, some of which were dominated by "taste" preferences and some by price overtones.

Within the taste category two distinct "taste images" were perceivable. One large group preferred a "pale, light, and dry" beer. This group, however, could not distinguish such a beer, in blindfold tests, from other varieties. The convictions on the part of these customers, nevertheless, were so strong that they would not likely be persuaded to purchase any product promoted otherwise. Perceivable attitudes about light, healthful foods, low calories, subtle taste, and gracious living were likewise exhibited.

The second homogeneous group of important size preferred a "hale, hearty, and full-bodied" beer but, like the first group, could not tell this taste from others in blindfold tests. This group also leaned toward the robust outdoor life, zestful humor, and more participative activity (fishing, hunting).

A third group was strongly price conscious, with cost transcending taste and with taste preference more undifferentiated. The pattern for the brewer to achieve a greater share of the overall beer market was first to introduce another product, different in physical form and promotional orientation, to cultivate more effectively the "pale, light, and dry" market. A second move was to acquire local breweries in order to offer a local, popular-priced product. This move replaced the dominant reliance on product differentiation in a single product with a plan to achieve better adjustment with markets through market segmentation based upon form, price, and motivational orientation.

It is important to keep in mind that the segmentation of markets and the matching of product-service offerings represent a highly creative aspect of marketing strategy planning. Since markets can be seen from a number of different vantage points, no two firms will view segmentation from the same perspective. Thus, market delineation, purchase behavior motivation, and product-service adjustment represent highly creative aspects of the overall management functions of marketing.

In summary, the selection of target markets involves identifying market segments, determining whether to follow a segmented or nonsegmented strategy, and evaluating market response. The planner should always remember that a segment must have the attributes of potential, stability, accessibility, and measurability to justify cultivation.[8] In the case of analyzing segmented strategy possibilities, it is necessary to evaluate the number of bases for segmentation and the ways in which the product, distribution, communications, and price mixes would be affected. In such evaluations, costs and market responses in terms of differential revenues must be assessed.

FORMULATION OF THE MARKETING MIX

The fourth step in marketing strategy planning is to formulate specific decisions concerning the managerial functions of channel selection, physical distribution, communications, and price. These four managerial functions combine with the product-service adjustment function to formulate the *marketing mix*. As noted earlier, the marketing mix to be executed governs the resources needed to meet the requirements of effective competition. In

---

[8] See Chapter 4.

the previous section, strategic aspects of product adjustment were discussed in the selection of target markets and in the determination of the degree to which a firm selects to engage in segmented marketing. In this section, we examine the finalization of the marketing mix from the perspective of decision making in each submix, as well as tradeoffs between individual subcombinations.

DECISION MAKING AT THE FUNCTIONAL LEVEL

Within each operational aspect of the overall marketing mix, the manager is faced with the need to select from among a number of alternatives. For example, there are several channels of distribution that could be used—which to choose is a critical question. The same could be said for which communication and pricing alternatives to follow. This section is meant to be illustrative and in no way covers all alternatives. It is hoped that we will demonstrate the care with which each of the individual decision areas must be handled.

Distribution Mix

The managerial functions of channel selection and physical distribution combine to formulate the distribution mix. The overall function of the distribution mix is to link highly specialized market segments with the producing firm. For successful marketing, a firm must develop an elaborate organization of institutions to assist the processes of ownership transfer and physical distribution. The operational structures through which the objectives of distribution are satisfied may be separate if specialization results in more effective marketing. The aspect of the distribution mix concerned with negotiation, contracting, and posttransaction administration of sales is referred to as the transaction channel structure. The aspect of the distribution mix concerned with physical delivery is referred to as the physical distribution channel structure.[9] This section considers decision tradeoffs within each of these subchannels of the distribution mix.

A common problem in selecting the transaction channel is to determine which alternative will satisfy market requirements for the selected product strategy. A variety of different channel considerations must be evaluated in the basic choice between direct and indirect channels.[10] The final selection must be based on an analysis of revenue and cost anticipated from serving the market through alternative channels. An example will illustrate the impact of the cost of aternative channels on profits.

[9] See Chapter 13.
[10] See Chapter 14.

FIGURE 19-9
Comparison of Profitability and Break-even Points of Three Alternative Channels

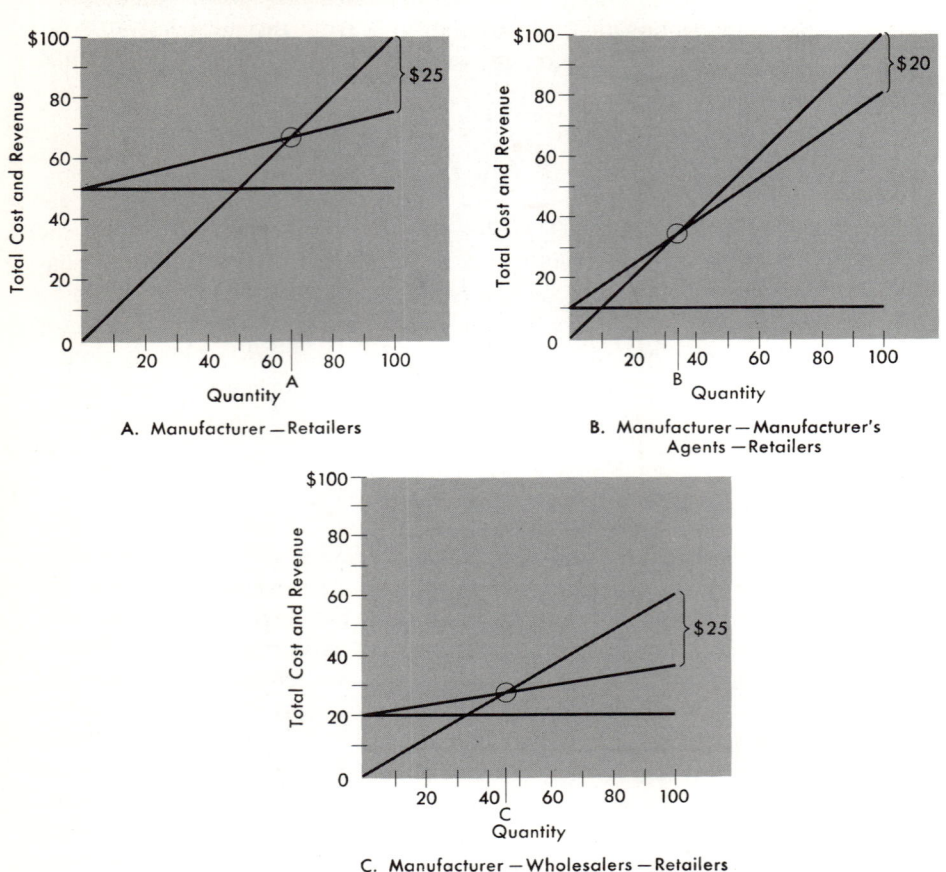

A. Manufacturer—Retailers

B. Manufacturer—Manufacturer's Agents—Retailers

C. Manufacturer—Wholesalers—Retailers

In Figure 19-9, the costs of the following three channels are shown: (1) manufacturer to retailers, (2) manufacturer to manufacturers' agents to retailers, and (3) manufacturer to wholesalers to retailers. In this hypothetical case the product is sold for $1. In the first case, direct from manufacturer to retailers, the revenues will be high because no trade discounts are given to middlemen for the performance of marketing functions. On the other hand, the fixed costs of maintaining a sales force to call upon thousands of retail outlets are high. The costs of selecting, training, and maintaining the sales force in the field are primarily fixed. The direct costs of such things as shipping, order assembly, and billing are substantial, as a large number of retailers must be serviced. In this alternative, profits are $25 at a capacity of 100 units. The break-even point with this cost structure is 65 units. In the second case, from manufacturer to manufacturers' agents to retailers, the revenues are the same as in the first case, since no trade discounts must be given. Fixed costs are materially smaller as the manufacturers' agents are a substitute for the firm's own sales force. Direct costs are somewhat higher than in the first case, as the agents' commissions must be paid. With this cost structure the profit is $20 at a capacity of 100 units, but notice how much less is required to break even—35 units. In the third case, from manufacturer to wholesalers to retailers, the revenues are sharply reduced because of the trade discounts, usually 40 percent, given to wholesalers. Fixed costs are less than in the first case, because not as many corporate salesmen are required to call upon the smaller number of wholesale establishments. They are higher than in the second case, however, as some salesmen are required. The direct costs, such as shipping, customer credit, order assembly, and billing costs, are less than in the other two cases because of the smaller number of customers. The profit in this case is $25 at a capacity of 100 units and the break-even point is 45 units.

In Figure 19-10 all three alternatives are superimposed on one break-even chart to demonstrate the variations in revenues, costs, profits, and break-even points.

With accurate cost and revenue information the decision as to which channel to use is dependent upon (1) the market coverage and market control requirements as perceived by the manufacturer, (2) the availability of a sufficient number of middlemen that will perform in the desired way, and (3) the risks inherent in using one channel versus another. Referring to Figure 19-10, it can be seen that if Channels B and C are equally effective, the volume at which the profitability of each channel is equal is between 60 and 65 units. If it is assumed that this volume can be reached easily, then the additional profits from higher volumes accrue much faster using Channel C than Channel B. This is so because the profit angle on Channel C is larger than the profit angle on Channel B. If the probability of reaching this volume is low, then Channel B, with the lower break-even point, may be the preferred choice. Or the analysis of potential revenues may be conducted on a market-by-market basis, demonstrating the need for different channels in different markets. If market control is perceived to be desirable and growth opportunities are present, it could be desirable to move toward Channel A as the profits accrue beyond the break-even point at an accelerated rate.

Once a channel is decided upon, effective implementation of the channel is crucial. Channel members must be selected with specific criteria in mind. These include "distributor sales strength (number of salesmen, their technical competence), distributor product lines already stocked (whether

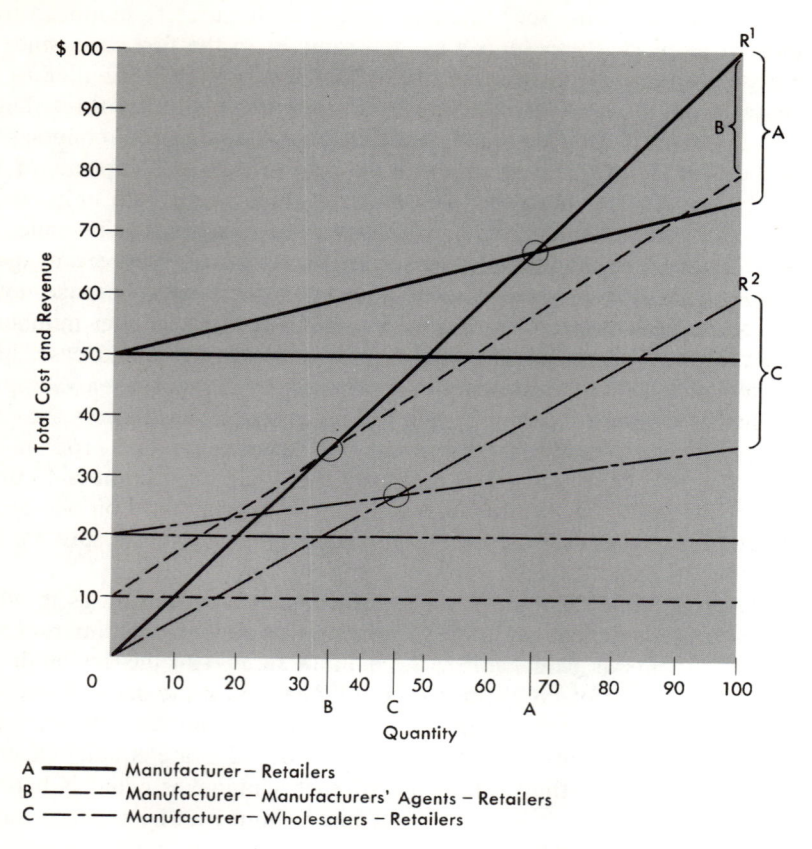

FIGURE 19-10
Profitability of Three Alternate Channels

```
A ———— Manufacturer – Retailers
B ---- Manufacturer – Manufacturers' Agents – Retailers
C —·— Manufacturer – Wholesalers – Retailers
```

they are competitive, compatible, complementary, and of high quality vis-à-vis the products of the investigating manufacturer), distributor reputation, market coverage (geographic, industrial), sales performance, inventory and warehousing, and management ability."

In the previous example, transaction and physical distribution functions of the distribution mix were combined to evaluate cost and revenue impact. In Option B, manufacturers' agents were used to assist in ownership transfer. The reader may recall that agents do not take possession of inventory, whereas wholesalers normally perform the physical distribution function. In the advent of selecting agents as participants in the transaction channel, provisions must be made to provide the physical distribution of merchandise.

Marketing Strategy Planning

In the selection among physical distribution alternatives, one example of an individual function tradeoff is to determine if a distribution warehouse is justified to support a specific market segment. The particular type of facility must also be selected as well as the ownership arrangement as to private or public operation. Figure 19-11 illustrates the economics of distribution warehouse establishment. It illustrates the differential freight rate per hundred pounds (CWT) between small shipments and truckload quantity shipments. Most transportation charges decrease in cost/cwt as the shipment size increases. On Figure 19-11 the cost/cwt from the plant location (PL) to the proposed distribution warehouse location (ML) is substantially lower if shipments can be combined in truckload quantities. This differential is reflected by the horizontal lines B (truckload—TL) and C (less-than-truckload—LTL). Providing that warehousing and breakbulk

FIGURE 19-11
Economic Justification of a Single Warehouse Facility Cost per CWT

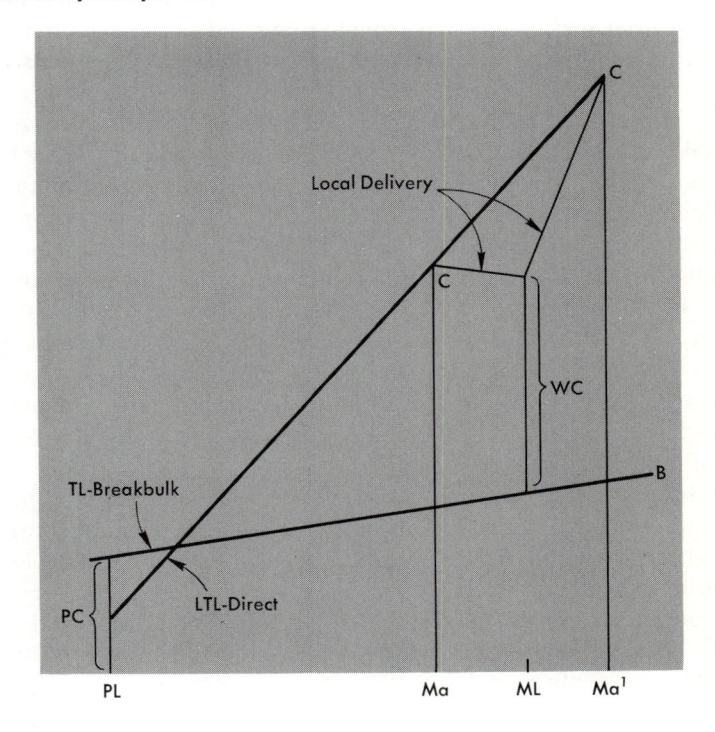

Source: Reprinted with permission of Macmillan Publishing Company, Inc., from *Logistical Management* by Donald J. Bowersox. Copyright 1974, Macmillan Publishing Co., Inc., p. 315.

can be performed at a cost per CWT less than the differential freight savings, the most economical method of physical distribution would be the establishment of the facility. In Figure 19-11, the lowest total cost method of physical distribution would be direct shipment to market point Ma with warehouse shipments in the market area defined as Ma to Ma^1.

The finalized channel mix could well result in the selection of a network of manufacturers' agents to perform the function of ownership transfer combined with a network of public warehouses for purposes of physical distribution operations.

Communication Mix

In communication a number of unique decisions must be faced. Should advertising be used and, if so, how much? Given a decision to advertise, a host of additional questions arise. Which media shall be used? Which products shall be advertised? What copy shall be used? When will advertising be placed and where? Similar questions can be asked regarding the other communications instruments—personal selling and sales promotion.

A common question is how many salesrepresentatives should be used relative to how much should be spent on advertising. Approaching the first question, the real problem is to determine the incremental sales that additional salesrepresentatives could be expected to generate. In order to make this determination it is necessary to know what happens to volume when the typical salesman spreads his effort over territories of varying potential. It can usually be expected that an increase in total sales volume results whenever another salesman is added. Usually, but not always, a substantial increase in the number of salesmen does not produce a *proportional* increase in sales. If the firm is operating above the break-even point, thereby already covering all fixed costs, but below plant capacity, an increase in sales can be very profitable. In order to know just how profitable, and how much volume can be anticipated, we must have estimates of market potentials.

In some instances, market potentials are relatively easy to compute; in other cases, complex analytical and statistical analysis must be employed. In the appliance industry, for instance, regular data are available on industry-wide sales by products for various geographic areas, making reasonably good indicators of market potentials of various territories readily available. If a particular firm has or can develop these kinds of data, and has a sufficient number of salesrepresentatives for reasonably reliable statistical analysis, the next task is to observe the volume of sales derived in the various territories in relation to the available potential. Table 19-1 shows such analysis. When these data are plotted on a graph (Figure 19-12), it is easy to see that sales are proportionately much higher in territories of small

Marketing Strategy Planning

potential, which immediately suggests that additional salesmen would be profitable. That is, more intensive coverage of markets is shown to produce sales above average levels for all territories. Sales (per 1 percent of market potential) increase as the size of territory in terms of market potential decreases. By graphing these data we can quickly compute the sales volume that could be expected from various numbers of salesrepresentatives, assuming the new salesrepresentatives would do relatively no better or no worse than the existing sales force. For example, we can see in the graph that if we had 50 salesmen, allocated to territories of even potentials of 2 percent, we could expect an average yield from each man of approximately $200,000 ($100,000 per 1 percent of potential) or a total sales revenue of $10 million, from the 50 representatives.

TABLE 19-1
Basic Factual Data Pertaining to
25 Salesmen's Territories (in thousands of dollars)

Territory Designation	Size of Territory (Percentage of Total Potential)	Total Sales per Territory	Sales per 1% of Potential
1	11.89%	$351	$ 29
2	9.53	300	31
3	7.68	244	32
4	6.36	179	28
5	6.07	393	65
6	4.78	200	42
7	4.75	192	40
8	4.64	312	67
9	4.58	169	37
10	4.10	187	45
11	3.75	218	58
12	3.42	210	61
13	3.33	151	45
14	3.08	186	60
15	2.65	234	89
16	2.61	235	90
17	2.56	194	76
18	2.50	398	160
19	2.16	208	97
20	1.86	344	185
21	1.83	288	158
22	1.80	140	78
23	1.43	252	177
24	1.39	346	250
25	1.25	257	206
	100.00%		

Source: Walter J. Semlow, "How Many Salesmen Do You Need?" in *Harvard Business Review,* vol. 37 (May–June 1959), 128.

FIGURE 19-12
Relationship between Sales Potential per Territory and Sales Volume per One Percent of Potential

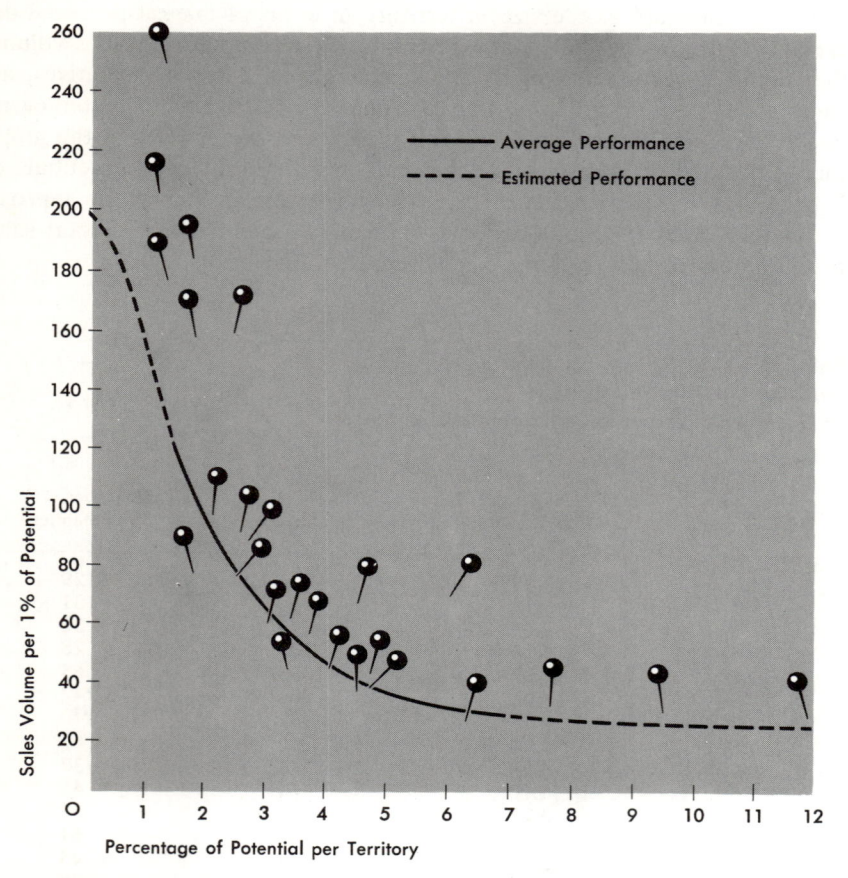

Source: Walter J. Semlow, "How Many Salesmen Do You Need?" in *Harvard Business Review,* 37 (May–June 1959), 129.

We must now develop data related to profit margins, so as to be able to determine the value of additional sales volume. This can be done by taking the average profit margin obtained by present salesmen on an average mix of products to obtain rough estimates, or we can derive more precise data by break-even analysis. Break-even analysis enables us to show fixed costs of production, direct and semidirect costs of production at various levels, "fixed" or "fully committed" costs of marketing, and finally, direct marketing costs. The difference between these totals and gross revenues at various levels would be the amount available to cover the addi-

Marketing Strategy Planning

tional costs of selling and profits. Costs of maintaining a salesman in the field are calculated to be $20,000 per year. A computation of operating profits before cost of salesmen is shown in Table 19-2.

Finally, to determine profitability in terms of return on investment, we must estimate any new investment in plant and working capital required at levels above present capacity. Assume that working capital is 40 percent of gross sales at any level, and that present plant investment of $3 million will support a maximum of $8,100,000 of sales volume, with $2 million additional investment to go to $12,300,000, another $3 million to go to $16,100,000, and finally an additional $2 million to go beyond $16,100,000.

These data show that *maximum dollar profit is at the level of 100 salesmen, maximum return on invested capital at 40 salesrepresentatives, and maximum profits to sales at 65 salesrepresentatives.* Since 65 salesmen produce almost as much operating profit as 100, and almost as good a return on investment as 40, and provide the maximum profit to sales, a compromise of the ideal number of representatives may be considered by many managements as 65. But since the firm might not be able to assimilate so many additional salesrepresentatives in any given year, it may decide to add 5 to 10 each year over a period of several years. This change can be undertaken with full confidence that the expenditure will be productive.

TABLE 19-2
Determination of Operating Profit with Varying Numbers of Salesmen (in Thousands of Dollars)

Number of Salesmen	Estimated Total Company Sales Volume	Operating Profit Before Variable Selling Cost	Variable Selling Cost	Operating Profit*	Total Investment	Operating Profit on Sales Volume	Operating Profit on Investment
200	$19,000	$5,350	$4,000	$1,350	$17,600	7.1%	7.7%
150	18,000	5,000	3,000	2,000	17,200	11.1	11.6
100	16,000	4,500	2,000	2,500	14,400	15.6	17.4
80	14,100	3,835	1,600	2,235	13,640	15.8	16.3
65	12,200	3,470	1,300	2,170	9,880	17.8	22.0
50	10,000	2,700	1,000	1,700	9,000	17.0	18.9
40	8,000	2,200	800	1,400	6,200	17.5	22.5
30	6,000	1,500	600	900	5,400	15.0	16.6
25	5,000	1,150	500	650	5,000	13.0	13.0
20	4,000	800	400	400	4,600	10.0	8.7
16	3,300	555	320	235	4,320	7.1	5.4
13	3,000	450	260	190	4,200	6.3	4.5
10	2,700	345	200	145	4,080	5.4	3.6

* Column 3 minus Column 4.
Source: Walter J. Semlow, "How Many Salesmen Do You Need?" in *Harvard Business Review*, vol. 37 (May–June 1959), 130.

FIGURE 19-13
Relationship Between Advertising Expenditures and Sales Volume

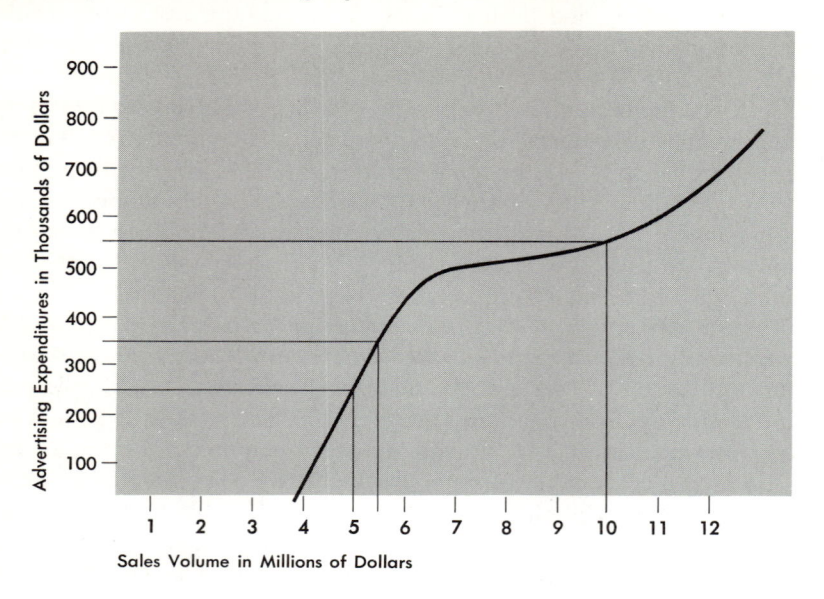

If funds are limited, which is the usual case, management must weigh the additional commitment of $100,000 (5 salesrepresentatives) in personal selling against the potential returns of the same commitment in another instrument—advertising, for example. Here the maximization rule applies in the selection of the alternative instruments. This requires some measure of marginal net returns. However, even if we have been able to develop these data, which is no easy matter, we still have some difficult choices and judgments to make. Using the applicable data from the previous illustration, let us assume that from historical data we have been able to graph the relationship between advertising expenditures and sales volume as shown in Figure 19-13. If the firm is currently spending $250,000 on advertising, an additional expenditure of $100,000 would not be as well spent as the same amount would be on increasing the sales force. The marginal profitability from the advertising expenditure would be $75,000 from generating a sales volume of $5,500,000. This compares with an expected $6 million in sales from 30 salesrepresentatives producing a marginal profitability of $250,000. On the basis of these two alternatives, the optimum decision is clear—add the salesrepresentatives.

Look at what happens, however, when the next increase in expenditures is considered. Adding 10 more salesrepresentatives (40 total) produces an expected profit increment of $500,000 from increasing sales to $8,000,000. Had the firm initially elected to increase advertising instead of the sales force, and then spent the equivalent monies in the second round of decisions on advertising, the $200,000 increase (plus the first $100,000) would produce sales of $10 million, and a profit increment of $1,175,000, compared with $500,000. Spending all the increase in both rounds on the sales force produces a total expected profit increment of $750,000, while spending it on advertising produces $1,250,000. This situation dramatizes the problem of long- and short-term moves, the judgment that must be exercised by executives in making these decisions, and the way objectives influence decisions.

Price Mix

The decision maker has a wide range of choices concerning the price or prices at which he wishes to offer products. The actual price selected is a function of the pricing objectives of the enterprise and the criterion used to measure the effect of different prices. For example, is the firm trying to "maximize" future earnings or the "present value" of future earnings, and over what time period? Is market penetration more important than recouping investment? These issues make a difference in pricing decisions. Likewise, what are the principal criteria for measuring profitability? For example, is the profit standard based on incremental profits, marginal profits, dollar profits on full costs, a return on tangible net worth, or what? Some decisions must be made on the above questions. Once made, the pricing choice is one of selecting from different results caused by different prices.

The task is one of making three predictions: (1) the effect of different marketing mixes (including price) on quantity,[11] (2) the effect of quantities on production costs, and (3) the effect of quantities on marketing cost. In Figure 19-14 cost and quantity measurements using a series of prices are combined. This is a modified break-even analysis. It assumes a constant variable cost both for production and the order-filling cost of marketing. It also assumes a step function for the other marketing costs. Fixed production costs are treated as "period costs," and disregarded.[12] The vertical axis is a range of quantities. The price lines are plotted by assuming a price and multiplying it by different quantities to determine total revenues. With such an analysis the effect of price can be evaluated against whatever objective has been set.

In this hypothetical case a manufacturer is selling 3,000 units without any changes in the cost structure. The manager plans to increase sales vol-

[11] See Roy G. Stout, "Developing Data to Estimate Price-Quantity Relationships," *Journal of Marketing,* 33 (April 1969), 34–36.

[12] "Period costs" are fixed costs, or costs which produce results only through the passage of time. Since nothing can be done about fixed costs in the short run, all price quantity adjustments should be carried out in terms of variable costs, or *product costs* as they are sometimes called by the accountant.

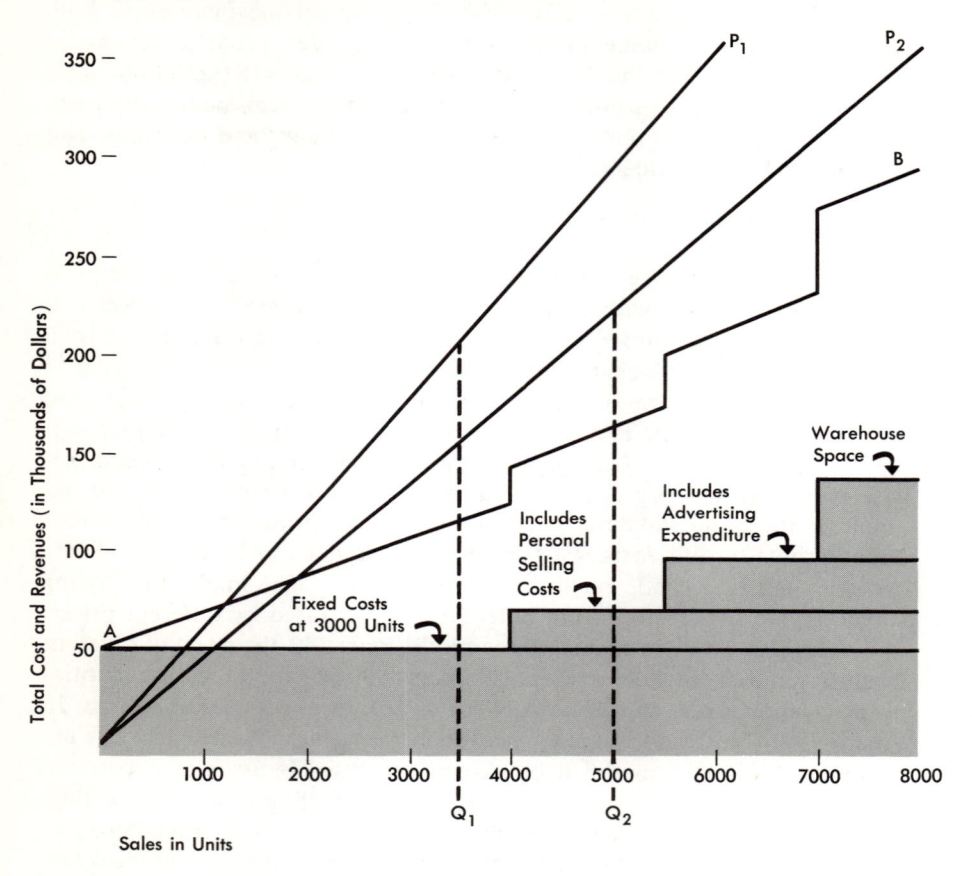

FIGURE 19-14
Combining Cost, Quantity, and Price Relationships

ume, and plans additional marketing effort in the form of more intense cultivation of the market. At 4,000 units the plans call for two new salesmen on a salary basis. Advertising expenditures are held constant until the spring campaign, and at 5,500 units, additional expenditures are made. At 7,000 units new warehouse space must be added.

With these assumptions as to marketing expenditures for the year, the total cost function is represented in the line AB. In reality the method of treating costs approaches a marginal cost calculation. Instead of dealing with the marginal cost associated with the last unit sold, attention is directed toward increases in marketing cost associated with additional chunks of sales volume.

With the marketing mix represented by the line AB, the quantity assumptions at different prices may now be taken into consideration. If with P_1, a quantity of Q_1 is forecast, certain profits result. If with P_2, Q_2 is forecast, another profit situation results. It is possible to speculate on the outcome of any price.

Of particular importance is the effect of the total cost step function. It creates pockets of profitability. Unless an additional cost input moves the volume beyond a cost peak on the total cost line, it may be more profitable to forego the additional volume.

The number of alternatives from which decisions may be made in each of these functional areas is staggering. Yet another set of considerations must also be examined. The various mixes are not independent of each other. For example, a direct channel of distribution with usually higher cost has an effect on pricing policy. Or a lower price might offset a smaller advertising expenditure. We now consider these questions of tradeoffs.

THE CONCEPT OF MARGINALISM

What combination of each of the individual decision areas will result in the optimum marketing mix? How might a physical scientist handle a similar problem?

Suppose the chemist wanted to determine the combination of ingredients that gave the greatest rust resistance to paint. He would conduct a series of experiments under controlled conditions in which he would hold all but one variable constant, observing the effects of different quantities of the particular ingredient being studied. After a series of such observations, he could determine the combination of quantities that produced the best result in terms of his objective—maximum resistance to rust.

The problem we face in marketing, and other social sciences for that matter, is that we cannot hold the variables constant for a series of controlled observations. We cannot keep competitors' actions, and market conditions and all the myriad of variables influencing effectiveness, constant. Moreover, as a practical business matter, we may not want to go too far in running experiments on products that are an important source of revenue. In the case of some products, for example, millions of dollars of sales volume are at stake, and management may well be reluctant to experiment on these products with already proven methods merely to come a bit closer to a theoretically optimum solution. The penalties of failure result in a risk not worth incurring if "good" profitability is being achieved.

Nevertheless, marketing mix formulation involves two basic decisions: (1) how much in total should be spent in each of the subcombinations, and (2) what the relative relationship should be between each of the techniques used in each mix. The theoretical solution to each of these problems involves a similar maximization rule: continue increasing expenditures until marginal cost equals marginal revenue.

How much in total should be spent on all forms of market cultivation? The objective here is to match total effort with market opportunity. Again this requires as clear a definition of market potential as can be secured and some indication of the returns that can be expected from any type of effort. Knowing these two factors would enable one to approximate the model solution, which would be to increase the total expenditure to the point where the last dollar spent on communication, for example, just pays for itself in additional revenues—which would be the point where marginal cost and marginal revenue are equal. The rule for any single communication instrument is to increase expenditures until the marginal revenue equals the marginal cost of the expenditure. The communication mix is optimum when the marginal revenue per dollar of cost is equal for each of the instruments used. This simply means that if there are differences in marginal revenues, expenditures should be increased or decreased until equal marginal revenues exist for all. Because of the tendency in business practice to think in terms of profit contributions resulting from additional expenditures, rather than marginal revenue or marginal cost, the optimum expenditure level is reached when the marginal net profit from an expenditure is equal to zero. This is the point at which marginal cost equals marginal revenue.

The practical problem, of course, is one of measurement, or knowing when expenditures are close to the point where marginal revenues are equal. In many cases management decisions are not so much oriented to perfection as to improvement; for example, can advertising be profitably increased? Is it desirable to add more salesmen? What results could we expect from a 20 percent increase in distributors?

There are a number of problems precluding the model solution. First, assets are fixed in the short run, and it is not possible to adjust the size, for example, of the sales force quickly or move out of a channel of distribution. Second, small incremental adjustments cannot be made in many of the mixes—a fact prohibiting a truly marginal solution. Third, measurement of the effects of elements in the total marketing mix is not always possible because of the interdependency of all mixes. Even though these factors preclude exact solutions, the planner is always striving toward such a model solution in the formulation of the marketing mix.

CHANGING THE MARKETING MIX THROUGH TIME

Because most firms produce a number of products, we must focus our attention on individual products as well as on the line as a whole. It is apparent that various products reaching different markets of special characteristics have individual marketing needs. Also, the same product has different marketing requirements as it passes through the various stages of market development. An increasingly common practice is to build marketing budgets product by product or by broad product lines.

Whereas up to now we have considered the marketing mix for the product line as a whole, let us now turn our attention to particular products. The basic models and decision rules are exactly the same for an individual product as for the total line. However, several additional complications set in when we attempt the same determination of marketing mix expenditures for particular products. The same difficulties exist in forecasting revenues from varying expenditures as existed before, but greater complications develop in cost and profit determination. The principal reason for this is that cost records are frequently inadequate for measuring the profitability of specific products; yet it is apparent that the marketing mix problem cannot be solved satisfactorily except on the basis of cost-versus-revenue relationships.

By way of illustration, let us consider the case of a company that had an average marketing expense ratio of 17 percent of sales. Without distribution cost analysis, product X, having a gross margin of 12 percent, showed a loss, and product Y, with a gross margin of 22 percent, showed a profit. However, when expenditures in the communications mix were allocated to individual products, it was found that the item with 12 percent gross margin actually showed a profit, and the item with 22 percent gross margin showed a loss. This is illustrative of the kind of misconceptions that can occur without adequate cost information. Unfortunately, this condition prevails in a great many firms. The role of cost and profit analysis is explored in Chapter 21.

A further matter that complicates the problem of mix decisions for individual products is the larger judgmental factors implicit in trying to develop cost data. For instance, in a specific case, a company does not allocate any of the time of salesmen to the promotion of old products, and therefore does not charge any of the costs of personal selling to these products. On the other hand, a part of the reason for the extensive use of personal selling is simply to develop a favorable relationship with the customer, to create a responsive environment for doing business with the account. If this is true, then a part of the cost of selling should be allocated to these older products even though the salesman does not mention them. But how much should be charged? What is the true "institutional value" of these calls that should be shared by all products? This is why this area is replete with "value judgments" as compared with exact data. The complexity of these problems and the inexactness of the data make careful analysis and judgment imperative. The basic objective in these assignments is to produce workable and effective results, as the performance of the executive is evaluated along these lines rather than on an "optimum standard." Therefore, it is necessary to develop the most adequate data possible and then apply the rules of decision outlined earlier.

Let us turn our attention now to the character of the changes in the marketing mix that takes place between old and new products. In new product introductions the total cost of marketing is exceptionally high. In the case of cold cereals the ratio of "marketing expenditures (of which advertising is about two-thirds) to sales during a product's first year is more than 3½ times as great as the corresponding ratio for cereal companies' total operations; in the second year, marketing expenditures are typically twice as high as the normal 'level'; and in the third year, about 1½ times normal."[13] The weighted average ratio of marketing costs to total sales of new cereals, cake mixes, dog foods, frozen dinners and specialties, and margarine, as well as a number of other product categories, was 57 percent during the first year and 37 percent during the second.[14]

Generally, the largest total marketing budget is given to new products of high potential, with the lowest total budget going to established older products. Many variations will exist among particular companies and different markets, but it is believed that the marketing mix must change as products pass through a cycle of growth and decline.

In summary, the development of the marketing mix is a matter of selecting from a myriad of alternative choices in each of the product, distribution, communications, and price mixes. As well, it requires judgments concerning the interdependent effect of the choices made when combined into a total marketing mix. Periodic review is then required to make adjustments throughout the product life cycle. The task is not simple. It requires a high level of research, analytical capability, and experienced judgment. It is, however, always developed. The question is merely one of how well the marketing mix is formulated.

SUMMARY

Marketing strategy planning follows a sequence of steps designed to match marketing effort with market opportunity to the end that selected objectives are achieved. Prior to the formulation of specific marketing objectives, the parameters of planning should be established through selection of a busi-

---

[13] Robert D. Buzzell and Robert E. Nourse, *Product Innovation, the Product Life Cycle and Competitive Behavior in Selected Food Processing Industries, 1947–1964* (Cambridge, Mass.: Arthur D. Little, Inc., 1966), p. 48.

[14] Ibid., p. 98.

ness rationale. Three rationales—a market, a supply, and a financial rationale—were presented for consideration. Using one or a combination of these, specific marketing objectives are identified through performance of the market delineation and purchase behavior motivation functions. In selecting target markets, segments must be identified and evaluated for ease of entry and profitability. Once identified, they must be examined from the point of view of whether they can be cultivated through segmented or nonsegmented marketing strategy. In the latter case, consideration should be given to broad-line segmentation strategy based on product form, quality, or price differentials, or limited-line segmentation strategy based on product image, communications, or minor product form adaptations. From this overall process the product-service adjustment is formulated.

Formulating the remainder of the marketing mix involves selecting from a wide array of alternatives in each of the distribution, communication, and price subcomponents. These decisions must be evaluated from the point of view of their interdependency. The concept of marginalism is introduced as a theoretical solution for achieving the optimum marketing mix. Ideally expenditures on each aspect of the mix should be increased until marginal cost equals marginal revenue. Expenditures must also be reviewed through time so that adjustments may be made to reflect differing requirements as products move through a cycle of growth and decline. Limitations such as the short-run permanence of assets, inability to make small incremental adjustments, and measurement difficulties preclude exact solutions. Nevertheless, the planner should strive to realize the best possible solution.

QUESTIONS AND PROBLEMS

1. What is the concept of a *business rationale?* How does this concept provide a nucleus for the formulation of marketing strategy?
2. Compare and contrast a market rationale with a supply rationale. Are each of these patterns of product diversification market oriented?
3. From a marketing point of view, what is the ideal product line, insofar as breadth of line is concerned? Why isn't this ideal realized?
4. What is meant by the *core* of the market?
5. What are the principal ways by which products may be matched with varying market segments?
6. Pick an example of a product assortment which, based upon psychological variables, seems to be matched with different market segments.
7. Describe the concept of *strategic marketing mix*. How does it relate to segmented marketing?

8. What is the *concept of marginalism?* How does this concept relate to the formulation of the marketing mix? What decisions are basic to formulation of a marketing mix?

BIBLIOGRAPHY

ALDERSON, WROE, "Marketing Efficiency and the Principle of Postponement," *Cost and Profit Outlook,* no. 3 (September 1950).
BALLOU, RONALD H., *Business Logistics Management.* Englewood Cliffs, N.J.: Prentice-Hall, Inc., 1973.
BERLO, DAVID K., *The Process of Communications.* New York: Holt, Rinehart & Winston, Inc., 1960, pp. 30–32.
BOONE, LOUIS E., and JAMES C. JOHNSON, eds., *Marketing Channels.* New Jersey: General Learning Press, 1973.
BORDEN, NEIL H., *The Economic Effects of Advertising.* Homewood, Ill.: Richard D. Irwin, Inc., 1942.
BOWERSOX, DONALD J., *Logistical Management.* New York: Macmillan Publishing Co., Inc., 1974.
————, "Physical Distribution Development, Current Status and Potential," *Journal of Marketing,* 33 (January 1969), 63–70.
————, "Showdown in the Magic Pipeline: A Call for New Priorities," Presidential Issue, *Handling & Shipping* (Fall 1973).
BUCKLIN, LOUIS P., "Postponement, Speculation and the Structure of Distribution Channels," *Journal of Marketing Research,* vol. 2 (February 1965).
CLEWETT, RICHARD M., ed., *Marketing Channels in Manufactured Products.* Homewood, Ill.: Richard D. Irwin, Inc., 1954.
CONLEY, PATRICK, "Experience Curves as a Planning Tool," *Spectrum* (June 1970), pp. 63–68.
DONNELLY, JAMES H., JR., and JOHN M. IVANCEVICH, "Role Clarity and the Salesman," *Journal of Marketing,* 39 (January 1975), 71–74.
FRANK, RONALD D., WILLIAM F. MASSY, and YORAM WIND, *Market Segmentation.* Englewood Cliffs, N.J.: Prentice-Hall, Inc., 1972.
FREY, ALBERT W., and JEAN C. HALTERMAN, *Advertising* (4th ed.). New York: The Ronald Press Company, 1971.
FRIEDMAN, WALTER F., "Physical Distribution: The Concept of Shared Services," *Harvard Business Review,* 53 (March–April 1975), 24–30.
HALL, MARGARET, *Distributive Trading.* London: Hutchinson's University Library, 1961.
HESKETT, JAMES L., "Sweeping Changes in Distribution," *Harvard Business Review* (March–April 1973), pp. 123–32.
HESKETT, JAMES L., ROBERT M. IVIE, and NICHOLAS A. GLASKOWSKY, *Business Logistics,* 2nd ed. New York: The Ronald Press Company, 1973.
KLEPPNER, OTTO. *Advertising Procedure* (6th ed.). Englewood Cliffs, N.J.: Prentice-Hall, Inc., 1973.

LITTLE, ROBERT W., "The Marketing Channel: Who Should Lead This Extracorporate Organization," *Journal of Marketing,* 34 (January 1970), 31–38.

MALLEN, BRUCE E., "Conflict and Cooperation in Marketing Channels," pp. 65–48, in *Reflections on Progress in Marketing,* ed. L. George Smith. Chicago: American Marketing Association, 1964.

MALLEN, BRUCE E., ed., *The Marketing Channel.* New York: John Wiley & Sons, Inc., 1967.

RIDGEWAY, VALENTINE P., "Administration of Manufacturer-Dealer Systems," *Administrative Science Quarterly,* vol. I (March 1957).

ROSENBERG, LARRY J., and LOUIS W. STERN, "Toward the Analysis of Conflict in Distribution Channels: A Descriptive Model," *Journal of Marketing,* 34 (October 1970), 40–46.

SCHIFF, MICHAEL, *Accounting and Cost in Physical Distribution Management.* Chicago: National Council of Physical Distribution Management, 1972.

SMYKAY, EDWARD W., *Physical Distribution Management,* 3rd ed. New York: Macmillan Publishing Co., Inc., 1973.

TAFF, CHARLES A., *Management of Traffic and Physical Distribution,* 5th ed. Homewood, Ill.: Richard D. Irwin, Inc., 1972.

THOMPSON, JOSEPH W., *Selling: A Managerial and Behavioral Science Analysis,* 2nd ed. New York: McGraw-Hill Book Company, 1973.

WEINER, NORBERT, *Cybernetics or Control and Communication in the Animal and the Machine.* New York: John Wiley & Sons, Inc., 1948.

Part V

EXECUTING THE MARKETING PLAN

Early in the text we viewed the enterprise as a production marketing system seeking its objectives in an environment characterized as competition for differential advantage. We stressed the need for the identification of corporate and specific marketing objectives. The starting point for marketing strategy planning is the selection of target markets through performance of the market delineation and purchase behavior motivation functions. Based upon precise target markets, the marketing mix—product mix, distribution mix, communication mix, and price mix—is developed.

The product mix of the firm should reflect its internal requirements in terms of the subtleties of the marketplace. The need for frequent adjustment of product mix to resolve the conflicts of internal efficiency with market change underscores the dynamic qualities of this aspect of the marketing mix.

Next, the distribution mix—the complex of intermediaries that provide the link between production and consumption—was examined. The activities necessary to make goods available to consumers in an efficient way matched with the intermediaries who offer services for hire, when establishing a distribution mix. Recognizing that, along with availability of goods, communication is needed to energize or precipitate the process of exchange, the communication mix was considered. The various elements of market cultivation—advertising, sales promotion, and personal selling—should be combined in such a way as to create a maximum impact at point of ultimate sale, within cost-revenue constraints. Then, the price mix brings into focus all cost and revenue implications of the other mixes so that financial objectives are achieved.

In combination, these mixes represent the marketing program of the enterprise. Based upon marketing strategy planning, resources are mobilized, allocated, and administered so that competitive superiority is maintained.

In Part V, we examine the allocation and mobilization of resources and how they are administered in the execution of the marketing strategy plan. Although the kind and capacity of physical facilities and human resources are extremely important to the success of the enterprise, they are in the short run a given for the marketing decision maker. In those situations where they are not, such as number of sales representatives or distribution facilities, they have been discussed in the appropriate chapters. In this part, we confine our treatment to the last two managerial functions of marketing—organization and administration.

In Chapter 20 we review the way in which the resources of the enterprise are organized to meet the requirements of effective competition. The need to develop organizational designs which accommodate a market orientation as a philosophy of business management is especially important. In Chapter 21 we explore the various aspects of marketing administration. Performance must be controlled. An integral part of administration are procedures and standards. They provide the operating guidelines by which the organizational actors carry out their responsibilities. At the same time, they provide the bench marks for evaluation of performance through time. Because the enterprise functions in a dynamic competitive environment, feedback is required to maintain a proper state of market adjustment.

Chapter 20

Organization

Market orientation as a philosophy of business management must be translated into an organizational structure that provides an operating mechanism to implement such a philosophy. The purpose of organizational design is to link people, facilities, and functions in the necessary sequential relationships. Market orientation focuses on the needs of the enterprise for growth and survival in competitive markets. It recognizes that corporate objectives are achieved through instrumental action in the marketplace. As a guide to organizational design, market orientation involves the structuring of planning, decision, and control points to insure that those responsible for the achievement of market results have the requisite organizational positioning to fulfill that responsibility.

This chapter explores organization as a function essential to the execution of marketing strategy. The objective here is to be diagnostic rather than prescriptive concerning persistent issues of organization. First, we review certain trends that have called for organizational modifications in many companies. Second, certain conceptual notions of organizational design are examined. Third, criteria of organizational efficiency are developed and applied to a reorganization of a large consumer goods enterprise embracing a market orientation as a philosophy of business management. Finally, certain organizational directions for the future are outlined.

MAJOR INFLUENCES LEADING TO ORGANIZATIONAL MODIFICATION

The evaluation of a managerial marketing philosophy as a way of corporate life has, in itself, called for organizational modification. The transition of an enterprise from production orientation to the intermediate stages of sales, then to promotion and, finally, to marketing orientation is accompanied by significant organizational change. When market forces and opportunities become the basis for designing whole systems and subsystems of action, the organization must be capable of accommodating the new structure.

MARKETING: A PROFIT CENTER IN THE ENTERPRISE

A change that is developing slowly, but nonetheless perceptibly, is the growing desire to make marketing a profit center in the enterprise. In general, line management has been preoccupied with sales volume rather than profitability. This is primarily because performance has been traditionally evaluated almost totally on sales volume. Other factors such as production costs and financial operations are recognized as influencing profitability and have tended to work *against* the idea of making marketing a profit center. These factors, along with the belief that "marketing profits" could not be fairly isolated, have led to excessive concern by marketing groups for structuring conditions favorable to volume attainment, sometimes at the expense of the welfare of the enterprise—as, for instance, pressure for low prices and big advertising budgets. More responsible administration may be achieved by making marketing a profit center through a system of intra-firm transfer prices. This has the effect of the factory selling to the marketing group and the marketing group having correspondingly greater freedom of action but more accountability for those actions. Organizational modifications and accompanying procedural changes are called for when such a system is introduced.

CENTRALIZATION OF MARKETING RESPONSIBILITES AT THE CORPORATE LEVEL

A tendency to centralize some responsibilities for marketing at the corporate level is evident. In the multiproduct or multidivisional firm, many decentralized marketing groups tend to come about as corporate growth takes place. This often reflects the widely divergent markets cultivated and the need for specialized sales forces and sales groups. As marketing divisions proliferate, a need is recognized for some degree of consistency in basic policy. Economies are recognized from having some centralized staff assistance available to all groups—as, for instance, economic forecasting and market research. Some areas require corporate-level decisions, such as the amount of money to be spent on institutional advertising. In order to accommodate these changes, a trend toward some degree of centralized marketing responsibility has taken place in the interest of tightening the administration and control of divergent marketing operations.

DELEGATION OF MORE DECISION-MAKING RESPONSIBILITY TO FIELD MANAGEMENT

At the same time that there has been a trend toward centralization of responsibility at the corporate level, a countering trend has occurred in the form of an increasing pressure to delegate more decision-making responsibility to field management. At first glance, these two trends might appear to be in conflict. This isn't actually the case. The desire in the latter case is to push more decisions toward the scene of action and allow those who have adequate information to make decisions which they are capable of making. This is in contrast to holding *all* decisions for unnecessarily high-level consideration. The desire to get decisions made at the right point in the organization can accommodate both trends. It has been recognized that those responsible for individual territorial management must have some degree of decision latitude in order to adjust to local competitive conditions quickly and decisively.

EMERGENCE OF LONG-RANGE PLANNING

Long-range planning has emerged in many companies as a formal procedure. Increasingly, recognition is given to the view that operating executives burdened with day-to-day work requirements may have neither the time nor the inclination for the development of comprehensive, long-term, strategic plans. When allocation of scarce decision-making resources requires a choice between attention to immediate problems and long-range considerations, the tendency is for the immediate issues to receive priority. The consequence is that long-range planning may never be done. For these reasons, companies are increasingly giving long-range planning separate organizational status and personnel.

NEW AND/OR INCREASINGLY SPECIALIZED STAFF GROUPS IN MARKETING

Related to the previously mentioned trend is the growth of increasingly specialized staff groups in marketing and, at the same time, the evolution of new groups in the organization. Examples of the former include such staff services as sales training, sales promotion, parts and service, and forecasting and research. Examples of the latter include marketing comptrollers and managers of physical distribution. The emergence of these numerous staff groups has occasioned shifts in organizational alignments and, for that matter, organizational climate. In moving from largely a line organization to one comprised of both line and staff, with a large number of staff groups, profound changes occur in the environment for decision. Most organizations undergo a rather extended "learning period" before understanding how to work effectively with staff groups.

THE IMPORTANCE OF LOGISTICAL PERFORMANCE

The growing recognition of logistics—material management and physical distribution—has required considerable change in organizational design. Logistical activities have been historically found in various functional units, with a tendency to house materials management under production and physical distribution under marketing. As an organization matures, there is a tendency to centralize all logistical activities in a separate functional unit with both line and staff responsibilities. In this way, better coordination is achieved among all affected parts of the enterprise.

The close relationship between customer service levels and marketing performance usually results in giving marketing a prominence in planning of physical distribution performance. Unless the two functional units are coordinated, attempts to achieve a least total cost system may be thwarted.

CORPORATE GROWTH

One of the principal factors that leads to reorganization is the expanded size and growth patterns of many firms. Organizational structure must be related to the scale of operations. What works well for a company of 500 employees will not work as effectively when growth to 5,000 employees occurs. To presume that ten times the same kind of effort will accommodate the growth is unrealistic.

It should be recognized that several, or conceivably all, of these factors and trends can be affecting a company simultaneously. It is when this happens that the greatest stress is placed on the organization and the most drastic reorganizations come about, which can change the whole fabric of an enterprise. One of the prices of such dramatic changes is often a substantial amount of tension and anxiety on the part of the many people affected in the organization.

CONCEPTS OF ORGANIZATIONAL DESIGN

It is helpful in understanding organizational arrangements and relationships to recognize differences in organizational orientation that exist between different companies. Two principal orientations are examined in this section: (1) orientations which relate to formal and informal organization and (2) orientations which relate to centralization or decentralization.

FORMAL AND INFORMAL ORGANIZATION

Every enterprise has two organizations, the formal and the informal, and the differences in orientation seem to relate more to the informal organization than to the formal. The formal organization is the one delineated by organization charts, job titles and descriptions, prescribed procedures, and the formal flow of information through the enterprise. It is the prescribed network of decision, power, and responsibility. The informal organization is what actually exists rather than what is intended. It is recognized by the operational pattern of power, decision, communication, and action. When persistent and fundamental variations exist between the formal and informal organizations, it usually signals the need for organizational realignment.

Objectives of individual decision makers should be as harmonious as possible with institutional objectives. Decisions are not likely to be optimum if the goals of the individuals making the decision are in conflict with the goals appropriate to the decision itself. For example, executives who are evaluated primarily on the basis of their *short-term* productivity are not placed in an ideal setting for making *long-run* corporate decisions.

The environment of modern corporate life seems to have resulted in an increased priority being given to short-run objectives by decision makers. Executive performance is frequently analyzed on the basis of a continuous evaluation of short-run results, as in the yearly evaluation of the sales manager. Where this method is used, it has a pronounced effect on decision making. One sales executive in a major industrial enterprise characterized this influence somewhat whimsically by saying, "Every time you get promoted in this company, you get closer to the street" (the executive offices were toward the front of the building with an outside view), "and, at this level, there is no way back, only out. I hold this office and position only so long as I produce results. Necessarily, I am far more concerned about sales in this model year than I honestly can be in any five- to ten-year forecast of corporate opportunities. If long-range marketing plans meant sacrificing short-run achievements, I would have to emphasize the short-run considerations; otherwise, I might not be around to have the opportunity of demonstrating the wisdom and judgment that went into the long-range plan." While one could place too much credence in this statement, it illustrates a friction point in decision making: often objectives of decision makers are not in harmony with decision objectives.

Concepts of leadership, authority, power, and decision are related to organizational structure. The informal organization is the structure within which these roles are played by participating personnel. We can distinguish at least three types of organizations with differences in their overall orientation. These are the *autocratically, bureaucratically,* and *democratically* oriented organizations. Within each, executives who are oriented to autocratic, bureaucratic, or democratic leadership can also be observed.[1]

The Autocratic Organization

The autocratic organization is one in which compelling leadership and power are exercised from the top. Decision making is held within a small cluster of personnel or by, perhaps, one individual. All but the most trivial decisions are made within this very powerful group. Such decisions as are made at lower levels are made on the basis of subordinates' interpretations of what the authoritarian leader would want or do. The image of the leader is continuously present in any subordinate consideration. Under these circumstances, formal organization is relatively less important as a basis for the focus of decision, authority, and responsibility. All significant actions will be taken by the authoritarian leader or, if taken by others, reviewed prior to their promulgation and permitted to take effect only when they are completely consistent with the leader's wishes.

While an organization that is predominately oriented to authoritarianism may sound sinister, evil, and inefficient, the reverse is often the case. Objectives, values, and policies are frequently clear-cut and consistent. Understandable direction is provided for subordinates. Endless debate in policy formulation is eliminated or drastically curtailed. Implementation of programs tends to be very much according to plan because of the pressures toward conformity.

When the authoritarian system is headed by an intelligent, keenly perceptive person with good insight, sound intuitive judgment, and the ability to inspire confidence and loyalty, the end result can be exceptionally good. Some of the famous early industrial complexes were built this way.

This organizational orientation is hard to sustain, however, as an organization becomes large and invades complex areas of operations. The lack of system, the delays caused by extreme centralization, the complexity

[1] For a detailed discussion of these leadership forms, see Eugene C. Jennings, *The Executive* (New York: Harper & Row, Publishers, 1962).

of decisions, and the morale problems among competent people who feel the lack of participation in decisions, all cause this form of organizational orientation to be self-defeating.

The Bureaucratic Organization

The bureaucratic organization is most easily recognized by the extreme role of systems and procedures. Standard operating procedures exist for almost any action, even the most routine. Policies are established as normative rules of behavior at all levels of the organization. Formal communications characterize the operation of the system. Standardization is desired, as is uniform treatment of personnel. Very complete records usually are required. Controls are established in almost every facet of operations, and policing is practiced when necessary to insure compliance with established procedures.

One usually associates government with bureaucracy. Moreover, it is common to associate bureaucracy directly with inefficiency, red tape, endless delay, excessive personnel, and a great deal of paper shuffling. This is hardly a fair characterization. Some of the model forms of organization are characterized by considerable bureaucracy—the Roman Catholic Church, the military forces and court system of the United States. In any large and complex organization, great reliance must be placed on system. A continuous array of *ad hoc* decisions would lead to chaos—operations would ultimately break down completely. Men cannot realistically dominate the system, as is feasible in small organizations. To do so would lead to inconsistency, conflicting values, discordant methods, great overlapping of responsibility, hopelessly tangled communications lines, and little coordination of a series of actions in a total program. A modern, large, complex organization must submit to orderly systems, policy formulation, and organized communications and coordination devices, hopefully, with able, motivated people to operate the system and make it work effectively.

The Democratic Organization

In recent years, a trend toward the democratic model as an organization form has taken place. Much has been made of the participative roles of personnel in the organization. Recognition has been given to the view that it is no longer feasible to publish policy directives and expect compliance—people respond with conviction only to that which they have had a part in determining. Respect for authority is not regarded as a right associated with organizational position; it is something that must be earned by the manager. In its most persuasive form, it is argued that a pooling of the best brains available should precede the making of complex decisions—two heads are better than one, so to speak. Consequently, the most conspicuous manifestation of this organizational orientation is the large number of committees which it tends to foster. A very prevalent procedure in the contemporary enterprise is for the executive to assemble all subordinates who would be affected by any decision, to solicit their views carefully, then to discuss all aspects of each of the alternatives proposed, and, on the basis of collective judgment, reach a joint decision—presumably one that all will carry out earnestly and enthusiastically.

The advantages of this organizational form are that strong motivation is aroused; the best resources within the firm are brought to bear on any particular decision; the heads of subordinate units all have an opportunity to participate; communication is increased through direct access and participation by the larger number of people involved in policy formulation; less control is required when subordinates carry out programs they themselves have participated in planning; and, finally, executive development is nurtured by the very nature of the participative roles played at all levels in the organization. For many companies, this "management by committees" has worked well. Executives often prefer to work in such an enterprise, both for its genuine merits and perhaps because of the collective security it provides them.

Offsetting considerations are several. The most important of these is the inability to pin down responsibility for decisions—to place appropriate blame for failures or to gain credit for success. "We decided" or "they decided" is a common retort when things go wrong. Other considerations are the inefficiencies from the point of view of the time involved in reaching a decision that such an approach entails: it presumes a large number of competent personnel participating—collective ignorance or incompetence can be disastrous; it can generate a severe pressure for group conformity and stifle creative solutions; it can foster dissipation of energies in politics through the subtleties of vote gathering.

The "Multicratic" Organization

Some organizations try to embrace all or more than two of the forms we have discussed, and for this reason are called *multicratic* organizations. The multicratic form has its own particular personality as well as elements of the others, and is increasingly the sought-after model of modern corporate enterprise. It is characterized by bold, aggressive, imaginative leadership that is particularly evident in times of stress and provides a strong sense of direction for the enterprise. It expresses itself in the form of rather clear-cut objectives, flowing from the top down. It relies on systems to economize decision making in the complex enterprise and seeks order and reasonable amounts of formal procedure to insure that work gets done according to program requirements, with adequate information provided for decision making. It encourages decentralized decision making for its participative value, motivation, and efficiency. It uses committees with restraint, where their coordinative and judgmental value is evident without diluting responsibility. Job descriptions are specific in order to formalize work responsibility. It encourages individual enterprise, but within a prescribed frame of reference. High morale is sought through the harmony of individual objectives and values and group objectives and values. It produces organizational unity through the formal organization's being very much in line with the informal organization.

CENTRALIZED VS. DECENTRALIZED ADMINISTRATION

A second area of conceptual importance in organizational understanding and design involves centralized and decentralized management. A tension exists between these extremes, which must be reconciled or embraced in any operating organization. For our purposes, we need only discern the major differences between the two in terms of administrative consequences, and then relate them to market orientation.

Systems vs. Results

In centralization, emphasis is placed on system and internal procedures. Operating personnel are expected to follow carefully formulated procedures, with higher levels of authority accepting proportionally greater responsibility for the effect of the procedures. In the decentralized enterprise the emphasis is on external considerations and results. The individual manager's performance is thus gauged on the results, in contrast with implementation skills.

Single vs. Multiple Methods

The centralized enterprise seeks the optimum or one best way of performing all operations. If careful analysis has gone into evaluating the promotional effectiveness of various layouts of toiletries in a food chain, for example, the optimum choice is extended to all units in the chain under centralized administrative concepts. In the decentralized organization, however, we find diverse and sometimes discordant methods being used. This is associated with the greater freedom of managers and the orientation to results rather than methods.

Relaxed vs. Close Control

Decisions tend to be made at the scene of action under decentralization and are not always coordinated throughout the company. Spontaneity of decision is more prevalent—controls are relaxed insofar as all but performance yardsticks are involved. In the centralized organization, more effective controls are exercised over the type of action taken, and prerogatives of individual managers are restricted. Coordination of effort is expected—through policing, if necessary.

Narrow vs. Broad Span of Control

The span of control refers to the number of subordinates reporting to a superior executive. A broader span of control is associated with decentralized administration. The number of subordinates an executive can have reporting to him effectively increases as the freedom of those subordinates increases. A district manager may have twenty-five store managers reporting if those store managers are held only for results and have great autonomy of decision. Or, a director of merchandising may have a large number of merchandise managers reporting if they have independence and need little coordination. Conversely, the centralized system has a narrow control span—a consistent feature in view of the system, control, and coordinative requirements of the individual manager's job.

Layers of Supervision

As a broader span of control exists in decentralized management, there are also fewer layers of supervision from the bottom to the top of the organization. While the manager at any level feels closer identity with top management, there are also fewer promotion opportunities. The opposite situation prevails in the centralized system.

Specialization

Centralization requires a large number of highly specialized personnel. More diverse staff groups tend to exist. Specialists can, with rather carefully defined fields of inquiry, be found in many areas. In decentralized organizations, more overlapping of job responsibilities occurs. It is common to find things never quite in order, as it might be somewhat unclear as to specifically what prerogatives are associated with various jobs. Individuals tend to "grow" in jobs for a period as compared with finding relatively comprehensive systems and job specifications. Informality is considerably more apparent. The system seems to breed more generalists than specialists.

Functions vs. Personnel

The organization is characteristically built on functions to be performed in centralized enterprises, whereas greater weight is placed on personnel in decentralized enterprises. The large enterprise is often considered to be more vulnerable when it fails to build the enterprise on a strong functional base which dominates individual executives. Many of the largest enterprises, such as government, the military, and the church, are built on a functional base rather than on individual personalities of the leaders involved. Critics of the functional view take the position that the quality of management resources is always of paramount consideration, and systems which foster the development of managerial personnel clearly enhance the long-run welfare of the enterprise.

There is no *pure* form of either centralized or decentralized administration. Companies tend toward one or the other form, and each presents mixed blessings and limitations. Perhaps this accounts for the heated debate over the years on the desirability of the two alternatives. It has been argued that decentralization is more compatible with market orientation and, in fact, is a natural outgrowth of market orientation. This view postulates that centralization is more oriented toward the internal aspects of managerial concern, while decentralization has a focus of external considerations and results.

Actually, such a forced choice of polar positions is not the relevant consideration. The really pertinent issues are, *what decisions can appropriately be decentralized* and *what decision areas must be taken to a higher level of centralized concern for efficient and effective administration?* This is especially true of marketing organizations. The vigorous debate over recent years of the merits of the two systems has hardly been a productive argument, for it has involved the shooting down of straw men. Every organization has, and needs, some degree of centralized *and* decentralized administration—the critical problem is to be sure that decision points are at appropriate levels throughout the organization.

EVOLUTION OF AN ORGANIZATION EMBRACING A CONCEPT OF MARKET ORIENTATION

Before interpreting the criteria of organizational efficiency, it is useful to observe various organizational stages of an enterprise which went through three distinct stages before it evolved into an organization embracing a concept of market orientation.[2]

Figure 20-1 conveys the arrangement of activities some years back when the enterprise had a heavy production orientation, reinforced with

[2] The illustrations are not precise. They are drawn, however, from an actual situation in a major United States corporation and reflect quite sharply the character of change. The first three exhibits are not organization charts; they are intended to convey the general arrangement of activities.

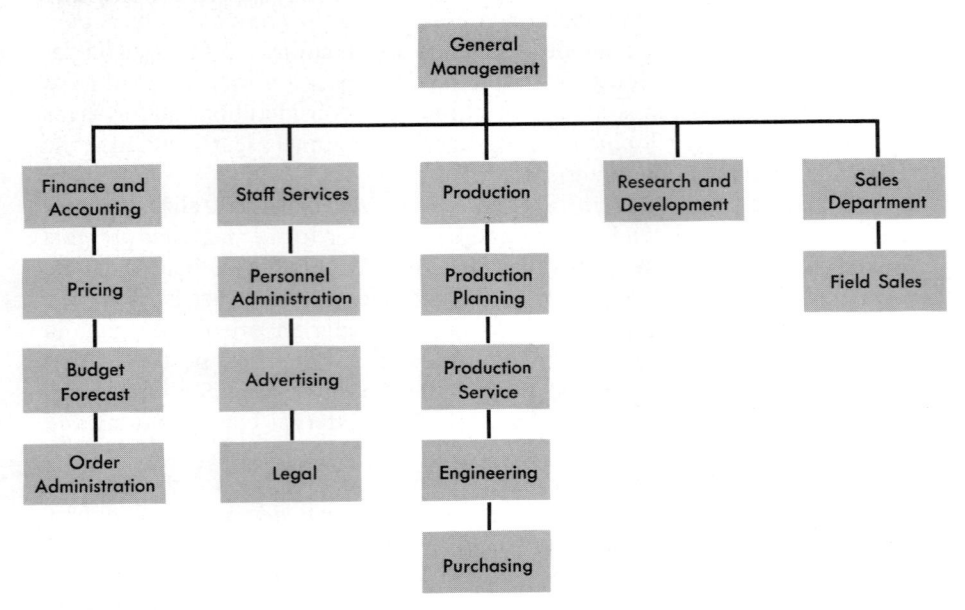

FIGURE 20-1
Production Orientation

```
                          General
                         Management
   ┌──────────┬──────────┬──────┴──────┬──────────────┬──────────┐
Finance and  Staff Services  Production  Research and   Sales
Accounting                              Development   Department
    │            │            │                           │
 Pricing     Personnel    Production                  Field Sales
           Administration   Planning
    │            │            │
  Budget     Advertising   Production
 Forecast                   Service
    │            │            │
  Order        Legal      Engineering
Administration                │
                           Purchasing
```

good technical research and engineering skills. The sales department was responsible solely for the activities of the sales force. Responsibilities of pricing, advertising, sales forecasting, order handling, product planning, product service, and sales personnel functions were located in other than the sales department. The sales department was, in effect, an order-obtaining group operating in the consumer durable goods field.

After several intermediate shifts, in Figure 20-2 the organization is at a point in its development which might be referred to as an orientation to sales. This shift came about as competitive selling became relatively more important. The pressure for more rapid disposal of goods and a larger volume of business resulted in the sales department's playing a more dominant role in the enterprise, receiving increased responsibilities, and being provided more "tools" to carry out effective selling. Product service was transferred from the production group, order administration from finance, and advertising from a central-staff services group. In addition, a sales training department and a sales analysis group were established. As an interesting aside, the general sales manager's title was changed to Vice-President—Sales.

This basic structure was maintained for some period of time, with a number of minor shifts. The next major organization change resulted from the recognition that much more was involved in sustaining a growing sales volume than just the quality of personal selling, which accounted for the bulk of time and attention within the sales department.

FIGURE 20-2
Sales Orientation

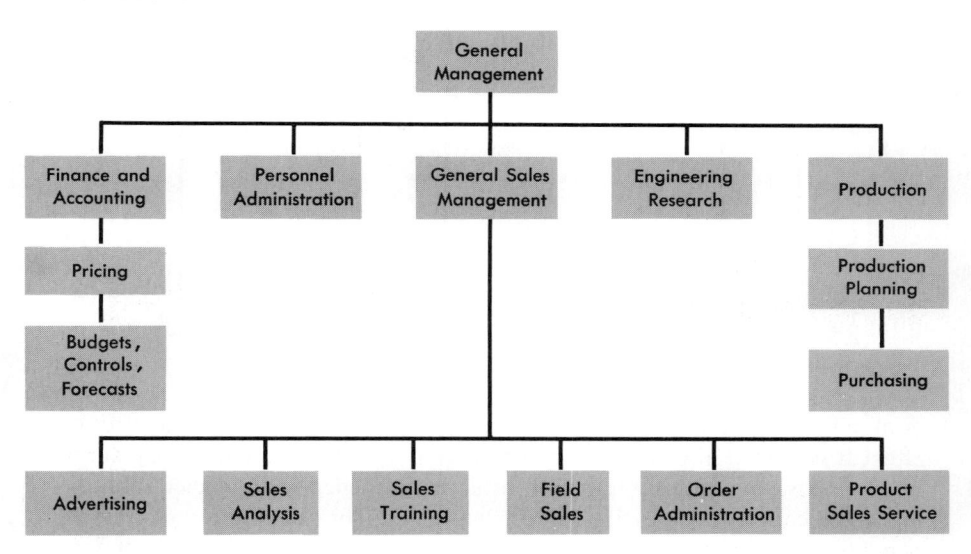

Other aspects of market cultivation were given increased attention and emphasis. Also, more scientific direction of marketing affairs was desired. This led to the creation of several new staff groups and the realignment of others as shown in Figure 20-3. The principal change, however, was the creation of separate but equal groups responsible for the conduct of market affairs. The one is composed of the line field-selling organization and closely related *operating* groups. The other is responsible for the creation of promotional programs to be *executed* by the sales organization, where the programs involve distributors and dealers or any part of the distribution system; the research, forecasting, and budgeting functions; and the conduct of advertising campaigns. These two major groupings report independently to the top level of corporate management.

The purpose of this arrangement was to prevent one group from

FIGURE 20-3
Promotional Orientation

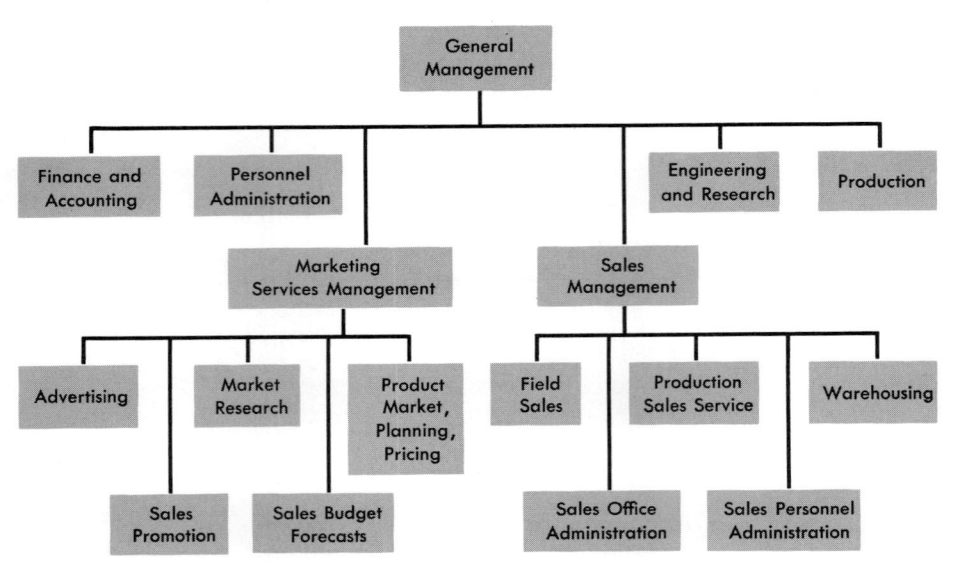

```
                            General
                           Management
        ┌──────────┬──────────┼──────────┬──────────┐
   Finance and  Personnel              Engineering    Production
   Accounting   Administration         and Research
                    │                      │
              Marketing                  Sales
              Services Management        Management
        ┌─────────┼─────────┐       ┌──────┼──────┐
   Advertising  Market   Product   Field  Production  Warehousing
                Research Market,   Sales  Sales Service
                         Planning,
                         Pricing
        │         │                    │         │
     Sales     Sales Budget         Sales Office  Sales Personnel
     Promotion Forecasts            Administration Administration
```

dominating the other and to prevent the bulk of expenditures for marketing effort from being allocated to the traditional area of personal selling activity. To provide a better integration of activities logically connected with the marketplace, several functions were transferred from elsewhere in the company or given formal participative roles in either of the two distribution groups. Forecasting was transferred from finance, and provision for product planning was made in the marketing services group, whereas it was previously the province of the production organization. Marketing and sales budgets were shifted from accounting and finance, and pricing recommendations were formally made a part of the responsibility of marketing services. Warehousing was shifted to the sales management group and the sales training function was broadened to include all aspects of sales personnel administration (recruiting, selection, and others). This activity had formerly been part of the corporate personnel function.

This organizational structure is, in fact, a modern design, characteristic of many large corporate enterprises today. It can work effectively when manned by proper personnel. Several aspects of the organizational structure regarded as serious defects, however, led to the most recent dramatic reorganization.

After a period of time with the divided marketing responsibility, there was a desire to centralize accountability for market results. Four reasons explain this desire for change. First, under the existing arrangement, the sales group could argue that advertising, promotion, product planning, and pricing policies and practices were responsible for disappointing market results. On the other hand, the marketing services group could take the position that difficulties in the distribution system, dealer structure, and personal selling effort accounted for the problem. Second, there was a desire to make the marketing area a "profit center" in the business by having this group "buy" its merchandise from the factory through intrafirm transfer pricing. This could not be done with the existence of the dual groups under the current organizational structure. Third was the desire to provide the senior sales executive with direct control over staff groups whose activities immediately affected his operations. Fourth was the desire to place in a headquarters capacity some staff groups whose specialized skills could be used advantageously in both the areas of advertising and promotion, and in personal selling operations, namely, marketing research. So to streamline information flows, ease the coordination problem, pin down accountability, provide better budget flexibility, and change the basis for evaluating operating performance in the marketplace, the third reorganization took place, as shown in Figure 20-4. We shall consider some of the features of this organization as we move on to consider the criteria for effective organizational design.

CRITERIA FOR EFFECTIVE ORGANIZATIONAL DESIGN

In this section we are seeking specific tests that can be applied to an organization to determine whether it needs modification and, if so, in what way. In auditing an existing organization for this purpose, careful consideration should be given to the criteria of effective organizational structure in the following areas.

ORGANIZATIONAL ORIENTATION

Often the organizational design for a particular company begins with the president's office and works down through successive layers of management and supervision until finally consideration is given to field-selling operations. This is not the appropriate design starting point, since the purpose is to structure the organization in such a way as to put it in the best possible position to compete effectively in the marketplace. Hence, we ought not to organize the factories, research, engineering, and product-development groups until we have established the basic approach to be taken to the market. Therefore, *we should start with the market and work back,* instead of from the president's office out. We want to mobilize, at each point behind the market, the necessary resources and appropriate authority for the effective conduct of operations.

In Figure 20-4 the product representatives and service-and-parts representatives were formed into two competing teams to make up a district. This clustering of products and specialization of selling effort was regarded as essential to effective market competition. Also decided at this time was the choice that all products would be handled by one integrated marketing organization, utilizing the same channel of distribution for all products rather than having separate divisions with specialized distribution facilities for smaller clusters of products.

One of the earliest decisions to be made, then, in organizational design is the degree to which specialized selling effort is required. When such specialization is necessary, it is usually either on a product or market basis. That is, the sales representative handles a specific product or group of products and covers all accounts in a particular geographic area that are potential purchasers of such products, or covers only specific markets in a given geographic area but handles all products purchased by that particular class of customer or industry. For instance, a petroleum company handling industrial lubricants could either have sales representatives specialize by industries, with one cultivating the aviation industry, another the marine industry, another the automotive industry, and so on; or it could have representatives handling only a specialized, narrow grouping of products but selling them in all the industries mentioned. This choice is usually made on the basis of judgment as to whether knowledge of users or knowledge of products is the most important in successful buyer cultivation. Where the user's production processes are particularly complicated and technical, market specialization tends to be preferred.

On the other hand, where technology surrounding a particular product is the critical variable in adapting it to a variety of market uses, the selling effort tends to be specialized around the product rather than around the type of customer purchasing the product. For instance, in marketing automated materials-handling equipment, market specialization might be generally preferred, with particular representatives calling on the steel industry, the rubber industry, the petroleum industry, and so on. To serve a particular customer most effectively in this instance, the representative would need to be intimately familiar with the production processes and methods of the firm and industry; and, obviously, could not be expert in a wide variety of diverse production technologies. Conversely, in industrial adhesives, the technology of the product itself is a more important variable than the particular application of the product to be made, and product specialization is preferred. Hence, the selling effort would need to have a high degree of specialized knowledge of product characteristics which could be applied in a wide variety of situations.

FIGURE 20-4
Market Orientation

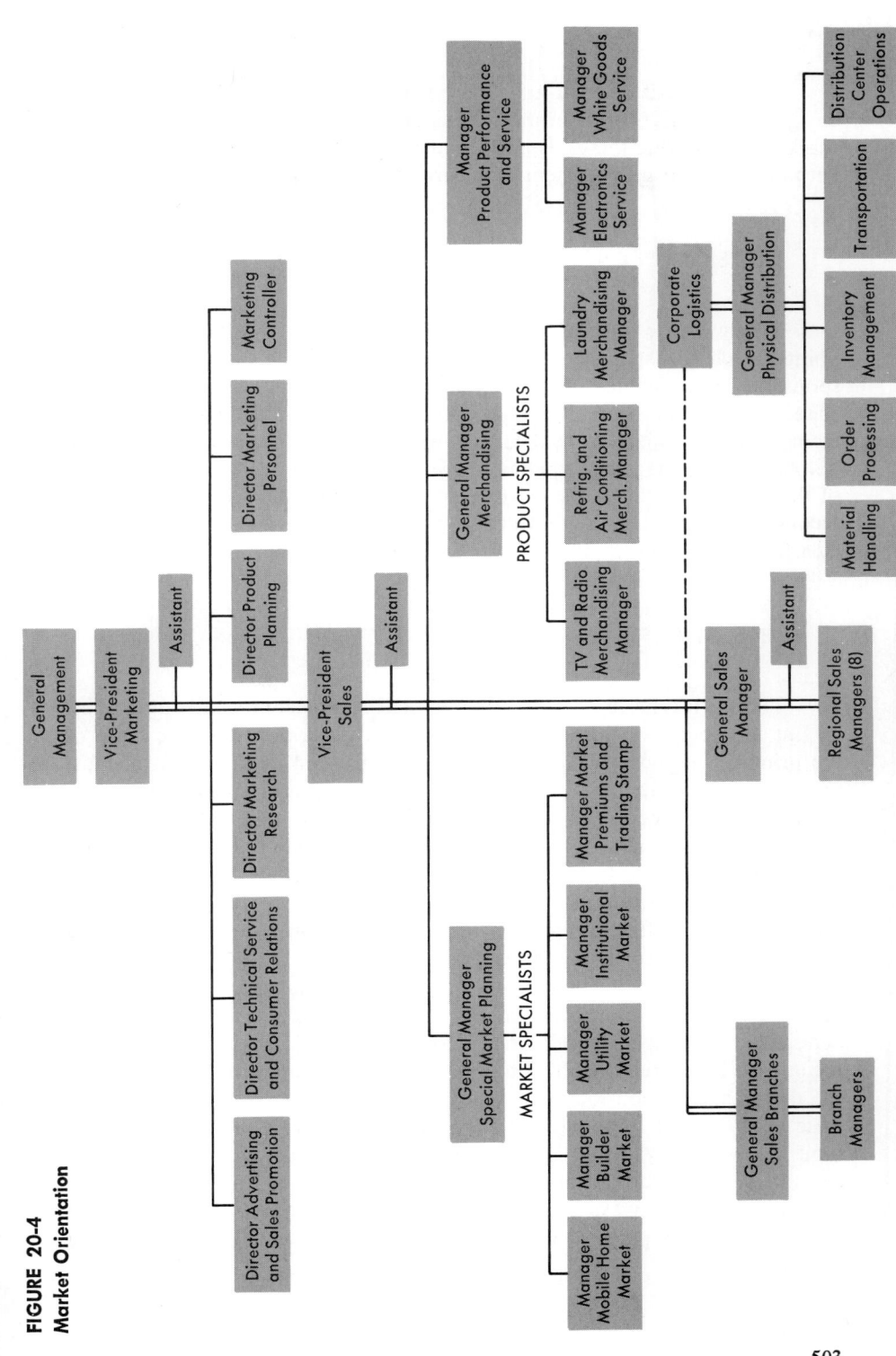

The first criterion of organizational effectiveness, then, is that the design must reflect, as a primary consideration, a sound approach to the market and provide the tools and resources at each point between the marketplace and top management to insure effective competition.

DECISION POINTS

Whatever the form of organization chosen, it is essential that decision points be clearly specified. If it is unclear as to which individuals are responsible for particular decisions, then operating difficulties are bound to arise. The organizational analyst should trace several major decisions through the organization to determine the clarity and precision of decision points and to determine whether there is uniformity in the point of view of the decision participants as to particular roles and final jurisdiction. The second criterion, then, is that decision points in the organization must be clearly specified and that the power to act must not be impaired.

LINE AND STAFF RELATIONSHIPS

The third criterion is that line and staff responsibilities for operations should be clearly distinct and separate. This criterion raises the issue of the primacy and sovereignty of the line organization. Staff personnel must not be in a position to usurp line management prerogatives, that is, the prerogatives of decision and implementation of programs. Notice in the organization chart shown in Figure 20-4 that the line organization is specified by double lines. Individuals in this chain of command are responsible for program decisions and implementation. Prior to reorganization, as many as twelve different people could give a field sales representative or a district manager directions and operating orders. In the bulk of the cases, these were staff personnel, such as merchandising managers, product managers, the market research manager, and director of sales training. This condition is untenable, for it simply does not provide for orderly management. This is one reason why job descriptions are so important; they specify the duties and responsibilities of the particular position and help to eliminate confusion of this kind. The organizational design should specifically limit the possibility of multiple direction and control at various levels in the organization. The broken line between the sales line organization and corporate logistics, conveys the close relationship between the two functions but also indicates physical distribution is directly responsible to corporate logistics.

ADEQUACY OF STAFF

The fourth design criterion is the adequacy of staff groups for long-term planning and specialized evaluation. A noticeable and limiting deficiency in many organizations is the lack of good long-range planning. This condition often exists because line executives are excessively burdened with day-to-day operations and do not have the time (and sometimes the inclination) to formulate longer-term plans and programs. It is a natural human tendency, when faced with the choice between dealing with immediate matters and dealing with longer-range considerations, to choose that which cannot be delayed or put off to a later date. Consequently, the organization must be structured to insure provision for adequate planning and evaluation.

One way to handle this problem is to maintain a sufficiently narrow span of control or number of subordinates reporting to one person, making time available for the manager to handle the planning function personally. A more current tendency is to provide executives carrying important responsibilities with sufficient staff resources for this purpose. The number and diversity of staff units is partially dependent on the size of the organization, its sales volume, the complexity of its markets, the nature of its products, the technology surrounding the production and application of the product in the market, and the degree to which the organization follows centralized versus decentralized organizational patterns. No specific rules of thumb can be applied to determine the adequacy of staff groups. Rather, this is a matter of judgment. A good organizational design, however, has this feature.

INFORMATION FLOWS

Two considerations are important in planning information flows. First, does information moving both up and down the organization consistently skip a level without undergoing some change in form? If this happens regularly, then it raises questions as to whether that level of supervision is essential and necessary in the organization. If, for instance, the information required from the various districts by a general sales manager is precisely the same as that needed by the regional managers, it raises a question as to whether the regional manager is an essential supervision intermediary between the general sales manager and the district managers.

The converse of this situation is equally valid. That is, if the district sales manager needs the same information from the general sales manager as that received by the regional managers, doubts would be raised as to the design effectiveness of the organizational structure. There are occasions when it is desirable for information to flow from the very bottom to the top (and vice versa) without undergoing any change in form whatsoever, but these should be exceptions rather than the rule. Presumably, as information flows upward, it becomes more general and less detailed or specific. As information flows downward, at each step or level of supervision it should become more specific, tailored to the particular needs of that level in the organization.

The second consideration in information flows is related to the clarity of decision points mentioned earlier. Decision points should be specified at the lowest level in organization at which the individual holding the position has all the relevant information to make an intelligent judgment as to the course of action to be followed. In other words, decisions should be made at the first level reached in the organization, beginning with the marketplace, where all relevant information pertaining to that decision has been assembled. If decisions are made either above or below this point, we have a situation where either an individual is forced into a position of making judgments without adequate information and data, or the individual is burdened with a number of decisions that he should not have to make and which could more appropriately be made at a lower level. This criterion of organizational efficiency, then, deals with the matter of whether decision patterns are compatible with information patterns, and whether responsibility flows are matched with appropriate information flows.

COORDINATION LEVELS

Activities requiring close coordination ideally should be on the same level of organization, or if this is not possible, as close to similar levels of organization as possible. This can be noticed in Figure 20-4, which shows market-planning managers and merchandising managers directly opposite each other on exactly the same organizational level. They are positioned thus because advertising and promotional programs for a particular product line, and the planning for variations in that particular product assortment, must be coordinated and integrated with the plans to develop a particular market. If one manager is subordinate to the other, a tendency will exist for the proposals of the higher-ranking manager to prevail.

We should not confuse this point with the situation wherein top-level, general plans are made and specific actions at lower levels necessarily must be coordinated with the broader plan or strategy. *This* coordination criterion refers to the situation wherein *simultaneous lateral* actions, rather than *vertically integrated* actions, are taking place. When responsibility for lateral activities is on widely different levels in the organization, the higher-ranking manager might not be particularly prone to report his ideas and actions to a substantially lower-ranked executive whose programs should dovetail, or at least should not be in conflict. Notice that in Figure 20-4 the managers responsible for selling effort through distributors and those responsible for selling effort through manufacturers' branches are again on the same level of organization, in an attempt to insure consistency of action between the two channels of distribution.

SPAN OF CONTROL

Earlier reference was made to the span of control (number of subordinates reporting to one superior). No arbitrary number can be established that is universally applicable under all conditions. The number varies from as few as three to as many as 50, depending on: the uniformity of the duties of subordinates (or the lack of it); the extent to which activities are routine or highly varied; the degree to which subordinates' activities must be coordinated; and the complexities and importance of decisions to be made. The Bible refers to units of ten in the organization of tax collectors and of the Roman army. A more current maximum seems to be seven at the upper levels of organization. This number may expand at the lower levels of supervision.

The problem of span of control is particularly difficult to deal with at the presidential level. Executives responsible for such areas as purchasing, personnel, labor relations, research, engineering, public relations, finance, comptrollership, legal counsel, manufacturing, international operations, and company acquisitions, all regard their functions as so important as to justify reporting to the company president. Inserting an executive vice-president hardly solves this problem—it merely transfers it from one level of responsibility to another. To a lesser degree, this same problem exists at lower levels of the organization. Notwithstanding the complexities involved, one of the criteria of good organizational design is that the appropriate span of control exist at all organizational levels.

AUTHORITY AND RESPONSIBILITY

One of the best known of the organizational design criteria is that authority and responsibility should be as closely matched as possible. This match can never be perfect, but there should not be great variances between the responsibilities of a position and the authority to act in such a way as to insure the proper discharge of that responsibility. This is a rather perplexing problem in marketing organization, because if the marketing manager is given responsibility for market results, then, according to the criterion, the manager should also be given commensurate authority to control the variables that make for market results. However, it is not possible to delegate authority to administer all the factors that make for market achievement. For instance, pricing decisions, channels of distribution, and the nature of product lines are only illustrative of the kinds of variables that cannot necessarily be delegated to an individual market manager, for they may deal with broad matters of corporate and overall marketing policy.

Another example of the difficulty in applying this criterion in the marketing organization deals with the authority given regional and district sales managers in the recruiting, selecting, and training of sales reresentatives. It may be uneconomical to have every district or regional sales manager perform these functions when they can be more efficiently handled at the central staff level. One sales training specialist or department can serve effectively the needs of a number of different district or regional offices. Similarly, college recruiting by a central staff may be more efficient than having six different regional managers all recruiting on the same campus. Yet, the criterion would indicate that if the district sales manager is to be held responsible for sales results in his area, then he or she should have authority over the hiring and training of people that represent capacity to achieve the desired results.

This problem can be handled by giving the district or regional sales manager an approval or rejection prerogative. When a vacancy occurs in a field-selling position, the individual manager has the prerogative of accepting or rejecting a candidate supplied by the headquarters or central office staff unit. This means that the individual manager is hiring a new sales person from the headquarters unit and, consequently, does have jurisdiction over who will be placed in the operating unit. This is a reasonable, but not exact, match of responsibility and authority. This same type of prerogative can be applied elsewhere to gain a realistic match of authority and responsibility.

PROVISION FOR CORPORATE GROWTH

Earlier in this chapter, corporate growth was mentioned as one of the principal factors accounting for the need for organizational modification. While the organization must be designed in such a way as to be consistent with the existing scale of operations, a good design provides some built-in flexibility for accommodating corporate growth. Growth within reasonable limits should not necessitate a basic change in the structure of the organization. Notice in Figure 20-4 the ease of adding district managers, regional managers, merchandising managers, branch managers, and market managers, as they are needed, and even new staff units. All of these positions can be added to the organization without changing basic structure or operating procedures and systems. Substantial corporate growth can, therefore, be accommodated readily. If, however, corporate growth comes about through widely divergent patterns of product diversification, then it is likely that some change in the structure of the organization will be required to accommodate this type of growth. A good organization, however, provides some inherent versatility and flexibility. This criterion, then, is a test of whether additional corporate growth can be accommodated with ease.

FORMAL-INFORMAL ORGANIZATION VARIANCES

The formal organization is the way in which the firm has been officially structured for operations. It is the organization as constituted by job descriptions, levels of authority, line and staff relationships, and the flow of information and decision. The informal organization describes the way the firm actually operates, not what is *supposed* to be but what in practice *is* the structure of decision and action. Because of flaws in organizational design, and variations in the abilities and personalities of executives, a separate power structure emerges as distinct from the organizational structure. The formal organization, as a result, is rarely an exact duplicate of the informal organization. One of the criteria of good organizational design, however, is that the formal and informal organizations be closely matched, if not exact duplicates. The organizational analyst should carefully observe the behavior of the organization to determine the degree of conformity between these two structures. If substantial variation is observed, one must judge as to whether the structure of the organization needs modification or whether the behavior patterns of individuals within the organization need to be altered.

ORGANIZATIONAL DIRECTIONS FOR THE FUTURE

While the discussion has stressed the criteria of good organizational design, certain directions for the future can be noted. Organizational evolution is continuous, and many firms find limitations implicit in any given structure; that is, there are certain advantages and limitations to each style of organizational arrangement. As firms grope for greater effectiveness in the future, directions for change might well lie along some of the following lines:

1. Organizations will be far more fluid than at present. Information will flow readily across organizational lines and up and down

vertical levels, available to all in whatever form is most useful.
2. "Modular organizational units" will appear which can be readily recombined in novel ways to meet fluctuating needs as markets and products change.
3. Personnel will be deployed on the basis of more loosely clustered "task packages" rather than highly structured job descriptions. Job descriptions tend to be more actively oriented; task packages are more results focused.
4. Electronic data processing will make feasible a clustering of key decisions within a small core of highly competent executives. Yet, many firms are recognizing the critical need for decentralizing decisions. The crosscurrents may lead to a new form of line and staff, with the high-talent corporate staff being given an official mandate to usurp operating line management prerogatives on the principle of the exception—that is, relatively infrequently when special strategic circumstances prevail.
5. Finally, organizational styles will shift far more readily than in the past. The blend of autocracy, bureaucracy, and democracy will be varied depending on the stage of corporate development, professional differences between particular organizational entities, and the newness of missions, this without the accompanying supposition that personnel are being subjected to a kind of corporate schizophrenia.

SUMMARY

Any enterprise is likely to prosper with three basic ingredients—vigorous, intelligent leadership; orderly systems; and capable, motivated personnel. But this obscures the complexities of organizational alignments which provide the structure for decision and action. Unfortunately, once designed, no matter how painstakingly and thoroughly done, organizational structure must be subjected to frequent modification and change. Business management is a continuous process of adaptive behavior to keep the firm in the proper state of adjustment to its environment.

This chapter has traced some of the influences that make organizational modification necessary. The special features of what may be referred to as the autocratic, bureaucratic, and democratic types of organization were outlined, leading to the conclusion that the most effective organization incorporates some features of each and may be characterized as the multicratic type of organization. Next, the tensions between centralized and decentralized organizations were considered; and finally, certain criteria of the effectiveness of organizational design were outlined in the context of some specific illustrations of marketing organization.

The relevant criteria for judging the effectiveness of an organization relate to: (1) organizational orientation, (2) decision points, (3) line and staff relationships, (4) adequacy of staff, (5) information flows, (6) coordination levels, (7) span of control, (8) authority and responsibility, (9) provision for corporate growth, and (10) formal-informal organizational variances. These criteria provide the basis for auditing an organization and for applying some specific tests of effectiveness against which to determine the suitability of the structure for the conduct of effective marketing operations.

Organizational design and style in the future are expected to evolve along the following lines: more fluid organizational arrangements with units that can more easily be recombined to meet changing product and market needs; greater flows of information vertically and horizontally within the organization; design around more results-focused task packages rather than highly activity structured job descriptions; new line-staff relationships for handling key operating decisions; and more varied blends of autocracy, bureaucracy, and democracy to reflect varied stages of organizational growth and development.

QUESTIONS AND PROBLEMS

1. What are some of the factors in marketing that have led to organizational modification in recent years?

2. How has the growing importance of logistics affected organizational design?

3. How would you distinguish between formal and informal organization? What relevance does this have for organizational design?

4. Why does there tend to be a higher degree of specialization in the centralized organization?

5. List the criteria that might be applied in judging organizational design effectiveness.

6. What are the limitations to dual marketing groups (marketing services and the field sales organization) reporting independently to top management?

7. How can information analysis be used to judge organizational design effectiveness?

8. In what ways may the use of electronic data processing change organizational design?

Chapter 21

Administration

In Part I the basic premise was established that a firm must be constantly engaged in the process of self-assessment in light of present and anticipated actions of competitive firms and purchasing units. The competitive setting is properly viewed as being in a state of "pervasive uncertainty." To maintain and perpetuate itself, a business enterprise must adjust to and capitalize upon such uncertainty.

In the competitive process, differential advantage is viewed as being best maintained by directing the enterprise as a total system of action guided by a philosophy of market orientation. That is, market opportunities are assessed; appropriate product strategies are tailored to opportunities; the commitments in the form of distribution, communications, and pricing are blended into a marketing mix strategy; human and physical resources are organized to achieve the specified objectives; and the plans are implemented. Throughout this process, the system must be monitored to assure desired results and to determine appropriate adjustments.

The final managerial function of marketing is administration, which, combined with organization, represents the managerial activity of executing the strategic marketing plan. Administration is an integral and continuous process within each of the other managerial functions of marketing. The administrative process provides the guidance system throughout the four-step marketing planning sequence.

After marketing plans have been finalized and organizational arrangements selected to execute such plans, two general areas of administrative concern remain: (1) to *control* performance through formulation and implementation of programs to guide pretransaction and transaction operations; and (2) to *measure* performance and provide posttransaction feedback to realize more effective marketing operations on a continuing basis. It is through marketing administration that closure is achieved for the total competitive effort of the enterprise.

In this chapter, we first review administrative control. The second section is concerned with performance measurement. The third section is devoted to recent technological advancements in automated marketing information systems. The final section describes an integrated approach to overall marketing administration. In total, the treatment of administrative effort guides the process of managerial marketing.

MARKETING CONTROL

Two views are held about the meaning of the word *control,* for our purposes usually referred to as *management control.* The differences in viewpoint are more related to the word *management* than to *control.* One view concentrates on the people who manage; consequently, "management control" means "management of (by) the manager." In this sense, evaluation of the manager's activities is the major idea. Control of this type is after the fact, as it cannot be exercised until the manager has done something or is supposed to have done something. In the other view, control is part of management, part of all the activities necessary to enable the enterprise to achieve its objectives.

This latter view of control is most useful to marketing administration. In this section we first review the control process. Next, a differential is presented between control efforts directed toward pretransaction and transaction activities. The final subsection is concerned with control devices and marketing information.

THE CONTROL PROCESS

The viewpoint that control is an integral part of management can be clarified by referring to our systems design approach developed in Chapter 3.[1] In the systems illustrated, no evaluation was necessary; the system worked automatically because the control mechanisms were built into it. In the simplest design a single thermostat automatically actuated the system and adjusted the system to a change in its environment. In the more complicated system a series of thermostats actuated the system in such a way that any number of preselected environments could be achieved. Let us examine again the way in which these systems work.

A disturbing element is introduced—a change in temperature. This triggers the thermostat, which in turn activates the system either to heat up or shut off, and the desired condition is restored. The thermostat is a con-

[1] See Chapter 3, p. 37.

trol device that enables the system automatically to adjust itself to a change in the environment. The system can be controlled after the fact as well. If it is not functioning as desired or a change is required, the thermostats can all be manually reprogrammed to provide a new set of environments.

In designing managerial systems, the need is also present to introduce control into the system and, at the same time, to provide a means to reprogram the system when desired. It is doubtful, however, whether it is possible to design a managerial system that will operate as smoothly as a temperature control system. The reasons are as follows: (1) the multiplicity of objectives may call for several subsystems within the general system. Since there may be a conflict between objectives, there is conflict between the subsystems, which prevents a smooth functioning of the general system. (2) The forces which call for change are so varied and so dynamic that it is difficult to incorporate control devices that are sufficiently sensitive to react to all changes in the environment. In the case of the heating system, the only change to be monitored continually is a change in temperature, whereas in a managerial system a change in competitors' actions, a change in consumers' desires, or a change in technology or labor efficiency all may call for a change in the system if it is to meet its ultimate goals. (3) The need for a change is not immediately evident. If a change is needed and is not made, sooner or later its need will become evident. This, however, is not satisfactory for the managerial system, since it may be too late to take the necessary steps to recoup its position. In the heating system analogy, it is clear that if the temperature fluctuates too widely and the system does not respond, this fact is immediately known and some action will be taken. In the managerial system a decline in sales volume or a mounting expense ratio will not become evident soon enough, unless some means are incorporated to measure these consequences periodically. (4) Managerial systems function through individuals. It is unreasonable to expect a human being to possess the knowledge or even have the intuitive sensitivity to identify minute changes in the environment calling for a change in the system. Even in the simple case of the heating system, an individual is not nearly as sensitive to changes in temperature as is the thermostat.

That there are control problems in the managerial system does not mean that control is or can be neglected. The managerial objective is to simplify the control process by developing performance procedures and standards for the strategic marketing plan. Regardless of how detailed a market plan is, events will not normally materialize as anticipated.

Through the implementation of soundly formulated performance procedures and standards, the organization is made to function smoothly. Operations relate functions, facilities, personnel, and the organizational structure, transforming these components into action systems. To insure the

Administration

effectiveness of operations, there must be procedures for completing specific projects, and standards against which to measure the results. Procedures for budgeting advertising appropriations, handling customers or sales inquiries, filling orders, and the like call for coordination among functions, facilities, and personnel.

Under ideal circumstances, each unit in an organization would know what standard its performance is measured against. Often this is not done, and although fair standards are sometimes difficult to determine, they are, nevertheless, important. Quotas for the sales force are a common form of standard, but standards should be extended into every aspect of operations —including such areas as warehousing, order filling, and credit extension. The proper use of job descriptions helps to facilitate the establishment of standards of performance. Also, it is important to note that if the basic job to be done changes, or operational procedures are adjusted, then standards must be modified accordingly. For instance, one of the telephone companies, in shifting to more of a market orientation with an objective of increasing the revenues from telephone service, developed a program for increasing the number of multiple phone installations in residences. It was believed that the installers were in an ideal position, on changing a number or the level of service from a two-party line to a private line, or in new installations, to persuade the housewife or home owner of the convenience of having several phones at different locations in the house. The installers' performance was evaluated, however, on the number of installations completed, and not on the sale of additional equipment. Until performance standards were changed to reflect the new job specifications for installers, the program was not very successful.

CONTROL ORIENTATION

The useful distinction in formulating control programs is to differentiate between pretransaction and transaction controllership. Each aspect of control is discussed in this subsection.

Pretransaction Controllership

The pretransaction aspect of marketing concerns all activities necessary to *create* a meeting of the minds among parties favorable to ownership transfer. Throughout the discussion of managerial functions, emphasis has been placed upon developing an integrated approach to achieve a favorable environment for purchase action. To assure the attainment of this objective is the purpose of pretransaction controllership. In reality, we have been dealing with this type of control in our earlier discussion of the product, distribution, communications, and pricing mixes. The following discussion elaborates the pervasiveness of pretransaction control throughout the marketing system.

Some of the most striking examples of pretransaction control was found in Part II dealing with product-service adjustment. The care exercised in adjusting products to specific segments of the market is an attempt to establish a product line that will achieve objectives. A heating plant with a 30,000 Btu heating unit will not produce a 70-degree temperature in zero weather if 120,000 Btu are needed. Similarly, if the firm is facing a saturated market and continues to attempt to achieve increased sales volume with the same product line it offered in an earlier period, it is not likely to achieve its objectives. By adjusting the product to specific segments of the market, however, management is introducing control in the development of the product line.

In the distribution mix, control is exercised at a number of points. One example is in the selection of a channel of distribution. Through analysis of the product, the market, and the manufacturing firm, channels which have the greatest chance of achieving objectives may be selected. The wrong channel, no matter how well it is managed afterward, will probably not achieve satisfactory results. Even the right channel, if improperly managed, will fall short. The actual channels selected and the means used to resolve the conflicts among participants are attempts to insure attainment of the goals of the firm, and are essentially elements of control.

A number of control devices are introduced into the system in all forms of communication. The analysis of the situation to determine the role of advertising in the total communications mix is an element of control. Selecting and training sales personnel are controls. It is hoped that if these functions are properly carried out, the representatives will perform in the desired manner. Recognizing that selection and training alone are not sufficient, management also uses supervision and compensation to motivate salespersons to perform in the desired way and sometimes imposes a penalty if they do not do so. These are all control devices.

No matter how carefully control has been introduced into the organization, improper delegation of authority and responsibility for execution will cause the system to malfunction. Organizational arrangement, therefore, is also a control device. This aspect of control is frequently overlooked, probably because it is too close to the activity we call planning. But every management would like to plan its mixes with 100 percent certainty that they were the correct mixes for all time; just as the heating engineer can design a heating system with the proper number and type of thermostats and the required capacity furnace to achieve a predetermined objective. If this were possible, the company would have perfect control through establishing the proper mixes.

Because the firm is operating in a competitive environment, in which

Administration

competitors' actions affect market shares, consumers' preferences are continually shifting, and channel members' objectives and modes of operation are changing, the managerial system must constantly adjust if objectives are to be met. The control built into the management system through product, distribution, and communication mixes is never fixed but must be changed frequently. An example will illustrate this situation.

A large paper manufacturer became concerned about its share of the cut-size bond paper market. The company was distributing its cut-size bond through full-service paper merchants, territorially protected by an exclusive franchise. An analysis of the cut-size market indicated that it had grown through the introduction and widespread use of business duplicating equipment—much of it by small firms. The paper merchants never called upon these small firms. However, through their service organizations, the business equipment manufacturers already had entry to the firms. By broadening their lines to include all accessories for use with their machines, the manufacturers could fill small orders at reasonable cost. By doing so, the business machine manufacturers had taken over about 50 percent of the cut-size bond market. This deviation from the paper manufacturer's expected results had its cause in a change in environment—the entry of another competitor. To its chagrin, the manufacturer learned that monitoring impending change is a most important aspect of control.

Even, however, if environmental changes were not present, management would rarely have sufficient information to make perfect decisions nor sufficient control to insure complete adherence to plans. For example, a regional insurance company was experiencing a higher than average lapse rate on new policies sold. Investigation showed that the sales force was using high pressure, misrepresentation, and near fraudulent means to sign up new policyholders. This deviation from expected policy retentions had its roots in poor selection and training of the field representatives—a malfunction in operations.

From a control point of view, the minimum the firm may settle for is a sufficient flow of information to signal deviations from expected results. For example, to indicate that the cut-size bond market is being taken over by the business equipment manufacturers or that the lapse rate experienced by the company is higher than industry average. Pinpointing the actual causes and effecting remedies are the result of another wave of effort designed to correct such deviations. Unfortunately this kind of information often comes too late or after the damage is done. As a management tool, control involves managing the flow of information that will aid in determining when and where changes must be made in the managerial system. Once the need is identified, a new round of planning begins to develop better control devices within the system.

A final aspect of pretransaction control concerns the dynamic inter-

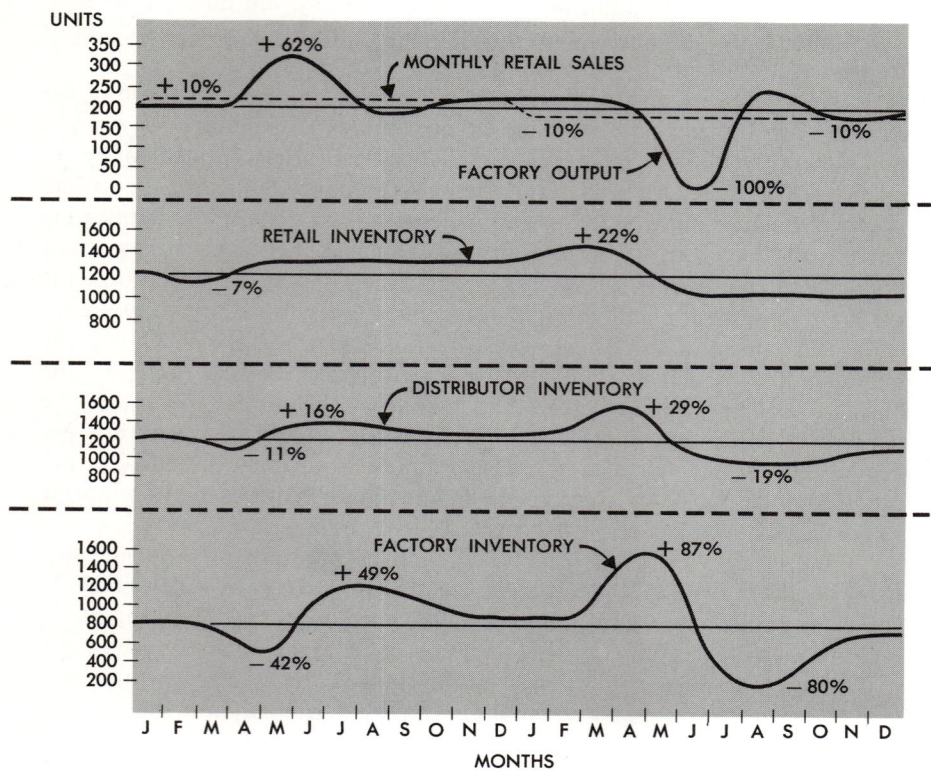

FIGURE 21-1
The Whiplash Effect: A Result of
Changes in Volume of Consumer Purchases

action of firms joined together in a distribution channel. While peaks and valleys in sales patterns can result from seasonal production or consumption, reverberations throughout the channel can also create a "whiplash," effect which complicates the control process. Figure 21-1 illustrates this form of channel dynamics.[2]

The top curve shows fluctuations in monthly retail sales, with maximum swings of plus and minus 10 percent from average sales over the two-year period. In the same period, factory production varied from a high of 62 percent to a low of minus 100 percent from the monthly average.

The retailer in this example delivers the product three days after purchase by the customer and orders from the wholesaler after a one-week

[2] J. W. Forrester, *Industrial Dynamics* (Cambridge, Mass. and New York: The M.I.T. Press, John Wiley & Sons, Inc., 1961), p. 24.

interval from time of delivery. Goods are received two weeks after the order is placed. The effect of the time lag on retail inventory is shown in the second curve, where retail inventory can be seen to decline 7 percent when sales increase, but then level off. When sales go down 10 percent, the retail inventory climbs 22 percent.

The distributor incurs even wider variations, ranging from 19 percent below average inventory to 29 percent above normal. The distributor's time lags result from shipping the retailer's order ten days after its receipt, and the receipt of replacement goods from manufacturers two and a half weeks after ordering. The resulting inventory changes for the distributor are shown by the third curve.

The whiplash effect at the factory is still greater. The distributor's order is processed and shipped within a week, but because the order for stock is about three weeks away from the retail sale, the accummulation of time lags produces swings as wide as 87 percent above normal levels and reductions below the average of 80 percent in factory inventory. This variation is accompanied by and tends to produce the wide swings in factory output shown in the top curve. Notice particularly how wide the variations are in factory output, in direct contrast to relatively minor fluctuations in retail sales in corresponding time periods.

The curves in Figure 21-1 illustrate two important points concerning pretransaction controllership. First, since a great deal of marketing is performed in anticipation of future transactions, the task of control is compounded by errors in forecasting, judgment, and appraisal. Second, since no firm is self-sufficient in the marketing process, controllership must view the interaction of total channel of distribution in terms of time lags and anticipation. The inventory imbalances, changes in production rates, and numerous adjustments made in the total system because of such a whiplash effect result in heavy cost penalties for the system as a whole. When information time lags are accompanied by changes in the level of inventory, the effect on the manufacturer is even more drastic.

Transaction Controllership

The *transaction* aspect of marketing concerns all activities that must be performed *between* the time a meeting of the minds occurs among the parties and the actual transfer of ownership. It includes all processes necessary to place goods under the responsibility of those who are to use them, other than manufacturing to order, or physical distribution. The principal domain of this function is the overt legal act of transferring title, and the facilitative activities necessary thereto. These facilitative activities are very important and often account for a sizable number of people in an organization. They include: order-handling systems, invoicing, billing, credit arrangements, determination of applicable discounts (if any), arrangements of time of delivery, effecting guarantees, and handling of any insurance policies applicable to the transfer of ownership. In the sale of industrial equipment other extensive services are often necessary before the buyer actually takes full custody of, and responsibility for, the goods. These include installation of the equipment, seeing that actual performance of the machine meets specifications, and training operators.

Let us look at an example of the transaction function in everyday life. A shopper entered a New York department store to find a Christmas gift for a friend. After reaching the housewares department, she selected a covered casserole dish in three minutes' time. At this point there was a meeting of the minds with regard to a market transaction. The preceding market functions had been effective in this instance—impact was sufficiently developed for purchase action favorable to the seller to take place. From the time the shopper announced her decision to the clerk until the transaction was completed and custody of the goods transferred, however, eighteen additional minutes were consumed.

Retailers, particularly, have devoted much time and effort to devising improved ways of carrying out the transaction function, but much work is yet to be done. When auditing a marketing system in order to appraise its overall effectiveness, careful consideration should be given to the efficiency of the mechanisms employed for facilitating the actual transaction and transferring custody of the goods. Systems for handling orders and service policies should come in for particular scrutiny.

It is apparent that the transaction phase of controllership is a critical aspect of total marketing effort. At the time of transaction, all activities leading to a buyer-seller match and their associated costs have been expended by the marketing organization. Loss of sale due to ineffective control of the transaction activities represents one of the most costly of all possible mistakes. Unfortunately, failure to culminate the final transaction is a common point of marketing breakdown.

CONTROL DEVICES AND MARKETING INFORMATION

The marketing decision maker is engaged in a series of decisions whose efficacy depends upon the quantity and quality of information available. Unlike production or personnel executives the kinds of information needed are more often external to the firm. Normally one relies on experience and the judgment of others to obtain critical information. This does not work, unfortunately. In an experiment conducted to determine the flow of information from customers through sales representatives to decision-making executives, six pieces of market information were planted among customers who agreed to pass them on. Of the six, only two were passed to top management by the sales representative. One arrived at the executive level in three days, greatly distorted, and the other in ten days in accurate form.[3] Information of the right kind and quality simply is not available to the decision maker through the informal means relied upon for providing it. There is a great need to formalize information flows.

One important aspect of marketing control is to maintain a proper perspective concerning the basic market segments and product strategy followed by the firm. If we had the good fortune to possess a magic wand that gave us the power to obtain any desired information about the market, what would we ask for? At first, the range of potential data staggers the imagination. However, the basic control program centers around three fundamental areas of information: (1) What did we expect the market to purchase? (2) How much, when, and where did we expect the market to purchase? (3) Under what conditions did we expect the market to purchase?

In part, the total answer to these three basic questions requires the input of performance measurement which results from posttransaction analysis. This will be discussed later in this chapter. At this point, it is sufficient to point out that we must be able to quantify our expectations if we expect to conduct a diagnostic review of the success of marketing strategy planning.

Some Difficulties in Information Flows

Marketing information for control purposes must flow vertically, that is, from the market (customers) through the channels to the sales force and through the sales force to the decision centers in the firm. It must flow in the reverse direction if management is to issue the kinds of instructions necessary to achieve the goals of the firm. It must also flow horizontally—between marketing, production, research and development, and finance and accounting executives. The free flow of market information is hampered by a number of special circumstances, some of which are peculiar to the market affairs of the firm.

As in the case of goods flow *time and space* too must be overcome. Almost always goods are produced far in advance of ultimate consumption in the marketplace. Results in the marketplace can only be ascertained after commitments of time, people, and money have taken place. It may be some time before any good reactions may be obtained regarding customer acceptance, and inventories will have piled up in the channel of distribution. By this time the second round of commitments will have been made,

---

[3] Gerald S. Albaum, "Horizontal Information Flow: An Exploratory Study," *Journal of the Academy of Management,* VII (March 1964), 21–33.

unless there have been special efforts to funnel information on inventory levels and customer acceptance to the decision centers almost continually. The space problem is also severe. Even with a reporting system for sales representatives there is no assurance that pertinent information will be passed through space to the decision maker thousands of miles away in the head office. The salesperson may not recognize the pertinence of a piece of information and thus fail to report. Even if the importance is recognized it makes a longer report task and human nature may result in excluding the information. Special efforts must be made to insure that the field sales force transmits information.

Organizational structures also are a hindrance to information flows. Because marketing systems are complex, there is usually some division of responsibility within the overall system. Responsibility and authority are allocated to particular units in the organization. Sometimes these units are called responsibility, or profit, centers. The organization may be structured on a product, geographic, customer, or channel of distribution base, or any combination of them. This division of responsibility is designed for efficiency and administrative ease. At the same time, it should not be forgotten that the firm is an integrated system, the various parts forming a complex whole. This organizational arrangement hampers the easy flow of information between the parts. The individual parts become so absorbed in their own activities that they are not concerned with the activities of other parts. For example, a product manager in a large soap company worked, as directed, to develop and commercialize a new product. The product met with success in the marketplace but was virtually stricken from the list of products earmarked for future support by top management. Unknown to the product manager the new item was gaining sales at the expense of other products that top management, for reasons unknown to the product manager, wished to maintain. Often the separate units become so autonomous that an aloofness from the remainder of the organization develops. Much internal information, for control purposes, must come from the accounting department. Sometimes this unit and market units are so far removed from each other, both in space and attitude, that it is almost impossible to get them together. And the kinds of information collected for financial and tax purposes are different from those needed for marketing control.

A complicating factor is found in the spatial and temporal dimensions of markets. Marketers generally do not deal with a single market but with a number of different markets, varying by geographic area and through time. Common to the key question we have asked is the matter of where the market will purchase certain products, in what quantities, and under what conditions. There may be slight variations in the product offered in order to find acceptance in different parts of the country. Brown eggs are far more popular along the Atlantic seaboard than in the Midwest. The quantities that will be taken vary considerably from section to section of the country.

In fact, market coverage may well be determined by the extent of market opportunity in different sections. Likewise, conditions of purchase will vary from section to section; in regions in which particular ethnic groups are predominant, the conditions of sale must be tailored to these groups.

Markets have a highly dynamic quality and relatively constant change is virtually certain. Because the desires of consumers are continually shifting, markets are in a constant state of flux, and last year's successful marketing plan cannot necessarily be expected to produce equally satisfactory results this year.

Another source of resistance to information flow is *executive fear*. Pertinent information is suppressed by administrative authority if the information is critical of past actions of individuals. This, of course, does not happen often, but it would be naive not to recognize that it exists. Closely allied to fear is jealousy. As individuals climb the management ladder, the positions to be filled begin to reduce in number; not all will occupy top positions. In the group dynamics of the process, frictions develop, and pertinent information is withheld to be used by individuals to enhance their own prestige at a later time.

We can recognize the importance of information flow for control purposes, and the difficulties in achieving adequate information flow are limited with informal arrangements. There is some justification for centralizing responsibility for information and systematizing routines for collection.

PERFORMANCE MEASUREMENT

A second vital aspect of marketing administration is performance measurement. A common viewpoint exists that, after custody of goods has been transferred, the marketing process has terminated. Managerially speaking, this is not a sound viewpoint. It implies that marketing systems are linear rather than circular. It does not contribute to achieving the continuing objective of management: an ever more entrenched market position and improved market share. The objective of the performance measurement aspect of marketing administration is to provide posttransaction feedback to increase future marketing effectiveness. In this section, we first review the nature of posttransaction analysis and feedback. The following three parts discuss and illustrate types of information required to provide an adequate fund of knowledge for effective marketing administration.

POSTTRANSACTION ANALYSIS

The posttransaction aspect of administration is concerned with the state of affairs that exist between buyer and seller *after* the ownership transfer is completed. Marketing responsibility does not stop with the ringing of the cash register at the retail level, at the point of ultimate sale, or even with actual delivery of goods. Management has a vital stake in seeing that goods give satisfactory performance. Unsatisfied customers can quickly destroy all that management has attempted to achieve in preceding marketing and production efforts. Carrying out guarantees and warranties on products, and maintaining repair parts and service facilities are obvious aspects of posttransaction. The adjustment departments and returned-goods privileges of retail stores also fall in this category. Proper marketing effort fully conceived should go beyond even this point. Marketers benefit from knowing who has purchased their goods, why, to what specific use they have been put, whether they are satisfactory, the limitations to their performance in use, and the features of the product that buyers like best.

The feedback of information should lead to a more precise delineation of the market, better understanding of the motivational elements in the market, improved adjustment of goods to market requirements, more effective communications—in short, more efficient performance of all the functions in the "next round of marketing effort" and in the continuous operations of the firm. Satisfied customers lead to new customers, and the circular flow keeps the firm in a better state of adjustment to the environment.

That effective use of the posttransaction performance measurement can result in good returns to the marketer can be seen in the following example. The owner of a new home visited a paint and wallpaper store in the community to select wallpaper and tools for repapering a bedroom. When the owner was in the store several weeks later to buy paint for another project, the proprietor inquired about the success of the paperhanging. The customer said the paper looked fine, except that the seams had darkened where the rolls were butted together. No complaint was registered against the product, because the buyer assumed the fault lay in the way the paper had been hung—particularly in the way the edges had been rolled. Puzzled because the paper should not darken that way, the proprietor offered to send an employee out to inspect the job. The employee was unable to find anything wrong with the job itself, and finally, the proprietor visited the home (at his own suggestion). After a careful inspection, he concluded that the paper was at fault. The customer was allowed to select new paper of the same grade without charge, and an allowance was made to pay for the cost of hanging the paper. Result: that customer purchased all other home decorating needs from that store, and was pleased to refer a number of new customers to the store. Sometime later, the customer received a note from the owner explaining that the problem had been traced to incorrect trimming of the paper, and steps had been taken to correct the situation.

Administration

As a consequence of concern for the posttransaction function, product adjustments were made, better understanding of application practices were developed, information modifications to future purchases were made on use of the material, and a more loyal customer following developed. The proprietor in this example knew that the marketing process was not necessarily completed with the ring of the cash register and the transfer of custody of the goods to the purchaser.

Posttransaction feedback represents an integral part of marketing administration in that it provides vital information to assist management in achieving competitive and buyer adjustment. Three kinds of information are desirable to complete performance measurement and evaluation: (1) information to measure performance against expectation, (2) information to determine the causes of deviations from expected results, and (3) information to signify impending changes in the environment. Each area of information is discussed separately.

MONITORING PAST PERFORMANCE

Standards of acceptable performance are established in relation to the specific objectives for achieving the overall goals of the organization. Some of the more common specific objectives are: (1) a designated share of the market, (2) profitability by product or product line, territories, and customer class, (3) a designated sales-expense ratio, (4) a given level of promotional activity in the channel, (5) stated standards of sales performance, and (6) competitive prices.

The kinds of analysis made to monitor past actions against standards, similar to those noted above, are usually divided into the following: (1) sales analysis, (2) market share analysis, (3) advertising effectiveness analysis, (4) sales force analysis, (5) distribution analysis, and (6) cost-revenue analysis.[4]

Sales Analysis

Analysis of sales has been placed first because the making of a sale is one of the major purposes of a firm's marketing system (secondary only to profits), and because it is the most common type of analysis carried out. Four questions must be answered before an adequate sales analysis program can be established. They are: (1) What is a sale? (2) How will sales

---

[4] The classification and the following presentation are based upon David J. Luck, Hugh G. Wales, and Donald A. Taylor, *Marketing Research*, 4th ed. (Englewood Cliffs, N.J.: Prentice-Hall, Inc., 1974).

be classified? (3) How shall the information be expressed? and (4) What standards of comparison will be used?

Generally, sales data are expressed in monetary or physical units. However, the way they are expressed depends somewhat on other kinds of analyses that will be made. If cost and profit analysis is to be performed, then sales data will be expressed in terms of profit contribution. If sales force analysis is made, it can be expressed relative to selling expenses, sales per call, sales to new customers, and so on.

Sales data alone, no matter how finely categorized, are of little value without standards of comparison. Past sales are often used as a basis. Their major weakness is that poor performance in the past makes it difficult to evaluate current performance. Accurate information on potential is needed for specific products in specific areas and for certain sizes or classes of customers.

Although the amount of historical data needed seems endless, most of it is available in the records of the average company. Later in the chapter we will discuss the retrieval of such data from a marketing information system.

Market Share Analysis

Pure sales analysis does not give information as to the share of the market the firm is getting. It is possible to experience an increasing sales volume and a declining market share. Whenever there is expansibility of demand for a product, each supplier generally seeks to participate in the expansion. Even though there is no expansion in demand, knowledge of market share is necessary to plan marketing strategy. The firm may be doing well overall but may have varied strengths and weaknesses in different geographic locations, different product lines, or different classes of customers.

The data necessary to assess the standing of different brands at the level of ultimate consumption are external to the organization and sometimes difficult to obtain. In those consumer goods industries in which there is high product turnover at the retail level, syndicated data services gather and sell brand-position data. The A. C. Nielsen Company conducts store audits in the grocery and drug fields and some others. These are conducted in a panel of stores presumed to be representative of all stores in the country. Table 21-1 shows the kind of information available to subscribers to the A. C. Nielsen service. The Market Research Corporation of America, through a panel of consuming units, gathers information on consumer expenditures, and in this way is able to make brand-position information available. An intermediate step in measuring product flow is the data available from Speedata, Inc. This company measures the flow of products, by brand, through 100 major warehouses, servicing 31,404 retail outlets in

TABLE 21-1
Complete List of Data Secured Every 60 Days in Food Stores*

1. Sales to customers
2. Purchases by retailers
3. Retail inventories
4. Days' supply
5. Store count distribution
6. All-commodity distribution
7. Out-of-stock
8. Prices (wholesale and retail)
9. Special factory packs
10. Dealer support (displays, local advertising, coupon redemption)
11. Special observations (order size, reorder, direct vs. wholesale)
12. Total food store sales (all commodities)
13. Major media advertising (from other sources)

Broken Down By:

	Brands	Territories	Your Own Territory		Counties Pop. Range	Stores	Package Size	Product Type
	Yours	New England	1	10	Metro. New York	Chain	Small	
	A	Metro. New York	2	11	Metro. Chicago			
								X
	B	Mid-Atlantic	3	12	Other Metro. 19 next largest mkts.	Independent:		
Competitors	C	East Central	4	13			Medium	
	D	Metro. Chicago	5	14	B counties Metro. areas over 100,000	Super		
						Large		Y
		West Central	6	15		Medium	Large	
		Southwest	7	16	C counties 30,000–100,000	Small		
	All others	Pacific	8	17			Giant	Z
		Southeast	9	18	Rural Others under 30,000			
	Total	Los Angeles						

* Substantially the same kinds of data are collected in all types of stores audited.

Retail Audit Data. The indicated types and breakdowns are provided to clients of the Nielsen services in food, drug, variety, and several other merchandise lines. *Courtesy of A. C. Nielsen Co.*

22 market areas. The data cover 259 product categories covering 18,000 grocery items.

Some newspapers and magazines also conduct studies in the markets they serve and periodically report the position of a number of brands in these markets. They usually do not disclose actual unit or dollar volume of different brands. These studies are conducted by the media to aid in selling space to prospective advertisers; they are available free of charge.

Trade associations often act as clearinghouses for industrywide information. Member firms periodically report sales to the association. These are analyzed on an industry basis, and the information is returned to the members. The association usually does not disclose the market share held by other members, but any single member can determine the share he is getting and identify trends in total sales volume.

In those product lines in which there is mandatory reporting of sales, such as insurance, liquor, and automobiles, it is possible to develop highly detailed information. One problem occasionally encountered in these areas is that the information is not made available rapidly enough to highlight growing problems in an early stage of development. When no data are available, the only recourse is to try to build estimates of sales opportunity through quantitative market investigation.

Advertising Effectiveness Analysis

The effectiveness of advertising must be evaluated for a number of reasons:

1. It is necessary to have some measure of the effect of advertising on sales to intelligently determine the size of succeeding advertising appropriations.
2. When one considers the alternatives in media and copy available, some measure of the effectiveness of different copy, different media, and frequency and seasonality of insertion is necessary for efficient management of this phase of advertising.
3. The market to which advertising is directed is in a steady state of change. The dynamic nature of the market is such that price reduction may produce a greater sales response in one period and advertising in another.
4. There is a saturation point in advertising beyond which sales response is negligible. It is necessary to know when this point has been reached.

Those charged with responsibility for all marketing effort will rarely engage directly in research studies designed to evaluate the effectiveness of advertising. Nevertheless, they will be exposed to those studies which have been conducted to ascertain effectiveness. For this reason, it is essential that they have some familiarity with the methods and, most important, that they understand precisely what these various methods measure. With this purpose in mind, the methods currently used to evaluate advertising effectiveness are presented.

With few exceptions, the overall objective of advertising research is to determine whether or not advertising is producing additional sales revenue that more than justifies its cost. On the other hand, for most companies sales are generated by a number of activities besides advertising. The multivariable character of the problem makes it almost impossible to measure those sales which can be attributed to advertising, those to personal selling, and those to sales promotional activities. Because of this, most advertising research concentrates on those characteristics of the advertisement which must be present if it is to be successful. That is, an advertisement cannot be successful if it is not seen or heard. Furthermore, it must be understood, believed, and remembered. If the advertiser can demonstrate exposure, comprehension, retention, and believability, it is inferred that the advertisement will produce more sales than one for which these characteristics cannot be demonstrated. Consequently, research done to evaluate advertising falls into four categories: (1) media research to determine exposure; (2) copy research to determine such characteristics as the ability of the consumer to comprehend, retain, and believe the message; (3) "image" studies to determine whether the customer's perception of the product and company has changed along desired lines; and (4) sales-results tests to determine the sales effectiveness of advertising.

MEDIA RESEARCH. As mentioned in Chapter 16, circulation figures are necessary to determine the economy of the various printed media. All printed media provide circulation data, and these, because of the objective of the media—selling space to the advertiser—are verified by such companies as the Audit Bureau of Circulation and Business Publications' Audit of Circulations, Inc. The advertiser, however, is forced to rely on the medium's claims for detailed analysis of the composition of its circulation. In broadcast media, such as radio or television, the measurement of audience size is more difficult. The problem is to determine how many radio and television sets are in use at any given time and to what program they are tuned. Current methods do not measure the number of *people* reached: audience size is expressed in terms of the number of *households* reached.

Two major methods are used in radio and television audience measurement: (1) coincidental and (2) postbroadcast. The *coincidental* method checks the number of households tuned in, either by making phone calls at the time of the broadcast or by using machines which record the time the set was turned on and the station tuned in. In both cases, probability samples are used, which are later projected to determine total audience size. A more recent development is an electronic device called the "Arbitron," used by the American Research Bureau. A controlled sample of approximately 500 homes is electronically linked with a scoreboard which records each set as it is tuned in to any station. The primary value of the coincidental method is that it does not rely upon recall by the respondent. On the other hand, it measures only the number of households tuned in. It does not measure whether anyone was listening or how many were viewing the message.

Most *postbroadcast* methods, in addition to measuring audience size, seek additional information about the respondent's attitude toward the advertising message. They are conducted with a probability sample and use either personal interviews with aided recall or a diary method. When aided recall is used, the respondent is shown a list of programs broadcast the previous day and asked to identify those heard. He may also be asked to identify the sponsor and indicate knowledge about the product advertised. In addition, information regarding the composition of the household, such as the size of the family, economic level, and education and occupation, is also acquired. The diary method provides an inexpensive means of getting information. A probability sample of families is provided by means of a diary, in which they record all programs listened to. The postbroadcast methods get more information, but they must rely on the respondent's ability to recall those programs viewed or listened to. In neither the coincidental nor the postbroadcast means of measurement is there any indication of sales effectiveness.

Copy Research. Copy research measures the effectiveness of different elements in an advertisement—that is, differences in theme, size, layout, illustration, and color that may be used in printed media. Almost as many variables are present in the preparation of both radio and television advertising messages. Research may try to measure the effectiveness of each element or of different elements in combination. Copy research is divided into prepublication and postpublication research. Among the prepublication tests which may be applied are the consumer-jury test, the arousal test, the eye-camera test, readability studies, the program analyzer, and the Schwerin test. A brief description of each follows.

The *consumer-jury test* is designed to test the preference of a group of representative customers for one advertisement over another or for several advertisements from a group. Advertisements are mocked up and shown to a representative group of customers, who are asked to select the preferred advertisement. If a group of advertisements is used, it is necessary to restrict the range of choice to enable the respondents to make a comparison easily. If eight advertisements are being tested, they are divided into fifty-six groups of two each in the number of combinations possible. This is known as a *paired-comparison test*. Another method often used is a *ranking scale,* on which the respondent lists in order his preferences of advertisements. The major limitations to this method are four: (1) The respondent may select his preference for an advertisement from the group, but none of the advertisements in the group may be desirable. (2) The respondent may react differently than would be the case if he were exposed to the advertisement under actual conditions of publication. (3) It is difficult to insure that the jury is representative of the potential customers for the product. (4) There is no indication of the sales power of the advertisement. At best, it may separate the stronger from the weaker advertisements.

Arousal tests use equipment similar to a lie detector to measure a respondent's emotional response when shown the advertisement. The subjects must represent typical potential customers. This method does not indicate whether the response is favorable or unfavorable to the advertiser. However, by questioning after the test, it may be useful in indicating the attention-getting power of different advertisements.

The *eye-camera test* mechanically records the movement of the eye across the advertisement, and the time spent on each element. The test does not indicate what the person thinks about the advertisement, nor can it determine whether a sustained look at a certain part of the advertisement is caused by difficulty in reading or in comprehending the copy or by the attention-getting power of the copy. There is a belief, however, that the most-read advertisements hold the eye the longest.

Readability studies test advertisements to determine if they are readable by people in different educational levels. Formulas have been developed which state the number of words per sentence, the number of affixes per hundred words, and the number of references to people per hundred words. Variations in these elements make the copy readable to people in different educational levels—which should match the educational levels of potential purchasers in the advertiser's market.

The *program analyzer* is used in broadcast media and is similar to a consumer-jury test. It is based on the premise that the program with which the advertisement is used determines, in part, the reviewer's response to the advertising. The jury member views the program and indicates those parts he likes or dislikes by pressing different colored buttons. These answers are recorded and crosstabulated with characteristics of the jury, such as age, sex, economic level, and educational level.

The *Schwerin test* uses a survey method to gather information about a large group of potential listeners or viewers. They are given lists of brand names and asked to select those brands they would choose if offered as a prize. Later, they are exposed to a program and commercials, usually in a theater, and afterward are asked to select those brands they would choose as a prize. Any shifting in preference is attributed to the effect of the commercial to which they have been exposed. This method still does not test the sales effectiveness of the advertisement, and a number of random variables are difficult to isolate.

The major postpublication tests are known as penetration or progress tests. *Penetration tests* measure such things as recognition and recall. There are many companies providing this service. Although there are differences in the methods used, many common characteristics exist. Practically all use a personal-interview technique in which the respondent is asked about an advertisement. The answer reveals the depth of his impressions. The major difference is the aid given to the respondent in recalling the advertisement. Some services use unaided recall, in which the respondent is asked, "What advertisements have you seen recently that impressed you most?" Aided recall can be of varying degrees. The respondent may be asked, "What brand of coffee do you remember seeing advertised lately?" The answer given indicates that the advertisements for the brand made a positive impression. It does not indicate any particular advertisement or medium and is, therefore, only a general test of brand dominance.

Another form of aided recall is to show the respondent a publication and ask if he has read any of the advertisements on each page. Then a series of questions are asked to determine the degree of penetration the advertisement has had. Wide differences in readership claims by different rating agencies result from differences in methods used. The Advertising Research Foundation, in comparing the different methods, found that one overstimulates the respondent to recall and results in a much larger number of presumed readers. Other methods greatly understimulate the reader and result in a much smaller number of readers being indicated than is actually the case.

Progress tests measure different stages in buyer awareness, preference, and intention to buy. Surveys are used which compare the proportion of those preferring a brand but who have not been exposed to advertising with those preferring a brand who have been exposed. If the two groups are identically matched, the difference in preference is attributed to the advertising. This can also be carried to the purchase level; a comparison of exposed purchasers and unexposed purchasers gives some measure of the sales-getting power of the advertisement.

Inquiry tests are those in which an invitation is made in the advertisement to write in to the sponsor for additional information. The number of inquiries resulting from one advertisement is compared with those resulting from another. There is an implication that the inquiry pulling power of the advertising is correlated with its selling power. This correlation may not always be valid. The inquiry pulling power of the advertisement is influenced by the offers made in the inquiry, and if these vary or the circumstances surrounding the offer vary, it is difficult to isolate net effects. Furthermore, the task of converting inquiries into prospects usually requires additional marketing effort of a different kind, such as personal selling. Nevertheless, the method has much validity, and is useful for comparing advertisements for this purpose.

IMAGE STUDIES. A new area of investigation for determining advertising effectiveness is called *image studies*. Presumably, if advertising is effective, it should change the attitude of the relevant public toward the product and sponsor in the desired way from the point of view of the advertiser. Before- and after-advertising studies are made using motivational research techniques to gain these customer perceptions. For example, an appliance manufacturer was having difficulty in trade relations, in that distributors and dealers were not giving products the aggressive marketing effort desired. The manufacturer, using motivational techniques, had a study made of the company image among the trade. The study showed that dealers believed the manufacturer was offering different prices to different accounts, that merchandise had substantial servicing difficulties, and that merchandise was not selling well—that there was a substantial carry-over of last year's goods still in the distribution channels. The appliance manufacturer then developed a trade advertising campaign to help alter this image. At the end of the program a similar image study was conducted which did not identify the client, and a noticeable improvement could be perceived. This procedure holds promise because it gives advertising and advertising research a specific problem-solving orientation.

SALES-RESULTS TESTS. As stated earlier, the multivariable nature of the influences affecting sales makes it difficult to measure the sales effectiveness of advertising alone. However, methods have been used to determine the effects of advertising when none has been used before or when there has been a change in campaigns, or a change in major media. The technique involves setting up an experiment by selecting test areas and control areas. These should be as near alike as possible; the factor tested is tried in the test area and sales results observed in each. The difference in results is attributed to the factor under test. Since the maintenance of complete uniformity between the test area and the control area is difficult, several areas are selected and the experiment rotated among them, in hopes that the differences in the areas will compensate for each other. The method does measure the sales effectiveness of major parts of the advertising, but it is of no value for measuring the sales effectiveness of minor variations in such areas as copy and layout.

Methods of evaluating advertising are far from utopian. There is still no satisfactory means for measuring sales effectiveness of advertising. At most, historical analysis gives some clues, but the dynamic nature of markets and competition makes it excessively risky to rely solely on historical, as compared with current or projected, conditions.

Sales Force Analysis

Since the field sales organization is the instrument through which sales are finally consummated, some evaluation of its activities is desirable. Whenever sales, brand-position, or distribution analyses are done on a territory basis, they are in part an evaluation of the efforts of the individual sales person, because the representative is the territory manager. Sales by products in a given territory, when compared to opportunity in that territory, are a measure of the way in which the territory has been managed. There are, however, a number of other analyses that may be made which are equally important in assessing the way in which the sales force is performing. It is necessary to determine precisely the functions that are expected to be performed in the field. Then it is necessary to collect information which will identify whether or not the functions were performed in the required way. Once the information is collected, care must be exercised in evaluating the findings through establishing fair standards of performance.

In Table 21-2, the basic items measured and the ways of measuring them are shown. Most of the information needed for measuring sales results and sales-related nonselling activities is already available and has been described in the analyses discussed. However, there are additional items of information not normally available. They are: (1) new account development, (2) investigation of complaints, (3) sales service and engineering, (4) sales promotion and engineering, (5) distribution assistance or training, (6) checks on distributors' stocks, and (7) price checks. The extent of the information collected depends on the kind of selling job being monitored.

This information may be obtained through establishing reporting systems for the sales force. These methods can usually be effective if any rewards are present in the compensation plan for performing these activities.

The determination of standards against which to compare results is important if this kind of information is going to permit effective control. All of the activities mentioned must be related to the opportunity to perform them. For example, the number of calls per day depends upon the length of call necessary and the number of outlets available to be called upon. Consequently, determination of standards may require original field studies to observe performance and relate it to opportunity.

Distribution Analysis

If thorough sales and market share analyses show company weaknesses, distribution analyses is one area that may uncover possible causes.

Administration

The most common type of distribution analysis is the number and quality of outlets in which the brand is distributed, relative to competition. This information may appear simple to obtain, but unless close control is exercised over the channels of distribution it frequently is not available. Where intermediaries are used, some loss in control is imminent, and it is difficult to know what outlets are handling the product. Retailers or wholesalers may sell to unauthorized dealers even when selective or exclusive distribution is used. Sales reports can be used to determine the outlets in which the products are sold. However, unless the sales representative calls on every single outlet—and it is not often profitable to do so—only a partial picture is given. Sales personnel can, however, be instructed to report the conditions of distribution in the markets in which they work.

The quality of performance throughout the channel is also important. A satisfactory level of product exposure is effective only if the intermediary handling the product perform in the desired way. Most performance evaluations of distributors are based upon three types of comparisons.[5]

1. Comparisons of the distributor's current sales with sales attainments in prior periods (analyzing historical performance).
2. Comparisons of the performances of various distribution outlets (usually classified by outlet type or geographic region).
3. Comparisons of sales figures with predetermined quotas and other gauges of territorial potential.

The data needed for these kinds of comparisons are found in the company's records and are usually a part of its sales analysis program.

Overall performance in terms of stock conditions, number of facings (the front packages on a shelf), location of facings, pricing, and use of point-of-purchase display material all should be checked periodically. Some of this information is provided by syndicated data services. If no service is available, the firm will have to find other ways to periodically assess performance. This usually involves establishing periodic research studies or developing some kind of reporting system utilizing the sales force.

Although much information may be collected about the conditions of distribution, without standards against which to judge results, little is achieved. It is in this area that distribution analysis is weakest. To establish standards of performance, some assessment must be made of what constitutes successful performance, both from the point of view of the intermediary and the manufacturer.

---

[5] *Selecting and Evaluating Distributors,* Studies in Business Policy, No. 116 (New York: National Industrial Conference Board, 1965), p. 109.

TABLE 21-2
How Companies Assess Their Salesmen's Performance

What Is Measured	Common Ways of Measuring
I. SALES RESULTS A. Sales volume (total, or by product, account, etc.)	I. Sales, expenses and/or profitability analyses: A. Sales analysis—Determination of absolute unit or dollar sales figures for the period; comparison with performance of other salesmen or salesman's own past performance
B. Quota attainment (unit or dollar sales—total, or by product, account, etc.; profitability of sales; new accounts; etc.)	B. Sales analysis—Comparison of actual achievement with predetermined quota(s) for the period; comparison of relative attainment of quota(s) with that of other salesmen
C. Selling expenses	C. Expense analysis—Determination of direct selling expenses for the period; computation of ratio of direct selling expenses to total dollar sales; comparison with predetermined standards or norms, with performance of other salesmen, or with past performance
D. Profitability of sales	D. Profitability analysis—Determination of profits on sales for the period; determination of relative profit contribution and assignment of profitability weights to product classes sold; comparison with predetermined standards or norms, with performance of other salesmen, or with salesman's own past performance
E. Product mix	E. Sales analysis—Determination of absolute unit or dollar sales figures by product for the period; determination of inclusion and/or relative importance of product classes in total sales; comparison with predetermined standards or norms, with performance of other salesmen, or with past performance

Administration

TABLE 21-2
How Companies Assess Their Salesmen's Performance—Continued

What Is Measured	Common Ways of Measuring

II. SALES-RELATED AND NONSELLING ACTIVITIES
  A. New account development
  B. Calls made (total, or by type customer, etc.)
  C. Matters discussed or handled during calls
  D. Investigation of complaints
  E. Sales service and engineering
  F. Sales promotion and merchandising
  G. Distributor assistance or training
  H. Check on distributor stocks
  I. Price checks
  J. Travel
  K. Filing of reports
  L. Time on job vs. time lost
  M. Time selling vs. time spent on other activities
	II. Sales and similar analysis—Determination of relevant numbers, time spent, or expense for given activity during the period; comparison with predetermined standards or norms, with performance of other salesmen, or with salesman's own past performance

III. PERSONAL QUALITIES, APTITUDES AND DEVELOPMENT	III. Personal observation by superior or other observer(s); self-evaluation; testing

Source: National Industrial Conference Board, "Measuring Salesmen's Performance," *Studies in Business Policy,* No. 114.

Cost-Revenue Analysis

Cost-revenue analysis, sometimes referred to as profitability analysis, was purposely left until last because it uses information from the other areas of past performance analysis. Further sales, share of market, distribution, and sales force analysis may all indicate acceptable performance, but the company may not be making satisfactory profits. The revenue part of profit analysis has been dealt with in sales analysis, but the cost phase must be analyzed to complete the equation. The following types of cost analysis are possible: (1) natural expense analysis, (2) functional cost analysis, (3) responsibility cost analysis, and (4) gross profit and net profit analysis.

NATURAL EXPENSE ANALYSIS. This method uses the normal accounts of most accounting systems. The accounts identify the goods or services received, such as heat, light and power, rent, advertising, and freight.

Hardly any diagnosis is possible with lump sum totals such as all freight charges during a period. From an analytical viewpoint, the major weakness with this form of analysis is that it is too aggregative and does not pinpoint those activities which are unprofitable to the company. At the same time, these aggregate figures must be compared against budgets to detect any items that are too far out of line.

FUNCTIONAL COST ANALYSIS. This method records cost in terms of the activity or task performed as a result of the expenditure, such as, direct selling, advertising and sales promotion, and physical distribution. Each cost outlay is charged to a natural expense. For example, a cash outlay is made for heat, light, and power, and it is charged first to its "natural" purpose. But heat, light, and power may be used by many parts of the total marketing function. Some of it must be charged to advertising and sales promotion, some to physical distribution, some to general marketing expense and some to nonmarketing activities. The difficulty with this kind of analysis is twofold. First a decision must be made on what functions are going to be used. They generally can be solved easily, but it will depend on the marketing operations of the particular firm.[6] Second, it is difficult to allocate natural expenses to the function benefiting from them. A logical basis for allocation may be found for some, but frequently the basis must be arbitrary.

RESPONSIBILITY COST ANALYSIS. For truly meaningful measures of profitability, costs must be assigned to those responsible for given functions in the organization. For management and control purposes the organization is divided into profit centers, with an individual responsible for the profitability of his domain. The normal profit centers used in business today are regions, branches or territories, products—single products or a group of products—sales to a given customer type or sales through a given channel of distribution. To determine profits for each of these managerial units, costs must be assigned to them; that is, the functional costs must be allocated to responsibility centers. Advertising and sales promotional expense must be allocated to territories if a territorial analysis is being made or to a product if a product profitability analysis is to be made.

Figures 21-2 through 21-5 are illustrative of the kinds of analyses that can be made.[7] These figures summarize the performance of a single product, Product X, both nationally and regionally. In Figure 21-2 the

[6] Charles H. Sevin, *Marketing Profitability Analysis* (New York: McGraw-Hill Book Company, 1965). For two early treatments, see J. Brooks Heckert and Robert B. Miner, *Distribution Costs* (New York: The Ronald Press Company, 1940), and Donald R. Longman and Michael Schiff, *Practical Distribution Cost Analysis* (Homewood, Ill.: Richard D. Irwin, Inc., 1955). See also Richard J. Lewis and Leo G. Erickson, "Distribution System Costing," unpublished paper presented at the James R. Riley Symposium, 1972.

[7] This example adapted from Michael Schiff, "Reporting for More Profitable Product Management," *The Journal of Accountancy* (May 1963), pp. 65–70.

Administration

FIGURE 21-2
Product X (National)

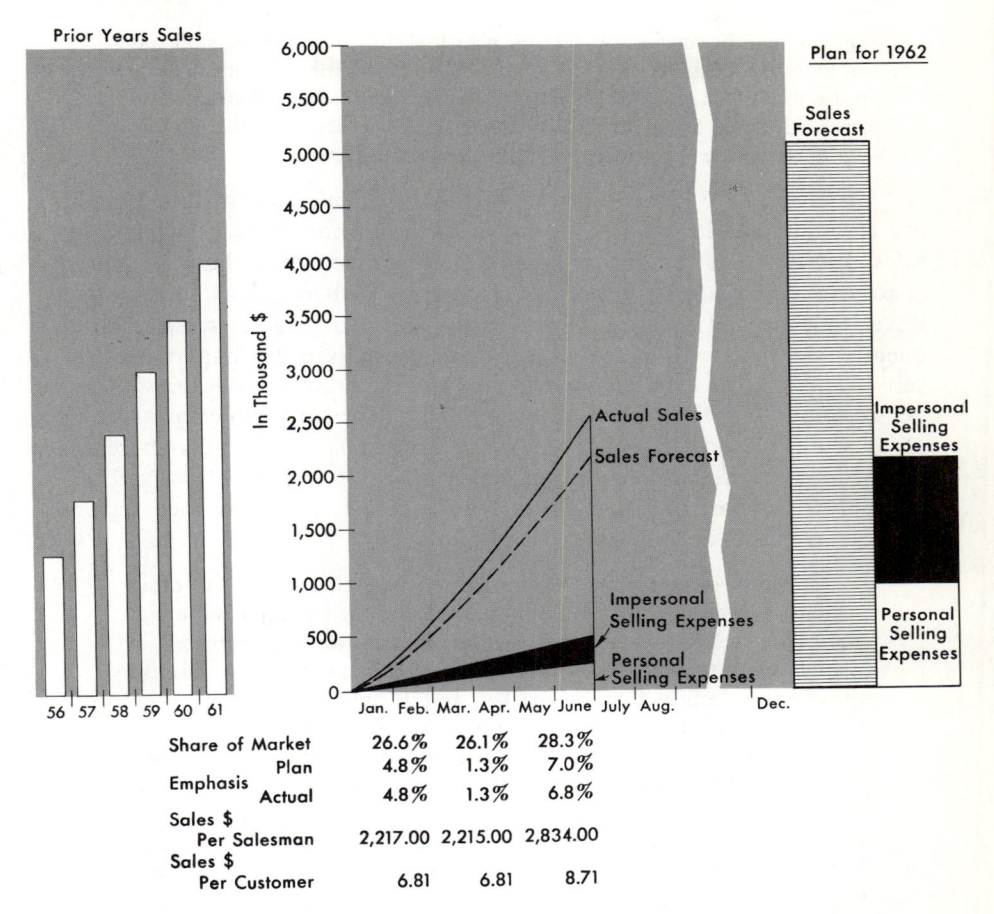

Source: Michael Schiff, "Reporting for More Profitable Product Management," *The Journal of Accountancy* (May 1963), p. 69. Copyrighted 1963 by the American Institute of CPAS.

product manager is supplied with prior years' sales to indicate the product's stage in the life cycle; actual and forecasted sales; actual and budgeted impersonal selling expenses (advertising and sales promotion) and personal selling expenses (field-selling costs); share of national market (supplied by an outside service); comparison of salesrepresentative's planned selling time on Product X versus actual selling time; and sales per salesrepresentative and sales per customer. At a glance several important bits of information are available. The figure is interpreted as follows:[8]

[8] Ibid., p. 68.

... it is apparent that sales exceeded forecast and that far less than one-half of the budgeted personal and impersonal expenses have been incurred. This could be the result of a seasonal pattern and is readily verified by reference to the budget. The field staff has apparently devoted time as planned, and the increase in sales is reflective of an increase in market penetration (share of market increased from 26.6 percent to 28.3 percent) accompanied by an increase in sales per salesman and sales per customer.

In Figure 21-3 share of market and sales per salesperson and customer are recorded for the six regions in which the company sells through fifty sales districts. The number of sales representatives varies because of the concentration in some regions of customers in urban areas and extended travel time needed in areas where customers are more scattered. Consequently, sales per customer and sales per salesperson are important measures. The southeastern region had the highest sales per salesperson and per customer and was second in market share. The poorest performance in all measures was in the western region. The reasons for these two extremes in performance are not known from this analysis. In Figures 21-4 and 21-5, an analysis similar to that made in Figure 21-2 is made for each region. These two charts are interpreted as follows:[9]

> The western region, despite its poor standing relative to other regions, shows sales above forecasted sales. Expenses incurred are at about the halfway point, and market penetration has increased in the last two months. It is well to note that in the second two months there was a drop in share of market, and this was followed by an increase in sales effort above plan (10.6 percent against 7.0 percent) with a sharp increase in sales and share of market. The product manager can now be rather specific in his discussions with the western regional manager relative to the shift in emphasis, the cost of the increased effort, and the products which as a result will receive less effort. Southwestern region shows increased sales, costs at less than half of the budgeted amount, increased market penetration but actual effort significantly below plan. The questions of why less effort was exerted by the sales force and its impact can now be reviewed. Perhaps greater sales and penetration would have resulted from applying the planned effort. Also what was the effect of the shift in effort from Product X to other products? Specific questions can be asked and the effects of alternative actions evaluated.

GROSS PROFIT VS. NET PROFIT ANALYSIS. An elementary form of profit analysis can be obtained through reviewing periodic data on gross profit, the amount left from revenues after paying for the cost of goods sold. The resulting gross profit is considered to be a contribution to marketing and general expenses, and profits. Sometimes the gross profit is

[9] Ibid., p. 69.

FIGURE 21-3
Comparison of Sales Data by Region

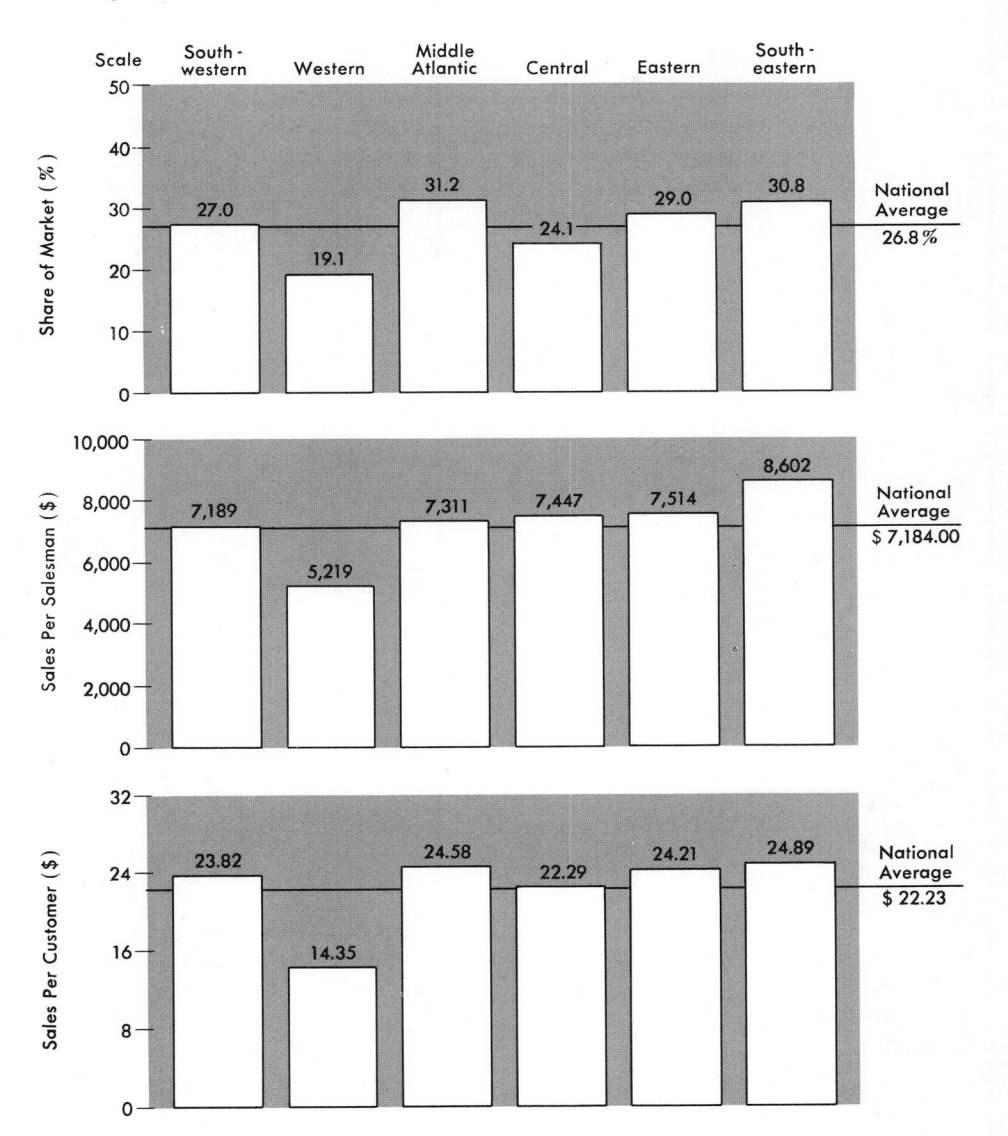

Scale	South-western	Western	Middle Atlantic	Central	Eastern	South-eastern	
Share of Market (%)	27.0	19.1	31.2	24.1	29.0	30.8	National Average 26.8%
Sales Per Salesman ($)	7,189	5,219	7,311	7,447	7,514	8,602	National Average $7,184.00
Sales Per Customer ($)	23.82	14.35	24.58	22.29	24.21	24.89	National Average $22.23

Source: Michael Schiff, "Reporting for More Profitable Product Management," *The Journal of Accountancy* (May 1963), p. 67. Copyrighted 1963 by the American Institute of CPAS.

FIGURE 21-4
Product X (Western Region)

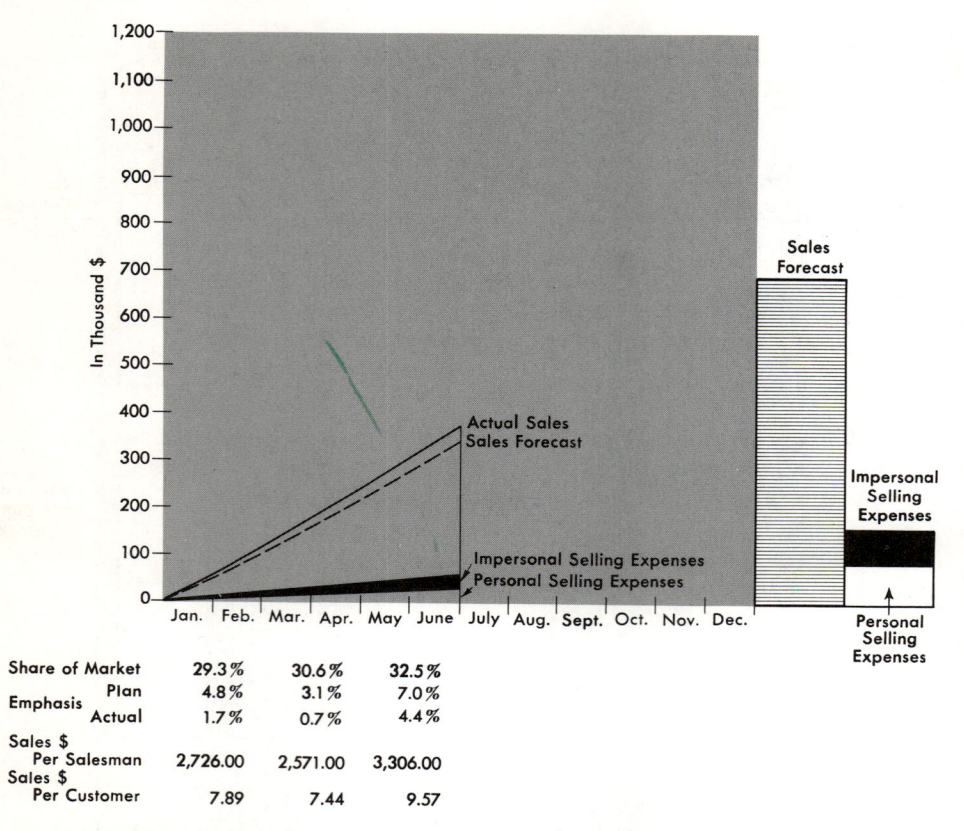

Share of Market	29.3%	30.6%	32.5%
Emphasis Plan	4.8%	3.1%	7.0%
Emphasis Actual	1.7%	0.7%	4.4%
Sales $ Per Salesman	2,726.00	2,571.00	3,306.00
Sales $ Per Customer	7.89	7.44	9.57

Source: Michael Schiff, "Reporting for More Profitable Product Management," *The Journal of Accountancy* (May 1963), p. 67. Copyrighted 1963 by the American Institute of CPAS.

adjusted by deducting direct selling expenses to arrive at an adjusted gross profit. If the cost of goods sold had been included in the analysis described in Figures 21-2 through 21-5 the adjusted gross profit would have been readily ascertainable.

When gross profit is calculated for specific responsibility centers, such as a territory, a product, a class of customer, or any other meaningful unit, it can be quite revealing. Often distinct differences between sales territories, products, or channels of distribution point toward the need for more complex research to determine causes.

Net profit for a responsibility center is the preferred measure. This, however, requires allocating every functional cost to every responsibility

FIGURE 21-5
Product X (Southwestern Region)

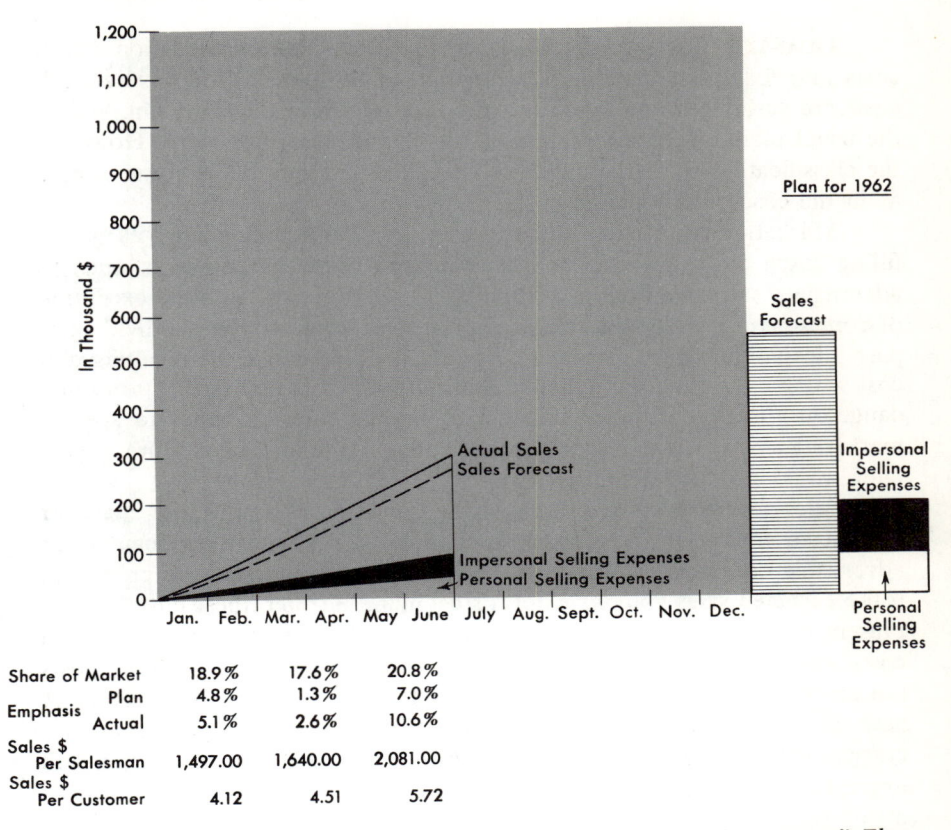

Share of Market	18.9%	17.6%	20.8%
Emphasis Plan	4.8%	1.3%	7.0%
Emphasis Actual	5.1%	2.6%	10.6%
Sales $ Per Salesman	1,497.00	1,640.00	2,081.00
Sales $ Per Customer	4.12	4.51	5.72

Source: Michael Schiff, "Reporting for More Profitable Product Management," *The Journal of Accountancy* (May 1963), p. 69. Copyrighted 1963 by the American Institute of CPAS.

center. In many instances there is no logical basis for doing so. Even though reasonable bases could be found, many executives argue that it is unfair to judge a responsibility center on costs over which those in authority in the center have no control. Because of the difficulty in allocation and the desire to judge fairly, most companies confine their analysis to adjusted gross profit. They vary the expenses deducted, depending upon ease of allocation and of controlling the responsibility center manager.

In the completion of costing performance measurement, it is often desirable to include the impact of alternative scales of potential operations. In the following subsection we briefly look at the impact of quantity on marketing costs. While such "scale" cost analysis is not strictly related to monitoring past performance, it does provide greater insight into cost-revenue analysis.

QUANTITY EFFECT ON MARKETING COST. The classification of all costs into fixed and variable is a function of the time period covered. All costs are variable in the long run, and all are fixed in the short run. Within the usual planning period of a year, the classification has merit. However, the classification of marketing costs into fixed and variable is not so simple as in the case of production costs.

Marketing costs are of three types: (1) sales-getting costs, (2) order-filling costs, and (3) sales-maintenance costs. Sales-getting costs, such as advertising, sales promotion, and personal selling costs, with the exception of commissions, cannot be related to any specific result. Simple dividing of past sales volume into historical cost data does not make the resulting unit cost variable. In fact, the dynamic nature of markets makes this procedure dangerous. Even if it were possible to impute sales revenues to specific marketing costs, there is no assurance that a similar expenditure a year later would produce a similar result.

Sales-getting costs are not variable. Once an expenditure is made or contracted for, such as sales representatives' employment agreements or advertising contracts awarded, it is most difficult to reverse the procedure if the expected sales volume is not forthcoming. Further, these costs are not present over the entire sales volume range, as is the case with those fixed costs associated with plant and production equipment. Sales-getting costs are made at different points in time over the entire sales volume range. A new cost situation exists each time additional sales-getting costs are incurred. They are fixed in nature and are analogous to the integration and aggregation of operating stages in production and must be represented as a step function.

Can they be disregarded, as in the case of fixed production costs? This would be a faulty approach, for two reasons. First, the sales-getting costs represent the greatest share of total marketing costs. Since marketing costs may represent almost 50 percent of selling price, to disregard them is to disregard a large proportion of cost. Second, it denies the opportunity to manage sales-getting costs in the short run.

Order-filling costs, such as packing, shipping, and transportation and delivery costs, are necessary because the sales-getting costs have been successful. In this case the cause-and-effect relationship between input and output is reversed. With order-filling costs the output, sales revenue, makes necessary the input, the order-filling costs. In most cases it is possible to relate these costs to specific sales. They are variable costs and can be assumed to be constant over a wide sales volume range.

Sales-maintenance costs are those which must be made to maintain a sales volume level. If sales-getting costs are successful in generating sales, it may be necessary to add additional sales personnel or new storage facilities or transportation equipment. These costs are closer to fixed rather than variable as are the sales-getting costs, and must be represented in a fixed-cost step function.

The greatest proportion of marketing costs are fixed for short periods of time. Since they are a substantial portion of total costs, they must be taken into consideration through a discontinuous cost function.

DIAGNOSTIC EVALUATION

One of the primary objectives in performance measurement is to arrive at the causal factors that caused operating deviations from expected results. Little is gained if all performance measurement does is indicate departures from expectations. To be meaningful, marketing administration must identify causes. Before we can say that the marketing program is properly administered, corrective action should be taken. The kinds of analyses discussed above sometimes do indicate the cause of a malfunction in the system; more often, however, they only indicate the departure from expectations, and specific studies must be made to get at the root causes. Most of these studies are conducted by market research, a unit in the organization whose prime responsibility is the gathering and analysis of information, generally to correct problem situations. An example will illustrate this aspect of control.[10]

Oceanic Industries (name fictitious) experienced a declining sales volume and deterioration of major accounts as measured against industry growths. The usual methods were used to jack up the sales force, a round of sales meetings, and a mass of written directives, with no appreciable improvement. Before effective control could be introduced, the company had to find out why there were deviations from expectations.

A review of the company's entire marketing program was made, and it revealed that the cause was poor planning and use of time by the sales force. They avoided systematic planning and spent most of their time with old accounts with whom they felt at home, and avoided the harder-to-sell, high-margin items in the line. It was decided that the solution to the problem lay in *changing the behavior of the sales representatives in the field.* At this point a new series of information-gathering forays was made and a plan devised to change the behavior. The steps in the plan were as follows:

[10] This example taken from Jon R. Katzenbach and R. R. Champion, "Linking Low-Level Planning to Salesman Performance," *Business Horizons,* 9 (Fall 1966), Graduate School of Business Administration, Indiana University, 91–100.

1. Translate corporate goals into specific performance criteria.
2. Determine the "opportunity gap," that is, the gap between actual and gross profit opportunity for each major account.
3. Establish gross profit potentials for each account for purpose of measuring current performance.
4. Establish other performance targets, such as sales expense targets, small order reduction targets for each account, and product-mix percentage goals for each major product category and each account.

Expectations on performance and actual performance for each salesperson were calculated in areas of: actual standing of each account against gross profit potential; sales expense ratio performance; ability to reduce orders below $20 for each account; and product-mix performance for each account. This information was made available monthly to each sales representative. Armed with up-to-date information on performance compared with company expectations, the sales representative could then plan his activities to correct deviations. With this added information it was relatively easy to determine how much time each account warranted.

Just where corrective action stops and a new phase of management planning begins in this case is difficult to determine. The remedy, however, is the establishment of a new system of control for monitoring past actions. It should be evident that control and information go hand in hand. Sometimes the information flow is on a continuous basis, such as that used to monitor past actions, and sometimes it results from specific studies designed to determine the causes of deviations from expectations.

MONITORING IMPENDING CHANGE

So far we have been discussing control in a passive sense. That is, provision has been made to monitor past actions on a continuous basis, and it was suggested that periodically specific information may be collected to remedy a malfunction in the system. In this sense control is passive and not anticipatory. Oftentimes indications of environmental change are present long before an actual change causes a deviation from expectations. Information on customers, channel members, competitors, and government actions should be collected and disseminated to decision-making executives on a continuous basis. The kind of market information discussed in Chapters 4, 5, 6, 7, and 8 should be carefully scrutinized for management use if it relates to an environmental change calling for a new direction in marketing effort. Information on channel members' actions, such as their sales volume, promotional activity, sales force quality, should be coming in continually, stored, and indexed for ready retrieval. Information on competitors' actions would seem to be essential. A carefully devised salesperson reporting system can supply information on competitors' moves in new product introductions, prices, and promotional activities. Last but not least, provisions must be made to keep abreast of the numerous actions of government that have an impact on markets and marketing activities. New laws, recent court decisions, government purchasing policies, and tax reforms are only a few of the many governmental actions which may affect the competitive environment.

Busy executives have little time to scan the thousands of bits of information that may be significant to them. Yet knowledge of the type suggested above would be helpful in many instances. Unless some means are found to provide this kind of information, the firm may find itself competitively displaced, even when the handwriting was on the wall years before deterioration set in in its market posture. In the next section attention is directed to a review of new technological developments in the area of marketing information systems.

MARKETING INFORMATION SYSTEMS

The term *marketing information system* is a general label used to describe the formal manner by which firms gather, process, and deploy information for purposes of marketing strategy planning and administration. Most firms have developed their own customized approach to information management to cope with the growing recognition of the need for orderly information in today's dynamic environment.

Given present technological development the computer hardware is available to process, manipulate, and store vast amounts of data. The potential of a computerized marketing information system lies in its speed in processing, its computational capability, and its tremendous data storage capacity, coupled with ease of retrieval. In this section we first direct our attention to the basic types of data normally included in a marketing information system. Next, the data structure and georeference systems available for organizing the information system structure are reviewed. The final subsection reviews recent developments in the field of management sciences closely related to the marketing information system.

WHAT CONSTITUTES THE BASIC DATA OF THE MARKETING INFORMATION SYSTEM?

The fundamental objective of a marketing information system is to collect the best possible data base for managerial use in planning and op-

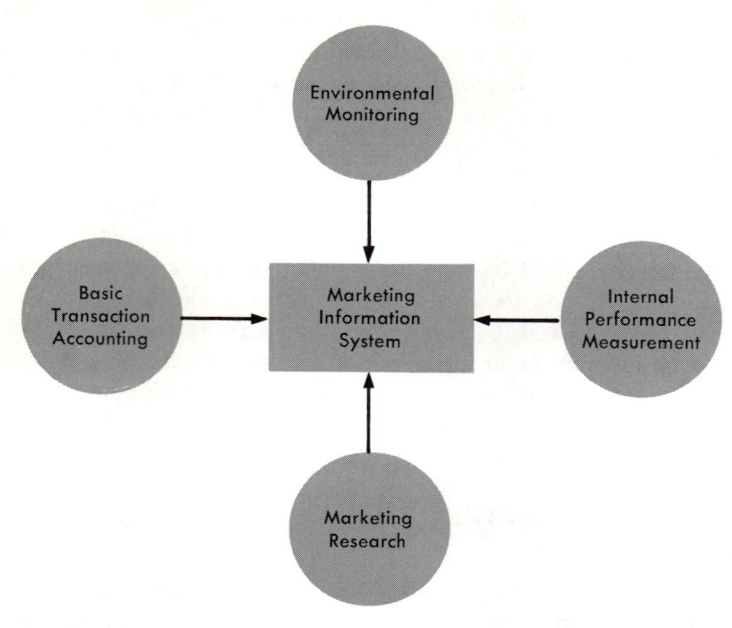

FIGURE 21-6
Components of Basic Marketing Information System

erational decision making. This means that the system must seek data related to all aspects of environmental monitoring and internal operations. The basic task is to provide management with a strategic assessment of where the firm has been, where it is, and the best possible estimate of where it is going.

The four basic sources of data which are integral to a marketing information system are detailed in Figure 21-6. Each is briefly discussed.

Environmental Monitoring

In Chapter 4 we discussed the importance of developing "sensing" devices to provide continued surveillance of the environment within which the firm must perpetuate itself. Environmental monitoring was defined as consisting of a "systematic review, appraisal, and projection of all aspects of the environment that involve existing and potential firm operations."[11] The data resulting from systematic environmental monitoring falls into six subenvironmental categories:

1. Economic.
2. Competitive.

[11] P. 57.

Administration

3. Technological.
4. Support.
5. Political and Legal.
6. Cultural and Social.

Basic trends in each area, coupled with an intelligence appraisal, should be regularly updated in the marketing information data base.

Internal Performance Measurement

The types of data included in the marketing information system based upon monitoring past performance were discussed earlier in this chapter. It is important that special analysis be included in the data base of the marketing information system in order to provide an accurate appraisal of the firm's present to expected position. No further elaboration is needed at this point of the importance of including performance analysis as an integral part of the marketing information system.

Marketing Research

Marketing research is the formal manner in which a firm conducts investigation and collection of data to support marketing strategy planning. The focal point of typical marketing research is the collection of data concerning market delineation and purchase behavior analysis for purposes of market segmentation and product-service matching. The input of marketing research into the marketing information system provides a selective source of data concerning an appraisal of opportunities which the firm can exploit in identification and attainment of objectives.

Basic Transaction Accounting

The prime source of data contained in the marketing information system is the routine recording and classification of sales transactions or invoices on a georeference basis. Computerized and centralized order processing results in a vast byproduct of information concerning basic demands being placed against a firm by its customers. The key in development of a comprehensive data base is to combine information available from orders and invoices with other informational flows within the enterprise. Table 21-3 provides a summary of data sources available from internal operations which represent important inputs to the marketing information system.

GEOREFERENCE CODING

Since marketing performance must be conducted in terms of the time and geographical aspects of competition, the most useful representation of

TABLE 21-3
Sources of Marketing Information

The source of most information about company sales is the order form and invoice, but various other documents, records, and reports also serve as raw material for sales reports, as the tabulation below indicates. Of course a single company is likely to draw on only two or three of these sources of sales information.

Document	Source Information Provided	Document	Source Information Provided
1. Order forms and invoices	Customer name, number, and location Product(s) or service(s) sold Volume and dollar amount of the transaction Salesman (or agent) responsible for the sale End use of product sold Location of customer facility where product is to be shipped Location of customer facility where product is to be used Customer's industry, class of trade and/or channel of distribution Terms of sales and applicable discount Freight paid and/or to be collected Shipment point for the order Transportation used in shipment	4. Salesmen's call reports (continued)	Products discussed Orders obtained Customer's product needs and usage Other significant information about customers Distribution of salesmen's time among customer calls, travel, and office work Sales related activities: meetings, conventions, etc.
2. Cash register receipts	Type (cash or credit) and dollar amount of transaction by department by sales person	5. Salesmen's expense accounts	Expenses by day by item, hotel, meals, travel, etc.
3. Salesmen's call reports	Customers and prospects called on (company and individual seen; planned or unplanned calls)	6. Individual customer (and prospect) records	Name and location and customer number Number of calls by company salesmen (agents) Sales by company (in dollars and/or units by product or service by location of customer facility) Customer's industry, class of trade, and/or trade channel Estimated total annual usage of each product or service sold by the company Estimated annual purchases from the company of each such product or service

550

TABLE 21-3
Sources of Marketing Information (Continued)

Document	Source Information Provided	Document	Source Information Provided
	Location (in terms of company sales territory)	10. Summary reports from distributors and dealers	Sales by product, geographic area, class of customer, etc.
7. Financial records	Sales revenue (by products, geographical markets, customers, class or trade, unit of sales organization, etc.) Direct sales expenses (similarly classified) Overhead sales costs (similarly classified) Profits (similarly classified)	11. Store audits	Unit and dollar volume and market share of consumer purchases of the company's brands in selected retail outlets
8. Credit memos	Returns and allowances	12. Consumer diaries (as a rule they cover only packaged foods and personal-care items)	Unit volume of purchases by package size of company's brand (and competing brands) made by selected families
9. Warranty cards	Indirect measures of dealer sales Customer service		Details about prices, special deals, and types of outlets in which the purchases were made

Source: National Industrial Conference Board, "Sales Analysis," *Studies in Business Policy*, No. 113.

data is in a coding structure which is referenced by geographical area. This form of data classification is referred to as *georeference coding*. Distribution of such data by geographical market and customer provides a structure of demand which the firm must cultivate to enjoy profitable growth.

A number of georeference classification structures have been developed. The six most commonly used are: (1) customer latitude and longitude point references, (2) county, (3) standard metropolitan statistical areas (SMSA), (4) economic trading areas, (5) ZIP codes, and (6) grid structures. It is not our objective here to elaborate these classification schemes in detail.[12] Some firms select to develop their own customized coding structures rather than use any standard system. However, since the 1970 census detail is available classified on a ZIP basis, coupled with the fact that ZIP codes are contained in almost all order processing files, this structure of coding is widely used.

MANAGEMENT SCIENCE DEVELOPMENTS (MIS)

Closely related to the development of marketing information systems is the fairly recent development of a wide variety of management science models available to assist in the performance of all managerial functions of marketing. Similar to the information system, management science developments have closely paralleled the advent of the computer. A *model* constitutes a body of information and restrictions about a unique situation accumulated for the purpose of systems analysis.[13]

Existing models can be grouped as analytical or simulation.[14] Analytical models strive to mathematically optimize the solution to a specific planning or operating problem. Simulation models replicate a process permitting repeated observation and experimental testing of solution to a planning or operating problem. While simulation does not optimize, its major benefit is that it allows an executive to change variables and assumptions systematically on a "what if" basis to observe a sensitivity measure of probable outcome in a matter of minutes.

[12] For detailed elaboration of geo-coding systems, see Pamela A. Werner, *A Survey of National Geo-Coding Systems* (Washington, D.C.: U.S. Department of Transportation, 1972), and Richard J. Lewis, *A Logistical Information System for Marketing Analysis* (Cincinnati, Ohio: Southwestern Publishing Co., 1970), pp. 33–34.

[13] The classical classification of model types is found in Jay W. Forrester, *Industrial Dynamics* (Cambridge, Mass.: The M.I.T. Press, 1961), Chapter 4.

[14] For an expanded discussion, see Donald J. Bowersox, *Logistical Management* (New York: Macmillan Publishing Co., Inc., 1974), Chapter 12.

Administration

The important point is to recognize that management science techniques have developed in conjunction with marketing information systems. In combination they provide aids or tools for more effective use of executive skill and judgment.

INTEGRATED MARKETING ADMINISTRATION

Figure 21-7 illustrates the overall perspective of integrated marketing administration. The total process of administration is concerned with keeping the enterprise in the desired state of competitive adjustment. Whenever the administrative process detects any indication of malfunction, management action must be initiated. Such action may vary from a flow of directives to

FIGURE 21-7
Integrated Marketing Administration

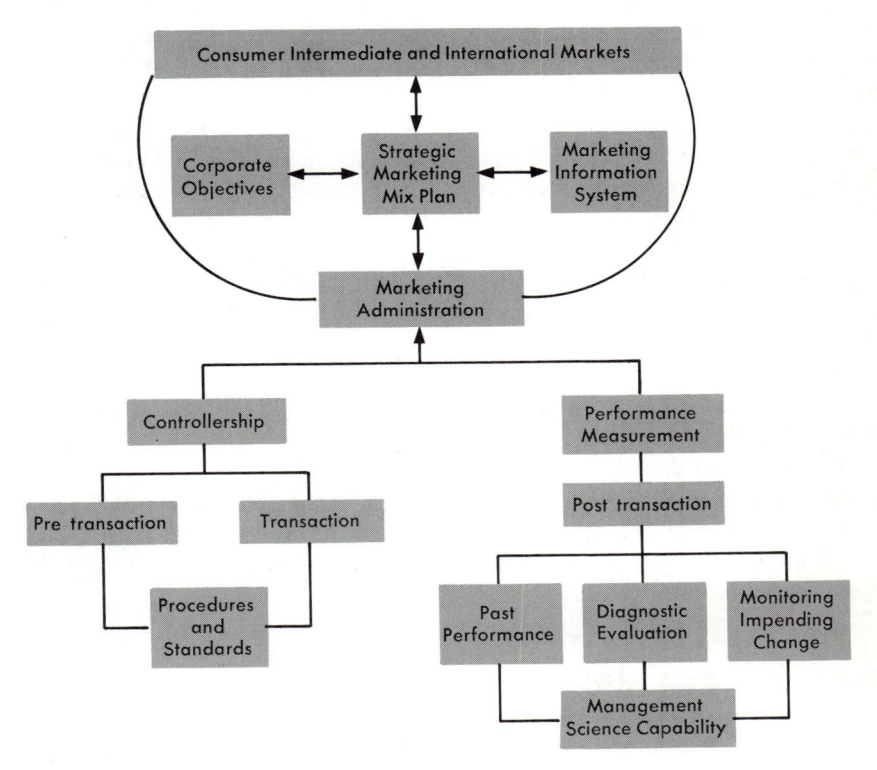

correct a specific problem, to conducting large-scale research in an effort to preplan various parts of the marketing mix to a basic change in corporate goals.

SUMMARY

Administration includes anything a firm is required to do to insure attainment of its specified objectives. The basic administrative function consists of control and performance measurement. Control is built into the operating system through programming product, distribution, and communication mixes and through mobilizing human and physical resources to execute the marketing strategy plan. Because of the impossibility of establishing exacting control devices, continuous performance measurement is required to determine whether the system is functioning as desired.

A great deal of difficulty can be experienced in collecting information for performance measurement. Three kinds of information are necessary if control is to be effective. The first is information to monitor past actions. This includes analyses of sales, market share, advertising, sales force, distribution, and cost and revenue. In each case the analysis should be made in such a way that it evaluates a responsibility or profit center. Although the firm functions as an integrated operating system, responsibility for activities is allocated to individuals. Control information must be assembled in such a way that performance of these responsibility centers is monitored. Second, information must be collected to determine the causes of malfunction so that the next round of reprogramming may begin. Generally this type of information is not collected on a continuous basis but rather in the form of separate studies. Third, information is needed which will indicate impending change in the environment.

The advent of marketing information systems is increasingly improving marketing administration. Utilizing the capability of electronic data processing, the marketing information system provides a synthesis of environmental monitoring, internal performance measurement, marketing research, and basic transaction accounting in a single data base. Closely coordinated to the development of marketing information has been a substantial advancement in the use of management science techniques for planning and administration.

QUESTIONS AND PROBLEMS

1. What is the meaning of control? Why are control devices needed for a sound program of marketing administration?

2. How does *transaction controllership* relate to *market programming?* Is the same relationship true of *pretransaction controllership?*
3. What is the *whiplash effect* in inventory control? What causes this effect?
4. To what extent do you feel marketing administration by necessity must be concerned with interorganizational behavior?
5. What is the significance of information in relationship to control?
6. What difficulties are present in collecting information and using it for control purposes? To what extent does georeference coding assist in this task?
7. Reflecting on your study of this book, why do you suppose it would be more difficult to precisely measure the marketing cost of a product than its production cost?
8. There is a current trend toward more emphasis on marketing profitability analysis as compared with marketing cost analysis. What difference do you see between the two? Which do you think would be more useful for the purposes of control devices? Why? What kinds of additional complexity are introduced by profitability analysis? Is one more suitable than the other for the emerging philosophy of this book? Why?

BIBLIOGRAPHY

BOWERSOX, DONALD J., *Logistical Management,* chapter 12. New York: Macmillan Publishing Co., Inc., 1974.

DEARDEN, JOHN, *Computers in Business Management.* Chicago: Dow Jones-Irwin, Inc., 1966.

DRUCKER, PETER F., "New Templates for Today's Organizations," *Harvard Business Review* (January–February 1974), pp. 45–53.

FORRESTER, JAY W., *Industrial Dynamics.* Cambridge, Mass.: The MIT Press, 1961.

GREINER, LARRY E., "What Managers Think of Participative Leadership," *Harvard Business Review* (March–April 1973), pp. 111–17.

KIRPALANI, V. H., and STANLEY S. SHAPIRO, "Financial Dimensions of Marketing Management," *Journal of Marketing,* 37 (July 1973).

KOCH, EDWARD G., "New Organization Patterns for Marketing," *Management Review* (February 1962), pp. 4–12.

LEWIS, RICHARD, *A Logistical Information System for Marketing Analysis,* Cincinnati, Ohio: Southwestern Publishing Co., 1970.

LUCK, DAVID J., HUGH WALES, and DONALD A. TAYLOR, *Marketing Research* (4th ed.), chapter 14. Englewood Cliffs, N.J.: Prentice-Hall, Inc., 1974.

MCLUHAN, MARSHALL, and JOHN MCLAUGHLIN, *Information Technology and Survival of the Firm.* Chicago: Dow Jones-Irwin, Inc., 1966.

SCHIFF, MICHAEL, "Reporting for More Profitable Product Management," *The Journal of Accountancy* (May 1963), pp. 65–70.

SEVIN, CHARLES H., *Marketing Profitability Analysis*. New York: McGraw-Hill Book Company, 1965.

VANCIL, RICHARD F., and PETER LORANGE, "Strategic Planning in Diversified Companies," *Harvard Business Review,* 53 (January–February 1975), 81–89.

WERNER, PAMELA A., *A Survey of National Geo-Coding Systems*. Washington, D.C.: U.S. Department of Transportation, 1972.

Part VI

THE UNIVERSALITY OF MARKETING

In Chapter 1 we established the relationship between competition and the way the firm conducts its market affairs. Our concern has been with the growth and survival of firms in competitive markets. As an organizing concept, marketing goes beyond the distribution of goods and services. It becomes a way of life for the enterprise. A free market system sanctions only those firms whose offerings are judged by the market to constitute a useful rendering of economic services. This establishes the rivalry of firms as the fundamental basis for the allocation of resources in the private sector of the economy. It is in meeting the requirements of effective competition that a firm attains the justification for its existence.

To avoid creating the impression that marketing is confined to institutions that function in a competitive system, we wish to explore differing degrees of competition and marketing's related role. There has been a discernible growth in institutions that do not function within the competitive system. An increasing number of members of the labor force have been employed by these institutions. It is our contention that marketing may be applied to the purposes of these noncompetitive entities. In fact, there is a universality to the application of marketing functions whenever there is an interphase, whether it be individual to individual, institution to institution, or individual to institution.

In terminating our discussion of marketing, we review in Chapter 23 the firm as a marketing and social entity. This final chapter is not presented as a rebuttal or a defense of contemporary marketing practice. Rather, the importance of adaptive behavior is elaborated in the context of today's social concerns.

Chapter 22

Marketing in Noncompetitive Systems

Throughout the book we have emphasized a philosophy of business management which conceives the firm as an entity in which market forces and opportunities provide the orientation for the design of whole systems of competitive action. We have purposely been concerned with the growth and survival of firms in competitive markets. Such firms make available to us the goods and services by which we measure our economic well-being. An important characteristic of the environment in which these enterprises engage is the free market system. It is the free market system that calculates the prices of inputs and outputs, and, as such, allocates resulting profits and losses which in turn energize economic activity.

Our treatment of marketing within such a free market system, however, is not dependent upon its application only in profit orientated enterprises. In this chapter, we examine the universality of the marketing approach by exploring its application to other types of institutions within our environment.

WHAT IS A NONPROFIT-MAKING INSTITUTION?

The assumption is frequently made that nonprofit institutions are not competitive and therefore do not require a marketing orientation. The distinction between profit-making and nonprofit-making institutions is not a valid basis for exploring differences in management orientation between institutions. A nonprofit institution is one in which the opportunity for profit is not essential to its initiation or the earning of profit essential to its continued existence. Many legal forms of organization, such as agricultural producer cooperatives and mutual insurance companies, do not rely on profit for existence. Nevertheless, such institutions represent many of the largest business enterprises in our economy. For example, Central Farmers System is owned by 20 regional farm supply cooperatives serving 42 states and parts of Canada. The system owns and operates four nitrogen manufacturing plants, two phosphate manufacturing plants, two potash manufacturing plants, a pipeline system, 11 strategically located storage terminals, and a retailer distribution system serving the needs of almost the entire United States argicultural market. Upon close examination, this cooperative functions precisely in the same manner as a profit-making organization. It probably should more appropriately be called a *corporative* rather than a *cooperative*.

Many mutual insurance companies chartered under various state laws are legally nonprofit institutions. These include The Prudential Insurance Company of America and the Metropolitan Life Insurance Company, two of the largest insurance companies in the United States.

In the public sector, the General Services Administration of the federal government is one of the largest business institutions in the country. It has been described as follows:

> GSA is the multibillion dollar business arm of the federal government, a conglomerate employing 40,000, controlling assets of $11.8 billion, and executing governmentwide policy and management activities. As one of the main construction arms of the government, it leases, owns, and maintains 10,000 buildings; procures over $2 billion annually in supplies and services; manages federal property disposal; provides computer and telecommunications service; develops governmentwide policies on procurement, federal property, automated data processing, management systems, and financial management; plans for the continuity of government operations in national emergencies; manages the national stockpile of critical and strategic materials; and keeps the records of the federal government through the National Archives system.

A regional warehouse of the General Services Administration located in Battle Creek, Michigan, operates as a wholesaling organization marketing millions of dollars worth of surplus government property per year. Management of the unit must perform each and all of the functions required by a profit-making wholesaler. It has extensive staff to perform the opportunity assessment activity, must match the product mix available with identified target markets, develop a marketing strategy plan including communications, selection of appropriate channels, and physical distribution capabilities, as well as price the products to be marketed. Execution of such a plan is no different from the administrative procedures followed in a profit-making organization.

In the above examples, it is difficult to differentiate the application of marketing practices from activities of profit-making institutions in the same lines of business. Whenever there are many nonprofit institutions operating in the same market, such as cooperatives and mutual insurance companies, they engage in a competition for differential advantage, just as do profit-making institutions. They must constantly renew their vitality through new product introductions and compete actively in the marketplace with all the skills they can develop. Finally, the success of this special type of institution is determined in a free market system.

In the case of the wholesale operations of the General Services Administration, the unit is compelled to function just as a profit-making institution because it competes with profit-making institutions. In developing countries where governments have entered the profit-making sector, it is a well-known fact that government-owned enterprises are much more successful when they must compete with nongovernment-owned profit-making enterprises. These nonprofit institutions differ only in that their existence is not solely dependent upon the free market system for survival. Paradoxically, they are competitive but they do not operate in a competitive system. Their continued existence is not dependent on profit. Their initiation and continuation is dependent upon administrative decision making by governmental, quasi-governmental, or institutional groups that are not a part of the competitive system.

On a continuum, we can recognize three states: (1) the *competitive state* engaged in only by profit-making institutions, (2) the *quasi-competitive state* engaged in by nonprofit institutions which must compete with similar institutions as well as profit-making institutions, and (3) the *noncompetitive state,* engaged in by nonprofit-making institutions that are created and continue to exist independent of the competitive system. These institutions may compete for consumers' attention or utilization of their services, but they are not competitive in the sense that the free market system is not the sole source of their survival.

Marketing as practiced by institutions in the competitive and quasi-competitive states is identical for all practical purposes. Marketing as a philosophy of managerial guidance may also be applied in the noncompetitive state. The remainder of this chapter is devoted to managerial marketing in a noncompetitive environment.

THE IMPORTANCE OF NONCOMPETITIVE INSTITUTIONS

Since the 1940s, the number of institutions that do not function in the competitive system has increased rapidly. In part, this has been caused by a reduction in the proportion of the labor force required in agriculture and manufacturing and the absorption of those released into the service sector. In 1973, 31 percent of the nonagricultural employed labor force was engaged in mining, contract construction and manufacturing; 5.9 percent in transportation and public utilities; and 63.1 percent in services.[1] This trend is continuing as a result of new technology introductions in manufacturing and the very large increase in the size of the labor force that occurred between 1964 and the mid-1970s. Because of the age composition of the population, 15 million entered the labor force between 1964 and 1975, the largest increase in any ten-year period in the history of the country. This represented a doubling of the number of workers in the 20 to 34 age group.[2] The majority of these new workers were absorbed in the service sector.

A closer look at the service sector shows that 32.5 percent of total services (20 percent of the total labor force) is engaged in federal, state, and local government. About 7.4 percent of the services sector (4.7 percent of the total labor force) is engaged in services such as "medical and other health services."[3] Many of these workers are employed in institutions such as hospitals or social agencies in the noncompetitive sector.

Current trends indicate that a large proportion of university graduates in the future will find employment in noncompetitive institutions. Marketing has an important role in the way these institutions conduct their affairs if they are to serve the purposes of society.

A FORMAT FOR NONCOMPETITIVE MARKETING

Whether the task is one of developing a marketing plan for a fund-raising program for a church, launching a family planning program, establishing an overseas trade mission for a state government, expanding a local hospital, developing and implementing a model cities program for a municipal government, or structuring a northeast corridor railroad system by the federal Department of Transportation, there is a common need to develop a support base.

Opportunity assessment through environmental monitoring is the starting point. Once the magnitude of the task is understood, the nature of the offering can be specified and the means used to gain receptivity can be formulated into a marketing strategy plan. Execution of the plan is constrained only by the plan's specifics, good management, and available re-

[1] Compiled from data in the *Statistical Abstract of the United States*, 1974, pp. 347–49.

[2] Seymour L. Wolfbein, "The Emerging Labor Force of the United States" (Unpublished report. Temple University).

[3] *Statistical Abstract of the United States*, 1974, p. 349.

sources. This format in principle is not much different from our steps in marketing strategy planning presented in Chapter 4: (1) environmental monitoring, (2) identification of objectives, (3) selection of target markets, (4) formulation of the marketing mix, and (5) resource allocation and mobilization (Figure 4-2). The specifics of each step, as we shall now examine, depart only slightly from our earlier treatment.

In the noncompetitive sector, at least two situations exist which may directly benefit from a marketing orientation to planning. The first is when the process requires the creation of a new institution or a restructuring of old institutions. This we call *noncompetitive institution building,* which includes such programs as building a new hospital, a community college, a church, or establishing an overseas office of a state government. A second situation occurs when the objective is to change a value system or precipitate new behavior patterns. This we call *behavior change,* which includes such programs as those associated with the United Community Chest campaign, a family planning program, or a reduction in drug use program. In the latter case, an existing institution may be established as part of the program, but if the change in behavior is accomplished the institution is no longer needed. Some examples of the application of marketing activities in each of these situations follow.

NONCOMPETITIVE INSTITUTION BUILDING

Any number of examples can illustrate marketing in the creation and operation of noncompetitive institutions. We have selected the establishment of an overseas trade office for a state government and a program of national market integration. The latter was very extensive and has resulted in the establishment of a number of institutions.

Establishing A Trade Mission

The first example to illustrate this situation is the establishment of a state overseas trade mission office.[4] In the early 1970s, the State of Michigan opened trade missions in Tokyo, Japan, and Brussels, Belgium. In early 1975, the state was considering opening an office in Sao Paulo, Brazil. The general purpose of such an office was: (1) to assist Michigan firms in acquiring information on foreign market opportunities for export of their products, (2) to inform foreign firms of investment opportunities in Michigan, and (3) to inform Michigan firms of investment opportunities abroad.

The first stage of a marketing program to establish an office is to

[4] Courtesy of P & G International, Kalamazoo, Michigan.

Marketing in Noncompetitive Systems

make an opportunity assessment of the area in which the office is to be located. In general terms, the future of Brazil could be assessed by the following data:

1. 10 percent annual level of real economic growth sustained for nine years.
2. Manufacturing increased 14 percent annually.
3. In 1973 savings at a rate of 23 percent of GNP.
4. Foreign capital inflow—$3.7 billion in 1973 with U.S. contributing 37.4 percent.
5. In 1973 total imports into Brazil $6 billion, and expected to double in 1974.
6. U.S. exports to Brazil in 1973 $1.9 billion.
7. Between 1971 and 1973 Michigan exports to Brazil increased $15.7 million.

The above data indicate that the Brazilian market represents an ideal opportunity for export of United States goods. The overall purpose of opportunity assessment for marketing strategy planning is to identify objectives and select target markets. In the Brazilian example, specific objectives and target markets of the proposed office were identified as follows:

A. Determination of Brazilian Export Targets
   1. Trend analysis and current volume of Michigan exports to Brazil in selected industries.
   2. Overall volume of Brazilian imports of comparable products and evaluation of capabilities to produce locally.
   3. Estimation of future potential by industry grouping based on findings in (1) and (2).
   4. Summary of existing and proposed legislation affecting imports or production in pertinent industries.
B. Determination of Michigan Investment Targets
   1. Assessment of magnitude and growth of Brazilian exports to the United States in selected industries.
   2. Determination of industry groupings or product lines representing the most favorable prospects for potential direct or indirect investment in Michigan.
   3. Summary of relevant Brazilian legislation affecting foreign investment outflows and anticipated modifications.

Once data are gathered, specific product groups can be identified for export cultivation. With the specific products selected, the development of the marketing mix to achieve the objectives is formulated and represented in the next phase of the program:

A. Comparative Evaluation of Representation Alternatives
1. Varying levels of representation will be presented and evaluated on the basis of activities performed, time schedules, and the cost-benefit considerations of each.
2. Determination of recommended informal and/or formal commitments to increased Brazilian activity consistent with the above findings and objectives and priorities of the Office of Economic Expansion.
B. Implementation of Designated Proposal
1. Assistance, through professional and personal contacts, in all phases of establishing informal or contractual agreements and/or field offices as deemed necessary by the anticipated level of involvement of the Office of Economic Expansion in the Brazilian market.
2. Development of recommendations regarding: possible location sites, negotiations, personnel requirements, operating cost estimates, operating objectives, and performance review criteria.

Instead of selecting a product, distribution, communications and price mix, concern is focused on linkages required to operationalize the program both in Michigan and Brazil. The formulation of the marketing mix necessitates the identification of information concerning operational practices in export-import trade which require dissemination and delineation of selling activities for involved Michigan manufacturing concerns. Once the marketing mix is developed, a number of alternatives concerning varying levels of representation, such as number of offices, personnel requirements, and legal requirements, require review. Upon selection of the best combination, resource requirements can be mobilized and allocated to implement the marketing strategy plan.

Institutional Building in Latin America

A second example is a program in national market integration developed in four Latin American countries. In 1965 Walt W. Rostow, counselor and chairman of the Policy Planning Council, United States Department of State, introduced the concept of *national market integration.* The problem visualized was one of "have and have not." In most developing countries more than half the labor force is engaged in agriculture at a very low level of subsistence. These people do not participate in the market economy. Most such economies suffer from food shortages. It was appropriate that any such program be initiated in the agricultural sector. The role of marketing toward stimulating such change was as follows:

First, the farmer must receive a reliable and fair price for his product. Second, credit must be made available at reasonable rates for him to make the change in the character of his output or the shift in productivity desired. Third, there must be available, on the spot, technical assistance that is relevant to his soil, his weather conditions, and his change in either output or in productivity.

Finally, there must be available at reasonable rates two types of industrial products: inputs such as chemical fertilizers, insecticides, and farm tools; and incentive goods—that is, the consumer goods of good quality he and his family would purchase in greater quantity or work harder to get if they were cheaper or if his income were higher.[5]

In this context, marketing was involved in a two-way flow from the urban to the rural sectors and vice versa. Environmental monitoring revealed that in the urban sectors a very small proportion of the population—the wealthy—pay high prices for the trickle of foodstuffs that do reach the market on an uncertain supply basis. Manufactured goods are out of reach of the majority of the rural sector and a large proportion of the urban sector as well. Incentives for increased investments and higher outputs in manufacturing are generally as dismal as in the agricultural sector. The inability to visualize a large market with effective demand is also a barrier to expansion in the nonfood sector. More specific environmental monitoring and marketing research was required to identify barriers to innovative action. It was hypothesized that a set of relationships which explain action or the lack of it exists among manufacturers, urban consumers, agricultural producers, agricultural consumers, wholesalers, and retailers.

Until the existing state of the market system was fully described, little could be accomplished concerning the development of concrete programs for improvement. In the Cauca Valley of Colombia these marketing research studies investigated the following:[6]

    A. Description of the Existing Market System.
        1. Volumes of production and direction of the flow of selected agricultural products.
        2. Outlines of the channels of distribution from the rural sec-

[5] Walt W. Rostow, "The Concept of a National Market and Its Economic Growth Implications," *Marketing and Economic Development,* ed. Peter D. Bennett. Proceedings of the Fiftieth Anniversary, International Symposium on Marketing, American Marketing Association, (September 1965), pp. 14–15.

[6] Unpublished documentation from a study described in Harold Riley, et al., *Market Coordination in the Development of the Cauca Valley Region—Colombia,* Research Report No. 5, Latin American Studies Center (East Lansing, Mich., 1970) Michigan State University.

tion to the urban section for five selected products. Outlines of the channels of distribution of agricultural inputs and consumption goods from the urban sector to the rural area. These outlines will include the wholesale levels as well as the retail, the stages of storage, transport, and warehousing, the number of middlemen with their respective functions. This description will be complemented in terms of physical volumes, value of the commercialized products, percentages of the flow of the commercialized production, and margins of commercialization.
3. Description and measurement of the structure of the process of urban marketing for some food products and durable and semidurable goods in terms of the characteristics of the products, volume commercialized, value of the products, margins of commercialization.
4. Description and measurement of the investment factors, consumption and urban and rural savings, and obtaining of adequate indicators for these variables.

B. Identification and Explanation of the Specific Obstacles for a Process of Efficient Marketing, a Greater Production, and a Betterment of the Consumption.
1. For rural areas
   a. System and forms of tenure.
   b. Problems and availability of credit.
   c. Degree of acceptance of modern agricultural practices.
   d. Problems of treatment and classification of products, storage, warehousing, transport, losses of quality, and other adverse conditions in the market.
   e. Cost-price relations in the production price policy.
   f. Availability of information on prices and of the market.
2. For urban areas.
   a. Structure of costs and margins according to participants within the process (wholesalers, transporters, retailers).
   b. Patrons of buying and preference of the consumers.
   c. Relations between size, organization, and coordination of the market with the efficiency of the process.

The number of barriers to innovative action were numerous, but perceptions of market risk seem to predominate. Often these perceptions by some participants are not based on fact, but a sufficient number are to rule out increased market participation moves. In northeast Brazil, among food and nonfood producers and the corresponding middlemen, it was found that invariably a very narrow concept of potential market size existed. No thought was given to remerchandising products in the nonfoods sector or establishing better price-income ratios to cater to those at the bottom level of the socioeconomic scale. The potential payoff of such a market orientation had been urged for some time by the Brazilian Ministry of Planning, but it was not heeded in spite of very favorable fiscal incentives to participate. A similar attitude prevailed among food producers, but the perceptions of market risk were more closely allied to structural problems within the channels of distribution. Instability of price because of poor communications, monopsony on the demand side, poor transportation and the risk of spoilage, and inadequate middlemen to handle a greatly increased output were common explanations. Middlemen's concepts of market risk were closely tied to perceptions of limited market size plus all of the market structure difficulties perceived by food producers. A number of other more personal perceptions, such as "live and let live," and "trust in God," and extended family considerations were also prevalent. But these were not strong among the high performers as measured by local standards of performance.

The number of obstacles identified in the above example were large, but only following such a thorough environmental monitoring was their articulation possible in terms of objectives and the selection of target markets for specific action. Illustrative of the shortage of food in the urban areas was the wholesale structure. Wholesalers were highly specialized to specific products and had capacity limited to stocking about two days' supply. One objective selected was improvement of the wholesale structure. Investigation revealed that there was extensive legislation concerning the size of inventory that wholesalers were permitted to carry. This legislation had its foundation on the assumption that wholesalers are speculators, parasites on the economy, and only drive prices up. A target market was to change governmental attitudes and win a repeal of such legislation. Another target market was the establishment of product-mixing or sorting warehouses in urban centers to achieve economies of scale and assure a larger available urban food supply.

In the rural areas, efficient assembly operations suffered from poor storage facilities and a lack of systematic standards or grades. Farmers brought their output to market in high-cost antiquated transportation resulting in small units of transport and extensive spoilage. Where assembly operations did exist, the lack of standard grading required separating each supplier's output for sale only by inspection. This investigation identified three target markets requiring action. First, a system of grading had to be established and implemented. Second, a more efficient rural storage system had to be planned, financed, and constructed. Third, a more efficient transportation network had to be planned and executed.

In each target market selected for action, a different marketing mix had to be established to achieve the identified objective. In each case, there is an element of matching a need with a service structure or behavioral change. The need for a distribution, communications, or price mix varies from target market to target market. In every case, there is a need to mobilize and allocate resources to remedy the situation.

We have purposely adopted the format recommended in Chapter 4 to guide marketing strategy planning in order to illustrate the use of marketing in noncompetitive institution building. The terminology may be changed but the analytical and action processes are identical to those used in the competitive and quasi-competitive systems.

BEHAVIOR CHANGE

If the objective is behavior change, more reliance is based on persuasion through communication than on institutional structure. A guiding concept underlies the process and directs the development of the marketing strategy plan. Establishment of a new set of ideas involves change—in attitudes, values, norms, and, possibly, structure. Existing attitudes, values, and norms determine how people will behave. The attitudes, values, and norms prevailing at any time are a result of relationships established between individuals and/or individuals and institutions. To change behavior, it is necessary to study the relationships to determine which establish attitudes, values, and norms hostile to the desired behavior pattern.[7] With this objective, environmental monitoring related to behavior change is slightly different than its counterpart in noncompetitive institution building.

Family planning will be used to illustrate the application of marketing toward the objective of behavior change. The treatment, however, is equally applicable to fund raising, gasoline conservation, or abortion reform.

Family Planning Program

In the case of family planning, a large number of relationships are involved which may or may not be hostile to the idea of smaller families. To select only a few, we can name the husband/wife relationship, the family/church relationship, the medical-service/family relationship, the relationship involved in the purchase of related products. These relationships can be examined by standard marketing research techniques. For example, in many countries, the husband/wife relationship is hostile. The wife wishes to practice family planning, but the husband does not concur in that his masculinity may be challenged by his peers. In the same environment, it was thought that the attitude of the Roman Catholic Church represented a hostile relationship. Study revealed that when Pope Paul VI delivered his encyclical on birth control, the vast majority of the target populace did not even know what an encyclical was, let alone how it related to birth

---

[7] See "The Guiding Concepts" (Unpublished paper. Inter-University Research Program in Institution Building, 1964).

control. The medical-service/family relationship can be a hostile one if the medical profession is dubious about the health complications of various contraceptives. The relationships involved in the acquisition of necessary products often may have a hostile environment. The marketing of such products in most countries has not come anywhere near the marketing of other pharmaceutical and health care products.

Once hostile relationships have been identified, it is necessary to identify objectives and select target markets for action. In the example above, the church/family relationship was considered important at first but was later discarded as a target for action. The husband/wife relationship represented a hostility which required attention. Likewise, the relationships existing in the purchase situation offered a desirable target market. In each case, additional research was necessary to identify the real causes of the hostility. How strong is the threat to masculinity drive, how is it expressed, who is the decision maker in the size of family, what is the leadership in peer groups? Similar questions arise in the typical marketer's study of purchase behavior motivation. How accessible is the desired product, is it displayed, is embarrassment present in purchase, is price acceptable? With answers to these and related questions it is possible to begin to develop a marketing strategy plan to weaken the attitudes, values, and norms that are hostile to the behavior change desired.

In this respect, the family planning agency generally must make linkages with the participants through the leadership existing in each set of relationships. The messages or doctrines that must be diffused should be developed on the basis of the findings uncovered in the environmental monitoring. The program which emerges must be aimed at reducing specific hostilities existing in the relationships selected for action. Resource mobilization and allocation in this type of behavior change must be maintained for a considerable length of time because anticipated change will be slow. Through time the nature of the activities and relationships evolving between participants in each target market must be studied. Constant monitoring of the program and appropriate feedback concerning the change in hostility are needed in order to modify programs as necessary to realize objectives. The marketing of behavior change, similar to private enterprise marketing strategy planning, is a circular process.

We have purposely once again adopted the format used to guide marketing strategy planning to illustrate the use of marketing in these kinds of noncompetitive settings. Similar to noncompetitive institution building, the terminology might be changed but the analytical and action processes need only be modified slightly over those used to create change in the competitive or quasi-competitive systems.

The opportunities to apply marketing in noncompetitive systems are numerous. An interesting exercise is to speculate on how marketing strategy planning can be applied to passing a new mill rate to finance a sewage disposal plant for a suburban community or how a strategy may be formulated to establish a marketing system for surgical transplants.

SUMMARY

The application of marketing is not confined to profit-making enterprises within a competitive system. In fact, there is little difference between marketing in the competitive system over the quasi-competitive system. Many nonprofit institutions, such as agricultural producer cooperatives and mutual insurance companies, follow a marketing orientation identical to profit-making institutions in the same lines of business. Likewise, some government-owned nonprofit-making institutions, because they are in competition with profit-making institutions, must apply the same marketing expertise as those with whom they compete. There is, however, a noncompetitive system composed of an increasing number of institutions whose existences are not dependent upon the free market system.

In the noncompetitive system, two situations were identified to which marketing can be applied. First, there are those in which a new institution, such as a hospital, a community college, a church, or a restructuring of an old institution, such as a northeast corridor railroad system, is desired to accomplish a specific objective. This activity we have identified as noncompetitive institution building. Second, there is a form of marketing activity which is targeted to changing existing values in an effort to precipitate new behavior patterns; for example, realizing a more successful United Community Chest Campaign or establishing a favorable attitude toward family planning. We called this form of noncompetitive marketing behavior change.

In each case, the format for marketing strategy planning is useful to guide executive action. Environmental monitoring, identification of objectives, selection of target markets, formulation of a marketing mix, and mobilization and allocation of resources are applicable to noncompetitive situations wherein change is the desired target with only slight modification as typically used in competitive and quasi-competitive situations.

QUESTIONS AND PROBLEMS

1. What is a nonprofit institution?
2. Give some examples of nonprofit institutions that engage in marketing in precisely the same way as do profit-making institutions.
3. What are the key elements of a competitive system?

4. Why is an understanding of the way in which noncompetitive institutions function important to the college graduate?

5. How might a marketing systems approach to national market integration work?

6. Explain the difference between noncompetitive institution building and behavior change situations as they relate to the application of marketing management.

7. What is meant by "centers of hostility" in those situations where a change in behavior is the objective?

8. Someone has said, "Sears, Roebuck has done more good in South America than the State Department." On what grounds might this be a plausible statement?

Chapter 23

The Firm as a Marketing and Social Entity

In concluding our treatment of managerial marketing, we summarize our exposition and explore some emerging social issues that either are directly related to marketing practice or may profoundly affect marketing practice in the future.

THE FIRM AS A MARKET ENTITY

Throughout this book you have been exposed to a philosophy of enterprise administration that conceives of the firm as a market entity in which market forces and opportunities provide the orientation systems and subsystems of competitive action. This concept is the fundamental meaning of a market orientation. It represents the focal point around which resources are mobilized and allocated to serve markets productively and efficiently in the achievement of corporate objectives.

Our concern has been with the growth and survival of firms in competitive markets. A free enterprise system sanctions only those firms whose market offerings are judged by the market to constitute a useful rendering of economic services. This establishes rivalry between firms as the fundamental basis for the allocation of resources throughout the economy. It is through this rivalry that we are confronted with competition and competitive strategies. In meeting the requirements of effective competition, a firm obtains the justification for its existence and derives its corporate vitality.

The level of uncertainty prevailing within the competitive system results in continuous fluctuations from an equilibrium state and leads the firm to seek superiority over its rivals. Thus, the firm seeks differential advantage—a form of competitive distinctiveness which separates it from its rivals and constitutes the basis for enduring economic strength. The firm is a market entity.

Because the market is the crucial point of action, we have dealt at some length with investigation of market forces and the measurement of market opportunity. The firm seeks a market offering that blends its competency in an optimum way with the complexity of market variables. Markets have important quantitative and qualitative dimensions. Each has its subtleties and obscure elements. The tools of measurement for the analysis of both components have advanced over the years, and we have attempted to show some of the methodology that can currently be brought to bear in this area.

The market offering, no matter how conceived, is only significant when placed in the complex of market forces operating at a particular time and place. This consideration provides the foundation for formulation of product strategy. Products are a large part, although not the total composition, of the market offering. Products and related services are the principal linkages of a firm with its markets.

The product mix is but one part of the broader marketing mix. There is a distribution mix that serves to move products through time and space into purchase and use. Consequently, the distribution network to be employed has both a logistical and a market cultivation element. It is through reconciling the cost-revenue capabilities of varying institutional arrangements that the ultimate channel of distribution is selected. These choices are of increasing complexity because of the conglomerate nature of competition that now prevails. We have recognized that entire production-marketing systems are in competition with other whole systems: one particular blend of manufacturer-distributor-dealer organizations competes with another. This sets up the conditions of both conflict and cooperation within the network itself. Within these conditions of interorganizational behavior, the complex issues of physical distribution must be resolved.

If the product offering, with its accompanying services, has been structured properly, the market or exchange process will be actuated through information flows. The offering must be communicated in a way that builds impact at the point of ultimate purchase. The market at any given time holds an inventory of information related to the solution of its own problems, which are solved through its procurement of goods and services. The marketer is most effective when he moves the potential purchaser along a path to his desired end purpose or self-image. The marketer needs therefore to close the gap between the information held in various parts of the market and the information it should hold if purchase action favorable to the seller is to be precipitated. Advertising, sales promotion, and personal selling are alternative methods for communicating with a market. To a degree, they can be substituted. This condition requires the formulation of a communications mix to be used in market cultivation. Determining appropriations for various forms of communication constitutes a most difficult problem. But it cannot be escaped.

The fact that we have treated pricing last has not been by accident. Neither does it necessarily reflect the significance of pricing. Price is a monetary expression of value and is the focal point of the entire exchange process. The customer can perceive the attractiveness of the market offering only through the price mechanism. In so doing he or she reflects a large number of objective and subjective evaluations in perception of the compatibility of the value represented with his or her own desired goals. On the other hand, price is a reflection of all the actions of the firm. Price serves to integrate supply with demand, and for this reason its theoretical, legal, and managerial aspects have been explored. Finally, price as a competitive instrument is an alternative to the use of other means of market cultivation that seek to insulate the firm from direct competitive forces. The end goals of managerial marketing must be combined and integrated into a marketing strategy plan. This involves environmental monitoring, identification of objectives, selection of target markets, and the formulation of the marketing mix. Resource allocation and mobilization is initialed through organizational alignments and measured by marketing administration.

If you now have an integrated philosophy of the managerial implications of the firm as a market entity, we have done our job well. The application of the approach to a number of institutions in the noncompetitive sector demonstrates the universality of marketing. Marketing will be increasingly called upon to contribute to the solutions of institutions outside the competitive system.

CONTEMPORARY ISSUES RELATED TO MARKETING PRACTICE

Just as managerial marketing serves the purposes of the enterprise, it is a party to concerns among those vitally interested in the overall welfare of society. Likewise, a number of other societal issues have emerged which may have a profound effect on the way in which the enterprise conducts its market affairs in the future. No extensive treatment is intended; rather, a scenario of vital concerns is reviewed.

MARKETING RELATED ISSUES

In this section, societal concerns that can be directly related to managerial marketing practice are examined under product strategy, communication strategy, and price, cost, and profit.

Product Strategy

A central focus of managerial marketing is the "maintenance of profitable market leadership through responding to buyers' needs and wants." With such a guiding concept, it is difficult to perceive how product strategies as developed by the firm can adversely affect society's welfare. Upon closer examination, however, it is evident that the continuous search for differential advantage coupled with the dynamics of rapid neutralization created the potential for planned *product obsolescence*. That is, consumers charge that products are either designed and produced to have a shorter life span than is desired or that products with additional useful lives are removed from the market because of reduced profitability resulting from excessive new product introductions.

Superfluous differentiation is equally spurned by large numbers of consumers and critics of the social scene. In the race for market leadership the enterprise frequently relies on cosmetic or nonfunctional differentiations to achieve objectives. The market response is critical of the additional social and economic cost of such proliferation.

More recent criticisms have been leveled at manufacturers for offering unsafe products. *Product safety* has become a major concern in the marketplace. To mention a few, automobiles, foods, drugs, and toys have been the targets of these criticisms. An elaborate regulatory structure has resulted to protect consumers. The supplier has been given the choice of a tradeoff between court-determined liability or the cost of more extensive testing before products are placed on the market.

In a more subtle vein, products that are indiscriminate in their use of depletable resources have come under attack. *Resource depletion* occurs when it is thought that the social cost is greater than the economic benefit to society. The large "gas-guzzling" automobiles have become increasingly repugnant to a substantial sector of the buying public. Closely allied is the excessive utilization of resources that pollute or endanger the environment. The use of freon in spray containers and packaging that is not biodegradable are thought by many to be excesses.

Communication Strategy

Communication, whether it be advertising, personal selling, sales promotion, or publicity is all persuasive. Although necessary to the functioning of a free economy, they are susceptible to *false and misleading representation*. In this sense, they do not serve a market purpose and are damaging, not only to the consumer but also to the enterprise which exerts care to avoid willful misrepresentation.

Of more recent origin is a concern over *cultural pollution* resulting from the excessive bombardment of messages that saturate and assault the dignity of mankind. Excessive reliance on sex and violence in the audio, printed, and visual media, as well as unwarranted interruption in communication, is of increasing concern to social critics. Not only is it annoying, but the charge has been made that it has had an affect in changing values, especially of the young.

Price, Cost, and Profit

The efficiency of the marketing system is judged by the consumer in terms of the price he must pay for products. If the price is thought to be too high, a normal reaction is to blame excessive costs or profits. The costs of superfluous differentiation, planned product obsolescence, and unwanted communications all have been villains in increasing prices to the consumer. Coupled with the cost element in the profit equation is the taking of unwarranted profits by the enterprise. To many, this is possible because of the capability of the firm to manipulate the consumer through marketing practices.

SOCIETAL RELATED ISSUES

In this section, we examine some contemporary social issues to which marketing practice is related. Although it cannot be said that marketing practice is responsible for these concerns, they do reflect an impact on the future of managerial marketing. Antigrowth mentality, resource depletion, and environmental concern are selected for examination.

Antigrowth Mentality

A large segment of society is becoming increasingly worried about worshiping economic growth as the cornerstone of our social objectives. The materialistic thrust of our culture, the general affluence already achieved, our declining population growth, and the failure to allocate resources to public goods all are given as reasons for re-examining our directions. Competition for differential advantage is a system in which market leadership is achieved through a cycle of innovation, neutralization, and reinnovation. Any change in our economic growth objectives strikes at the very heart of current marketing practice.

Resource Depletion

Selected groups place limits on our growth potential based on the available supply of resources. A conservation mode is the recommended solution. To the extent that a limited growth policy is sought, the effect is similar to the impact of an antigrowth mentality. On the other hand, additional implications are present for marketing practice. Concern over resource depletion cannot help but result in stricter controls on the freedom of production. Freedom of choice in production is an integral part of the competitive system, of which marketing is more than an incidental segment.

Environmental Concern

Although all environmental concerns are not related directly to the marketing of goods and services, the procedures used to protect and improve environmental quality can be expected to have a direct effect on marketing practice. The Environmental Protection Agency and the Office of Technology Assessment, with their rights of approval on selected products, greatly increase the risks of new product innovation. As well, the tendency to set standards for products may reduce the scope of substantive product differentiation and may inadvertently cause superfluous differentiation.

CONCLUSION

These, then, are some of the issues facing marketers in the contemporary business scene. Many of the issues directly related to marketing practice have intensified the consumerism movement and, in part, have resulted in a critical attitude concerning economic growth, the establishment of the Environmental Protection Agency, and the Office of Technology Assessment, and even the articulation of social indicators to measure the quality of life.

No rebuttal is or should be offered to these developments. In many instances, the concern is genuine, warranted, and more or less correct. In other, the charges can be answered and society must make its own choices between insatiable wants, scarce resources, and political and economic freedoms. The central and significant point is that a free market society has the right to make such a choice.

The marketing professional is not discouraged by the possible impact of these and related developments on enterprise management. They may precipitate change in marketing practice but they are not barriers to the exercise of the principles of marketing management developed throughout this book. The enterprise that truly follows *a market orientation as a philosophy of business management* is ideally suited to cope with change. In fact, such societal concerns represent market opportunities for the alert enterprise. The willingness and capability of an enterprise to adapt to market needs and wants as reflected in contemporary social concerns are reflections of its marketing vitality. The successful enterprise is an adaptive institution. Marketing can only be understood as a scheme of adaptive behavior.

BIBLIOGRAPHY

EL-ANSARY, ADEL I., and OSCAR E. KRAMER, JR., "Social Marketing: The Family Planning Experience," *Journal of Marketing*, 37 (July 1973), 1–7.

FULMER, VINCENT A., "Cost Benefit Analysis in Fund Raising," *Harvard Business Review* (March–April 1973), pp. 103–10.

FURUHASHI, Y. HUGH, and JEROME E. MCCARTHY. *Social Issues of Marketing in the American Economy.* Columbus, Ohio: Grid, Inc., 1971.

GIST, RONALD R., *Marketing and Society: A Conceptual Introduction.* New York: Holt, Rinehart and Winston, Inc., 1971.

HARTLEY, ROBERT F., *Marketing: Management and Social Change.* Scranton, Pa.: Intext Educational Publishers, 1972.

KELLEY, EUGENE J., "Marketing's Changing Social/Environmental Role," *Journal of Marketing*, 35 (July 1971), 1–2.

KOTLER, PHILIP, *Non-Profit Marketing.* Englewood Cliffs, N.J.: Prentice-Hall, Inc., 1975.

LAZER, WILLIAM, and EUGENE KELLEY. *Social Marketing: Perspectives and Viewpoints.* Homewood, Ill.: Richard D. Irwin, Inc., 1973.

LUCK, DAVID J., "Social Marketing: Confusion Compounded," *Journal of Marketing*, 38 (October 1974), 70–72.

ZALTMAN, GERALD, and ILAN VERTINSKY, "Health Service Marketing: A Suggested Model," *Journal of Marketing*, 35 (July 1971), 19–27.

Appendix A

Retail and Wholesale Trade

This appendix examines some aspects of retail and wholesale trade, including size, different methods of retailing and wholesaling, and different classes of retailers and wholesalers.

RETAILING

Retail trade is defined by the Bureau of the Census as "all establishments engaged in selling merchadise for personal or household consumption and rendering services incident to the sale of such goods."[1]

In 1972 the last complete Census of Business reported retail trade amounted to $459 billion conducted by 1.9 million establishments, employing about 11.2 million people.

Table A-1 shows retail trade by method of retailing, and Table A-2 retail trade by kind of business.

TABLE A-1
Methods of Retailing, 1972

Method of Retailing	Number of Establishments	Retail Sales (In $ Millions)
Mail-order houses	7,982	4,574
Automatic merchandising machine operators	12,845	3,010
Direct selling establishments	141,294	3,984
Retail establishments	1,750,750	447,472
TOTAL	1,912,871	459,040

Source: U.S. Bureau of the Census, Census of Retail Trade, 1972, United States Summary.

[1] U.S. Bureau of the Census, Census of Retail Trade, 1972, Summary Statistics.

TABLE A-2
Retail Sales and Retail Establishments By Kind of Business, 1972

Kind of Business	Retail Sales (In $ Millions)	Number of Establishments
Building materials, hardware, garden supply and mobile home dealers	23,844	83,842
General merchandise group	65,091	56,245
Food stores	100,719	267,352
Automotive dealers	90,030	121,369
Gasoline service stations	33,655	226,459
Apparel, accessory stores	24,741	129,201
Furniture, home furnishings, equipment stores	22,533	116,857
Eating and drinking places	36,868	359,524
Drugstores, proprietary stores	15,599	51,542
Miscellaneous retail stores	34,391	338,359
Nonstore retailers	11,569	162,121
TOTAL	459,040	1,912,871

Source: U.S. Bureau of the Census, Census of Retail Trade, 1972, Summary Statistics.

METHODS OF RETAILING[2]

The different methods of retailing are defined as follows:

Mail-Order Houses: "Establishments primarily engaged in the retail sale of products by catalog and mail order."

Automatic Merchandising Machine Operators: "Establishments primarily engaged in the retail sale of products by means of automatic merchandising units, also referred to as vending machines."

Direct Selling Establishments: "Establishments primarily engaged in the retail sale of merchandise by house-to-house canvas. Included in this industry are individuals who sell products by this method and who are not employees of the organization which they represent, and establishments which are retail sales offices from which employees operate to sell merchandise from door-to-door."

Retail establishments is the most important method of retailing, accounting for approximately 97 percent of retail trade in 1972. Table A-3 shows retail sales and retail establishment by kind of business and ownership. Table A-4 shows retail sales by retail establishments by kind of business and sales volume size.

[2] *Standard Industrial Classification Manual,* 1967, Executive Office of the President, Bureau of the Budget (Washington, D.C.: Government Printing Office, 1967), pp. 240–241.

TABLE A-3
Retail Trade by Single Units and Multiunits
By Kind of Business: 1972

Kind of Business	All Establishments Number	All Establishments Sales ($1,000)	Establishment of Firms in Business December 31, 1972 Total Number	Total Sales ($1,000)	Single Units Number	Single Units Sales ($1,000)	Multiunits Number	Multiunits Sales ($1,000)
Retail trade, total	1,912,871	459,040,436	1,912,871	447,006,077	1,621,373	245,167,966	291,498	201,838,111
Building materials, hardware, garden supply and mobile home dealers	83,842	23,844,148	83,842	23,151,761	69,704	15,259,818	14,138	7,891,943
General merchandise group stores	56,245	65,090,832	56,245	64,766,481	31,711	5,190,973	24,534	59,575,509
Food stores	267,352	100,718,864	267,352	98,604,703	213,335	34,918,696	54,017	63,686,007
Automotive dealers	121,369	90,030,255	121,369	88,149,157	109,712	79,457,181	11,657	8,691,976
Gasoline service stations	226,459	33,655,378	226,459	31,378,051	197,755	24,776,441	28,704	6,601,610
Apparel and accessory stores	129,201	24,741,375	129,201	24,077,225	88,823	10,709,914	40,378	13,367,311
Furniture, home furnishings, and equipment stores	116,857	22,533,328	116,857	21,846,076	98,734	14,592,278	18,123	7,253,798
Eating and drinking places	359,524	36,867,707	359,524	35,252,540	320,552	25,885,782	38,972	9,366,758
Drug stores and proprietary stores	51,542	15,598,952	51,542	15,344,110	39,627	7,835,222	11,915	7,508,888
Miscellaneous retail stores	500,480	45,959,597	500,480	44,316,804	457,874	29,095,110	42,606	15,220,694

Source: U.S. Bureau of the Census, Census of Retail Trades, 1972, Establishment and Firm Size (RC72-S-1).

TABLE A-4
Retail Trade by Sales Size and Kind of Business: 1972

Kind of Business	All Establishments Number	All Establishments Sales ($1,000)	Total Number	Total Sales ($1,000)	Less than $100,000 Number	Less than $100,000 Sales ($1,000)	$100,000 or More Number	$100,000 or More Sales ($1,000)
Retail trade, total	1,912,871	459,040,436	1,709,555	427,639,607	1,008,066	35,998,918	701,489	391,640,689
Building materials, hardware, garden supply and mobile home dealers	83,842	23,844,148	77,837	22,411,699	35,090	1,426,163	42,747	20,985,536
General merchandise group stores	56,245	65,090,832	52,363	62,155,466	20,504	831,694	31,859	61,323,772
Food stores	267,352	100,718,864	243,543	94,070,275	123,732	5,065,552	119,811	89,004,723
Automotive dealers	121,369	90,030,255	111,284	85,932,336	42,760	1,535,924	68,524	84,396,412
Gasoline service stations	226,459	33,655,378	197,220	29,136,145	88,796	4,461,089	108,424	24,675,056
Apparel and accessory stores	129,201	24,741,375	118,466	22,775,907	60,283	2,665,418	58,183	20,110,489
Furniture, home furnishings, and equipment stores	116,857	22,533,328	107,403	21,001,598	57,308	2,104,418	50,095	18,897,180
Eating and drinking places	359,524	36,867,707	316,328	33,138,994	227,103	8,915,344	89,225	24,223,650
Drug stores and proprietary stores	51,542	15,598,952	48,899	14,742,105	11,950	648,562	36,949	14,093,543
Miscellaneous retail stores	500,480	45,959,597	436,212	42,275,082	340,540	8,344,754	95,672	33,930,328

Source: U.S. Bureau of the Census, Census of Retail Trades, 1972, Establishment and Firm Size (RC72-S-1).

WHOLESALING

Wholesale trade is defined as including "all establishments or places of business primarily engaged in selling merchandise to retailers; to industrial, commercial, institutional, or professional users; or to other wholesalers; or acting as agents in buying merchandise for or selling merchandise to such persons or companies."[3]

In 1972, the last complete Census of Business reported wholesale trade amounted to $695.8 billion conducted by 369,792 establishments employing about four million people.

Table A-5 shows wholesale sales and establishments by kind of business and Table A-6 shows wholesale trade by method of wholesaling.

TABLE A-5
Wholesale Establishments and Sales By Kind of Business, 1972

Kind of Business	Establishments Number	Wholesale Sales (In $ Millions)
DURABLE GOODS	204,126	341,830
Motor vehicles and automotive supplies	36,486	83,016
Furniture and home furnishings	9,530	12,359
Lumber and other construction materials	15,888	28,095
Sporting, recreational, photographic, and hobby goods, toys, and supplies	6,721	11,146
Metals and minerals, except petroleum	7,967	43,488
Electrical goods	21,172	49,349
Hardware, plumbing, heating equipment, and supplies	17,398	18,600
Machinery, equipment, and supplies	73,752	80,692
Miscellaneous durable goods	15,212	15,085

[3] U.S. Bureau of the Census, Census of Wholesale Trade, 1972, Summary Statistics.

TABLE A-5, continued

Kind of Business	Establishments Number	Wholesale Sales (In $ Millions)
NONDURABLE GOODS	165,666	354,000
Paper and paper products	10,714	17,280
Drugs, drug proprietaries, druggists' sundries	4,024	12,666
Apparel, piece goods, and notions	12,383	27,933
Groceries and related products	38,533	107,374
Farm product raw materials	14,820	53,313
Chemicals and allied products	6,397	24,621
Petroleum and petroleum products	31,277	46,284
Beer, wine, and distilled alcoholic beverages	7,012	19,884
Miscellaneous nondurable goods	40,506	44,645
TOTAL	369,792	695,830

Source: U.S. Bureau of the Census, Census of Wholesale Trade, 1972, Summary Statistics.

TABLE A-6
Wholesale Trade by Type of Operation, 1972

Type of Operation	Establishments Number	Percentage of Total	Wholesale Sales $ Millions	Percentage of Total
MERCHANT WHOLESALERS	289,980	78.4	353,316	50.8
Wholesale merchant and distributors	274,733	74.3	305,182	43.9
Grain elevators (Terminal and country)	5,811	1.6	11,441	1.6
Importers	6,786	1.8	23,092	3.3
Exporters	2,650	.7	13,601	2.0
MANUFACTURERS' SALES BRANCHES AND OFFICES	47,191	12.8	255,562	36.7
Manufacturers' sales branches with stocks	32,611	8.9	124,458	17.9
Manufacturers' sales offices without stocks	14,580	3.9	131,104	18.8
MERCHANDISE AGENTS AND BROKERS	32,621	8.8	86,952	12.5
Merchandise brokers for buyers or sellers	4,770	1.3	20,398	2.9
Commission merchants	6,940	1.9	18,971	2.7
Manufacturers' agents	16,529	4.4	23,345	3.4
Selling agents	1,723	.4	6,990	1.0
Auction companies	1,769	.5	8,170	1.2
Import agents	265	.1	3,619	.5
Export agents	440	.1	4,694	.7
Purchasing agents and resident buyers	185	.1	765	.1
TOTAL	369,792	100.0	695,830	100.0

Source: U.S. Bureau of the Census, Census of Wholesale Trade, 1972, Summary Statistics.

TYPE OF OPERATION CLASSIFICATIONS[4]

In addition to kind of business, each wholesale establishment is classified by *type of operation,* according to the ownership of the business, ownership of the goods sold, or character of principal transactions. Establishments in wholesale trade are grouped into three major type-of-operation groups and further classified as outlined below.

Merchant Wholesalers

This type group consists of wholesale establishments primarily engaged in buying and selling merchandise on their own account. Included here are such types of establishments as wholesale merchants or jobbers, industrial distributors, voluntary group wholesalers, exporters, importers, cash-and-carry wholesalers, wagon distributors, retailer cooperative warehouses, terminal and country grain elevators, farm products assemblers, wholesale cooperative associations, and petroleum bulk plants and terminals operated by non-refining companies.

>*Wholesale merchants, distributors.* Establishments primarily engaged in buying and selling merchandise in the domestic market and performing the principal wholesale functions—buying, stocking, selling, and the like. Included here are establishments, except country grain elevators, which are primarily engaged in purchasing from farmers and assembling and marketing farm products at wholesale.
>
>*Importers.* Establishments buying and selling goods at wholesale on own account, whose principal source of purchases is foreign.
>
>*Exporters.* Establishments primarily engaged in purchasing goods in the United States and selling to foreign customers.
>
>*Terminal grain elevators.* Grain elevators primarily engaged in buying and selling grain received from country grain elevators and grain marketing establishments. These elevators have sizable space for grain storage and products are received primarily by rail or barge rather than by truck.
>
>*Country grain elevators.* Grain elevators, cooperative or other, buying and receiving grain direct from farmers by truck and selling at wholesale.

Manufacturers' Sales Branches, and Sales Offices

Establishments maintained by manufacturing, refining, and mining companies apart from their plants or mines for marketing their products at wholesale. Branch stores selling to household consumers and individual

[4] Ibid.

users are classified in retail trade. Sales branches and sales offices located at plants and at administrative offices are included when separate records are available. In some tables data are shown separately for manufacturers' sales branches and for sales offices. These two types of establishments differ in that sales offices normally do not carry stocks of merchandise for delivery to consumers.

Merchandise Agents and Brokers

Establishments whose operators are in business for themselves and are primarily engaged in selling or buying goods for others. Included here are such types of operations as auction companies, commission merchants, export agents, import agents, selling agents, and merchandise brokers. "Sales," as shown in census publications for agents and brokers, represent the gross sales (or purchase) value of the goods in the transactions negotiated.

Auction companies. Wholesale establishments primarily engaged in selling merchandise on an agency basis by the auction method.

Merchandise brokers. Wholesale establishments primarily engaged in buying or selling merchandise in the domestic market on a brokerage basis, but not receiving the goods on consignment.

Commission merchants. Wholesale establishments operating in the domestic market receiving goods for sale on consignment.

Import agents. Merchandise agents and brokers in the domestic market buying merchandise from or selling merchandise for foreign firms.

Export agents. Merchandise agents and brokers in the domestic market selling to or buying for foreign customers.

Manufacturers' agents. Wholesale establishments in the domestic market selling for a limited number of manufacturers on a continuing agency basis.

Selling agents. Wholesale establishments primarily engaged in selling, on an agency basis in the domestic market, all or the major portion of the output of clients.

Purchasing agents, resident buyers. Wholesale establishments primarily engaged in buying merchandise on an agency basis, in the domestic market, for a limited number of customers on a continuing basis.

INDEX

A

Acceptance stage of product life cycle, 227–30
Accounting, 549
Administration
 execution and, 47–49
 integrated, 553–54
Advertising, 344–72
 analyzing effectiveness of, 528–34
 communication model of, 345–47
 cost of, to customers, 368–70
 factors affecting successful use of, 356–63
 media for, 363–68
 objectives of, 352–56
 terminology of, 348–52
Advertising agencies, 351–52
Affluence, effects of, 93–95
Agents, 275, 373, 393–99
Arousal tests, 531
Audio media, 363
Authority, 507–8
Autocratic organization, 492–93
Automation, 298
Availability of transportation, 331

B

Basing-point pricing, 435–37
Bonuses, 390–91
Brand-choice decisions, defined, 115
Brand loyalty, 140–41, 232
Brand names, 141
Brand preference, institutional, 232
Brands
 defined, 359
 effects of conglomerate market competition on, 299–300
Broad-line segmentation strategy, 76, 206–7, 457–59

Buildup method for objective identification, 105–6
Bureaucratic organization, 493
Business logistics, 316, 490
Business management, 20–34
 application of marketing philosophy to, 25–28
 competition for differential advantage and, 28–29
 market veto power and, 24–25
 marketing leadership and, 31–32
 profits as guide to effective functioning of, 21–24
Buyers of intermediate goods, 153–54, 159–60

C

Capability of transportation, 331
Capital availability, 186–87
Capital goods, 155–56
Capital risk in product planning, 200
Centralized organization, 488–89
 decentralized vs., 495–97
Channel jumping, defined, 320
Channel leadership, 289–90
Channel roles, 289
Channel selection function, 41–42; see also Intermediaries; Physical distribution channels; Transaction channels
Closed-circuit system, 50–51
Closed society, defined, 125
Cognitive foundation of consumer choice decisions, 133–36
Coincidental method of media research, 529–30
Commercialization stage, 265–66
Commissions, 390–91
Common carriers, 331
Communication function, 43–44
 issues related to, 575–76

587

Communication function (Cont'd.)
  limited-line segmentation based on, 461–62
  See also Advertising
Communication mix, 73, 74, 449, 470–75
Communication model of advertising, 345–47
Compensation of sales personnel, 390–92
Competition, 3–19
  behavior of, 10–12
  conglomerate market, 60, 290–301
  decision making and, 16–17
  for differential advantage, 28–29
  full-line, 215–16
  monitoring, 59–60
  monopolistic, 8, 9, 417–21
  physical distribution and, 319–22
  as process of adjustment, 4–10
  product life cycle and, 223–39
  test marketing and, 259–60
  uncertainty and, 12–16
Component, defined, 156
Conglomerate market competition, 60, 290–301
Consumer behavior
  effects of, on transaction channels, 293
  on international markets, 183–84
  See also Consumer choice decisions; Purchase motivation
Consumer choice decisions, 113–37
  classification of, 113–16
  framework for understanding, 116–37
Consumer credit, 296–97
Consumer goods market, 87–111
  identifying objectives for, 95–106
  monitoring, 88–95
  target market selection for, 107–11
Consumer-jury tests, 531
Consumption equipment, ownership of, on international markets, 182–83
Contract carriers, 331
Control, 513–23
  over agent sales force, 398
  in centralized and decentralized organization, 495–96
  marketing information and devices of, 520–23
  orientation of, 515–20
  span of, 496, 507
Convergent marketing, 207–12
  convergent production and, 207–8
  divergent production and, 211–12
Convergent production, 207–11
  convergent marketing and, 207–8
  divergent marketing and, 209–11
Cooperative marketing, 29–30
Coordination in effective organization, 506–7

Copy research, advertising effectiveness analyzed through, 530–34
Corporate growth, 65–67, 490–91
  provisions for, 508–9
Corporate objectives, 421–23
Corporate research, 247–56
Cost analysis
  functional, 538
  responsibility, 538–41
  total, 325–27, 336–38
Cost-revenue analysis, 537–45
Costs
  of advertising to customers, 368–70
  of agents, 397
  buildups of, 424–26
  of physical distribution, 319
  prices, profits and, 576
Creative selling, defined, 375
Credit availability
  consumer credit, 296–97
  in international markets, 182
Cultural environment
  consumer choice decisions and, 128
  of international markets, 187
  monitoring, 65
Cultural pollution, 575–76
Cumulative quantity discounts, 433
Customer service
  distribution channels and, 338–40
  effects of, on transaction channels, 297–98

D

Dealers, 373, 407
Dealerships, structure of, 399–403
Decentralized organization, centralized vs., 495–97
Decision making, 16–17, 489
Decision points, 504
Deep product mix, defined, 204
Delineation function, 37–38, 169–71
Demand
  defined, 6
  expansion of, 352–55
  inelasticity of, 355
  interconnectedness of, 293–94
  on intermediate markets, 160–63
  manufacturer's responsibility for creation of, 300
  plasticity of, 205
  primary, *see* Primary demand
  selective, *see* Selective demand
  supply and, 6
Democratic organization, 493–94
Dependability of transportation, 331
Diminishing marginal utility, law of, 118
Discounts, 433, 434

Discrimination, defined, 140
Distribution
  in acceptance stage, 228
  channels of, defined, 41, 62; *see also* Physical distribution channels
  intensive, selective and exclusive, 302–4
  measuring effectiveness of, 534–36
  physical, 41–43
  in saturation stage, 235–36
  use of agents and, 397
Distribution centers, 327–29
Distribution mix, 73, 74, 449, 465–70
Divergent marketing
  convergent production and, 209–11
  divergent production and, 212–13
Divergent production, 211–13
  convergent marketing and, 211–12
  divergent marketing and, 212–13
Diversification, transaction channels and, 297

E

Earnings per share, 68
Economic environment, 58–59
Economic equilibrium analysis, 7–8
Economic growth, opposed, 576
Economic theory, contributions of, to pricing, 416–21
Educational factor in international markets, 180
Ego involvement, defined, 124
Emotional appeals in purchase of intermediate goods, 165
Employees, 373, 380–92
Employment application blanks, 386
Enabling conditions of consumer choice decisions, 116–20
Enterprise, as total system of action, 2
Environment
  concerns over, 577
  consumer choice decisions and, 120–29
Environmental monitoring, 55–67, 449
  as basic data of information systems, 548–49
  competitive environment, 59–60
  consumer goods market, 88–95
  cultural and social environment, 65
  defined, 57
  economic environment, 58–59
  legal and political environment, 63–65
  product planning and, 201
  support environment, 62–63
  technological environment, 60–62
Equal marginal utility per dollar spent, law of, 118
Equilibrium price, defined, 413
Ethical pricing, 422, 423

Evaluation of sales personnel, 392
Exchange function, importance of, 5
Execution
  of managerial activity, 31, 32
  managerial functions related to, 46–49
Executive fear, as source of resistance to information flows, 523
Exempt carriers, 331
Exporting, 176
Eye-camera test, 531

F

False and misleading representation, defined, 575
Family formation, 89–91
Family income, 91–93
Family planning programs, 568–70
Family unit, consumer choice decisions and, 121–23
Feasibility research, 256–59
Federal Trade Commission Act (1914), 438, 441–42
Feedback, 50, 52
Financial objectives, identifying, 68–69; *see also* Profits
Financial rationale in formation of marketing objectives, 454–56
Firms
  function of, 20
  as marketing social entities, 572–78
Foreign markets, *see* International markets
Formal organization, 491–97
Formula pricing, 424–32
  from cost buildups, 424–26
  limitations to, 426–27
  variations from, 427–32
Franchising, 176–77, 403, 408–10
Freight absorption, 435–36
Frequency of transportation, defined, 331
Full-line competition, 215–16
Full-line pricing, 422, 423
Functional cost analysis, 438

G

Generalization, defined, 140
Geographic selectivity of media, 364
Georeference coding, 549–52
Gross profit analysis, 541–44

H

Heterogeneity in supply and demand, 6
Historical method, 99–104

Homogeneity of intermediate goods, 157–58
Horizontal cooperative advertising, 351
Human resources, defined, 74

I

Image matching, defined, 135–36
Impact of media, defined, 363
Income
    as factor in international markets, 181
    family, 91–93
Indifference approach, 118–19
Individual motivation, 129–33, 136
Industrial goods, defined, 152
Industrial marketing, defined, 379
Inelasticity of demand on intermediate markets, 162–63
Informal organization, 491–97
Information flows
    as control devices, 521–23
    in effective organization, 505–6
Information systems, 547–54
Inquiry tests, 532–33
Institutional brand preference, 232
Institutional loyalty, 140
Integration, as cooperative action, 30
Intermediaries (middlemen), 273
    classified, 274–76
    defined, 62
    merchant middlemen, 244, 378
    role of, 278–82
Intermediate goods, 155–69
    classification of, 155–57
    defined, 152
    purchase of, 163–69
    special characteristics of, 157–64
Intermediate markets, 152–74
    nature of, 153–55
    opportunity assessment in, 169–73
    special characteristics of, 157–64
International companies, 178–79
International markets, 175–95
    characteristics of, 179–84
    opportunity assessment in, 184–93
    participation in, 175–79
Interviews of sales personnel, 386–87
Inventory, 333–34
Investments
    in international markets, 187–93
    product planning and, 200–201

J

Joint ventures, 177–78

K

Kinked demand curve, defined, 10

L

Labor-intensive systems, 200
Latin America, noncompetitive institutions in, 564–68
Lead times, product planning and, 202
Learned behavior, purchase action as, 139–40
Leasing arrangements, 434–35
Legal environment
    monitoring, 63–65
    product planning and, 201
Legislation
    on conglomerate market competition, 300–301
    on franchise agreements, 408–10
    on price determination, 437–45
Life span factor in international markets, 180–81
Limited-line segmentation strategy, 76, 205–6, 459–63
Limited product mix, defined, 204
Linear system, described, 49–50
Line-staff relations, 505
Literacy, as factor in international markets, 180
Long-range planning, 489

M

Managerial functions of marketing, 34–54
    related to execution, 46–49
    related to opportunity assessment, 36–39
    related to product-service market matching, 39–40
    related to programming, 41–46
    systems integration of, 49–52
Manufacturers
    advantages of resale price maintenance to, 442–43
    sales to, 379–80
Marginal utility approach, 117–18
Marginalism, 477–78
Market
    business management and veto power of, 24–25
    choice of transaction channels affected by characteristics of, 308–12
    delineation of, 37–38, 169–71
    leadership in, 25–28, 31–32
    See also specific types of markets
Market entry
    agents and, 397
    in saturation stage, 236–37
Market introduction stage, 264–65
Market province, defined, 451
Market rationale, 451–53
Market segmentation, 71–73

Index

Market segmentation (Cont'd.)
  broad-line, 76, 206–7, 457–59
  limited-line, 76, 205–6, 459–63
Market share analysis, 526–28
Marketing
  as center of profits, 488
  contemporary issues related to, 574–77
  defined, 1, 31
  research in, as basic data of information systems, 549
Marketing channels, 273–86
  nature of, 274–76
  problem of sorting, 276–78
  separation of, 282–85
  See also Intermediaries; Physical distribution channels; Transaction channels
Marketing mix, 72–74, 449, 464–80
Marketing objectives
  behavior change as, 568–70
  identifying, 67–71, 95–106
  strategy planning and, 449–56
Marketing strategy, 67–83
  in action, 76–81
  development of, 67–75
  kinds of, 75–76
  selecting target markets in, 71–75
  See also Environmental monitoring; Strategy planning
Mass coverage, defined, 363
Massed reserves, principle of, 280–81
Mass production economies, 214–15
Material handling, 334–35
Materials, defined, 156
Media
  advertising, 363–68
  in international markets, 181–82
  research by, to analyze effectiveness of advertising, 529–30
Merchandising, scrambled, 60, 320
Merchant middlemen, 274, 378
Milline rate, formula for, 366
Minimization-of-loss pricing, 422, 423
Minimum total transactions, principle of, 279–80
Missionary selling, defined, 378
Modern, defined, 218
Monetary compensation of sales personnel, 390–91
Monitoring, *see* Environmental monitoring
Monopolistic competition, 8, 9, 417–21
Multicratic organization, 494–95
Multinational companies, 178

N

National market integration, defined, 564
Natural expense analysis, 537–38

Need satisfaction, 131–32
Negotiations, 25–26, 432–33
Net profit analysis, 541–44
Neutralization, defined, 15
New products
  development of, defined, 247
  effects of, on transaction channels, 295–96
  physical distribution channels for, 320
  pricing of, 423–32
Noise, defined, 345
Noncompetitive marketing, 558–71
  when behavior change is the objective, 568–70
  building of noncompetitive institutions, 562–68
  format for, 561–70
  nonprofit institutions, 558–61
Noncumulative quantity discounts, 433
Nonmonetary compensation, 391–92
Nonrational consumer behavior, 129–31
Nonsegmented marketing, 75, 76
Nonvariable-price policy, 433

O

Objectives
  advertising, 352–56
  corporate, 421–23
  product planning and definition of, 250
  See also Marketing objectives
Obsolescence, 237–39, 575
Oligopoly, 10, 421
Open-circuit feedback, defined, 52
Open-circuit system, described, 51–52
Open society, defined, 125
Operating objectives, 69–71
Opportunity assessment
  for intermediate markets, 169–73
  for international markets, 184–93
  as managerial activity, 31–32
  managerial functions related to, 36–39
Order processing, 334
Organization, 487–511
  concepts of, 491–97
  control and, 522; *see also* Control
  effective, 501–9
  execution and, 46–47
  future, 509–10
  influences leading to modifications in, 487–90
  market orientation and, 497–501
Organized purchasing units, 164

P

Paired-comparison tests, 531
Payback periods, 201
Penetration pricing, defined, 422
Penetration tests, 532

Performance measurement, 523–47
  control and, 48
  evaluation of, 545–47
  past performance, 525–45
  posttransaction analysis of, 523–25
Perishable distinctiveness cycle, 221
Personal selling, 373–411
  agents in, 393–99; *see also* Agents
  employee sales force in, 373, 380–92
  by franchise agreements, 176–77, 403, 408–10
  manufacturer-dealer arrangements in, 399–410
  nature of, 374–80
Physical distribution channels, 314–43
  customer service performance and, 338–40
  operating areas of, 327–36
  in perspective, 315–17
  pressures for improved, 317–27
  total cost analysis and, 325–27, 336–38
Physical distribution function, defined, 41–43
Physical facilities, defined, 75
Pioneering state of product life cycle, elements of, 223–26
Plant and equipment, 155–56
Political environment
  international markets and, 185
  monitoring, 63–65
Population characteristics, 84–89
Postbroadcast method, 529, 530
Postponement, principle of, 281–82
Posttransaction aspect of marketing, 48
Pretransaction controllership, 515–19
Price determination
  legal implications of, 437–45
  theoretical concepts of, 415–21
Price mix, 73, 74, 449, 475–77
Prices
  in acceptance stage, 228
  alternative price structures, 432–37
  broad-line segmentation strategy based on, 458–59
  cost, profits and, 576
  effects of conglomerate market competition on, 299
  in obsolescence stage, 238–39
  in pioneering stage, 225
  resale, 442–45
  See also Price determination; Pricing
Pricing, 44–46
  to achieve corporate objectives, 421–23
  contributions of economic theory to, 416–21
  of new products, 423–32
  role of, 412–15
  zone, 436

Primary demand
  advertising affected by, 356–59
  defined, 226
  in obsolescence stage, 238
Private carriers, 331
Product changes
  in obsolescence stage, 237–38
  in saturation stage, 234–35
  in turbulence stage, 230
Product characteristics, 305–8
Product criteria, 254
Product form
  broad-line segmentation strategy based on, 457–58
  limited-line segmentation based on, 462–63
Product image
  limited-line segmentation based on, 459–61
  overextension of, 217–18
Product life cycle
  competition and, 223–39
  concept of, 221–23
  limitations and benefits of concept, 243–44
Product-market development, 239–44
Product-market matching, 73, 204–7
Product mix, 73, 204, 449
Product-mix decision, defined, 114–15
Product planning, 199–220, 246–70
  case study in, 266–69
  commercialization stage in, 265–66
  corporate research for, 247–56
  elements of risk in, 199–204
  feasibility research for, 256–59
  patterns of product diversity and, 207–13
  problems of, 213–18
  product development as stage in, 258–59
  product-market matching and, 73, 204–7
  test marketing and, 259–64
Product-service adjustment, 39–40, 457
Product-service market matching, 31, 32, 39–40
Product strategy, 574–75
Production
  in acceptance stage, 228
  costs of, in pioneering stage, 225
  mass production economies, 214–15
  uncertainty and freedom of choice in, 14–15
  See also Convergent production; Divergent production
Profit analysis, gross vs. net, 541–44
Profits
  earnings per share, 68

Index

Profits (Cont'd.)
  as guide to effective functioning, 21–24
  marketing as center of, 488
  price, costs and, 576
  in turbulence stage, 231–32
Profits-to-sales volume ratio, as measure of profitability, 68
Program analyzer, uses of, 531
Programming
  as managerial activity, 31, 32
  managerial functions related to, 41–46; *see also* Communication; Physical distribution channels; Pricing
Program tests, 532
Proximity, principle of, 281
Psychoanalytic foundation of consumer choice decisions, 132–33
Purchase conditions decisions, 115–16
Purchase motivation, 38–39, 138–51
  in intermediate markets, 171–73
  learning perspective on, 138–41
  practical considerations on, 148–50
  qualitative market investigation in, 142–44
  study of, 144–48
Purchasing unit preferences, 13–14
Pure competition, 8–9, 417
Pure monopoly, 8, 9, 417

Q

Quality, 458–59
Quantity discounts, 433

R

Rational consumer behavior, 129–31
Rationales for marketing objectives, 451–56
Readability studies, 531
Recession, effects of, 229
Reciprocity in purchase of intermediate goods, 167–69
Reference groups, 123–25
References for sales personnel selection, 386
Reinforcement, purchase actions and, 140
Resale price, 442–45
Resources
  allocation and mobilization of, 74–75
  depletion of, 575–77
  human, 74
  for product planning, appraised, 253–54
Responsibility cost analysis, 538–41
Responsibility in effective organization, 507–8

Responsiveness in manufacturer-dealer arrangements, 403–8
Retail trade, 479–83
Retailers
  advantages of resale price maintenance to, 443
  defined, 275
  sales to, 377–78
Return-on-investment pricing, 422
Returns, *see* Profits
Risk, 12–16, 199–204
Robinson-Patman Act (1936), 438–41

S

Salaries of sales personnel, 390–91
Sale value of intermediate goods, 159
Sales
  in acceptance stage, 227
  analysis of, 525–26
  assisted by advertising, 355–56
  classification of, 376–80
  obsolescence and, 237–38
  in pioneering stage, 223–24
  in saturation stage, 234
  in turbulence stage, 230
  See also Personal selling
Sales force, 380–99
  agents in, 275, 373, 393–99
  analysis of, 534
  employee, 373, 380–92
  motivation of, 389–92
  selection and training of, 382–89
Sales-results tests, 533–34
Sales-service situations, defined, 375
Saturation stage of product life cycle, 233–37
Schwerin test, 531–32
Scrambled merchandising, 60, 320
Search and selection, 254–56
Selection of sales personnel, 382–88, 393–94
Selective coverage, defined, 363
Selective demand
  in acceptance stage, 228–29
  advertising affected by, 359–63
  defined, 226
Self-image, concept of, 134
Segmentation strategy, 75–76
  broad-line, 275, 373, 393–99
  limited-line, 76, 205–6, 459–63
  in saturation stage, 235
Sellers of intermediate goods, 152–54
Single-line stores, 299
Single-price policy, defined, 433
Situational analysis, 250–53
Skimming pricing, defined, 422–23
Social class, 125–27

Social environment
  international markets and, 187
  monitoring, 65
Span of control, 496, 507
Specialization, 496
Speed of transportation, defined, 331
Spend-save decisions, 114
Staff groups, 489–90, 505
Status roles, consumer choice decisions and, 125
Stimuli (information cues), 139
Strategic product adjustment, 73, 204
Strategy planning, 448–83
  format for, 448–49
  marketing mix and, 72–74, 449, 464–80
  marketing objectives and, 449–56
  selection of target markets for, 456–64
Superfluous differentiation, defined, 575
Supervision, 389–90, 496
Supply, defined, 6
Supply and demand, characteristics of, 6
Supply rationale, 453–54
Support environment, 62–63
Symbols, purpose of, 141
Systems concept, 324–25
Systems integration, 49–52

T

Tactical product adjustment, 73, 204
Target markets, 449
  selection of, 71–75, 107–11, 456–64
Taxes, 186
Technical sales, defined, 378
Technological environment, 60–62
Technology, 203–4, 298, 322–27
Territory structure, 381–82, 395
Test marketing, 259–64
Time compression, described, 322–23
Total cost analysis, 325–27, 336–38
Trade discounts, 434
Trade missions, 562–64
Trademarks, 141, 359

Trading down, 216–17
Trading up, 216–17
Training, 388, 407
Transaction accounting, 549
Transaction aspect of marketing, 48
Transaction channels, 287–314
Transaction controllership, 519–20
Transactional companies, 177
Transportation, 332–39
Turbulence stage of product life cycle, 230–33
Type selectivity of media, 364

U

Uniform delivered prices, 435–37

V

Variable-price policy, 432
Vertical cooperative advertising, 351, 361–63, 407
Vertical integration, defined, 290
Visual media, 363

W

Wantingness, 5–6
Wholesale trade, 583–87
Wholesalers
  advantages of resale price maintenance to, 443
  defined, 276
  sales to, 378–79
Wide (broad) product mix, defined, 204

Y

Youth, 93–95

Z

Zone pricing, 436